Crafting and Executing Strategy

Concepts and Readings

Crafting and Executing Strategy

Concepts and Readings

EIGHTEENTH EDITION

Arthur A. Thompson
The University of Alabama

Margaret A. Peteraf
Dartmouth College

John E. Gamble
University of South Alabama

A. J. Strickland III
The University of Alabama

McGraw-Hill Irwin

McGraw-Hill Irwin

CRAFTING & EXECUTING STRATEGY: CONCEPTS AND READINGS: GLOBAL EDITION

Published by McGraw-Hill/Irwin, a business unit of The McGraw-Hill Companies, Inc., 1221 Avenue of the Americas, New York, NY, 10020. Copyright © 2012, 2010, 2007, 2005, 2003, 2001 by The McGraw-Hill Companies, Inc. All rights reserved. Printed in the United States of America. No part of this publication may be reproduced or distributed in any form or by any means, or stored in a database or retrieval system, without the prior written consent of The McGraw-Hill Companies, Inc., including, but not limited to, in any network or other electronic storage or transmission, or broadcast for distance learning.

Some ancillaries, including electronic and print components, may not be available to customers outside the United States.

This book is printed on acid-free paper.

1 2 3 4 5 6 7 8 9 0 DOW/DOW 1 0 9 8 7 6 5 4 3 2 1

ISBN   978-0-07-131699-6
MHID   0-07-131699-X

Photo Credits

Chapter 1: page 55, © Yu Chu Di/Redlink/Redlink/Corbis; **Chapter 2:** page 90, © Jason Reed/Reuters/Corbis; page 90, Bloomberg via Getty Images; **Chapter 4:** page 160, Just Coffee Cooperative; **Chapter 5:** page 191, Courtesy of Walmart; page 203, Pichi Chuang/Reuters/Corbis; page 207, 2010 Toyota Motor Sales, USA, Inc.; **Chapter 6:** page 224, Amazon.com, Inc.; **Chapter 7:** page 282, MARK/epa/Corbis; page 285, Bloomberg Via Getty Images; **Chapter 8:** page 329, AP Photo/Mike Derer; **Chapter 9:** page 341, Courtesy of Apple; page 350, Aaron M. Sprecher/Corbis; page 353, CLARO CORTESIV/Reuters/Corbis; **Chapter 10:** page 383, AFP/Getty Images; page 387, Courtesy of Toyota; **Chapter 11:** page 417, Paulo Fridman/Corbis; page 426, Courtesy of Lincoln Electric; page 429, Bloomberg Via Getty Images

www.mhhe.com

To our families and especially our spouses:
Hasseline, Paul, and Kitty.

ABOUT THE AUTHORS

Arthur **A. Thompson, Jr.,** earned his B.S. and Ph.D. degrees in economics from The University of Tennessee, spent three years on the economics faculty at Virginia Tech, and served on the faculty of The University of Alabama's College of Commerce and Business Administration for 24 years. In 1974 and again in 1982, Dr. Thompson spent semester-long sabbaticals as a visiting scholar at the Harvard Business School.

His areas of specialization are business strategy, competition and market analysis, and the economics of business enterprises. In addition to publishing over 30 articles in some 25 different professional and trade publications, he has authored or co-authored five textbooks and six computer-based simulation exercises. His textbooks and strategy simulations have been used at well over 1,000 college and university campuses worldwide.

Dr. Thompson and his wife of 49 years have two daughters, two grandchildren, and a Yorkshire Terrier.

Margaret **Peteraf** is the Leon E. Williams Professor of Management at the Tuck School of Business at Dartmouth College. She is an internationally recognized scholar of strategic management, with a long list of publications in top management journals. She has earned myriad honors and prizes for her contributions, including the 1999 Strategic Management Society Best Paper Award recognizing the deep influence of her work on the field of Strategic Management. Professor Peteraf is on the Board of Directors of the Strategic Management Society and has been elected as a Fellow of the Society. She served previously as a member of the Academy of Management's Board of Governors and as Chair of the Business Policy and Strategy Division of the Academy. She has also served in various editorial roles and is presently on 9 editorial boards, including the *Strategic Management Journal,* the *Academy of Management Review,* and *Organization Science.* She has taught in Executive Education programs in various programs around the world and has won teaching awards at the MBA and Executive level.

Professor Peteraf earned her Ph.D., M.A., and M.Phil. at Yale University and held previous faculty appointments at Northwestern University's Kellogg Graduate School of Management and at the University of Minnesota's Carlson School of Management.

John E. Gamble is currently a Professor of Management in the Mitchell College of Business at the University of South Alabama. His teaching specialty at USA is strategic management and he also conducts a course in strategic management in Germany, which is sponsored by the University of Applied Sciences in Worms.

Dr. Gamble's research interests center on strategic issues in entrepreneurial, health care, and manufacturing settings. His work has been published in various scholarly journals and he is the author or co-author of more than 50 case studies published in an assortment of strategic management and strategic marketing texts. He has done consulting on industry and market analysis for clients in a diverse mix of industries.

Professor Gamble received his Ph.D. in management from The University of Alabama in 1995. Dr. Gamble also has a Bachelor of Science degree and a Master of Arts degree from The University of Alabama.

Dr. A. J. (Lonnie) Strickland is the Thomas R. Miller Professor of Strategic Management at the Culverhouse School of Business at The University of Alabama. He is a native of North Georgia, and attended the University of Georgia, where he received a Bachelor of Science degree in math and physics; Georgia Institute of Technology, where he received a Master of Science in industrial management; and Georgia State University, where he received his Ph.D. in business administration.

Lonnie's experience in consulting and executive development is in the strategic management arena, with a concentration in industry and competitive analysis. He has developed strategic planning systems for numerous firms all over the world. He served as Director of Marketing and Strategy at Bell-South, has taken two companies to the New York Stock Exchange, is one of the founders and directors of American Equity Investment Life Holding (AEL), and serves on numerous boards of directors. He is a very popular speaker in the area of Strategic Management.

Lonnie and his wife, Kitty, have been married for 44 years; they have two children, and two grandchildren. Each summer Lonnie and his wife live on their private game reserve in South Africa where they enjoy taking their friends on safaris.

PREFACE

This 18th edition represents one of our most important and thoroughgoing revisions ever. The newest member of the author team, Margie Peteraf, played the lead role in conducting a thorough reexamination of every paragraph on every page of the 17th-edition chapters. The overriding objective was to give all the chapters a major facelift by injecting new perspectives and the best academic thinking, strengthening linkages to the latest research findings, and modifying the coverage and exposition as needed to ensure squarely on-target content. The 18th edition features an attractive new collection of contemporary readings that amplify important topics in managing a company's strategy-making, strategy-executing process and help drive the chapter lessons home.

This edition retains the 12-chapter organization of the prior edition, but topical coverage and discussions have been trimmed in some areas and expanded in others. New material has been added here and there. The presentations of some topics were recast, others fine-tuned, and still others left largely intact. As with past editions, scores of new examples have been added, along with fresh Illustration Capsules, to make the content come alive and to provide students with a ringside view of strategy in action. The result is a major step forward in terms of punch, up-to-date coverage, clarity, and classroom effectiveness. But none of the changes have altered the fundamental character that has driven the text's success over three decades. The chapter content continues to be solidly mainstream and balanced, mirroring *both* the penetrating insight of academic thought and the pragmatism of real-world strategic management. And, as always, painstaking attention has been paid to keeping the chapters very reader-friendly and exceptionally teachable.

Through our experiences as business school faculty members, we fully understand the assessment demands on faculty teaching strategic management and business policy courses. In many institutions, capstone courses have emerged as the logical home for assessing student achievement of program learning objectives. The 18th edition includes a set of Assurance of Learning Exercises at the end of each chapter that link to the specific learning objectives appearing at the beginning of each chapter and highlighted throughout the text. *An important new instructional feature of the 18th edition is the linkage of selected chapter-end Assurance of Learning Exercises to the publisher's Web-based assignment and assessment platform called Connect.* Your students will be able to use the online Connect supplement to complete an Assurance of Learning Exercise for each of the 12 chapters and also to complete chapter-end self-quizzes, each consisting of 20 multiple-choice questions. All of the Connect exercises are automatically graded, thereby enabling you to easily assess the learning that has occurred.

For some years now, growing numbers of strategy instructors at business schools worldwide have been transitioning to a course structure that includes use of a strategy simulation. Incorporating a competition-based strategy simulation has the strong appeal of providing class members with *an immediate and engaging opportunity to apply the concepts and analytical tools covered in the chapters and to become personally involved in crafting and executing a strategy for a virtual company that they have been assigned to manage and that competes head-to-head with companies run by other class members.* Two widely used and pedagogically effective online strategy simulations, *The Business Strategy Game* and *GLO-BUS,* are optional companions for this text. Both simulations were created by this text's senior author and are closely linked to the content of each chapter in the text. The Exercises for Simulation Participants, found at the end of each chapter, provide clear guidance to class members in applying the concepts and analytical tools covered in the chapters to the issues and decisions that they have to wrestle with in managing their simulation company.

REVITALIZED AND EFFECTIVE CONTENT: THE SIGNATURE OF THE 18TH EDITION

Our objective in undertaking a major revision of this text was to ensure that its content was current, with respect to both scholarship and managerial practice, and was presented in as clear and compelling a fashion as possible. We established four criteria for meeting this objective, namely, that the final product must:

- Explain core concepts in language that students can grasp and provide first-rate examples of their relevance and use by actual companies.
- Thoroughly describe the tools of strategic analysis, how they are used, and where they fit into the managerial process of crafting and executing strategy.
- Incorporate the latest developments in the theory and practice of strategic management in every chapter to keep the content solidly in the mainstream of contemporary strategic thinking.
- Focus squarely on what every student needs to know about crafting, implementing, and executing business strategies in today's market environments.

We believe the 18th edition measures up on all four criteria. Chapter discussions cut straight to the chase about what students really need to know. At the same time, our explanations of core concepts and analytical tools are covered in enough depth to make them understandable and usable, since a shallow explanation carries little punch and almost no instructional value. Chapter content is driven by the imperative of including well-settled strategic management principles, fresh examples that illustrate the principles through the practices of real-world companies, recent research findings and contributions to the literature on strategic management, and the latest thinking of prominent academics and practitioners. There's a logical flow from one chapter to the next, as well as a complementary set of readings with which to spark discussions and drive the lessons home. And we have worked hard to hammer home the whys and hows of successfully crafting and executing strategy in an engaging, cogent, and convincing fashion.

Three standout features strongly differentiate our 12-chapter presentation:

1. *Our coverage of the resource-based theory of the firm in the 18th edition is unsurpassed by any other leading strategy text.* RBV principles and concepts are prominently and comprehensively integrated into our coverage of crafting both single-business and multibusiness strategies. In Chapters 3 through 8 it is repeatedly emphasized that a company's strategy must be matched *not only* to

its external market circumstances *but also* to its internal resources and competitive capabilities. Moreover, an RBV perspective is thoroughly integrated into the presentation on strategy execution (Chapters 10, 11, and 12) to make it unequivocally clear how and why the tasks of assembling intellectual capital and building core competencies and competitive capabilities are absolutely critical to successful strategy execution and operating excellence.

2. *Our coverage of the relational view, which focuses on cooperative strategies and the role that interorganizational activity can play in the pursuit of competitive advantage, is similarly unsurpassed by other leading texts.* The topics of alliances, joint ventures, franchising, and other types of cooperative and collaborative relationships are featured prominently in a number of chapters and are integrated into other material throughout the text as well. We show how strategies of this nature can contribute to the success of single business companies as well as multibusiness enterprises. And while we begin with coverage of such topics with respect to firms operating in domestic markets, we extend our discussion of this material to the international realm as well.

3. *In addition, our coverage of business ethics, core values, social responsibility, and environmental sustainability is unsurpassed by any other leading strategy text.* In this new edition, we have embellished the highly important chapter "Ethics, Corporate Social Responsibility, Environmental Sustainability, and Strategy" with fresh content so that it can better fulfill the important functions of (1) alerting students to the role and importance of ethical and socially responsible decision making and (2) addressing the accreditation requirement of the AACSB International that business ethics be visibly and thoroughly embedded in the core curriculum. Moreover, discussions of the roles of values and ethics are integrated into portions of other chapters to further reinforce why and how considerations relating to ethics, values, social responsibility, and sustainability should figure prominently into the managerial task of crafting and executing company strategies.

ORGANIZATION, CONTENT, AND FEATURES OF THE 18TH-EDITION TEXT CHAPTERS

The following rundown summarizes the noteworthy features and topical emphasis in this new edition:

- Although Chapter 1 continues to focus on the central questions of *"What is strategy?"* and *"Why is it important?"* the presentation of this material has been sharpened considerably, with more concise definitions of the key concepts and significant updating to improve the currency of the material. We introduce students to the primary approaches to building competitive advantage and the key elements of business-level strategy. Following Henry Mintzberg's process approach, we explain why a company's strategy is partly planned and partly reactive and why a strategy and its environment tend to co-evolve over time. We discuss the importance of a viable business model that outlines the company's customer value proposition and its profit formula, framing this discussion in terms of key elements of value, price, and cost. We show how the mark of a winning strategy is its ability to pass three tests: (1) the *fit test* (for internal and external fit), (2) the *competitive advantage test,* and (3) the *performance test.* And we explain why good company performance depends upon good strategy execution as well as a sound strategy. In short, this brief chapter is a perfect accompaniment for your opening-day lecture on what the course is all about and why it matters.

- Chapter 2 delves more deeply into the managerial process of actually crafting and executing a strategy—it makes a great assignment for the second day of class and provides a smooth transition into the heart of the course. The focal point of the chapter is the five-step managerial process of crafting and executing strategy: (1) forming a strategic vision of where the company is headed and why, (2) developing strategic as well as financial objectives with which to measure the company's progress, (3) crafting a strategy to achieve these targets and move the company toward its market destination, (4) implementing and executing the strategy, and (5) monitoring progress and making corrective adjustments as needed. Students are introduced to such core concepts as strategic visions, mission statements and core values, the balanced scorecard, strategic intent, and business-level versus corporate-level strategies. There's a robust discussion of why *all managers are on a company's strategy-making, strategy-executing team* and why a company's strategic plan is a collection of strategies devised by different managers at different levels in the organizational hierarchy. The chapter winds up with a section on how to exercise good corporate governance and examines the conditions that led to recent high-profile corporate governance failures.

- Chapter 3 sets forth the now-familiar analytical tools and concepts of industry and competitive analysis and demonstrates the importance of tailoring strategy to fit the circumstances of a company's industry and competitive environment. The standout feature of this chapter is a presentation of Michael Porter's "five-forces model of competition" *that has long been the clearest, most straightforward discussion of any text in the field.* This edition also provides expanded coverage of a company's macro-environment to enable students to conduct what some call *Pestel analysis* of *p*olitical, *e*conomic, *s*ocial, *t*echnological, *e*nvironmental, and *l*egal factors.

- Chapter 4 presents the resource-based view of the firm and convincingly argues why a company's strategy must be built around its most competitively valuable resources and capabilities. We provide students with a simple taxonomy for identifying a company's resources and capabilities and frame our discussion of how a firm's resources and capabilities can provide a sustainable competitive advantage with the *VRIN model.* We introduce the notion of a company's *dynamic capabilities* and cast SWOT analysis as a simple, easy-to-use way to assess a company's overall situation in terms of its ability to seize market opportunities and ward off external threats. There is solid coverage of value chain analysis, benchmarking, and competitive strength assessments—standard tools for appraising a company's relative cost position and customer value proposition vis-à-vis rivals. *An important feature of this chapter is a table showing how key financial and operating ratios are calculated and how to interpret them;* students will find this table handy in doing the number crunching needed to evaluate whether a company's strategy is delivering good financial performance.

- Chapter 5 deals with the basic approaches used to compete successfully and gain a competitive advantage over market rivals. This discussion is framed around the five generic competitive strategies—low-cost leadership, differentiation, best-cost provider, focused differentiation, and focused low cost. We emphasize that regardless of a company's choice, competitive success depends upon a company's capacity to deliver more customer value—one way or another. We provide a fuller treatment of *cost drivers* and *uniqueness drivers* as the keys to bringing down a company's cost and enhancing its differentiation, respectively, in support of this overall goal.

- Chapter 6 continues the theme of competitive strategies for single-business firms with its spotlight on *strategic actions (offensive and defensive) and their timing,* including blue-ocean strategies and first-mover advantages and disadvantages. It also serves to segue into the material covered in the next two chapters (on international and diversification strategies) by introducing the topic of *strategies that alter a company's scope of operations.* The chapter features sections on the strategic benefits and risks of horizontal mergers and acquisitions, vertical integration, and outsourcing of certain value chain activities. The concluding section of this chapter covers the advantages and drawbacks of using strategic alliances and cooperative arrangements to alter a company's scope of operations, with some pointers on how to make strategic alliances work.

- Chapter 7 explores the full range of strategy options for expanding a company's geographic scope and competing in foreign markets: export strategies, licensing, franchising, establishing a wholly owned subsidiary via acquisition or "greenfield" venture, and alliance strategies. In the 18th edition, we've added new coverage of topics such as Porter's *Diamond of National Advantage;* the choice between *multidomestic, global, and transnational strategies; profit sanctuaries* and cross-border strategic moves; and *the quest for competitive advantage via sharing, transferring, or accessing valuable resources and capabilities across national borders.* The chapter concludes with a discussion of the special issues of competing in the markets of developing countries and the strategies that local companies can use to defend against global giants.

- Chapter 8 introduces the topic of corporate-level strategy—a topic of concern for multibusiness companies pursuing diversification. This chapter begins by explaining why successful diversification strategies must create shareholder value and lays out the three essential tests that a strategy must pass to achieve this goal *(the industry attractiveness, cost-of-entry, and better-off tests).* We discuss alternative means of entering new businesses (acquisition, internal start-up, or joint venture) and offer a method for discerning which choice is a firm's best option. Then we turn our attention to a comparison of related versus unrelated diversification strategies, showing that they differ in terms of the nature of their critical resources *(specialized versus general parenting capabilities)* and whether they can exploit cross-business strategic fit for competitive gain. The chapter's analytical spotlight is trained on the techniques and procedures for assessing the strategic attractiveness of a diversified company's business portfolio—the relative attractiveness of the various industries the company has diversified into, the company's competitive strength in each of its lines of business, and the extent to which there is *strategic fit* and *resource fit* among its different businesses. The chapter concludes with a brief survey of a company's four main postdiversification strategy alternatives: (1) sticking closely with the existing business lineup, (2) broadening the diversification base, (3) divesting some businesses and retrenching to a narrower diversification base, and (4) restructuring the makeup of the company's business lineup.

- Chapter 9 reflects the very latest in the literature on (1) a company's duty to operate according to ethical standards, (2) a company's obligation to demonstrate socially responsible behavior and corporate citizenship, and (3) why more companies are limiting strategic initiatives to those that meet the needs of consumers in a manner that protects natural resources and ecological support systems needed by future generations. The discussion includes approaches to ensuring consistent ethical standards for companies with international operations. The contents of this chapter will definitely give students some things to ponder and will help to make them more *ethically aware* and conscious of *why all companies should conduct their business in a socially responsible and sustainable manner*. Chapter 9 has been written as a stand-alone chapter that can be assigned in the early, middle, or late part of the course.

- Chapter 10 begins a three-chapter module on executing strategy (Chapters 10 to 12), anchored around a pragmatic, compelling conceptual framework. Chapter 10 presents an overview of this 10-step framework and then develops the first three pieces of it: (1) *staffing the organization* with capable managers and employees, (2) *marshaling the resources and building the organizational capabilities* required for successful strategy execution, and (3) *creating a strategy-supportive organizational structure* and structuring the work effort. We discuss three approaches to building and strengthening a company's capabilities, ranging from internal development to acquisitions to collaborative arrangements, and consider outsourcing as an option for structuring the work effort. We argue for matching a company's organizational structure to its strategy execution requirements, describe four basic types of organizational structures (simple, functional, multidivisional, and matrix), and discuss centralized versus decentralized decision making. We conclude with some further perspectives on facilitating collaboration with external partners and structuring the company's work effort.

- Chapter 11 covers five important topics concerning strategy execution: (1) *allocating ample resources* to strategy-critical activities, (2) ensuring that *policies and procedures* facilitate rather than impede strategy execution, (3) employing *process management tools* and adopting *best practices* to drive continuous improvement in the performance of value chain activities, (4) installing *information and operating systems* that enable company personnel to better carry out their strategic roles proficiently, and (5) tying *rewards and incentives* directly to good strategy execution and the achievement of performance targets.

- Chapter 12 concludes the text with a discussion of corporate culture and leadership in relation to good strategy execution. The recurring theme throughout the final three chapters is that implementing strategy entails figuring out the specific actions, behaviors, and conditions that are needed for a smooth strategy-supportive operation and then following through to get things done and deliver results. The goal here is to ensure that students understand that the strategy-executing phase is a make-things-happen and make-them-happen-right kind of managerial exercise—one that is critical for achieving operating excellence and reaching the goal of strong company performance.

We have done our best to ensure that the 12 chapters convey the best thinking of academics and practitioners in the field of strategic management and hit the bull's-eye in topical coverage for senior- and MBA-level strategy courses. The ultimate test of the text, of course, is the positive pedagogical impact it has in the classroom. If this edition sets a more effective stage for your lectures and does a better job of helping you persuade students that the discipline of strategy merits their rapt attention, then it will have fulfilled its purpose.

THE COLLECTION OF READINGS

The readings that accompany the chapter presentations were chosen with three criteria in mind: relevance, readability, and recency of publication. The *relevance* criterion led us to seek out articles that connected clearly to the material in the text chapters and either extended the chapter coverage or expanded on a topic of strategic importance. The *readability* criterion helped us identify articles that were clearly written, engaging, practically oriented, and relatively short. The *recency* criterion limited our selections to those that appeared in the 2007–2011 period. We endeavored to be highly selective in our choices, deciding that a manageable number of on-target readings was a better fit with the teaching/learning objectives of most senior and MBA courses in strategy than a more sweeping collection of readings. The 15 readings we chose came from recent issues of *Academy of Management Perspectives, McKinsey Quarterly, MIT Sloan Management Review, Business Strategy Review, Business Horizons, Harvard Business Review, Journal of Business Strategy, Ivey Business Journal, Strategy & Leadership,* and *IESE Insight.*

The first reading, by Matthew Eyring, Mark Johnson, and Hari Nair, "New Business Models in Emerging Markets," is an article that appeared in *Harvard Business Review* in 2011 that provides an outstanding discussion of the connection between a good business model and a successful strategy, especially for companies competing in emerging markets. With its rich discussion of business model innovations that allow companies to identify and meet unsatisfied customer needs at prices customers are willing to pay, this reading is the perfect accompaniment to our introductory chapter "What Is Strategy and Why Is It Important?" Reading 2, "The Power of Vision: Statements That Resonate," is a practically oriented article that ties tightly to the material in Chapter 2. It offers explicit advice on how to develop a powerful vision and shows how effective vision statements can produce results.

The next four readings connect to Chapters 3 and 4, with their presentations of the basic concepts and analytical tools for conducting external (industry environment) and internal (single-business firm) analyses. Hugh Courtney and his co-authors argue in Reading 3 that, because the business world is increasingly interdependent, the success of a company's strategy often depends upon the strategies of its rivals. Therefore those companies that can most accurately predict their competitors' moves have a distinct competitive advantage. Reading 3 provides step-by-step advice on how managers can improve their competitive intelligence skills.

Reading 4, "Operational Capabilities: Hidden in Plain View," adds considerable depth to the coverage of the resource-based view of the firm that dominates the presentation in Chapter 4 (and that is integral to other chapters as well). Reading 4's extended example from a restaurant's kitchen provides a concrete and easy-to-follow illustration of exactly what we mean by the terms *resources* and *capabilities,* and how they apply to everyday business operations. Reading 5 by Amy Shuen and Sandra Sieber, "Orchestrating the New Dynamic Capabilities," provides a nice counterpart to this, showing how the advent of Web 2.0 is making the development of dynamic capabilities for orchestrating knowledge and ecosystems across multiple industry and geographic boundaries a top strategic priority. Reading 6, "The Battle of Value Chains," also complements the material in Chapter 4 and will give students additional insight into why the value chain concept is such a critically important analytical tool.

There are three readings that complement and expand on topics covered in Chapters 5 through 7. The timely reading "Low-cost Strategy through Product Architecture: Lessons from China" will provide students with some insight on how upstart Chinese car makers, such as Chery and BYD, have been able to follow a low-cost strategy while still producing cars that are roughly equivalent to those of their higher cost foreign rivals. The next reading pairs nicely with Chapter 6. Prashant Kale and Harbir Singh identify the primary drivers of alliance success in their article, "Managing Strategic Alliances: What Do We Know Now, and Where Do We Go from Here?" They offer advice on how companies can develop the capabilities needed to enhance the success of their strategic alliances and suggest that these capabilities can improve the success of acquisitions and other cooperative arrangements as well. Reading 9, "How to Win in Emerging Markets," adds breadth and depth to the discussion of the same topic in Chapter 7.

We included one reading to be assigned in conjunction with Chapter 8 on diversification strategies. It is titled "Why Is Synergy So Difficult in Mergers of Related Businesses?" It is a perfect fit with the content of this chapter. We chose two articles to complement and expand on the topics of ethical business strategies, social responsibility, and environmental sustainability covered in Chapter 9. "When Managers Pressure Employees to Behave Badly: Toward a Comprehensive Response" discusses managerial pressure on employees to behave unethically and a comprehensive approach to reducing the frequency with which managers place such pressure on employees. Reading 12, "How to Do Well *and* Do Good," by Rosabeth Moss Kanter shows that companies can boost both bottom-line performance and societal benefits by creating synergistic benefits between their business mission and efforts to benefit society.

Four readings were chosen for use with the three chapters on executing strategy (Chapters 10–12). The Nelson, Martin, and Powers article, "The Secrets to Successful Strategy Execution," from the *Harvard Business Review* is a splendid treatise on how to avoid breakdowns in strategy execution, while "Six Sigma at Your Service" and "Mismanaging Pay and Performance" are good fits with the material in Chapter 11.

TWO ACCOMPANYING ONLINE, FULLY AUTOMATED SIMULATION EXERCISES: *THE BUSINESS STRATEGY GAME* AND *GLO-BUS*

The Business Strategy Game and *GLO-BUS: Developing Winning Competitive Strategies*—two competition-based strategy simulations that are delivered online and that feature automated processing of decisions and grading of performance—are being marketed by the publisher as companion supplements for use with this book (and other texts in the field).

- *The Business Strategy Game* is the world's most popular strategy simulation, having been used in courses involving over 600,000 students at more than 700 university campuses in over 40 countries.
- *GLO-BUS*, a somewhat simpler strategy simulation introduced in 2004, has been used at more than 400 university campuses worldwide in courses involving over 120,000 students.

How the Strategy Simulations Work

In both *The Business Strategy Game (BSG)* and *GLO-BUS*, class members are divided into teams of one to five persons and assigned to run a company that competes head-to-head against companies run by other class members.

- In *BSG*, team members run an athletic footwear company, producing and marketing both branded and private-label footwear.
- In *GLO-BUS*, team members operate a digital camera company that designs, assembles, and markets entry-level digital cameras and upscale, multifeatured cameras.

In both simulations, companies compete in a global market arena, selling their products in four geographic regions—Europe-Africa, North America, Asia-Pacific, and Latin America. Each management team is called upon to craft a strategy for their company and make decisions relating to plant operations, workforce compensation, pricing and marketing, social responsibility/citizenship, and finance.

Company co-managers are held accountable for their decision making. Each company's performance is scored on the basis of earnings per share, return on equity investment, stock price, credit rating, and image rating. Rankings of company performance, along with a wealth of industry and company statistics, are available to company co-managers after each decision round to use in making strategy adjustments and decisions for the next competitive round. You can be certain that the market environment, strategic issues, and operating challenges that company co-managers must contend with are *very tightly linked* to what your class members will be reading about in the text chapters. The circumstances that co-managers face in running their simulation company embrace the very concepts, analytical tools, and strategy options they encounter in the text chapters (this is something you can quickly confirm by skimming through some of the Exercises for Simulation Participants that appear at the end of each chapter).

We suggest that you schedule 1 or 2 practice rounds and anywhere from 4 to 10 regular (scored) decision rounds (more rounds are better than fewer rounds). Each decision round represents a year of company operations and will entail roughly two hours of time for company co-managers to complete. In traditional 13-week, semester-long courses, there is merit is scheduling one decision round per week. In courses that run 5 to 10 weeks, it is wise to schedule two decision rounds per week for the last several weeks of the term (sample course schedules are provided for courses of varying length and varying numbers of class meetings).

When the instructor-specified deadline for a decision round arrives, the simulation server automatically accesses the saved decision entries of each company, determines the competitiveness and buyer appeal of each company's product offering relative to the other companies being run by students in your class, and then awards sales and market shares to the competing companies, geographic region by geographic region. The unit sales volumes awarded to each company *are totally governed by:*

- How its prices compare against the prices of rival brands.,
- How its product quality compares against the quality of rival brands.,
- How its product line breadth and selection compare.
- How its advertising effort compares.
- And so on, for a total of 11 competitive factors that determine unit sales and market shares.

The competitiveness and overall buyer appeal of each company's product offering *in comparison to the product offerings of rival companies* is all-decisive—this algorithmic feature is what makes *BSG* and *GLO-BUS* "competition-based" strategy simulations. Once each company's sales and market shares are awarded based on the competitiveness of its respective overall product offering, the various company and industry reports detailing the outcomes of the decision round are then generated. Company co-managers can access the results of the decision round 15 to 20 minutes after the decision deadline.

The Compelling Case for Incorporating Use of a Strategy Simulation

There are *three exceptionally important benefits* associated with using a competition-based simulation in strategy courses taken by seniors and MBA students:

- *A three-pronged text-case-simulation course model delivers significantly more teaching-learning power than the traditional text-case model.* Using *both* cases and a strategy simulation to drill students in thinking strategically and applying what they read in the text chapters is a stronger, more effective means of helping them connect theory with practice and develop better business judgment. What cases do that a simulation cannot is give class members broad exposure to a variety of companies and industry situations and insight into the kinds of strategy-related problems managers face. But what a competition-based strategy simulation does far better than case analysis is thrust class members squarely into *an active, hands-on managerial role* where they are totally responsible for assessing market conditions, determining how to respond to the actions of competitors, forging a long-term direction and strategy for their company, and making all kinds of operating decisions. Because they are held fully accountable for their decisions and their company's performance, *co-managers are strongly motivated* to dig deeply into company operations, probe for ways to be more cost-efficient and competitive, and ferret out strategic moves and decisions calculated to boost company performance. *Consequently, incorporating both case assignments and a strategy simulation to develop the skills of class members in thinking strategically and applying the concepts and tools of strategic analysis turns out to be more pedagogically powerful than relying solely on case assignments—there's stronger retention of the lessons learned and better achievement of course learning objectives.*

  To provide you with quantitative evidence of the learning that occurs with using *The Business Strategy Game* or *GLO-BUS*, there is a built-in Learning

Assurance Report showing how well each class member performs on nine skills/learning measures versus tens of thousands of students worldwide who have completed the simulation in the past 12 months.

• *The competitive nature of a strategy simulation arouses positive energy and steps up the whole tempo of the course by a notch or two.* Nothing sparks class excitement quicker or better than the concerted efforts on the part of class members at each decision round to achieve a high industry ranking and avoid the perilous consequences of being outcompeted by other class members. Students really enjoy taking on the role of a manager, running their own company, crafting strategies, making all kinds of operating decisions, trying to outcompete rival companies, and getting immediate feedback on the resulting company performance. Lots of back-and-forth chatter occurs when the results of the latest simulation round become available and co-managers renew their quest for strategic moves and actions that will strengthen company performance. Co-managers become *emotionally invested* in running their company and figuring out what strategic moves to make to boost their company's performance. Interest levels climb. All this stimulates learning and causes students to see the practical relevance of the subject matter and the benefits of taking your course.

As soon as your students start to say "Wow! Not only is this fun but I am learning a lot," *which they will,* you have won the battle of engaging students in the subject matter and moved the value of taking your course to a much higher plateau in the business school curriculum. This translates into *a livelier, richer learning experience from a student perspective and better instructor-course evaluations.*

• *Use of a fully automated online simulation reduces the time instructors spend on course preparation, course administration, and grading.* Since the simulation exercise involves a 20- to 30-hour workload for student teams (roughly 2 hours per decision round times 10 to 12 rounds, plus optional assignments), simulation adopters often compensate by trimming the number of assigned cases from, say, 10 to 12 to perhaps 4 to 6. This significantly reduces the time instructors spend reading cases, studying teaching notes, and otherwise getting ready to lead class discussion of a case or grade oral team presentations. Course preparation time is further cut because you can use several class days to have students meet in the computer lab to work on upcoming decision rounds or a three-year strategic plan (in lieu of lecturing on a chapter or covering an additional assigned case). Not only does use of a simulation permit assigning fewer cases, but it also permits you to eliminate at least one assignment that entails considerable grading on your part. Grading one less written case or essay exam or other written assignment saves enormous time. With *BSG* and *GLO-BUS,* grading is effortless and takes only minutes; once you enter percentage weights for each assignment in your online grade book, a suggested overall grade is calculated for you. You'll be pleasantly surprised—and quite pleased—at how little time it takes to gear up for and to administer *The Business Strategy Game* or *GLO-BUS.*

In sum, incorporating use of a strategy simulation turns out to be *a win-win proposition for both students and instructors.* Moreover, a very convincing argument can be made that a competition-based strategy simulation is *the single most effective teaching/learning tool that instructors can employ to teach the discipline of business and competitive strategy, to make learning more enjoyable, and to promote better achievement of course learning objectives.*

A Bird's-Eye View of *The Business Strategy Game*

The setting for *The Business Strategy Game (BSG)* is the global athletic footwear industry (there can be little doubt in today's world that a globally competitive strategy simulation is *vastly superior* to a simulation with a domestic-only setting). Global market demand for footwear grows at the rate of 7 to 9 percent annually for the first five years and 5 to 7 percent annually for the second five years. However, market growth rates vary by geographic region—North America, Latin America, Europe-Africa, and Asia-Pacific.

Companies begin the simulation producing branded and private-label footwear in two plants, one in North America and one in Asia. They have the option to establish production facilities in Latin America and Europe-Africa, either by constructing new plants or by buying previously constructed plants that have been sold by competing companies. Company co-managers exercise control over production costs on the basis of the styling and quality they opt to manufacture, plant location (wages and incentive compensation vary from region to region), the use of best practices and Six Sigma programs to reduce the production of defective footwear and to boost worker productivity, and compensation practices.

All newly produced footwear is shipped in bulk containers to one of four geographic distribution centers. All sales in a geographic region are made from footwear inventories in that region's distribution center. Costs at the four regional distribution centers are a function of inventory storage costs, packing and shipping fees, import tariffs paid on incoming pairs shipped from foreign plants, and exchange rate impacts. At the start of the simulation, import tariffs average $4 per pair in Europe-Africa, $6 per pair in Latin America, and $8 in the Asia-Pacific region. However, the Free Trade Treaty of the Americas allows tariff-free movement of footwear between North America and Latin America. Instructors have the option to alter tariffs as the game progresses.

Companies market their brand of athletic footwear to footwear retailers worldwide and to individuals buying online at the company's Web site. Each company's sales and market share in the branded footwear segments hinge on its competitiveness on 11 factors: attractive pricing, footwear styling and quality, product line breadth, advertising, use of mail-in rebates, appeal of celebrities endorsing a company's brand, success in convincing footwear retailers to carry its brand, number of weeks it takes to fill retailer orders, effectiveness of a company's online sales effort at its Web site, and customer loyalty. Sales of private-label footwear hinge solely on being the low-price bidder.

All told, company co-managers make as many as 53 types of decisions each period that cut across production operations (up to 10 decisions per plant, with a maximum of four plants), plant capacity additions/sales/upgrades (up to 6 decisions per plant), worker compensation and training (3 decisions per plant), shipping (up to 8 decisions per plant), pricing and marketing (up to 10 decisions in four geographic regions), bids to sign celebrities (2 decision entries per bid), financing of company operations (up to 8 decisions), and corporate social responsibility and environmental sustainability (up to 6 decisions).

Each time company co-managers make a decision entry, an assortment of on-screen calculations instantly shows the projected effects on unit sales, revenues, market shares, unit costs, profit, earnings per share, ROE, and other operating statistics. The on-screen calculations help team members evaluate the relative merits of one decision entry versus another and put together a promising strategy.

Companies can employ any of the five generic competitive strategy options in selling branded footwear—low-cost leadership, differentiation, best-cost provider, focused low cost, and focused differentiation. They can pursue essentially the same strategy worldwide or craft slightly or very different strategies for the Europe-Africa, Asia-Pacific, Latin America, and North America markets. They can strive for competitive advantage based on more advertising, a wider selection of models, more appealing styling/quality, bigger rebates, and so on.

Any well-conceived, well-executed competitive approach is capable of succeeding, provided it is not overpowered by the strategies of competitors or defeated by the presence of too many copycat strategies that dilute its effectiveness. The challenge for each company's management team is to craft and execute a competitive strategy that produces good performance on five measures: earnings per share, return on equity investment, stock price appreciation, credit rating, and brand image.

All activity for *The Business Strategy Game* takes place at www.bsg-online.com.

A Bird's-Eye View of *GLO-BUS*

The industry setting for *GLO-BUS* is the digital camera industry. Global market demand grows at the rate of 8 to 10 percent annually for the first five years and 4 to 6 percent annually for the second five years. Retail sales of digital cameras are seasonal, with about 20 percent of consumer demand coming in each of the first three quarters of each calendar year and 40 percent coming during the big fourth-quarter retailing season.

Companies produce entry-level and upscale, multifeatured cameras of varying designs and quality in a Taiwan assembly facility and ship assembled cameras directly to retailers in North America, Asia-Pacific, Europe-Africa, and Latin America. All cameras are assembled as retail orders come in and are shipped immediately upon completion of the assembly process—companies maintain no finished-goods inventories, and all parts and components are delivered on a just-in-time basis (which eliminates the need to track inventories and simplifies the accounting for plant operations and costs). Company co-managers exercise control over production costs on the basis of the designs and components they specify for their cameras, workforce compensation and training, the length of warranties offered (which affects warranty costs), the amount spent for technical support provided to buyers of the company's cameras, and their management of the assembly process.

Competition in each of the two product market segments (entry-level and multifeatured digital cameras) is based on 10 factors: price, camera performance and quality, number of quarterly sales promotions, length of promotions in weeks, size of the promotional discounts offered, advertising, number of camera models, size of retail dealer network, warranty period, and amount/caliber of technical support provided to camera buyers. Low-cost leadership, differentiation strategies, best-cost provider strategies, and focus strategies are all viable competitive options. Rival companies can strive to be the clear market leader in either entry-level cameras or upscale multifeatured cameras or both. They can focus on one or two geographic regions or strive for geographic balance. They can pursue essentially the same strategy worldwide or craft slightly or very different strategies for the Europe-Africa, Asia-Pacific, Latin America, and North America markets. Just as with *The Business Strategy Game,* almost any well-conceived, well-executed competitive approach is capable of succeeding, *provided it is not overpowered by the strategies of competitors or defeated by the presence of too many copycat strategies that dilute its effectiveness.*

Company co-managers make 49 types of decisions each period, ranging from R&D, camera components, and camera performance (10 decisions) to production operations and worker compensation (15 decisions) to pricing and marketing (15 decisions) to the financing of company operations (4 decisions) to corporate social responsibility (5 decisions). Each time participants make a decision entry, an assortment of on-screen calculations instantly shows the projected effects on unit sales, revenues, market shares, unit costs, profit, earnings per share, ROE, and other operating statistics. These on-screen calculations help team members evaluate the relative merits of one decision entry versus another and stitch the separate decisions into a cohesive and promising strategy. Company performance is judged on five criteria: earnings per share, return on equity investment, stock price, credit rating, and brand image.

All activity for *GLO-BUS* occurs at www.glo-bus.com.

Administration and Operating Features of the Two Simulations

The Internet delivery and user-friendly designs of both *BSG* and *GLO-BUS* make them incredibly easy to administer, even for first-time users. And the menus and controls are so similar that you can readily switch between the two simulations or use one in your undergraduate class and the other in a graduate class. If you have not yet used either of the two simulations, you may find the following of particular interest:

- Setting up the simulation for your course is done online and takes about 10 to 15 minutes. Once setup is completed, no other administrative actions are required beyond those of moving participants to a different team (should the need arise) and monitoring the progress of the simulation (to whatever extent desired).
- Participant's Guides are delivered at the Web site—students can read the guide on their monitors or print out a copy, as they prefer.
- There are 2- to 4-minute Video Tutorials scattered throughout the software (including each decision screen and each page of each report) that provide on-demand guidance to class members who may be uncertain about how to proceed.
- Complementing the Video Tutorials are detailed and clearly written Help sections explaining "all there is to know" about (a) each decision entry and the relevant cause-effect relationships, (b) the information on each page of the Industry Reports, and (c) the numbers presented in the Company Reports. *The Video Tutorials and the Help screens allow company co-managers to figure things out for themselves, thereby curbing the need for students to ask the instructor "how things work."*
- Built-in chat capability on each screen enables company co-managers to collaborate online in the event that a face-to-face meeting to review results and make decision entries is not convenient (or feasible, as is usually the case for class members taking an online course). Company co-managers can also use their cell phones to talk things over while online looking at the screens.
- Both simulations are quite suitable for use in distance-learning or online courses (and are currently being used in such courses on numerous campuses).
- Participants and instructors are notified via e-mail when the results are ready (usually about 15 to 20 minutes after the decision round deadline specified by the instructor/game administrator).

- Following each decision round, participants are provided with a complete set of reports—a six-page Industry Report, a one-page Competitive Intelligence report for each geographic region that includes strategic group maps and bulleted lists of competitive strengths and weaknesses, and a set of Company Reports (income statement, balance sheet, cash flow statement, and assorted production, marketing, and cost statistics).

- Two "open-book" multiple-choice tests of 20 questions are built into each simulation. The quizzes, which you can require or not as you see fit, are taken online and automatically graded, with scores reported instantaneously to participants and automatically recorded in the instructor's electronic grade book. Students are automatically provided with three sample questions for each test.

- Both simulations contain a three-year strategic plan option that you can assign. Scores on the plan are automatically recorded in the instructor's online grade book.

- At the end of the simulation, you can have students complete online peer evaluations (again, the scores are automatically recorded in your online grade book).

- Both simulations have a Company Presentation feature that enables each team of company co-managers to easily prepare PowerPoint slides for use in describing their strategy and summarizing their company's performance in a presentation to either the class, the instructor, or an "outside" board of directors.

- *A Learning Assurance Report provides you with hard data concerning how well your students performed vis-à-vis students playing the simulation worldwide over the past 12 months.* The report is based on nine measures of student proficiency, business know-how, and decision-making skill and can also be used in evaluating the extent to which your school's academic curriculum produces the desired degree of student learning insofar as accreditation standards are concerned.

For more details on either simulation, please consult Section 2 of the Instructor's Manual accompanying this text or register as an instructor at the simulation Web sites (www.bsg-online.com and www.glo-bus.com) to access even more comprehensive information. Using Internet conferencing technology, the simulation authors conduct seminars several times each month (sometimes each week) to demonstrate how the software works, walk you through the various features and menu options, and answer any questions. By all means, please feel free to call the senior author of this text at (205) 722-9145 to arrange a personal demonstration or talk about how one of the simulations might work in one of your courses. We think you'll be quite impressed with the capabilities that have been programmed into *The Business Strategy Game* and *GLO-BUS,* the simplicity with which both simulations can be administered, and their exceptionally tight connection to the text chapters, core concepts, and standard analytical tools.

RESOURCES AND SUPPORT MATERIALS FOR THE 18TH EDITION

For Students

Key Points Summaries   At the end of each chapter is a synopsis of the core concepts, analytical tools, and other key points discussed in the chapter. These chapter-end synopses, along with the core concept definitions and margin notes scattered throughout each chapter, help students focus on basic strategy principles, digest the messages of each chapter, and prepare for tests.

Two Sets of Chapter-End Exercises   Each chapter concludes with two sets of exercises. The *Assurance of Learning Exercises* can be used as the basis for class discussion, oral presentation assignments, short written reports, and substitutes for case assignments. The *Exercises for Simulation Participants* are designed expressly for use by adopters who have incorporated use of a simulation and want to go a step further in tightly and explicitly connecting the chapter content to the simulation company their students are running. The questions in both sets of exercises (along with those Illustration Capsules that qualify as "mini-cases") can be used to round out the rest of a 75-minute class period should your lecture on a chapter last for only 50 minutes.

A Value-Added Web Site   The student section of the Online Learning Center (OLC) at Web site www.mhhe.com/thompson contains a number of helpful aids:

- Ten-question self-scoring chapter tests that students can take to measure their grasp of the material presented in each of the 12 chapters.
- The "Guide to Case Analysis," containing sections on what a case is, why cases are a standard part of courses in strategy, preparing a case for class discussion, doing a written case analysis, doing an oral presentation, and using financial ratio analysis to assess a company's financial condition. We suggest having students read this guide before the first class discussion of a case.
- PowerPoint slides for each chapter.

The *Connect*™ Management Web-Based Assignment and Assessment Platform   Beginning with this edition, we have taken advantage of the publisher's innovative *Connect*™ assignment and assessment platform and created several features that simplify the task of assigning and grading three types of exercises for students:

- There are self-scoring chapter tests consisting of 20 multiple-choice questions that students can take to measure their grasp of the material presented in each of the 12 chapters.
- There are author-developed Assurance of Learning Exercises for each of the 12 chapters that drill students in the use and application of the concepts and tools of strategic analysis.

All of the *Connect*™ exercises are automatically graded (with the exception of a few exercise components that entail student entry of essay answers), thereby simplifying the task of evaluating each class member's performance and monitoring the learning outcomes. The progress-tracking function built into the *Connect*™ *Management* system enables you to:

- View scored work immediately and track individual or group performance with assignment and grade reports.
- Access an instant view of student or class performance relative to learning objectives.
- Collect data and generate reports required by many accreditation organizations, such as AACSB or EQUIS.

For Instructors

Online Learning Center (OLC)
In addition to the student resources, the instructor section of www.mhhe.com/thompson includes an Instructor's Manual and other support materials. Your McGraw-Hill representative can arrange delivery of instructor support materials in a format-ready Standard Cartridge for Blackboard, WebCT, and other Web-based educational platforms.

Instructor's Manual
The accompanying IM contains a section on suggestions for organizing and structuring your course, sample syllabi and course outlines, a set of lecture notes on each chapter and a copy of the test bank.

Test Bank and EZ Test Online
There is a test bank containing over 900 multiple-choice questions and short-answer/essay questions. It has been tagged with AACSB and Bloom's Taxonomy criteria. All of the test bank questions are also accessible within a computerized test bank powered by McGraw-Hill's flexible electronic testing program EZ Test Online (www.eztestonline.com). Using EZ Test Online allows you to create paper and online tests or quizzes. With EZ Test Online, instructors can select questions from multiple McGraw-Hill test banks or author their own and then either print the test for paper distribution or give it online.

PowerPoint Slides
To facilitate delivery preparation of your lectures and to serve as chapter outlines, you'll have access to approximately 500 colorful and professional-looking slides displaying core concepts, analytical procedures, key points, and all the figures in the text chapters.

Instructor's Resource CD-ROM
All of our instructor supplements are available in this one-stop multimedia resource, which includes the complete Instructor's Manual, computerized test bank (EZ Test), accompanying PowerPoint slides, and the Digital Image Library with all of the figures from the text. It is a useful aid for compiling a syllabus and daily course schedule, preparing customized lectures, and developing tests on the text chapters.

The Business Strategy Game and GLO-BUS Online Simulations
Using one of the two companion simulations is a powerful and constructive way of emotionally connecting students to the subject matter of the course. We know of no more effective and interesting way to stimulate the competitive energy of students and prepare them for the rigors of real-world business decision making than to have them match strategic wits with classmates in running a company in head-to-head competition for global market leadership.

ACKNOWLEDGMENTS

A great number of colleagues and students at various universities, business acquaintances, and people at McGraw-Hill provided inspiration, encouragement, and counsel during the course of this project. Like all text authors in the strategy field, we are intellectually indebted to the many academics whose research and writing have blazed new trails and advanced the discipline of strategic management. In addition, we'd like to thank the following reviewers who provided seasoned advice and splendid suggestions for improving the chapters in this 18th edition:

Joan H. Bailar, Lake Forest Graduate School of Management
David Blair, University of Nebraska at Omaha
Jane Boyland, Johnson & Wales University
William J. Donoher, Missouri State University
Stephen A. Drew, Florida Gulf Coast University
Jo Ann Duffy, Sam Houston State University
Alan Ellstrand, University of Arkansas
Susan Fox-Wolfgramm, Hawaii Pacific University
Rebecca M. Guidice, University of Nevada–Las Vegas
Mark Hoelscher, Illinois State University
Sean D. Jasso, University of California–Riverside
Xin Liang, University of Minnesota–Duluth
Paul Mallette, Colorado State University
Dan Marlin, University of South Florida–St. Petersburg
Raza Mir, William Paterson University
Mansour Moussavi, Johnson & Wales University
James D. Spina, University of Maryland
Monica A. Zimmerman, West Chester University

We also express our thanks to Dennis R. Balch, Jeffrey R. Bruehl, Edith C. Busija, Donald A. Drost, Randall Harris, Mark Lewis Hoelscher, Phyllis Holland, James W. Kroeger, Sal Kukalis, Brian W. Kulik, Paul Mallette, Anthony U. Martinez, Lee Pickler, Sabine Reddy, Thomas D. Schramko, V. Seshan, Charles Strain, Sabine Turnley, S. Stephen Vitucci, Andrew Ward, Sibin Wu, Lynne Patten, Nancy E. Landrum, Jim Goes, Jon Kalinowski, Rodney M. Walter, Judith D. Powell, Seyda Deligonul, David Flanagan, Esmerlda Garbi, Mohsin Habib, Kim Hester, Jeffrey E. McGee, Diana J. Wong, F. William Brown, Anthony F. Chelte, Gregory G. Dess, Alan B. Eisner, John George, Carle M. Hunt, Theresa Marron-Grodsky, Sarah Marsh, Joshua D. Martin, William L. Moore, Donald Neubaum, George M. Puia, Amit Shah, Lois M. Shelton, Mark Weber, Steve Barndt, J. Michael Geringer, Ming-Fang Li, Richard Stackman, Stephen Tallman, Gerardo R. Ungson, James Boulgarides, Betty Diener, Daniel F. Jennings, David Kuhn, Kathryn Martell, Wilbur Mouton, Bobby Vaught, Tuck Bounds, Lee Burk, Ralph Catalanello, William Crittenden, Vince Luchsinger, Stan Mendenhall, John Moore, Will Mulvaney, Sandra Richard, Ralph Roberts, Thomas Turk, Gordon Von Stroh, Fred Zimmerman, S. A. Billion, Charles Byles, Gerald L. Geisler, Rose Knotts, Joseph Rosenstein, James B. Thurman, Ivan Able, W. Harvey Hegarty, Roger Evered, Charles B. Saunders, Rhae M. Swisher, Claude I. Shell, R. Thomas Lenz, Michael C. White, Dennis Callahan, R. Duane Ireland, William E. Burr II, C. W. Millard, Richard Mann, Kurt Christensen, Neil W. Jacobs, Louis W. Fry, D. Robley Wood, George J. Gore, and William R. Soukup. These reviewers provided valuable guidance in steering our efforts to improve earlier editions.

We owe a special debt of gratitude to Catherine Maritan, for her detailed comments on a number of chapters, and to Richard S. Shreve and Anant K. Sundaram, who gave us sage advice regarding the material in Chapter 9. We'd like to thank the following students of the Tuck School of Business for their assistance with the chapter revisions: C. David Morgan, Amy E. Florentino, John R. Moran, Mukund Kulashakeran, Jeffrey L. Boyink, Jonathan D. Keith, Anita Natarajan, Alison F. Connolly, and Melissa E. Vess. And we'd like to acknowledge the help of Dartmouth students Catherine Wu, Jack McNeily, and Jenna Pfeffer, as well as Feldberg librarians Karen Sluzenski and Sarah J. Buckingham and Tuck staff members Annette Lyman, Mary Biathrow, Doreen Aher, and Karen H. Summer.

As always, we value your recommendations and thoughts about the book. Your comments regarding coverage and contents will be taken to heart, and we always are grateful for the time you take to call our attention to printing errors, deficiencies, and other shortcomings. Please e-mail us at athompso@cba.ua.edu, mpeteraf@dartmouth.edu, jgamble@usouthal.edu, or astrickl@cba.ua.edu.

Arthur A. Thompson

Margaret A. Peteraf

John E. Gamble

A. J. Strickland

Chapter Structure and Organization

Part II: Readings in Crafting and Executing Strategy

Section A: What Is Strategy and How Is the Process of Crafting and Executing Strategy Managed? (2 readings)
Section B: Crafting Strategy in Single-Business Companies (7 readings)
Section C: Crafting Strategy in Diversified Companies (1 reading)
Section D: Strategy, Ethics, Social Responsibility, and Sustainability (2 readings)
Section E: Executing Strategy (3 readings)

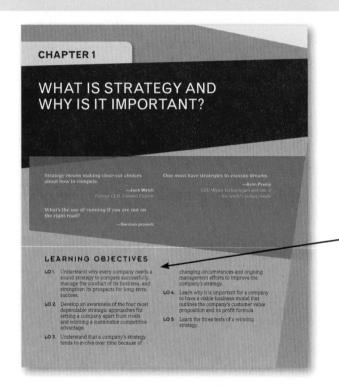

Learning Objectives are listed at the beginning of each chapter; corresponding numbered indicators in the margins show where learning objectives are covered in the text.

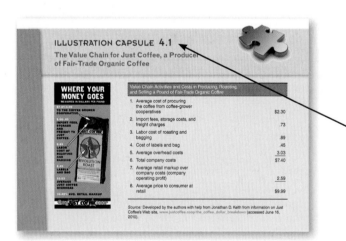

Illustration Capsules appear in boxes throughout each chapter to provide in-depth examples, connect the text presentation to real-world companies, and convincingly demonstrate "strategy in action." Some are appropriate for use as mini-cases.

Margin Notes define core concepts and call attention to important ideas and principles.

and changes taking place in the business environment that might affect the company. The answer to the question *"Where do we want to go from here?"* lies within management's vision of the company's future direction—what new customer groups and customer needs to endeavor to satisfy and what new capabilities to build or acquire. The question *"How are we going to get there?"* challenges managers to craft and execute a strategy capable of moving the company in the intended direction.

Developing clear answers to the question *"How are we going to get there?"* is the essence of managing strategically. Rather than relying on the status quo as a road map and dealing with new opportunities or threats as they emerge, managing strategically involves developing a full-blown game plan that spells out the competitive moves and business approaches that will be employed to compete successfully, attract and please customers, conduct operations, achieve targeted levels of performance, and grow the business. Thus, a company's strategy is all about *how*:

- *How* to outcompete rivals.
- *How* to respond to changing economic and market conditions and capitalize on growth opportunities.
- *How* to manage each functional piece of the business (e.g., R&D, supply chain activities, production, sales and marketing, distribution, finance, and human resources).
- *How* to improve the company's financial and market performance.

CORE CONCEPT

A company's **strategy** consists of the competitive moves and business approaches that managers are employing to compete successfully, improve performance, and grow the business.

The specific elements that constitute management's answer to the question *"How are we going to get there?"* define a company's business strategy. Thus, a company's **strategy** is management's *action plan* for competing successfully and operating profitably, based on an integrated array of considered choices.[1] The crafting of a strategy represents a managerial commitment to pursuing a particular set of actions. In choosing a strategy, management is in effect saying, "Among all the many different business approaches and ways of competing we could have chosen, we have decided to employ this particular combination of approaches in moving the company in the intended direction, strengthening its market position and competitiveness, and boosting performance." The strategic choices a company

22 **Part 1** Concepts and Techniques for Crafting and Executing Strategy

Figure 2.1 **The Strategy-Making, Strategy-Executing Process**

Figure 2.1 displays this five-stage process, which we examine next in some detail.

STAGE 1: DEVELOPING A STRATEGIC VISION, A MISSION, AND A SET OF CORE VALUES

Figures scattered throughout the chapters provide conceptual and analytical frameworks.

KEY POINTS

The strategic management process consists of five interrelated and integrated stages:

1. *Developing a strategic vision* of the company's future, a *mission* that defines the company's current purpose, and a set of *core values* to guide the pursuit of the vision and mission. This managerial step provides direction for the company, motivates and inspires company personnel, aligns and guides actions throughout the organization, and communicates to stakeholders management's aspirations for the company's future.

2. *Setting objectives* to convert the vision and mission into performance targets and using the targeted results as yardsticks for measuring the company's performance. Objectives need to spell out *how much* of *what kind* of performance *by when*. Two broad types of objectives are required: *financial objectives* and *strategic objectives*. A *balanced-scorecard* approach provides a popular method for linking financial objectives to specific, measurable strategic objectives.

3. *Crafting a strategy* to achieve the objectives and move the company along the strategic course that management has charted. Crafting deliberate strategy calls for strategic analysis, based on the business model. Crafting emergent strategy is a learning-by-doing process involving experimentation. Who participates in the process of crafting strategy depends on (1) whether the process is emergent or deliberate and (2) the level of strategy concerned. Deliberate strategies are mostly top-down, while emergent strategies are bottom-up, although both cases require two-way interaction between different types of managers. In large, diversified companies, there are four levels of strategy, each of which involves a corresponding level of management: corporate strategy (multibusiness strategy), business strategy (strategy for individual businesses that compete in a single industry), functional-area strategies within each business (e.g., marketing, R&D, logistics), and operating strategies (for key operating units, such as manufacturing plants). Thus, strategy making is an inclusive, collaborative activity involving not only senior company executives but also the heads of major business divisions, functional-area managers, and operating managers on the frontlines. The larger and more diverse the operations of an enterprise, the more points of strategic initiative it has and the more levels of management that play a significant strategy-making role.

Key Points at the end of each chapter provide a handy summary of essential ideas and things to remember.

ENDNOTES

[1] For a more extended discussion of the problems with the life-cycle hypothesis, see Michael E. Porter, *Competitive Strategy: Techniques for Analyzing Industries and Competitors* (New York: Free Press, 1980), pp. 157–62.
[2] The five-forces model of competition is the creation of Professor Michael Porter of the Harvard Business School. See Michael E. Porter, "How Competitive Forces Shape Strategy," *Harvard Business Review* 57, no. 2 (March–April 1979), pp. 137–45; Porter, *Competitive Strategy*, chap. 1; and Porter's most recent discussion of the model, "The Five Competitive Forces That Shape Strategy," *Harvard Business Review* 86, no. 1 (January 2008), pp. 78–93.
[3] For a discussion of how a company's actions to counter the moves of rival firms tend to escalate competitive pressures, see Pamela J. Derfus, Patrick G. Maggitti, Curtis M.Grimm, and Ken G. Smith, "The Red Queen Effect: Competitive Actions and Firm Performance," *Academy of Management Journal* 51, no. 1 (February 2008), pp. 61–80.
[4] Many of these indicators of whether rivalry produces intense competitive pressures are based on Porter, *Competitive Strategy*, pp. 17–21.

[5] Porter, *Competitive Strategy*, p. 7; Porter, "The Five Competitive Forces That Shape Strategy," p. 81.
[6] The role of entry barriers in shaping the strength of competition in a particular market has long been a standard topic in the literature of microeconomics. For a discussion of how entry barriers affect competitive pressures associated with potential entry, see J. S. Bain, *Barriers to New Competition* (Cambridge, MA: Harvard University Press, 1956); F. M. Scherer, *Industrial Market Structure and Economic Performance*

Exercises at the end of each chapter, linked to learning objectives, provide a basis for class discussion, oral presentations, and written assignments. Several chapters have exercises that qualify as mini-cases.

Web site: www.mhhe.com/thompson The student portion of the Web site features 10-question self-scoring chapter tests, the "Guide to Case Analysis," and PowerPoint slides for each chapter.

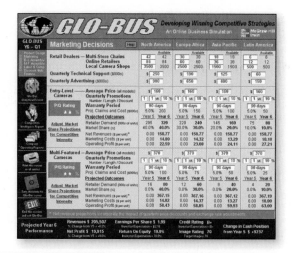

The Business Strategy Game or ***GLO-BUS*** **Simulation Exercises** Either one of these text supplements involves teams of students managing companies in a head-to-head contest for global market leadership. Company co-managers have to make decisions relating to product quality, production, workforce compensation and training, pricing and marketing, and financing of company operations. The challenge is to craft and execute a strategy that is powerful enough to deliver good financial performance despite the competitive efforts of rival companies. Each company competes in North America, Latin America, Europe-Africa, and Asia-Pacific.

BRIEF CONTENTS

PART ONE Concepts and Techniques for Crafting and Executing Strategy

Section A: Introduction and Overview

1 What Is Strategy and Why Is It Important? 50

2 Charting a Company's Direction: Vision and Mission, Objectives, and Strategy 68

Section B: Core Concepts and Analytical Tools

3 Evaluating a Company's External Environment 96

4 Evaluating a Company's Resources, Capabilities, and Competitiveness 138

Section C: Crafting a Strategy

5 The Five Generic Competitive Strategies: Which One to Employ? 182

6 Strengthening a Company's Competitive Position: Strategic Moves, Timing, and Scope of Operations 214

7 Strategies for Competing in International Markets 250

8 Corporate Strategy: Diversification and the Multibusiness Company 292

9 Ethics, Corporate Social Responsibility, Environmental Sustainability, and Strategy 338

Section D: Executing the Strategy

10 Building an Organization Capable of Good Strategy Execution: People, Capabilities, and Structure 374

11 Managing Internal Operations: Actions That Promote Good Strategy Execution 406

12 Corporate Culture and Leadership: Keys to Good Strategy Execution 436

PART TWO Readings in Crafting and Executing Strategy

Section A: What Is Strategy and How Is the Process of Crafting and Executing Strategy Managed?

1 New Business Models in Emerging Markets   R-2

2 The Power of Vision: Statements That Resonate   R-9

Section B: Crafting Strategy in Single-Business Companies

3 Getting into Your Competitor's Head   R-16

4 Operational Capabilities: Hidden in Plain View   R-22

5 Orchestrating the New Dynamic Capabilities   R-33

6 The Battle of the Value Chains: New Specialized versus Old Hybrids   R-41

7 Low-Cost Strategy through Product Architecture: Lessons from China   R-47

8 Managing Strategic Alliances: What Do We Know Now, and Where Do We Go from Here?   R-55

9 How to Win in Emerging Markets   R-73

Section C: Crafting Strategy in Diversified Companies

10 Why Is Synergy So Difficult in Mergers of Related Businesses?   R-79

Section D: Strategy, Ethics, Social Responsibility, and Sustainability

11 When Managers Pressure Employees to Behave Badly: Toward a Comprehensive Response   R-85

12 How to Do Well *and* Do Good   R-94

Section E: Executing Strategy

13 The Secrets to Successful Strategy Execution   R-96

14 Six Sigma at Your Service   R-107

15 Mismanaging Pay and Performance   R-113

Indexes

Company   I1

Name   I7

Subject   I13

TABLE OF CONTENTS

PART ONE Concepts and Techniques for Crafting and Executing Strategy

Section A: Introduction and Overview

1 WHAT IS STRATEGY AND WHY IS IT IMPORTANT? 50

What Do We Mean by *Strategy?* 52

Strategy and the Quest for Competitive Advantage 53
Why a Company's Strategy Evolves over Time 57
A Company's Strategy Is Partly Proactive and Partly Reactive 58

The Relationship between a Company's Strategy and Its Business Model 59

What Makes a Strategy a Winner? 60

Why Crafting and Executing Strategy Are Important Tasks 62

Good Strategy + Good Strategy Execution = Good Management 62

The Road Ahead 63

ILLUSTRATION CAPSULES

1.1 McDonald's Strategy in the Quick-Service Restaurant Industry 55

1.2 Microsoft and Red Hat Linux: Two Contrasting Business Models 61

2 CHARTING A COMPANY'S DIRECTION: VISION AND MISSION, OBJECTIVES, AND STRATEGY 68

What Does the Strategy-Making, Strategy-Executing Process Entail? 69

Stage 1: Developing a Strategic Vision, a Mission, and a Set of Core Values 70

Developing a Strategic Vision 70
Communicating the Strategic Vision 71
Crafting a Mission Statement 74
Linking the Vision and Mission with Company Values 75

Stage 2: Setting Objectives 76

What Kinds of Objectives to Set 76

Stage 3: Crafting a Strategy 81

Strategy Making Involves Managers at All Organizational Levels 81
A Strategic Vision + Objectives + Strategy = A Strategic Plan 85

Stage 4: Executing the Strategy 86

Stage 5: Evaluating Performance and Initiating Corrective Adjustments   87

Corporate Governance: The Role of the Board of Directors in the Strategy-Crafting, Strategy-Executing Process   88

ILLUSTRATION CAPSULES

2.1   Examples of Strategic Visions—How Well Do They Measure Up?   73

2.2   Royal Dutch Shell Mission, Core Values, and Business Principles   77

2.3   Examples of Company Objectives   80

2.4   Corporate Governance Failures at Fannie Mae and Freddie Mac   90

Section B: Core Concepts and Analytical Tools

3 EVALUATING A COMPANY'S EXTERNAL ENVIRONMENT   96

The Strategically Relevant Components of a Company's Macro-Environment   98

Thinking Strategically about a Company's Industry and Competitive Environment   100

Question 1: Does the Industry Offer Attractive Opportunities for Growth?   101

Question 2: What Kinds of Competitive Forces Are Industry Members Facing, and How Strong Are They?   102

Competitive Pressures Created by the Rivalry among Competing Sellers   102
Competitive Pressures Associated with the Threat of New Entrants   107
Competitive Pressures from the Sellers of Substitute Products   111
Competitive Pressures Stemming from Supplier Bargaining Power   112
Competitive Pressures Stemming from Buyer Bargaining Power and Price Sensitivity   115
Is the Collective Strength of the Five Competitive Forces Conducive to Good Profitability?   118

Question 3: What Factors Are Driving Industry Change, and What Impacts Will They Have?   120

Analyzing Industry Dynamics   120
Identifying an Industry's Drivers of Change   120
Assessing the Impact of the Factors Driving Industry Change   124
Developing a Strategy That Takes the Changes in Industry Conditions into Account   125

Question 4: How Are Industry Rivals Positioned—Who Is Strongly Positioned and Who Is Not?   125

Using Strategic Group Maps to Assess the Market Positions of Key Competitors   126
What Can Be Learned from Strategic Group Maps?   127

Question 5: What Strategic Moves Are Rivals Likely to Make Next?   128

Question 6: What Are the Key Factors for Future Competitive Success?   130

Question 7: Does the Industry Offer Good Prospects for Attractive Profits?   131

ILLUSTRATION CAPSULE

3.1   Comparative Market Positions of Selected Retail Chains: A Strategic Group Map Example   127

4 EVALUATING A COMPANY'S RESOURCES, CAPABILITIES, AND COMPETITIVENESS   138

Question 1: How Well Is the Company's Present Strategy Working?   140

Question 2: What are the Company's Competitively Important Resources and Capabilities?   141

Identifying the Company's Resources and Capabilities   144
Determining Whether a Company's Resources and Capabilities Are Potent Enough to Produce a Sustainable Competitive Advantage   147

Question 3: Is the Company Able To Seize Market Opportunities and Nullify External Threats?   150

Identifying a Company's Internal Strengths   151
Identifying Company Weaknesses and Competitive Deficiencies   152
Identifying a Company's Market Opportunities   152
Identifying the Threats to a Company's Future Profitability   153
What Do the SWOT Listings Reveal?   155

Question 4: Are the Company's Prices and Costs Competitive with Those of Key Rivals, and Does It Have an Appealing Customer Value Proposition?   156

The Concept of a Company Value Chain   157
The Value Chain System for an Entire Industry   161
Benchmarking: A Tool for Assessing Whether the Costs and Effectiveness of a Company's Value Chain Activities Are in Line   162
Strategic Options for Remedying a Disadvantage in Costs or Effectiveness   163
Translating Proficient Performance of Value Chain Activities into Competitive Advantage   166

Question 5: Is the Company Competitively Stronger or Weaker than Key Rivals?   168

Strategic Implications of Competitive Strength Assessments   172

Question 6: What Strategic Issues and Problems Merit Front-Burner Managerial Attention?   173

ILLUSTRATION CAPSULES

4.1   The Value Chain for Just Coffee, a Producer of Fair-Trade Organic Coffee   160
4.2   Benchmarking and Ethical Conduct   164

Section C: Crafting a Strategy

5 THE FIVE GENERIC COMPETITIVE STRATEGIES: WHICH ONE TO EMPLOY?   182

The Five Generic Competitive Strategies   183

Low-Cost Provider Strategies   185

The Two Major Avenues for Achieving a Cost Advantage   185
The Keys to Being a Successful Low-Cost Provider   190
When a Low-Cost Provider Strategy Works Best   192
Pitfalls to Avoid in Pursuing a Low-Cost Provider Strategy   193

Broad Differentiation Strategies   193

Managing the Value Chain to Create the Differentiating Attributes   194
Delivering Superior Value via a Broad Differentiation Strategy   197
When a Differentiation Strategy Works Best   199
Pitfalls to Avoid in Pursuing a Differentiation Strategy   199

Focused (Or Market Niche) Strategies   201

A Focused Low-Cost Strategy   201
A Focused Differentiation Strategy   201
When a Focused Low-Cost or Focused Differentiation Strategy Is Attractive   202
The Risks of a Focused Low-Cost or Focused Differentiation Strategy   203

Best-Cost Provider Strategies   205

When a Best-Cost Provider Strategy Works Best   206
The Big Risk of a Best-Cost Provider Strategy   207

The Contrasting Features of the Five Generic Competitive Strategies: A Summary   208

Successful Competitive Strategies Are Resource-Based   210

ILLUSTRATION CAPSULES

5.1 How Walmart Managed Its Value Chain to Achieve a Huge Low-Cost Advantage over Rival Supermarket Chains   191

5.2 Vizio's Focused Low-Cost Strategy   203

5.3 Nestlé Nespresso's Focused Differentiation Strategy in the Coffee Industry   204

5.4 Toyota's Best-Cost Provider Strategy for Its Lexus Line   207

6 STRENGTHENING A COMPANY'S COMPETITIVE POSITION: STRATEGIC MOVES, TIMING, AND SCOPE OF OPERATIONS   214

Going on the Offensive—Strategic Options to Improve a Company's Market Position   215

Choosing the Basis for Competitive Attack   216
Choosing Which Rivals to Attack   218
Blue-Ocean Strategy—A Special Kind of Offensive   219

Defensive Strategies—Protecting Market Position and Competitive
Advantage   220

   Blocking the Avenues Open to Challengers   220
   Signaling Challengers That Retaliation Is Likely   221

Timing a Company's Offensive and Defensive Strategic Moves   221

   The Potential for First-Mover Advantages   221
   *The Potential for First-Mover Disadvantages or Late-Mover
   Advantages   223*
   To Be a First Mover or Not   224

Strengthening a Company's Market Position via Its Scope of
Operations   225

Horizontal Merger and Acquisition Strategies   226

   *Why Mergers and Acquisitions Sometimes Fail to Produce Anticipated
   Results   229*

Vertical Integration Strategies   229

   The Advantages of a Vertical Integration Strategy   231
   The Disadvantages of a Vertical Integration Strategy   233
   Weighing the Pros and Cons of Vertical Integration   234

Outsourcing Strategies: Narrowing the Scope of Operations   235

   The Big Risk of Outsourcing Value Chain Activities   236

Strategic Alliances and Partnerships   237

   Why and How Strategic Alliances Are Advantageous   240
   Capturing the Benefits of Strategic Alliances   241
   *The Drawbacks of Strategic Alliances
   and Partnerships   242*
   How to Make Strategic Alliances Work   243

ILLUSTRATION CAPSULES

6.1   Amazon.com's First-Mover Advantage in Online Retailing   224
6.2   Clear Channel Communications: Using Mergers and Acquisitions
    to Become a Global Market Leader in Radio Broadcasting   230

**7 STRATEGIES FOR COMPETING IN
INTERNATIONAL MARKETS**   250

Why Companies Decide to Enter Foreign Markets   252

Why Competing across National Borders Makes Strategy Making More
Complex   253

   *Cross-Country Variation in Factors That Affect Industry
   Competitiveness   253*
   Locating Value Chain Activities for Competitive Advantage   255
   *The Impact of Government Policies and Economic Conditions in Host
   Countries   256*
   The Risks of Adverse Exchange Rate Shifts   257
   *Cross-Country Differences in Demographic, Cultural, and Market
   Conditions   259*

The Concepts of Multidomestic Competition and Global Competition   260

Strategic Options for Entering and Competing in International Markets   262

Export Strategies   262
Licensing Strategies   263
Franchising Strategies   263
Acquisition Strategies   264
Greenfield Venture Strategies   264
Alliance and Joint Venture Strategies   265

Competing Internationally: The Three Main Strategic Approaches   268

Multidomestic Strategy—Think Local, Act Local   269
Global Strategy—Think Global, Act Global   271
Transnational Strategy—Think Global, Act Local   272

The Quest for Competitive Advantage in the International Arena   273

Using Location to Build Competitive Advantage   273
Sharing and Transferring Resources and Capabilities across Borders to Build Competitive Advantage   275
Using Cross-Border Coordination for Competitive Advantage   277

Profit Sanctuaries and Cross-Border Strategic Moves   277

Using Cross-Market Subsidization to Wage a Strategic Offensive   279
Using Cross-Border Tactics to Defend against International Rivals   280

Strategies for Competing in the Markets of Developing Countries   280

Strategy Options for Competing in Developing-Country Markets   281

Defending against Global Giants: Strategies for Local Companies In Developing Countries   284

ILLUSTRATION CAPSULES

7.1   Four Examples of Cross-Border Strategic Alliances   267
7.2   Yum! Brands' Strategy for Becoming the Leading Food Service Brand in China   282
7.3   How Ctrip Successfully Defended against International Rivals to Become China's Largest Online Travel Agency   285

8 **CORPORATE STRATEGY: DIVERSIFICATION AND THE MULTIBUSINESS COMPANY**   292

When to Diversify   294

Building Shareholder Value: The Ultimate Justification for Diversifying   295

Strategies for Entering New Businesses   296

Acquisition of an Existing Business   296
Internal Development   297
Joint Ventures   298
Choosing a Mode of Entry   298

Choosing the Diversification Path: Related versus Unrelated Businesses   300

Strategic Fit and Diversification into Related Businesses   300

Identifying Cross-Business Strategic Fit along the Value Chain   304
Strategic Fit, Economies of Scope, and Competitive Advantage   306

Diversification into Unrelated Businesses   307

Building Shareholder Value via Unrelated Diversification   308
The Path to Greater Shareholder Value through Unrelated Diversification   310
The Drawbacks of Unrelated Diversification   311
Inadequate Reasons for Pursuing Unrelated Diversification   312

Combination Related-Unrelated Diversification Strategies   313

Evaluating the Strategy of a Diversified Company   313

Step 1: Evaluating Industry Attractiveness   314
Step 2: Evaluating Business-Unit Competitive Strength   317
Step 3: Checking the Competitive Advantage Potential of Cross-Business Strategic Fit   321
Step 4: Checking for Resource Fit   322
Step 5: Ranking the Performance Prospects of Business Units and Assigning a Priority for Resource Allocation   325
Step 6: Crafting New Strategic Moves to Improve Overall Corporate Performance   326

ILLUSTRATION CAPSULE

8.1   Managing Diversification at Johnson & Johnson: The Benefits of Cross-Business Strategic Fit   329

9 ETHICS, CORPORATE SOCIAL RESPONSIBILITY, ENVIRONMENTAL SUSTAINABILITY, AND STRATEGY   338

What Do We Mean by *Business Ethics*?   339

Where Do Ethical Standards Come From—Are They Universal or Dependent on Local Norms?   340

The School of Ethical Universalism   340
The School of Ethical Relativism   342
Ethics and Integrative Social Contracts Theory   345

How and Why Ethical Standards Impact the Tasks of Crafting and Executing Strategy   346

What Are the Drivers of Unethical Strategies and Business Behavior?   348

Why Should Company Strategies Be Ethical?   352

The Moral Case for an Ethical Strategy   354
The Business Case for Ethical Strategies   354

Strategy, Corporate Social Responsibility, and Environmental Sustainability   356

What Do We Mean by Corporate Social Responsibility?   356
What Do We Mean by Sustainability and Sustainable Business Practices?   362
Crafting Corporate Social Responsibility and Sustainability Strategies   364
The Moral Case for Corporate Social Responsibility and Environmentally Sustainable Business Practices   365
The Business Case for Corporate Social Responsibility and Environmentally Sustainable Business Practices   366

ILLUSTRATION CAPSULES

9.1   Many of Apple's Suppliers Flunk the Ethics Test   341

9.2   Investment Fraud at Bernard L. Madoff Investment Securities and Stanford Financial Group   350

9.3   How General Electric's Top Management Built a Culture That Fuses High Performance with High Integrity   353

9.4   John Deere's Approach to Corporate Social Responsibility   359

Section D: Executing the Strategy

10 BUILDING AN ORGANIZATION CAPABLE OF GOOD STRATEGY EXECUTION: PEOPLE, CAPABILITIES, AND STRUCTURE   374

A Framework for Executing Strategy   376
The Principal Components of the Strategy Execution Process   377

Building an Organization Capable of Good Strategy Execution: Where to Begin   379

Staffing the Organization   381
Putting Together a Strong Management Team   381
Recruiting, Training, and Retaining Capable Employees   382

Building and Strengthening Core Competencies and Competitive Capabilities   385
Three Approaches to Building and Strengthening Capabilities   385
Upgrading Employee Skills and Knowledge Resources   389
Strategy Execution Capabilities and Competitive Advantage   390

Organizing the Work Effort with a Supportive Organizational Structure   390
Deciding Which Value Chain Activities to Perform Internally and Which to Outsource   391
Aligning the Firm's Organizational Structure with Its Strategy   393
Determining How Much Authority to Delegate   397
Facilitating Collaboration with External Partners and Strategic Allies   400
Further Perspectives on Structuring the Work Effort   401

ILLUSTRATION CAPSULES

10.1 How General Electric Develops a Talented and Deep Management Team   383

10.2 Toyota's Legendary Production System: A Capability That Translates into Competitive Advantage   387

11 MANAGING INTERNAL OPERATIONS: ACTIONS THAT PROMOTE GOOD STRATEGY EXECUTION   406

Allocating Resources to the Strategy Execution Effort   407

Instituting Policies and Procedures That Facilitate Strategy Execution   409

Using Process Management Tools to Strive for Continuous Improvement   411

How the Process of Identifying and Incorporating Best Practices Works   411
Business Process Reengineering, Total Quality Management, and Six Sigma Quality Programs: Tools for Promoting Operating Excellence   413
Capturing the Benefits of Initiatives to Improve Operations   419

Installing Information and Operating Systems   420

Instituting Adequate Information Systems, Performance Tracking, and Controls   422

Tying Rewards and Incentives to Strategy Execution   423

Incentives and Motivational Practices That Facilitate Good Strategy Execution   424
Striking the Right Balance between Rewards and Punishment   425
Linking Rewards to Strategically Relevant Performance Outcomes   427

ILLUSTRATION CAPSULES

11.1 Whirlpool's Use of Six Sigma to Promote Operating Excellence   417
11.2 What Companies Do to Motivate and Reward Employees   426
11.3 Nucor Corporation: Tying Incentives Directly to Strategy Execution   429

12 CORPORATE CULTURE AND LEADERSHIP: KEYS TO GOOD STRATEGY EXECUTION   436

Instilling a Corporate Culture That Promotes Good Strategy Execution   437

Identifying the Key Features of a Company's Corporate Culture   438
Company Cultures Can Be Strongly or Weakly Embedded   443
Why Corporate Cultures Matter to the Strategy Execution Process   445
Healthy Cultures That Aid Good Strategy Execution   446
Unhealthy Cultures That Impede Good Strategy Execution   448
Changing a Problem Culture: The Role of Leadership   450

Leading the Strategy Execution Process   454

Staying on Top of How Well Things Are Going   455

Putting Constructive Pressure on Organizational Units to Execute the Strategy Well and Achieve Operating Excellence 455
Leading the Process of Making Corrective Adjustments 457

A Final Word on Leading the Process of Crafting and Executing Strategy 458

ILLUSTRATION CAPSULE

12.1 The Corporate Cultures at Google and Alberto-Culver 439

PART TWO Readings in Crafting and Executing Strategy

Section A: What Is Strategy and How Is the Process of Crafting and Executing Strategy Managed?

1 New Business Models in Emerging Markets R-2

Matthew J. Eyring, Innosight
Mark W. Johnson, Innosight
Hari Nair, Innosight Venture Partner

2 The Power of Vision: Statements That Resonate R-9

Sooksan Kantabutra, Madihol University, Bangkok, Thailand
Gayle C. Avery, Macquarie University, Sydney, Australia

Section B: Crafting Strategy in Single-Business Companies

3 Getting into Your Competitor's Head R-16

Hugh Courtney, University of Maryland
John T. Horn, McKinsey & Company
Jayanti Kar, McKinsey & Company

4 Operational Capabilities: Hidden in Plain View R-22

Barbara B. Flynn, Indiana University
Sarah Jinhui Wu, Fordham University
Steven Melnyk, Michigan State University

5 Orchestrating the New Dynamic Capabilities R-33

Amy Shuen, CEIBS (China Europe International Business School)
Sandra Sieber, IESE Business School, University of Navarra, Spain

6 The Battle of the Value Chains: New Specialized versus Old Hybrids R-41

Gillis Jonk, A. T. Kearney
Martin Handschuh, A. T. Kearney
Sandra Niewiem, A. T. Kearney

7 Low-Cost Strategy through Product Architecture: Lessons from China R-47

Hua Wang, Euromed Management Ecole de Marseille, France
Chris Kimble, Euromed Management Ecole de Marseille, France

8   Managing Strategic Alliances: What Do We Know Now, and Where Do We Go from Here?   R-55
      Prashant Kale, Rice University
      Harbir Singh, University of Pennsylvania

9   How to Win in Emerging Markets   R-73
      Satish Shankar, Bain & Co.
      Charles Ormiston, Bain & Co.
      Nicolas Bloch, Bain & Co.
      Robert Schaus, Bain & Co.
      Vijay Vishwanath, Bain & Co.

Section C: Crafting Strategy in Diversified Companies

10   Why Is Synergy So Difficult in Mergers of Related Businesses?   R-79
      Sayan Chatterjee, Case Western Reserve University

Section D: Strategy, Ethics, Social Responsibility, and Sustainability

11   When Managers Pressure Employees to Behave Badly: Toward a Comprehensive Response   R-85
      Bennett J. Tepper, Georgia State University

12   How to Do Well *and* Do Good   R-94
      Rosabeth Moss Kanter, Harvard Business School

Section E: Executing Strategy

13   The Secrets to Successful Strategy Execution   R-96
      Gary L. Neilson, Booz & Company
      Karla L. Martin, Booz & Company
      Elizabeth Powers, Booz & Company

14   Six Sigma at Your Service   R-107
      Peter Guarraia, Bain and Company
      Gib Carey, Bain and Company
      Alistair Corbett, Bain and Company
      Klaus Neuhaus, Bain and Company

15   Mismanaging Pay and Performance   R-113
      Rupert Merson, London Business School

INDEXES

Company   I1

Name   I7

Subject   I13

PART 1

Concepts and Techniques for Crafting and Executing Strategy

CHAPTER 1

WHAT IS STRATEGY AND WHY IS IT IMPORTANT?

Strategy means making clear-cut choices about how to compete.

—Jack Welch
Former CEO, General Electric

What's the use of running if you are not on the right road?

—German proverb

One must have strategies to execute dreams.

—Azim Premji
CEO Wipro Technologies and one of the world's richest people

LEARNING OBJECTIVES

LO 1. Understand why every company needs a sound strategy to compete successfully, manage the conduct of its business, and strengthen its prospects for long-term success.

LO 2. Develop an awareness of the four most dependable strategic approaches for setting a company apart from rivals and winning a sustainable competitive advantage.

LO 3. Understand that a company's strategy tends to evolve over time because of changing circumstances and ongoing management efforts to improve the company's strategy.

LO 4. Learn why it is important for a company to have a viable business model that outlines the company's customer value proposition and its profit formula.

LO 5. Learn the three tests of a winning strategy.

In any given year, a group of companies will stand out as the top performers, in terms of metrics such as profitability, sales growth, or growth in shareholder value. Some of these companies will find that their star status fades quickly, due to little more than a fortuitous constellation of circumstances, such as being in the right business at the right time. But other companies somehow manage to rise to the top and stay there, year after year, pleasing their customers, shareholders, and other stakeholders alike in the process. Companies such as Apple, Google, Coca-Cola, Procter & Gamble, McDonald's, and Microsoft come to mind—but long-lived success is not just the province of U.S. companies. Diverse kinds of companies, both large and small, from many different countries have been able to sustain strong performance records, including Sweden's IKEA (in home furnishings), Australia's BHP Billiton (in mining), Korea's Hyundai Heavy Industries (in shipbuilding and construction), Mexico's America Movil (in telecommunications), and Japan's Nintendo (in video game systems).

What can explain the ability of companies like these to beat the odds and experience prolonged periods of profitability and growth? Why is it that some companies, like Southwest Airlines and Walmart, continue to do well even when others in their industry are faltering? Why can some companies survive and prosper even through economic downturns and industry turbulence?

Many factors enter into a full explanation of a company's performance, of course. Some come from the external environment; others are internal to the firm. But only one thing can account for the kind of long-lived success records that we see in the world's greatest companies—and that is a cleverly crafted and well executed *strategy*, one that facilitates the capture of emerging opportunities, produces enduringly good performance, is adaptable to changing business conditions, and can withstand the competitive challenges from rival firms.

In this opening chapter, we define the concept of strategy and describe its many facets. We will explain what is meant by a competitive advantage, discuss the relationship between a company's strategy and its business model, and introduce you to the kinds of competitive strategies that can give a company an advantage over rivals in attracting customers and earning above-average profits. We will look at what sets a winning strategy apart from others and why the caliber of a company's strategy determines whether it will enjoy a competitive advantage over other firms or be burdened by competitive disadvantage. By the end of this chapter, you will have a clear idea of why the tasks of crafting and executing strategy are core management functions and why excellent execution of an excellent strategy is the most reliable recipe for turning a company into a standout performer over a long-term horizon.

WHAT DO WE MEAN BY *STRATEGY*?

LO 1

Understand why
every company
needs a sound
strategy to compete
successfully,
manage the conduct
of its business,
and strengthen its
prospects for long-
term success.

In moving a company forward, managers of all types of organizations—small family-owned businesses, rapidly growing entrepreneurial firms, not-for-profit organizations, and the world's leading multinational corporations—face the same three central questions:

- What is our present situation?
- Where do we want to go from here?
- How are we going to get there?

The first question, *"What is our present situation?"* prompts managers to evaluate industry conditions, the company's current financial performance and market standing, its resources and capabilities, its competitive strengths and weaknesses, and changes taking place in the business environment that might affect the company. The answer to the question *"Where do we want to go from here?"* lies within management's vision of the company's future direction—what new customer groups and customer needs to endeavor to satisfy and what new capabilities to build or acquire. The question *"How are we going to get there?"* challenges managers to craft and execute a strategy capable of moving the company in the intended direction.

Developing clear answers to the question *"How are we going to get there?"* is the essence of managing strategically. Rather than relying on the status quo as a road map and dealing with new opportunities or threats as they emerge, managing strategically involves developing a full-blown game plan that spells out the competitive moves and business approaches that will be employed to compete successfully, attract and please customers, conduct operations, achieve targeted levels of performance, and grow the business. Thus, a company's strategy is all about *how:*

- *How* to outcompete rivals.
- *How* to respond to changing economic and market conditions and capitalize on growth opportunities.
- *How* to manage each functional piece of the business (e.g., R&D, supply chain activities, production, sales and marketing, distribution, finance, and human resources).
- *How* to improve the company's financial and market performance.

CORE CONCEPT

A company's **strategy**
consists of the competi-
tive moves and business
approaches that managers
are employing to compete
successfully, improve performance, and grow the
business.

The specific elements that constitute management's answer to the question *"How are we going to get there?"* define a company's business strategy. Thus, a company's **strategy** is management's *action plan* for competing successfully and operating profitably, based on an integrated array of considered choices.[1] The crafting of a strategy represents a managerial commitment to pursuing a particular set of actions. In choosing a strategy, management is in effect saying, "Among all the many different business approaches and ways of competing we could have chosen, we have decided to employ this particular combination of approaches in moving the company in the intended direction, strengthening its market position and competitiveness, and boosting performance." The strategic choices a company makes are seldom easy decisions and often involve difficult trade-offs—but that does not excuse failure to pursue a concrete course of action.[2]

In most industries, there are many different avenues for outcompeting rivals and boosting company performance, thus giving managers considerable freedom in choosing the specific elements of their company's strategy.[3] Consequently, some companies strive to improve their performance by employing strategies aimed at achieving lower costs than rivals, while others pursue strategies aimed at achieving product superiority or personalized customer service or quality dimensions that rivals cannot match. Some companies opt for wide product lines, while others concentrate their energies on a narrow product lineup. Some position themselves in only one part of the industry's chain of production/distribution activities (preferring to be just in manufacturing or wholesale distribution or retailing), while others are partially or fully integrated, with operations ranging from components production to manufacturing and assembly to wholesale distribution and retailing. Some competitors deliberately confine their operations to local or regional markets; others opt to compete nationally, internationally (several countries), or globally (all or most of the major country markets worldwide). Some companies decide to operate in only one industry, while others diversify broadly or narrowly into related or unrelated industries.

There is no shortage of opportunity to fashion a strategy that both tightly fits a company's own particular situation and is discernibly different from the strategies of rivals. In fact, competitive success requires a company's managers to make strategic choices about the key building blocks of its strategy that differ from the choices made by competitors—not 100 percent different but at least different in several important respects. A strategy stands a better chance of succeeding when it is predicated on actions, business approaches, and competitive moves aimed at appealing to buyers *in ways that set a company apart from rivals.* Simply trying to mimic the strategies of the industry's successful companies rarely works. Rather, every company's strategy needs to have some distinctive element that draws in customers and produces a competitive edge. Strategy, at its essence, is about competing differently—doing what rival firms *don't* do or what rival firms *can't* do.[4]

> Strategy is about competing differently from rivals—doing what competitors *don't* do or, even better, doing what they *can't* do! Every strategy needs a distinctive element that attracts customers and produces a competitive edge.

A company's strategy provides direction and guidance, in terms of not only what the company *should* do but also what it *should not* do. Knowing what not to do can be as important as knowing what to do, strategically. At best, making the wrong strategic moves will prove a distraction and a waste of company resources. At worst, it can bring about unintended long-term consequences that put the company's very survival at risk.

Figure 1.1 illustrates the broad types of actions and approaches that often characterize a company's strategy in a particular business or industry. For a more concrete example of the specific actions constituting a firm's strategy, see Illustration Capsule 1.1, describing McDonald's strategy in the quick-service restaurant industry.

Strategy and the Quest for Competitive Advantage

The heart and soul of any strategy is the actions and moves in the marketplace that managers are taking to gain a competitive edge over rivals. A creative, distinctive strategy that sets a company apart from rivals and

CORE CONCEPT

A company achieves **sustainable competitive advantage** when it can meet customer needs more effectively or efficiently than rivals and when the basis for this is durable, despite the best efforts of competitors to match or surpass this advantage.

Figure 1.1   **Identifying a Company's Strategy—What to Look For**

Actions to gain sales and market share via more performance features, more appealing design, better quality or customer service, wider product selection, or other such actions

Actions to strengthen the firm's bargaining position with suppliers, distributors, and others

Actions to gain sales and market share with lower prices based on lower costs

Actions to upgrade, build, or acquire competitively important resources and capabilities

Actions to enter new product or geographic markets or to exit existing ones

THE PATTERN OF ACTIONS AND BUSINESS APPROACHES THAT DEFINE A COMPANY'S STRATEGY

Actions and approaches used in managing R&D, production, sales and marketing, finance, and other key activities

Actions to capture emerging market opportunities and defend against external threats to the company's business prospects

Actions to strengthen competitiveness via strategic alliances and collaborative partnerships

Actions to strengthen market standing and competitiveness by acquiring or merging with other companies

provides a competitive advantage is a company's most reliable ticket for earning above-average profits. Competing in the marketplace on the basis of a competitive advantage tends to be more profitable than competing with no advantage. And a company is almost certain to earn significantly higher profits when it enjoys a competitive advantage as opposed to when it is hamstrung by competitive disadvantage.

Competitive advantage comes from an ability to meet customer needs more *effectively,* with products or services that customers value more highly, or more *efficiently,* at lower cost. Meeting customer needs more effectively can translate into the ability to command a higher price (e.g., Godiva chocolate), which can improve profits by boosting revenues. Meeting customer needs more cost-effectively can translate into being able to charge lower prices and achieve higher sales volumes (e.g., Walmart), thereby improving profits on the revenue side as well as the cost side. Furthermore, if a company's competitive edge holds promise for being sustainable (as opposed to just temporary), then so much the better for both the strategy and the company's future profitability. What makes a competitive advantage **sustainable** (or durable), as opposed to temporary, are elements of the strategy that give buyers *lasting reasons to prefer* a company's products or services over those of competitors—reasons that competitors are unable to nullify or overcome despite their best efforts.

LO 2

Develop an awareness of the four most-dependable strategic approaches for setting a company apart from rivals and winning a sustainable competitive advantage.

ILLUSTRATION CAPSULE 1.1

McDonald's Strategy in the Quick-Service Restaurant Industry

In 2010, McDonald's was setting new sales records despite a global economic slowdown and declining consumer confidence in the United States. More than 60 million customers visited one of McDonald's 32,000 restaurants in 117 countries each day, which allowed the company to record 2009 revenues and earnings of more than $22.7 billion and $6.8 billion, respectively. McDonald's performance in the marketplace made it one of only two companies listed on the Dow Jones Industrial Average (the other was Walmart Stores, Inc.) that actually increased in share value in spite of the economic meltdown. The company's sales were holding up well amid the ongoing economic uncertainty in early 2010, with global sales as measured in constant currencies increasing by more than 4 percent in the first quarter. Its combined operating margin had risen to nearly 30 percent. The company's success was a result of its well-conceived and executed Plan-to-Win strategy that focused on "being better, not just bigger." Key initiatives of the Plan-to-Win strategy included:

- *Improved restaurant operations.* McDonald's global restaurant operations improvement process involved employee training programs ranging from on-the-job training for new crew members to college-level management courses offered at the company's Hamburger University. The company also sent nearly 200 high-potential employees annually to its McDonald's Leadership Institute to build the leadership skills needed by its next generation of senior managers. McDonald's commitment to employee development earned the company a place on *Fortune*'s list of Top 25 Global Companies for Leaders in 2010. The company also trained its store managers to closely monitor labor, food, and utility costs.

- *Affordable pricing.* In addition to tackling operating costs in each of its restaurants, McDonald's kept its prices low by closely scrutinizing administrative costs and other corporate expenses. McDonald's saw the poor economy in the United States as an opportunity to renegotiate its advertising contracts with newspapers and television networks in early 2009. The company also began

to replace its company-owned vehicles with more fuel-efficient models when gasoline prices escalated dramatically in the United States during 2008. However, McDonald's did not choose to sacrifice product quality in order to offer lower prices. The company implemented extensive supplier monitoring programs to ensure that its suppliers did not change product specifications to lower costs. For example, the company's chicken breasts were routinely checked for weight when arriving from suppliers' production facilities. The company's broad approach to minimizing non-value-adding expenses allowed it to offer more items on its Dollar Menu in the United States, its Ein Mal Eins menu in Germany, and its 100 Yen menu in Japan.

- *Wide menu variety and beverage choices.* McDonald's has expanded its menu beyond the popular-selling Big Mac and Quarter Pounder to include such new, healthy quick-service items as grilled chicken salads, chicken snack wraps, and premium chicken sandwiches in the United States, Lemon Shrimp Burgers in Germany, and Ebi shrimp wraps in Japan. The company has also added an extensive line of premium coffees that include espressos,

(continued)

cappuccinos, and lattes sold in its McCafe restaurant locations in the United States, Europe, and the Asia/Pacific region. McDonald's latte was judged "as good [as] or better" than lattes sold by Starbucks or Dunkin' Donuts in a review by the *Chicago Tribune*'s Good Eating and Dining staff in December 2008.

• *Convenience and expansion of dining opportunities.* The addition of McCafes helped McDonald's increase same store sales by extending traditional dining hours. Customers wanting a midmorning coffee or an afternoon snack helped keep store traffic high after McDonald's had sold its last Egg McMuffin, McGriddle, or chicken biscuit and before the lunch crowd arrived to order Big Macs, Quarter Pounders, chicken sandwiches, or salads. The company also extended its drive-thru hours to 24 hours in more than 25,000 locations in cities around the world where consumers tended to eat at all hours of the day and night. At many high-traffic locations in the United States, double drive-thru lanes were added to serve customers more quickly.

• *Ongoing restaurant reinvestment and international expansion.* With more than 14,000 restaurants in the United States, the focus of McDonald's expansion of units was in rapidly growing emerging markets such as Russia and China. The company opened 125 new restaurants in China and 40 new restaurants in Russia in 2008. The company also refurbished about 10,000 of its locations in the United States between 2004 and 2008 as a part of its McCafe rollout and as a way to make its restaurants pleasant places for both customers to dine and employees to work.

Sources: Janet Adamy, "McDonald's Seeks Way to Keep Sizzling," *Wall Street Journal Online,* March 10, 2009; various annual reports; various company press releases.

Four of the most frequently used and dependable strategic approaches to setting a company apart from rivals, building strong customer loyalty, and winning a competitive advantage are:

1. *Striving to be the industry's low-cost provider, thereby aiming for a cost-based competitive advantage over rivals.* Walmart and Southwest Airlines have earned strong market positions because of the low-cost advantages they have achieved over their rivals and their consequent ability to underprice competitors. These advantages in meeting customer needs *efficiently* have translated into volume advantages, with Walmart as the world's largest discount retailer and Southwest as the largest U.S. air carrier, based on the number of domestic passengers.[5]

2. *Outcompeting rivals on the basis of differentiating features, such as higher quality, wider product selection, added performance, value-added services, more attractive styling, and technological superiority.* Successful adopters of differentiation strategies include Apple (innovative products), Johnson & Johnson in baby products (product reliability), Rolex (top-of-the-line prestige), and Mercedes (engineering design). These companies have achieved a competitive advantage because of their ability to meet customer needs more effectively than rivals can, thus driving up their customers' willingness to pay higher prices. One way to sustain this type of competitive advantage is to be sufficiently innovative to thwart the efforts of clever rivals to copy or closely imitate the product offering.

3. *Focusing on a narrow market niche and winning a competitive edge by doing a better job than rivals of serving the special needs and tastes of buyers in the niche.* Firms using a focus strategy can achieve an advantage through either greater efficiency in serving the niche or greater effectiveness in meeting the special needs. Prominent companies that enjoy competitive success in a specialized market niche include eBay in online auctions, Jiffy Lube International

in quick oil changes, McAfee in virus protection software, and The Weather Channel in cable TV.

4. *Aiming to offer the lowest (best) prices for differentiated goods that at least match the features and performance of higher-priced rival brands.* This is known as a *best-cost provider strategy,* and it rests on the ability to be the most cost-effective provider of an upscale product or service. This option is a hybrid strategy that blends elements of the previous approaches. Target is an example of a company that is known for its hip product design (a reputation it built by featuring cheap-chic designers such as Isaac Mizrahi), as well as a more appealing shopping ambience than other "big-box" discounters, such as Walmart and Kmart. It offers the perfect illustration of a best-cost provider strategy.

Winning a *sustainable* competitive edge over rivals with any of the above four strategies generally hinges as much on building competitively valuable expertise and capabilities that rivals cannot readily match as it does on having a distinctive product offering. Clever rivals can nearly always copy the attributes of a popular product or service, but for rivals to match the experience, know-how, and specialized capabilities that a company has developed and perfected over a long period of time is substantially harder to do and takes much longer. FedEx, for example, has superior capabilities in next-day delivery of small packages. Walt Disney has hard-to-beat capabilities in theme park management and family entertainment. In recent years, Apple has demonstrated impressive product innovation capabilities in digital music players, smart phones, and e-readers. Hyundai has become the world's fastest-growing automaker as a result of its advanced manufacturing processes and unparalleled quality control system. Ritz Carlton and Four Seasons have uniquely strong capabilities in providing their hotel guests with an array of personalized services. Each of these capabilities has proved hard for competitors to imitate or best.

The tight connection between competitive advantage and profitability means that the quest for sustainable competitive advantage always ranks center stage in crafting a strategy. The key to successful strategy making is to come up with one or more strategy elements that act as a magnet to draw customers and that produce a lasting competitive edge over rivals. Indeed, what separates a powerful strategy from a run-of-the-mill or ineffective one is management's ability to forge a series of moves, both in the marketplace and internally, that sets the company apart from its rivals, tilts the playing field in the company's favor by giving buyers reason to prefer its products or services, and produces a sustainable competitive advantage over rivals. The bigger and more sustainable the competitive advantage, the better are a company's prospects for winning in the marketplace and earning superior long-term profits relative to its rivals. Without a strategy that leads to competitive advantage, a company risks being outcompeted by stronger rivals and locked into mediocre financial performance.

Why a Company's Strategy Evolves over Time

The appeal of a strategy that yields a sustainable competitive advantage is that it offers the potential for an enduring edge over rivals. However, managers of every company must be willing and ready to modify the strategy in response to changing market conditions, advancing technology, the fresh moves of competitors, shifting buyer needs, emerging market opportunities, and new ideas for improving the strategy. In some industries, conditions change at a fairly slow pace, making it feasible for the major components of a good strategy to remain in place for long

LO 3

Understand that a company's strategy tends to evolve over time because of changing circumstances and ongoing management efforts to improve the company's strategy.

periods. But in industries where industry and competitive conditions change frequently and in sometimes dramatic ways, the life cycle of a given strategy is short. Industry environments characterized by high-velocity change require companies to repeatedly adapt their strategies.[6] For example, companies in industries with rapid-fire advances in technology like medical equipment, electronics, and wireless devices often find it essential to adjust key elements of their strategies several times a year, sometimes even finding it necessary to "reinvent" their approach to providing value to their customers.

Regardless of whether a company's strategy changes gradually or swiftly, the important point is that the task of crafting strategy is not a one-time event but always a work in progress. Adapting to new conditions and constantly evaluating what is working well enough to continue and what needs to be improved are normal parts of the strategy-making process, resulting in an *evolving strategy.*[7]

> Changing circumstances and ongoing management efforts to improve the strategy cause a company's strategy to evolve over time—a condition that makes the task of crafting strategy *a work in progress,* not a one-time event.

A Company's Strategy Is Partly Proactive and Partly Reactive

The evolving nature of a company's strategy means that the typical company strategy is a blend of (1) *proactive* actions to improve the company's financial performance and secure a competitive edge and (2) *adaptive* reactions to unanticipated developments and fresh market conditions. In most cases, much of a company's current strategy flows from previously initiated actions and business approaches that are working well enough to merit continuation and from newly launched initiatives aimed at boosting financial performance and edging out rivals. This part of management's action plan for running the company is its **deliberate strategy,** consisting of strategy elements that are both planned and realized as planned (while other planned strategy elements may not work out).

> A company's strategy is shaped partly by management analysis and choice and partly by the necessity of adapting and learning by doing.

But managers must always be willing to supplement or modify the proactive strategy elements with as-needed reactions to unanticipated conditions. Inevitably, there will be occasions when market and competitive conditions take an unexpected turn that calls for some kind of strategic reaction or adjustment. Hence, *a portion of a company's strategy is always developed on the fly,* coming as a response to fresh strategic maneuvers on the part of rival firms, unexpected shifts in customer requirements, fast-changing technological developments, newly appearing market opportunities, a changing political or economic climate, or other unanticipated happenings in the surrounding environment. Under conditions of high uncertainty, strategy elements are more likely to emerge from experimentation, trial-and-error, and adaptive learning processes than from a proactive plan. These unplanned, reactive, and adaptive strategy adjustments make up the firm's **emergent strategy,** consisting of the new strategy elements that emerge as changing conditions warrant. A company's strategy in toto (its *realized* strategy) thus tends to be a *combination* of proactive and reactive elements, with certain strategy elements being *abandoned* because they have become obsolete or ineffective—see Figure 1.2.[8] A company's realized strategy can be observed in the pattern of its actions over time—a far better indicator than any of its strategic plans on paper or public pronouncements about its strategy.

> A company's **proactive (or deliberate) strategy** consists of strategy elements that are both planned and realized as planned; its **reactive (or emergent) strategy** consists of new strategy elements that emerge as changing conditions warrant.

Figure 1.2   A Company's Strategy Is a Blend of Proactive Initiatives and Reactive Adjustments

THE RELATIONSHIP BETWEEN A COMPANY'S STRATEGY AND ITS BUSINESS MODEL

Closely related to the concept of strategy is the company's **business model.** A company's business model is management's blueprint for delivering a valuable product or service to customers in a manner that will generate ample revenues to cover costs and yield an attractive profit.[9] It is management's story line for how the strategy will be a moneymaker. Without the ability to deliver good profitability, the strategy is not viable and the survival of the business is in doubt.

The two crucial elements of a company's business model are (1) its *customer value proposition* and (2) its *profit formula*. The customer value proposition lays out the company's approach to satisfying buyer wants and needs at a price customers will consider a good value. The greater the value provided (V) and the lower the price (P), the more attractive the value proposition is to customers. The profit formula describes the company's approach to determining a cost structure that will allow for acceptable profits, given the pricing tied to its customer value proposition. More specifically, a company's profit formula depends on three basic elements: V—the *value* provided to customers, in terms of how effectively the goods or services of the company meet customers' wants and needs; P—the *price* charged to customers; and C—the company's *costs*. The lower the costs (C), given the customer value proposition ($V - P$), the greater the ability of the business model to be a moneymaker. Thus

CORE CONCEPT

A company's **business model** sets forth the economic logic for making money in a business, given the company's strategy. It describes two critical elements: (1) the customer value proposition and (2) the profit formula.

the profit formula reveals how efficiently a company can meet customer wants and needs and deliver on the value proposition.

Magazines and newspapers employ a business model keyed to delivering information and entertainment they believe readers will find valuable and a profit formula aimed at securing sufficient revenues from subscriptions and advertising to more than cover the costs of producing and delivering their products to readers. Mobile phone providers, satellite radio companies, and broadband providers also employ a subscription-based business model. The business model of network TV and radio broadcasters entails providing free programming to audiences but charging advertising fees based on audience size. Gillette's business model in razor blades involves selling a "master product"—the razor—at an attractively low price and then making money on repeat purchases of razor blades that can be produced very cheaply and sold at high profit margins. Printer manufacturers like Hewlett-Packard, Lexmark, and Epson pursue much the same business model as Gillette—selling printers at a low (virtually break-even) price and making large profit margins on the repeat purchases of printer supplies, especially ink cartridges.

The nitty-gritty issue surrounding a company's business model is whether it can execute its customer value proposition profitably. Just because company managers have crafted a strategy for competing and running the business, this does not automatically mean that the strategy will lead to profitability—it may or it may not. The relevance of a company's business model is to clarify *how the business will (1) provide customers with value and (2) generate revenues sufficient to cover costs and produce attractive profits.*[10] Illustration Capsule 1.2 discusses the contrasting buisness models of Microsoft and Redhat.

WHAT MAKES A STRATEGY A WINNER?

Three tests can be applied to determine whether a strategy is a *winning strategy:*

1. ***The Fit Test:*** *How well does the strategy fit the company's situation?* To qualify as a winner, a strategy has to be well matched to industry and competitive conditions, a company's best market opportunities, and other pertinent aspects of the business environment in which the company operates. No strategy can work well unless it exhibits good *external fit* and is in sync with prevailing market conditions. At the same time, a winning strategy has to be tailored to the company's resources and competitive capabilities and be supported by a complementary set of functional activities (i.e., activities in the realms of supply chain management, operations, sales and marketing, and so on). That is, it must also exhibit *internal fit* and be compatible with a company's ability to execute the strategy in a competent manner. Unless a strategy exhibits good fit with both the external and internal aspects of a company's overall situation, it is likely to be an underperformer and fall short of producing winning results. Winning strategies also exhibit *dynamic fit* in the sense that they evolve over time in a manner that maintains close and effective alignment with the company's situation even as external and internal conditions change.[11]

A **winning strategy** must pass three tests:

1. The Fit Test
2. The Competitive Advantage Test
3. The Performance Test

ILLUSTRATION CAPSULE 1.2

Microsoft and Red Hat Linux: Two Contrasting Business Models

The strategies of rival companies are often predicated on strikingly different business models. Consider, for example, the business models for Microsoft and Red Hat Linux in operating system software for PCs. Microsoft's business model—sell proprietary code software and give service away free—is a proven money maker that generates billions in profits annually. On the other hand, the jury is still out on Red Hat's business model of selling subscriptions to open-source software to large corporations and deriving substantial revenues from the sales of technical support, training, consulting, software customization, and engineering to generate revenues sufficient to cover costs and yield a profit. Red Hat's fiscal 2010 revenues of $748 million and net income of $87 million are quite meager in comparison.

	Microsoft	Red Hat
Customer value proposition	• Employ a cadre of highly skilled programmers to develop proprietary code for the Windows operating system and software package. • Keep the source code hidden so as to keep the inner-workings of the software proprietary. • Provide a modest level of technical support to users at no cost. • Sell the Windows operating system and software package to personal computer PC makers and to PC users at relatively attractive prices.	• Rely on the collaborative efforts of volunteer programmers from all over the world who contribute bits and pieces of code to improve and polish the Linux system. • Collect and test enhancements and new applications submitted by the open-source community of volunteer programmers. Linux's originator, Linus Torvalds, and a team of 300-plus Red Hat engineers and software developers evaluate which incoming submissions merit inclusion in new releases of Red Hat Linux. • Make the source code open and available to all users, allowing them to create a customized version of Linux.
Profit formula	***Revenue generation:*** • Strive to maintain a 90 percent or more market share of the 350 million PCs sold annually worldwide. • Charge licensing fees to PC makers and users ranging from $50 to $100 per installation. • Keep rejuvenating revenues by periodically introducing next-generation software versions with features that will induce PC users to upgrade the operating system on previously purchased PCs to the new version. ***Profit margin:*** • Most of Microsoft's costs arise on the front end in developing the software and are thus "fixed"; the variable costs of producing and packaging the CDs provided to users are only a couple of dollars per copy—once the break-even volume is reached, Microsoft's revenues from additional sales are almost pure profit.	***Revenue generation:*** • Market the upgraded and tested family of Red Hat Linux products to large enterprises and charge them a subscription fee that includes 24/7 support within one hour in seven languages. Provide subscribers with updated versions of Red Hat Linux every 12–18 months to maintain the subscriber base. • Capitalize on the specialized expertise required to use Linux in multiserver, multiprocessor applications by providing fees-based training, consulting, software customization, and client-directed engineering to Red Hat Linux users. Red Hat offers Linux certification training programs at all skill levels at more than 60 global locations—Red Hat certification in the use of Linux is considered the best in the world. ***Profit margin:*** • Most of Red Hat's development costs arise from the evaluation and integration of new submissions for modifications to Linux; the company also incurs substantial variable costs related to its customer service, training, consulting, software customization, and client-directed engineering activities. The company's profit margin is dependent on sufficient subscription revenues and consulting fees to cover the costs of these activities.

Source: Company documents and information posted on their Web sites.

2. ***The Competitive Advantage Test:*** *Can the strategy help the company achieve a sustainable competitive advantage?* Strategies that fail to achieve a durable competitive advantage over rivals are unlikely to produce superior performance for more than a brief period of time. Winning strategies enable a company to achieve a competitive advantage over key rivals that is long-lasting. The bigger and more durable the competitive advantage, the more powerful it is.

3. ***The Performance Test:*** *Is the strategy producing good company performance?* The mark of a winning strategy is strong company performance. Two kinds of performance indicators tell the most about the caliber of a company's strategy: (1) profitability and financial strength and (2) competitive strength and market standing. Above-average financial performance or gains in market share, competitive position, or profitability are signs of a winning strategy.

Strategies that come up short on one or more of the above tests are plainly less appealing than strategies passing all three tests with flying colors. Managers should use the same questions when evaluating either proposed or existing strategies. New initiatives that don't seem to match the company's internal and external situations should be scrapped before they come to fruition, while existing strategies must be scrutinized on a regular basis to ensure they have good fit, offer a competitive advantage, and are contributing to above-average performance or performance improvements.

WHY CRAFTING AND EXECUTING STRATEGY ARE IMPORTANT TASKS

Crafting and executing strategy are top-priority managerial tasks for a very big reason. A clear and reasoned strategy is management's prescription for doing business, its road map to competitive advantage, its game plan for pleasing customers, and its formula for improving performance. High-achieving enterprises are nearly always the product of astute, creative, proactive strategy making. Companies don't get to the top of the industry rankings or stay there with illogical strategies, copy-cat strategies, or timid attempts to try to do better. Only a handful of companies can boast of hitting home runs in the marketplace due to lucky breaks or the good fortune of having stumbled into the right market at the right time with the right product. And even then, unless they subsequently craft a strategy that capitalizes on their luck, building in what's working and discarding the rest, success of this sort will be fleeting. So there can be little argument that a company's strategy matters—and matters a lot.

The chief executive officer of one successful company put it well when he said:

> In the main, our competitors are acquainted with the same fundamental concepts and techniques and approaches that we follow, and they are as free to pursue them as we are. More often than not, the difference between their level of success and ours lies in the relative thoroughness and self-discipline with which we and they develop and execute our strategies for the future.

Good Strategy + Good Strategy Execution = Good Management

Crafting and executing strategy are thus core management functions. Among all the things managers do, nothing affects a company's ultimate success or failure more fundamentally than how well its management team charts the company's direction, develops competitively effective strategic moves and business approaches, and pursues what needs to be done internally to produce good day-in, day-out strategy execution and operating excellence. Indeed, *good strategy and good strategy execution are the most telling signs of good management.* Managers don't deserve a gold star for designing a potentially brilliant strategy but failing to put the organizational means in place to carry it out in high-caliber fashion. Competent execution of a mediocre strategy scarcely merits enthusiastic applause for management's efforts either. The rationale for using the twin standards of good strategy making and good strategy execution to determine whether a company is well managed is therefore compelling: *The better conceived a company's strategy and the more competently it is executed, the more likely that the company will be a standout performer in the marketplace.* In stark contrast, a company that lacks clear-cut direction, has a flawed strategy, or can't execute its strategy competently is a company whose financial performance is probably suffering, whose business is at long-term risk, and whose management is sorely lacking.

> How well a company performs is directly attributable to the caliber of its strategy and the proficiency with which the strategy is executed.

THE ROAD AHEAD

Throughout the chapters to come and the accompanying case collection, the spotlight is trained on the foremost question in running a business enterprise: *What must managers do, and do well, to make a company a winner in the marketplace?* The answer that emerges, and that becomes the message of this book, is that doing a good job of managing inherently requires good strategic thinking and good management of the strategy-making, strategy-executing process.

The mission of this book is to provide a solid overview of what every business student and aspiring manager needs to know about crafting and executing strategy. We will explore what good strategic thinking entails, describe the core concepts and tools of strategic analysis, and examine the ins and outs of crafting and executing strategy. The accompanying cases will help build your skills both in diagnosing how well the strategy-making, strategy-executing task is being performed and in prescribing actions for how the strategy in question or its execution can be improved. In the process, we hope to convince you that first-rate capabilities in crafting and executing strategy are basic to managing successfully and are skills every manager needs to possess.

As you tackle the following pages, ponder the following observation by the essayist and poet Ralph Waldo Emerson: "Commerce is a game of skill which many people play, but which few play well." If the content of this book helps you become a savvy player and equips you to succeed in business, then your journey through these pages will indeed be time well spent.

KEY POINTS

The tasks of crafting and executing company strategies are the heart and soul of managing a business enterprise and winning in the marketplace. The key points to take away from this chapter include the following:

1. A company's strategy is the *game plan* management is using to stake out a market position, conduct its operations, attract and please customers, compete successfully, and achieve the desired performance targets.

2. The central thrust of a company's strategy is undertaking moves to build and strengthen the company's long-term competitive position and financial performance by *competing differently* from rivals and gaining a sustainable competitive advantage over them.

3. A company achieves a sustainable competitive advantage when it can meet customer needs more effectively or efficiently than rivals and when the basis for this is durable, despite the best efforts of competitors to match or surpass this advantage.

4. A company's strategy typically evolves over time, emerging from a blend of (1) proactive and deliberate actions on the part of company managers to improve the strategy and (2) reactive, as-needed adaptive responses to unanticipated developments and fresh market conditions.

5. A company's business model is management's story line for how the strategy will be a moneymaker. It contains two crucial elements: (1) the *customer value proposition*—a plan for satisfying customer wants and needs at a price customers will consider good value, and (2) the *profit formula*—a plan for a cost structure that will enable the company to deliver the customer value proposition profitably. In effect, a company's business model sets forth the economic logic for making money in a particular business, given the company's current strategy.

6. A winning strategy will pass three tests: (1) *Fit* (external, internal, and dynamic consistency), (2) *Competitive Advantage* (durable competitive advantage), and (3) *Performance* (outstanding financial and market performance).

7. Crafting and executing strategy are core management functions. How well a company performs and the degree of market success it enjoys are directly attributable to the caliber of its strategy and the proficiency with which the strategy is executed.

ASSURANCE OF LEARNING EXERCISES

LO 1, LO 2

1. Go to www.ikea.com, choose your country, and click on the About Ikea section, and explore Ikea's latest Yearly Summary and Other Facts & Figures to see if you can identify the key elements of Ikea's strategy. Use the framework provided in Figure 1.1 to help identify these key elements. What approach toward winning a competitive advantage does Ikea seem to be pursuing?

LO 1, LO 2, LO 5

2. On the basis of what you know about the quick-service restaurant industry, does McDonald's strategy as described in Illustration Capsule 1.1 seem to be well matched to industry and competitive conditions? Does the strategy seem to be keyed to having a cost-based advantage, offering differentiating features, serving the unique needs of a narrow market niche, or being the best-cost provider? What is there about the action elements of McDonald's strategy that is consistent with its approach to competitive advantage? From the information provided, which tests of a winning strategy does McDonald's strategy pass?

LO 3, LO 4

3. Go to www.redhat.com and check whether the company's recent financial reports indicate that its business model is working. Is the company sufficiently profitable to validate its business model and strategy? Is its revenue stream from selling training and consulting and engineering services growing or declining as a percentage of total revenues? Does your review of the company's recent financial performance suggest that its business model and strategy are changing? Read the company's latest statement about its business model and about why it is pursuing the subscription approach (as compared to Microsoft's approach of selling copies of its operating software directly to PC manufacturers and individuals).

EXERCISE FOR SIMULATION PARTICIPANTS

This chapter discusses three questions that must be answered by managers of organizations of all sizes:

- What is our present situation?
- Where do we want to go from here?
- How are we going to get there?

After you read the Participant's Guide or Player's Manual for the strategy simulation exercise that you will participate in this academic term, you and your co-managers should come up with brief one- or two-paragraph answers to these three questions *before* entering your first set of decisions. While the management team's answer to the first of the three questions can be developed from your reading of the manual, the second and third questions will require a collaborative discussion among the members of your company's management team about how you intend to manage the company you have been assigned to run.

LO 1, LO 2

1. *What is our company's current situation?* A substantive answer to this question should cover the following issues:

   - Is your company in a good, average, or weak competitive position vis-à-vis rival companies?
   - Does your company appear to be in sound financial condition?
   - What problems does your company have that need to be addressed?

LO 3, LO 5

2. *Where do we want to take the company during the time we are in charge?* A complete answer to this question should say something about each of the following:

   - What goals or aspirations do you have for your company?
   - What do you want the company to be known for?
   - What market share would you like your company to have after the first five decision rounds?

- By what amount or percentage would you like to increase total profits of the company by the end of the final decision round?
- What kinds of performance outcomes will signal that you and your co-managers are managing the company in a successful manner?

LO 3, LO 4

3. *How are we going to get there?* Your answer should cover these issues:

- Which of the basic strategic and competitive approaches discussed in this chapter do you think makes the most sense to pursue?
- What kind of competitive advantage over rivals will you try to achieve?
- How would you describe the company's business model?
- What kind of actions will support these objectives?

ENDNOTES

[1] Jan Rivkin, "An Alternative Approach to Making Strategic Choices," Harvard Business School, 9-702-433, 2001.

[2] Costas Markides, "What Is Strategy and How Do You Know If You Have One?" *Business Strategy Review* 15, no. 2 (Summer 2004), pp. 5–6. See also David J. Collis and Michael F. Rukstad, "Can You Say What Your Strategy Is?" *Harvard Business Review* 86, no. 4 (April 2008), pp. 82–90.

[3] For a discussion of the different ways that companies can position themselves in the marketplace, see Michael E. Porter, "What Is Strategy?" *Harvard Business Review* 74, no. 6 (November–December 1996), pp. 65–67.

[4] Ibid.

[5] Walmartstores.com/download/2230.pdf; Southwest Airlines Fact Sheet, July 16, 2009.

[6] For more on the strategic challenges posed by high-velocity changes, see Shona L. Brown and Kathleen M. Eisenhardt, *Competing on the Edge: Strategy as Structured Chaos* (Boston, MA: Harvard Business School Press, 1998), chap. 1.

[7] For an excellent discussion of strategy as a dynamic process involving continuous, unending creation and re-creation of strategy, see Cynthia A. Montgomery, "Putting Leadership Back into Strategy," *Harvard Business Review* 86, no. 1 (January 2008), pp. 54–60.

[8] See Henry Mintzberg and Joseph Lampel, "Reflecting on the Strategy Process," *Sloan Management Review* 40, no. 3 (Spring 1999), pp. 21–30; Henry Mintzberg and J. A. Waters, "Of Strategies, Deliberate and Emergent," *Strategic Management Journal* 6 (1985), pp. 257–72; Costas Markides, "Strategy as Balance: From 'Either-Or' to 'And,'" *Business Strategy Review* 12, no. 3 (September 2001), pp. 1–10.

[9] Mark W. Johnson, Clayton M. Christensen, and Henning Kagermann, "Reinventing Your Business Model," *Harvard Business Review* 86, no. 12 (December 2008), pp. 52–53; Joan Magretta, "Why Business Models Matter," *Harvard Business Review* 80, no. 5 (May 2002), p. 87.

[10] For further discussion of the meaning and role of a company's customer value proposition and profit proposition, see W. Chan Kim and Renée Mauborgne, "How Strategy Shapes Structure," *Harvard Business Review* 87, no. 9 (September 2009), pp. 74–75.

[11] For a discussion of the three types of fit, see Rivkin, "An Alternative Approach to Making Strategic Choices." For an example of managing internal fit dynamically, See M. Peteraf and R. Reed, "Managerial Discretion and Internal Alignment under Regulatory Constraints and Change," *Strategic Management Journal* 28 (2007), pp. 1089–1112.

CHAPTER 2

CHARTING A COMPANY'S DIRECTION: VISION AND MISSION, OBJECTIVES, AND STRATEGY

The vision we have . . . determines what we do and the opportunities we see or don't see.

—Charles G. Koch
CEO of Koch Industries, the second-largest privately held company in the U.S.

A good goal is like a strenuous exercise—it makes you stretch.

—Mary Kay Ash
Founder of Mary Kay Cosmetics

If you don't know where you are going, any road will take you there.

—Cheshire Cat to Alice
Lewis Carroll, Alice in Wonderland

LEARNING OBJECTIVES

LO 1. Grasp why it is critical for company managers to have a clear strategic vision of where a company needs to head and why.

LO 2. Understand the importance of setting both strategic and financial objectives.

LO 3. Understand why the strategic initiatives taken at various organizational levels must be tightly coordinated to achieve companywide performance targets.

LO 4. Become aware of what a company must do to achieve operating excellence and to execute its strategy proficiently.

LO 5. Become aware of the role and responsibility of a company's board of directors in overseeing the strategic management process.

Crafting and executing strategy are the heart and soul of managing a business enterprise. But exactly what is involved in developing a strategy and executing it proficiently? What are the various components of the strategy-making, strategy-executing process and to what extent are company personnel—aside from senior management—involved in the process? In this chapter we present an overview of the ins and outs of crafting and executing company strategies. Special attention will be given to management's direction-setting responsibilities—charting a strategic course, setting performance targets, and choosing a strategy capable of producing the desired outcomes. We will also explain why strategy making is a task for a company's entire management team and discuss which kinds of strategic decisions tend to be made at which levels of management. The chapter concludes with a look at the roles and responsibilities of a company's board of directors in the strategy-making, strategy-executing process and how good corporate governance protects shareholder interests and promotes good management.

WHAT DOES THE STRATEGY-MAKING, STRATEGY-EXECUTING PROCESS ENTAIL?

The process of crafting and executing a company's strategy consists of five interrelated managerial stages:

1. *Developing a strategic vision* of the company's long-term direction, a *mission* that describes the company's purpose, and a set of *values* to guide the pursuit of the vision and mission.
2. *Setting objectives* and using them as yardsticks for measuring the company's performance and progress.
3. *Crafting a strategy* to achieve the objectives and move the company along the strategic course that management has charted.
4. *Executing the chosen strategy* efficiently and effectively.
5. *Monitoring developments, evaluating performance, and initiating corrective adjustments* in the company's vision and mission, objectives, strategy, or execution in light of actual experience, changing conditions, new ideas, and new opportunities.

Figure 2.1   The Strategy-Making, Strategy-Executing Process

Figure 2.1 displays this five-stage process, which we examine next in some detail.

STAGE 1: DEVELOPING A STRATEGIC VISION, A MISSION, AND A SET OF CORE VALUES

LO 1

Grasp why it is critical for company managers to have a clear strategic vision of where a company needs to head and why.

Very early in the strategy-making process, a company's senior managers must wrestle with the issue of what directional path the company should take. Can the company's prospects be improved by changing its product offerings and/or the markets in which it participates and/or the customers it caters to and/or the technologies it employs? Deciding to commit the company to one path versus another pushes managers to draw some carefully reasoned conclusions about whether the company's present strategic course offers attractive opportunities for growth and profitability or whether changes of one kind or another in the company's strategy and long-term direction are needed.

Developing a Strategic Vision

Top management's views and conclusions about the company's long-term direction and what product-customer-market-technology mix seems optimal for the road ahead constitute a **strategic vision** for the company. A strategic vision delineates management's aspirations for the business, providing a panoramic view of "where we are going" and a convincing rationale for why this makes good business sense for the company. A strategic vision thus points an organization in a particular direction, charts a strategic path for it to follow in preparing for the future, and builds commitment to the future course of action. A clearly articulated strategic vision communicates management's aspirations to stakeholders and helps steer the energies of company personnel in a common direction.

Well-conceived visions are *distinctive* and *specific* to a particular organization; they avoid generic, feel-good statements like "We will become a global leader and the first choice of customers in every market we serve"—which could apply to hundreds of organizations.[1] And they are not the product of a committee charged with coming up with an innocuous but well-meaning one-sentence vision that wins consensus approval from various stakeholders. Nicely worded vision statements with no specifics about the company's product-market-customer-technology focus fall well short of what it takes for a vision to measure up.

A sampling of vision statements currently in use shows a range from strong and clear to overly general and generic. A surprising number of the vision statements found on company Web sites and in annual reports are vague and unrevealing, saying very little about the company's future direction. Some could apply to almost any company in any industry. Many read like a public relations statement—high-sounding words that someone came up with because it is fashionable for companies to have an official vision statement.[2] But the real purpose of a vision statement is to serve as a management tool for giving the organization a sense of direction. Like any tool, it can be used properly or improperly, either clearly conveying a company's future strategic path or not.

For a strategic vision to function as a valuable managerial tool, it must convey what management wants the business to look like and provide managers with a reference point in making strategic decisions and preparing the company for the future. It must say something definitive about how the company's leaders intend to position the company beyond where it is today. Table 2.1 provides some dos and don'ts in composing an effectively worded vision statement. Illustration Capsule 2.1 provides a critique of the strategic visions of several prominent companies.

> **CORE CONCEPT**
>
> A **strategic vision** describes management's aspirations for the future and delineates the company's strategic course and long-term direction.

Communicating the Strategic Vision

Effectively communicating the strategic vision down the line to lower-level managers and employees is as important as the strategic soundness of the long-term direction top management has chosen. Company personnel can't be expected to unite behind managerial efforts to get the organization moving in the intended direction until they understand why the strategic course that management has charted is reasonable and beneficial. It is particularly important for executives to provide a compelling rationale for a dramatically *new* strategic vision and company direction. When company personnel don't understand or accept the need for redirecting organizational efforts, they are prone to resist change. Hence, reiterating the basis for the new direction, addressing employee concerns head-on, calming fears, lifting spirits, and providing updates and progress reports as events unfold all become part of the task in mobilizing support for the vision and winning commitment to needed actions.

> An effectively communicated vision is a tool for enlisting the commitment of company personnel to actions that move the company forward in the intended direction.

Winning the support of organization members for the vision nearly always means putting "where we are going and why" in writing, distributing the statement organizationwide, and having executives personally explain the vision and its

Table 2.1   Wording a Vision Statement—the Dos and Don'ts

The Dos	The Don'ts
Be graphic. Paint a clear picture of where the company is headed and the market position(s) the company is striving to stake out.	**Don't be vague or incomplete.** Never skimp on specifics about where the company is headed or how the company intends to prepare for the future.
Be forward-looking and directional. Describe the strategic course that management has charted and the kinds of product-market-customer-technology changes that will help the company prepare for the future.	**Don't dwell on the present.** A vision is not about what a company once did or does now; it's about "where we are going."
Keep it focused. Be specific enough to provide managers with guidance in making decisions and allocating resources.	**Don't use overly broad language.** All-inclusive language that gives the company license to head in almost any direction, pursue almost any opportunity, or enter almost any business must be avoided.
Have some wiggle room. Language that allows some flexibility is good. The directional course may have to be adjusted as market-customer-technology circumstances change, and coming up with a new vision statement every one to three years signals rudderless management.	**Don't state the vision in bland or uninspiring terms.** The best vision statements have the power to motivate company personnel and inspire shareholder confidence about the company's direction and business outlook.
Be sure the journey is feasible. The path and direction should be within the realm of what the company can pursue and accomplish; over time, a company should be able to demonstrate measurable progress in achieving the vision.	**Don't be generic.** A vision statement that could apply to companies in any of several industries (or to any of several companies in the same industry) is incapable of giving a company its own unique identity.
Indicate why the directional path makes good business sense. The directional path should be in the long-term interests of stakeholders (especially shareowners, employees, and customers).	**Don't rely on superlatives only.** Visions that claim the company's strategic course is one of being the "best" or "the most successful" or "a recognized leader" or the "global leader" usually shortchange the essential and revealing specifics about the path the company is taking to get there.
Make it memorable. To give the organization a sense of direction and purpose, the vision needs to be easily communicated. Ideally, it should be reducible to a few choice lines or a memorable "slogan" (like Henry Ford's famous vision of "a car in every garage").	**Don't run on and on.** Vison statements that are overly long tend to be unfocused and meaningless. A vision statement that is not short and to-the-point will tend to lose its audience.

Sources: John P. Kotter, *Leading Change* (Boston: Harvard Business School Press, 1996), p. 72; Hugh Davidson, *The Committed Enterprise* (Oxford: Butterworth Heinemann, 2002), chap. 2; and Michel Robert, *Strategy Pure and Simple II* (New York: McGraw-Hill, 1992), chaps. 2, 3, and 6.

Strategic visions become real only when the vision statement is imprinted in the minds of organization members and then translated into hard objectives and strategies.

rationale to as many people as feasible. *A strategic vision can usually be stated adequately in one to two paragraphs, and managers should be able to explain it to company personnel and outsiders in 5 to 10 minutes.* Ideally, executives should present their vision for the company in a manner that reaches out and grabs people. An engaging and convincing strategic vision has enormous motivational value—for the same reason that a stonemason is more inspired by building a great cathedral for the ages than simply laying stones to create floors and walls. When managers articulate a vivid and compelling case for where the company is headed, organization members begin to say "This is interesting and has a lot of merit. I want to be involved and do my part to help make it happen." The more that a vision evokes positive support and excitement, the greater its impact in terms of arousing a committed organizational effort and getting company personnel to move in a common direction.[3] Thus executive ability to paint a convincing and inspiring picture of a company's journey and destination is an important element of effective strategic leadership.

Examples of Strategic Visions—How Well Do They Measure Up?

Vision Statement	Effective Elements	Shortcomings
Samsung Samsung is dedicated to developing innovative technologies and efficient processes that create new markets, enrich people's lives, and continue to make Samsung a digital leader.	• Directional • Focused • Flexible • Desirable • Easy to communicate	• Bland or uninspiring
UBS We are determined to be the best global financial services company. We focus on wealth and asset management, and on investment banking and securities businesses. We continually earn recognition and trust from clients, shareholders, and staff through our ability to anticipate, learn and shape our future. We share a common ambition to succeed by delivering quality in what we do. Our purpose is to help our clients make financial decisions with confidence. We use our resources to develop effective solutions and services for our clients. We foster a distinctive, meritocratic culture of ambition, performance and learning as this attracts, retains and develops the best talent for our company. By growing both our client and our talent franchises, we add sustainable value for our shareholders.	• Focused • Feasible • Desirable	• Not forward-looking • Bland or uninspiring • Hard to communicate
Caterpillar Be the global leader in customer value.	• Directional • Desirable • Easy to communicate	• Vague or incomplete • Could apply to many companies in many industries

Sources: Company documents and Web sites (accessed April 23, 2010, June 6, 2010, and February 4, 2011).

Expressing the Essence of the Vision in a Slogan   The task of effectively conveying the vision to company personnel is assisted when management can capture the vision of where to head in a catchy or easily remembered slogan. A number of organizations have summed up their vision in a brief phrase:

- Levi Strauss & Company: "We will clothe the world by marketing the most appealing and widely worn casual clothing in the world."
- Nike: "To bring innovation and inspiration to every athlete in the world."
- Mayo Clinic: "The best care to every patient every day."
- Scotland Yard: "To make London the safest major city in the world."
- Greenpeace: "To halt environmental abuse and promote environmental solutions."

Creating a short slogan to illuminate an organization's direction and purpose helps rally organization members to hurdle whatever obstacles lie in the company's path and maintain their focus.

The Payoffs of a Clear Vision Statement   A well-conceived, forcefully communicated strategic vision pays off in several respects: (1) It crystallizes senior executives' own views about the firm's long-term direction; (2) it reduces the risk of rudderless decision making; (3) it is a tool for winning the support of organization members for internal changes that will help make the vision a reality; (4) it provides a beacon for lower-level managers in setting departmental objectives and crafting departmental strategies that are in sync with the company's overall strategy; and (5) it helps an organization prepare for the future. When management is able to demonstrate significant progress in achieving these five benefits, the first step in organizational direction setting has been successfully completed.

Crafting a Mission Statement

The defining characteristic of a strategic vision is what it says about the company's *future strategic course*—"the direction we are headed and our aspirations for the future." In contrast, a **mission statement** describes the enterprise's *current business and purpose*—"who we are, what we do, and why we are here." The mission statements that one finds in company annual reports or posted on company Web sites are typically quite brief; some do a better job than others of conveying what the enterprise is all about. Consider for example, the mission statement of Sony:

> Sony is committed to developing a wide range of innovative products and multimedia services that challenge the way consumers access and enjoy digital entertainment. By ensuring synergy between businesses within the organization, Sony is constantly striving to create exciting new worlds of entertainment that can be experienced on a variety of different products.

Note that Sony's mission statement does a good job of conveying "who we are, what we do, and why we are here," but it says nothing about the company's long-term direction.

Another example of a well-stated mission statement with ample specifics about what the organization does is that of the Nestlé Research Center:

The distinction between a strategic vision and a mission statement is fairly clear-cut: A **strategic vision** portrays a company's aspirations for its *future* ("where we are going"), whereas a company's **mission** describes its *purpose* and its *present* business ("who we are, what we do, and why we are here").

> At Nestlé, we believe that research can help us make better food so that people live a better life.
>
> Good Food is the primary source of Good Health throughout life. We strive to bring consumers foods that are safe, of high quality and provide optimal nutrition to meet physiological needs. In addition to Nutrition, Health and Wellness, Nestlé products bring consumers the vital ingredients of taste and pleasure.
>
> As consumers continue to make choices regarding foods and beverages they consume, Nestlé helps provide selections for all individual taste and lifestyle preferences.
>
> Research is a key part of our heritage at Nestlé and an essential element of our future. We know there is still much to discover about health, wellness and the role of food in our lives, and we continue to search for answers to bring consumers Good Food for Good Life.

Microsoft's grandiloquent mission statement—"To help people and businesses throughout the world realize their full potential"—says so little about the customer needs it is satisfying that it could be applied to almost any firm. A well-conceived mission statement should employ language specific enough to give the company its own identity.

Ideally, a company mission statement is sufficiently descriptive to:

- Identify the company's product or services.
- Specify the buyer needs it seeks to satisfy.
- Identify the customer groups or markets it is endeavoring to serve.
- Specify its approach to pleasing customers.
- Give the company its own identity.

Not many company mission statements fully reveal *all* these facets of the business or employ language specific enough to give the company an identity that is distinguishably different from those of other companies in much the same business or industry. A few companies have worded their mission statements so obscurely as to mask what they are all about. Occasionally, companies couch their mission in terms of making a profit. This is misguided. Profit is more correctly an *objective* and a *result* of what a company does. Moreover, earning a profit is the obvious intent of every commercial enterprise. Such companies as BMW, McDonald's, Shell Oil, Procter & Gamble, Nintendo, and Nokia are each striving to earn a profit for shareholders; but plainly the fundamentals of their businesses are substantially different when it comes to "who we are and what we do." It is management's answer to "make a profit doing what and for whom?" that reveals the substance of a company's true mission and business purpose.

> **CORE CONCEPT**
>
> A well-conceived **mission statement** conveys a company's *purpose* in language specific enough to give the company its own identity.

Linking the Vision and Mission with Company Values

The **values** of a company (sometimes called *core values*) are the beliefs, traits, and behavioral norms that management has determined should guide the pursuit of its vision and mission. They relate to such things as fair treatment, integrity, ethical behavior, innovativeness, teamwork, top-notch quality, superior customer service, social responsibility, and community citizenship. Many companies have developed a statement of values to emphasize the expectation that the values be reflected in the conduct of company operations and the behavior of company personnel.

Most companies have identified four to eight core values. At FedEx, the six core values concern people (valuing employees and promoting diversity), service (putting customers at the heart of all it does), innovation (inventing services and technologies to improve what it does), integrity (managing with honesty, efficiency, and reliability), and loyalty (earning the respect of the FedEx people, customers, and investors every day, in everything it does). Samsung embraces five values—giving employees opportunities to reach their full potential; an unyielding passion for excellence; anticipating change in market needs and demands; operating in an ethical way; and being a socially and environmentally responsible corporate citizen—in its quest to be among the world's leading consumer electronics companies.

> **CORE CONCEPT**
>
> A company's **values** are the beliefs, traits, and behavioral norms that company personnel are expected to display in conducting the company's business and pursuing its strategic vision and mission.

Do companies practice what they preach when it comes to their professed values? Sometimes no, sometimes yes—it runs the gamut. At one extreme are companies with window-dressing values; the values are given lip service by top executives but have little discernible impact on either how company personnel behave or how the company operates. Such companies have value statements because they are in vogue and make the company look good. At the other extreme are companies whose executives are committed to infusing the company with the desired character, traits, and behavioral norms so that they are ingrained in the company's corporate culture—the core values thus become an integral part of the company's DNA and what makes it tick. At such value-driven companies, executives "walk the talk" and company personnel are held accountable for displaying the stated values.

At companies where the stated values are real rather than cosmetic, managers connect values to the pursuit of the strategic vision and mission in one of two ways. In companies with long-standing values that are deeply entrenched in the corporate culture, senior managers are careful to craft a vision, mission, and strategy that match established values; they also reiterate how the value-based behavioral norms contribute to the company's business success. If the company changes to a different vision or strategy, executives take care to explain how and why the core values continue to be relevant. In new companies or companies having unspecified values, top management has to consider what values, behaviors, and business conduct should characterize the company and then draft a value statement that is circulated among managers and employees for discussion and possible modification. A final value statement that incorporates the desired behaviors and traits and that connects to the vision and mission is then officially adopted. Some companies combine their vision, mission, and values into a single statement or document, circulate it to all organization members, and in many instances post the vision, mission, and value statement on the company's Web site. Illustration Capsule 2.2 describes how core values and business principles drive the company's mission and approach to conducting business at Royal Dutch Shell.

STAGE 2: SETTING OBJECTIVES

The managerial purpose of setting **objectives** is to convert the vision and mission into specific performance targets. Well-stated objectives are *specific, quantifiable* or *measurable,* and contain a *deadline for achievement.* As Bill Hewlett, cofounder of Hewlett-Packard, shrewdly observed, "You cannot manage what you cannot measure. . . . And what gets measured gets done."[4] Concrete, measurable objectives are managerially valuable for three reasons: (1) They focus efforts and align actions throughout the organization, (2) they serve as *yardsticks* for tracking a company's performance and progress, and (3) they provide motivation and inspire employees to greater levels of effort. Ideally, managers should develop challenging yet achievable objectives that *stretch* an organization to perform at its full potential.

What Kinds of Objectives to Set

Two very distinct types of performance targets are required: those relating to financial performance and those relating to strategic performance. **Financial objectives** communicate management's targets for financial

ILLUSTRATION CAPSULE 2.2

Royal Dutch Shell Mission, Core Values, and Business Principles

The mission of the Shell Group is to engage efficiently, responsibly and profitably in oil, gas, chemicals and other selected businesses and to participate in the search for and development of other sources of energy to meet evolving customer needs and the world's growing demand for energy. Our shared core values of honesty, integrity and respect for people underpin all the work we do and are the foundation of our Business Principles. The Business Principles drive the behavior expected of every employee in every Shell company in the conduct of its business at all times and living by them is crucial to our continued success.

OUR VALUES

Shell employees share a set of core values—honesty, integrity and respect for people. We also firmly believe in the fundamental importance of trust, openness, teamwork and professionalism, and pride in what we do.

OUR BUSINESS PRINCIPLES

1. **Economic:** Long-term profitability is essential to achieving our business goals and to our continued growth. It is a measure both of efficiency and of the value that customers place on Shell products and services. It supplies the necessary corporate resources for the continuing investment that is required to develop and produce future energy supplies to meet customer needs. Without profits and a strong financial foundation, it would not be possible to fulfill our responsibilities.

2. **Competition:** Shell companies support free enterprise. We seek to compete fairly and ethically and within the framework of applicable competition laws; we will not prevent others from competing freely with us.

3. **Business Integrity:** Shell companies insist on honesty, integrity and fairness in all aspects of our business and expect the same in our relationships with all those with whom we do business. The direct or indirect offer, payment, soliciting or acceptance of bribes in any form is unacceptable. Facilitation payments are also bribes and must not be made. Employees must avoid conflicts of interest between their private

activities and their part in the conduct of company business. Employees must also declare to their employing company potential conflicts of interest. All business transactions on behalf of a Shell company must be reflected accurately and fairly in the accounts of the company in accordance with established procedures and are subject to audit and disclosure.

4. **Political Activities:** Shell companies act in a socially responsible manner within the laws of the countries in which we operate in pursuit of our legitimate commercial objectives. Shell companies do not make payments to political parties, organizations or their representatives. Shell companies do not take part in party politics. However, when dealing with governments, Shell companies have the right and the responsibility to make our position known on any matters, which affect us, our employees, our customers, our shareholders or local communities in a manner, which is in accordance with our values and the Business Principles.

5. **Health, Safety, Security and the Environment:** Shell companies have a systematic approach to health, safety, security and environmental management in order to achieve continuous performance improvement. To this end, Shell companies manage these matters as critical business activities, set standards and targets for improvement, and measure, appraise and report performance externally. We continually look for ways to reduce the environmental impact of our operations, products and services.

6. **Local Communities:** Shell companies aim to be good neighbors by continuously improving the ways in which we contribute directly or indirectly to the general well-being of the communities within which we work. We manage the social impacts of our business activities carefully and work with others to enhance the benefits to local communities, and to mitigate any negative impacts from our activities. In addition, Shell companies take a constructive interest in societal matters, directly or indirectly related to our business.

7. **Communication and Engagement:** Shell companies recognise that regular dialogue and engagement with our stakeholders is essential.

We are committed to reporting of our performance by providing full relevant information to legitimately interested parties, subject to any overriding considerations of business confidentiality. In our interactions with employees, business partners and local communities, we

seek to listen and respond to them honestly and responsibly.

8. **Compliance:** We comply with all applicable laws and regulations of the countries in which we operate.

Source: Information posted at www.shell.com/home/content/aboutshell/who_we_are/our_values/sgbp/ (accessed March 15, 2011).

performance. **Strategic objectives** are related to a company's marketing standing and competitive vitality. Examples of commonly used financial and strategic objectives include the following:

Financial Objectives	Strategic Objectives
• An x percent increase in annual revenues	• Winning an x percent market share
• Annual increases in after-tax profits of x percent	• Achieving lower overall costs than rivals
• Annual increases in earnings per share of x percent	• Overtaking key competitors on product performance or quality or customer service
• Annual dividend increases of x percent	• Deriving x percent of revenues from the sale of new products introduced within the past five years
• Profit margins of x percent	
• An x percent return on capital employed (ROCE) or return on shareholders' equity investment (ROE)	• Having broader or deeper technological capabilities than rivals
	• Having a wider product line than rivals
• Increased shareholder value—in the form of an upward-trending stock price	• Having a better-known or more powerful brand name than rivals
• Bond and credit ratings of x	• Having stronger national or global sales and distribution capabilities than rivals
• Internal cash flows of x dollars to fund new capital investment	• Consistently getting new or improved products to market ahead of rivals

The importance of setting and achieving financial objectives is intuitive. Without adequate profitability and financial strength, a company's long-term health and ultimate survival are jeopardized. Furthermore, subpar earnings and a weak balance sheet alarm shareholders and creditors and put the jobs of senior executives at risk. However, good financial performance, by itself, is not enough.

The Balanced Scorecard: Improved Strategic Performance Fosters Better Financial Performance

A company's financial performance measures are really *lagging indicators* that reflect the results of past decisions and organizational activities.[5] But a company's past or current financial performance is not a reliable indicator of its future prospects—poor financial performers often turn things around and do better, while good financial performers can fall upon hard times. The best and most reliable *leading indicators* of a company's future financial performance and business prospects are strategic outcomes that indicate whether the company's competitiveness and market position are stronger or weaker. The accomplishment of strategic objectives signals that the company is well positioned to sustain or improve its performance. For instance, if a company is achieving ambitious strategic objectives such that its competitive strength and market position are on the rise, then there's reason to expect that its *future* financial performance will be better than its current or past performance. If a company begins to lose competitive strength and fails to achieve important strategic objectives, then its ability to maintain its present profitability is highly suspect.

Consequently, utilizing a performance measurement system that strikes a *balance* between financial objectives and strategic objectives is optimal.[6] Just tracking a company's financial performance overlooks the fact that what ultimately enables a company to deliver better financial results from its operations is the achievement of strategic objectives that improve its competitiveness and market strength. Indeed, *the surest path to boosting company profitability* quarter after quarter and year after year *is to relentlessly pursue strategic outcomes* that strengthen the company's market position and produce a growing competitive advantage over rivals.

The most widely used framework for balancing financial objectives with strategic objectives is known as the **Balanced Scorecard**.[7] This is a method for linking financial performance objectives to specific strategic objectives that derive from a company's business model. It provides a company's employees with clear guidelines about how their jobs are linked to the overall objectives of the organization, so they can contribute most productively and collaboratively to the achievement of these goals. In 2008, nearly 60 percent of global companies used a balanced-scorecard approach to measuring strategic and financial performance.[8] Examples of organizations that have adopted a balanced-scorecard approach to setting objectives and measuring performance include UPS, UK Ministry of Defense, Caterpillar, Daimler AG, Hilton Hotels, and Siemens AG.[9] Illustration Capsule 2.3 provides selected strategic and financial objectives of three prominent companies.

> **CORE CONCEPT**
>
> The **Balanced Scorecard** is a tool that is widely used to help a company achieve its *financial objectives* by linking them to specific *strategic objectives* derived from the company's business model.

The Merits of Setting Stretch Objectives

Ideally, managers ought to use the objective-setting exercise as a tool for *stretching an organization to perform at its full potential and deliver the best possible results.* Challenging company personnel to go all out and deliver "stretch" gains in performance pushes an enterprise to be more inventive, to exhibit more urgency in improving both its financial performance and its business position, and to be more intentional and focused in its actions. Stretch objectives spur exceptional performance and help build a firewall against contentment with modest gains in organizational performance.

Why Both Short-Term and Long-Term Objectives Are Needed

A company's set of financial and strategic objectives should include both near-term and longer-term performance targets. Short-term (quarterly or annual) objectives focus attention on delivering performance improvements in the current period and satisfy shareholder expectations for near-term progress. Longer-term targets (three to five years off) force managers to consider what to do *now* to put the company in position to perform better later. Long-term objectives are critical for achieving optimal long-term performance and stand as a barrier to a nearsighted management philosophy and an undue focus on short-term results. When trade-offs have to be made between achieving long-run objectives and achieving short-run objectives, long-run objectives should

YUM! BRANDS (KFC, PIZZA HUT, TACO BELL, LONG JOHN SILVER'S)

Increase operating profit derived from international operations from 65% in 2010 to 75% in 2010; Increase operating profit derived from operations in emerging markets from 48% in 2010 to 60 percent in 2015; increase number of KFC units in Africa from 655 in 2010 to 2,100 in 2020; increase KFC revenues in Africa from $865 million in 2010 to $1.94 billion in 2014; increase number of KFC units in India from 101 in 2010 to 1,250 in 2020; increase number of KFC units in Vietnam from 87 in 2010 to 500 in 2020; increase number of KFC units in Russia from 150 in 2010 to 500 in 2020; open 100+ new Taco Bell units in international markets in 2015; increase annual cash flows from operations from $1.5 billion in 2010 to $2+ billion in 2015.

MICROSOFT

On a broad level, deliver end-to-end experiences that connect users to information, communications, entertainment, and people in new and compelling ways across their lives at home, at work, and the broadest-possible range of mobile scenarios. Given the dramatic changes in the way people interact with technology, as touch, gestures, handwriting, and speech recognition become a normal part of how we control devices, focus on making technology more accessible and simpler to use, which will create opportunities to reach new markets and deliver new kinds of computing experiences.

More specifically, grow revenue in the PC Division slightly faster than the overall PC market fueled especially by emerging market trends. Launch Office 2010 for the business market and promote adoption followed by a 2011 launch of the WindowsPhone 7 in the Entertainment and Devices Division. Grow annuity revenue between 4–6% in the Server and Tools Business segment. Target overall gross margin increases of 1% fueled in part by improved operational efficiency. Operating expenses are targeted at $26.1–$26.3 billion for the year with projected capital spending at $2 billion.

MCDONALD'S

Reinvest $2.4 billion in the business; 50% of this will be spent on opening 1,000 new restaurants around the world, including roughly 500 in Asia Pacific, 250 in Europe, and 150 in the U.S. The other half will be allocated toward "re-imagining" the décor and menu of over 2,000 existing locations. Re-imagining has a direct positive impact on sales as market share increases after re-imagining restaurants in the U.S., France and Australia demonstrate. Continue to expand refranchising; 80% of restaurants have been refranchised and this will be augmented by 200–300 restaurants in the next year. Focus on menu choice with a balance of familiar and popular core products as well as new items to keep products relevant.

Developed with C. David Morgan.

Sources: www.yum.com/investors/; "Microsoft Annual Report" www.microsoft.com/msft/reports/default.mspx (accessed April 23, 2010); "Microsoft Third Quarter Earnings Call," www.microsoft.com/msft/earnings/fy10/earn_rel_q3_10.mspx (accessed April 30, 2010); Thompson Reuters Street Events, "MCD – Q4 2009 McDonald's Corporate Earnings Conference Call," www.streetevents.com, January 2010 (transcribed version of Webcast accessed April 30, 2010, through InvesText database).

take precedence (unless the achievement of one or more short-run performance targets has unique importance).

The Need for Objectives at All Organizational Levels   Objective setting should not stop with top management's establishing of companywide performance targets. Company objectives need to be broken down into performance targets for each of the organization's separate businesses, product lines, functional departments, and individual work units. Company performance can't reach full potential unless each organizational unit sets and pursues performance targets that contribute directly to the desired companywide outcomes and results. Objective-setting is thus a *top-down process* that must extend to the lowest organizational levels. And it means that each organizational unit must take care to set performance targets that support—rather than conflict with or negate—the achievement of companywide strategic and financial objectives.

The ideal situation is a team effort in which each organizational unit strives to produce results in its area of responsibility that contribute to the achievement of the company's performance targets and strategic vision. Such consistency signals that organizational units know their strategic role and are on board in helping the company move down the chosen strategic path and produce the desired results.

STAGE 3: CRAFTING A STRATEGY

The task of stitching a strategy together entails addressing a series of hows: *how* to grow the business, *how* to please customers, *how* to outcompete rivals, *how* to respond to changing market conditions, *how* to manage each functional piece of the business, *how* to develop needed capabilities, and *how* to achieve strategic and financial objectives. It also means choosing among the various strategic alternatives—proactively searching for opportunities to do new things or to do existing things in new or better ways.[10] The faster a company's business environment is changing, the more critical it becomes for its managers to be good entrepreneurs in diagnosing the direction and force of the changes under way and in responding with timely adjustments in strategy. Strategy makers have to pay attention to early warnings of future change and be willing to experiment with dare-to-be-different ways to establish a market position in that future. When obstacles appear unexpectedly in a company's path, it is up to management to adapt rapidly and innovatively. *Masterful strategies come from doing things differently from competitors where it counts—out-innovating them, being more efficient, being more imaginative, adapting faster—rather than running with the herd.* Good strategy making is therefore inseparable from good business entrepreneurship. One cannot exist without the other.

Strategy Making Involves Managers at All Organizational Levels

A company's senior executives obviously have important strategy-making roles. The chief executive officer (CEO), as captain of the ship, carries the mantles of chief direction setter, chief objective setter, chief strategy maker, and chief strategy implementer for the total enterprise. Ultimate responsibility for *leading* the strategy-making, strategy-executing process rests with the CEO. In some

LO 3

Understand why the strategic initiatives taken at various organizational levels must be tightly coordinated to achieve companywide performance targets.

enterprises the CEO or owner functions as strategic visionary and chief architect of strategy, personally deciding what the key elements of the company's strategy will be, although others may well assist with data gathering and analysis and the CEO may seek the advice of senior executives or board members. A CEO-centered approach to strategy development is characteristic of small owner-managed companies and sometimes large corporations that were founded by the present CEO or that have a CEO with strong strategic leadership skills. Steve Jobs at Apple, Andrea Jung at Avon, Carlos Ghosn at Nissan, and Howard Schultz at Starbucks are prominent examples of corporate CEOs who have wielded a heavy hand in shaping their company's strategy.

Even here, however, it is a mistake to view strategy making as a *top* management function, the exclusive province of owner-entrepreneurs, CEOs, other senior executives, and board members. The more a company's operations cut across different products, industries, and geographic areas, the more that headquarters executives have little option but to delegate considerable strategy-making authority to down-the-line managers in charge of particular subsidiaries, divisions, product lines, geographic sales offices, distribution centers, and plants. On-the-scene managers who oversee specific operating units can be reliably counted on to have more detailed command of the strategic issues and choices for the particular operating unit under their supervision—knowing the prevailing market and competitive conditions, customer requirements and expectations, and all the other relevant aspects affecting the several strategic options available. Managers with day-to-day familiarity of, and authority over, a specific operating unit thus have a big edge over headquarters executives in making wise strategic choices for their operating unit.

CORE CONCEPT

In most companies, crafting and executing strategy is a *collaborative team effort* in which every manager has a role for the area he or she heads. It is flawed thinking to view crafting and executing strategy as something only high-level managers do.

Take, for example, a company like General Electric, a $183 billion global corporation with 325,000 employees, operations in some 100 countries, and businesses that include jet engines, lighting, power generation, electric transmission and distribution equipment, housewares and appliances, medical equipment, media and entertainment, locomotives, security devices, water purification, and financial services. While top-level headquarters executives may well be personally involved in shaping GE's *overall* strategy and fashioning *important* strategic moves, it doesn't follow that a few senior executives in GE's headquarters have either the expertise or a sufficiently detailed understanding of all the relevant factors to wisely craft all the strategic initiatives taken for hundreds of subsidiaries and thousands of products. They simply cannot know enough about the situation in every GE organizational unit to decide on every strategy detail and direct every strategic move made in GE's worldwide organization. Rather, it takes involvement on the part of GE's whole management team—top executives, business group heads, the heads of specific business units and product categories, and key managers in plants, sales offices, and distribution centers—to craft the thousands of strategic initiatives that end up constituting the whole of GE's strategy.

The *level* of strategy also has a bearing on who participates in crafting strategy. In diversified companies, where multiple businesses have to be managed, the strategy-making task involves four distinct levels of strategy. Each of these involves different facets of the company's overall strategy and calls for the participation of different types of managers, as shown in Figure 2.2.

1. *Corporate strategy* is strategy at the multibusiness level—how to achieve a competitive edge through a multibusiness, multimarket strategy. It concerns

Figure 2.2   A Company's Strategy-Making Hierarchy

Orchestrated by the CEO and other senior executives

Corporate Strategy

Multibusiness Strategy—how to gain advantage from managing a group of businesses

Two-Way Influence

In the case of a single-business company, these two levels of the strategy-making pyramid merge into one level— *business strategy*—that is orchestrated by the company's CEO and other top executives

Orchestrated by the general managers of each of the company's different lines of business, often with advice and input from more senior executives and the heads of functional-area activities within each business

Business Strategy (one for each business the company has diversified into)
- How to strengthen market position and gain competitive advantage
- Actions to build competitive capabilitiesbusinesses

Two-Way Influence

Orchestrated by the heads of major functional activities within a particular business, often in collaboration with other key people

Functional Area Strategies (within each business)
- Add relevant detail to the hows of the business strategy
- Provide a game plan for managing a particular activity in ways that support the business strategy

Two-Way Influence

Orchestrated by brand managers, the operating managers of plants, distribution centers, and purchasing centers, and the managers of strategically important activities like Web site operations, often in collaboration with other key people

Operating Strategies within Each Business
- Add detail and completeness to business and functional strategies
- Provide a game plan for managing specific lower-echelon activities with strategic significance

how to boost the combined performance of *the set of businesses* the company has diversified into and the means of capturing cross-business synergies and turning them into competitive advantage. It addresses the questions of what businesses to hold or divest, which new markets to enter, and what mode of entry to employ (e.g., through an acquisition, strategic alliance, or franchising). It concerns the *scope* of the firm and thus includes diversification strategies, vertical integration strategies, and geographic expansion strategies. Senior corporate executives normally have lead responsibility for devising corporate strategy and for choosing among whatever recommended actions bubble up from the organization below. Key business-unit heads may also be influential regarding issues related to the businesses they head. Major strategic decisions are usually reviewed and approved by the company's board of directors. We will look deeper into crafting corporate strategy in Chapter 8.

2. *Business strategy* is strategy at the level of a single line of business—one that competes in a relatively well-defined industry or market domain. The key focus is on crafting responses to changing market circumstances and initiating actions to develop strong competitive capabilities, build competitive advantage, strengthen market position, and enhance performance. Orchestrating the development of business-level strategy is typically the responsibility of the manager in charge of the business, although corporate-level managers may be influential. The business head has at least two other strategy-related roles: (1) seeing that lower-level strategies are well conceived, consistent, and adequately matched to the overall business strategy and (2) getting major business-level strategic moves approved by corporate-level officers and keeping them informed of emerging strategic issues. In diversified companies, business-unit heads have the additional obligation of making sure business-level objectives and strategy conform to corporate-level objectives and strategy themes.

3. *Functional-area strategies* concern the actions and approaches employed in managing particular functions within a business—like R&D, production, sales and marketing, customer service, and finance. A company's marketing strategy, for example, represents the managerial game plan for running the sales and marketing part of the business. A company's product development strategy represents the game plan for keeping the company's product lineup in tune with what buyers are looking for. The primary role of functional strategies is to flesh out the details of a company's business strategy. Lead responsibility for functional strategies within a business is normally delegated to the heads of the respective functions, with the general manager of the business having final approval. Since the different functional-level strategies must be compatible with the overall business strategy and with one another to have beneficial impact, the general business manager may at times exert stronger influence on the content of the functional strategies.

4. *Operating strategies* concern the relatively narrow strategic initiatives and approaches for managing key operating units (e.g., plants, distribution centers, purchasing centers) and specific operating activities with strategic significance (e.g., quality control, materials purchasing, brand management, Internet sales). A distribution center manager of a company promising customers speedy delivery must have a strategy to ensure that finished goods are rapidly turned around and shipped out to customers once they are received from the company's manufacturing facilities. Operating strategies, while of limited scope, add further detail to functional strategies and to the overall

business strategy. Lead responsibility for operating strategies is usually delegated to frontline managers, subject to review and approval by higher-ranking managers.

Even though operating strategy is at the bottom of the strategy-making hierarchy, its importance should not be downplayed. A major plant that fails in its strategy to achieve production volume, unit cost, and quality targets can damage the company's reputation for quality products and undercut the achievement of company sales and profit objectives. Frontline managers are thus an important part of an organization's strategy-making team. One cannot reliably judge the strategic importance of a given action simply by the strategy level or location within the managerial hierarchy where it is initiated.

In single-business enterprises, the corporate and business levels of strategy making merge into one level—business strategy—because the strategy for the whole company involves only one distinct line of business. Thus a single-business enterprise has three levels of strategy: business strategy for the company as a whole, functional-area strategies for each main area within the business, and operating strategies undertaken by lower-echelon managers to flesh out strategically significant aspects of the company's business and functional-area strategies. Proprietorships, partnerships, and owner-managed enterprises may have only one or two strategy-making levels since their strategy-making process can be handled by just a few key people. The larger and more diverse the operations of an enterprise, the more points of strategic initiative it has and the more levels of management that have a significant strategy-making role.

The overall point is this: Regardless of the type of enterprise and whether the strategy is primarily deliberate or primarily emergent, crafting strategy involves managers in various positions and at various organizational levels. And while managers farther down in the managerial hierarchy obviously have a narrower, more specific strategy-making role than managers closer to the top, the important understanding is that in most of today's companies *every company manager typically has a strategy-making role—ranging from minor to major—for the area he or she heads.* Hence any notion that an organization's strategists are at the top of the management hierarchy and that midlevel and frontline personnel merely carry out the strategic directives of senior managers needs to be cast aside. In companies with wide-ranging operations, it is far more accurate to view strategy making as a *collaborative team effort* involving managers (and sometimes other key employees) down through the whole organizational hierarchy. A valuable strength of collaborative strategy making is that the team of people charged with crafting the strategy include the very people who will also be charged with implementing and executing it. Giving people an influential stake in crafting the strategy they must later help execute not only builds motivation and commitment but also enhances accountability at multiple levels of management—the excuse of "It wasn't my idea to do this" won't fly.

In most companies, crafting strategy is a *collaborative team effort* that includes managers in various positions and at various organizational levels. Crafting strategy is rarely something only high-level executives do.

A Strategic Vision + Objectives + Strategy = A Strategic Plan

Developing a strategic vision and mission, setting objectives, and crafting a strategy are basic direction-setting tasks. They map out where a company is headed, its purpose, the targeted strategic and financial outcomes, the basic business model, and the competitive moves and internal action approaches to be used in achieving the desired business results. Together, they constitute a **strategic plan** for coping with industry conditions, outcompeting rivals, meeting objectives, and making progress toward the strategic vision.[11] Typically, a strategic plan includes a commitment to allocate resources to the plan and specifies a time period for achieving goals (usually three to five years).

In some companies, the strategic plan is focused around achieving exceptionally bold strategic objectives—stretch goals requiring resources that are well beyond the current means of the company. This type of strategic plan is more the expression of a **strategic intent** to rally the organization through an *unshakable—often obsessive—commitment* to do whatever it takes to acquire the resources and achieve the goals. Nike's strategic intent during the 1960s was to overtake Adidas—an objective far beyond Nike's means at the time. Starbucks strategic intent is to make the Starbucks brand the world's most recognized and respected brand.

In companies that do regular strategy reviews and develop explicit strategic plans, the strategic plan usually ends up as a written document that is circulated to most managers and perhaps selected employees. Near-term performance targets are the part of the strategic plan most often spelled out explicitly and communicated to managers and employees. A number of companies summarize key elements of their strategic plans in the company's annual report to shareholders, in postings on their Web sites, or in statements provided to the business media, whereas others, perhaps for reasons of competitive sensitivity, make only vague, general statements about their strategic plans.[12] In small, privately owned companies, it is rare for strategic plans to exist in written form. Small-company strategic plans tend to reside in the thinking and directives of owners/executives, with aspects of the plan being revealed in meetings and conversations with company personnel, and in the understandings and commitments among managers and key employees about where to head, what to accomplish, and how to proceed.

STAGE 4: EXECUTING THE STRATEGY

Managing the implementation of a strategy is an operations-oriented, make-things-happen activity aimed at performing core business activities in a strategy-supportive manner. It is easily the most demanding and time-consuming part of the strategy management process. Converting strategic plans into actions and results tests a manager's ability to direct organizational action, motivate people, build and strengthen company competencies and competitive capabilities, create and nurture a strategy-supportive work climate, and meet or beat performance targets. Initiatives to put the strategy in place and execute it proficiently have to be launched and managed on many organizational fronts.

Management's action agenda for executing the chosen strategy emerges from assessing what the company will have to do to achieve the targeted financial and strategic performance. Each company manager has to think through the answer to "What has to be done in my area to execute my piece of the strategic plan, and what actions should I take to get the process under way?" How much internal change is needed depends on how much of the strategy is new, how far internal practices and competencies deviate from what the strategy requires, and how well the present work climate/culture supports good strategy execution. Depending on the amount of internal change involved, full implementation and proficient execution of company strategy (or important new pieces thereof) can take several months to several years.

In most situations, managing the strategy execution process includes the following principal aspects:

- Staffing the organization with the needed skills and expertise.
- Building and strengthening strategy-supporting resources and competitive capabilities.
- Organizing the work effort along the lines of best practice.
- Allocating ample resources to the activities critical to strategic success.
- Ensuring that policies and procedures facilitate rather than impede effective strategy execution.
- Installing information and operating systems that enable company personnel to carry out their roles effectively and efficiently.
- Motivating people and tying rewards and incentives directly to the achievement of performance objectives.
- Creating a company culture and work climate conducive to successful strategy execution.
- Exerting the internal leadership needed to propel implementation forward and drive continuous improvement of the strategy execution processes.

Good strategy execution requires diligent pursuit of operating excellence. It is a job for a company's whole management team. Success hinges on the skills and cooperation of operating managers who can push for needed changes in their organizational units and consistently deliver good results. Management's handling of the strategy implementation process can be considered successful if things go smoothly enough that the company meets or beats its strategic and financial performance targets and shows good progress in achieving management's strategic vision.

STAGE 5: EVALUATING PERFORMANCE AND INITIATING CORRECTIVE ADJUSTMENTS

The fifth component of the strategy management process—monitoring new external developments, evaluating the company's progress, and making corrective adjustments—is the trigger point for deciding whether to continue or change the company's vision and mission, objectives, strategy, and/or strategy execution methods.[13] As long as the company's strategy continues to pass the three tests of a winning strategy (good fit, competitive advantage, strong performance), company executives may well decide to stay the course. Simply fine-tuning the strategic plan and continuing with efforts to improve strategy execution are sufficient.

However, whenever a company encounters disruptive changes in its environment, questions need to be raised about the appropriateness of its direction and strategy. If a company experiences a downturn in its market position or

> A company's vision and mission, objectives, strategy, and approach to strategy execution are never final; managing strategy is an ongoing process.

persistent shortfalls in performance, then company managers are obligated to ferret out the causes—do they relate to poor strategy, poor strategy execution, or both?—and take timely corrective action. A company's direction, objectives, and strategy have to be revisited anytime external or internal conditions warrant. It is to be expected that a company will modify its strategic vision, direction, objectives, and strategy over time.

Likewise, it is not unusual for a company to find that one or more aspects of its strategy execution are not going as well as intended. Proficient strategy execution is always the product of much organizational learning. It is achieved unevenly—coming quickly in some areas and proving nettlesome in others. It is both normal and desirable to periodically assess strategy execution to determine which aspects are working well and which need improving. Successful strategy execution entails vigilantly searching for ways to improve and then making corrective adjustments whenever and wherever it is useful to do so.

CORPORATE GOVERNANCE: THE ROLE OF THE BOARD OF DIRECTORS IN THE STRATEGY-CRAFTING, STRATEGY-EXECUTING PROCESS

LO 5

Become aware of the role and responsibility of a company's board of directors in overseeing the strategic management process.

Although senior managers have *lead responsibility* for crafting and executing a company's strategy, it is the duty of a company's board of directors to exercise strong oversight and see that the five tasks of strategic management are conducted in a manner that is in the best interests of shareholders and other stakeholders.[14] A company's board of directors has four important obligations to fulfill:

1. *Critically appraise the company's direction, strategy, and business approaches.* Board members must ask probing questions and draw on their business acumen to make independent judgments about whether strategy proposals have been adequately analyzed and whether proposed strategic actions appear to have greater promise than alternatives. Asking incisive questions is usually sufficient to test whether the case for management's proposals is compelling and to exercise vigilant oversight. However, when the company's strategy is failing or is plagued with faulty execution, and certainly when there is a precipitous collapse in profitability, board members have a duty to be more proactive, expressing their concerns about the validity of the strategy and/or operating methods, initiating debate about the company's strategic path, having one-on-one discussions with key executives and other board members, and perhaps directly intervening as a group to alter the company's executive leadership and, ultimately, its strategy and business approaches.

2. *Evaluate the caliber of senior executives' strategic leadership skills.* The board is always responsible for determining whether the current CEO is doing a good job of strategic leadership.[15] The board must also evaluate the leadership skills of other senior executives, since the board must elect a successor when the incumbent CEO steps down, either going with an insider

or deciding that an outsider is needed. Evaluation of senior executives' skills is enhanced when outside directors visit company facilities and talk with company personnel to personally evaluate whether the strategy is on track, how well the strategy is being executed, and how well issues and problems are being addressed. Independent board members at GE visit operating executives at each major business unit once a year to assess the company's talent pool and stay abreast of emerging strategic and operating issues affecting the company's divisions.

3. *Institute a compensation plan for top executives that rewards them for actions and results that serve stakeholder interests—especially those of shareholders.* A basic principle of corporate governance is that the owners of a corporation (the shareholders) delegate managerial control to a team of executives who are compensated for their efforts on behalf of the owners. In their role as an *agent* of shareholders, corporate managers have a clear and unequivocal duty to make decisions and operate the company in accord with shareholder interests. (This does not mean disregarding the interests of other stakeholders—employees, suppliers, the communities in which the company operates, and society at large.) Most boards of directors have a compensation committee, composed entirely of directors from *outside* the company, to develop a salary and incentive compensation plan that rewards senior executives for boosting the company's *long-term* performance and growing the economic value of the enterprise on behalf of shareholders; the compensation committee's recommendations are presented to the full board for approval. But during the past 10 to 15 years, many boards of directors have done a poor job of ensuring that executive salary increases, bonuses, and stock option awards are tied tightly to performance measures that are truly in the long-term interests of shareholders. Rather, compensation packages at many companies have increasingly rewarded executives for short-term performance improvements that led to undue risk taking and compensation packages that, in the view of many people, were obscenely large. This has proved damaging to long-term company performance and has worked against shareholder interests—witness the huge loss of shareholder wealth that occurred at many financial institutions in 2008–2009 because of executive risk taking in subprime loans, credit default swaps, and collateralized mortgage securities in 2006–2007. As a consequence, the need to overhaul and reform executive compensation has become a hot topic in both public circles and corporate boardrooms. Illustration Capsule 2.4 discusses how weak governance at the U.S. mortgage companies Fannie Mae and Freddie Mac allowed opportunistic senior managers to boost their compensation while making decisions that imperiled the futures of the companies they managed.

4. *Oversee the company's financial accounting and financial reporting practices.* While top executives, particularly the company's CEO and CFO (chief financial officer), are primarily responsible for seeing that the company's financial statements fairly and accurately report the results of the company's operations, board members have a fiduciary duty to protect shareholders by exercising oversight of the company's financial practices. In addition, corporate boards must ensure that generally acceptable accounting principles are properly used in preparing the company's financial statements and that proper financial controls are in place to

Corporate Governance Failures at Fannie Mae and Freddie Mac

Executive compensation in the financial services industry during the mid-2000s ranks high among examples of failed corporate governance. Corporate governance at the U.S. government-sponsored mortgage giants Fannie Mae and Freddie Mac was particularly weak. The politically appointed boards at both enterprises failed to understand the risks of the subprime loan strategies being employed, did not adequately monitor the decisions of the CEO, did not exercise effective oversight of the accounting principles being employed (which led to inflated earnings), and approved executive compensation systems that allowed management to manipulate earnings to receive lucrative performance bonuses. The audit and compensation committees at Fannie Mae were particularly ineffective in protecting shareholder interests, with the audit committee allowing the company's financial officers to audit reports prepared under their direction and used to determine performance bonuses. Fannie Mae's audit committee also was aware of management's use of questionable accounting practices that reduced losses and recorded one-time gains to achieve financial targets linked to bonuses. In addition, the audit committee failed to investigate formal charges of accounting improprieties filed by a manager in the U.S. Office of the Controller.

Fannie Mae's compensation committee was equally ineffective. The committee allowed the company's CEO, Franklin Raines, to select the consultant employed to design the mortgage firm's executive compensation plan and agreed to a tiered bonus plan that would permit Raines and other senior managers to receive maximum bonuses without great difficulty. The compensation plan allowed Raines to earn performance-based bonuses of $52 million and total compensation of $90 million between 1999 and 2004. Raines was forced to resign in December 2004 when the U.S. Office of Federal Housing Enterprise Oversight found that Fannie Mae executives had fraudulently inflated earnings to receive bonuses linked to financial performance. Securities and Exchange Commission investigators also found evidence of improper accounting at Fannie Mae and required the company to restate its earnings between 2002 and 2004 by $6.3 billion.

Poor governance at Freddie Mac allowed its CEO and senior management to manipulate financial data to receive performance-based compensation as well. Freddie Mac CEO Richard Syron received 2007 compensation of $19.8 million while the mortgage company's share price declined from a high of $70 in 2005 to $25 at year-end 2007. During Syron's tenure as CEO, the company became embroiled in a multibillion-dollar accounting scandal, and Syron personally disregarded internal reports dating to 2004 that cautioned of an impending financial crisis at the company. Forewarnings within Freddie Mac and by federal regulators and outside industry observers proved to be correct, with loan underwriting policies at Freddie Mac and Fannie Mae leading to combined losses at the two firms in 2008 of more than $100 billion. The price of

(continued)

Freddie Mac's shares had fallen to below $1 by the time of Syron's resignation in September 2008.

Both organizations were placed into a conservatorship under the direction of the U.S. government in September 2008 and were provided bailout funds of nearly $60 billion by April 2009. In May 2009, Fannie Mae requested another $19 billion of the $200 billion committed by the U.S. government to cover the operating losses of the two government-sponsored mortgage firms. By June 2010, the bill for bailing out the two enterprises had risen to $145 billion, with the expectation that still more aid would be required to get them back on sound financial footing.

Sources: "Adding Up the Government's Total Bailout Tab," New York Times Online, February 4, 2009; Eric Dash, "Fannie Mae to Restate Results by $6.3 Billion because of Accounting," New York Times Online, December 7, 2006; Annys Shin, "Fannie Mae Sets Executive Salaries," Washington Post, February 9, 2006, p. D4; Scott DeCarlo, Eric Weiss, Mark Jickling, James R. Cristie, Fannie Mae and Freddie Mac: Scandal in U.S. Housing (Nova, 2006), pp. 266–86; "Chaffetz, Conyers, Smith, Issa and Bachus Call for FOIA to Apply to Fannie-Freddie," June 17, 2010 (June 2010 Archives), http://chaffetz.house.gov/2010/06/ (accessed June 24, 2010).

prevent fraud and misuse of funds. Virtually all boards of directors have an audit committee, always composed entirely of *outside directors* (*inside directors* hold management positions in the company and either directly or indirectly report to the CEO). The members of the audit committee have lead responsibility for overseeing the decisions of the company's financial officers and consulting with both internal and external auditors to ensure that financial reports are accurate and that adequate financial controls are in place. Faulty oversight of corporate accounting and financial reporting practices by audit committees and corporate boards during the early 2000s resulted in the investigation of more than 20 major corporations between 2000 and 2002. The investigations of such well-known companies as Global Crossing, Enron, Qwest Communications, Parmalat, and WorldCom found that upper management had employed fraudulent or unsound accounting practices to artificially inflate revenues, overstate assets, and reduce expenses.

Every corporation should have a strong, independent board of directors that (1) is well informed about the company's performance, (2) guides and judges the CEO and other top executives, (3) has the courage to curb management actions the board believes are inappropriate or unduly risky, (4) certifies to shareholders that the CEO is doing what the board expects, (5) provides insight and advice to management, and (6) is intensely involved in debating the pros and cons of key decisions and actions.[16] Boards of directors that lack the backbone to challenge a strong-willed or "imperial" CEO or that rubber-stamp almost anything the CEO recommends without probing inquiry and debate (perhaps because the board is stacked with the CEO's cronies) abdicate their duty to represent and protect shareholder interests.

Effective corporate governance requires the board of directors to oversee the company's strategic direction, evaluate its senior executives, handle executive compensation, and oversee financial reporting practices.

KEY POINTS

The strategic management process consists of five interrelated and integrated stages:

1. *Developing a strategic vision* of the company's future, a *mission* that defines the company's current purpose, and a set of *core values* to guide the pursuit of the vision and mission. This managerial step provides direction for the company, motivates and inspires company personnel, aligns and guides actions throughout the organization, and communicates to stakeholders management's aspirations for the company's future.

2. *Setting objectives* to convert the vision and mission into performance targets and using the targeted results as yardsticks for measuring the company's performance. Objectives need to spell out *how much* of *what kind* of performance *by when*. Two broad types of objectives are required: *financial objectives* and *strategic objectives*. A *balanced-scorecard* approach provides a popular method for linking financial objectives to specific, measurable strategic objectives.

3. *Crafting a strategy* to achieve the objectives and move the company along the strategic course that management has charted. Crafting deliberate strategy calls for strategic analysis, based on the business model. Crafting emergent strategy is a learning-by-doing process involving experimentation. Who participates in the process of crafting strategy depends on (1) whether the process is emergent or deliberate and (2) the level of strategy concerned. Deliberate strategies are mostly top-down, while emergent strategies are bottom-up, although both cases require two-way interaction between different types of managers. In large, diversified companies, there are four levels of strategy, each of which involves a corresponding level of management: corporate strategy (multibusiness strategy), business strategy (strategy for individual businesses that compete in a single industry), functional-area strategies within each business (e.g., marketing, R&D, logistics), and operating strategies (for key operating units, such as manufacturing plants). Thus, strategy making is an inclusive, collaborative activity involving not only senior company executives but also the heads of major business divisions, functional-area managers, and operating managers on the frontlines. The larger and more diverse the operations of an enterprise, the more points of strategic initiative it has and the more levels of management that play a significant strategy-making role.

4. *Executing the chosen strategy* and converting the strategic plan into action. Managing the execution of strategy is an operations-oriented, make-things-happen activity aimed at shaping the performance of core business activities in a strategy-supportive manner. Management's handling of the strategy implementation process can be considered successful if things go smoothly enough that the company meets or beats its strategic and financial performance targets and shows good progress in achieving management's strategic vision.

5. *Monitoring developments, evaluating performance, and initiating corrective adjustments* in light of actual experience, changing conditions, new ideas, and new opportunities. This stage of the strategy management process is the trigger point for deciding whether to continue or change the company's vision and mission, objectives, strategy, and/or strategy execution methods.

The sum of a company's strategic vision and mission, objectives, and strategy constitutes a *strategic plan* for coping with industry conditions, outcompeting rivals, meeting objectives, and making progress toward the strategic vision. A company whose strategic plan is based around ambitious *stretch goals* that require an unwavering commitment to do whatever it takes to achieve them is said to have *strategic intent.*

Boards of directors have a duty to shareholders to play a vigilant role in overseeing management's handling of a company's strategy-making, strategy-executing process. This entails four important obligations: (1) Critically appraise the company's direction, strategy, and strategy execution, (2) evaluate the caliber of senior executives' strategic leadership skills, (3) institute a compensation plan for top executives that rewards them for actions and results that serve stakeholder interests—*especially those of shareholders,* and (4) ensure that the company issues accurate financial reports and has adequate financial controls.

ASSURANCE OF LEARNING EXERCISES

LO 1

1. Using the information in Table 2.1, critique the adequacy and merit of the following vision statements, listing effective elements and shortcomings. Rank the vision statements from best to worst once you complete your evaluation.

Vision Statement	Effective Elements	Shortcomings
BASF We are "The Chemical Company" successfully operating in all major markets. • Our customers view BASF as their partner of choice. • Our innovative products, intelligent solutions and services make us the most competent worldwide supplier in the chemical industry. • We generate a high return on assets. • We strive for Sustainable Development. • We welcome change as an opportunity. • We, the employees of BASF, together ensure our success.		
Hilton Hotels Corporation Our vision is to be the first choice of the world's travelers. Hilton intends to build on the rich heritage and strength of our brands by: • Consistently delighting our customers • Investing in our team members • Delivering innovative products and services • Continuously improving performance • Increasing shareholder value • Creating a culture of pride • Strengthening the loyalty of our constituents		
Bank of China To be customer's premier bank.		

(continued)

Vision Statement	Effective Elements	Shortcomings
Rio Tinto Our vision of being the global mining leader means maintaining or achieving sector leadership, including operational excellence, sustainable development, exploration and innovation.		
Chevron To be *the* global energy company most admired for its people, partnership and performance. Our vision means we: • provide energy products vital to sustainable economic progress and human development throughout the world; • are people and an organization with superior capabilities and commitment; • are the partner of choice; • deliver world-class performance; • earn the admiration of all our stakeholders—investors, customers, host governments, local communities and our employees—not only for the goals we achieve but how we achieve them.		

Source: Company Web sites and annual reports.

LO 2

2. Review the analyst presentations and other reports at the company investor relations Web sites for Intel (www.intc.com), Lufthansa (http://investor-relations.lufthansa.com), and Tata Motors (http://ir.tatamotors.com) to find some examples of strategic and financial objectives. Make a list of four objectives for each company, and indicate which of these are strategic and which are financial.

LO 5

3. Go to www.dell.com/leadership, and read the sections dedicated to Dell's board of directors and corporate governance. Is there evidence of effective governance at Dell in regard to (1) accurate financial reports and controls, (2) a critical appraisal of strategic action plans, (3) evaluation of the strategic leadership skills of the CEO, and (4) executive compensation?

EXERCISES FOR SIMULATION PARTICIPANTS

LO 1, LO 2, LO 3

1. Meet with your co-managers and prepare a strategic vision statement for your company. It should be at least one sentence long and no longer than a brief paragraph. When you are finished, check to see if your vision statement is in compliance with the dos and don'ts set forth in Table 2.1. If not, revise it accordingly. What would be a good slogan that captures the essence of your strategic vision and that could be used to help communicate the vision to company personnel, shareholders, and other stakeholders?

2. What is your company's strategic intent? Write a sentence that expresses your company's strategic intent.

3. What are your company's financial objectives?

4. What are your company's strategic objectives?

5. What are the three or four key elements of your company's strategy?

ENDNOTES

[1] For a more in-depth discussion of the challenges of developing a well-conceived vision, as well as some good examples, see Hugh Davidson, *The Committed Enterprise: How to Make Vision and Values Work* (Oxford: Butterworth Heinemann, 2002), chap. 2; W. Chan Kim and Renée Mauborgne, "Charting Your Company's Future," *Harvard Business Review* 80, no. 6 (June 2002), pp. 77–83; James C. Collins and Jerry I. Porras, "Building Your Company's Vision," *Harvard Business Review* 74, no. 5 (September–October 1996), pp. 65–77; Jim Collins and Jerry Porras, *Built to Last: Successful Habits of Visionary Companies* (New York: HarperCollins, 1994), chap. 11; Michel Robert, *Strategy Pure and Simple II: How Winning Companies Dominate Their Competitors* (New York: McGraw-Hill, 1998), chaps. 2, 3 and 6.

[2] Davidson, *The Committed Enterprise*, pp. 20 and 54.

[3] Ibid., pp. 36, 54.

[4] As quoted in Charles H. House and Raymond L. Price, "The Return Map: Tracking Product Teams," *Harvard Business Review* 60, no. 1 (January–February 1991), p. 93.

[5] Robert S. Kaplan and David P. Norton, *The Strategy-Focused Organization* (Boston: Harvard Business School Press, 2001), p. 3. Also see Robert S. Kaplan and David P. Norton, *The Balanced Scorecard: Translating Strategy into Action* (Boston: Harvard Business School Press, 1996), chap. 1.

[6] Kaplan and Norton, p.7. Also see Kevin B. Hendricks, Larry Menor, and Christine Wiedman, "The Balanced Scorecard: To Adopt or Not to Adopt," *Ivey Business Journal* 69, no. 2 (November–December 2004), pp. 1–7; Sandy Richardson, "The Key Elements of Balanced Scorecard Success," *Ivey Business Journal* 69, no. 2 (November–December 2004), pp.7–9.

[7] Kaplan and Norton, *The Balanced Scorecard*.

[8] Information posted on the Web site of Bain and Company, www.bain.com (accessed May 27, 2009).

[9] Information posted on the Web site of Balanced Scorecard Institute, http://www.balancedscorecard.org/ (accessed May 27, 2009).

[10] For a fuller discussion of strategy as an entrepreneurial process, see Henry Mintzberg, Bruce Ahlstrand, and Joseph Lampel, *Strategy Safari: A Guided Tour through the Wilds of Strategic Management* (New York: Free Press, 1998), chap. 5. Also see Bruce Barringer and Allen C. Bluedorn, "The Relationship between Corporate Entrepreneurship and Strategic Management," *Strategic Management Journal* 20 (1999), pp. 421–44; Jeffrey G. Covin and Morgan P. Miles, "Corporate Entrepreneurship and the Pursuit of Competitive Advantage," *Entrepreneurship: Theory and Practice* 23, no. 3 (Spring 1999), pp. 47–63; David A. Garvin and Lynned C. Levesque, "Meeting the Challenge of Corporate Entrepreneurship," *Harvard Business Review* 84, no. 10 (October 2006), pp. 102–12.

[11] For an excellent discussion of why a strategic plan needs to be more than a list of bullet points and should in fact tell an engaging, insightful, stage-setting story that lays out the industry and competitive situation as well as the vision, objectives, and strategy, see Gordon Shaw, Robert Brown, and Philip Bromiley, "Strategic Stories: How 3M Is Rewriting Business Planning," *Harvard Business Review* 76, no. 3 (May–June 1998), pp. 41–50.

[12] In many companies, there is often confusion or ambiguity about exactly what a company's strategy is; see David J. Collis and Michael G. Rukstad, "Can You Say What Your Strategy Is?" *Harvard Business Review* 86, no. 4 (April 2008), pp. 82–90.

[13] For an excellent discussion of why effective strategic leadership on the part of senior executives involves continuous re-creation of a company's strategy, see Cynthia A. Montgomery, "Putting Leadership Back into Strategy," *Harvard Business Review* 86, no. 1 (January 2008), pp. 54–60.

[14] For a timely and insightful discussion of the strategic and leadership functions of a company's board of directors, see Jay W. Lorsch and Robert C. Clark, "Leading from the Boardroom," *Harvard Business Review* 86, no. 4 (April 2008), pp. 105–11.

[15] For a deeper discussion of this function, see Stephen P. Kaufman, "Evaluating the CEO," *Harvard Business Review* 86, no. 10 (October 2008), pp. 53–57.

[16] For a discussion of what it takes for the corporate governance system to function properly, see David A. Nadler, "Building Better Boards," *Harvard Business Review* 82, no. 5 (May 2004), pp. 102–5; Cynthia A. Montgomery and Rhonda Kaufman, "The Board's Missing Link," *Harvard Business Review* 81, no. 3 (March 2003), pp. 86–93; John Carver, "What Continues to Be Wrong with Corporate Governance and How to Fix It," *Ivey Business Journal* 68, no. 1 (September–October 2003), pp. 1–5. See also Gordon Donaldson, "A New Tool for Boards: The Strategic Audit," *Harvard Business Review* 73, no. 4 (July–August 1995), pp. 99–107.

CHAPTER 3

EVALUATING A COMPANY'S EXTERNAL ENVIRONMENT

> Analysis is the critical starting point of strategic thinking.
>
> **—Kenichi Ohmae**
> *Consultant and Author*

> In essence, the job of a strategist is to understand and cope with competition.
>
> **—Michael Porter**
> *Harvard Business School professor and Cofounder of Monitor Consulting*

> Things are always different—the art is figuring out which differences matter.
>
> **—Laszlo Birinyi**
> *Investments Manager*

LEARNING OBJECTIVES

LO 1. Gain command of the basic concepts and analytical tools widely used to diagnose the competitive conditions in a company's industry.

LO 2. Learn how to diagnose the factors shaping industry dynamics and to forecast their effects on future industry profitability.

LO 3. Become adept at mapping the market positions of key groups of industry rivals.

LO 4. Understand why in-depth evaluation of a business's strengths and weaknesses in relation to the specific industry conditions it confronts is an essential prerequisite to crafting a strategy that is well-matched to its external situation.

In Chapter 1, we learned that one of the three central questions that managers must address in evaluating their business prospects is "What's the company's present situation?" Two facets of a company's situation are especially pertinent: (1) competitive conditions in the industry in which the company operates—its external environment; and (2) the company's resources and organizational capabilities—its internal environment.

Insightful diagnosis of a company's external and internal environments is a prerequisite for managers to succeed in crafting a strategy that is an excellent *fit* with the company's situation—the first test of a winning strategy. As depicted in Figure 3.1, the task of crafting a strategy should always begin with an appraisal of the company's external environment and internal environment (as a basis for deciding on a long-term direction and developing a strategic vision), then move toward an evaluation of the most promising alternative strategies and business models, and culminate in choosing a specific strategy.

This chapter presents the concepts and analytical tools for zeroing in on those aspects of a company's external environment that should be considered in making strategic choices about where and how to compete. Attention centers on the competitive arena in which a company operates, the drivers of market change, the market positions of rival companies, and the factors that determine competitive success. In Chapter 4 we explore the methods of evaluating a company's internal circumstances and competitive capabilities.

Figure 3.1   **From Thinking Strategically about the Company's Situation to Choosing a Strategy**

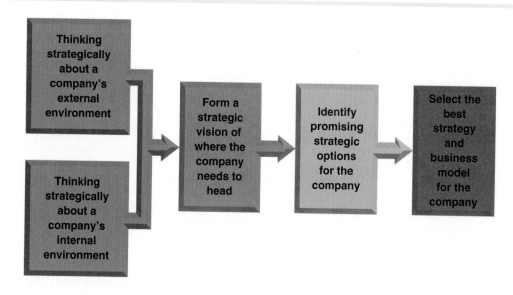

THE STRATEGICALLY RELEVANT COMPONENTS OF A COMPANY'S MACRO-ENVIRONMENT

Every company operates in a larger environment that goes well beyond just the industry in which it operates; this **"macro-environment"** includes seven principal components: population demographics; societal values and lifestyles; political, legal, and regulatory factors; the natural environment and ecological factors; technological factors; general economic conditions; and global forces. Each of these components has the potential to affect the firm's more immediate industry and competitive environment, although some are likely to have a more important effect than others (see Figure 3.2). Since macroeconomic factors affect different industries in different ways and to different degrees, it is important for managers to determine which of these represent the most *strategically relevant factors* outside the firm's industry boundaries. By *strategically relevant,* we mean important enough to have a bearing on the decisions the company ultimately makes about its direction, objectives, strategy, and business model. Strategically relevant influences coming from the outer ring of the external environment can sometimes have a high impact on a company's business situation and have a very significant impact on the company's direction and strategy. For example, the strategic opportunities of cigarette producers to grow their businesses are greatly reduced by antismoking ordinances, the decisions of governments to impose higher cigarette taxes, and the growing cultural stigma attached to smoking. Motor vehicle companies must adapt their strategies to customer concerns about high gasoline prices and to environmental concerns about

> **CORE CONCEPT**
>
> The **macro-environment** encompasses the broad environmental context in which a company's industry is situated.

Figure 3.2 **The Components of a Company's Macro-Environment**

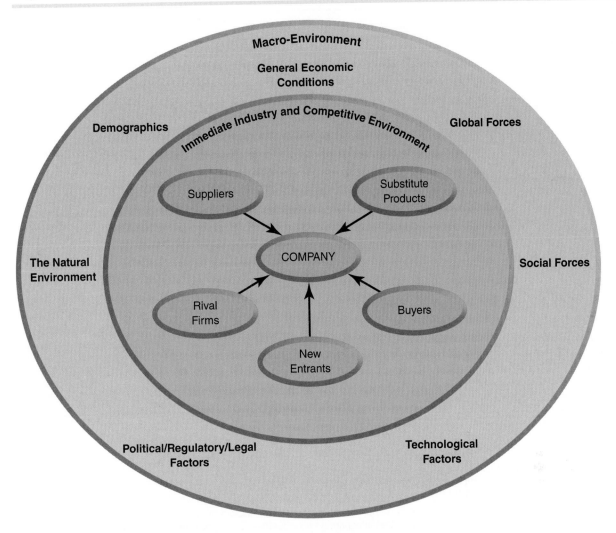

carbon emissions. Companies in the food processing, restaurant, sports, and fitness industries have to pay special attention to changes in lifestyles, eating habits, leisure-time preferences, and attitudes toward nutrition and fitness in fashioning their strategies. Table 3.1 provides a brief description of the components of the macro-environment and some examples of the industries or business situations that they might affect.

Happenings in the outer ring of the environment may occur rapidly or slowly, with or without advance warning. As company managers scan the external environment, they must be alert for potentially important outer-ring developments, assess their impact and influence, and adapt the company's direction and strategy as needed. However, the factors and forces in a company's environment having the *biggest* strategy-shaping impact typically pertain to the company's immediate industry and competitive environment—competitive pressures, the actions of rival firms, buyer behavior, supplier-related considerations, and so on. Consequently, it is on a company's industry and competitive environment that we concentrate the bulk of our attention in this chapter.

Table 3.1   The Seven Components of the Macro-Environment

Component	Description
Demographics	Demographics includes the size, growth rate, and age distribution of different sectors of the population. It includes the geographic distribution of the population, the distribution of income across the population, and trends in these factors. Population demographics can have large implications for industries such as health care, where costs and service needs vary with demographic factors such as age and income distribution.
Social forces	Social forces include the societal values, attitudes, cultural factors, and lifestyles that impact businesses. Social forces vary by locale and change over time. An example includes the attitudes toward gender roles and diversity in the workforce. Another example is the trend toward healthier lifestyles, which can shift spending toward exercise equipment and health clubs and away from alcohol and snack foods.
Political, legal, and regulatory factors	These factors include political policies and processes, as well as the regulations and laws with which companies must comply. Examples include labor laws, antitrust laws, tax policy, regulatory policies, the political climate, and the strength of institutions such as the court system. Some political factors, such as banking deregulation, are industry-specific. Others, such as minimum wage legislation, affect certain types of industries (low-wage, labor-intensive industries) more than others.
Natural environment	This includes ecological and environmental forces such as weather, climate, climate change, and associated factors like water shortages. These factors can directly impact industries such as insurance, farming, energy production, and tourism. They may have an indirect but substantial effect on other industries such as transportation and utilities.
Technological factors	Technological factors include the pace of technological change and technical developments that have the potential for wide-ranging effects on society, such as genetic engineering, the rise of the Internet, and changes in communication technologies. They include activities and institutions involved in creating new knowledge and controlling the use of technology, such as R&D consortia, university-sponsored technology incubators, patent and copyright laws, and government control over the Internet. Technological change can encourage the birth of new industries, such as those based on nanotechnology, and disrupt others, such as the recording industry.
Global forces	Global forces include conditions and changes in global markets, including political events and policies toward international trade. They also include sociocultural practices and the institutional environment in which global markets operate. Global forces influence the degree of international trade and investment through such mechanisms as trade barriers, tariffs, import restrictions, and trade sanctions. Their effects are often industry-specific, such as import restrictions on steel.
General economic conditions	General economic conditions include economic factors at the local, state, national, or international level that affect firms and industries. These include the rate of economic growth, unemployment rates, inflation rates, interest rates, trade deficits or surpluses, savings rates, and per capita domestic product. Economic factors also include conditions in the markets for stocks and bonds, which can affect consumer confidence and discretionary income. Some industries, such as construction, are particularly vulnerable to economic downturns but are positively affected by factors such as low interest rates. Others, such as discount retailing, may benefit when general economic conditions weaken, as consumers become more price-conscious.

THINKING STRATEGICALLY ABOUT A COMPANY'S INDUSTRY AND COMPETITIVE ENVIRONMENT

To gain a deep understanding of a company's industry and competitive environment, managers do not need to gather all the information they can find and spend lots of time digesting it. Rather, they can focus more directly on using some well-defined concepts and analytical tools to get clear answers to seven questions:

1. Does the industry offer attractive opportunities for growth?
2. What kinds of competitive forces are industry members facing, and how strong is each force?
3. What factors are driving changes in the industry, and what impact will these changes have on competitive intensity and industry profitability?
4. What market positions do industry rivals occupy—who is strongly positioned and who is not?
5. What strategic moves are rivals likely to make next?
6. What are the key factors for competitive success in the industry?
7. Does the industry offer good prospects for attractive profits?

Analysis-based answers to these seven questions provide managers with the understanding needed to craft a strategy that fits the company's external situation and positions the company to best meet its competitive challenges. The remainder of this chapter is devoted to describing the methods of obtaining solid answers to the seven questions and explaining how the nature of a company's industry and competitive environment weighs upon the strategic choices of company managers.

QUESTION 1: DOES THE INDUSTRY OFFER ATTRACTIVE OPPORTUNITIES FOR GROWTH?

Answering the question of whether or not an industry will offer the prospect of attractive profits begins with a consideration of whether it offers good opportunities for growth. Growth, of course, cannot guarantee profitability—a lesson that too many firms that have pursued growth for growth's sake have learned the hard way. But it is an indicator of how much customers value the industry's products (or services) and whether the industry demand is strong enough to support profitable sales growth.

Key economic indicators of an industry's growth prospects include market size, in terms of overall unit sales and sales volume, as well as the industry growth rate. Assessing the market size and growth rate will depend, however, on whether the industry is defined broadly or narrowly, in terms of its product or service characteristics. For example, the freight transport industry is far more inclusive than the air freight industry, and market size will vary accordingly. Market size and growth rates will also depend on where the geographic boundary lines are drawn (local, regional, national, or global). In addition, market size and growth rates often vary markedly by region (e.g., Europe versus Asia) and by demographic market segment (e.g., Gen Y versus baby boomers). Looking at the market in a variety of ways can help managers assess the various opportunities for growth and its limits.

One reason for differences among industries in the size of the market and the rate of growth stems from what is known as the "industry life cycle." This is the notion that industries commonly follow a general pattern of development and maturation, consisting of four stages: emergence, rapid growth, maturity, and decline.[1] The size of a market and its growth rate, then, depend on which stage of the life cycle best characterizes the industry in question.

QUESTION 2: WHAT KINDS OF COMPETITIVE FORCES ARE INDUSTRY MEMBERS FACING, AND HOW STRONG ARE THEY?

LO 1

Gain command of the basic concepts and analytical tools widely used to diagnose the competitive conditions in a company's industry.

The character and strength of the competitive forces operating in an industry are never the same from one industry to another. Far and away the most powerful and widely used tool for systematically diagnosing the principal competitive pressures in a market is the *five-forces model of competition.*[2] This model holds that the competitive forces affecting industry profitability go beyond rivalry among competing sellers and include pressures stemming from four coexisting sources. As depicted in Figure 3.3, the five competitive forces include (1) competition from *rival sellers,* (2) competition from *potential new entrants* to the industry, (3) competition from producers of *substitute products,* (4) *supplier* bargaining power, and (5) *customer* bargaining power.

Using the five-forces model to determine the nature and strength of competitive pressures in a given industry involves building the picture of competition in three steps:

- *Step 1:* For each of the five forces, identify the different parties involved, along with the specific factors that bring about competitive pressures.
- *Step 2:* Evaluate how strong the pressures stemming from each of the five forces are (strong, moderate to normal, or weak).
- *Step 3:* Determine whether the strength of the five competitive forces, overall, is conducive to earning attractive profits in the industry.

Competitive Pressures Created by the Rivalry among Competing Sellers

The strongest of the five competitive forces is often the market maneuvering for buyer patronage that goes on among rival sellers of a product or service. In effect, *a market is a competitive battlefield* where the contest among competitors is ongoing and dynamic. Each competing company endeavors to deploy whatever means in its business arsenal it believes will attract and retain buyers, strengthen its market position, and yield good profits. The challenge is to craft a competitive strategy that, at the very least, allows a company to hold its own against rivals and that, ideally, *produces a competitive edge over rivals.* But when one firm deploys a strategy or makes a new strategic move that produces good results, its rivals typically respond with offensive or defensive countermoves of their own. This pattern of action and reaction, move and countermove, produces a continually evolving competitive landscape where the market battle ebbs and flows, sometimes takes unpredictable twists and turns, and produces winners and losers.[3]

Competitive battles among rival sellers can assume many forms that extend well beyond lively price competition. For example, rivalrous firms may resort to such marketing tactics as special sales promotions, heavy advertising, rebates, or low-interest-rate financing to drum up additional sales. Active rivals may race one another to differentiate their products by offering better performance

Figure 3.3 The Five-Forces Model of Competition: A Key Analytical Tool

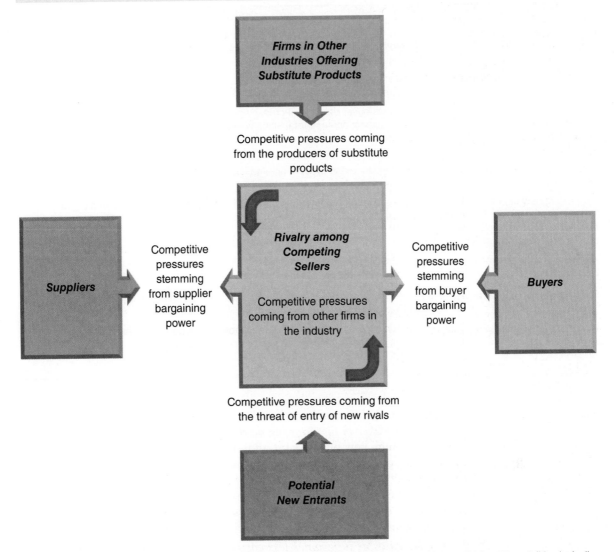

Sources: Adapted from Michael E. Porter, "How Competitive Forces Shape Strategy," *Harvard Business Review* 57, no. 2 (March–April 1979), pp. 137–45, and Michael E. Porter, "The Five Competitive Forces That Shape Strategy," *Harvard Business Review* 86, no. 1 (January 2008), pp. 80–86.

features or higher quality or improved customer service or a wider product selection. Rivals may also compete through the rapid introduction of next-generation products, frequent introduction of new or improved products, and efforts to build stronger dealer networks, establish positions in foreign markets, or otherwise expand distribution capabilities and market presence. Table 3.2 provides a sampling of the types of competitive weapons available to rivals, along with their primary effects.

The intensity of rivalry varies from industry to industry and depends on a number of identifiable factors. Figure 3.4 summarizes these factors, identifying those that intensify or weaken rivalry among direct competitors in an industry. A brief explanation of why these factors affect the degree of rivalry is in order:[4]

Table 3.2   Common "Weapons" for Competing with Rivals

Types of Competitive Weapons	Primary Effects
Price discounting, clearance sales, "blowout" sales	Lowers price (P), acts to boost total sales volume and market share, lowers profit margins per unit sold when price cuts are big and/or increases in sales volume are relatively small
Couponing, advertising items on sale	Acts to increase unit sales volume and total revenues, lowers price (P), increases unit costs (C), may lower profit margins per unit sold ($P − C$)
Advertising product or service characteristics, using ads to enhance a company's image or reputation	Boosts buyer demand, increases product differentiation and perceived value (V), acts to increase total sales volume and market share, may increase unit costs (C) and/or lower profit margins per unit sold
Innovating to improve product performance and quality	Acts to increase product differentiation and value (V), boosts buyer demand, acts to boost total sales volume, likely to increase unit costs (C)
Introducing new or improved features, increasing the number of styles or models to provide greater product selection	Acts to increase product differentiation and value (V), strengthens buyer demand, acts to boost total sales volume and market share, likely to increase unit costs (C)
Increasing customization of product or service	Acts to increase product differentiation and value (V), increases switching costs, acts to boost total sales volume, often increases unit costs (C)
Building a bigger, better dealer network	Broadens access to buyers, acts to boost total sales volume and market share, may increase unit costs (C)
Improving warranties, offering low-interest financing	Acts to increase product differentiation and value (V), increases unit costs (C), increases buyer costs to switch brands, acts to boost total sales volume and market share

- *Rivalry is stronger in markets where buyer demand is growing slowly or declining, and it is weaker in fast-growing markets.* Rapidly expanding buyer demand produces enough new business for all industry members to grow without using volume-boosting sales tactics to draw customers away from rival enterprises. But in markets where buyer demand is growing only 1 to 2 percent or is shrinking, companies anxious (or perhaps desperate) to gain more business typically employ price discounts, sales promotions, and other tactics to boost their sales volumes, sometimes to the point of igniting a fierce battle for market share.

- *Rivalry increases as it becomes less costly for buyers to switch brands.* The less expensive it is for buyers to switch their purchases from the seller of one brand to the seller of another brand, the easier it is for sellers to steal customers away from rivals. But the higher the costs buyers incur to switch brands, the less prone they are to brand switching. Switching costs include not only monetary costs but also the time, inconvenience, and psychological costs involved in switching brands. For example distributors and retailers may not switch to the brands of rival manufacturers because they are hesitant to sever long-standing supplier relationships, incur any technical support costs or retraining expenses in making the switchover, go to the trouble of testing the quality and reliability of the rival brand, or devote resources to marketing the new brand (especially if the brand is not well known).

- *Rivalry increases as the products of rival sellers become more alike, and it diminishes as the products of industry rivals become more strongly differentiated.* When the offerings of rivals are identical or weakly differentiated, buyers have less reason to be brand-loyal—a condition that makes it easier for rivals to convince

Figure 3.4   Factors Affecting the Strength of Rivalry

Substitutes

Suppliers

Rivalry among Competing Sellers:
How strong is seller-related competition?

Rivalry is stronger when:

- Buyer demand is growing slowly
- Buyer demand is falling off and sellers find themselves with excess capacity and/or inventory
- Buyer costs to switch brands are low
- The products of industry members are commodities or else weakly differentiated
- The firms in the industry have high fixed costs or high storage costs
- Competitors are numerous or are of roughly equal size and competitive strength
- Rivals have diverse objectives, strategies, and/or countries of origin
- Rivals have emotional stakes in the business or face high exit barriers

Rivalry is weaker when:

- Buyer demand is growing rapidly
- Buyer costs to switch brands are high
- The products of rival sellers are strongly differentiated and customer loyalty is high
- Fixed and storage costs are low
- Sales are concentrated among a few large sellers
- Industry members are relatively homogeneous in size, strength, objectives, strategy, and country of origin
- Exit barriers are low

Buyers

New Entrants

buyers to switch to their offerings. And since the brands of different sellers have comparable attributes, buyers can shop the market for the best deal and switch brands at will. On the other hand, strongly differentiated product offerings among rivals breed high brand loyalty on the part of buyers—because many buyers view the attributes of certain brands as more appealing or better suited to their needs. Strong brand attachments make it tougher for sellers to draw customers away from rivals. Unless meaningful numbers of buyers are open to considering new or different product attributes being offered by rivals, the high degree of brand loyalty that accompanies strong product differentiation works against fierce rivalry among competing sellers. *The degree of product differentiation also affects switching costs.* When the offerings of rivals are identical or weakly differentiated, it is usually easy and inexpensive for buyers to switch their purchases from one seller to another. But in the case of strongly differentiated brands with quite different features and functionality (like rival brands of cell phones), buyers may be reluctant to go through the brand-switching hassle.

- *Rivalry is more intense when there is unused production capacity, especially if the industry's product has high fixed costs or high storage costs.* Whenever a market is oversupplied (such that sellers have unutilized production capacity and/or too much inventory), the result is a "buyer's market" that intensifies rivalry perhaps even to the point of threatening the survival of competitively weak firms. A similar effect occurs when a product is perishable, seasonal, or costly to hold in inventory, since firms often engage in aggressive price cutting to ensure that they are not left with unwanted or costly inventories. Likewise, whenever fixed costs account for a large fraction of total cost so that unit costs are significantly lower at full capacity, firms come under significant pressure to cut prices to boost sales whenever they are operating below full capacity. Unused capacity imposes a significant cost-increasing penalty because there are fewer units over which to spread fixed costs. The pressure of high fixed or high storage costs can push rival firms into price concessions, special discounts, rebates, and other volume-boosting competitive tactics.

- *Rivalry intensifies as the number of competitors increases and as competitors become more equal in size and competitive strength.* The greater the number of competitors, the higher the probability that one or more companies will be busily engaged in a strategic offensive intended to enhance their market standing, thereby heating up competition and putting new pressures on rivals to respond with offensive or defensive moves of their own. In addition, when rivals are of comparable size and competitive strength, they can usually compete on a fairly equal footing—an evenly matched contest tends to be fiercer than a contest in which one or more industry members have commanding market shares and substantially greater resources and capabilities than their much smaller rivals.

- *Rivalry often becomes more intense—as well as more volatile and unpredictable— as the diversity of competitors increases in terms of long-term directions, objectives, strategies, and countries of origin.* A diverse group of sellers often contains one or more mavericks willing to try novel or rule-breaking market approaches, thus generating a livelier and less predictable competitive environment. Globally competitive markets usually boost the intensity of rivalry, especially when aggressors having lower costs or products with more attractive features are intent on gaining a strong foothold in new country markets.

- *Rivalry is stronger when high exit barriers keep unprofitable firms from leaving the industry.* In industries where the assets cannot easily be sold or transferred to other uses, where workers are entitled to job protection, or where owners are committed to remaining in business for personal reasons, failing firms tend to hold on longer than they might otherwise—even when they are bleeding red ink. This increases rivalry in two ways. Firms that are losing ground or in financial trouble often resort to deep price discounting that can trigger a price war and destabilize an otherwise attractive industry. In addition, high exit barriers result in an industry being more overcrowded than it would otherwise be, and this boosts rivalry and forces the weakest companies to scramble (often pushing them into desperate maneuvers of all kinds) to win sufficient sales and revenues to stay in business.

Rivalry can be characterized as *cutthroat* or *brutal* when competitors engage in protracted price wars or habitually undertake other aggressive strategic moves that prove mutually destructive to profitability. Rivalry can be considered *fierce* to *strong* when the battle for market share is so vigorous that the profit margins of most industry members are squeezed to bare-bones levels. Rivalry can be characterized as *moderate* or *normal* when the maneuvering among industry members, while lively and healthy, still allows most industry members to earn acceptable profits. Rivalry is *weak* when most companies in the industry are relatively well satisfied with their sales growth and market shares, rarely undertake offensives to steal customers away from one another, and—because of weak competitive forces—earn consistently good profits and returns on investment.

Competitive Pressures Associated with the Threat of New Entrants

New entrants to a market bring new production capacity, the desire to establish a secure place in the market, and sometimes substantial resources. Just how serious the competitive threat of entry is in a particular market depends on two classes of factors: *barriers to entry* and the *expected reaction of incumbent firms to new entry.*[5]

Industry incumbents that are willing and able to launch strong defensive maneuvers to maintain their positions can make it hard for a new entrant to gain a sufficient market foothold to survive and eventually become profitable. Entry candidates may have second thoughts if they conclude that existing firms are likely to give newcomers a hard time by offering price discounts (especially to the very customer groups a newcomer is seeking to attract), spending more on advertising, running frequent sales promotions, adding attractive new product features (to match or beat the newcomer's product offering), or providing additional services to customers. Such defensive maneuvers on the part of incumbents raise an entrant's costs and risks and have to be considered likely if one or more incumbents have previously tried to strongly contest the entry of new firms into the marketplace.

A barrier to entry exists whenever it is hard for a newcomer to break into the market and/or the economics of the business put a potential entrant at a disadvantage. The most widely encountered such barriers that entry candidates must hurdle include the following:[6]

- *Sizable economies of scale in production, distribution, advertising, or other areas of operation.* When incumbent companies enjoy cost advantages associated with large-scale operations, outsiders must either enter on a large scale (a costly and perhaps risky move) or accept a cost disadvantage and consequently lower profitability.
- *Significant cost advantages held by existing firms due to experience and learning curve effects.* In many industries, incumbent firms are favored by learning-based cost savings that accrue from experience in performing certain activities such as manufacturing or new product development or inventory management. This gives incumbent firms a first-mover advantage over new entrants that may be difficult to overcome.

- *Other cost advantages enjoyed by industry incumbents.* Existing industry members may also have other types of cost advantages that are hard for a newcomer to replicate. These can stem from (1) preferential access to raw materials, components, or other inputs, (2) cost savings accruing from patents or proprietary technology, (3) favorable locations, and (4) low fixed costs (because they have older facilities that have been mostly depreciated). The bigger the cost advantages of industry incumbents, the more risky it becomes for outsiders to attempt entry (since they will have to accept thinner profit margins or even losses until the cost disadvantages can be overcome).

- *Strong brand preferences and high degrees of customer loyalty.* The stronger the attachment of buyers to established brands, the harder it is for a newcomer to break into the marketplace. In such cases, a new entrant must have the financial resources to spend enough on advertising and sales promotion to overcome customer loyalties and build its own clientele. Establishing brand recognition and building customer loyalty can be a slow and costly process. In addition, if it is difficult or costly for a customer to switch to a new brand, a new entrant may have to offer buyers a discounted price or an extra margin of quality or service. Such barriers discourage new entry because they act to boost financial requirements and lower expected profit margins for new entrants.

- *Strong "network effects" in customer demand.* In industries where buyers are more attracted to a product when there are many other users of the product, there are said to be "network effects," since demand is higher the larger the network of users. Video game systems are an example, since users prefer to have the same systems as their friends so that they can play together on systems they all know and share games. When incumbents have a larger base of users, new entrants with comparable products face a serious disadvantage in attracting buyers.

- *High capital requirements.* The larger the total dollar investment needed to enter the market successfully, the more limited the pool of potential entrants. The most obvious capital requirements for new entrants relate to manufacturing facilities and equipment, introductory advertising and sales promotion campaigns, working capital to finance inventories and customer credit, and sufficient cash to cover start-up costs.

- *The difficulties of building a network of distributors or dealers and securing adequate space on retailers' shelves.* A potential entrant can face numerous distribution channel challenges. Wholesale distributors may be reluctant to take on a product that lacks buyer recognition. Retailers must be recruited and convinced to give a new brand ample display space and an adequate trial period. When existing sellers have strong, well-functioning distributor-dealer networks, a newcomer has an uphill struggle in squeezing its way into existing distribution channels. Potential entrants sometimes have to "buy" their way into wholesale or retail channels by cutting their prices to provide dealers and distributors with higher markups and profit margins or by giving them big advertising and promotional allowances. As a consequence, a potential entrant's own profits may be squeezed unless and until its product gains enough consumer acceptance that distributors and retailers are anxious to carry it.

- *Restrictive government policies.* Regulated industries like cable TV, telecommunications, electric and gas utilities, radio and television broadcasting, liquor retailing, and railroads entail government-controlled entry. Government agencies can also limit or even bar entry by requiring licenses and permits, such as the medallion required to drive a taxicab in New York City. Government-mandated safety regulations and environmental pollution standards also create entry barriers because they raise entry costs. In international markets, host governments commonly limit foreign entry and must approve all foreign investment applications. National governments commonly use tariffs and trade restrictions (antidumping rules, local content requirements, quotas, etc.) to raise entry barriers for foreign firms and protect domestic producers from outside competition.

The threat of entry changes as the industry's prospects grow brighter or dimmer and as entry barriers rise or fall. For example, in the pharmaceutical industry the expiration of a key patent on a widely prescribed drug virtually guarantees that one or more drug makers will enter with generic offerings of their own. Use of the Internet for shopping is making it much easier for e-tailers to enter into competition against some of the best-known retail chains. Moreover, new strategic actions by incumbent firms to increase advertising, strengthen distributor-dealer relations, step up R&D, or improve product quality can erect higher roadblocks to entry.

> High entry barriers and weak entry threats today do not always translate into high entry barriers and weak entry threats tomorrow.

Additional Entry Threat Considerations   There are two additional factors that need to be considered in evaluating whether the threat of entry is strong or weak. The first concerns how attractive the growth and profit prospects are for new entrants. *Rapidly growing market demand and high potential profits act as magnets, motivating potential entrants to commit the resources needed to hurdle entry barriers.*[7] When growth and profit opportunities are sufficiently attractive, certain types of entry barriers are unlikely to provide an effective entry deterrent. At most, they limit the pool of candidate entrants to enterprises with the requisite competencies and resources and with the creativity to fashion a strategy for competing with incumbent firms. Hence, *the best test of whether potential entry is a strong or weak competitive force in the marketplace is to ask if the industry's growth and profit prospects are strongly attractive to potential entry candidates with sufficient expertise and resources to hurdle prevailing entry barriers.* When the answer is no, potential entry is a weak competitive force. When the answer is yes, then potential entry adds significantly to competitive pressures in the marketplace.

A second factor concerns the pool of potential entrants and their capabilities in relation to the particular entry barriers in place. Companies with sizable financial resources, proven competitive capabilities, and a respected brand name may be able to marshal the resources to hurdle certain types of entry barriers rather easily, while small start-up enterprises may find the same entry barriers insurmountable. Thus, how hard it will be for potential entrants to compete on a level playing field is always relative to the financial resources and competitive capabilities of likely entrants. The big take-away is this: *Whether an industry's entry barriers ought to be considered high or low depends on the resources and capabilities possessed by the pool of potential entrants.*[8] As a rule, the bigger the pool of entry candidates that have what it takes, the stronger is the threat of entry.

> The threat of entry is stronger when entry barriers are low, when incumbent firms are unable or unwilling to vigorously contest a newcomer's entry, and when there's a sizable pool of entry candidates with resources and capabilities well suited for competing in the industry.

For example, when Honda opted to enter the U.S. lawn mower market in competition against Toro, Snapper, Craftsman, John Deere, and others, it was easily able to hurdle entry barriers that would have been formidable to other newcomers because it had long-standing expertise in gasoline engines; its well-known reputation for quality and durability in automobiles gave it instant credibility with homeowners. In fact, the strongest competitive pressures associated with potential entry frequently come not from outsiders but from current industry participants with strong capabilities looking for growth opportunities. *Existing industry members are often strong candidates to enter market segments or geographic areas where they currently do not have a market presence.* Companies already well established in certain product categories or geographic areas often possess the resources, competencies, and competitive capabilities to hurdle the barriers of entering a different market segment or new geographic area.

Figure 3.5 summarizes the factors that cause the overall competitive threat from potential new entrants to be strong or weak.

Figure 3.5   Factors Affecting the Threat of Entry

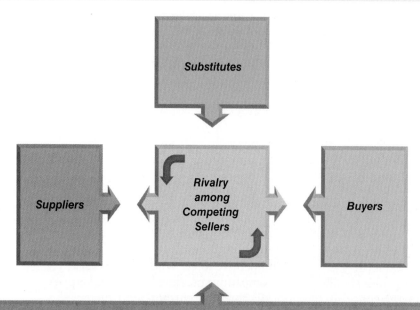

Substitutes

Suppliers

Rivalry among Competing Sellers

Buyers

Potential New Entrants

How strong are the competitive pressures coming from the threat of entry of new rivals?

Entry threats are stronger when:
- Entry barriers are low
- Industry members are unwilling or unable to strongly contest the entry of newcomers
- There is a large pool of potential entrants, some of which have the capabilities to overcome high entry barriers
- Existing industry members are looking to expand their market reach by entering product segments or geographic areas where they do not have a presence
- Buyer demand is growing rapidly and newcomers can expect to earn attractive profits without inviting a strong reaction from incumbents

Entry threats are weaker when:
- Entry barriers are high
  - High economies of scale
  - Significant experience-based cost advantages
  - Other cost advantages held by industry members (e.g., access to inputs, technology, favorable location) or low fixed costs
  - Strong product differentiation and brand loyalty
  - Strong network effects
  - High capital requirements
  - Limited new access to distribution channels
  - Restrictive government policies
- Industry members are willing and able to contest new entry
- Industry outlook is risky and uncertain, discouraging entry

Competitive Pressures from the Sellers of Substitute Products

Companies in one industry come under competitive pressure from the actions of companies in a closely adjoining industry whenever buyers view the products of the two industries as good substitutes. For instance, the producers of sugar experience competitive pressures from the sales and marketing efforts of the makers of sucralose and aspartame. Newspapers are struggling to maintain their relevance to subscribers who can watch the news on any of numerous TV channels and use Internet sources to get information about sports results, stock quotes, and job opportunities. The retailers of music CDs are experiencing competitive pressure from downloadable digital music on sites such as iTunes.

As depicted in Figure 3.6, whether the competitive pressures from substitute products are strong, moderate, or weak depends on three factors:

1. *Whether substitutes are readily available.* The presence of readily available substitutes creates competitive pressure by placing a ceiling on the prices industry members can charge without giving customers an incentive to switch to substitutes and risking sales erosion.[9] This price ceiling, at the same time, puts a lid on the profits that industry members can earn unless they find ways to cut costs.

2. *Whether buyers view the substitutes as attractively priced in relation to their quality, performance, and other relevant attributes.* In deciding whether to switch to a substitute product, customers compare its performance, features, ease of use, and other attributes as well as price to see if the substitute offers more value for the money than the industry's product. The users of paper cartons constantly weigh the price/performance trade-offs with plastic containers and metal cans, for example.

3. *Whether the costs that buyers incur in switching to the substitutes are low or high.* Low switching costs make it easier for the sellers of attractive substitutes to lure buyers to their offerings; high switching costs deter buyers from purchasing substitute products.[10] Typical switching costs include the time and inconvenience involved in switching, payments for technical help in making the changeover, the cost of any additional equipment needed, employee retraining costs, the cost of testing the quality and reliability of the substitute, and the psychological costs of severing old supplier relationships and establishing new ones.

Before assessing the competitive pressures coming from substitutes, company managers must identify the substitutes, which is less easy than it sounds since it involves (1) determining where the industry boundaries lie and (2) figuring out which other products or services can address the same basic customer needs as those produced by industry members. Deciding on the industry boundaries is necessary for determining which firms are direct rivals and which produce substitutes. This is a matter of perspective—there are no hard-and-fast rules, other than to say that other brands of the same basic product constitute rival products and not substitutes.

As a rule, *the lower the price of substitutes, the higher their quality and performance; and the lower the user's switching costs, the more intense the competitive pressures posed by substitute products.* Other market indicators of the competitive strength of substitute products include (1) whether the sales of substitutes are growing faster than the sales of the industry being analyzed (a sign that the

Figure 3.6   Factors Affecting Competition from Substitute Products

Firms in Other Industries Offering Substitute Products

How strong are competitive pressures coming from substitute products from outside the industry?

Competitive pressures from substitutes are stronger when:

- Good substitutes are readily available or new ones are emerging
- Substitutes are attractively priced
- Substitutes have comparable or better performance features
- Buyers have low costs in switching to substitutes

Competitive pressures from substitutes are weaker when:

- Good substitutes are not readily available or don't exist
- Substitutes are higher-priced relative to the performance they deliver
- Buyers have high costs in switching to substitutes

Signs That Competition from Substitutes Is Strong

- Sales of substitutes are growing faster than sales of the industry being analyzed
- Producers of substitutes are moving to add new capacity
- Profits of the producers of substitutes are on the rise

Suppliers

Rivalry among Competing Sellers

Buyers

New Entrants

sellers of substitutes may be drawing customers away from the industry in question), (2) whether the producers of substitutes are moving to add new capacity, and (3) whether the profits of the producers of substitutes are on the rise.

Competitive Pressures Stemming from Supplier Bargaining Power

Whether the suppliers of industry members represent a weak or strong competitive force depends on the degree to which suppliers have sufficient *bargaining power* to influence the terms and conditions of supply in their favor. Suppliers with strong bargaining power can erode industry profitability by charging industry members higher prices, passing costs on to them, and limiting their opportunities to find better deals. For instance, Microsoft and Intel, both of whom supply PC makers with essential components, have been known to use their dominant market status not only to charge PC makers premium prices but also to leverage PC makers in other ways. The bargaining power of these two companies over their customers is so great that both companies have faced antitrust charges on numerous occasions. Before a legal agreement ending the practice, Microsoft pressured PC makers to load only Microsoft products on the screens of new computers that come with factory-loaded software. Intel has also defended against antitrust charges but continues to give PC makers who use the biggest percentages of Intel chips in their PC models top priority in filling orders for newly introduced Intel chips. Being on Intel's list of preferred customers helps a PC maker get an allocation of the first production runs of Intel's latest chips and thus get new PC models to market ahead of rivals. Microsoft's and Intel's pressuring of PC makers has helped them maintain their dominant positions in their industries.

Small-scale retailers often must contend with the power of manufacturers whose products enjoy well-known brand names, since consumers expect to find these products on the shelves of the retail stores where they shop. This provides the manufacturer with a degree of pricing power and often the ability to push hard for favorable shelf displays. Similarly, the operators of franchised units of such chains as McDonald's, KFC, Pizza Hut, 7-Eleven, Mr. Rooter, and Radisson Hotels must frequently agree to source some of their supplies from the franchisor at prices and terms favorable to that franchisor. Supplier bargaining power is also a competitive factor in industries where unions have been able to organize the workforce (which supplies labor). Air pilot unions, for example, have employed their bargaining power to increase pilots' wages and benefits in the air transport industry.

As shown in Figure 3.7, a variety of factors determines the strength of suppliers' bargaining power:[11]

- *Whether suppliers' products are in short supply.* Suppliers of items in short supply have pricing power and bargaining leverage, whereas a surge in the available supply of particular items shifts the bargaining power to the industry members.
- *Whether suppliers provide a differentiated input that enhances the performance or quality of the industry's product.* The more differentiated and valuable a particular input is in terms of enhancing the performance or quality of the products of industry members, the more bargaining leverage and pricing power suppliers have.
- *Whether the item being supplied is a standard item or a commodity that is readily available from a host of suppliers.* The suppliers of commodities (like copper or steel reinforcing rods or shipping cartons) are in a weak position to demand a premium price or insist on other favorable terms because industry members can readily obtain essentially the same item at the same price from many other suppliers eager to win their business.
- *Whether it is difficult or costly for industry members to switch their purchases from one supplier to another.* The higher the switching costs of industry members, the stronger the bargaining power of their suppliers. Low switching costs limit supplier bargaining power by enabling industry members to change suppliers if any one supplier attempts to raise prices by more than the costs of switching.
- *Whether there are good substitutes available for the suppliers' products.* The ready availability of substitute inputs lessens the bargaining power of suppliers by reducing the dependence of industry members on the suppliers. The better

Figure 3.7   Factors Affecting the Bargaining Power of Suppliers

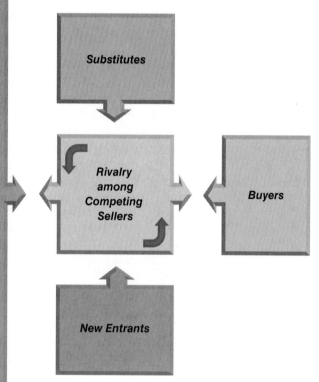

Suppliers

How strong are the competitive pressures stemming from supplier bargaining power?

Supplier bargaining power is stronger when:

- Supplier products/services are in short supply (which gives suppliers leverage in setting prices)
- Supplier products/services are differentiated
- Supplier products/services are critical to industry members' production processes
- Industry members incur high costs in switching their purchases to alternative suppliers
- There are no good substitutes for what the suppliers provide
- Suppliers are not dependent on the industry for a large portion of their revenues
- The supplier industry is more concentrated than the industry it sells to and is dominated by a few large companies

Supplier bargaining power is weaker when:

- There is a surge in the availability of supplies
- The item being supplied is a "commodity" that is readily available from many suppliers at the going market price
- Industry members' switching costs to alternative suppliers are low
- Good substitutes for supplier products/services exist
- Industry members account for a big fraction of suppliers' sales
- The number of suppliers is large relative to the number of industry members and there are no suppliers with large market shares
- Industry members have the potential to integrate backward into the business of suppliers and to self-manufacture their own requirements

the price and performance characteristics of the substitute inputs, the weaker the bargaining power of suppliers.

- *Whether industry members account for a sizable fraction of suppliers' total sales.* As a rule, suppliers have less bargaining leverage when their sales to members of the industry constitute a big percentage of their total sales. In such cases, the well-being of suppliers is closely tied to the well-being of their major customers. Suppliers have a big incentive to protect and enhance the competitiveness of their major customers via reasonable prices, exceptional quality, and ongoing advances in the technology of the items supplied.
- *Whether the supplier industry is dominated by a few large companies and whether it is more concentrated than the industry it sells to.* Suppliers with sizable market

shares and strong demand for the items they supply generally have sufficient bargaining power to charge high prices and deny requests from industry members for lower prices or other concessions.

- *Whether it makes good economic sense for industry members to integrate backward and self-manufacture items they have been buying from suppliers.* The make-or-buy issue generally boils down to whether suppliers who specialize in the production of particular parts or components and make them in volume for many different customers have the expertise and scale economies to supply as-good or better components at a lower cost than industry members could achieve via self-manufacture. Frequently, it is difficult for industry members to self-manufacture parts and components more economically than they can obtain them from suppliers who specialize in making such items. For instance, most producers of outdoor power equipment (lawn mowers, rotary tillers, leaf blowers, etc.) find it cheaper to source the small engines they need from outside manufacturers that specialize in small-engine manufacture than to make their own engines, because the quantity of engines they need is too small to justify the investment in manufacturing facilities, master the production process, and capture scale economies. Specialists in small-engine manufacture, by supplying many kinds of engines to the whole power equipment industry, can obtain a big-enough sales volume to fully realize scale economies, become proficient in all the manufacturing techniques, and keep costs low. As a rule, suppliers are safe from the threat of self-manufacture by their customers *until* the volume of parts a customer needs becomes large enough for the customer to justify backward integration into self-manufacture of the component.

In identifying the degree of supplier power in an industry, it is important to recognize that different types of suppliers are likely to have different amounts of bargaining power. Thus, the first step is for managers to identify the different types of suppliers, paying particular attention to those that provide the industry with important inputs. The next step is to assess the bargaining power of each type of supplier separately. Figure 3.7 summarizes the conditions that tend to make supplier bargaining power strong or weak.

Competitive Pressures Stemming from Buyer Bargaining Power and Price Sensitivity

Whether buyers are able to exert strong competitive pressures on industry members depends on (1) the degree to which buyers have bargaining power and (2) the extent to which buyers are price-sensitive. Buyers with strong bargaining power can limit industry profitability by demanding price concessions, better payment terms, or additional features and services that increase industry members' costs. Buyer price sensitivity limits the profit potential of industry members by restricting the ability of sellers to raise prices without losing revenue.

The strength of buyers as a competitive force depends on a set of factors that predict the degree of bargaining power and price sensitivity, which may vary according to buyer group (e.g., wholesalers, large retail chains, small retailers, consumers). Retailers tend to have greater bargaining power over industry sellers if they have influence over the purchase decisions of the end user or if they are critical in providing sellers with access to the end user. For example, large retail chains like Walmart, Carrefour, Metro AG, Tesco, and Woolworths typically have considerable negotiating leverage in purchasing products from manufacturers because of manufacturers' need for broad retail exposure and the most appealing shelf locations. Retailers may stock two or three competing brands of a product but rarely all competing brands, so competition among rival manufacturers for visibility on the shelves of popular multistore retailers gives such retailers significant bargaining strength. Major supermarket chains like Walmart, Ahold, Kroger, Aldi, and Carrefour have sufficient bargaining power to demand promotional allowances and lump-sum payments (called slotting fees) from food products manufacturers in return for stocking certain brands or putting them in the best shelf locations. Motor vehicle manufacturers have strong bargaining power in negotiating to buy original-equipment tires from Goodyear, Michelin, Bridgestone/Firestone, Continental, and Pirelli not only because they buy in large quantities but also because tire makers believe they gain an advantage in supplying replacement tires to vehicle owners if their tire brand is original equipment on the vehicle.

In contrast, individual consumers rarely have any real bargaining power in negotiating price concessions or other favorable terms with sellers. While an individual with other purchase options may refuse to buy a high-priced item, her actions will have no discernible   effect on industry profitability. As a buyer group, however, consumers can limit the profit potential of an industry for the same reasons that other buyer groups exert competitive pressure. These reasons are discussed below and summarized in Figure 3.8:[12]

- *Buyers' bargaining power is greater when their costs of switching to competing brands or substitutes are relatively low.* Buyers who can readily switch brands have more leverage than buyers who have high switching costs. Switching costs limit industry profitability, in essence, by putting a cap on how much producers can raise price or reduce quality before they will lose the buyer's business.

- *Buyer power increases when industry goods are standardized or differentiation is weak.* In such circumstances, buyers make their selections on the basis of price, which increases price competition among vendors. When products are differentiated, buyers' options are more limited and they are less focused on obtaining low prices, which may signal poor quality.

- *Buyers have more power when they are large and few in number relative to the number of sellers.* The smaller the number of buyers, the more sellers have to compete for their business and the less easy it is for sellers to find alternative buyers when a customer is lost to a competitor. The prospect of losing a customer not easily replaced often makes a seller more willing to grant concessions of one kind or another. The larger the buyer, the more important their business is to the seller and the more sellers will be willing to grant concessions.

- *Buyer power increases when buyer demand is weak and industry members are scrambling to sell more units.* Weak or declining demand creates a "buyers' market," in which bargain-hunting buyers are able to press for better deals and special treatment; conversely, strong or rapidly growing demand creates a "sellers' market" and shifts bargaining power to sellers.

- *Buyers gain leverage if they are well informed about sellers' products, prices, and costs.* The more information buyers have, the better bargaining position they are in. The mushrooming availability of product information on the Internet is giving added bargaining power to consumers. Buyers can easily use the Internet to compare prices and features of vacation packages, shop for the best interest rates on mortgages and loans, and find the best prices on big-ticket items such as digital cameras. Bargain hunters can shop around for the best deal on the Internet and use that information to negotiate better deals

Figure 3.8   Factors Affecting the Bargaining Power of Buyers

Buyers

How strong are competitive pressures stemming from buyer bargaining power?

Buyer bargaining power is stronger when:

- Buyer costs of switching to competing products are low
- The industry's products are standardized or undifferentiated
- Buyers are large and few in number relative to the number of industry sellers
- Buyer demand is weak in relation to industry supply
- Buyers are well informed about the quality, prices, and costs of sellers
- Buyers have the ability to integrate backward into the business of sellers
- Buyers have the ability to postpone purchases
- Buyers are price-sensitive
  - Buyers earn low profits or low income
  - The product represents a significant fraction of their purchases
  - Product quality has limited consequences

Buyer bargaining power is weaker when:

- Buyer costs of switching to competing brands or substitutes are high
- Sellers' products are differentiated
- Buyers are small and numerous relative to sellers
- Industry supply is insufficient to satisfy buyer demand
- Buyers information regarding sellers is limited in quantity and quality
- Buyers are not very price-sensitive (high profits or income; small part of cost structure or total purchases; product performance really matters)

from local retailers; this method is becoming commonplace in buying new and used motor vehicles.

- *Buyers' bargaining power is greater when they pose a credible threat of integrating backward into the business of sellers.* Companies like Anheuser-Busch, Coors, and Heinz have integrated backward into metal can manufacturing to gain bargaining power in obtaining the balance of their can requirements from otherwise powerful metal can manufacturers. Retailers gain bargaining power by stocking and promoting their own private-label brands alongside manufacturers' name brands.

- *Buyer leverage increases if buyers have discretion to delay their purchases or perhaps even not make a purchase at all.* Consumers often have the option to delay purchases of durable goods, such as major appliances, or discretionary goods, such as hot tubs and home entertainment centers, if they are not happy with the prices offered. Business customers may also be able to defer their purchases of certain items, such as plant equipment or maintenance services. This puts pressure on sellers to provide concessions to buyers so that the sellers can keep their sales numbers from dropping off.

- *Buyer price sensitivity increases when buyers are earning low profits or have low income.* Price is a critical factor in the purchase decisions of low-income consumers and companies that are barely scraping by. In such cases, their high price sensitivity limits the ability of sellers to charge high prices.

- *Buyers are more price-sensitive if the product represents a large fraction of their total purchases.* When a purchase eats up a large portion of a buyer's budget or represents a significant part of his or her cost structure, the buyer cares more about price than might otherwise be the case. When the item is a small fraction of total purchases, buyers are less likely to feel that negotiating or shopping for a better deal is worth the time and trouble.

- *Buyers are more price-sensitive if product performance has limited consequences.* When product performance has limited consequences for the buyer, then purchase decisions are based mostly on price. On the other hand, when product quality is important, such as when it materially affects the quality of an intermediate buyer's goods, then price becomes a less important factor. Price is particularly unimportant to intermediate buyers when a good has the potential to pay for itself by reducing a buyer's other production costs.

The starting point for the analysis of buyers as a competitive force is to identify the different types of buyers along the value chain—then proceed to analyzing the bargaining power and price sensitivity of each type separately. Overall, buyers exert strong competitive pressures and force industry profitability downward if the majority of industry member sales are made to buyer groups that have either strong bargaining power or high price sensitivity. Buyers are able to exert only moderate competitive pressures on sellers when the majority of sellers' revenues come from buyers with intermediate levels of power or price sensitivity. Competitive pressures exerted by buyers are weak when a big portion of sellers' sales revenues comes from buyers with weak bargaining power and price sensitivity.

Is the Collective Strength of the Five Competitive Forces Conducive to Good Profitability?

Assessing whether each of the five competitive forces gives rise to strong, moderate, or weak competitive pressures sets the stage for evaluating whether, overall, the strength of the five forces is conducive to good profitability. Is the state of competition in the industry stronger than "normal"? Can companies in this industry reasonably expect to earn decent profits in light of the prevailing competitive forces? Are some of the competitive forces sufficiently powerful to undermine industry profitability?

The most extreme case of a "competitively unattractive" industry occurs when all five forces are producing strong competitive pressures: Rivalry among sellers is vigorous, low entry barriers allow new rivals to gain a market foothold, competition from substitutes is intense, and both suppliers and buyers are able to exercise considerable leverage. Fierce to strong competitive pressures coming from all five directions drive industry profitability to unacceptably low levels, frequently producing losses for many industry members and forcing some out of business. But an industry can be competitively unattractive without all five competitive forces being strong. In fact, intense competitive pressures *from just one or two* of the five forces may suffice to destroy the conditions for good profitability and prompt some companies to exit the business.

As a rule, *the strongest competitive forces determine the extent of the competitive pressure on industry profitability.*[13] Thus, in evaluating the strength of the five forces overall and their effect on industry profitability, managers should look to the strongest forces. Having more than one strong force will not worsen the effect on industry profitability, but it does mean that the industry has multiple competitive challenges with which to cope. In that sense, an industry with three to five strong forces is even more "unattractive" as a place to compete. Especially intense competitive conditions seem to be the norm in tire manufacturing, apparel, and commercial airlines, three industries where profit margins have historically been thin.

In contrast, when the overall impact of the five competitive forces is moderate to weak, an industry is "attractive" in the sense that the *average* industry member can reasonably expect to earn good profits and a nice return on investment. The ideal competitive environment for earning superior profits is one in which both suppliers and customers are in weak bargaining positions, there are no good substitutes, high barriers block further entry, and rivalry among present sellers generates only limited competitive pressures. Weak competition is the best of all possible worlds for also-ran companies because even they can usually eke out a decent profit—if a company can't make a decent profit when competition is weak, then its business outlook is indeed grim.

In most industries, the collective strength of the five competitive forces is somewhere near the middle of the two extremes of very intense and very weak, typically ranging from slightly stronger than normal to slightly weaker than normal and typically allowing well-managed companies with sound strategies to earn moderately attractive profits.

Matching Company Strategy to Competitive Conditions

Working through the five-forces model step by step not only aids strategy makers in assessing whether the intensity of competition allows good profitability but also promotes sound strategic thinking about how to better match company strategy to the specific competitive character of the marketplace. Effectively matching a company's business strategy to prevailing competitive conditions has three aspects:

A company's strategy is increasingly effective the more it provides some insulation from competitive pressures, shifts the competitive battle in the company's favor, and positions firms to take advantage of attractive growth opportunities.

1. Pursuing avenues that shield the firm from as many of the different competitive pressures as possible.
2. Initiating actions calculated to shift the competitive forces in the company's favor by altering the underlying factors driving the five forces.
3. Spotting attractive arenas for expansion, where competitive pressures in the industry are somewhat weaker.

But making headway on these three fronts first requires identifying competitive pressures, gauging the relative strength of each of the five competitive forces, and gaining a deep enough understanding of the state of competition in the industry to know which strategy buttons to push.

QUESTION 3: WHAT FACTORS ARE DRIVING INDUSTRY CHANGE, AND WHAT IMPACTS WILL THEY HAVE?

LO 2

Learn how to diagnose the factors shaping industry dynamics and to forecast their effects on future industry profitability.

While it is critical to understand the nature and intensity of the competitive forces in an industry, it is just as important to understand that the intensity of these forces and the level of an industry's attractiveness are fluid and subject to change. All industries are affected by new developments and ongoing trends that alter industry conditions, some more speedily than others. Many of these changes are important enough to require a strategic response. Since the five competitive forces have such significance for an industry's profit potential, it is critical that managers remain alert to the changes most likely to affect the strength of the five forces. Environmental scanning for changes of this nature will enable managers to forecast changes in the expected profitability of the industry and to adjust their company's strategy accordingly.

Changes that affect the competitive forces in a positive manner may present opportunities for companies to reposition themselves to take advantage of these forces. Changes that affect the five forces negatively may require a defensive strategic response. Regardless of the direction of change, managers will be able to react in a more timely fashion, with lower adjustment costs, if they have advance notice of the coming changes. Moreover, with early notice, managers may be able to influence the direction or scope of environmental change and improve the outlook.

Analyzing Industry Dynamics

CORE CONCEPT

Dynamic industry analysis involves determining how the **drivers of change** are affecting industry and competitive conditions.

Managing under changing conditions begins with a strategic analysis of the industry dynamics. This involves three steps: (1) identifying the **drivers of change,** (2) assessing whether the drivers of change are, individually or collectively, acting to make the industry more or less attractive, and (3) determining what strategy changes are needed to prepare for the impacts of the anticipated change. All three steps merit further discussion.

Identifying an Industry's Drivers of Change

While many types of environmental change can affect industries in one way or another, it is important to focus on the most powerful agents of change— those with the biggest influence in reshaping the industry landscape and altering competitive conditions. Many drivers of change originate in the outer ring of the company's external environment (see Figure 3.2), but others originate in the company's more immediate industry and competitive environment. Although some drivers of change are unique and specific to a particular industry situation, most drivers of industry and competitive change fall into one of the following categories:[14]

- *Changes in an industry's long-term growth rate.* Shifts in industry growth up or down are a key driver of industry change, affecting the balance between industry supply and buyer demand, entry and exit, and the character and strength of competition. Whether demand is growing or declining is one of the key factors influencing the intensity of rivalry in an industry, as explained earlier. But the strength of this effect will depend on how changes in the industry growth rate affect entry and exit in the industry. If entry barriers are low, then growth in demand will attract new entrants, increasing the number of industry rivals. If exit barriers are low, then shrinking demand will induce exit, resulting in fewer remaining rivals. Since the numbers of firms in an industry also affects the strength of rivalry, these secondary effects via entry and exit would counteract the more direct effects of the change in demand on rivalry. Depending on how much entry or exit takes place, the net result might be that the overall force of rivals remains the same. A change in the long-term growth rate may affect industry conditions in other ways as well. For example, if growth prospects induce the entry of a large, established firm with ambitious growth goals, the intensity of rivalry may increase markedly due to the added diversity or changes in the size mix of incumbents. The exact effect of growth rate changes will vary depending on the specific industry situation. In analyzing the effects of any change driver, managers need to keep in mind the various factors that influence the five forces.

- *Increasing globalization.* Globalization can be precipitated by the blossoming of consumer demand in more and more countries and by the actions of government officials in many countries to reduce trade barriers or open up once-closed markets to foreign competitors, as is occurring in many parts of Europe, Latin America, and Asia. Significant differences in labor costs among countries give manufacturers a strong incentive to locate plants for labor-intensive products in low-wage countries and use these plants to supply market demand across the world. Wages in China, India, Singapore, Mexico, and Brazil, for example, are about one-fourth those in the United States, Germany, and Japan. Because globalization is a complex phenomenon that affects different industries in different ways, analyzing its effects on industry dynamics is a challenging task that requires a consideration of how each of the five forces may be affected. For example, globalization increases the diversity and number of competitors, and this in turn increases the force of rivalry in an industry. At the same time, the lowering of trade barriers increases the threat of entry, putting further pressure on industry profitability. On the other hand, globalization is likely to weaken supplier power by increasing the number of suppliers and increasing the possibility of substituting cheap labor for other inputs. The specific effects vary by industry and will impact some industries more than others. Globalization is very much a driver of industry change in such industries as motor vehicles, steel, petroleum, personal computers, video games, public accounting, and textbook publishing.

- *Changes in who buys the product and how they use it.* Shifts in buyer demographics and the ways products are used can greatly alter industry and competitive conditions. Longer life expectancies and growing percentages of relatively well-to-do retirees, for example, are driving demand growth in such industries as health care, prescription drugs, recreational living, and vacation travel. This is the most common effect of changes in buyer demographics, and it affects industry rivalry, as observed above. But other effects are possible as well. Dell's "buy direct" strategy lessened the buyer power of big-box middlemen in the PC industry by cutting out the intermediate buyers and selling directly to end users. Buyer power increased in the pharmaceutical industry when large health care insurers and other large payers created lists of approved drugs, reducing the role of individual (powerless) doctors in the choice process.

- *Technological change.* Advances in technology can cause disruptive change in an industry by introducing substitutes that offer buyers an irresistible price/performance combination. At the least, this increases the power of substitutes; it may change the business landscape in more fundamental ways if it has a devastating effect on demand. Technological change can also impact the manufacturing process in an industry. This might lead to greater economies of scale, for example, which would increase industry entry barriers. Or it could lead to greater product differentiation, as did the introduction of "mass-customization" techniques. Increasing product differentiation tends to lower buyer power, increase entry barriers, and reduce rivalry—all of which have positive implications for industry profitability.

- *Emerging new Internet capabilities and applications.* The emergence of high-speed Internet service and Voice-Over-Internet-Protocol technology, along with an ever-growing series of Internet applications, provides a special case of technological change that has been a major driver of change in industry after industry. It has reshaped many aspects of the business landscape and can affect the five forces in various ways. The ability of companies to reach consumers via the Internet increases the number of rivals a company faces and often escalates rivalry by pitting pure online sellers against combination brick-and-click sellers against pure brick-and-mortar sellers (increasing diversity and size mix). The Internet gives buyers increasing power through unprecedented ability to research the product offerings of competitors and shop the market for the best value (making buyers better informed). Widespread use of e-mail has forever eroded the business of providing fax services and the first-class-mail delivery revenues of government postal services worldwide (substitute power). Video-conferencing via the Internet erodes the demand for business travel (increasing rivalry in the travel market). The Internet of the future will feature faster speeds, dazzling applications, and over a billion connected gadgets performing an array of functions, thus driving further industry and competitive changes. But Internet-related impacts vary from industry to industry. The challenges here are to assess precisely how emerging Internet developments are altering a particular industry's landscape and to factor these impacts into the strategy-making equation.

- *Product and marketing innovation.* An ongoing stream of product innovations tends to alter the pattern of competition in an industry by attracting more first-time buyers, rejuvenating industry growth, and/or increasing product differentiation, with concomitant effects on rivalry, entry threat, and buyer power. Product innovation has been a key driving force in such industries as digital cameras, golf clubs, video games, toys, and prescription drugs. Similarly, when firms are successful in introducing *new ways* to market their products, they can spark a burst of buyer interest, widen industry demand, increase or lower entry barriers, and increase product differentiation—any or all of which can alter the competitiveness of an industry.

- *Entry or exit of major firms.* The entry of one or more foreign companies into a geographic market once dominated by domestic firms nearly always changes the balance between demand and supply and shakes up competitive conditions by adding diversity. Likewise, when an established domestic firm from another industry attempts entry either by acquisition or by launching its own start-up venture, it usually applies its skills and resources in some innovative fashion that pushes competition in new directions. Entry by a major firm thus often produces a new ball game, with greater rivalry as the result. Similarly, exit of a major firm changes the competitive structure by reducing the number of market leaders and increasing the dominance of the leaders who remain. The primary effect is on the degree of rivalry in the industry, through changes in industry concentration.

- *Diffusion of technical know-how across more companies and more countries.* As knowledge about how to perform a particular activity or execute a particular manufacturing technology spreads, products tend to become more commodity-like. This increases the intensity of rivalry, buyer power, and the threat of entry into an industry, as described earlier.

- *Improvements in cost and efficiency in closely adjoining markets.* Big changes in the costs of substitute producers can dramatically alter the state of competition by changing the price/performance trade-off between an industry's products and that of substitute goods. For example, lower production costs and longer-life products have allowed the makers of super-efficient, fluorescent-based spiral lightbulbs to cut deeply into the sales of incandescent lightbulbs. This has occurred because the spiral lightbulbs, despite being priced two to three times higher than incandescent bulbs, are still far cheaper to use because of their energy-saving efficiency (as much as $50 per bulb) and longer lives (up to eight years between replacements).

- *Reductions in uncertainty and business risk.* Many companies are hesitant to enter industries with uncertain futures or high levels of business risk, and firms already in these industries may be cautious about making aggressive capital investments to expand—often because it is unclear how much time and money it will take to overcome various technological hurdles and achieve acceptable production costs (as is the case in the infant solar power industry). Likewise, firms entering foreign markets where demand is just emerging or where political conditions are volatile may be cautious and limit their downside exposure by using less risky strategies. Over time, however, diminishing risk levels and uncertainty tend to stimulate new entry and capital investments on the part of growth-minded companies seeking new opportunities. This can dramatically alter industry and competitive conditions by increasing rivalry, as the numbers of firms in the industry and their diversity increases.

- *Regulatory influences and government policy changes.* Changes in regulations and government policies can affect competitive conditions in industries in a variety of ways. For example, regulatory actions can affect barriers to entry directly, as they have in industries such as airlines, banking, and broadcasting. Regulations regarding product quality, safety, and environmental protection can affect entry barriers more indirectly, by altering capital requirements or economies of scale. Government actions can also affect rivalry through antitrust policies, as they have in soft-drink bottling, where exclusive territorial rights were granted, and in automobile parts, where a loosening of restrictions led to increasing supplier power.[15] In international markets, host governments can affect industry rivalry or supplier and buyer power by opening their domestic markets to foreign participation or closing them to protect domestic companies.

- *Changing societal concerns, attitudes, and lifestyles.* Emerging social issues and changing attitudes and lifestyles can be powerful instigators of industry change. Growing concerns about global warming have emerged as a major driver of change in the energy industry, changing the rate of industry growth in different sectors. The greater attention and care being given to household pets has driven growth across the whole pet industry. Changes in the industry growth rate, as we have seen, can affect the intensity of industry rivalry and entry conditions.

Table 3.3 lists these 12 most common drivers of change. That there are so many different *potential* drivers of change explains why a full understanding of all types of change drivers is a fundamental part of analyzing industry dynamics. However, for each industry no more than three or four of these drivers are likely to be powerful enough to qualify as the *major determinants* of why and how an industry's competitive conditions are changing. The true analytical task is to evaluate the forces of industry and competitive change carefully enough to separate major factors from minor ones.

Assessing the Impact of the Factors Driving Industry Change

Just identifying the factors driving industry change is not sufficient, however. The second, and more important, step in dynamic industry analysis is to determine whether the prevailing change drivers, on the whole, are acting to make the industry environment more or less attractive. Answers to three questions are needed:

1. Overall, are the factors driving change causing demand for the industry's product to increase or decrease?
2. Is the collective impact of the drivers of change making competition more or less intense?
3. Will the combined impacts of the change drivers lead to higher or lower industry profitability?

Getting a handle on the collective impact of the factors driving industry change requires looking at the likely effects of each factor separately, since the drivers of change may not all be pushing change in the same direction. For example, one change driver may be acting to spur demand for the industry's product while

Table 3.3   The Most Common Drivers of Industry Change

1. Changes in the long-term industry growth rate
2. Increasing globalization
3. Changes in who buys the product and how they use it
4. Technological change
5. Emerging new Internet capabilities and applications
6. Product and marketing innovation
7. Entry or exit of major firms
8. Diffusion of technical know-how across companies and countries
9. Improvements in efficiency in adjacent markets
10. Reductions in uncertainty and business risk
11. Regulatory influences and government policy changes
12. Changing societal concerns, attitudes, and lifestyles

another is working to curtail demand. Whether the net effect on industry demand is up or down hinges on which driver of change is the more powerful. Similarly, the effects of the drivers of change on each of the five forces should be looked at individually first, and then collectively, to view the overall effect. In summing up the overall effect of industry change on the five forces, it is important to recall that it is the *strongest* of the five forces that determines the degree of competitive pressure on industry profitability and therefore the industry's profit potential. The key question, then, is whether a new strong force is emerging or whether forces that are strong presently are beginning to weaken.

> The most important part of dynamic industry analysis is to determine whether the collective impact of the change drivers will be to increase or decrease market demand, make competition more or less intense, and lead to higher or lower industry profitability.

Developing a Strategy That Takes the Changes in Industry Conditions into Account

The third step in the strategic analysis of industry dynamics—where the real payoff for strategy making comes—is for managers to draw some conclusions about *what strategy adjustments will be needed to deal with the impacts of the changes in industry conditions.* The value of analyzing industry dynamics is to gain better understanding of what strategy adjustments will be needed to cope with the drivers of industry change and the impacts they are likely to have on competitive intensity and industry profitability. Indeed, without understanding the forces driving industry change and the impacts these forces will have on the character of the industry environment and on the company's business over the next one to three years, managers are ill-prepared to craft a strategy tightly matched to emerging conditions. To the extent that managers are unclear about the drivers of industry change and their impacts, or if their views are off-base, the chances of making astute and timely strategy adjustments are slim. So dynamic industry analysis is not something to take lightly; it has practical value and is basic to the task of thinking strategically about where the industry is headed and how to prepare for the changes ahead.

> Dynamic industry analysis, when done properly, pushes company managers to think about what's around the corner and what the company needs to be doing to get ready for it.

QUESTION 4: HOW ARE INDUSTRY RIVALS POSITIONED—WHO IS STRONGLY POSITIONED AND WHO IS NOT?

Since competing companies commonly sell in different price/quality ranges, emphasize different distribution channels, incorporate product features that appeal to different types of buyers, have different geographic coverage, and so on, it stands to reason that some companies enjoy stronger or more attractive market positions than other companies. Understanding which companies are strongly positioned and which are weakly positioned is an integral part of analyzing an industry's competitive structure. The best technique for revealing the market positions of industry competitors is **strategic group mapping.**[16]

LO 3

Become adept at mapping the market positions of key groups of industry rivals.

Using Strategic Group Maps to Assess the Market Positions of Key Competitors

A **strategic group** consists of those industry members with similar competitive approaches and positions in the market.[17] Companies in the same strategic group can resemble one another in any of several ways: They may have comparable product-line breadth, sell in the same price/quality range, emphasize the same distribution channels, use essentially the same product attributes to appeal to similar types of buyers, depend on identical technological approaches, or offer buyers similar services and technical assistance.[18] An industry contains only one strategic group when all sellers pursue essentially identical strategies and have similar market positions. At the other extreme, an industry may contain as many strategic groups as there are competitors when each rival pursues a distinctively different competitive approach and occupies a substantially different market position.

The procedure for constructing a *strategic group map* is straightforward:

- Identify the competitive characteristics that differentiate firms in the industry. Typical variables are price/quality range (high, medium, low), geographic coverage (local, regional, national, global), product-line breadth (wide, narrow), degree of service offered (no frills, limited, full), use of distribution channels (retail, wholesale, Internet, multiple), degree of vertical integration (none, partial, full), and degree of diversification into other industries (none, some, considerable).
- Plot the firms on a two-variable map using pairs of these differentiating characteristics.
- Assign firms occupying about the same map location to the same strategic group.
- Draw circles around each strategic group, making the circles proportional to the size of the group's share of total industry sales revenues.

This produces a two-dimensional diagram like the one for the retail chain store industry in Illustration Capsule 3.1.

Several guidelines need to be observed in creating strategic group maps.[19] First, the two variables selected as axes for the map should *not* be highly correlated; if they are, the circles on the map will fall along a diagonal and reveal nothing more about the relative positions of competitors than would be revealed by comparing the rivals on just one of the variables. For instance, if companies with broad product lines use multiple distribution channels while companies with narrow lines use a single distribution channel, then looking at broad versus narrow product lines reveals just as much about industry positioning as looking at single versus multiple distribution channels; that is, one of the variables is redundant.

Second, the variables chosen as axes for the map should reflect key approaches to offering value to customers and expose big differences in how rivals position themselves to compete in the marketplace. This, of course, means analysts must identify the characteristics that differentiate rival firms and use these differences as variables for the axes and as the basis for deciding which firm belongs in which strategic group. Third, the variables used as axes don't have to be either quantitative or continuous; rather, they can be discrete variables, defined in terms of distinct classes and combinations. Fourth, drawing the sizes of the circles on the map proportional to the combined sales of the firms in each strategic group allows the map to reflect the relative sizes of each strategic

ILLUSTRATION CAPSULE 3.1

Comparative Market Positions of Selected Retail Chains: A Strategic Group Map Example

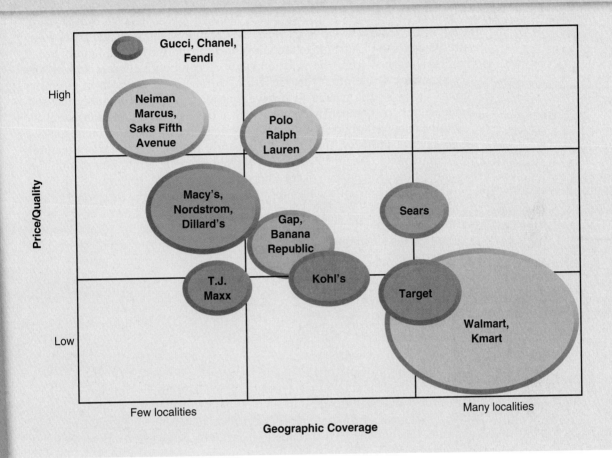

Note: Circles are drawn roughly proportional to the sizes of the chains, based on revenues.

group. Fifth, if more than two good variables can be used as axes for the map, then it is wise to draw several maps to give different views of the relationships among the competitive positions present in the industry's structure—there is not necessarily one best map for portraying how competing firms are positioned.

What Can Be Learned from Strategic Group Maps?

Strategic group maps are revealing in several respects. The most important has to do with identifying which industry members are close rivals and which are distant rivals. Firms in the same strategic group are the closest rivals; the next closest rivals are in the immediately adjacent groups. Often, firms in strategic groups that are far apart on the map hardly compete at all. For instance, Walmart's clientele, merchandise selection, and pricing points are much too different to justify calling Walmart a close

> Strategic group maps reveal which companies are close competitors and which are distant competitors.

competitor of Neiman Marcus or Saks Fifth Avenue. For the same reason, Timex is not a meaningful competitive rival of Rolex.

The second thing to be gleaned from strategic group mapping is that *not all positions on the map are equally attractive.*[20] Two reasons account for why some positions can be more attractive than others:[21]

1. *Prevailing competitive pressures in the industry and drivers of change favor some strategic groups and hurt others.* Discerning which strategic groups are advantaged and disadvantaged requires scrutinizing the map in light of what has been learned from the prior analyses of competitive forces and industry dynamics. Quite often the strength of competition varies from group to group—there's little reason to believe that all firms in an industry feel the same degrees of competitive pressure, since their strategies and market positions may well differ in important respects. For instance, in the ready-to-eat cereal industry, there are significantly higher entry barriers (capital requirements, brand loyalty, etc.) for the strategic group comprising the large branded-cereal makers than for the group of generic-cereal makers or the group of small natural-cereal producers. Furthermore, industry dynamics may affect different groups in different ways. For example, the long-term growth in demand may be increasing for some strategic groups and shrinking for others—as is the case in the news industry, where Internet news services and cable news networks are gaining ground at the expense of newspapers and network television. The industry driving forces of emerging Internet capabilities and applications, changes in who buys the product and how they use it, and changing societal concerns, attitudes, and lifestyles are making it increasingly difficult for traditional media to increase audiences and attract new advertisers.

> Some strategic groups are more favorably positioned than others because they confront weaker competitive forces and/or because they are more favorably impacted by the drivers of industry change.

2. *Profit prospects vary from strategic group to strategic group.* The profit prospects of firms in different strategic groups can vary from good to poor because of differing growth rates for the principal buyer segments served by each group, differing degrees of competitive rivalry within strategic groups, differing pressures from potential entrants to each group, differing degrees of exposure to competition from substitute products outside the industry, differing degrees of supplier or customer bargaining power from group to group, and differing impacts from the industry's drivers of change.

Thus, part of strategic group map analysis always entails drawing conclusions about where on the map is the "best" place to be and why. Which companies/strategic groups are destined to prosper because of their positions? Which companies/strategic groups seem destined to struggle because of their positions? What accounts for why some parts of the map are better than others?

QUESTION 5: WHAT STRATEGIC MOVES ARE RIVALS LIKELY TO MAKE NEXT?

Unless a company pays attention to the strategies and situations of competitors and has some inkling of what moves they will be making, it ends up flying blind into competitive battle. As in sports, scouting the opposition is an essential part of game plan development. **Competitive intelligence** about rivals' strategies, their latest actions and announcements, their financial performance, their strengths and weaknesses, and the thinking and leadership styles of their executives is valuable for anticipating the strategic moves competitors are likely to make next. Having good information about the strategic direction and likely moves of key competitors allows a company to prepare defensive countermoves, to craft its own strategic moves with some confidence about what market maneuvers to expect from rivals in response, and to exploit any openings that arise from competitors' missteps.

> Good **competitive intelligence** helps managers avoid the damage to sales and profits that comes from being caught napping by the surprise moves of rivals.

One indicator of the types of moves a rival is likely to make is its financial performance—how much pressure it is under to improve. Rivals with good financial performance are likely to continue their present strategy with only minor fine-tuning. Poorly performing rivals are virtually certain to make fresh strategic moves. Ambitious rivals looking to move up in the industry ranks are strong candidates for launching new strategic offensives to pursue emerging market opportunities and exploit the vulnerabilities of weaker rivals.

Other good clues about what actions a specific company is likely to undertake can often be gleaned from what its management is saying in company press releases, information posted on the company's Web site (especially the presentations management has recently made to securities analysts), and such public documents as annual reports and other financial reports. (Figure 1.1 in Chapter 1 indicates what to look for in identifying a company's strategy.) Many companies have a competitive intelligence unit that sifts through the available information to construct up-to-date strategic profiles of rivals—their current strategies, resources, competitive capabilities, and competitive shortcomings. Such profiles are typically updated regularly and made available to managers and other key personnel.

There are several useful questions that company managers can pose to help predict the likely actions of important rivals:

1. Which competitors have strategies that are producing good results—and thus are likely to make only minor strategic adjustments?

2. Which competitors are losing ground in the marketplace or otherwise struggling to come up with a good strategy—and thus are strong candidates for altering their prices, improving the appeal of their product offerings, moving to a different part of the strategic group map, and otherwise adjusting important elements of their strategy?

3. Which competitors are poised to gain market share, and which ones seem destined to lose ground?

4. Which competitors are likely to rank among the industry leaders five years from now? Do the up-and-coming competitors have strong ambitions and the resources needed to overtake the current industry leader?

5. Which rivals badly need to increase their unit sales and market share? What strategic options are they most likely to pursue: lowering prices, adding new models and styles, expanding their dealer networks, entering additional geographic markets, boosting advertising to build better brand-name awareness, acquiring a weaker competitor, or placing more emphasis on direct sales via their Web sites?

6. Which rivals are likely to enter new geographic markets or make major moves to substantially increase their sales and market share in a particular geographic region?

7. Which rivals are strong candidates to expand their product offerings and enter new product segments where they do not currently have a presence?

8. Which rivals are good candidates to be acquired? Which rivals may be looking to make an acquisition and are financially able to do so?

To succeed in predicting a competitor's next moves, company strategists need to have a good understanding of each rival's situation, its pattern of behavior in the past, how its managers think, and what the rival's best strategic options are. Doing the necessary detective work can be time-consuming, but scouting competitors well enough to anticipate their next moves allows managers to prepare effective countermoves (perhaps even beat a rival to the punch) and to take rivals' probable actions into account in crafting their own best course of action.

QUESTION 6: WHAT ARE THE KEY FACTORS FOR FUTURE COMPETITIVE SUCCESS?

An industry's **key success factors (KSFs)** are those competitive factors that affect industry members' ability to survive and prosper in the marketplace—the particular strategy elements, product attributes, operational approaches, resources, and competitive capabilities that spell the difference between being a strong competitor and a weak competitor—and between profit and loss. KSFs by their very nature are so important to competitive success that *all firms* in the industry must pay close attention to them or risk becoming an industry laggard or failure. To indicate the significance of KSFs another way, how well the elements of a company's strategy measure up against an industry's KSFs determines just how financially and competitively successful that company will be. Identifying KSFs, in light of the prevailing and anticipated industry and competitive conditions, is therefore always a top priority in analytical and strategy-making considerations. Company strategists need to understand the industry landscape well enough to separate the factors most important to competitive success from those that are less important.

Key success factors vary from industry to industry, and even from time to time within the same industry, as drivers of change and competitive conditions change. But regardless of the circumstances, an industry's key success factors can always be deduced by asking the same three questions:

1. On what basis do buyers of the industry's product choose between the competing brands of sellers? That is, what product attributes and service characteristics are crucial?

2. Given the nature of competitive rivalry and the competitive forces prevailing in the marketplace, what resources and competitive capabilities must a company have to be competitively successful?

3. What shortcomings are almost certain to put a company at a significant competitive disadvantage?

Only rarely are there more than five key factors for competitive success. When there appear to be more, usually some are of greater importance

CORE CONCEPT

Key success factors are the strategy elements, product and service attributes, operational approaches, resources, and competitive capabilities with the greatest impact on competitive success in the marketplace.

than others. Managers should therefore bear in mind the purpose of identifying key success factors—to determine which factors are most important to competitive success—and resist the temptation to label a factor that has only minor importance as a KSF. Compiling a list of every factor that matters even a little bit defeats the purpose of concentrating management attention on the factors truly critical to long-term competitive success.

In the beer industry, for example, although there are many types of buyers (wholesale, retail, end consumer), it is most important to understand the preferences and buying behavior of the beer drinkers. Their purchase decisions are driven by price, taste, convenient access, and marketing. Thus the KSFs include a *strong network of wholesale distributors* (to get the company's brand stocked and favorably displayed in retail outlets, bars, restaurants, and stadiums, where beer is sold) and *clever advertising* (to induce beer drinkers to buy the company's brand and thereby pull beer sales through the established wholesale/retail channels). Because there is a potential for strong buyer power on the part of large distributors and retail chains, competitive success depends on some mechanism to offset that power, of which advertising (to create demand pull) is one. Thus the KSFs also include *superior product differentiation* (as in microbrews) or *superior firm size and branding capabilities* (as in national brands). The KSFs also include *full utilization of brewing capacity* (to keep manufacturing costs low and offset the high advertising, branding, and product differentiation costs).

Correctly diagnosing an industry's KSFs raises a company's chances of crafting a sound strategy. The key success factors of an industry point to those things that every firm in the industry needs to attend to in order to retain customers and weather the competition. If the company's strategy cannot deliver on the key success factors of its industry, it is unlikely to earn enough profits to remain a viable business. The goal of strategists, however, should be to do more than just meet the KSFs, since all firms in the industry need to clear this bar to survive. The goal of company strategists should be to design a strategy that allows it to compare favorably vis-à-vis rivals on each and every one of the industry's KSFs and that aims at being *distinctively better* than rivals on one (or possibly two) of the KSFs.

LO 4

Understand why in-depth evaluation of a business's strengths and weaknesses in relation to the specific industry conditions it confronts is an essential prerequisite to crafting a strategy that is well-matched to its external situation.

QUESTION 7: DOES THE INDUSTRY OFFER GOOD PROSPECTS FOR ATTRACTIVE PROFITS?

The final step in evaluating the industry and competitive environment is to use the results of the analyses performed in answering Questions 1 to 6 to determine whether the industry presents the company with strong prospects for attractive profits. The important factors on which to base a conclusion include:

- The industry's growth potential.
- Whether strong competitive forces are squeezing industry profitability to subpar levels.
- Whether industry profitability will be favorably or unfavorably affected by the prevailing drivers of change in the industry (i.e., whether the industry growth potential and competition appear destined to grow stronger or weaker).

- Whether the company occupies a stronger market position than rivals (one more capable of withstanding negative competitive forces) and whether this is likely to change in the course of competitive interactions.
- How well the company's strategy delivers on the industry key success factors.

As a general proposition, if a company can conclude that its overall profit prospects are above average in the industry, then the industry environment is basically attractive *(for that company);* if industry profit prospects are below average, conditions are unattractive *(for the company).* However, it is a mistake to think of a particular industry as being equally attractive or unattractive to all industry participants and all potential entrants.[22] Attractiveness is relative, not absolute, and conclusions one way or the other have to be drawn from the perspective of a particular company. For instance, a favorably positioned competitor may see ample opportunity to capitalize on the vulnerabilities of weaker rivals even though industry conditions are otherwise somewhat dismal. And even if an industry has appealing potential for growth and profitability, a weak competitor (one that may be part of an unfavorably positioned strategic group) may conclude that having to fight a steep uphill battle against much stronger rivals holds little promise of eventual market success or good return on shareholder investment. Similarly, industries attractive to insiders may be unattractive to outsiders because of the difficulty of challenging current market leaders with their particular resources and competencies or because they have more attractive opportunities elsewhere.

> The degree to which an industry is attractive or unattractive is not the same for all industry participants and all potential entrants.

When a company decides an industry is fundamentally attractive and presents good opportunities, a strong case can be made that it should invest aggressively to capture the opportunities it sees and to improve its long-term competitive position in the business. When a strong competitor concludes an industry is becoming less attractive, it may elect to simply protect its present position, investing cautiously if at all and looking for opportunities in other industries. A competitively weak company in an unattractive industry may see its best option as finding a buyer, perhaps a rival, to acquire its business.

KEY POINTS

Thinking strategically about a company's external situation involves probing for answers to the following seven questions:

1. *Does the industry offer attractive opportunities for growth?* Industries differ significantly on such factors as market size and growth rate, geographic scope, life-cycle stage, the number and sizes of sellers, industry capacity, and other conditions that describe the industry's demand-supply balance and opportunities for growth. Identifying the industry's basic economic features and growth potential sets the stage for the analysis to come, since they play an important role in determining an industry's potential for attractive profits.

2. *What kinds of competitive forces are industry members facing, and how strong is each force?* The strength of competition is a composite of five forces: (1) competitive pressures stemming from the competitive jockeying among industry rivals, (2) competitive pressures associated with the market inroads

being made by the sellers of substitutes, (3) competitive pressures associated with the threat of new entrants into the market, (4) competitive pressures stemming from supplier bargaining power, and (5) competitive pressures stemming from buyer bargaining. The nature and strength of the competitive pressures have to be examined force by force and their collective strength must be evaluated. The strongest forces, however, are the ultimate determinant of the intensity of the competitive pressure on industry profitability. Working through the five-forces model aids strategy makers in assessing how to insulate the company from the strongest forces, identify attractive arenas for expansion, or alter the competitive conditions so that they offer more favorable prospects for profitability.

3. *What factors are driving changes in the industry, and what impact will these changes have on competitive intensity and industry profitability?* Industry and competitive conditions change because of a variety of forces, some coming from the industry's macro-environment and others originating within the industry. The most common change drivers include changes in the long-term industry growth rate, increasing globalization, changing buyer demographics, technological change, Internet-related developments, product and marketing innovation, entry or exit of major firms, diffusion of know-how, efficiency improvements in adjacent markets, reductions in uncertainty and business risk, government policy changes, and changing societal factors. Once an industry's change drivers have been identified, the analytical task becomes one of determining whether they are acting, individually and collectively, to make the industry environment more or less attractive. Are the change drivers causing demand for the industry's product to increase or decrease? Are they acting to make competition more or less intense? Will they lead to higher or lower industry profitability?

4. *What market positions do industry rivals occupy—who is strongly positioned and who is not?* Strategic group mapping is a valuable tool for understanding the similarities, differences, strengths, and weaknesses inherent in the market positions of rival companies. Rivals in the same or nearby strategic groups are close competitors, whereas companies in distant strategic groups usually pose little or no immediate threat. The lesson of strategic group mapping is that some positions on the map are more favorable than others. The profit potential of different strategic groups varies due to strengths and weaknesses in each group's market position. Often, industry competitive pressures and change drivers favor some strategic groups and hurt others.

5. *What strategic moves are rivals likely to make next?* Scouting competitors well enough to anticipate their actions can help a company prepare effective countermoves (perhaps even beating a rival to the punch) and allows managers to take rivals' probable actions into account in designing their own company's best course of action. Managers who fail to study competitors risk being caught unprepared by the strategic moves of rivals.

6. *What are the key factors for competitive success?* An industry's key success factors (KSFs) are the particular strategy elements, product attributes, operational approaches, resources, and competitive capabilities that all industry members must have in order to survive and prosper in the industry. KSFs vary by industry and may vary over time as well. For any industry, however, they can be deduced by answering three basic questions: (1) On what basis do buyers of the industry's product choose between the competing brands of

sellers, (2) what resources and competitive capabilities must a company have to be competitively successful, and (3) what shortcomings are almost certain to put a company at a significant competitive disadvantage? Correctly diagnosing an industry's KSFs raises a company's chances of crafting a sound strategy.

7. *Does the outlook for the industry present the company with sufficiently attractive prospects for profitability?* The last step in industry analysis is summing up the results from answering questions 1 to 6. If the answers reveal that a company's overall profit prospects in that industry are above average, then the industry environment is basically attractive *for that company;* if industry profit prospects are below average, conditions are unattractive for them. What may look like an attractive environment for one company may appear to be unattractive from the perspective of a different company.

Clear, insightful diagnosis of a company's external situation is an essential first step in crafting strategies that are well matched to industry and competitive conditions. To do cutting-edge strategic thinking about the external environment, managers must know what questions to pose and what analytical tools to use in answering these questions. This is why this chapter has concentrated on suggesting the right questions to ask, explaining concepts and analytical approaches, and indicating the kinds of things to look for.

ASSURANCE OF LEARNING EXERCISES

LO 1, LO 2

1. Prepare a brief analysis of the bottled water industry using the information provided on industry trade association Web sites. On the basis of information provided on these Web sites, draw a five-forces diagram for the bottled water industry and briefly discuss the nature and strength of each of the five competitive forces. What factors are driving change in the industry?

LO 1, LO 3

2. Based on the strategic group map in Illustration Capsule 3.1, who are Nordstrom's closest competitors? Between which two strategic groups is competition the strongest? Why do you think no retail chains are positioned in the upper right corner of the map? Which company/strategic group faces the weakest competition from the members of other strategic groups?

LO 1, LO 4

3. Using your knowledge as a bottled water consumer and your analysis of the five forces in that industry (from question 1), describe the key success factors for the bottled water industry. Your list should contain no more than six industry KSFs. In deciding on your list, it's important to distinguish between factors critical for the success of *any* firm in the industry and factors that pertain only to specific companies.

EXERCISES FOR SIMULATION PARTICIPANTS

LO 1

1. Which of the five competitive forces is creating the strongest competitive pressures for your company?
2. What are the "competitive weapons" that rival companies in your industry can use to gain sales and market share? See Table 3.2 to help you identify possible competitive tactics. (You may be able to think of others.)
3. What are the factors affecting the intensity of rivalry in the industry in which your company is competing. Use Figure 3.4 and the accompanying discussion to help you pinpoint the specific factors most affecting competitive intensity. Would you characterize the rivalry among the companies in your industry as brutal, strong, moderate, or relatively weak? Why?

LO 2

4. Are there any factors driving change in the industry in which your company is competing? What impact will these drivers of change have? How will they change demand or supply? Will they cause competition to become more or less intense? Will they act to boost or squeeze profit margins? List at least two actions your company should consider taking in order to combat any negative impacts of the factors driving change.

LO 3

5. Draw a strategic group map showing the market positions of the companies in your industry. Which companies do you believe are in the most attractive position on the map? Which companies are the most weakly positioned? Which companies do you believe are likely to try to move to a different position on the strategic group map?

LO 4

6. What do you see as the key factors for being a successful competitor in your industry? List at least three.

ENDNOTES

[1] For a more extended discussion of the problems with the life-cycle hypothesis, see Michael E. Porter, *Competitive Strategy: Techniques for Analyzing Industries and Competitors* (New York: Free Press, 1980), pp. 157–62.
[2] The five-forces model of competition is the creation of Professor Michael Porter of the Harvard Business School. See Michael E. Porter, "How Competitive Forces Shape Strategy," *Harvard Business Review* 57, no. 2 (March–April 1979), pp. 137–45; Porter, *Competitive Strategy*, chap. 1; and Porter's most recent discussion of the model, "The Five Competitive

Forces That Shape Strategy," *Harvard Business Review* 86, no. 1 (January 2008), pp. 78–93.
[3] For a discussion of how a company's actions to counter the moves of rival firms tend to escalate competitive pressures, see Pamela J. Derfus, Patrick G. Maggitti, Curtis M. Grimm, and Ken G. Smith, "The Red Queen Effect: Competitive Actions and Firm Performance," *Academy of Management Journal* 51, no. 1 (February 2008), pp. 61–80.
[4] Many of these indicators of whether rivalry produces intense competitive pressures are based on Porter, *Competitive Strategy*, pp. 17–21.

[5] Porter, *Competitive Strategy*, p. 7; Porter, "The Five Competitive Forces That Shape Strategy," p. 81.
[6] The role of entry barriers in shaping the strength of competition in a particular market has long been a standard topic in the literature of microeconomics. For a discussion of how entry barriers affect competitive pressures associated with potential entry, see J. S. Bain, *Barriers to New Competition* (Cambridge, MA: Harvard University Press, 1956); F. M. Scherer, *Industrial Market Structure and Economic Performance*

(Chicago: Rand McNally, 1971), pp. 216–20, 226–33; Porter, *Competitive Strategy,* pp. 7–17; Porter, "The Five Competitive Forces That Shape Strategy," pp. 80–82.

[7] For a good discussion of this point, see George S. Yip, "Gateways to Entry," *Harvard Business Review* 60, no. 5 (September–October 1982), pp. 85–93.

[8] C. A. Montgomery and S. Hariharan, "Diversified Expansion by Large Established Firms," *Journal of Economic Behavior & Organization* 15, no. 1 (January 1991), pp. 71–89.

[9] Porter, "How Competitive Forces Shape Strategy," p. 142; Porter, *Competitive Strategy,* pp. 23–24.

[10] Porter, *Competitive Strategy,* p. 10.

[11] Ibid., pp. 27–28.

[12] Ibid., pp. 24–27.

[13] Porter, "The Five Competitive Forces That Shape Strategy," p. 80.

[14] Most of the candidate driving forces described here are based on the discussion in Porter, *Competitive Strategy,* pp. 164–83.

[15] D. Yoffie, "Cola Wars Continue: Coke and Pepsi in 2006," Harvard Business School case 9-706-447, rev. April 2, 2007; B. C. Lynn, "How Detroit Went Bottom-Up," *American Prospect,* October 2009, pp. 21–24.

[16] Porter, *Competitive Strategy,* chap. 7.

[17] Ibid., pp. 129–30.

[18] For an excellent discussion of how to identify the factors that define strategic groups, see Mary Ellen Gordon and George R. Milne, "Selecting the Dimensions That Define Strategic Groups: A Novel Market-Driven Approach," *Journal of Managerial Issues* 11, no. 2 (Summer 1999), pp. 213–33.

[19] Porter, *Competitive Strategy,* pp. 152–54.

[20] For other benefits of strategic group analysis, see Avi Fiegenbaum and Howard Thomas, "Strategic Groups as Reference Groups: Theory, Modeling and Empirical Examination of Industry and Competitive Strategy," *Strategic Management Journal* 16 (1995), pp. 461–76; S. Ade Olusoga, Michael P. Mokwa, and Charles H. Noble, "Strategic Groups, Mobility Barriers, and Competitive Advantage," *Journal of Business Research* 33 (1995), pp. 153–64.

[21] Porter, *Competitive Strategy,* pp. 130, 132–38, and 152–55.

[22] B. Wernerfelt and C. Montgomery, "What Is an Attractive Industry?" *Management Science* 32, no. 10 (October 1986), pp. 1223–30.

CHAPTER 4

EVALUATING A COMPANY'S RESOURCES, CAPABILITIES, AND COMPETITIVENESS

Before executives can chart a new strategy, they must reach common understanding of the company's current position.

—W. Chan Kim and Renée Mauborgne
Consultants and INSEAD Professors

Organizations succeed in a competitive marketplace over the long run because they can do certain things their customers value better than can their competitors.

—Robert Hayes, Gary Pisano, and David Upton
Harvard Business School Professors

You have to learn to treat people as a resource ... you have to ask not what do they cost, but what is the yield, what can they produce?

—Peter F. Drucker
Business Thinker and Management Consultant

Only firms who are able to continually build new strategic assets faster and cheaper than their competitors will earn superior returns over the long term.

—C. C. Markides and P. J. Williamson
London Business School Professors and Consultants

LEARNING OBJECTIVES

LO 1. Learn how to take stock of how well a company's strategy is working.

LO 2. Understand why a company's resources and capabilities are central to its strategic approach and how to evaluate their potential for giving the company a competitive edge over rivals.

LO 3. Discover how to assess the company's strengths and weaknesses in light of market opportunities and external threats.

LO 4. Grasp how a company's value chain activities can affect the company's cost structure, degree of differentiation, and competitive advantage.

LO 5. Understand how a comprehensive evaluation of a company's competitive situation can assist managers in making critical decisions about their next strategic moves.

I n Chapter 3 we described how to use the tools of industry analysis to assess the profit potential and key success factors of a company's external environment. This laid the groundwork for matching a company's strategy to its external situation. In this chapter we discuss techniques for evaluating a company's internal situation, including its collection of resources and capabilities and the activities it performs along its value chain. Internal analysis enables managers to determine whether their strategy has appealing prospects for giving the company a significant competitive edge over rival firms. Combined with external analysis, it facilitates an understanding of how to reposition a firm to take advantage of new opportunities and to cope with emerging competitive threats. The analytical spotlight will be trained on six questions:

1. How well is the company's present strategy working?

2. What are the company's competitively important resources and capabilities?

3. Is the company able to take advantage of market opportunities and overcome external threats to its external well-being?

4. Are the company's prices and costs competitive with those of key rivals, and does it have an appealing customer value proposition?

5. Is the company competitively stronger or weaker than key rivals?

6. What strategic issues and problems merit front-burner managerial attention?

In probing for answers to these questions, five analytical tools—resource and capability analysis, SWOT analysis, value chain analysis, benchmarking, and competitive strength assessment—will be used. All five are valuable techniques for revealing a company's competitiveness and for helping company managers match their strategy to the company's own particular circumstances.

QUESTION 1: HOW WELL IS THE COMPANY'S PRESENT STRATEGY WORKING?

LO 1

Learn how to take stock of how well a company's strategy is working.

In evaluating how well a company's present strategy is working, the best way to start is with a clear view of what the strategy entails. Figure 4.1 shows the key components of a single-business company's strategy. The first thing to examine is the company's competitive approach. What moves has the company made recently to attract customers and improve its market position—for instance, has it cut prices, improved the design of its product, added new features, stepped up advertising, entered a new geographic market (domestic or foreign), or merged with a competitor? Is it striving for a competitive advantage based on low costs or an appealingly different or better product offering? Is it concentrating on serving a broad spectrum of customers or a narrow market niche? The company's functional strategies in R&D, production, marketing, finance, human resources, information technology, and so on further characterize company strategy, as do any efforts to establish competitively valuable alliances or partnerships with other enterprises.

The two best indicators of how well a company's strategy is working are (1) whether the company is achieving its stated financial and strategic objectives and (2) whether the company is an above-average industry performer. Persistent shortfalls in meeting company performance targets and weak performance relative to rivals are reliable warning signs that the company has a weak strategy or suffers from poor strategy execution or both. Other indicators of how well a company's strategy is working include:

- Whether the firm's sales are growing faster than, slower than, or about the same pace as the market as a whole, thus resulting in a rising, eroding, or stable market share.
- Whether the company is acquiring new customers at an attractive rate as well as retaining existing customers.
- Whether the firm's profit margins are increasing or decreasing and how well its margins compare to rival firms' margins.
- Trends in the firm's net profits and return on investment and how they compare to the same trends for other companies in the industry.
- Whether the company's overall financial strength and credit rating are improving or declining.
- How shareholders view the company on the basis of trends in the company's stock price and shareholder value (relative to the stock price trends at other companies in the industry).
- Whether the firm's image and reputation with its customers are growing stronger or weaker.
- How well the company stacks up against rivals on technology, product innovation, customer service, product quality, delivery time, price, getting newly developed products to market quickly, and other relevant factors on which buyers base their choices.
- Whether key measures of operating performance (such as days of inventory, employee productivity, unit cost, defect rate, scrap rate, order-filling accuracy, delivery times, and warranty costs) are improving, remaining steady, or deteriorating.

Figure 4.1 Identifying the Components of a Single-Business Company's Strategy

Planned, proactive moves to attract customers and outcompete rivals via improved product design, better features, higher quality, wider selection, lower prices, and so on

Moves to respond to changing conditions in the macro-environment or in industry and competitive conditions

Initiatives to build competitive advantage based on
- Lower costs relative to rivals?
- A different or better product offering?
- Superior ability to serve a market niche or specific group of buyers?

Efforts to expand or narrow geographic coverage

Efforts to build competitively valuable partnerships and strategic alliances with other enterprises

BUSINESS STRATEGY (The action plan for managing a single business)

KEY FUNCTIONAL STRATEGIES

R&D, technology, product design strategy

Supply chain management strategy

Production strategy

Sales, marketing, and distribution strategies

Information technology strategy

Human resource strategy

Finance strategy

The stronger a company's current overall performance, the less likely the need for radical changes in strategy. The weaker a company's financial performance and market standing, the more its current strategy must be questioned. Weak performance is almost always a sign of weak strategy, weak execution, or both.

Evaluating how well a company's strategy is working should include quantitative as well as qualitative assessments. Table 4.1 provides a compilation of the financial ratios most commonly used to evaluate a company's financial performance and balance sheet strength.

> The stronger a company's financial performance and market position, the more likely it has a well-conceived, well-executed strategy.

QUESTION 2: WHAT ARE THE COMPANY'S COMPETITIVELY IMPORTANT RESOURCES AND CAPABILITIES?

Regardless of how well the strategy is working, it is important for managers to understand the underlying reasons. Clearly, this is critical if strategy changes are needed. But even when the strategy is working well, this can help managers to bolster a

Table 4.1   Key Financial Ratios: How to Calculate Them and What They Mean

Ratio	How Calculated	What It Shows
Profitability Ratios		
1. Gross profit margin	$$\frac{\text{Revenues} - \text{Cost of goods sold}}{\text{Revenues}}$$	Shows the percentage of revenues available to cover operating expenses and yield a profit. Higher is better, and the trend should be upward.
2. Operating profit margin (or return on sales)	$$\frac{\text{Revenues} - \text{Operating expenses}}{\text{Revenues}}$$ or $$\frac{\text{Operating income}}{\text{Revenues}}$$	Shows how much profit is earned on each dollar of sales, before paying interest charges and income taxes. Earnings before interest and taxes is known as *EBIT* in financial and business accounting. Higher is better, and the trend should be upward.
3. Net profit margin (or net return on sales)	$$\frac{\text{Profits after taxes}}{\text{Revenues}}$$	Shows after-tax profits per dollar of sales. Higher is better, and the trend should be upward.
4. Return on total assets	$$\frac{\text{Profits after taxes} + \text{Interest}}{\text{Total assets}}$$	A measure of the return on total investment in the enterprise. Interest is added to after-tax profits to form the numerator, since total assets are financed by creditors as well as by stockholders. Higher is better, and the trend should be upward.
5. Return on stockholder's equity	$$\frac{\text{Profits after taxes}}{\text{Total stockholders' equity}}$$	Shows the return stockholders are earning on their investment in the enterprise. A return in the 12% to 15% range is "average," and the trend should be upward.
6. Return on invested capital	$$\frac{\text{Profits after taxes}}{\text{Long-term debt} + \text{total equity}}$$	Shows how effectively a company uses the monetary capital invested in its operations and the returns to those investments. Higher is better, and the trend should be upward.
7. Earnings per share	$$\frac{\text{Profits after taxes}}{\text{Number of shares of common stock outstanding}}$$	Shows the earnings for each share of common stock outstanding. The trend should be upward, and the bigger the annual percentage gains, the better.
Liquidity Ratios		
1. Current ratio	$$\frac{\text{Current assets}}{\text{Current liabilities}}$$	Shows a firm's ability to pay current liabilities using assets that can be converted to cash in the near term. The ratio should definitely be higher than 1.0; a ratio of 2.0 or higher is better still.
2. Working capital	Current assets − Current liabilities	Shows the cash available for a firm's day-to-day operations. Bigger amounts are better because the company has more internal funds available to (1) pay its current liabilities on a timely basis and (2) finance inventory expansion, additional accounts receivable, and a larger base of operations without resorting to borrowing or raising more equity capital.

(Continued)

Ratio	How Calculated	What It Shows
Leverage Ratios		
1. Debt-to-assets ratio	$$\frac{\text{Total debt}}{\text{Total assets}}$$	Measures the extent to which borrowed funds have been used to finance the firm's operations. A low fraction or ratio is better—a high fraction indicates overuse of debt and greater risk of bankruptcy.
2. Long-term debt-to-capital ratio	$$\frac{\text{Long-term debt}}{\text{Long-term debt} + \text{Total stockholders' equity}}$$	An important measure of creditworthiness and balance sheet strength. It indicates the percentage of capital investment that has been financed by creditors and bondholders. A ratio below 0.25 is usually preferable since monies invested by stockholders account for 75% or more of the company's total capital. The lower the ratio, the greater the capacity to borrow additional funds. A debt-to capital ratio above 0.50 and certainly above 0.75 indicates a heavy and perhaps excessive reliance on debt, lower creditworthiness, and weak balance sheet strength.
3. Debt-to-equity ratio	$$\frac{\text{Total debt}}{\text{Total stockholders' equity}}$$	Should usually be less than 1.0. A high ratio (especially above 1.0) signals excessive debt, lower creditworthiness, and weaker balance sheet strength.
4. Long-term debt-to-equity ratio	$$\frac{\text{Long-term debt}}{\text{Total stockholders' equity}}$$	Shows the balance between debt and equity in the firm's *long-term* capital structure. A low ratio indicates greater capacity to borrow additional funds if needed.
5. Times-interest-earned (or coverage) ratio	$$\frac{\text{Operating income}}{\text{Interest expenses}}$$	Measures the ability to pay annual interest charges. Lenders usually insist on a minimum ratio of 2.0, but ratios above 3.0 signal better creditworthiness.
Activity Ratios		
1. Days of inventory	$$\frac{\text{Inventory}}{\text{Cost of goods sold} \div 365}$$	Measures inventory management efficiency. Fewer days of inventory are usually better.
2. Inventory turnover	$$\frac{\text{Cost of goods sold}}{\text{Inventory}}$$	Measures the number of inventory turns per year. Higher is better.
3. Average collection period	$$\frac{\text{Accounts receivable}}{\text{Total sales} \div 365}$$ *or* $$\frac{\text{Accounts receivable}}{\text{Average daily sales}}$$	Indicates the average length of time the firm must wait after making a sale to receive cash payment. A shorter collection time is better.
Other Important Measures of Financial Performance		
1. Dividend yield on common stock	$$\frac{\text{Annual dividends per share}}{\text{Current market price per share}}$$	A measure of the return to owners received in the form of dividends.

(Continued)

Ratio	How Calculated	What It Shows
2. Price-earnings ratio	$$\frac{\text{Current market price per share}}{\text{Earnings per share}}$$	A P/E ratio above 20 indicates strong investor confidence in a firm's outlook and earnings growth. Firms whose future earnings are at risk or likely to grow slowly typically have ratios below 12.
3. Dividend payout ratio	$$\frac{\text{Annual dividends per share}}{\text{Earnings per share}}$$	Indicates the percentage of after-tax profits paid out as dividends.
4. Internal cash flow	After tax profits + Depreciation	A quick and rough estimate of the cash a company's business is generating after payment of operating expenses, interest, and taxes. Such amounts can be used for dividend payments or funding capital expenditures.
5. Free cash flow	After tax profits + Depreciation − Capital Expenditures − Dividends	A quick and rough estimate of the cash a company's business is generating after payment of operating expenses, interest, taxes, dividends, and desirable reinvestments in the business. The larger a company's free cash flow, the greater is its ability to internally fund new strategic initiatives, repay debt, make new acquisitions, repurchase shares of stock, or increase dividend payments.

LO 2

Understand why a company's resources and capabilities are central to its strategic approach and how to evaluate their potential for giving the company a competitive edge over rivals.

successful strategy and avoid harmful missteps. How well a strategy works depends a great deal on the relative strengths and weaknesses of a company's resources and capabilities. A company's resources and capabilities are its **competitive assets** and determine whether its competitive power in the marketplace will be impressively strong or disappointingly weak. Companies with minimal or only ordinary competitive assets nearly always are relegated to a trailing position in the industry.

Resource and capability analysis provides managers with a powerful tool for sizing up the company's competitive assets and determining whether they can provide the foundation necessary for competitive success in the marketplace. This is a two step process. The first step is for managers to identify the company's resources and capabilities so that they have a better idea of what they have to work with in crafting the company's competitive strategy. The second step is to examine the company's resources and capabilities more closely to ascertain which of them are the most competitively valuable and to determine whether the best of them can help the firm attain a sustainable competitive advantage over rival firms.[1] This step involves applying the *four tests of a resource's competitive power.*

Identifying the Company's Resources and Capabilities

A firm's resources and capabilities are the fundamental building blocks of its competitive strategy. In crafting strategy, it is essential for managers to be able to recognize a resource or an organizational capability for what it is and to know how to take stock of the company's full complement of resources and capabilities.

To do a good job with this, managers and strategists need to start with a basic understanding of what these terms mean.

In brief, a **resource** is a productive input or competitive asset that is owned or controlled by the firm. Firms have many different types of resources at their disposal that vary not only in kind but in quality as well. Some are higher-quality than others, and some are more competitively valuable, having greater potential to give a firm a competitive advantage over its rivals. For example, a company's brand is a resource, as is an R&D team—yet some brands such as Coca-Cola and Danone are well known, with enduring value, while others have little more name recognition than generic products. In similar fashion, some R&D teams are far more innovative and productive than others due to the outstanding talents of the individual team members, the team's composition, and its chemistry.

A **capability** is the capacity of a firm to perform some activity proficiently. Capabilities also vary in form, quality, and competitive importance, with some being more competitively valuable than others. Apple's product innovation capabilities are widely recognized as being far superior to those of its competitors; BMW is known for its engineering capabilities; PepsiCo is admired for its marketing and brand management capabilities.

> **Resource and capability analysis** is a powerful tool for sizing up a company's competitive assets and determining if they can support a sustainable competitive advantage over market rivals.

> **CORE CONCEPT**
>
> A **resource** is a competitive asset that is owned or controlled by a company; a **capability** is the capacity of a firm to perform some activity proficiently.

Types of Company Resources A useful way to identify a company's resources is to look for them within categories, as shown in Table 4.2. Broadly speaking, resources can be divided into two main categories:

Table 4.2 Types of Company Resources

Tangible Resources
• *Physical resources:* ownership of or access rights to natural resources (such as mineral deposits); state-of-the-art manufacturing plants, equipment, and/or distribution facilities; land and real estate; the locations of stores, manufacturing plants, or distribution centers, including the overall pattern of their physical locations
• *Financial resources:* cash and cash equivalents; marketable securities; other financial assets such as the borrowing capacity of the firm (as indicated from its balance sheet and credit rating)
• *Technological assets:* patents, copyrights, and trade secrets; production technology, stock of other technologies, technological processes
• *Organizational resources:* IT and communication systems (servers, workstations, etc.); other planning, coordination, and control systems; the company's organizational design and reporting structure
Intangible Resources
• *Human assets and intellectual capital:* the experience, cumulative learning, and tacit knowledge of employees; the education, intellectual capital, and know-how of specialized teams and work groups; the knowledge of key personnel concerning important business functions (e.g., skills in keeping operating costs low, improving product quality, and providing customer service); managerial talent; the creativity and innovativeness of certain personnel
• *Brands, company image, and reputational assets:* brand names, trademarks, product image, buyer loyalty and goodwill; company image, reputation for quality, service, and reliability; reputation with suppliers and partners for fair dealing
• *Relationships:* alliances or joint ventures that provide access to technologies, specialized know-how, or geographic markets; partnerships with suppliers that reduce costs and/or enhance product quality and performance; networks of dealers or distributors; the trust established with various partners
• *Company culture and incentive system:* the norms of behavior, business principles, and ingrained beliefs within the company; the attachment of personnel to the company's ideals; the compensation system and the motivation level of company personnel

tangible and **intangible** resources. Although *human resources* make up one of the most important parts of a company's resource base, we include them in the intangible category to emphasize the role played by the skills, talents, and knowledge of a company's human resources.

Tangible resources are the most easily identified, since tangible resources are those that can be touched or quantified readily. Obviously, they include various types of *physical resources* such as manufacturing facilities and mineral resources, but they also include a company's *financial resources, technological resources,* and *organizational resources* such as the company's communication and control systems.

Intangible resources are harder to discern, but they are often among the most important of a firm's competitive assets. They include various sorts of *human assets and intellectual capital,* as well as a company's *brands, image, and reputational assets.* While intangible resources have no material existence on their own, they are often embodied in something material. Thus the skills and knowledge resources of a firm are embodied in its managers and employees; a company's brand name is embodied in the company logo or product labels. Other important kinds of intangible resources include a company's *relationships* with suppliers, buyers, or partners of various sorts, and the *company's culture and incentive system.* A more detailed listing of the various types of tangible and intangible resources is provided in Table 4.2.

Listing a company's resources category by category can prevent managers from inadvertently overlooking some company resources that might be competitively important. At times, it can be difficult to decide exactly how to categorize certain types of resources. For example, resources such as a work group's specialized expertise in developing innovative products can be considered to be technological assets or human assets or intellectual capital and knowledge assets; the work ethic and drive of a company's workforce could be included under the company's human assets or its culture and incentive system. In this regard, it is important to remember that *it is not exactly how a resource is categorized that matters but, rather, that all of the company's different types of resources are included in the inventory.* The real purpose of using categories in identifying a company's resources is to ensure that none of a company's resources go unnoticed when sizing up the company's competitive assets.

Identifying Capabilities   Organizational capabilities are more complex entities than resources; indeed, they are built up through the use of resources and draw on some combination of the firm's resources as they are exercised.[2] Virtually all organizational capabilities are *knowledge-based, residing in people and in a company's intellectual capital or in organizational processes and systems, which embody tacit knowledge.* For example, Nestlé's brand management capabilities draw on the knowledge of the company's brand managers, the expertise of its marketing department, and the company's relationships with retailers, since brand building is a cooperative activity requiring retailer support. The capability in video game design for which Electronic Arts is known derives from the creative talents and technological expertise of its highly talented game developers, the company's culture of creativity, and a compensation system that generously rewards talented developers for creating best-selling video games.

Because of their complexity, capabilities are harder to categorize than resources and more challenging to search for as a result. There are, however, two approaches that can make the process of uncovering and identifying a firm's capabilities more systematic. The first method takes the completed listing of a firm's resources as its starting point. Since capabilities are built from resources and utilize resources as they are exercised, a firm's resources can provide a strong set of clues about the types of capabilities the firm is likely to have accumulated. This approach simply involves looking over the firm's resources and considering whether (and to what extent) the firm has built up any related capabilities. So, for example, a fleet of trucks, the latest RFID tracking technology, and a set of large automated distribution centers may be indicative of sophisticated capabilities in logistics and distribution. R&D teams composed of top scientists with expertise in genomics may suggest organizational capabilities in developing new gene therapies or in biotechnology more generally.

The second method of identifying a firm's capabilities takes a functional approach. Many capabilities relate to fairly specific functions; these draw on a limited set of resources and typically involve a single department or organizational unit. Capabilities in injection molding or continuous casting or metal stamping are manufacturing-related; capabilities in direct selling, promotional pricing, or database marketing all connect to the sales and marketing functions; capabilities in basic research, strategic innovation, or new product development link to a company's R&D function. This approach requires managers to survey the various functions a firm performs to find the different capabilities associated with each function.

A problem with this second method is that many of the most important capabilities of firms are inherently *cross-functional.* Cross-functional capabilities draw on a number of different kinds of resources and are generally multidisciplinary in nature—they spring from the effective collaboration among people with different expertise working in different organizational units. An example is the capability for fast-cycle, continuous product innovation that comes from teaming the efforts of groups with expertise in market research, new product R&D, design and engineering, advanced manufacturing, and market testing. Cross-functional capabilities and other complex capabilities involving numerous linked and closely integrated competitive assets are sometimes referred to as **resource bundles.** Although resource bundles are not as easily pigeonholed as other types of resources and capabilities, they can still be identified by looking for company activities that link different types of resources, functions, and departmental units. It is important not to miss identifying a company's resource bundles, since they can be the most competitively important of a firm's competitive assets. Unless it includes a company's cross-functional capabilities and resource bundles, no identification of a company's resources and capabilities can be considered complete.

> **CORE CONCEPT**
>
> A **resource bundle** is a linked and closely integrated set of competitive assets centered around one or more cross-functional capabilities.

Determining Whether a Company's Resources and Capabilities Are Potent Enough to Produce a Sustainable Competitive Advantage

To determine the strategic relevance and competitive power of a firm's resources and capabilities, it is necessary to go beyond merely identifying a company's resources and capabilities. The second step in resource and capability analysis is designed to ascertain which of a company's resources and capabilities are competitively valuable and to what extent they can support a company's quest for a sustainable competitive advantage over market rivals. This involves probing the *caliber* of a firm's competitive assets relative to those of its competitors.[3] When a company has competitive assets that are central to its strategy and superior to those of rival firms, it has a competitive advantage over other firms. If this advantage proves durable despite the best efforts of competitors to overcome it, then the company is said to have a *sustainable* **competitive advantage.** While it may be difficult for a company to achieve a sustainable competitive advantage, it is an important strategic objective because it imparts a potential for attractive and long-lived profitability.

The Four Tests of a Resource's Competitive Power

The competitive power of a resource or capability is measured by how many of the following four tests it can pass.[4] The first two tests determine whether a resource or capability can support a competitive advantage. The last two determine whether the competitive advantage can be sustained in the face of active competition.

1. *Is the resource (or capability) competitively valuable?* To be competitively valuable, a resource or capability must be directly relevant to the company's strategy, making the company a more effective competitor, able to exploit market opportunities and ward off external threats. Unless the resource contributes to the effectiveness of the company's strategy, it cannot pass this first test. An indicator of its effectiveness is whether the resource enables the company to strengthen its business model through a better customer value proposition and/or profit formula. Companies have to guard against contending that something they do well is necessarily competitively valuable. Apple's operating system for its PCs is by most accounts a world beater (compared to Windows Vista and Windows 7), but Apple has failed miserably in converting its strength in operating system design into competitive success in the global PC market—it is an also-ran with a paltry 3 to 5 percent market share worldwide.

2. *Is the resource rare—is it something rivals lack?* Resources and capabilities that are common among firms and widely available cannot be a source of competitive advantage. All makers of branded cereals have valuable marketing capabilities and brands, since the key success factors in the ready-to-eat cereal industry demand this. They are not rare. The brand strength of Pillsbury, however, is uncommon and has provided General Mills with greater market share as well as the opportunity to benefit from brand extensions like Pillsbury Grands! Biscuits, Pillsbury Ready to Bake! Cookies, and Pillsbury Simply . . . Cookies. A resource or capability is considered rare if it is held by only a small number of firms in an industry or specific competitive domain. Thus, while general management capabilities are not rare in an absolute sense, they are relatively rare in some of the less developed regions of the world and in some business domains.

3. *Is the resource hard to copy?* If a resource or capability is both valuable and rare, it will be competitively superior to comparable resources of rival firms. As such, it is a source of competitive advantage for the company. The more difficult and more costly it is for competitors to imitate, the more likely that it can also provide a *sustainable* competitive advantage. Resources tend to be difficult to copy when they are unique (a fantastic real estate location, patent-protected technology, an unusually talented and motivated labor force), when they must be built over time in ways that are difficult to imitate (a well-known brand name, mastery of a complex process technology, a global network of dealers and distributors), and when they entail financial outlays or large-scale operations that few industry members can undertake. Imitation is also difficult for resources that

reflect a high level of *social complexity* (company culture, interpersonal relationships among the managers or R&D teams, trust-based relations with customers or suppliers) and *causal ambiguity,* a term that signifies the hard-to-disentangle nature of the complex resources, such as a web of intricate processes enabling new drug discovery. Hard-to-copy resources and capabilities are important competitive assets, contributing to the longevity of a company's market position and offering the potential for sustained profitability.

4. *Can the resource be trumped by different types of resources and capabilities—are there good substitutes available for the resource?* Even resources and capabilities that are valuable, rare, and hard to copy can lose much of their competitive power if rivals have other types of resources and capabilities that are of equal or greater competitive power. A company may have the most technologically advanced and sophisticated plants in its industry, but any efficiency advantage it enjoys may be nullified if rivals are able to produce equally good products at lower cost by locating their plants in countries where wage rates are relatively low and a labor force with adequate skills is available.

The vast majority of companies are not well endowed with standout resources or capabilities, capable of passing all four tests with high marks. Most firms have a mixed bag of resources—one or two quite valuable, some good, many satisfactory to mediocre. Resources and capabilities that are valuable pass the first of the four tests. As key contributors to the efficiency and effectiveness of the strategy, they are relevant to the firm's competitiveness but are no guarantee of competitive advantage. They may offer no more than competitive parity with competing firms.

Passing both of the first two tests requires more—it requires resources and capabilities that are not only valuable but also rare. This is a much higher hurdle that can be cleared only by resources and capabilities that are *competitively superior.* Resources and capabilities that are competitively superior are the company's true strategic assets.[5] They provide the company with a competitive advantage over its competitors, if only in the short run.

To pass the last two tests, a resource must be able to maintain its competitive superiority in the face of competition. It must be resistant to imitative attempts and efforts by competitors to find equally valuable substitute resources. Assessing the availability of substitutes is the most difficult of all the tests since substitutes are harder to recognize, but the key is to look for resources or capabilities held by other firms that *can serve the same function* as the company's core resources and capabilities.[6]

Very few firms have resources and capabilities that can pass these tests, but those that do enjoy a sustainable competitive advantage with far greater profit potential. Walmart is a notable example, with capabilities in logistics and supply chain management that have surpassed those of its competitors for over 30 years. Lincoln Electric Company, less well known but no less notable in its achievements, has been the world leader in welding products for over 100 years as a result of its unique piecework incentive system for compensating production workers and the unsurpassed worker productivity and product quality that this system has fostered.

A Company's Resources and Capabilities Must Be Managed Dynamically
Even companies like Walmart and Lincoln Electric cannot afford to rest on their laurels. Rivals that are initially unable to replicate a key resource may develop better and better substitutes over time. Resources and

capabilities can depreciate like other assets if they are managed with benign neglect. Disruptive environmental change can also destroy the value of key strategic assets, turning resources and capabilities "from diamonds to rust."[7] Some resources lose their clout quickly when there are rapid changes in technology, customer preferences, distribution channels, or other competitive factors.

> A company requires a dynamically evolving portfolio of resources and capabilities to sustain its competitiveness and help drive improvements in its performance.

For a company's resources and capabilities to have *durable* value, they must be continually refined, updated, and sometimes augmented with altogether new kinds of expertise. Not only are rival companies endeavoring to sharpen and recalibrate their capabilities, but customer needs and expectations are also undergoing constant change. Organizational capabilities grow stale unless they are kept freshly honed and on the cutting edge.[8] A company's resources and capabilities are far more competitively potent when they are (1) in sync with changes in the company's own strategy and its efforts to achieve a resource-based competitive advantage and (2) fully supportive of company efforts to attract customers and combat competitors' newly launched offensives to win bigger sales and market shares. Management's challenge in managing the firm's resources and capabilities dynamically has two elements: attending to ongoing recalibration of existing competitive assets and casting a watchful eye for opportunities to develop totally new kinds of capabilities.

The Role of Dynamic Capabilities

> **CORE CONCEPT**
>
> A **dynamic capability** is the capacity of a company to modify its existing resources and capabilities or create new ones.

Companies that know the importance of recalibrating and upgrading their most valuable resources and capabilities ensure that these activities are done on a continual basis. By incorporating these activities into their routine managerial functions, they gain the experience necessary to be able to do them consistently well. At that point, their ability to freshen and renew their competitive assets becomes a capability in itself—a **dynamic capability.** A dynamic capability is the ability to modify or augment the company's existing resources and capabilities.[9] This includes the capacity to improve existing resources and capabilities incrementally, in the way that 3M continually upgrades the R&D resources driving its product innovation strategy. It also includes the capacity to add new resources and capabilities to the company's competitive asset portfolio. An example is Pfizer's acquisition capabilities, which have enabled it to replace degraded resources such as expiring patents with newly acquired capabilities in biotechnology.

QUESTION 3: IS THE COMPANY ABLE TO SEIZE MARKET OPPORTUNITIES AND NULLIFY EXTERNAL THREATS?

An essential element in evaluating a company's overall situation entails examining the company's resources and competitive capabilities in terms of the degree to which they enable it to pursue its best market opportunities and defend against the external threats to its future well-being. The simplest and most easily applied tool for conducting this examination is widely known as *SWOT analysis,* so named because it zeros in on a company's internal **S**trengths and **W**eaknesses, market **O**pportunities, and external **T**hreats. Just as important, a first-rate SWOT analysis provides the basis for crafting a strategy that capitalizes on the company's resource strengths, overcomes its resource weaknesses, aims squarely at capturing the company's best opportunities, and defends against the threats to its future well-being.

Identifying a Company's Internal Strengths

A *strength* is something a company is good at doing or an attribute that enhances its competitiveness in the marketplace. A company's strengths depend on the quality of its resources and capabilities. Resource and capability analysis provides a way for managers to assess the quality objectively. While resources and capabilities that pass the four tests of sustainable competitive advantage are among the company's greatest strengths, other types can be counted among the company's strengths as well. A capability that is not potent enough to produce a sustainable advantage over rivals may yet enable a series of temporary advantages if used as a basis for entry into a new market or market segment. A resource bundle that fails to match those of top-tier competitors may still allow a company to compete successfully against the second tier.

Assessing a Company's Competencies—What Activities Does It Perform Well?   One way to appraise the degree of a company's strengths has to do with the company's competence level in performing key pieces of its business—such as supply chain management, R&D, production, distribution, sales and marketing, and customer service. Which activities does it perform especially well? And are there any activities it performs better than rivals? A company's proficiency in conducting different facets of its operations can range from a mere competence in performing an activity to a core competence to a distinctive competence.

A **competence** is an internal activity an organization performs with proficiency—a capability, in other words. A **core competence** is a proficiently performed internal activity that is *central* to a company's strategy and competitiveness. Ben & Jerry's Ice Cream, a subsidiary of Unilever, has a core competence in creating unusual flavors of ice cream and marketing them with catchy names like Chunky Monkey, Chubby Hubby, Cherry Garcia, Karamel Sutra, Imagine Whirled Peace, and Phish Food. A core competence is a more competitively valuable company strength than a competence because of the activity's key role in the company's strategy and the contribution it makes to the company's market success and profitability. Often, core competencies can be leveraged to create new markets or new product demand, as the engine behind a company's growth. 3M Corporation has a core competence in product innovation—its record of introducing new products goes back several decades and new product introduction is central to 3M's strategy of growing its business.

A **distinctive competence** is a competitively valuable activity that a company *performs better than its rivals*. A distinctive competence thus signifies greater proficiency than a core competence. Because a distinctive competence represents a level of proficiency that rivals do not have, it qualifies as a *competitively superior strength* with competitive advantage potential. This is particularly true when the distinctive competence enables

SWOT analysis is a simple but powerful tool for sizing up a company's strengths and weaknesses, its market opportunities, and the external threats to its future well-being.

Basing a company's strategy on its most competitively valuable resource and capability strengths gives the company its best chance for market success.

CORE CONCEPT

A **competence** is an activity that a company has learned to perform with proficiency—a capability, in other words.

a company to deliver standout value to customers (in the form of lower prices, better product performance, or superior service). For instance, Apple has a distinctive competence in product innovation, as exemplified by its iPod, iPhone, and iPad products.

The conceptual differences between a competence, a core competence, and a distinctive competence draw attention to the fact that a company's strengths and competitive assets are not all equal.[10] Some competencies merely enable market survival because most rivals have them—indeed, not having a competence or capability that rivals have can result in competitive disadvantage. If an apparel company does not have the competence to produce its apparel items very cost-efficiently, it is unlikely to survive given the intensely price-competitive nature of the apparel industry. Every Web retailer requires a basic competence in designing an appealing and user-friendly Web site. Core competencies are *competitively* more important strengths than competencies because they are central to the company's strategy. Distinctive competencies are even more competitively important. Because a distinctive competence is a competitively valuable capability that is unmatched by rivals, it can propel the company to greater market success and profitability. A distinctive competence is thus potentially the mainspring of a company's success—unless it is trumped by other, even more powerful types of competencies that rivals hold.

Identifying Company Weaknesses and Competitive Deficiencies

A **weakness,** or *competitive deficiency,* is something a company lacks or does poorly (in comparison to others) or a condition that puts it at a competitive disadvantage in the marketplace. A company's internal weaknesses can relate to (1) inferior or unproven skills, expertise, or intellectual capital in competitively important areas of the business; (2) deficiencies in competitively important physical, organizational, or intangible assets; or (3) missing or competitively inferior capabilities in key areas. *Company weaknesses are thus internal shortcomings that constitute competitive liabilities.* Nearly all companies have competitive liabilities of one kind or another. Whether a company's internal weaknesses make it competitively vulnerable depends on how much they matter in the marketplace and whether they are offset by the company's strengths.

Table 4.3 lists many of the things to consider in compiling a company's strengths and weaknesses. Sizing up a company's complement of strengths and deficiencies is akin to constructing a *strategic balance sheet,* where strengths represent *competitive assets* and weaknesses represent *competitive liabilities.* Obviously, the ideal condition is for the company's competitive assets to outweigh its competitive liabilities by an ample margin—a 50-50 balance is definitely not the desired condition!

Identifying a Company's Market Opportunities

Market opportunity is a big factor in shaping a company's strategy. Indeed, managers can't properly tailor strategy to the company's situation without first identifying its market opportunities and appraising the growth and profit potential each one holds. Depending on the prevailing circumstances, a company's opportunities can be plentiful or scarce, fleeting or lasting, and can range from wildly attractive (an absolute "must" to pursue) to marginally interesting (because of the high risks or questionable profit potentials) to unsuitable (because the company's strengths are ill-suited to successfully capitalizing on the opportunities). A sampling of potential market opportunities is shown in Table 4.3.

Newly emerging and fast-changing markets sometimes present stunningly big or "golden" opportunities, but it is typically hard for managers at one company to peer into "the fog of the future" and spot them much ahead of managers at other companies.[11] But as the fog begins to clear, golden opportunities are nearly always seized rapidly—and the companies that seize them are usually those that have been actively waiting, staying alert with diligent market reconnaissance, and preparing themselves to capitalize on shifting market conditions by patiently assembling an arsenal of competitively valuable resources—talented personnel, technical know-how, strategic partnerships, and a war chest of cash to finance aggressive action when the time comes.[12] In mature markets, unusually attractive market opportunities emerge sporadically, often after long periods of relative calm—but future market conditions may be more predictable, making emerging opportunities easier for industry members to detect.

> A company is well advised to pass on a particular market opportunity unless it has or can acquire the competencies needed to capture it.

In evaluating a company's market opportunities and ranking their attractiveness, managers have to guard against viewing every *industry* opportunity as a *company* opportunity. Not every company is equipped with the competencies to successfully pursue each opportunity that exists in its industry. Some companies are more capable of going after particular opportunities than others, and a few companies may be hopelessly outclassed. *The market opportunities most relevant to a company are those that match up well with the company's competitive assets, offer the best growth and profitability, and present the most potential for competitive advantage.*

Identifying the Threats to a Company's Future Profitability

Often, certain factors in a company's external environment pose *threats* to its profitability and competitive well-being. Threats can stem from the emergence of cheaper or better technologies, rivals' introduction of new or improved products, the entry of lower-cost foreign competitors into a company's market stronghold, new regulations that are more burdensome to a company than to its competitors, vulnerability to a rise in interest rates or tight credit conditions, the potential of a hostile takeover, unfavorable demographic shifts, adverse changes in foreign exchange rates, political upheaval in a foreign country where the company has facilities, and the like. A list of potential threats to a company's future profitability and market position is shown in Table 4.3.

External threats may pose no more than a moderate degree of adversity (all companies confront some threatening elements in the course of doing business), or they may be so imposing as to make a company's situation and outlook quite tenuous. On rare occasions, market shocks can give birth to a *sudden-death* threat that throws a company into an immediate crisis and a battle to survive. Many of the world's major airlines were plunged into an unprecedented financial crisis by the perfect storm of 9/11, rising prices for jet fuel, mounting competition

Table 4.3   What to Look For in Identifying a Company's Strengths, Weaknesses, Opportunities, and Threats

Potential Strengths and Competitive Assets	Potential Weaknesses and Competitive Deficiencies
• Competencies that are well matched to industry key success factors • Strong financial condition; ample financial resources to grow the business • Strong brand-name image/company reputation • Attractive customer base • Proprietary technology/superior technological skills/ important patents • Superior intellectual capital • Skills in advertising and promotion • Strong bargaining power over suppliers or buyers • Product innovation capabilities • Proven capabilities in improving production processes • Good supply chain management capabilities • Good customer service capabilities • Superior product quality • Wide geographic coverage and/or strong global distribution capability • Alliances/joint ventures that provide access to valuable technology, competencies, and/or attractive geographic markets • A product that is strongly differentiated from those of rivals • Cost advantages over rivals • Core competencies in _____ • A distinctive competence in _____ • Resources that are hard to copy and for which there are no good substitutes	• Competencies that are not well-matched to industry key success factors • In the wrong strategic group • Losing market share because _____ • Lack of attention to customer needs • Weak balance sheet, short on financial resources to grow the firm, too much debt; • Higher overall unit costs relative to those of key competitors • Weak or unproven product innovation capabilities • A product/service with ho-hum attributes or features inferior to the offerings of rivals • Too narrow a product line relative to rivals • Weak brand image or reputation • Weaker dealer network than key rivals and/or lack of adequate global distribution capability • Behind on product quality, R&D, and/or technological know-how • Lack of management depth • Inferior intellectual capital relative to rivals • Plagued with internal operating problems or obsolete facilities • Too much underutilized plant capacity • No well-developed or proven core competencies • No distinctive competencies or competitively superior resources • Resources that are readily copied or for which there are good substitutes • No clear strategic direction
Potential Market Opportunities	Potential External Threats to a Company's Future Profitability
• Openings to win market share from rivals • Sharply rising buyer demand for the industry's product • Serving additional customer groups or market segments • Expanding into new geographic markets • Expanding the company's product line to meet a broader range of customer needs • Utilizing existing company skills or technological know-how to enter new product lines or new businesses • Online sales via the Internet • Integrating forward or backward • Falling trade barriers in attractive foreign markets • Acquiring rival firms or companies with attractive technological expertise or capabilities • Entering into alliances or joint ventures to expand the firm's market coverage or boost its competitive capability • Openings to exploit emerging new technologies	• Increasing intensity of competition among industry rivals—may squeeze profit margins • Slowdowns in market growth • Likely entry of potent new competitors • Loss of sales to substitute products • Growing bargaining power of customers or suppliers • Vulnerability to industry driving forces • Shift in buyer needs and tastes away from the industry's product • Adverse demographic changes that threaten to curtail demand for the industry's product • Adverse economic conditions that threaten critical suppliers or distributers • Changes in technology—particularly disruptive technology that can undermine the company's distinctive competencies • Restrictive foreign trade policies • Costly new regulatory requirements • Tight credit conditions • Rising prices on energy or other key inputs

from low-fare carriers, shifting traveler preferences for low fares as opposed to lots of in-flight amenities, and higher labor costs. Similarly, the global economic crisis that began with the mortgage lenders, banks, and insurance companies has produced shock waves from which few industries have been insulated, causing even strong performers like General Electric to falter. While not all crises can be anticipated, it is management's job to identify the threats to the company's future prospects and to evaluate what strategic actions can be taken to neutralize or lessen their impact.

What Do the SWOT Listings Reveal?

SWOT analysis involves more than making four lists. The two most important parts of SWOT analysis are *drawing conclusions* from the SWOT listings about the company's overall situation and *translating these conclusions into strategic actions* to better match the company's strategy to its internal strengths and market opportunities, to correct important weaknesses, and to defend against external threats. Figure 4.2 shows the steps involved in gleaning insights from SWOT analysis.

> Simply making lists of a company's strengths, weaknesses, opportunities, and threats is not enough; the payoff from SWOT analysis comes from the conclusions about a company's situation and the implications for strategy improvement that flow from the four lists.

Figure 4.2   **The Steps Involved in SWOT Analysis: Identify the Four Components of SWOT, Draw Conclusions, Translate Implications into Strategic Actions**

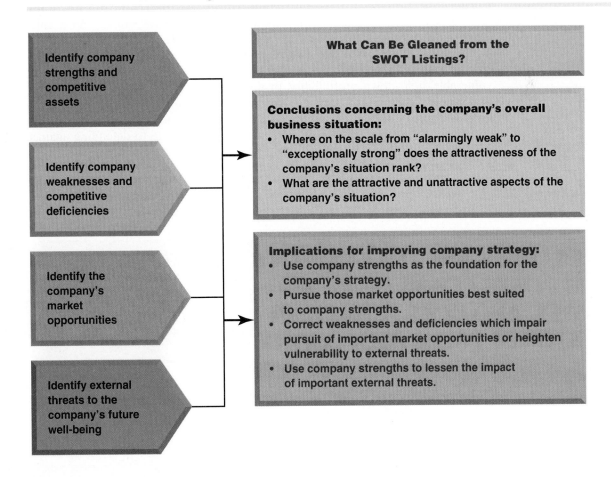

Just what story the SWOT listings tell about the company's overall situation is often revealed in the answers to the following set of questions:

- What aspects of the company's situation are particularly attractive?
- What aspects are of the most concern?
- All things considered, where on a scale of 1 to 10 (where 1 is alarmingly weak and 10 is exceptionally strong) do the company's overall situation and future prospects rank?
- Are the company's internal strengths and competitive assets powerful enough to enable it to compete successfully?
- Are the company's weaknesses and competitive deficiencies mostly inconsequential and readily correctable, or could one or more prove fatal if not remedied soon?
- Do the company's strengths and competitive assets outweigh its weaknesses and competitive liabilities by an attractive margin?
- Does the company have attractive market opportunities that are well suited to its internal strengths? Does the company lack the competitive assets to pursue any of the most attractive opportunities?
- Are the threats alarming, or are they something the company appears able to deal with and defend against?

The final piece of SWOT analysis is to translate the diagnosis of the company's situation into actions for improving the company's strategy and business prospects. *A company's internal strengths should always serve as the basis of its strategy—placing heavy reliance on a company's best competitive assets is the soundest route to attracting customers and competing successfully against rivals.*[13] As a rule, strategies that place heavy demands on areas where the company is weakest or has unproven competencies are suspect and should be avoided. Plainly, managers have to look toward correcting competitive weaknesses that make the company vulnerable, hold down profitability, or disqualify it from pursuing an attractive opportunity. Furthermore, strategy has to be aimed squarely at capturing those market opportunities that are most attractive and suited to the company's collection of competencies. How much attention to devote to defending against external threats to the company's market position and future performance hinges on how vulnerable the company is, whether there are attractive defensive moves that can be taken to lessen their impact, and whether the costs of undertaking such moves represent the best use of company competitive assets.

QUESTION 4: ARE THE COMPANY'S PRICES AND COSTS COMPETITIVE WITH THOSE OF KEY RIVALS, AND DOES IT HAVE AN APPEALING CUSTOMER VALUE PROPOSITION?

Company managers are often stunned when a competitor cuts its price to "unbelievably low" levels or when a new market entrant comes on strong with a very low price. The competitor may not, however, be "dumping" (an economic term for selling at prices that are below cost), buying its way into the market with a super-low price, or waging a desperate move to gain sales—it may simply have substantially lower costs. One of the most telling signs of whether a company's business position is strong or precarious is whether its prices and costs can remain competitive with industry rivals. For a company to retain its market share, its costs must be *in line* with those of close rivals selling similar quality products.

LO 4

Grasp how a company's value chain activities can affect the company's cost structure, degree of differentiation, and competitive advantage.

While less common, new entrants can also storm the market with a product that ratchets the quality level up so high that customers will abandon competing sellers even if they have to pay more for the new product. With its vastly greater storage capacity and lightweight, cool design, Apple's iPod left other makers of portable digital music players in the dust when it was first introduced. By introducing new models with even more attractive features, Apple has continued its worldwide dominance of this market. Apple's new iPad appears to be doing the same in the market for e-readers and tablet PCs.

The higher a company's costs are above those of close rivals, the more competitively vulnerable it becomes.

Regardless of where on the quality spectrum a company competes, it must also remain competitive in terms of its customer value proposition in order to stay in the game. Tiffany's value proposition, for example, remains attractive to customers who want customer service, the assurance of quality, and a high-status brand despite the availability of cut-rate diamond jewelry online. Target's customer value proposition has withstood the Walmart low-price juggernaut by attention to product design, image, and attractive store layouts in addition to efficiency.

The value provided to the customer depends on how well a customer's needs are met for the price paid. How well customer needs are met depends on the perceived quality of a product or service as well as other, more tangible attributes. The greater the amount of customer value that the company can offer profitably compared to its rivals, the less vulnerable it will be to competitive attack. For managers, the key is to keep close track of how *cost effectively* the company can deliver value to customers relative to its competitors. If they can deliver the same amount of value with lower expenditures (or more value at the same cost), they will maintain a competitive edge.

The greater the amount of customer value that a company can offer profitably relative to close rivals, the less competitively vulnerable it becomes.

Two analytical tools are particularly useful in determining whether a company's prices, costs, and customer value proposition are competitive: value chain analysis and benchmarking.

The Concept of a Company Value Chain

Every company's business consists of a collection of activities undertaken in the course of designing, producing, marketing, delivering, and supporting its product or service. All the various activities that a company performs internally combine to form a **value chain**—so called because the underlying intent of a company's activities is to do things that ultimately *create value for buyers.*

CORE CONCEPT

A company's **value chain** identifies the primary activities that create customer value and the related support activities.

As shown in Figure 4.3, a company's value chain consists of two broad categories of activities: the *primary activities* that are foremost in creating value for customers and the requisite *support activities* that facilitate and enhance the performance of the primary activities.[14] The exact nature of the primary and secondary activities that make up a company's value chain vary according to the specifics of a company's business; hence, the listing of the primary and support activities in Figure 4.3 is illustrative rather than definitive. For example, the primary value-creating activities for a manufacturer of bakery goods, such as Grupo Bimbo, include supply chain management, baking and packaging operations, distribution, and sales and marketing but are unlikely to include service. Its support activities include quality control as well as product R&D, human resource management, and administration. For a department store retailer, such as Saks Fifth Avenue, customer service is included among its primary activities, along with merchandise selection and buying, store layout and product display, and advertising; its support activities include site selection, hiring and training, and store maintenance, plus the usual assortment of administrative activities. For a hotel chain like Marriot, the primary activities and costs are in site selection and construction, reservations, operation of its hotel properties, and marketing; principal support activities include accounting, hiring and training hotel staff, supply chain management, and general administration.

With its focus on value-creating activities, the value chain is an ideal tool for examining how a company delivers on its customer value proposition. It permits a deep look at the company's cost structure and ability to offer low prices. It reveals the emphasis that a company places on activities that enhance differentiation and support higher prices, such as service and marketing. Note that there is also a profit margin component to the value chain; this is because profits are necessary to compensate the company's owners/shareholders and investors, who bear risks and provide capital. Tracking the profit margin along with the value-creating activities is critical because unless an enterprise succeeds in delivering customer value profitably (with a sufficient return on invested capital), it can't survive for long. This is the essence of a sound business model.

Illustration Capsule 4.1 shows representative costs for various activities performed by Just Coffee, a cooperative producer and roaster of fair-trade organic coffee.

Comparing the Value Chains of Rival Companies The primary purpose of value chain analysis is to facilitate a comparison, activity-by-activity, of how effectively and efficiently a company delivers value to its customers, relative to its competitors. Segregating the company's operations into different types of primary and secondary activities is the first step in this comparison. The next is to do the same for the company's most significant competitors.

Even rivals in the same industry may differ significantly in terms of the activities they perform. For instance, the "operations" component of the value chain for a manufacturer that makes all of its own parts and components and assembles them into a finished product differs from the "operations" of a rival producer that buys the needed parts and components from outside suppliers and only performs assembly operations. How each activity is performed may affect a company's relative cost position as well as its capacity for differentiation. Thus, even a simple comparison of how the activities of rivals' value chains differ can be revealing of competitive differences.

A Company's Primary and Secondary Activities Identify the Major Components of Its Internal Cost Structure Each activity in the value chain gives rise to costs and ties up assets. For a company to remain competitive, it is critical for it to perform its activities cost-effectively,

Figure 4.3   A Representative Company Value Chain

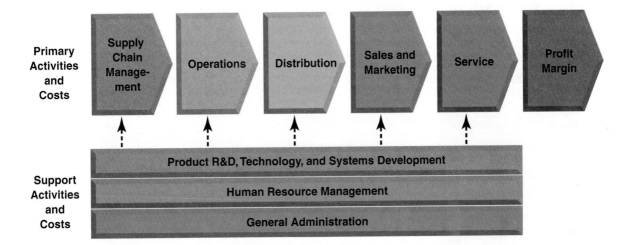

PRIMARY ACTIVITIES

- **Supply Chain Management**—Activities, costs, and assets associated with purchasing fuel, energy, raw materials, parts and components, merchandise, and consumable items from vendors; receiving, storing, and disseminating inputs from suppliers; inspection; and inventory management.

- **Operations**—Activities, costs, and assets associated with converting inputs into final product form (production, assembly, packaging, equipment maintenance, facilities, operations, quality assurance, environmental protection).

- **Distribution**—Activities, costs, and assets dealing with physically distributing the product to buyers (finished goods warehousing, order processing, order picking and packing, shipping, delivery vehicle operations, establishing and maintaining a network of dealers and distributors).

- **Sales and Marketing**—Activities, costs, and assets related to sales force efforts, advertising and promotion, market research and planning, and dealer/distributor support.

- **Service**—Activities, costs, and assets associated with providing assistance to buyers, such as installation, spare parts delivery, maintenance and repair, technical assistance, buyer inquiries, and complaints.

SUPPORT ACTIVITIES

- **Product R&D, Technology, and Systems Development**—Activities, costs, and assets relating to product R&D, process R&D, process design improvement, equipment design, computer software development, telecommunications systems, computer-assisted design and engineering, database capabilities, and development of computerized support systems.

- **Human Resources Management**—Activities, costs, and assets associated with the recruitment, hiring, training, development, and compensation of all types of personnel; labor relations activities; and development of knowledge-based skills and core competencies.

- **General Administration**—Activities, costs, and assets relating to general management, accounting and finance, legal and regulatory affairs, safety and security, management information systems, forming strategic alliances and collaborating with strategic partners, and other "overhead" functions.

Source: Based on the discussion in Michael E. Porter, *Competitive Advantage* (New York: Free Press, 1985), pp. 37–43.

ILLUSTRATION CAPSULE 4.1

The Value Chain for Just Coffee, a Producer of Fair-Trade Organic Coffee

Value Chain Activities and Costs in Producing, Roasting, and Selling a Pound of Fair-Trade Organic Coffee	
1. Average cost of procuring the coffee from coffee-grower cooperatives	$2.30
2. Import fees, storage costs, and freight charges	.73
3. Labor cost of roasting and bagging	.89
4. Cost of labels and bag	.45
5. Average overhead costs	3.03
6. Total company costs	$7.40
7. Average retail markup over company costs (company operating profit)	2.59
8. Average price to consumer at retail	$9.99

Source: Developed by the authors with help from Jonathan D. Keith from information on Just Coffee's Web site, www.justcoffee.coop/the_coffee_dollar_breakdown (accessed June 16, 2010).

regardless of which it chooses to emphasize. Once the major value chain activities are identified, the next step is to evaluate the company's cost competitiveness using what accountants call *activity-based costing* to determine the costs of performing each value chain activity (and assets required, including working capital).[15] The degree to which a company's costs should be disaggregated into specific activities depends on how valuable it is to develop cost data for narrowly defined activities as opposed to broadly defined activities. Generally speaking, cost estimates are needed at least for each broad category of primary and secondary activities, but finer classifications may be needed if a company discovers that it has a cost disadvantage vis-à-vis rivals and wants to pin down the exact source or activity causing the disadvantage. Quite often, there are links between activities such that the manner in which one activity is done can affect the costs of performing other activities. For instance, how an automobile is designed has a huge impact on the number of different parts and components, their respective manufacturing costs, and the expense of assembling the various parts and components into a finished product.

The combined costs of all the various activities in a company's value chain define the company's internal cost structure. Further, the cost of each activity contributes to whether the company's overall cost position relative to rivals is favorable or unfavorable. But a company's own internal costs are insufficient to assess whether its costs are competitive with those of rivals. Cost and price differences among competing companies can have their origins in activities performed by suppliers or by distribution allies involved in getting the product to the final customer or end user of the product, in which case the company's entire value chain system becomes relevant.

The Value Chain System for an Entire Industry

A company's value chain is embedded in a larger system of activities that includes the value chains of its suppliers and the value chains of whatever wholesale distributors and retailers it utilizes in getting its product or service to end users. This *value chain system* has implications that extend far beyond the company's costs. It can affect attributes like product quality that enhance differentiation and have importance for the company's customer value proposition as well as its profitability.[16] Suppliers' value chains are relevant because suppliers perform activities and incur costs in creating and delivering the purchased inputs utilized in a company's own value-creating activities. The costs, performance features, and quality of these inputs influence a company's own costs and product differentiation capabilities. Anything a company can do to help its suppliers' drive down the costs of their value chain activities or improve the quality and performance of the items being supplied can enhance its own competitiveness—a powerful reason for working collaboratively with suppliers in managing supply chain activities.[17]

> A company's cost competitiveness depends not only on the costs of internally performed activities (its own value chain) but also on costs in the value chains of its suppliers and distribution channel allies.

Similarly, the value chains of a company's distribution channel partners are relevant because (1) the costs and margins of a company's distributors and retail dealers are part of the price the ultimate consumer pays and (2) the activities that distribution allies perform affect sales volumes and customer satisfaction. For these reasons, companies normally work closely with their distribution allies (who are their direct customers) to perform value chain activities in mutually beneficial ways. For instance, motor vehicle manufacturers have a competitive interest in working closely with their automobile dealers to promote higher sales volumes and better customer satisfaction with dealers' repair and maintenance services. Producers of bathroom fixtures are heavily dependent on the sales and promotional activities of their distributors and building supply retailers and on whether distributors/retailers operate cost-effectively enough to be able to sell at prices that lead to attractive sales volumes.

As a consequence, *accurately assessing a company's competitiveness entails scrutinizing the nature and costs of value chain activities throughout the entire value chain system for delivering its products or services to end-use customers.* A typical industry value chain system that incorporates the value chains of suppliers and forward channel allies (if any) is shown in Figure 4.4. As was the case with company value chains, the specific activities constituting industry value chains also vary significantly. The primary value chain system activities in the pulp and paper industry (timber farming, logging, pulp mills, and papermaking) differ from the primary value chain system activities in the home appliance industry (parts and components manufacture, assembly, wholesale distribution, retail sales). The value chain system in the soft-drink industry (syrup manufacture, bottling and can filling, wholesale distribution, advertising, and retail merchandising) differs from that in the computer software industry (programming, disk loading, marketing, distribution).

Figure 4.4   **Representative Value Chain System for an Entire Industry**

Supplier-Related Value Chains

Company's Own Value Chain

Forward Channel Value Chains

Activities, costs, and margins of suppliers

Internally performed activities, costs, and margins

Activities, costs, and margins of forward channel allies and strategic partners

Buyer or end-user value chains

Source: Based in part on the single-industry value chain displayed in Michael E. Porter, *Competitive Advantage* (New York: Free Press, 1985), p. 35.

Benchmarking: A Tool for Assessing Whether the Costs and Effectiveness of a Company's Value Chain Activities Are in Line

Once a company has developed good estimates for the costs and effectiveness of each of the major activities in its own value chain and has sufficient data relating to the value chain activities of suppliers and distribution allies, then it is ready to explore how it compares on these dimensions with key rivals. This is where benchmarking comes in. **Benchmarking** entails comparing how different companies perform various value chain activities—how inventories are managed, how products are assembled, how fast the company can get new products to market, how customer orders are filled and shipped—and then making cross-company comparisons of the costs and effectiveness of these activities.[18] The objectives of benchmarking are to identify the best practices in performing an activity, to learn how other companies have actually achieved lower costs or better results in performing benchmarked activities, and to take action to improve a company's competitiveness whenever benchmarking reveals that its costs and results of performing an activity are not on a par with what other companies have achieved.

Xerox became one of the first companies to use benchmarking in 1979 when Japanese manufacturers began selling midsize copiers in the United States for $9,600 each—less than Xerox's production costs.[19] Xerox management suspected its Japanese competitors were dumping, but it sent a team of line managers to Japan, including the head of manufacturing, to study competitors' business processes and costs. With the aid of Xerox's joint venture partner in Japan, Fuji-Xerox, which knew the competitors well, the team found that Xerox's costs were excessive due to gross inefficiencies in the company's manufacturing processes and business practices. The findings triggered a major internal effort at Xerox to become cost-competitive and prompted Xerox to begin benchmarking 67 of its key work processes against companies identified as employing the best practices. Xerox quickly decided not to restrict its benchmarking efforts to its office equipment rivals but to extend them to any company regarded as "world class" in performing *any activity* relevant to Xerox's business. Other companies quickly picked up on Xerox's approach. Toyota managers got their idea for just-in-time inventory deliveries by studying how U.S. supermarkets replenished their shelves. Southwest Airlines reduced the turnaround time of its aircraft at each scheduled stop by studying pit crews on the auto racing circuit. Over 80 percent of Fortune 500 companies reportedly use benchmarking for comparing themselves against rivals on cost and other competitively important measures.

The tough part of benchmarking is not whether to do it but rather how to gain access to information about other companies' practices and costs. Sometimes benchmarking can be accomplished by collecting information from published reports, trade groups, and industry research firms or by talking to knowledgeable industry analysts, customers, and suppliers. Sometimes field trips to the facilities of competing or noncompeting companies can be arranged to observe how things are done, ask questions, compare practices and processes, and perhaps exchange data on productivity, staffing levels, time requirements, and other cost components—but the problem here is that such companies, even if they agree to host facilities tours and answer questions, are unlikely to share competitively sensitive cost information. Furthermore, comparing one company's costs to another's costs may not involve comparing apples to apples if the two companies employ different cost accounting principles to calculate the costs of particular activities.

> Benchmarking the costs of company activities against rivals provides hard evidence of whether a company is cost-competitive.

However, a third and fairly reliable source of benchmarking information has emerged. The explosive interest of companies in benchmarking costs and best practices has prompted numerous consulting firms and business organizations (e.g., Accenture, A.T. Kearney, Benchnet—The Benchmarking Exchange, Best Practices LLC, and the Strategic Planning Institute's Council on Benchmarking and Best Practices, LLC) to gather benchmarking data, distribute information about best practices, and provide comparative cost data without identifying the names of particular companies. Having an independent group gather the information and report it in a manner that disguises the names of individual companies protects competitively sensitive data and lessens the potential for unethical behavior on the part of company personnel in gathering their own data about competitors. Illustration Capsule 4.2 presents a widely recommended code of conduct for engaging in benchmarking.

Strategic Options for Remedying a Disadvantage in Costs or Effectiveness

Examining the costs of a company's own value chain activities and comparing them to rivals' indicates who has how much of a cost advantage or disadvantage and which cost components are responsible. Similarly, much can be learned by comparisons at the activity level of how effectively a company delivers on its value proposition relative to its competitors and which elements in its value chain system are responsible. Such information is vital in strategic actions to eliminate a cost disadvantage, deliver more customer value, enhance differentiation, and improve profitability. Such information can also help a company to recognize and reinforce activities in which it has a comparative advantage and to find

Because discussions between benchmarking partners can involve competitively sensitive data, conceivably raising questions about possible restraint of trade or improper business conduct, many benchmarking organizations urge all individuals and organizations involved in benchmarking to abide by a code of conduct grounded in ethical business behavior. One of the most widely used codes of conduct is the one developed by APQC (formerly the American Productivity and Quality Center) and advocated by the Qualserve Benchmarking Clearinghouse; it is based on the following principles and guidelines:

- Avoid discussions or actions that could lead to or imply an interest in restraint of trade, market and/or customer allocation schemes, price fixing, dealing arrangements, bid rigging, or bribery. Don't discuss costs with competitors if costs are an element of pricing.

- Refrain from the acquisition of trade secrets from another by any means that could be interpreted as improper, including the breach of any duty to maintain secrecy. Do not disclose or use any trade secret that may have been obtained through improper means or that was disclosed by another in violation of duty to maintain its secrecy or limit its use.

- Be willing to provide to your benchmarking partner the same type and level of information that you request from that partner.

- Communicate fully and early in the relationship to clarify expectations, avoid misunderstanding, and establish mutual interest in the benchmarking exchange.

- Be honest and complete with the information submitted.

- The use or communication of a benchmarking partner's name with the data obtained or practices observed requires the prior permission of the benchmarking partner.

- Honor the wishes of benchmarking partners regarding how the information that is provided will be handled and used.

- In benchmarking with competitors, establish specific ground rules up front. For example, "We don't want to talk about things that will give either of us a competitive advantage, but rather we want to see where we both can mutually improve or gain benefit."

- Check with legal counsel if any information-gathering procedure is in doubt. If uncomfortable, do not proceed. Alternatively, negotiate and sign a specific nondisclosure agreement that will satisfy the attorneys representing each partner.

- Do not ask competitors for sensitive data or cause benchmarking partners to feel they must provide data to continue the process.

- Use an ethical third party to assemble and "blind" competitive data, with inputs from legal counsel in direct competitor sharing. (Note: When cost is closely linked to price, sharing cost data can be considered to be the same as sharing price data.)

- Any information obtained from a benchmarking partner should be treated as internal, privileged communications. If "confidential" or proprietary material is to be exchanged, then a specific agreement should be executed to specify the content of the material that needs to be protected, the duration of the period of protection, the conditions for permitting access to the material, and the specific handling requirements necessary for that material.

Sources: APQC, www.apqc.org; Qualserve Benchmarking Clearinghouse, www.awwa.org (accessed October 8, 2010).

new avenues for enhancing its competitiveness through lower costs, greater differentiation, or a more attractive customer value proposition. There are three main areas in a company's total value chain system where company managers can try to improve its efficiency and effectiveness: (1) a company's own activity segments, (2) suppliers' part of the overall value chain, and (3) the distribution channel portion of the chain.

Improving the Efficiency and Effectiveness of Internally Performed Value Chain Activities   Managers can pursue any of several strategic approaches to reduce the costs of internally performed value chain activities and improve a company's cost competitiveness:[20]

1. Implement the use of best practices throughout the company, particularly for high-cost activities.
2. Redesign the product and/or some of its components to eliminate high-cost components or facilitate speedier and more economical manufacture or assembly—computer chip makers regularly design around the patents held by others to avoid paying royalties; automakers have substituted lower-cost plastic and rubber for metal at many exterior body locations.
3. Relocate high-cost activities (such as manufacturing) to geographic areas like Southeast Asia or Latin America or eastern Europe where they can be performed more cheaply.
4. See if certain internally performed activities can be outsourced from vendors or performed by contractors more cheaply than they can be done in-house.
5. Shift to lower-cost technologies and/or invest in productivity-enhancing, cost-saving technological improvements (robotics, flexible manufacturing techniques, state-of-the-art information systems).
6. Stop performing activities that add little or no customer value. Examples include seldom-used customer services, employee training programs that are of marginal value, and maintaining large raw-material or finished-goods inventories.

How successfully a company competes depends on more than low costs. It also depends on how effectively it delivers value to the customer and on its ability to differentiate itself from rivals. To improve the effectiveness of its customer value proposition and enhance differentiation, there are several approaches a manager can take:[21]

1. Implement the use of best practices for quality throughout the company, particularly for high-value activities (those that are important for creating value for the customer).
2. Adopt best practices and technologies that spur innovation, improve design, and enhance creativity.
3. Implement the use of best practices in providing customer service.
4. Reallocate resources to devote more to activities that will have the biggest impact on the value delivered to the customer and that address buyers' most important purchase criteria.
5. For intermediate buyers (distributors or retailers, for example), gain an understanding of how the activities the company performs impact the buyer's value chain. Improve the effectiveness of company activities that have the greatest impact on the efficiency or effectiveness of the buyer's value chain.
6. Adopt best practices for signaling the value of the product and for enhancing customer perceptions.

Improving the Efficiency and Effectiveness of Supplier-Related Value Chain Activities   Improving the efficiency and effectiveness of the value chain activities of suppliers can also address a company's competitive weaknesses with respect to costs and differentiation. On the cost side, a company can gain savings in suppliers' part of the overall value chain by pressuring suppliers for lower prices, switching to lower-priced substitute inputs, and collaborating closely with suppliers to identify mutual cost-saving opportunities.[22] For example, just-in-time deliveries from suppliers can lower a company's inventory and internal logistics costs and may also allow suppliers to economize on their warehousing, shipping, and production scheduling costs—a win-win outcome for both. In a few instances, companies may find that it is cheaper to integrate backward into the business of high-cost suppliers and make the item in-house instead of buying it from outsiders.

Similarly, a company can enhance its differentiation by working with or through its suppliers to do so. Some methods include selecting and retaining suppliers who meet higher-quality standards, coordinating with suppliers to enhance design or other features desired by customers, providing incentives to encourage suppliers to meet higher-quality standards, and assisting suppliers in their efforts to improve. Fewer defects in parts from suppliers not only improve quality and enhance differentiation throughout the value chain system but can lower costs as well since there is less waste and disruption to the production processes.

Improving the Efficiency and Effectiveness of Distribution-Related Value Chain Activities   Taking actions aimed at improvements with respect to the forward or downstream portion of the value chain system can also help to remedy a company's competitive disadvantage with respect to either costs or differentiation. Any of three means can be used to achieve better cost competitiveness in the forward portion of the industry value chain: (1) Pressure distributors, dealers, and other forward channel allies to reduce their costs and markups so as to make the final price to buyers more competitive with the prices of rivals; (2) collaborate with forward channel allies to identify win-win opportunities to reduce costs—a chocolate manufacturer, for example, learned that by shipping its bulk chocolate in liquid form in tank cars instead of as 10-pound molded bars, it could not only save its candy-bar manufacturing customers the costs associated with unpacking and melting but also eliminate its own costs of molding bars and packing them; and (3) change to a more economical distribution strategy, including switching to cheaper distribution channels (perhaps direct sales via the Internet) or perhaps integrating forward into company-owned retail outlets.

The means to enhance differentiation through activities at the forward end of the value chain system include (1) engaging in cooperative advertising and promotions with forward allies (dealers, distributors, retailers, etc.), (2) creating exclusive arrangements with downstream sellers or other mechanisms that increase their incentives to enhance delivered customer value, and (3) creating and enforcing standards for downstream activities and assisting in training channel partners in business practices. Harley-Davidson, for example, enhances the shopping experience and perceptions of buyers by selling through retailers that sell Harley-Davidson motorcycles exclusively and meet Harley-Davidson standards.

Translating Proficient Performance of Value Chain Activities into Competitive Advantage

Value chain analysis and benchmarking are not only useful for identifying and remedying competitive disadvantages; they can also be used to uncover and strengthen competitive advantages. A company's value-creating activities can offer a competitive advantage in one of two ways: (1) They can contribute to greater efficiency and lower costs relative to competitors, or (2) they can provide a basis for differentiation, so customers are willing to pay relatively more for the company's goods and services. A company that does a *first-rate job* of managing its value chain activities *relative to competitors* stands a good chance of profiting from its competitive advantage.

Achieving a cost-based competitive advantage requires determined management efforts to be cost-efficient in performing value chain activities. Such efforts have to be ongoing and persistent, and they have to involve each and every value chain activity. The goal must be continuous cost reduction, not a one-time or on-again–off-again effort. Companies whose managers are truly committed to low-cost performance of value chain activities and succeed in engaging company personnel to discover innovative ways to drive costs out of the business have a real chance of gaining a durable low-cost edge over rivals. It is not as easy as it seems to imitate a company's low-cost practices. Companies like Nucor Steel, Ryanair, and Carrefour have been highly successful in managing their values chains in a low-cost manner.

Ongoing and persistent efforts are also required for a competitive advantage based on differentiation. Superior reputations and brands are built up slowly over time, through continuous investment and activities that deliver consistent, reinforcing messages. Differentiation based on quality requires vigilant management of activities for quality assurance throughout the value chain. While the basis for differentiation (e.g., status, design, innovation, customer service, reliability, image) may vary widely among companies pursuing a differentiation advantage, companies that succeed do so on the basis of a commitment to coordinated value chain activities aimed purposefully at this objective. Examples include Chopin Vodka (status), IKEA (design), FedEx (reliability), 3M (innovation), Louis Vuitton (image), and Ritz Carlton (customer service).

How Activities Relate to Resources and Capabilities

There is a close relationship between the value-creating activities that a company performs and its resources and capabilities. An organizational capability or competence implies a *capacity* for action; in contrast, a value-creating activity *is* the action. With respect to resources and capabilities, activities are "where the rubber hits the road." When companies engage in a value-creating activity, they do so by drawing on specific company resources and capabilities that underlie and enable the activity. For example, brand-building activities depend on human resources, such as experienced brand managers (including their knowledge and expertise in this arena), as well as organizational capabilities in advertising and marketing. Cost-cutting activities may derive from organizational capabilities in inventory management, for example, and resources such as inventory tracking systems.

Because of this correspondence between activities and supporting resources and capabilities, value chain analysis can complement resource and capability analysis as tools for assessing a company's competitive advantage. Resources and capabilities that are *both valuable and rare* provide a company with *what it takes* for competitive advantage. For a company with competitive assets of this sort, the potential is there. When these assets are deployed in the form of a value-creating activity, that potential is realized due to their competitive superiority. Resource analysis is one tool for identifying competitively superior resources and capabilities. But their value and the competitive superiority of that value can only be assessed objectively *after* they are deployed. Value chain analysis and benchmarking provide the type of data needed to make that objective assessment.

There is also a dynamic relationship between a company's activities and its resources and capabilities. Value-creating activities are more than just the embodiment of a resource's or capability's potential. They also contribute to the formation and development of capabilities. The road to competitive advantage begins with management efforts to build organizational expertise in performing certain competitively important value chain activities. With consistent practice and continuous investment of company resources, these activities rise to the level of a reliable organizational capability or a competence. To the extent that top management makes the growing capability a cornerstone of the company's strategy, this capability becomes a core competence for the company. Later, with further organizational learning and gains in proficiency, the core competence may evolve into a distinctive competence, giving the company superiority over rivals in performing an important value chain activity. Such superiority, if it gives the company significant competitive clout in the marketplace, can produce an attractive competitive edge over rivals. Whether the resulting competitive advantage is on the cost side or on the differentiation side (or both) will depend on the company's choice of which types of competence-building activities to engage in over this time period, as shown in Figure 4.5.

> Performing value chain activities in ways that give a company the capabilities to either outmatch rivals on differentiation or beat them on costs will help the company to secure a competitive advantage.

QUESTION 5: IS THE COMPANY COMPETITIVELY STRONGER OR WEAKER THAN KEY RIVALS?

LO 5

Understand how a comprehensive evaluation of a company's competitive situation can assist managers in making critical decisions about their next strategic moves.

Resource and capability analysis together with value chain analysis and benchmarking will reveal whether a company has a competitive advantage over rivals on the basis of *individual* resources, capabilities, and activities. These tools can also be used to assess the competitive advantage attributable to a *bundle* of resources and capabilities. Resource bundles can sometimes pass the four tests of a resource's competitive power even when the individual components of the resource bundle cannot. For example, although Callaway Golf Company's engineering capabilities and market research capabilities are matched relatively well by rivals Cobra Golf and Ping Golf, the company's bundling of resources used in its product development process (including cross-functional development systems, technological capabilities, knowledge of consumer preferences, and a collaborative organizational culture) gives it a competitive advantage that has allowed it to remain the largest seller of golf equipment for more than a decade.

Resource analysis and value chain/benchmarking analysis of the company's resources, capabilities, and activities (both as individual entities and as bundles) are necessary for determining whether the company is competitively stronger or weaker than key rivals. But they are not sufficient for gaining a complete picture

Figure 4.5   Translating Company Performance of Value Chain Activities into Competitive Advantage

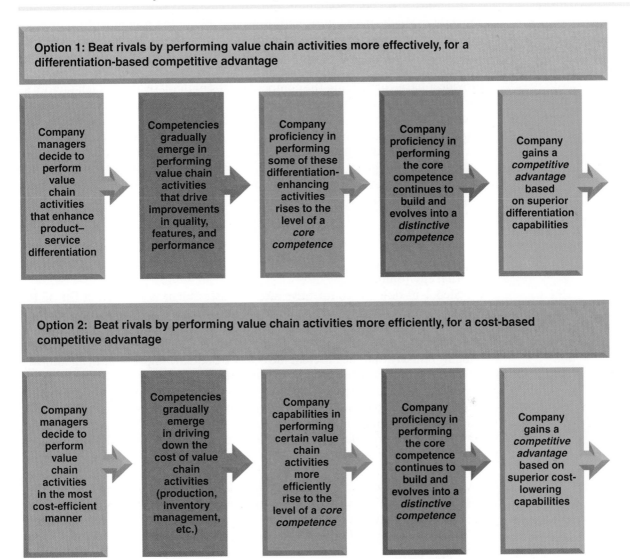

of a company's competitive situation. A more comprehensive assessment needs to be made of the company's *overall* competitive strengths and weaknesses since a competitive advantage along one part of its value chain can be overwhelmed by competitive disadvantages along other parts of the chain. In making an overall assessment of a company's competitiveness, the answers to two questions are of particular interest: First, how does the company rank relative to competitors on each of the important factors that determine market success? Second, all things considered, does the company have a *net* competitive advantage or disadvantage versus major competitors?

An easy-to-use method for answering these two questions involves developing quantitative strength ratings for the company and its key competitors on each industry key success factor and each competitively pivotal resource and capability. Much of the information needed for doing a competitive strength assessment comes from previous analyses. Industry and five-forces analyses reveal the key success factors and competitive forces that separate industry winners from losers. Analyzing benchmarking data and scouting key competitors provide a basis for judging the competitive strength of rivals on such factors as cost, key product attributes, customer service, image and reputation, financial strength, technological skills, distribution capability, and other resources and capabilities. Resource and capability analysis reveals which factors are competitively important, given the external situation. Together with value chain analysis, it also shines a light on the competitive strengths of the company. That is, it reveals whether the company or its rivals have the advantage with respect to competitively important resources, capabilities, and activities. The four tests of a resource's competitive power indicate, further, whether any of these advantages are sustainable. SWOT analysis provides a more comprehensive and forward-looking picture of the company's overall situation by surveying the entire set of its strengths and weaknesses in relation to rivals and the external environment.

Step 1 in doing a competitive strength assessment is to make a list of the industry's key success factors and most telling measures of competitive strength or weakness (6 to 10 measures usually suffice). Step 2 is to assign weights to each of the measures of competitive strength based on their perceived importance—it is highly unlikely that the different measures are equally important. In an industry where the products/services of rivals are virtually identical, for instance, having low unit costs relative to rivals is nearly always the most important determinant of competitive strength. In an industry with strong product differentiation, the most significant measures of competitive strength may be brand awareness, brand image and reputation, product attractiveness, and distribution capability. A weight could be as high as 0.75 (maybe even higher) in situations where one particular competitive variable is overwhelmingly decisive, or a weight could be as low as 0.20 when two or three strength measures are more important than the rest. Lesser competitive strength indicators can carry weights of 0.05 or 0.10. Whether the differences between the importance weights are big or little, *the sum of the weights must add up to 1.*

Step 3 is to rate the firm and its rivals on each competitive strength measure. Numerical rating scales (e.g., from 1 to 10) are best to use, although ratings of stronger (+), weaker (−), and about equal (=) may be appropriate when information is scanty and assigning numerical scores conveys false precision. Step 4 is to multiply each strength rating by its importance weight to obtain weighted strength scores (a strength rating of 4 times a weight of 0.20 gives a weighted strength score of 0.80). Step 5 is to sum the weighted scores on each measure to get overall weighted competitive strength ratings for each company. Step 6 is to use the overall strength ratings to draw conclusions about the size and extent of the company's net competitive advantage or disadvantage and to take specific note of areas of strength and weakness.

Table 4.4 provides an example of competitive strength assessment in which a hypothetical company (ABC Company) competes against two rivals. In the

Table 4.4   A Representative Weighted Competitive Strength Assessment

Key Success Factor/Strength Measure	Importance Weight	Competitive Strength Assessment (Rating scale: 1 = very weak; 10 = very strong)					
		ABC Co.		Rival 1		Rival 2	
		Strength Rating	Weighted Score	Strength Rating	Weighted Score	Strength Rating	Weighted Score
Quality/product performance	0.10	8	0.80	5	0.50	1	0.10
Reputation/image	0.10	8	0.80	7	0.70	1	0.10
Manufacturing capability	0.10	2	0.20	10	1.00	5	0.50
Technological skills	0.05	10	0.50	1	0.05	3	0.15
Dealer network/distribution capability	0.05	9	0.45	4	0.20	5	0.25
New product innovation capability	0.05	9	0.45	4	0.20	5	0.25
Financial resources	0.10	5	0.50	10	1.00	3	0.30
Relative cost position	0.30	5	1.50	10	3.00	1	0.30
Customer service capabilities	0.15	5	0.75	7	1.05	1	0.15
Sum of importance weights	**1.00**						
Overall weighted competitive strength rating			**5.95**		**7.70**		**2.10**

example, relative cost is the most telling measure of competitive strength, and the other strength measures are of lesser importance. The company with the highest rating on a given measure has an implied competitive edge on that measure, with the size of its edge reflected in the difference between its weighted rating and rivals' weighted ratings. For instance, Rival 1's 3.00 weighted strength rating on relative cost signals a considerable cost advantage versus ABC Company (with a 1.50 weighted score on relative cost) and an even bigger cost advantage against Rival 2 (with a weighted score of 0.30). The measure-by-measure ratings reveal the competitive areas where a company is strongest and weakest, and against whom.

The overall competitive strength scores indicate how all the different strength measures add up—whether the company is at a net overall competitive advantage or disadvantage against each rival. The higher a company's *overall weighted strength rating,* the stronger its *overall competitiveness* versus rivals. The bigger the difference between a company's overall weighted rating and the scores of *lower-rated* rivals, the greater is its implied *net competitive advantage.* Thus, Rival 1's overall weighted score of 7.70 indicates a greater net competitive advantage over Rival 2 (with a score of 2.10) than over ABC Company (with a score of 5.95). Conversely, the bigger the difference between a company's overall rating and the scores of *higher-rated* rivals, the greater its implied *net competitive disadvantage.* Rival 2's score of 2.10 gives it a smaller net competitive disadvantage against ABC Company (with an overall score of 5.95) than against Rival 1 (with an overall score of 7.70).

> High weighted competitive strength ratings signal a strong competitive position and possession of competitive advantage; low ratings signal a weak position and competitive disadvantage.

Strategic Implications of Competitive Strength Assessments

Competitive strength assessments provide useful conclusions about a company's competitive situation. The ratings show how a company compares against rivals, factor by factor (or capability by capability), thus revealing where it is strongest and weakest, and against whom. Moreover, the overall competitive strength score indicates how all the different factors add up—whether the company is at a net competitive advantage or disadvantage against each rival. The firm with the largest overall competitive strength rating enjoys the strongest competitive position, with the size of its net competitive advantage reflected by how much its score exceeds the scores of rivals.

In addition, the strength ratings provide guidelines for designing wise offensive and defensive strategies. For example, if ABC Co. wants to go on the offensive to win additional sales and market share, such an offensive probably needs to be aimed directly at winning customers away from Rival 2 (which has a lower overall strength score) rather than Rival 1 (which has a higher overall strength score). Moreover, while ABC has high ratings for technological skills (a 10 rating), dealer network/distribution capability (a 9 rating), new product innovation capability (a 9 rating), quality/product performance (an 8 rating), and reputation/image (an 8 rating), these strength measures have low importance weights—meaning that ABC has strengths in areas that don't translate into much competitive clout in the marketplace. Even so, it outclasses Rival 2 in all five areas, plus it enjoys substantially lower costs than Rival 2 (ABC has a 5 rating on relative cost position versus a 1 rating for Rival 2)—and relative cost position carries the highest importance weight of all the strength measures. ABC also has greater competitive strength than Rival 3 as concerns customer service capabilities (which carries the second-highest importance weight). Hence, because ABC's strengths are in the very areas where Rival 2 is weak, ABC is in a good position to attack Rival 2—it may well be able to persuade a number of Rival 2's customers to switch their purchases over to ABC's product.

> A company's competitive strength scores pinpoint its strengths and weaknesses against rivals and point directly to the kinds of offensive/defensive actions it can use to exploit its competitive strengths and reduce its competitive vulnerabilities.

But ABC should be cautious about cutting price aggressively to win customers away from Rival 2, because Rival 1 could interpret that as an attack by ABC to win away Rival 1's customers as well. And Rival 1 is in far and away the best position to compete on the basis of low price, given its high rating on relative cost in an industry where low costs are competitively important (relative cost carries an importance weight of 0.30). Rival 1's very strong relative cost position vis-à-vis both ABC and Rival 2 arms it with the ability to use its lower-cost advantage to thwart any price cutting on ABC's part; clearly ABC is vulnerable to any retaliatory price cuts by Rival 1—Rival 1 can easily defeat both ABC and Rival 2 in a price-based battle for sales and market share. If ABC wants to defend against its vulnerability to potential price cutting by Rival 1, then it needs to aim a portion of its strategy at lowering its costs.

The point here is that a competitively astute company should utilize the strength scores in deciding what strategic moves to make—what strengths to exploit in winning business away from rivals, which rivals to attack, and which competitive weaknesses to try to correct. When a company has important competitive strengths in areas where one or more rivals are weak, it makes sense to consider offensive moves to exploit rivals' competitive weaknesses. When a company has important competitive weaknesses in areas where one or more rivals are strong, it makes sense to consider defensive moves to curtail its vulnerability.

QUESTION 6: WHAT STRATEGIC ISSUES AND PROBLEMS MERIT FRONT-BURNER MANAGERIAL ATTENTION?

The final and most important analytical step is to zero in on exactly what strategic issues company managers need to address—and resolve—for the company to be more financially and competitively successful in the years ahead. This step involves drawing on the results of both industry analysis and the evaluations of the company's own competitiveness. The task here is to get a clear fix on exactly what strategic and competitive challenges confront the company, which of the company's competitive shortcomings need fixing, what obstacles stand in the way of improving the company's competitive position in the marketplace, and what specific problems merit front-burner attention by company managers.

> Zeroing in on the strategic issues a company faces and compiling a "worry list" of problems and roadblocks creates a strategic agenda of problems that merit prompt managerial attention.

The "worry list" of issues and problems that have to be wrestled with can include such things as:

- *How* to stave off market challenges from new foreign competitors.
- *How* to combat the price discounting of rivals.
- *How* to reduce the company's high costs and pave the way for price reductions.
- *How* to sustain the company's present rate of growth in light of slowing buyer demand.
- *Whether* to expand the company's product line.
- *Whether* to correct the company's competitive deficiencies by acquiring a rival company with the missing strengths.
- *Whether* to expand into foreign markets rapidly or cautiously.
- *Whether* to reposition the company and move to a different strategic group.
- *What to do* about growing buyer interest in substitute products.
- *What to do* to combat the aging demographics of the company's customer base.

The worry list thus always centers on such concerns as "how to … ," "what to do about … ," and "whether to… ." The purpose of the worry list is to identify the specific issues/problems that management needs to address, not to figure out what specific actions to take. Deciding what to do—which strategic actions to take and which strategic moves to take—comes later (when it is time to craft the strategy and choose among the various strategic alternatives).

> Actually deciding on a strategy and what specific actions to take is what comes *after* developing the list of strategic issues and problems that merit front-burner management attention.

If the items on the worry list are relatively minor—which suggests that the company's strategy is mostly on track and reasonably well matched to the company's overall situation, company managers seldom need to go much beyond fine-tuning the present strategy. If, however, the issues and problems confronting the company are serious and indicate the present strategy is not well suited for the road ahead, the task of crafting a better strategy has got to go to the top of management's action agenda.

> A good strategy must contain ways to deal with all the strategic issues and obstacles that stand in the way of the company's financial and competitive success in the years ahead.

KEY POINTS

There are six key questions to consider in evaluating a company's ability to compete successfully against market rivals:

1. *How well is the present strategy working?* This involves evaluating the strategy from a qualitative standpoint (completeness, internal consistency, rationale, and suitability to the situation) and also from a quantitative standpoint (the strategic and financial results the strategy is producing). The stronger a company's current overall performance, the less likely the need for radical strategy changes. The weaker a company's performance and/or the faster the changes in its external situation (which can be gleaned from industry and competitive forces analysis), the more its current strategy must be questioned.

2. *Do the company's resources and capabilities have sufficient competitive power to give it a sustainable advantage over competitors?* The answer to this question comes from conducting the four tests of a resource's competitive power. If a company has resources and capabilities that are competitively valuable and rare, the firm will have a competitive advantage over market rivals. If its resources and capabilities are also hard to copy, with no good substitutes, then the firm may be able to sustain this advantage even in the face of active efforts by rivals to overcome it.

3. *Is the company able to seize market opportunities and overcome external threats to its future well-being?* The answer to this question comes from performing a SWOT analysis. The two most important parts of SWOT analysis are (1) drawing conclusions about what story the compilation of strengths, weaknesses, opportunities, and threats tells about the company's overall situation and (2) acting on the conclusions to better match the company's strategy to its internal strengths and market opportunities, to correct the important internal weaknesses, and to defend against external threats. A company's strengths and competitive assets are strategically relevant because they are the most logical and appealing building blocks for strategy; internal weaknesses are important because they may represent vulnerabilities that need correction. External opportunities and threats come into play because a good strategy necessarily aims at capturing a company's most attractive opportunities and at defending against threats to its well-being.

4. *Are the company's prices, costs, and value proposition competitive?* One telling sign of whether a company's situation is strong or precarious is whether its prices and costs are competitive with those of industry rivals. Another sign is how it compares with rivals in terms of differentiation—how effectively it delivers on its customer value proposition. Value chain analysis and benchmarking are essential tools in determining whether the company is performing particular functions and activities efficiently and effectively, learning whether its costs are in line with competitors, whether it is differentiating in ways that really enhance customer value, and deciding which internal activities and business processes need to be scrutinized for improvement. They complement resource and capability analysis by providing data at the level of individual activities that provides more objective evidence of whether individual resources and capabilities, or bundles of resources and linked activity sets, are competitively superior.

5. *On an overall basis, is the company competitively stronger or weaker than key rivals?* The key appraisals here involve how the company matches up against key rivals on industry key success factors and other chief determinants of competitive success and whether and why the company has a *net* competitive advantage or disadvantage. Quantitative competitive strength assessments, using the method presented in Table 4.4, indicate where a company is competitively strong and weak and provide insight into the company's ability to defend or enhance its market position. As a rule, a company's competitive strategy should be built around its competitive strengths and should aim at shoring up areas where it is competitively vulnerable. When a company has important competitive strengths in areas where one or more rivals are weak, it makes sense to consider offensive moves to exploit rivals' competitive weaknesses. When a company has important competitive weaknesses in areas where one or more rivals are strong, it makes sense to consider defensive moves to curtail its vulnerability.

6. *What strategic issues and problems merit front-burner managerial attention?* This analytical step zeros in on the strategic issues and problems that stand in the way of the company's success. It involves using the results of industry analysis as well as resource and value chain analysis of the company's competitive situation to identify a "worry list" of issues to be resolved for the company to be financially and competitively successful in the years ahead. The worry list always centers on such concerns as "how to ... ," "what to do about ... ," and "whether to ... "—the purpose of the worry list is to identify the specific issues/problems that management needs to address. Actually deciding on a strategy and what specific actions to take is what comes after the list of strategic issues and problems that merit front-burner management attention is developed.

Solid analysis of the company's competitive situation vis-à-vis its key rivals, like good industry analysis, is a valuable precondition for good strategy making. A competently done evaluation of a company's resources, capabilities, and competitive strengths exposes strong and weak points in the present strategy and how attractive or unattractive the company's competitive position is and why. Managers need such understanding to craft a strategy that is well suited to the company's competitive circumstances.

ASSURANCE OF LEARNING EXERCISES

LO 2, LO 3, LO 4

1. Review the information in Illustration Capsule 4.1 concerning the average costs of producing and selling fair-trade coffee. Then answer the following questions:

   a. Companies that do not sell fair-trade coffee can buy coffee direct from small farmers for as little as $0.75 per pound. By paying substandard wages, they can also reduce their labor costs of roasting and bagging coffee to $0.70 per pound and reduce their overhead by 20 percent. If they sell their coffee at the same average price as Just Coffee, what would their profit margin be and how would this compare to Just Coffee's?

b. How can Just Coffee respond to this type of competitive threat? Does it have any valuable competitive assets that can help it respond, or will it need to acquire new ones. Would your answer change the company's value chain in any way?

LO 1

2. Using the information in Table 4.1 and the financial statement information for Avon Products below, calculate the following ratios for Avon for both 2008 and 2009:

a. Gross profit margin

b. Operating profit margin

c. Net profit margin.

d. Times interest earned coverage

e. Return on shareholders' equity

f. Return on assets

g. Debt-to-equity ratio

h. Days of inventory

i. Inventory turnover ratio

j. Average collection period

Based on these ratios, did Avon's financial performance improve, weaken, or remain about the same from 2008 to 2009?

Consolidated Statements of Income for Avon Products, Inc., 2008–2009 (in millions, except per-share data)

	Years ended December 31	
	2009	**2008**
Net sales	$10,284.7	$10,588.9
Other revenue	98.1	101.2
Total revenue	10,382.8	10,690.1
Costs, expenses, and other:		
Cost of sales	3,888.3	3,949.1
Selling, general and administrative expenses	5,476.3	5,401.7
Operating profit	1,018.2	1,339.3
Interest expense	104.8	100.4
Interest income	(20.2)	(37.1)
Other expense, net	7.1	37.7
Total other expenses	91.7	101.0
Income before taxes	926.5	1,238.3
Income taxes	298.3	362.7
Net income	628.2	875.6

(Continued)

	Years ended December 31	
	2009	2008
Net income attributable to noncontrolling interests	(2.4)	(.3)
Net income attributable to Avon	$ 625.8	$ 875.3
Earnings per share:		
Basic	$ 1.45	$ 2.04
Diluted	$ 1.45	$ 2.03

Consolidated Balance Sheets for Avon Products, Inc., 2008–2009 (in millions, except per-share data)

	As of Dec. 31, 2009	As of Dec. 31, 2008
Assets		
Cash and cash equivalents	$ 1,311.6	$ 1,104.7
Accounts receivable (less allowances of $165.5 and $127.9)	779.7	687.8
Inventories	1,067.5	1,007.9
Prepaid expenses and other	1,030.5	756.5
Total current assets	4,189.3	3,556.9
Property, plant, and equipment, at cost		
Land	144.3	85.3
Buildings and improvements	1,048.1	1,008.1
Equipment	1,506.9	1,346.5
Total property, plant, and equipment, at cost	2,699.3	2,439.9
Less accumulated depreciation	(1,169.7)	(1,096.0)
Net property, plant, and equipment	1,529.6	1,343.9
Other assets	1,113.8	1,173.2
Total assets	$ 6,832.7	$ 6,074.0
Liabilities and Shareholders' Equity		
Debt maturing within 1 year	$ 138.1	$1,031.4
Accounts payable	754.7	724.3
Accrued compensation	291.0	234.4
Other accrued liabilities	697.1	581.9
Sales and taxes other than income	259.2	212.2
Income taxes	134.7	128.0
Total current liabilities	2,274.8	2,912.2
Long-term debt	2,307.8	1,456.2
Employee benefit plans	588.9	665.4
Long-term income taxes	173.8	168.9
Other liabilities	174.8	159.0
Total liabilities	$ 5,520.1	$ 5,361.7

Commitments and contingencies

(Continued)

Shareholders' equity

Common stock, par value $.25—authorized 1,500 shares; issued 740.9 and 739.4 shares	$ 186.1	$ 185.6
Additional paid-in capital	1,941.0	1,874.1
Retained earnings	4,383.9	4,118.9
Accumulated other comprehensive loss	(692.6)	(965.9)
Treasury stock, at cost (313.4 and 313.1 shares)	(4,545.8)	(4,537.8)
Total Avon shareholders' equity	1,272.6	674.9
Noncontrolling interest	40.0	37.4
Total shareholders' equity	**$ 1,312.6**	**$ 712.3**
Total liabilities and shareholders' equity	**$ 6,832.7**	**$ 6,074.0**

Source: Avon Products, Inc., 2009 10-K.

LO 3

3. Prepare a SWOT analysis for Singapore Airlines after reviewing the company's latest Annual Reports, Financial Results, Analyst Briefings, and Operating Statistics at its Web site (www.singaporeair.com). Using the steps in Figure 4.2, create a list of important company strengths and competitive assets, weaknesses and competitive deficiencies, market opportunities, and threats to the company's future well-being. Also, summarize your conclusions concerning the company's overall business situation and implications for improving the company's strategy.

EXERCISES FOR SIMULATION PARTICIPANTS

LO 1

1. Using the formulas in Table 4.1 and the data in your company's latest financial statements, calculate the following measures of financial performance for your company:

   a. Operating profit margin

   b. Return on total assets

   c. Current ratio

   d. Working capital

   e. Long-term debt-to-capital ratio

   f. Price-earnings ratio

LO 1

2. On the basis of your company's latest financial statements and all the other available data regarding your company's performance that appear in the Industry Report, list the three measures of financial performance on which

your company did "best" and the three measures on which your company's financial performance was "worst."

LO 1, LO 2, LO 3, LO 4, LO 5

3. What hard evidence can you cite that indicates your company's strategy is working fairly well (or perhaps not working so well, if your company's performance is lagging that of rival companies)?

LO 3

4. What internal strengths and weaknesses does your company have? What external market opportunities for growth and increased profitability exist for your company? What external threats to your company's future well-being and profitability do you and your co-managers see? What does the preceding SWOT analysis indicate about your company's present situation and future prospects—where on the scale from "exceptionally strong" to "alarmingly weak" does the attractiveness of your company's situation rank?

LO 2, LO 3

5. Does your company have any core competencies? If so, what are they?

LO 4

6. What are the key elements of your company's value chain? Refer to Figure 4.3 in developing your answer.

LO 5

7. Using the methodology presented in Table 4.4, do a weighted competitive strength assessment for your company and two other companies that you and your co-managers consider to be very close competitors.

ENDNOTES

[1] In recent years, considerable research has been devoted to the role a company's resources and competitive capabilities play in determining its competitiveness, shaping its strategy, and impacting its profitability. Following the trailblazing article by Birger Wernerfelt, "A Resource-Based View of the Firm," *Strategic Management Journal* 5, no. 5 (September–October 1984), pp. 171–80, the findings and conclusions have merged into what is now referred to as the resource-based view of the firm. Other very important contributions include Jay Barney, "Firm Resources and Sustained Competitive Advantage," *Journal of Management* 17, no. 1 (1991), pp. 99–120; Margaret A. Peteraf, "The Cornerstones of Competitive Advantage: A Resource-Based View," *Strategic Management Journal* 14, no. 3 (March 1993), pp. 179–91; Birger Wernerfelt, "The Resource-Based View of the Firm: Ten Years After," *Strategic Management Journal* 16, no. 3 (March 1995), pp. 171–74. A full-blown overview of the resource-based view of the firm, in its most current form, is presented in Jay B. Barney and Delwyn N. Clark, *Resource-Based Theory: Creating and Sustaining Competitive Advantage* (New York: Oxford University Press, 2007).

[2] A more detailed explanation of the relationship between resources and capabilities can be found in R. Amit and P. Schoemaker, "Strategic Assets and Organizational Rent," *Strategic Management Journal* 14 (1993), pp. 33–46.

[3] See, for example, Jay B. Barney, "Looking Inside for Competitive Advantage," *Academy of Management Executive* 9, no. 4 (November 1995), pp. 49–61; Christopher A. Bartlett and Sumantra Ghoshal, "Building Competitive Advantage through People," *MIT Sloan Management Review* 43, no. 2 (Winter 2002), pp. 34–41; Danny Miller, Russell Eisenstat, and Nathaniel Foote, "Strategy from the Inside Out: Building Capability-Creating Organizations," *California Management Review* 44, no. 3 (Spring 2002), pp. 37–54.

[4] See Barney , "Firm Resources and Sustained Competitive Advantage," pp. 105–9; M. Peteraf and J. Barney, "Unraveling the Resource-Based Tangle," *Managerial and Decision Economics* 24, no. 4 (June–July 2003), pp. 309–23.

[5] See Amit and Schoemaker, Strategic Assets and Organizational Rent, for more on the power of strategic assets to improve a company's profitability.

[6] For a discussion of how to recognize powerful substitute resources, see Margaret A. Peteraf and Mark E. Bergen, "Scanning Dynamic Competitive Landscapes: A Market-Based and Resource-Based Framework," *Strategic Management Journal* 24 (2003), pp. 1027–42.

[7] See C. Montgomery, "Of Diamonds and Rust: A New Look at Resources," in C. Montgomery (ed.), *Resource-Based and Evolutionary Theories of the Firm* (Boston: Kluwer Academic, 1995), pp. 251–68.

[8] For a good discussion of what happens when a company's capabilities grow stale and obsolete, see D. Leonard-Barton, "Core Capabilities and Core Rigidities: A Paradox in Managing New Product Development," *Strategic Management Journal* 13 (Summer 1992), pp. 111–25; Montgomery, "Of Diamonds and Rust."

[9] The concept of dynamic capabilities was introduced by D. Teece, G. Pisano, and A. Shuen, "Dynamic Capabilities and Strategic Management," *Strategic Management Journal* 18, no. 7 (1997), pp. 509–33. Other important contributors to the concept include K. Eisenhardt and J. Martin, "Dynamic Capabilities: What Are They?" *Strategic Management Journal* 21, nos. 10–11 (2000), pp. 1105–21; M. Zollo and S. Winter, "Deliberate Learning and the Evolution of Dynamic Capabilities," *Organization Science* 13 (2002), pp. 339–51; C. Helfat et al., *Dynamic Capabilities: Understanding Strategic Change in Organizations* (Malden, MA: Blackwell, 2007).

[10] For a more extensive discussion of how to identify and evaluate the competitive power of a company's capabilities, see David W. Birchall and George Tovstiga, "The Strategic Potential of a Firm's Knowledge Portfolio," *Journal of General Management* 25, no. 1 (Autumn 1999), pp. 1–16; Nick Bontis, Nicola C. Dragonetti, Kristine Jacobsen, and Goran Roos, "The Knowledge Toolbox: A Review of the Tools Available to Measure and Manage Intangible Resources," *European Management Journal* 17, no. 4 (August 1999), pp. 391–401. Also see David Teece, "Capturing Value from Knowledge Assets: The New Economy, Markets for Know-How, and Intangible Assets," *California Management Review* 40, no. 3 (Spring 1998), pp. 55–79.

[11] Donald Sull, "Strategy as Active Waiting," *Harvard Business Review* 83, no. 9 (September 2005), pp. 121–22.

[12] Ibid., pp. 124–26.

[13] See M. Peteraf, "The Cornerstones of Competitive Advantage: A Resource-Based View," *Strategic Management Journal,* March 1993, pp. 179–91.

[14] The value chain concept was developed and articulated by Michael Porter in his 1985 best-seller, *Competitive Advantage* (New York: Free Press).

[15] For discussions of the accounting challenges in calculating the costs of value chain activities, see John K. Shank and Vijay Govindarajan, *Strategic Cost Management* (New York: Free Press, 1993), especially chaps. 2–6, 10, and 11; Robin Cooper and Robert S. Kaplan, "Measure Costs Right: Make the Right Decisions," *Harvard Business Review* 66, no. 5 (September–October 1988), pp. 96–103; Joseph A. Ness and Thomas G. Cucuzza, "Tapping the Full Potential of ABC," *Harvard Business Review* 73, no. 4 (July–August 1995), pp. 130–38.

[16] Porter, *Competitive Advantage,* p. 34.

[17] The strategic importance of effective supply chain management is discussed in Hau L. Lee, "The Triple-A Supply Chain," *Harvard Business Review* 82, no. 10 (October 2004), pp. 102–12.

[18] For more details, see Gregory H. Watson, *Strategic Benchmarking: How to Rate Your Company's Performance Against the World's Best* (New York: Wiley, 1993); Robert C. Camp, *Benchmarking: The Search for Industry Best Practices That Lead to Superior Performance* (Milwaukee: ASQC Quality Press, 1989); Dawn Iacobucci and Christie Nordhielm, "Creative Benchmarking," *Harvard Business Review* 78 no. 6 (November–December 2000), pp. 24–25.

[19] Jeremy Main, "How to Steal the Best Ideas Around," *Fortune,* October 19, 1992, pp. 102–3.

[20] Some of these options are discussed in more detail in Porter, *Competitive Advantage,* chap. 3.

[21] Porter discusses options such as these in *Competitive Advantage,* chap. 4.

[22] An example of how Whirlpool Corporation transformed its supply chain from a competitive liability to a competitive asset is discussed in Reuben E. Stone, "Leading a Supply Chain Turnaround," *Harvard Business Review* 82, no. 10 (October 2004), pp. 114–21.

CHAPTER 5

THE FIVE GENERIC COMPETITIVE STRATEGIES

Which One to Employ?

> I'm spending my time trying to understand our competitive position and how we're serving customers.
>
> **—Lou Gerstner**
> *Former CEO credited with IBM's turnaround*

> Competitive strategy is about being different. It means deliberately choosing to perform activities differently or to perform different activities than rivals to deliver a unique mix of value.
>
> **—Michael E. Porter**
> *Harvard Business School professor and Cofounder of Monitor Consulting*

> The essence of strategy lies in creating tomorrow's competitive advantages faster than competitors mimic the ones you possess today.
>
> **—Gary Hamel and C. K. Prahalad**
> *Professors, authors, and consultants*

LEARNING OBJECTIVES

LO 1. Understand what distinguishes each of the five generic strategies and why some of these strategies work better in certain kinds of industry and competitive conditions than in others.

LO 2. Gain command of the major avenues for achieving a competitive advantage based on lower costs.

LO 3. Learn the major avenues to a competitive advantage based on differentiating a

company's product or service offering from the offerings of rivals.

LO 4. Recognize the attributes of a best-cost provider strategy and the way in which some firms use a hybrid strategy to go about building a competitive advantage and delivering superior value to customers.

There are several basic approaches to competing successfully and gaining a competitive advantage over rivals, but they all involve the capacity to deliver more customer value than rivals can. Superior value can mean a good product at a lower price, a superior product that is worth paying more for, or a best-value offering that represents an attractive combination of price, features, quality, service, and other appealing attributes. But whatever form delivering superior value takes, it nearly always requires performing value chain activities differently than rivals and building competitively valuable resources and capabilities that rivals cannot readily match or trump.

This chapter describes the five *generic competitive strategy options*. Which of the five to employ is a company's first and foremost choice in crafting an overall strategy and beginning its quest for competitive advantage.

THE FIVE GENERIC COMPETITIVE STRATEGIES

A company's competitive strategy *deals exclusively with the specifics of management's game plan for competing successfully*—its specific efforts to please customers, its offensive and defensive moves to counter the maneuvers of rivals, its responses to shifting market conditions, its initiatives to strengthen its market position, and the specific kind of competitive advantage it is trying to achieve. The chances are remote that any two companies—even companies in the same industry—will employ competitive strategies that are exactly alike in every detail. Why? Because managers at different companies always have a slightly different spin on how best to deal with competitive pressures and industry driving forces, what future market conditions will be like, and what strategy specifics make the most sense for their particular company in light of the company's strengths and weaknesses, its most promising market opportunities, and the external threats to its future well-being.

LO 1

Understand what
distinguishes each
of the five generic
strategies and
why some of these
strategies work
better in certain
kinds of industry
and competitive
conditions than in
others.

However, when one strips away the details to get at the real substance, the two factors that most distinguish one competitive strategy from another boil down to (1) whether a company's market target is broad or narrow and (2) whether the company is pursuing a competitive advantage linked to low costs or product differentiation. As shown in Figure 5.1, these two factors give rise to five competitive strategy options for staking out a market position, operating the business, and delivering value to customers:[1]

1. *A low-cost provider strategy:* striving to achieve lower overall costs than rivals on products that attract a broad spectrum of buyers.

2. *A broad differentiation strategy:* seeking to differentiate the company's product offering from rivals' with attributes that will appeal to a broad spectrum of buyers.

3. *A focused (or market niche) low-cost strategy:* concentrating on a narrow buyer segment and outcompeting rivals on costs, thus being in position to win buyer favor by means of a lower-priced product offering.

4. *A focused (or market niche) differentiation strategy:* concentrating on a narrow buyer segment and outcompeting rivals with a product offering that meets the specific tastes and requirements of niche members better than the product offerings of rivals.

5. *A best-cost provider strategy:* giving customers *more value for the money* by offering upscale product attributes at a lower cost than rivals. Being the "best-cost" producer of an upscale product allows a company to underprice rivals whose products have similar upscale attributes. This option is a *hybrid* strategy that *blends elements of differentiation and low-cost strategies* in a unique way.

The remainder of this chapter explores the ins and outs of these five generic competitive strategies and how they differ.

Figure 5.1   **The Five Generic Competitive Strategies: Each Stakes Out a Different Market Position**

Source: This is an author-expanded version of a three-strategy classification discussed in Michael E. Porter, *Competitive Strategy* (New York: Free Press, 1980), pp. 35–40.

LOW-COST PROVIDER STRATEGIES

Striving to be the industry's overall low-cost provider is a powerful competitive approach in markets with many price-sensitive buyers. A company achieves **low-cost leadership** when it becomes the industry's lowest-cost provider rather than just being one of perhaps several competitors with comparatively low costs. A low-cost provider's strategic target is to have lower costs than rivals on products of comparable quality. In striving for a cost advantage over rivals, company managers must take care to incorporate features and services that buyers consider essential—*a product offering that is too frills-free sabotages the attractiveness of the company's product and can turn buyers off even if it is cheaper than competing products.* For maximum effectiveness, a low-cost provider needs to pursue cost-saving approaches that are difficult for rivals to copy. When it is relatively easy or inexpensive for rivals to imitate the low-cost firm's methods, then any resulting cost advantage evaporates too quickly to gain a very valuable edge in the marketplace.

A low-cost advantage over rivals has enormous competitive power, sometimes enabling a company to achieve faster rates of growth (by using price cuts to draw customers away from rivals) and frequently helping to boost a company's profitability. A company can translate a low-cost advantage over rivals into attractive profit performance in either of two ways:

1. By using its lower-cost edge to underprice competitors and attract price-sensitive buyers in great enough numbers to increase total profits.
2. By refraining from using price cuts to steal sales away from rivals (which runs the risk of starting a price war) and, instead, charging a price roughly equal to those of other low-priced rivals. While this strategy will not increase the company's market share, it will enable the company to earn a bigger profit margin per unit sold (because the company's costs per unit are below the unit costs of rivals) and thereby propel it to higher total profits and return on investment than rivals are able to earn.

While many companies are inclined to exploit a low-cost advantage by attacking rivals with lower prices (in hopes that the expected gains in sales and market share will lead to higher total profits), this strategy can backfire if rivals respond with retaliatory price cuts of their own (in order to protect their customer base) and the aggressor's price cuts fail to produce sales gains that are big enough to offset the profit erosion associated with charging a lower price. The bigger the risk that rivals will respond with matching price cuts, the more appealing it becomes to employ the second option for using a low-cost advantage to achieve higher profitability.

The Two Major Avenues for Achieving a Cost Advantage

To achieve a low-cost edge over rivals, a firm's cumulative costs across its overall value chain must be lower than competitors' cumulative costs. There are two ways to accomplish this:[2]

CORE CONCEPT

A **low-cost leader**'s basis for competitive advantage is lower overall costs than competitors. Successful low-cost leaders are exceptionally good at finding ways to drive costs out of their businesses and still provide a product or service that buyers find acceptable.

A low-cost advantage over rivals can translate into better profitability than rivals attain.

1. Do a better job than rivals of performing value chain activities more cost-effectively.
2. Revamp the firm's overall value chain to eliminate or bypass some cost-producing activities.

Let's look at each of the two approaches to securing a cost advantage.

Cost-Efficient Management of Value Chain Activities

CORE CONCEPT

A **cost driver** is a factor that has a strong influence on a company's costs.

For a company to do a more cost-efficient job of managing its value chain than rivals, managers must launch a concerted, ongoing effort to ferret out cost-saving opportunities in every part of the value chain. No activity can escape cost-saving scrutiny, and all company personnel must be expected to use their talents and ingenuity to come up with innovative and effective ways to keep costs down. All avenues for performing value chain activities at a lower cost than rivals have to be explored. Particular attention, however, needs to be paid to a set of factors known as **cost drivers,** which have an especially strong effect on a company's costs and which managers can use as levers to push costs down. (Figure 5.2 provides a list of important cost drivers.) Cost-cutting methods that demonstrate an effective use of the cost drivers include:

1. *Striving to capture all available economies of scale.* Economies of scale stem from an ability to lower unit costs by increasing the scale of operation, and they can affect the unit costs of many activities along the value chain, including manufacturing, R&D, advertising, distribution, and general administration. For example, PepsiCo and Anheuser-Busch have the ability to afford the $3 million cost of a 30-second Super Bowl ad because the cost of such an ad can be spread out over the hundreds of millions of units they sell. In contrast, a small company with a sales volume of only 1 million units would find the $3 million cost of a Super Bowl ad prohibitive—just one ad would raise costs over $2 per unit even if the ad was unusually effective and caused sales volume to jump 25 percent, to 1.25 million units. Similarly, a large manufacturing plant can be more economical to operate than a smaller one. In global industries, making separate products for each country market instead of selling a mostly standard product worldwide tends to boost unit costs because of lost time in model changeover, shorter production runs, and inability to reach the most economic scale of production for each country model.

2. *Taking full advantage of experience and learning-curve effects.* The cost of performing an activity can decline over time as the learning and experience of company personnel build. Learning/experience economies can stem from debugging and mastering newly introduced technologies, using the experiences and suggestions of workers to install more efficient plant layouts and assembly procedures, and the added speed and effectiveness that accrues from repeatedly picking sites for and building new plants, retail outlets, or distribution centers. Aggressively managed low-cost providers pay diligent attention to capturing the benefits of learning and experience and to keeping these benefits proprietary to whatever extent possible.

3. *Trying to operate facilities at full capacity.* Whether a company is able to operate at or near full capacity has a big impact on units costs when

Figure 5.2 Cost Drivers: The Keys to Driving Down Company Costs

Sources: Adapted by the authors from M. Porter, *Competitive Advantage: Creating and Sustaining Competitive Advantage* (New York: Free Press, 1985).

its value chain contains activities associated with substantial fixed costs. Higher rates of capacity utilization allow depreciation and other fixed costs to be spread over a larger unit volume, thereby lowering fixed costs per unit. The more capital-intensive the business and the higher the fixed costs relative to total costs, the greater the unit-cost penalty for underutilizing existing capacity.

4. *Improving supply chain efficiency.* Partnering with suppliers to streamline the ordering and purchasing process, to reduce inventory carrying costs via just-in-time inventory practices, to economize on shipping and materials handling, and to ferret out other cost-saving opportunities is a much-used approach to cost reduction. A company with a distinctive competence in cost-efficient supply chain management can sometimes achieve a sizable cost advantage over less adept rivals.

5. *Using lower cost inputs wherever doing so will not entail too great a sacrifice in quality.* Some examples include lower-cost raw materials or component parts, nonunion labor "inputs," and lower rental fees due to differences in location. If the costs of certain factors are "too high," a company may even design the high-cost inputs out of the product altogether.

6. *Using the company's bargaining power vis-à-vis suppliers or others in the value chain system to gain concessions.* Home Depot, for example, has sufficient bargaining clout with suppliers to win price discounts on large-volume purchases. PepsiCo similarly uses its bargaining power to win concessions from supermarkets, mass merchandisers, and other forward channel allies.

7. *Using communication systems and information technology to achieve operating efficiencies.* For example, data sharing, starting with customer orders and going all the way back to components production, coupled with the use of enterprise resource planning (ERP) and manufacturing execution system (MES) software, can greatly reduce production times and labor costs. Numerous companies now have online systems and software that turn formerly time-consuming and labor-intensive tasks like purchasing, inventory management, invoicing, and bill payment into speedily performed mouse clicks.

8. *Employing advanced production technology and process design to improve overall efficiency.* Examples range from highly automated robotic production technology to computer-assisted design (CAD) techniques to design for manufacture (DFM) procedures that enable more integrated and efficient production. Dell's highly automated PC assembly plant in Austin, Texas, is a prime example of the use of advanced product and process technologies. Other manufacturers have pioneered the use of production or processing technology that eliminates the need for costly investments in facilities or equipment and that requires fewer employees. Companies can also achieve substantial efficiency gains through process innovation or through approaches such as business process management, business process reengineering, and total quality management that aim to coordinate production activities and drive continuous improvement in productivity and quality.[3] Procter & Gamble is an example of a company known for its successful application of business process reengineering techniques.

9. *Being alert to the cost advantages of outsourcing or vertical integration.* Outsourcing the performance of certain value chain activities can be more economical than performing them in-house if outside specialists, by virtue of their expertise and volume, can perform the activities at lower cost. Indeed, outsourcing has, in recent years, become a widely used cost reduction approach. On the other hand, there can be times when integrating into the activities of either suppliers or distribution channel allies can lower costs through greater production efficiencies, reduced transaction costs, or a better bargaining position.

10. *Motivating employees through incentives and company culture.* A company's incentive system can encourage not only greater worker productivity but also cost-saving innovations that come from worker suggestions. The culture of a company can also spur worker pride in productivity and continuous improvement. Companies that are well known for their cost-reducing incentive systems and culture include Nucor Steel, which characterizes itself as a company of "11,900 teammates," Southwest Airlines, and Walmart.

In addition to the above means of performing value chain activities more efficiently than rivals, managers can also achieve important cost savings by deliberately opting for an inherently economical strategy. For instance, a company can often open up a significant cost advantage over rivals by:

- Having lower specifications for purchased materials, parts, and components than do rivals. Thus, a maker of personal computers can use the cheapest hard drives, microprocessors, monitors, and other components so as to end up with lower production costs than rival PC makers.

- Stripping frills and features from its product offering that are not highly valued by price-sensitive or bargain-hunting buyers. Deliberately restricting the company's product offering to "the essentials" can help a company cut costs associated with snazzy attributes and a full lineup of options and extras. Activities and costs can also be eliminated by offering buyers fewer services.

- Offering a limited product line as opposed to a full product line. Pruning slow-selling items from the product lineup and being content to meet the needs of most buyers rather than all buyers can eliminate activities and costs associated with numerous product versions and wide selection.

- Distributing the company's product only through low-cost distribution channels and avoiding high-cost distribution channels.

- Choosing to use the most economical method for delivering customer orders (even if it results in longer delivery times).

The point here is that a low-cost provider strategy entails not only performing value chain activities cost-effectively but also judiciously choosing cost-saving strategic approaches.

Revamping the Value Chain System to Lower Costs   Dramatic cost advantages can often emerge from redesigning the company's value chain system in ways that eliminate costly work steps and entirely bypass certain cost-producing value chain activities. While using communication technologies and information systems or business process reengineering to drive down costs often involves activities that span the value chain system, other approaches to revamping the value chain system can include:

- *Selling direct to consumers and bypassing the activities and costs of distributors and dealers.* To circumvent the need for distributors-dealers, a company can (1) create its own direct sales force (which adds the costs of maintaining and supporting a sales force but which may well be cheaper than utilizing independent distributors and dealers to access buyers) and/or (2) conduct sales operations at the company's Web site (incurring costs for Web site operations and shipping may be a substantially cheaper way to make sales to customers than going through distributor-dealer channels). Costs in the wholesale/retail portions of the value chain frequently represent 35 to 50 percent of the price final consumers pay, so establishing a direct sales force or selling online may offer big cost savings.

- *Coordinating with suppliers to bypass the need to perform certain value chain activities, speed up their performance, or otherwise increase overall efficiency.* Examples include having suppliers combine particular parts and components into preassembled modules, thus permitting a manufacturer to assemble its own product in fewer work steps and with a smaller workforce, and sharing real-time sales information to lower costs through improved inventory management. At Walmart, some items supplied by manufacturers are delivered directly to retail stores rather than being routed through Walmart's distribution centers and delivered by Walmart trucks; in other instances, Walmart unloads incoming shipments from manufacturers' trucks arriving at its distribution centers directly onto outgoing Walmart trucks headed to particular stores without ever moving the goods into the distribution center. Many supermarket chains have greatly reduced in-store meat butchering and cutting activities by shifting to meats that are cut and packaged at the meatpacking plant and then delivered to their stores in ready-to-sell form.

- *Reducing materials handling and shipping costs by having suppliers locate their plants or warehouses close to the company's own facilities.* Having suppliers locate their plants or warehouses very close to a company's own plant facilitates just-in-time deliveries of parts and components to the exact work station where they will be utilized in assembling the company's product. This not only lowers incoming shipping costs but also curbs or eliminates the need for a company to build and operate storerooms for incoming parts and components and have plant personnel move the inventories to the work stations as needed for assembly.

Illustration Capsule 5.1 describes how Walmart has managed its value chain in the retail grocery portion of its business to achieve a dramatic cost advantage over rival supermarket chains and become the world's biggest grocery retailer.

Examples of Companies That Revamped Their Value Chains to Reduce Costs
Nucor Corporation, the most profitable steel producer in the United States and one of the largest steel producers worldwide, drastically revamped the value chain process for manufacturing steel products by using relatively inexpensive electric arc furnaces where scrap steel and directly reduced iron ore are melted and then sent to a continuous caster and rolling mill to be shaped into steel bars, steel beams, steel plate, and sheet steel. Using electric arc furnaces to make new steel products by recycling scrap steel eliminated many of the steps used by traditional steel mills that made their steel products from iron ore, coke, limestone, and other ingredients using costly coke ovens, basic oxygen blast furnaces, ingot casters, and multiple types of finishing facilities—plus Nucor's value chain system required far few employees. As a consequence, Nucor was able to make steel with a far lower capital investment, a far smaller workforce, and far lower operating costs than traditional steel mills. Nucor's strategy to replace the traditional steelmaking value chain with its simpler, quicker value chain approach has made it one of the lowest-cost producers of steel in the world and enabled Nucor to take huge volumes of sales and market share away from traditional steel companies and earn attractive profits. (Nucor has reported profits for every quarter in every year during the 1966–2008 period—a remarkable accomplishment in a mature and cyclical industry notorious for poor profitability.) While the recession-plagued year of 2009 was not a good one for Nucor, it returned to profits quickly in 2010.

Southwest Airlines has achieved considerable cost savings by reconfiguring the traditional value chain of commercial airlines, thereby allowing it to offer travelers dramatically lower fares. Its mastery of fast turnarounds at the gates (about 25 minutes versus 45 minutes for rivals) allows its planes to fly more hours per day. This translates into being able to schedule more flights per day with fewer aircraft, allowing Southwest to generate more revenue per plane on average than rivals. Southwest does not offer assigned seating, baggage transfer to connecting airlines, or first-class seating and service, thereby eliminating all the cost-producing activities associated with these features. The company's fast and user-friendly online reservation system facilitates e-ticketing and reduces staffing requirements at telephone reservation centers and airport counters. Its use of automated check-in equipment reduces staffing requirements for terminal check-in.

The Keys to Being a Successful Low-Cost Provider

To succeed with a low-cost provider strategy, company managers have to scrutinize each cost-creating activity and determine what factors cause costs to be high or low. Then they have to use this knowledge to streamline or reengineer how activities are performed, exhaustively pursuing cost efficiencies throughout the value chain. Normally, low-cost producers try to engage all company personnel in continuous cost improvement efforts, and they strive to operate with exceptionally small corporate staffs to keep administrative costs to a minimum. Many successful low-cost

ILLUSTRATION CAPSULE 5.1

How Walmart Managed Its Value Chain to Achieve a Huge Low-Cost Advantage over Rival Supermarket Chains

Walmart has achieved a very substantial cost and pricing advantage over rival supermarket chains both by revamping portions of the grocery retailing value chain and by outmanaging its rivals in efficiently performing various value chain activities. Its cost advantage stems from a series of initiatives and practices:

- Instituting extensive information sharing with vendors via online systems that relay sales at its checkout counters directly to suppliers of the items, thereby providing suppliers with real-time information on customer demand and preferences (creating an estimated 6 percent cost advantage). It is standard practice at Walmart to collaborate extensively with vendors on all aspects of the purchasing and store delivery process to squeeze out mutually beneficial cost savings. Procter & Gamble, Walmart's biggest supplier, went so far as to integrate its enterprise resource planning (ERP) system with Walmart's.

- Pursuing global procurement of some items and centralizing most purchasing activities so as to leverage the company's buying power (creating an estimated 2.5 percent cost advantage).

- Investing in state-of-the-art automation at its distribution centers, efficiently operating a truck fleet that makes daily deliveries to Walmart's stores, and putting other assorted cost-saving practices into place at its headquarters, distribution centers, and stores (resulting in an estimated 4 percent cost advantage).

- Striving to optimize the product mix and achieve greater sales turnover (resulting in about a 2 percent cost advantage).

- Installing security systems and store operating procedures that lower shrinkage rates (producing a cost advantage of about 0.5 percent).

- Negotiating preferred real estate rental and leasing rates with real estate developers and owners of its store sites (yielding a cost advantage of 2 percent).

- Managing and compensating its workforce in a manner that produces lower labor costs (yielding an estimated 5 percent cost advantage).

Altogether, these value chain initiatives give Walmart an approximately 22 percent cost advantage over Kroger, Safeway, and other leading supermarket chains. With such a sizable cost advantage, Walmart has been able to underprice its rivals and rapidly become the world's leading supermarket retailer.

Sources: Developed by the authors from information at www.walmart.com and in Marco Iansiti and Roy Levien, "Strategy as Ecology," *Harvard Business Review* 82, no. 3 (March 2004), p. 70.

leaders also use benchmarking to keep close tabs on how their costs compare with those of rivals and firms performing comparable activities in other industries.

But while low-cost providers are champions of frugality, they seldom hesitate to spend aggressively on resources and capabilities *that promise to drive costs out of the business.* Indeed, having resources or capabilities of this type and ensuring that they remain competitively superior is essential for achieving competitive advantage as a low-cost provider. Walmart, one of the world's foremost

> Success in achieving a low-cost edge over rivals comes from out-managing rivals in finding ways to perform value chain activities faster, more accurately, and more cost-effectively.

low-cost providers, has been an early adopter of state-of-the-art technology throughout its operations—its distribution facilities are an automated showcase, it has developed sophisticated online systems to order goods from suppliers and manage inventories, it equips its stores with cutting-edge sales-tracking and checkout systems, and it sends daily point-of-sale data to 4,000 vendors, *but Walmart carefully estimates the cost savings of new technologies before it rushes to invest in them.* By continuously investing in complex technologies that are hard for rivals to match, Walmart has sustained its competitive advantage for over 30 years.

Other companies noted for their successful use of low-cost provider strategies include Haier in home appliances, Toyota in automobiles, Bata in footwear, and Acer in computers.

When a Low-Cost Provider Strategy Works Best

A low-cost provider strategy becomes increasingly appealing and competitively powerful when:

1. *Price competition among rival sellers is vigorous.* Low-cost providers are in the best position to compete offensively on the basis of price, to use the appeal of lower price to grab sales (and market share) from rivals, to win the business of price-sensitive buyers, to remain profitable despite strong price competition, and to survive price wars.

2. *The products of rival sellers are essentially identical and readily available from many eager sellers.* Look-alike products and/or overabundant product supply set the stage for lively price competition; in such markets, it is the less efficient, higher-cost companies whose profits get squeezed the most.

3. *There are few ways to achieve product differentiation that have value to buyers.* When the differences between product attributes or brands do not matter much to buyers, buyers are nearly always very sensitive to price differences and market share winners will tend to be those with the lowest-priced brands.

4. *Most buyers use the product in the same ways.* With common user requirements, a standardized product can satisfy the needs of buyers, in which case low selling price, not features or quality, becomes the dominant factor in causing buyers to choose one seller's product over another's.

5. *Buyers incur low costs in switching their purchases from one seller to another.* Low switching costs give buyers the flexibility to shift purchases to lower-priced sellers having equally good products or to attractively priced substitute products. A low-cost leader is well positioned to use low price to induce its customers not to switch to rival brands or substitutes.

6. *Buyers are large and have significant power to bargain down prices.* Low-cost providers have partial profit-margin protection in bargaining with high-volume buyers, since powerful buyers are rarely able to bargain price down past the survival level of the next most cost-efficient seller.

7. *Industry newcomers use introductory low prices to attract buyers and build a customer base.* A low-cost provider can use price cuts of its own to make it harder for a new rival to win customers. Moreover, the pricing power of a low-cost provider acts as a barrier for new entrants.

As a rule, the more price-sensitive buyers are, the more appealing a low-cost strategy becomes. A low-cost company's ability to set the industry's price floor and still earn a profit erects protective barriers around its market position.

Pitfalls to Avoid in Pursuing a Low-Cost Provider Strategy

Perhaps the biggest mistake a low-cost provider can make to spoil the profitability of its low-cost advantage is getting carried away with overly aggressive price cutting to win sales and market share away from rivals. *Higher unit sales and market shares do not automatically translate into higher total profits.* A low-cost/low-price advantage results in superior profitability only if (1) prices are cut by less than the size of the unit cost advantage or (2) the added gains in unit sales are large enough to bring in a bigger total profit despite lower margins per unit sold. A company with a 5 percent per-unit cost advantage cannot cut prices 20 percent, end up with a volume gain of only 10 percent, and still expect to earn higher profits!

> A low-cost provider is in the best position to win the business of price-sensitive buyers, set the floor on market price, and still earn a profit.

A lower price improves total profitability only if the price cuts lead to total revenues that are big enough to *more than cover* all the added costs associated with selling more units. When the incremental gains in total revenues flowing from a lower price exceed the incremental increases in total costs associated with a higher sales volume, then cutting price is a profitable move. But if a lower selling price results in revenue gains that are smaller than the increases in total costs, company profits end up lower than before and the price cut ends up reducing profits rather than raising them.

> Reducing price does not lead to higher total profits unless the incremental gain in total revenues exceeds the incremental increase in total costs.

A second pitfall of a low-cost provider strategy is failing to emphasize avenues of cost advantage that can be kept proprietary or that relegate rivals to playing catch-up. The real value of a cost advantage depends on its sustainability. Sustainability, in turn, hinges on whether the company achieves its cost advantage in ways difficult for rivals to copy or otherwise overcome.

A third pitfall is becoming too fixated on cost reduction. Low cost cannot be pursued so zealously that a firm's offering ends up being too features-poor to generate buyer appeal. Furthermore, a company driving hard to push its costs down has to guard against misreading or ignoring increased buyer interest in added features or service, declining buyer sensitivity to price, or new developments that start to alter how buyers use the product. Otherwise, it risks losing market ground if buyers start opting for more upscale or feature-rich products.

> A low-cost provider's product offering must always contain enough attributes to be attractive to prospective buyers—low price, by itself, is not always appealing to buyers.

Even if these mistakes are avoided, a low-cost provider strategy still entails risk. An innovative rival may discover an even lower-cost value chain approach. Important cost-saving technological breakthroughs may suddenly emerge. And if a low-cost provider has heavy investments in its present means of operating, then it can prove very costly to quickly shift to the new value chain approach or a new technology.

BROAD DIFFERENTIATION STRATEGIES

Differentiation strategies are attractive whenever buyers' needs and preferences are too diverse to be fully satisfied by a standardized product offering. Successful product differentiation requires careful study of buyers' needs and behaviors to learn what buyers consider important, what they think has value, and what they are willing to pay for.[4] Then the trick is for a company to incorporate certain buyer-desired attributes into its product offering such that its offering will not only appeal to a broad range of buyers but also be different enough to stand apart from the product offerings of rivals—in regard to the latter, a strongly differentiated product offering is always preferable to a weakly differentiated one. A differentiation strategy calls for a customer value proposition that is *unique*. The strategy achieves its aim when an attractively large number of buyers find the customer value proposition appealing and become strongly attached to a company's differentiated attributes.

Successful differentiation allows a firm to do one or more of the following:

- Command a premium price for its product.
- Increase unit sales (because additional buyers are won over by the differentiating features).
- Gain buyer loyalty to its brand (because some buyers are strongly bonded to the differentiating features of the company's product offering).

Differentiation enhances profitability whenever a company's product can command a sufficiently higher price or produce sufficiently bigger unit sales *to more than cover the added costs of achieving the differentiation.* Company differentiation strategies fail when buyers don't value the brand's uniqueness and/or when a company's approach to differentiation is easily copied or matched by its rivals.

Companies can pursue differentiation from many angles: a unique taste (Red Bull); multiple features (Microsoft Office, the iPhone); superior service (FedEx); engineering design and performance (Mercedes, BMW); prestige and distinctiveness (Rolex); product reliability (Johnson & Johnson in baby products); quality manufacture (Michelin in tires, Honda in automobiles); technological leadership (3M Corporation in bonding and coating products); a full range of services (ING in banking, investments, and insurance); wide product selection (Ikea, Amazon.com); and high fashion design (Gucci and Chanel).

CORE CONCEPT

The essence of a **broad differentiation strategy** is to offer unique product attributes that a wide range of buyers find appealing and worth paying for.

Managing the Value Chain to Create the Differentiating Attributes

Differentiation is not something hatched in marketing and advertising departments, nor is it limited to the catchalls of quality and service. Differentiation opportunities can exist in activities all along an industry's value chain. The most systematic approach that managers can take, however, involves focusing on the **uniqueness drivers,** a set of factors—analogous to cost drivers—that are particularly effective in creating differentiation. Figure 5.3 contains a list of important uniqueness drivers. Ways that managers can enhance differentiation based on these drivers include the following:

CORE CONCEPT

A **uniqueness driver** is a factor that can have a strong differentiating effect.

1. *Striving to create superior product features, design, and performance.* This applies to the physical and well as functional attributes of a product, including features such as expanded end uses and applications, added user safety, greater recycling capability, or enhanced environmental protection. Design features can be important in enhancing the aesthetic appeal of a product. Ducati's motorcycles, for example, are prized for their designs and have been exhibited in the Guggenheim art museum in New York City.[5]

Figure 5.3   Uniqueness Drivers: The Keys to Creating a Differentiation Advantage

Source: Adapted from M. Porter, *Competitive Advantage: Creating and Sustaining Competitive Advantage* (New York: Free Press, 1985).

2. *Improving customer service or adding additional services.* Better customer services, in areas such as delivery, returns, and repair, can be as important in creating differentiation as superior product features. Examples include superior technical assistance to buyers, higher-quality maintenance services, more and better product information provided to customers, more and better training materials for end users, better credit terms, quicker order processing, or greater customer convenience.

3. *Pursuing production R&D activities.* Engaging in production R&D may permit custom-order manufacture at an efficient cost, provide wider product variety and selection through product "versioning," improve product quality, or make production methods safer for the environment. Many manufacturers have developed flexible manufacturing systems that allow different models and product versions to be made on the same assembly line. Being able to provide buyers with made-to-order products can be a potent differentiating capability.

4. *Striving for innovation and technological advances.* Successful innovation is the route to more frequent first-on-the-market victories and is a powerful differentiator. If the innovation proves hard to replicate, through patent protection or other means, it can provide a company with a first mover advantage that is sustainable.

5. *Pursuing continuous quality improvement.* Perceived quality differences can be an important differentiator in the eyes of customers. Quality control processes can be applied throughout the value chain, including postsale customer service activities. They can reduce product defects, prevent premature product failure, extend product life, make it economical to offer longer warranty

coverage, improve economy of use, result in more end-user convenience, or enhance product appearance. Companies whose quality management systems meet certification standards, such as the ISO 9001 standards, can enhance their reputation for quality with customers.

6. *Increasing the intensity of marketing and sales activities.* Marketing and advertising can have a tremendous effect on the value perceived by buyers and therefore their willingness to pay more for the company's offerings. They can create differentiation even when little tangible differentiation exists otherwise. For example, blind taste tests show that even the most loyal Pepsi or Coke drinkers have trouble telling one cola drink from another.[6] Brands create customer loyalty, which increases the perceived "cost" of switching to another product. Brand management activities are therefore also important in supporting differentiation.

7. *Seeking out high-quality inputs.* Input quality can ultimately spill over to affect the performance or quality of the company's end product. Starbucks, for example, gets high ratings on its coffees partly because it has very strict specifications on the coffee beans purchased from suppliers.

8. *Improving employee skill, knowledge, and experience through human resource management activities.* Hiring, training, and retaining highly skilled and experienced employees is important since such employees are often the source of creative, innovative ideas that are behind new product development. Moreover, they are essential to performing differentiating activities such as design, engineering, marketing, and R&D. Company culture and reward systems can help unleash the potential contribution of high-value employees to a differentiation strategy.

Managers need keen understanding of the sources of differentiation and the activities that drive uniqueness to evaluate various differentiation approaches and design durable ways to set their product offering apart from rival brands.

Revamping the Value Chain System to Increase Differentiation

Just as pursuing a cost advantage can involve the entire value chain system, the same is true for a differentiation advantage. Activities performed upstream by suppliers or downstream by distributors and retailers can have a meaningful effect on customers' perceptions of a company's offerings and its value proposition. Approaches to enhancing differentiation through changes in the value chain system include:[7]

• *Coordinating with channel allies to enhance customer perceptions of value.* Coordinating with downstream partners such as distributors, dealers, brokers, and retailers can contribute to differentiation in a variety of ways. Methods that companies use to influence the value chain activities of their channel allies include setting standards for downstream partners to follow, providing them with templates to standardize the selling environment or practices, training channel personnel, or cosponsoring promotions and advertising campaigns. Coordinating with retailers is important for enhancing the buying experience and building a company's image. Coordinating with distributors or shippers can mean quicker delivery to customers, more accurate order filling, and/or lower shipping costs. The Coca-Cola Company considers coordination with its bottler/distributors so important that it has at times taken over a troubled bottler for the purpose of improving its management and upgrading its plant and equipment before releasing the product to the market.[8]

- *Coordinating with suppliers to better address customer needs.* Collaborating with suppliers can also be a powerful route to a more effective differentiation strategy. Coordinating and collaborating with suppliers can improve many dimensions affecting product features and quality. This is particularly true for companies that only engage in assembly operations, such as Dell in PCs and Ducati in motorcycles. Close coordination with suppliers can also enhance differentiation by speeding up new product development cycles or speeding delivery to end customers. Strong relationships with suppliers can also mean that the company's supply requirements are prioritized when industry supply is insufficient to meet overall demand.

Delivering Superior Value via a Broad Differentiation Strategy

Differentiation strategies depend on meeting customer needs in unique ways or creating new needs, through activities such as innovation or persuasive advertising. The objective is to offer customers something that rivals can't—at least in terms of the level of satisfaction. There are four basic routes to achieving this aim.

The first route is to incorporate product attributes and user features that *lower the buyer's overall costs* of using the company's product. This is the least obvious and most overlooked route to a differentiation advantage. It is a differentiating factor since it can help business buyers be more competitive in their markets and more profitable. Producers of materials and components often win orders for their products by reducing a buyer's raw-material waste (providing cut-to-size components), reducing a buyer's inventory requirements (providing just-in-time deliveries), using online systems to reduce a buyer's procurement and order processing costs, and providing free technical support. This route to differentiation can also appeal to individual consumers who are looking to economize on their overall costs of consumption. Making a company's product more economical for a buyer to use can be done by incorporating energy-efficient features (energy-saving appliances and lightbulbs help cut buyers' utility bills; fuel-efficient vehicles cut buyer costs for gasoline) and/or by increasing maintenance intervals and product reliability so as to lower buyer costs for maintenance and repairs.

A second route is to incorporate *tangible* features that increase customer satisfaction with the product, such as product specifications, functions, and styling. This can be accomplished by including attributes that add functionality, enhance the design, expand the range of uses, save time for the user, are more reliable, or make the product cleaner, safer, quieter, simpler to use, portable, more convenient, or longer-lasting than rival brands. Mobile phone manufacturers are in a race to introduce next-generation devices capable of being used for more purposes and having simpler menu functionality.

A third route to a differentiation-based competitive advantage is to incorporate *intangible* features that enhance buyer satisfaction in noneconomic ways. Toyota's Prius appeals to environmentally conscious motorists not only because these drivers want to help reduce global carbon dioxide emissions but also because they identify with the image conveyed. Rolls-Royce, Ralph Lauren, Tiffany, Rolex, and Prada have differentiation-based competitive advantages linked to buyer desires for status, image, prestige, upscale fashion, superior craftsmanship, and the finer things in life.

> Differentiation can be based on *tangible* or *intangible* attributes.

Intangibles that contribute to differentiation can extend beyond product attributes to the reputation of the company and to customer relations or trust.

The fourth route is to *signal the value* of the company's product offering to buyers. Typical signals of value include a high price (in instances where high price implies high quality and performance), more appealing or fancier packaging than competing products, ad content that emphasizes a product's standout attributes, the quality of brochures and sales presentations, the luxuriousness and ambience of a seller's facilities (important for high-end retailers and for offices or other facilities frequented by customers). They make potential buyers aware of the professionalism, appearance, and personalities of the seller's employees and/or make potential buyers realize that a company has prestigious customers. Signaling value is particularly important (1) when the nature of differentiation is based on intangible features and is therefore subjective or hard to quantify, (2) when buyers are making a first-time purchase and are unsure what their experience with the product will be, and (3) when repurchase is infrequent and buyers need to be reminded of a product's value.

Regardless of the approach taken, achieving a successful differentiation strategy requires, first, that the company have strengths in capabilities, such as customer service, marketing, brand management, and technology, that can create and support differentiation. That is, the resources, competencies, and value chain activities of the company must be well matched to the requirements of the strategy. For the strategy to result in competitive advantage, the company's competencies must also be sufficiently unique in delivering value to buyers that they help set its product offering apart from those of rivals. They must be competitively superior. There are numerous examples of companies that have differentiated themselves on the basis of distinctive competencies and capabilities. Apple has set itself apart from rivals on the basis of its capabilities to develop innovative new products and speed next-generation products to market ahead of competitors. When a major new event occurs, many people turn to Sky News and BBC because they have the capability to devote more airtime to breaking news stories and get reporters on the scene very quickly. Avon has differentiated itself from other cosmetics and personal care companies by assembling a sales force numbering in the hundreds of thousands that gives it a direct sales capability—its sales associates personally demonstrate products to interested buyers, take their orders on the spot, and deliver the items to buyers' homes.

The most successful approaches to differentiation are those that are hard or expensive for rivals to duplicate. Indeed, this is the route to a sustainable differentiation advantage. While resourceful competitors can, in time, clone almost any tangible product attribute, socially complex intangible attributes, such as company reputation, long-standing relationships with buyers, and image are much harder to imitate. Differentiation that creates switching costs that lock in buyers also provides a route to sustainable advantage. For example, if a buyer makes a substantial investment in learning to use one type of system, that buyer is less likely to switch to a competitor's system. (This has kept many users from switching away from Microsoft Office products, despite the fact that there are other applications with superior features.) As

Easy-to-copy differentiating features cannot produce sustainable competitive advantage.

a rule, differentiation yields a longer-lasting and more profitable competitive edge when it is based on a well-established brand image, patent-protected product innovation, complex technical superiority, a reputation for superior product quality and reliability, relationship-based customer service, and unique competitive capabilities. Such differentiating attributes are generally tougher and take longer for rivals to match, and buyers widely perceive them as offering superior value.

When a Differentiation Strategy Works Best

Differentiation strategies tend to work best in market circumstances where:

- *Buyer needs and uses of the product are diverse.* Diverse buyer preferences present competitors with a bigger window of opportunity to do things differently and set themselves apart with product attributes that appeal to particular buyers. For instance, the diversity of consumer preferences for menu selection, ambience, pricing, and customer service gives restaurants exceptionally wide latitude in creating a differentiated product offering. Similar opportunities exist for the publishers of magazines, the makers of motor vehicles, and the manufacturers of cabinetry and countertops.

- *There are many ways to differentiate the product or service that have value to buyers.* There's plenty of room for retail apparel competitors to stock different styles and quality of apparel merchandise but very little room for the makers of paper clips or copier paper or sugar to set their products apart. Likewise, the sellers of different brands of gasoline or orange juice have little differentiation opportunity compared to the sellers of high-definition TVs or patio furniture or breakfast cereal. Basic commodities, such as chemicals, mineral deposits, and agricultural products, provide few opportunities for differentiation.

- *Few rival firms are following a similar differentiation approach.* The best differentiation approaches involve trying to appeal to buyers on the basis of attributes that rivals are not emphasizing. A differentiator encounters less head-to-head rivalry when it goes its own separate way in creating uniqueness and does not try to outdifferentiate rivals on the very same attributes. When many rivals are all claiming "ours tastes better than theirs" or "ours gets your clothes cleaner than theirs," the most likely result is weak brand differentiation and "strategy overcrowding"— competitors end up chasing much the same buyers with much the same product offerings.

- *Technological change is fast-paced and competition revolves around rapidly evolving product features.* Rapid product innovation and frequent introductions of next-version products not only provide space for companies to pursue separate differentiating paths but also heighten buyer interest. In video game hardware and video games, golf equipment, PCs, and smartphones, competitors are locked into an ongoing battle to set themselves apart by introducing the best next-generation products; companies that fail to come up with new and improved products and distinctive performance features quickly lose out in the marketplace. In U.S. network TV broadcasting, NBC, ABC, CBS, Fox, and several others are always scrambling to develop a lineup of TV shows that will win higher audience ratings and pave the way for charging higher advertising rates and boosting ad revenues.

Pitfalls to Avoid in Pursuing a Differentiation Strategy

Differentiation strategies can fail for any of several reasons. *A differentiation strategy is always doomed when competitors are able to quickly copy most or all of the appealing product attributes a company comes up with.* Rapid imitation means that no rival achieves differentiation, since whenever one firm introduces some aspect of uniqueness that strikes the fancy of buyers, fast-following copycats quickly reestablish similarity. This is

Any differentiating feature that works well is a magnet for imitators, although imitation attempts are not always successful.

why a firm must seek out sources of uniqueness that are time-consuming or burdensome for rivals to match if it hopes to use differentiation to win a lasting competitive edge over rivals.

A second pitfall is that *the company's attempt at differentiation produces an unenthusiastic response on the part of buyers.* Thus even if a company succeeds in setting its product apart from those of rivals, its strategy can result in disappointing sales and profits if buyers find other brands more appealing. Any time many potential buyers look at a company's differentiated product offering and conclude "so what," the company's differentiation strategy is in deep trouble.

The third big pitfall of a differentiation strategy is *overspending on efforts to differentiate the company's product offering, thus eroding profitability.* Company efforts to achieve differentiation nearly always raise costs, often substantially since marketing and R&D are expensive undertakings. The trick to profitable differentiation is either to keep the unit cost of achieving differentiation below the price premium that the differentiating attributes can command in the marketplace (thus increasing the profit margin per unit sold) or to offset thinner profit margins per unit by selling enough additional units to increase total profits. If a company goes overboard in pursuing costly differentiation efforts and then unexpectedly discovers that buyers are unwilling to pay a sufficient price premium to cover the added costs of differentiation, it ends up saddled with unacceptably thin profit margins or even losses. The need to contain differentiation costs is why many companies add little touches of differentiation that add to buyer satisfaction but are inexpensive to institute. Upscale restaurants often provide valet parking. Laundry detergent and soap manufacturers add pleasing scents to their products. Ski resorts provide skiers with complimentary coffee or hot apple cider at the base of the lifts in the morning and late afternoon.

Other common mistakes in crafting a differentiation strategy include:[9]

- *Being timid and not striving to open up meaningful gaps in quality, service, or performance features vis-à-vis the products of rivals.* Tiny differences between rivals' product offerings may not be visible or important to buyers. If a company wants to generate the fiercely loyal customer following needed to earn superior profits and open up a differentiation-based competitive advantage over rivals, then its strategy must result in *strong rather than weak product differentiation.* In markets where differentiators do no better than achieve weak product differentiation (because the attributes of rival brands are fairly similar in the minds of many buyers), customer loyalty to any one brand is weak, the costs of brand switching are fairly low, and no one company has enough of a market edge that it can get by with charging a price premium over rival brands.

- *Adding so many frills and extra features that the product exceeds the needs and use patterns of most buyers.* A dazzling array of features and options not only drives up costs (and therefore product price) but also runs the risk that many buyers will conclude that a less deluxe and lower-priced brand is a better value since they have little occasion or reason to use some of the deluxe attributes.

  - *Charging too high a price premium.* While buyers may be intrigued by a product's deluxe features, they may nonetheless see it as being overpriced relative to the value delivered by the differentiating attributes. A company must guard against turning off would-be buyers with what is perceived as "price gouging." Normally, the bigger the price premium for the differentiating extras, the harder it is to keep buyers from switching to the lower-priced offerings of competitors.

> Overdifferentiating and overcharging can be fatal strategy mistakes.

A low-cost provider strategy can defeat a differentiation strategy when buyers are sat-
isfied with a basic product and don't think "extra" attributes are worth a higher price.

FOCUSED (OR MARKET NICHE) STRATEGIES

What sets focused strategies apart from low-cost provider and broad differentiation strategies is concentrated attention on a narrow piece of the total market. The
target segment, or niche, can be defined by geographic uniqueness, by specialized
requirements in using the product, or by special product attributes that appeal
only to niche members. Examples of firms that concentrate on a well-defined
market niche keyed to a particular product or buyer segment include Motobecane
(in racing bicycles); eBay (in online auctioning); Aston Martin (in automobiles);
Red Bull GmbH (in energy drinks); and Facebook (in social networking). Local
owner–managed hotels, restaurants, and retail boutiques have also scaled their
operations to serve narrow or local customer segments.

A Focused Low-Cost Strategy

A focused strategy based on low cost aims at securing a competitive advantage by
serving buyers in the target market niche at a lower cost and lower price than those
of rival competitors. This strategy has considerable attraction when a firm can lower
costs significantly by limiting its customer base to a well-defined buyer segment.
The avenues to achieving a cost advantage over rivals also serving the target market
niche are the same as those for low-cost leadership: outmanage rivals in keeping the
costs of value chain activities contained to a bare minimum and search for innovative ways to bypass certain value chain activities. The only real difference between
a low-cost provider strategy and a focused low-cost strategy is the size of the buyer
group that a company is trying to appeal to—the former involves a product offering
that appeals broadly to almost all buyer groups and market segments, whereas the
latter aims at just meeting the needs of buyers in a narrow market segment.

Focused low-cost strategies are fairly common. Producers of private-label
goods are able to achieve low costs in product development, marketing, distribution, and advertising by concentrating on making generic items imitative of
name-brand merchandise and selling directly to retail chains wanting a low-priced
store brand. The Perrigo Company has become a leading manufacturer of over-
the-counter health care products, with 2010 sales of more than $2.2 billion, by
focusing on producing private-label brands for U.S. retailers such as Walmart,
CVS, Walgreens, Rite-Aid, and Safeway. Budget motel chains, like Hometel in
India, cater to price-conscious travelers who just want to pay for a clean, no-frills
place to spend the night. Illustration Capsule 5.2 describes how Vizio's low costs
and focus on big-box retailers has allowed it to become the largest seller of flat-
panel HDTVs in the United States in less than six years from its startup.

A Focused Differentiation Strategy

A focused strategy keyed to differentiation aims at securing a competitive advantage with a product offering carefully designed to appeal to the unique preferences and needs of a narrow, well-defined group of buyers (as opposed to a broad

differentiation strategy aimed at many buyer groups and market segments). Successful use of a focused differentiation strategy depends on the existence of a buyer segment that is looking for special product attributes or seller capabilities and on a firm's ability to stand apart from rivals competing in the same target market niche.

Companies like Godiva Chocolates, Rolls-Royce, Haägen-Dazs, and W. L. Gore (the maker of Gore-Tex) employ successful differentiation-based focused strategies targeted at upscale buyers wanting products and services with world-class attributes. Indeed, most markets contain a buyer segment willing to pay a big price premium for the very finest items available, thus opening the strategic window for some competitors to pursue differentiation-based focused strategies aimed at the very top of the market pyramid. Ferrari markets its 1,500 cars sold in North America each year to a list of just 20,000 highly affluent car enthusiasts. Only the highest echelon of this exclusive group were contacted by Ferrari for a chance to put their names on the waiting list for one of the 29 $1.9 million FXX models planned for sale in North America.

Another successful focused differentiator is "fashion food retailer" Trader Joe's, a 300-store, 25-state chain that is a combination gourmet deli and food warehouse. Customers shop Trader Joe's as much for entertainment as for conventional grocery items—the store stocks out-of-the-ordinary culinary treats like raspberry salsa, salmon burgers, and jasmine fried rice, as well as the standard goods normally found in supermarkets. What sets Trader Joe's apart is not just its unique combination of food novelties and competitively priced grocery items but also its capability to turn an otherwise mundane grocery excursion into a whimsical treasure hunt that is just plain fun. Illustration Capsule 5.3 describes Nestlé's focused differentiation strategy for Nespresso.

When a Focused Low-Cost or Focused Differentiation Strategy Is Attractive

A focused strategy aimed at securing a competitive edge based either on low cost or differentiation becomes increasingly attractive as more of the following conditions are met:

- The target market niche is big enough to be profitable and offers good growth potential.
- Industry leaders do not see that having a presence in the niche is crucial to their own success—in which case focusers can often escape battling head to head against some of the industry's biggest and strongest competitors.
- It is costly or difficult for multisegment competitors to put capabilities in place to meet the specialized needs of buyers constituting the target market niche and at the same time satisfy the expectations of their mainstream customers.
- The industry has many different niches and segments, thereby allowing a focuser to pick a competitively attractive niche suited to its most valuable resources and capabilities. Also, with more niches there is more room for focusers to avoid each other in competing for the same customers.
- Few, if any, other rivals are attempting to specialize in the same target segment—a condition that reduces the risk of segment overcrowding.
- The focuser has a reservoir of customer goodwill and loyalty (accumulated from having catered to the specialized needs and preferences of niche members over many years) that it can draw on to help stave off ambitious challengers looking to horn in on its business.

California-based Vizio, Inc., designs flat-panel LCD and plasma TVs that range in size from 20 to 55 inches and are sold only by big-box discount retailers such as Walmart, Sam's Club, Costco Wholesale, and Best Buy. If you've shopped for a flat-panel TV recently, you've probably noticed that Vizio is among the lowest-priced brands and that its picture quality is surprisingly good considering the price. The company is able to keep its cost low by only designing TVs and then sourcing its production to a limited number of contract manufacturers in Taiwan. In fact, 80 percent of its production is handled by a company called AmTran Technology. Such a dependence on a supplier can place a buyer in a precarious situation by making it vulnerable to price increases or product shortages, but Vizio has countered this possible threat by making AmTran a major stockholder. AmTran Technology owns a 23 percent stake in Vizio and earns about 80 percent of its revenues from its sales of televisions to Vizio. Vizio's close relationship with its major supplier and its focus on a single product category sold through limited distribution channels allows it to offer its customers deep price discounts.

Vizio's first major account was landed in 2003 when it approached buyers for Costco with a 46-inch plasma TV whose wholesale price was half that of the next lowest-price competitor. Within two months, Costco was carrying Vizio flat-panel TVs in 320 of its warehouse stores in the United States. In October 2007, Vizio approached buyers for Sam's Club with a 20-inch LCD TV that could be sold at retail for under $350. The price and quality of the 20-inch TV led Sam's Club buyers to place an order for 20,000 TVs for March 2008 delivery. By 2009, Vizio had become the largest seller of flat-panel HDTVs in the United States, with a market share of 21.6 percent.

Sources: "Picture Shift: U.S. Upstart Takes On TV Giants in Price War," Wall Street Journal, April 15, 2008, p. A1; Vizio, Inc., "Vizio Achieves #1 LCD HDTV Ranking in North America and #1 Ranking in U.S. Flat Panel HDTV Shipments," press release, May 11, 2009.

The advantages of focusing a company's entire competitive effort on a single market niche are considerable, especially for smaller and medium-size companies that may lack the breadth and depth of resources to tackle going after a broad customer base with a "something for everyone" lineup of models, styles, and product selection. YouTube has become a household name by concentrating on short video clips posted online. Papa John's and Domino's Pizza have created impressive businesses by focusing on the home delivery segment. Porsche and Ferrari have done well catering to wealthy sports car enthusiasts.

The Risks of a Focused Low-Cost or Focused Differentiation Strategy

Focusing carries several risks. One is the chance that competitors will find effective ways to match the focused firm's capabilities in serving the target niche—perhaps by coming up with products or brands specifically designed to appeal to buyers in the target niche or by developing expertise and capabilities that offset the focuser's strengths. In the lodging business, large chains like Accor have launched multibrand strategies that allow them to compete effectively in several

Nestlé's strategy in the gourmet coffee industry has allowed its Nespresso brand of espresso coffee to become the fastest growing billion dollar brand in its broad lineup of chocolates and confectionery, bottled waters, coffee, ready-to-eat cereals, frozen food, dairy products, ice cream, and baby foods. The Nespresso concept was developed in 1986 to allow consumers to create a perfect cup of espresso coffee, equal to that of a skilled barista, with the use of a proprietary line of coffee makers designed to accommodate Nespresso's single-serving coffee capsules. Nespresso capsules are available in 16 different roasts and aromatic profiles and can be purchased online at Nestlé's Nespresso Club Web site, in any of Nestlé's 200 lavish Nespresso boutiques located in the world's most exclusive shopping districts, and in select upscale retailers across the globe. Nespresso coffee machines are designed for ease-of-use while having advanced technological features that maximize the aroma of the coffee and automate the entire process even down to creating a thick and creamy froth from cold milk for cappuccinos. Nespresso coffee makers also set standards for aesthetics with classic, sleek models, avant-garde models, and retro-modern models.

The ease-of-use of the stylish Nespresso coffee makers and the high quality coffee selected by Nestlé for its single-serving coffee pods allow coffee drinkers with little experience in preparing gourmet coffees to master great-tasting lattes, cappuccinos, and espresso drinks. Nespresso was sold in more than 50 countries in 2011 and had averaged annual growth in revenues of 30 percent since 2000 to reach sales of more than $3 billion Swiss Francs in 2010.

Nestlé's focused differentiation strategy for Nespresso includes the following primary elements:

- **Unsurpassed product quality and proven coffee expertise**—Through its unique business model, Nespresso has the ability to guarantee highest quality at every stage of the coffee value chain. Nespresso's team of passionate green coffee experts, agronomists, and supply partners regularly crisscross the globe in search of highest quality beans from specialty farms in the finest countries of origin. They in turn work with a variety of other Nespresso coffee experts including coffee sensory, aroma and flavor experts who create the exquisite Nespresso Grand Crus at state-of-the-art coffee production facilities in Orbe and Avenches, Switzerland.

- **Unstoppable drive for innovation and distinctive design**—Obsessed about innovation, compulsive about the fine details and passionate about the fusion between technology and design, the Nespresso in-house Research and Development Team has pioneered many award winning machine innovations and cutting edge designs, in collaboration with external design and machine experts. These breakthroughs have resulted in more than 1,700 patents.

- **Inspirational, iconic global reputation of the brand**—Nespresso is continually infusing itself with original ideas, flavors and innovations from around the world to define its own unique lifestyle. Its journey toward becoming an iconic brand has made it a well recognized, loved and respected reference for highest quality around the world. Through Nespresso's network of more than 200 exclusive boutiques in key cities around the world, coffee lovers can come together to experience the brand with all senses, such as tasting Nespresso's luxurious coffees or learning more about the coffee countries of origin. These stylish sanctuaries are the perfect destinations for people who love the very best coffee.

- **Global brand community thanks to direct customer relationships**—Much of the success Nespresso has enjoyed in recent years can be attributed to the privileged relationships the brand has developed with its consumers and the reciprocal enthusiasm consumers have consistently shown for the brand. Currently, more than 50% of all new Nespresso Club Members first experience the brand through existing members. Between 2001 and 2009, the number of Nespresso Club Members worldwide has jumped from 600,000 to more than 6 million.

- **Exclusive routes-to-market**—The unique Nespresso business model enables the company to maintain direct relationships with its customers

(continued)

through three channels: a global Internet boutique available 24/7 at http://www.nespresso.com; a global retail boutique network, which gives consumers the opportunity to experience the brand with all senses; and Customer Relationship Centers which help consumers connect with friendly coffee specialists by phone.

- **Expertise in Sustainable Quality development**—Nespresso and its key suppliers work closely with more than 30,000 farmers who are part of the AAA Sustainable Quality™ Program to ensure they are implementing farming practices that lead to highest quality beans and economic viability, whilst respecting the environment. Coffee farmers who are part of the program are rewarded not only with higher compensation but also with a long-term partnership with Nespresso. Approximately 50% of the coffee Nespresso buys is AAA Sustainable Quality™.

Source: Nestlé press releases, June 9, 2009, September 21, 2009 and August 11, 2010.

lodging segments simultaneously. Accor has 120 Sofitel luxury hotels on all five continents that offer business travelers and vacationers elegant accommodations and world-class service; its 15 Thalassa sea & spa resorts are among the finest resorts in the Mediterranean; Pullman, MGallery, and Grand Mercure offer travelers upscale amenities in prime locations around the world; Novotel and Mercure midscale hotels are located in nearly 50 countries and offer a comfortable setting and personalized service to business and leisure travelers; ibis is the worldwide economy hotel brand of Accor with 879 hotels in 45 countries; and its Etap hotels in Europe, its Formule1 hotels in the southern hemisphere, and Motel 6 hotels in the U.S. and Canada offer budget-minded travelers affordable rates and comfortable rooms. Multibrand strategies are attractive to large companies like Accor precisely because they enable a company to enter a market niche and siphon business away from companies that employ a focused strategy.

A second risk of employing a focused strategy is the potential for the preferences and needs of niche members to shift over time toward the product attributes desired by the majority of buyers. An erosion of the differences across buyer segments lowers entry barriers into a focuser's market niche and provides an open invitation for rivals in adjacent segments to begin competing for the focuser's customers. A third risk is that the segment may become so attractive that it is soon inundated with competitors, intensifying rivalry and splintering segment profits.

BEST-COST PROVIDER STRATEGIES

Best-cost provider strategies stake out a middle ground between pursuing a low-cost advantage and a differentiation advantage and between appealing to the broad market as a whole and a narrow market niche—see Figure 5.1. Such a middle ground allows a company to aim squarely at the sometimes great mass of value-conscious buyers looking for a good to very good product or service at an economical price. Value-conscious buyers frequently shy away from both cheap low-end products and expensive high-end products, but they are quite willing to pay a "fair" price for extra

LO 4

Recognize the attributes of a best-cost provider strategy and the way in which some firms use a hybrid strategy to go about building a competitive advantage and delivering superior value to customers.

features and functionality they find appealing and useful. The essence of a best-cost provider strategy is giving customers more *value for the money* by satisfying buyer desires for appealing features/performance/quality/service and charging a lower price for these attributes compared to rivals with similar caliber product offerings.[10] From a competitive-positioning standpoint, best-cost strategies are thus a *hybrid,* balancing a strategic emphasis on low cost against a strategic emphasis on differentiation (desirable features delivered at a relatively low price).

To profitably employ a best-cost provider strategy, a company *must have the resources and capabilities to incorporate attractive or upscale attributes into its product offering at a lower cost than rivals.* When a company can incorporate appealing features, good to excellent product performance or quality, or more satisfying customer service into its product offering *at a lower cost than rivals,* then it enjoys "best-cost" status—it is the low-cost provider of a product or service with *desirable attributes.* A best-cost provider can use its low-cost advantage to underprice rivals whose products or services have similarly desirable attributes and still earn attractive profits. It is usually not difficult to entice buyers away from rivals with an equally good product at a more economical price.

Being a best-cost provider is different from being a low-cost provider because the additional attractive attributes entail additional costs (which a low-cost provider can avoid by offering buyers a basic product with few frills). Moreover, the two strategies aim at a distinguishably different market target. *The target market for a best-cost provider is value-conscious buyers*—buyers who are looking for appealing extras and functionality at an appealingly low price. Value-hunting buyers (as distinct from *price-conscious buyers* looking for a basic product at a bargain-basement price) often constitute a very sizable part of the overall market. Normally, value-conscious buyers are willing to pay a "fair" price for extra features, but they shy away from paying top dollar for items having all the bells and whistles. It is the desire to cater to *value-conscious buyers* as opposed to *budget-conscious buyers* that sets a best-cost provider apart from a low-cost provider—the two strategies aim at distinguishably different market targets.

When a Best-Cost Provider Strategy Works Best

A best-cost provider strategy works best in markets where product differentiation is the norm and there is an attractively large number of value-conscious buyers who prefer midrange products to cheap, basic products or expensive top-of-the-line products. A best-cost provider needs to position itself near the middle of the market with either a medium-quality product at a below-average price or a high-quality product at an average or slightly higher price. The objective is to provide the *best value* for better-quality, differentiated products. Best-cost provider strategies also work well in recessionary times when great masses of buyers become value-conscious and are attracted to economically priced products and services with appealing attributes. *But unless a company has the resources, know-how, and capabilities to incorporate upscale product or service attributes at a lower cost than rivals, adopting a best-cost strategy is ill-advised*—a winning strategy must always be matched to a company's most valuable resources and capabilities.

Illustration Capsule 5.4 describes how Toyota has applied the principles of the best-cost provider strategy in producing and marketing its Lexus brand.

ILLUSTRATION CAPSULE 5.4

Toyota's Best-Cost Provider Strategy for Its Lexus Line

Toyota Motor Company is widely regarded as a low-cost producer among the world's motor vehicle manufacturers. Despite its emphasis on product quality, Toyota has achieved low-cost leadership because it has developed considerable skills in efficient supply chain management and low-cost assembly capabilities and because its models are positioned in the low-to-medium end of the price spectrum, where high production volumes are conducive to low unit costs. But when Toyota decided to introduce its new Lexus models to compete in the luxury-car market segment, it employed a classic best-cost provider strategy. Toyota took the following four steps in crafting and implementing its Lexus strategy:

- Designing an array of high-performance characteristics and upscale features into the Lexus models to make them comparable in performance and luxury to other high-end models and attractive to Mercedes, BMW, Audi, Jaguar, Cadillac, and Lincoln buyers.

- Transferring its capabilities in making high-quality Toyota models at low cost to making premium-quality Lexus models at costs below other luxury-car makers. Toyota's supply chain capabilities and low-cost assembly know-how allowed it to incorporate high-tech performance features and upscale quality into Lexus models at substantially less cost than Mercedes, BMW, and other luxury-vehicle makers have been able to achieve in producing their models.

- Using its relatively lower manufacturing costs to underprice comparable Mercedes, BMW, Audi, and Jaguar models. Toyota believed that with its cost advantage it could price attractively equipped Lexus cars low enough to draw price-conscious buyers away from comparable high-end brands. Toyota's pricing policy also allowed it to induce Toyota, Honda, Ford, or GM owners desiring more luxury to switch to a Lexus. Lexus's pricing advantage has typically been quite significant. For example, in 2009 the Lexus RX 350, a midsize SUV, carried a sticker price in the $38,000 to $48,000 range (depending on how it was equipped), whereas comparable Mercedes M-class SUVs had price tags in the $45,000 to $63,000 range and a comparable BMW X5 SUV could range anywhere from $47,000 to $65,000.

- Establishing a new network of Lexus dealers, separate from Toyota dealers, dedicated to providing a level of personalized, attentive customer service unmatched in the industry.

Toyota's best-cost strategy has resulted in growing sales of Lexus models (now over 400,000 vehicles annually). Lexus has consistently ranked first in the widely watched J. D. Power & Associates quality survey, and Lexus owners enjoy both top-notch dealer service and product quality.

The Big Risk of a Best-Cost Provider Strategy

A company's biggest vulnerability in employing a best-cost provider strategy is getting squeezed between the strategies of firms using low-cost and high-end differentiation strategies. Low-cost providers may be able to siphon customers away with the appeal of a lower price (despite less appealing product attributes). High-end differentiators may be able to steal customers away with the appeal of better product attributes (even though their products carry a higher price tag). Thus, to be successful, a best-cost provider must offer buyers *significantly* better product attributes in order to justify a price above what low-cost leaders are charging. Likewise, it has to achieve significantly lower costs in providing upscale features so that it can outcompete high-end differentiators on the basis of a *significantly lower price*.

THE CONTRASTING FEATURES OF THE FIVE GENERIC COMPETITIVE STRATEGIES: A SUMMARY

Deciding which generic competitive strategy should serve as the framework on which to hang the rest of the company's strategy is not a trivial matter. Each of the five generic competitive strategies *positions* the company differently in its market and competitive environment. Each establishes a central theme for how the company will endeavor to outcompete rivals. Each creates some boundaries or guidelines for maneuvering as market circumstances unfold and as ideas for improving the strategy are debated. Each points to different ways of experimenting and tinkering with the basic strategy—for example, employing a low-cost leadership strategy means experimenting with ways that costs can be cut and value chain activities can be streamlined, whereas a broad differentiation strategy means exploring ways to add new differentiating features or to perform value chain activities differently if the result is to add value for customers in ways they are willing to pay for. Each entails differences in terms of product line, production emphasis, marketing emphasis, and means of maintaining the strategy, as shown in Table 5.1.

Thus a choice of which generic strategy to employ spills over to affect many aspects of how the business will be operated and the manner in which value chain activities must be managed. Deciding which generic strategy to employ is perhaps the most important strategic commitment a company makes—it tends to drive the rest of the strategic actions a company decides to undertake.

Table 5.1   Distinguishing Features of the Five Generic Competitive Strategies

	Low-Cost Provider	Broad Differentiation	Focused Low-Cost Provider	Focused Differentiation	Best-Cost Provider
Strategic target	• A broad cross-section of the market.	• A broad cross-section of the market.	• A narrow market niche where buyer needs and preferences are distinctively different.	• A narrow market niche where buyer needs and preferences are distinctively different.	• Value-conscious buyers. • A middle market range.
Basis of competitive strategy	• Lower overall costs than competitors.	• Ability to offer buyers something attractively different from competitors' offerings.	• Lower overall cost than rivals in serving niche members.	• Attributes that appeal specifically to niche members.	• Ability to offer better goods at attractive prices.

(Continued)

	Low-Cost Provider	Broad Differentiation	Focused Low-Cost Provider	Focused Differentiation	Best-Cost Provider
Product line	• A good basic product with few frills (acceptable quality and limited selection).	• Many product variations, wide selection; emphasis on differentiating features.	• Features and attributes tailored to the tastes and requirements of niche members.	• Features and attributes tailored to the tastes and requirements of niche members.	• Items with appealing attributes; assorted features; better quality, not best.
Production emphasis	• A continuous search for cost reduction without sacrificing acceptable quality and essential features.	• Build in whatever differentiating features buyers are willing to pay for; strive for product superiority.	• A continuous search for cost reduction for products that meet basic needs of niche members.	• Small-scale production or custom-made products that match the tastes and requirements of niche members.	• Build in appealing features and better quality at lower cost than rivals.
Marketing emphasis	• Low prices, good value. • Try to make a virtue out of product features that lead to low cost.	• Tout differentiating features. • Charge a premium price to cover the extra costs of differentiating features.	• Communicate attractive features of a budget-priced product offering that fits niche buyers' expectations.	• Communicate how product offering does the best job of meeting niche buyers' expectations.	• Tout delivery of *best* value. • Either deliver comparable features at a lower price than rivals or else match rivals on prices and provide better features.
Keys to maintaining the strategy	• Economical prices, good value. • Strive to manage costs down, year after year, in every area of the business.	• Stress constant innovation to stay ahead of imitative competitors. • Concentrate on a few key differentiating features.	• Stay committed to serving the niche at the lowest overall cost; don't blur the firm's image by entering other market segments or adding other products to widen market appeal.	• Stay committed to serving the niche better than rivals; don't blur the firm's image by entering other market segments or adding other products to widen market appeal.	• Unique expertise in simultaneously managing costs down while incorporating upscale features and attributes.
Resources and capabilities required	• Capabilities for driving costs out of the value chain system. • *Examples:* large-scale automated plants, an efficiency-oriented culture, bargaining power.	• Capabilities concerning quality, design, intangibles, and innovation. • *Examples:* marketing capabilities, R&D teams, technology.	• Capabilities to lower costs on niche goods. • *Examples:* lower input costs for the specific product desired by the niche, batch production capabilities.	• Capabilities to meet the highly specific needs of niche members. • *Examples:* custom production, close customer relations.	• Capabilities to simultaneously deliver lower cost and higher-quality/differentiated features. • *Examples:* TQM practices, mass customization.

Successful Competitive Strategies Are Resource-Based

A company's competitive strategy is unlikely to succeed unless it is predicated on leveraging a competitively valuable collection of resources and capabilities that match the strategy.

For a company's competitive strategy to succeed in delivering good performance and the intended competitive edge over rivals, it has to be underpinned by an appropriate set of resources, know-how, and competitive capabilities. To succeed in employing a low-cost provider strategy, a company has to have the resources and capabilities needed to keep its costs below those of its competitors; this means having the expertise to cost-effectively manage value chain activities better than rivals and/or having the innovative capability to bypass certain value chain activities being performed by rivals. Successful focused strategies require the capability to do an outstanding job of satisfying the needs and expectations of niche buyers. Success in employing a best-cost strategy requires the resources and capabilities to simultaneously incorporate desirable product or service attributes and deliver them at a lower cost than rivals. To succeed in strongly differentiating its product in ways that are appealing to buyers, a company must have the resources and capabilities to incorporate unique attributes into its product offering that a broad range of buyers will find appealing and worth paying for. This is easier said than done because, given sufficient time, competitors can clone almost any product feature buyers find quite appealing. Hence, long-term differentiation success is usually dependent on having a hard-to-imitate portfolio of resource capabilities (like patented technology; strong, socially complex skills in product innovation; expertise in relationship-based customer service) that allow a company to sustain its differentiation-based competitive advantage. Likewise, sustaining the competitive edge inherent in any generic strategy depends on resources, capabilities, and competences that rivals have a hard time duplicating and for which there are no good substitutes.

KEY POINTS

The key points to take away from this chapter include the following:

1. Deciding which of the five generic competitive strategies to employ—overall low-cost, broad differentiation, focused low-cost, focused differentiation, or best-cost—is perhaps the most important strategic commitment a company makes. It tends to drive the remaining strategic actions a company undertakes and sets the whole tone for pursuing a competitive advantage over rivals.

2. In employing a low-cost provider strategy and trying to achieve a low-cost advantage over rivals, a company must do a better job than rivals of cost-effectively managing value chain activities and/or it must find innovative ways to eliminate cost-producing activities. Low-cost provider strategies work particularly well when the products of rival sellers are virtually identical or very weakly differentiated and supplies are readily available from eager sellers, when there are not many ways to differentiate that have value to buyers, when many buyers are price-sensitive and shop the market for the lowest price, and when buyer switching costs are low.

3. Broad differentiation strategies seek to produce a competitive edge by incorporating tangible and intangible attributes that set a company's product/service offering apart from rivals in ways that buyers consider valuable and worth

paying for. Successful differentiation allows a firm to (1) command a premium price for its product, (2) increase unit sales (because additional buyers are won over by the differentiating features), and/or (3) gain buyer loyalty to its brand (because some buyers are strongly attracted to the differentiating features and bond with the company and its products). Differentiation strategies work best when diverse buyer preferences open up windows of opportunity to strongly differentiate a company's product offering from those of rival brands, in situations where few other rivals are pursuing a similar differentiation approach, and in circumstances where companies are racing to bring out the most appealing next-generation product. A differentiation strategy is doomed when competitors are able to quickly copy most or all of the appealing product attributes a company comes up with, when a company's differentiation efforts fail to interest many buyers, and when a company overspends on efforts to differentiate its product offering or tries to overcharge for its differentiating extras.

4. A focused strategy delivers competitive advantage either by achieving lower costs than rivals in serving buyers constituting the target market niche or by developing a specialized ability to offer niche buyers an appealingly differentiated offering that meets their needs better than rival brands do. A focused strategy based on either low cost or differentiation becomes increasingly attractive when the target market niche is big enough to be profitable and offers good growth potential, when it is costly or difficult for multisegment competitors to put capabilities in place to meet the specialized needs of the target market niche and at the same time satisfy the expectations of their mainstream customers, and when few other rivals are attempting to specialize in the same target segment.

5. Best-cost provider strategies combine a strategic emphasis on low cost with a strategic emphasis on more than minimal quality, service, features, or performance. The aim is to create competitive advantage by giving buyers *more value for the money for midrange products*—an approach that entails (1) matching close rivals on key quality/service/features/performance attributes, (2) beating them on the costs of incorporating such attributes into the product or service, and (3) charging a more economical price. A best-cost provider strategy works best in markets with large numbers of value-conscious buyers desirous of purchasing appealingly good products and services for less money.

6. In all cases, competitive advantage depends on having competitively superior resources and capabilities that are a good match for the chosen generic strategy. A sustainable advantage depends on maintaining that competitive superiority with resources, capabilities, and value chain activities that rivals have trouble matching and for which there are no good substitutes.

ASSURANCE OF LEARNING EXERCISES

LO 1, LO 2

1. Haier is the world's fourth largest appliance manufacturer and one of China's 100 largest companies. The company's four leading product categories—refrigerators, refrigerating cabinets, air conditioners, and washing machines—hold over 30 percent market shares and are available in 12 of the top

15 chain stores in Europe and 10 leading chains stores in the U.S. Review its Corporate Profile at http://www.haier.com/abouthaier/corporateprofile/ and list specific elements of its low cost provider strategy that have yielded its advantage in the marketplace.

LO 3

2. Stihl is the world's leading manufacturer and marketer of chain saws, with annual sales exceeding $2 billion. With innovations dating to its 1929 invention of the gasoline-powered chain saw, the company holds over 1,000 patents related to chain saws and outdoor power tools. The company's chain saws, leaf blowers, and hedge trimmers sell at price points well above competing brands and are sold only by its network of over 8,000 independent dealers. The company boasts in its advertisements that its products are rated number one by consumer magazines and are *not* sold at Lowe's or Home Depot. How does Stihl's choice of distribution channels and advertisements contribute to its differentiation strategy?

LO 3

3. Explore BMW's Web site (www.bmw.com), and then click on the link for www.bmwgroup.com. The site you find provides an overview of the company's key functional areas, including research and development and production activities (see the page headings). Under Research and Development, click on Innovation & Technology and explore the links at the sidebar to better understand the types of resources and capabilities that underlie BMW's approach to innovation. Also review the statements under Production focusing on automobile production worldwide and sustainable production. How do the resources, capabilities, and activities of BMW contribute to its differentiation strategy and the unique position in the industry that it has achieved?

EXERCISES FOR SIMULATION PARTICIPANTS

LO 1, LO 2, LO 3, LO 4

1. Which one of the five generic competitive strategies best characterizes your company's strategic approach to competing successfully?
2. Which rival companies appear to be employing a low-cost provider strategy?
3. Which rival companies appear to be employing a broad differentiation strategy?
4. Which rival companies appear to be employing some type of focused strategy?
5. Which rival companies appear to be employing a best-cost provider strategy?
6. What is your company's action plan to achieve a sustainable competitive advantage over rival companies? List at least three (preferably more) specific kinds of decision entries on specific decision screens that your company has made or intends to make to win this kind of competitive edge over rivals.

ENDNOTES

[1] This classification scheme is an adaptation of a narrower three-strategy classification presented in Michael E. Porter, *Competitive Strategy: Techniques for Analyzing Industries and Competitors* (New York: Free Press, 1980). For a discussion of the different ways that companies can position themselves in the marketplace, see Michael E. Porter, "What Is Strategy?" *Harvard Business Review* 74, no. 6 (November–December 1996), pp. 65–67.

[2] M. Porter, *Competitive Advantage: Creating and Sustaining Superior Performance* (New York: Free Press, 1985), p. 97.

[3] Michael Hammer and James Champy were the main proponents of business process reengineering. See M. Hammer and J. Champy, *Reengineering the Corporation: A Manifesto for Business Revolution,* rev. and updated (New York: HarperBusiness, 2003).

[4] For a discussion of how unique industry positioning and resource combinations are linked to consumers' perspectives of value and their willingness to pay more for differentiated products or services, see Richard L. Priem, "A Consumer Perspective on Value Creation," *Academy of Management Review* 32, no. 1 (2007), pp. 219–35.

[5] G. Gavetti, "Ducati," Harvard Business School case 9-701-132, rev. March 8, 2002.

[6] http://jrscience.wcp.muohio.edu/nsfall01/FinalArticles/Final-IsitWorthitBrandsan.html.

[7] This section expands on the section on value chain linkages found in Porter, *Competitive Advantage,* p. 125.

[8] D. Yoffie, "Cola Wars Continue: Coke and Pepsi in 2006," Harvard Business School case 9-706-447.

[9] Porter, *Competitive Advantage,* pp. 160–62.

[10] For an excellent discussion of best-cost provider strategies, see Peter J. Williamson and Ming Zeng, "Value-for-Money Strategies for Recessionary Times," *Harvard Business Review* 87, no. 3 (March 2009), pp. 66–74.

CHAPTER 6

STRENGTHENING A COMPANY'S COMPETITIVE POSITION

Strategic Moves, Timing, and Scope of Operations

> Competing in the marketplace is like war. You have injuries and casualties, and the best strategy wins.
>
> **—John Collins**
> *NHL executive*

> It was our duty to expand.
>
> **—Ingvar Kamprad**
> *Founder of IKEA*

> In the virtual economy, collaboration is a new competitive imperative.
>
> **—Michael Dell**
> *CEO of Dell Inc.*

> In this new wave of technology, you can't do it all yourself, you have to form alliances.
>
> **—Carlos Slim**
> *CEO of Telmex, Telcel and América Móvil and the wealthiest person in the world*

LEARNING OBJECTIVES

LO 1. Learn whether and when to pursue offensive or defensive strategic moves to improve a company's market position.

LO 2. Recognize when being a first mover or a fast follower or a late mover is most advantageous.

LO 3. Become aware of the strategic benefits and risks of expanding a company's horizontal scope through mergers and acquisitions.

LO 4. Learn the advantages and disadvantages of extending the company's scope of operations via vertical integration.

LO 5. Become aware of the conditions that favor farming out certain value chain activities to outside parties.

LO 6. Understand when and how strategic alliances can substitute for horizontal mergers and acquisitions or vertical integration and how they can facilitate outsourcing.

Once a company has settled on which of the five generic competitive strategies to employ, attention turns to how strategic choices along several other dimensions can complement its competitive approach and maximize the power of its overall strategy. The first dimension concerns competitive actions—both offensive and defensive; the second concerns competitive dynamics and the timing of strategic moves; and the third concerns the breadth of a company's activities (or its *scope* of operations along an industry's entire value chain). All in all, the following measures to strengthen a company's competitive position and create a full-blown business strategy have to be considered:

- Whether and when to go on the offensive and initiate aggressive strategic moves to improve the company's market position.

- Whether and when to employ defensive strategies to protect the company's market position.

- When to undertake strategic moves—whether advantage or disadvantage lies in being a first mover, a fast follower, or a late mover.

- Whether to bolster the company's market position by merging with or acquiring another firm in the same industry.

- Whether to integrate backward or forward into more stages of the vertical chain of activities that (typically) begins with raw-material production and ends with sales to the end consumer.

- Whether to outsource certain value chain activities or perform them in-house.

- Whether to enter into strategic alliances or partnership arrangements with other enterprises.

This chapter presents the pros and cons of each of these strategy-enhancing measures.

GOING ON THE OFFENSIVE—STRATEGIC OPTIONS TO IMPROVE A COMPANY'S MARKET POSITION

No matter which one of the five generic competitive strategies a firm employs, there are times when it makes sense for the company to *go on the offensive* to strengthen its market position and improve its overall business performance. Strategic offensives are called for when a company spots opportunities to gain profitable market share at the expense of rivals or when a company has no choice but to try to whittle away at a strong rival's competitive advantage. Companies like Walmart, Apple, and Google play hardball, aggressively pursuing competitive advantage and trying to reap the benefits of a leading market share, superior profit margins, and more rapid growth, as well as the reputational rewards of being known as a winning company on the move.[1] The best offensives tend to incorporate several principles: (1) focusing relentlessly on building competitive advantage and then striving to convert it into sustainable advantage (as described in Chapter 4), (2) creating and deploying company resources in ways that cause rivals to struggle to defend themselves, (3) employing the element of surprise as opposed to doing what rivals expect and are prepared for, and (4) displaying a strong bias for swift, decisive, and overwhelming actions to overpower rivals.[2]

Choosing the Basis for Competitive Attack

As a rule, challenging rivals on competitive grounds where they are strong is an uphill struggle.[3] Offensive initiatives that exploit competitor weaknesses stand a far better chance of succeeding than do those that challenge competitor strengths, especially if the weaknesses represent important vulnerabilities and if weak rivals can be caught by surprise with no ready defense.[4]

Strategic offensives should, as a general rule, be based on exploiting a company's strongest strategic assets—its most valuable resources and capabilities, such as a better-known brand name, a more efficient production or distribution system, greater technological capability, or a superior reputation for quality. But a consideration of the company's strengths should not be made without also considering the rival's strengths and weaknesses. A strategic offensive should be based on those areas of strength where the company has its greatest competitive advantage over the targeted rivals. If a company has especially good customer service capabilities, it can make special sales pitches to the customers of those rivals that provide subpar customer service. Aggressors with a recognized brand name and strong marketing skills can launch efforts to win customers away from rivals with weak brand recognition. There is considerable appeal in emphasizing sales to buyers in geographic regions where a rival has a weak market share or is exerting less competitive effort. Likewise, it may be attractive to pay special attention to buyer segments that a rival is neglecting or is weakly equipped to serve.

Ignoring the need to tie a strategic offensive to a company's resources where they are competitively stronger than rivals' is like going to war with a popgun—the prospects for success are dim. For instance, it is foolish for a company with relatively high costs to employ a price-cutting offensive—price-cutting offensives are best left to financially strong companies whose costs are relatively low in comparison to those of the companies being attacked. Likewise, it is ill-advised to pursue a product innovation offensive without having competitively superior expertise in R&D, new product development, and speeding new products to market.

The principal offensive strategy options include the following:

> The best offensives use a company's most competitively potent resources to attack rivals in the areas where they are weakest.

> Sometimes a company's best strategic option is to seize the initiative, go on the attack, and launch a strategic offensive to improve its market position.

1. *Using a cost-based advantage to attack competitors on the basis of price or value.* A price-cutting offensive can involve offering customers an equally good or better product at a lower price or offering a low-priced, lower-quality product that gives customers more value for the money. This is the classic offensive for improving a company's market position vis-à-vis rivals, but it works well only

under certain circumstances. Lower prices can produce market share gains if competitors don't respond with price cuts of their own and if the challenger convinces buyers that its product offers them a better value proposition. However, such a strategy increases total profits only if the gains in additional unit sales are enough to offset the impact of lower prices and thinner margins per unit sold. Price-cutting offensives are generally successful only when a company *first achieves a cost advantage and then hits competitors with a lower price.*[5] Walmart's rise to dominance in discount retailing and supermarkets was based on just this type of strategic offensive. Ryanair also used this strategy successfully against rivals such as British Air and Aer Lingus, by first cutting costs to the bone and then targeting leisure passengers who care more about low price than in-flight amenities and service.[6] While some companies have used price-cutting offensives as a means of obtaining the cost advantages associated with greater market share (economies of scale or experience), this has proved to be a highly risky strategy. More often than not, such price-cutting offensives are met with retaliatory attacks that can mire the entire industry in a costly price war.

2. *Leapfrogging competitors by being the first adopter of next-generation technologies or being first to market with next-generation products.* In technology-based industries, the opportune time to overtake an entrenched competitor is when there is a shift to the next generation of the technology. Microsoft got its next-generation Xbox 360 to market a full 12 months ahead of Sony's PlayStation 3 and Nintendo's Wii, helping it convince video gamers to buy an Xbox rather than wait for the new PlayStation 3 and Wii to hit the market. This type of offensive strategy is high-risk, however, since it requires costly investment at a time when consumer reactions to the new technology are yet unknown.

3. *Pursuing continuous product innovation to draw sales and market share away from less innovative rivals.* Ongoing introductions of new and improved products can put rivals under tremendous competitive pressure, especially when rivals' new product development capabilities are weak. But such offensives can be sustained only if a company has sufficient product innovation skills to keep its pipeline full and maintain buyer enthusiasm for its new and better product offerings.

4. *Adopting and improving on the good ideas of other companies (rivals or otherwise).*[7] The idea of warehouse-type home improvement centers did not originate with Home Depot cofounders Arthur Blank and Bernie Marcus; they got the "big-box" concept from their former employer Handy Dan Home Improvement. But they were quick to improve on Handy Dan's business model and take Home Depot to the next plateau in terms of product line breadth and customer service. Casket maker Hillenbrand greatly improved its market position by adapting Toyota's production methods to casket making. Offense-minded companies are often quick to take any good idea (not nailed down by a patent or other legal protection), make it their own, and then aggressively apply it to create competitive advantage for themselves.

5. *Using hit-and-run or guerrilla warfare tactics to grab sales and market share from complacent or distracted rivals.* Options for "guerrilla offensives" include occasional lowballing on price (to win a big order or steal a key account from a rival), surprising key rivals with sporadic but intense bursts of promotional activity (offering a special trial offer for new customers to draw them away

from rival brands), or undertaking special campaigns to attract buyers away from rivals plagued with a strike or problems in meeting buyer demand.[8] Guerrilla offensives are particularly well suited to small challengers that have neither the resources nor the market visibility to mount a full-fledged attack on industry leaders and that may not merit a full retaliatory response from larger rivals.[9]

6. *Launching a preemptive strike to secure an advantageous position that rivals are prevented or discouraged from duplicating.*[10] What makes a move preemptive is its one-of-a-kind nature—whoever strikes first stands to acquire competitive assets that rivals can't readily match. Examples of preemptive moves include (1) securing the best distributors in a particular geographic region or country; (2) obtaining the most favorable sites in terms of customer demographics, cost characteristics, or access to transportation, raw-material supplies, or low-cost inputs; (3) tying up the most reliable, high-quality suppliers via exclusive partnerships, long-term contracts, or acquisition; and (4) moving swiftly to acquire the assets of distressed rivals at bargain prices. To be successful, a preemptive move doesn't have to totally block rivals from following; it merely needs to give a firm a prime position that is not easily replicated or circumvented.

How long it takes for an offensive to yield good results varies with the competitive circumstances.[11] It can be short if buyers respond immediately (as can occur with a dramatic cost-based price cut, an imaginative ad campaign, or an especially appealing new product). Securing a competitive edge can take much longer if winning consumer acceptance of an innovative product will take some time or if the firm may need several years to debug a new technology, put new production capacity in place, or develop and perfect new competitive capabilities. But how long it takes for an offensive move to improve a company's market standing (and whether it can do so) also depends on whether market rivals recognize the threat and begin a counterresponse. And whether rivals will respond depends on whether they are capable of making an effective response and if they believe that a counterattack is worth the expense and the distraction.[12]

Choosing Which Rivals to Attack

Offensive-minded firms need to analyze which of their rivals to challenge as well as how to mount the challenge. The following are the best targets for offensive attacks:[13]

- *Market leaders that are vulnerable.* Offensive attacks make good sense when a company that leads in terms of size and market share is not a true leader in terms of serving the market well. Signs of leader vulnerability include unhappy buyers, an inferior product line, a weak competitive strategy with regard to low-cost leadership or differentiation, strong emotional commitment to an aging technology the leader has pioneered, outdated plants and equipment, a preoccupation with diversification into other industries, and mediocre or declining profitability. Toyota's massive product recalls in the U.S. during 2009 and 2010 due to safety concerns presented other car companies with a prime opportunity to attack a vulnerable and distracted market leader. GM and Ford used incentives and low-financing offers aimed at winning over Toyota buyers to increase their market share during this period. Offensives to erode the positions of vulnerable market leaders have real promise when the challenger is also able to revamp its value chain or innovate to gain a fresh cost-based or differentiation-based competitive advantage.[14] To be judged successful, attacks on leaders don't have to result in making the aggressor the new leader; a challenger may "win" by simply becoming a stronger runner-up. Caution is well advised in challenging strong market leaders—there's a significant risk of squandering valuable resources in a futile effort or precipitating a fierce and profitless industrywide battle for market share.

- *Runner-up firms with weaknesses in areas where the challenger is strong.* Runner-up firms are an especially attractive target when a challenger's resources and capabilities are well suited to exploiting their weaknesses.

- *Struggling enterprises that are on the verge of going under.* Challenging a hard-pressed rival in ways that further sap its financial strength and competitive position can weaken its resolve and hasten its exit from the market. In this type of situation, it makes sense to attack the rival in the market segments where it makes the most profits, since this will threaten its survival the most.

- *Small local and regional firms with limited capabilities.* Because small firms typically have limited expertise and resources, a challenger with broader and/or deeper capabilities is well positioned to raid their biggest and best customers—particularly those that are growing rapidly, have increasingly sophisticated requirements, and may already be thinking about switching to a supplier with more full-service capability.

Blue-Ocean Strategy—A Special Kind of Offensive

A **blue-ocean strategy** seeks to gain a dramatic and durable competitive advantage by abandoning efforts to beat out competitors in existing markets and, instead, inventing a new industry or distinctive market segment that renders existing competitors largely irrelevant and allows a company to create and capture altogether new demand.[15] This strategy views the business universe as consisting of two distinct types of market space. One is where industry boundaries are defined and accepted, the competitive rules of the game are well understood by all industry members, and companies try to outperform rivals by capturing a bigger share of existing demand; in such markets, lively competition constrains a company's prospects for rapid growth and superior profitability since rivals move quickly to either imitate or counter the successes of competitors. The second type of market space is a "blue ocean" where the industry does not really exist yet, is untainted by competition, and offers wide-open opportunity for profitable and rapid growth if a company can come up with a product offering and strategy that allows it to create new demand.

> **CORE CONCEPT**
>
> A **blue-ocean strategy** is based on discovering or inventing new industry segments that create altogether new demand, thereby positioning the firm in uncontested market space offering superior opportunities for profitability and growth.

A terrific example of such wide-open or blue-ocean market space is the online auction industry that eBay created and now dominates. Other examples of companies that have achieved competitive advantages by creating blue-ocean market spaces include Starbucks in the U.S. espresso bar industry, FedEx in overnight package delivery, and Cirque du Soleil in live entertainment. Cirque du Soleil "reinvented the circus" by creating a distinctively different market space for its performances (Las Vegas nightclubs and theater-type settings) and pulling in a whole new group of customers—adults and corporate clients—who were willing to pay several times more than the price of a conventional circus ticket to have an "entertainment experience" featuring sophisticated clowns and star-quality acrobatic acts in a comfortable atmosphere. Companies that create blue-ocean market spaces can usually sustain their initial competitive advantage without encountering a major competitive challenge for 10 to 15 years because of high barriers to imitation and the strong brand-name awareness that a blue-ocean strategy can produce.

Zipcar Inc. is presently using a blue-ocean strategy to compete against entrenched rivals in the rental-car industry. It rents cars by the hour or day (rather than by the week) to members who pay a yearly fee for access to cars parked in designated spaces located conveniently throughout large cities. By allowing drivers under 25 years of age to rent cars and by targeting city dwellers who need to supplement their use of public transportation with short-term car rentals, Zipcar entered uncharted waters in the rental-car industry, growing rapidly in the process. Founded in 2000, Zipcar filed to go public in mid-2010.

DEFENSIVE STRATEGIES—PROTECTING MARKET POSITION AND COMPETITIVE ADVANTAGE

> Good defensive strategies can help protect a competitive advantage but rarely are the basis for creating one.

In a competitive market, all firms are subject to offensive challenges from rivals. The purposes of defensive strategies are to (1) lower the risk of being attacked, (2) weaken the impact of any attack that occurs, and (3) influence challengers to aim their efforts at other rivals. While defensive strategies usually don't enhance a firm's competitive advantage, they can definitely help fortify the firm's competitive position, protect its most valuable resources and capabilities from imitation, and defend whatever competitive advantage it might have. Defensive strategies can take either of two forms: actions to block challengers and actions to signal the likelihood of strong retaliation.

Blocking the Avenues Open to Challengers

The most frequently employed approach to defending a company's present position involves actions that restrict a challenger's options for initiating a competitive attack. There are any number of obstacles that can be put in the path of would-be challengers.[16] A defender can participate in alternative technologies as a hedge against rivals attacking with a new or better technology. A defender can introduce new features, add new models, or broaden its product line to close off

> There are many ways to throw obstacles in the path of would-be challengers.

gaps and vacant niches to opportunity-seeking challengers. It can thwart the efforts of rivals to attack with a lower price by maintaining economy-priced options of its own. It can try to discourage buyers from trying competitors' brands by lengthening warranties, offering free training and support services, developing the capability to deliver spare parts to users faster than rivals can, providing coupons and sample giveaways to buyers most prone to experiment, and making early announcements about impending new products or price changes to induce potential buyers to postpone switching. It can challenge the quality or safety of rivals' products. Finally, a defender can grant volume discounts or better financing terms to dealers and distributors to discourage them from experimenting with other suppliers, or it can convince them to handle its product line *exclusively* and force competitors to use other distribution outlets.

Signaling Challengers That Retaliation Is Likely

The goal of signaling challengers that strong retaliation is likely in the event of an attack is either to dissuade challengers from attacking at all or to divert them to less threatening options. Either goal can be achieved by letting challengers know the battle will cost more than it is worth. Signals to would-be challengers can be given by:[17]

- Publicly announcing management's commitment to maintaining the firm's present market share.
- Publicly committing the company to a policy of matching competitors' terms or prices.
- Maintaining a war chest of cash and marketable securities.
- Making an occasional strong counterresponse to the moves of weak competitors to enhance the firm's image as a tough defender.

Signaling is most likely to be an effective defensive strategy if the signal is accompanied by a credible commitment to follow through.

TIMING A COMPANY'S OFFENSIVE AND DEFENSIVE STRATEGIC MOVES

When to make a strategic move is often as crucial as *what* move to make. Timing is especially important when **first-mover advantages** or **disadvantages** exist.[18] Under certain conditions, being first to initiate a strategic move can have a high payoff in the form of a competitive advantage that later movers can't dislodge. Moving first is no guarantee of success, however, since first movers also face some significant disadvantages. Indeed, there are circumstances in which it is more advantageous to be a fast follower or even a late mover. Because the timing of strategic moves can be consequential, it is important for company strategists to be aware of the nature of first-mover advantages and disadvantages and the conditions favoring each type.[19]

> **CORE CONCEPT**
>
> Because of **first-mover advantages** and **disadvantages,** competitive advantage can spring from *when* a move is made as well as from *what* move is made.

The Potential for First-Mover Advantages

Market pioneers and other types of first movers typically bear greater risks and greater development costs than firms that move later. If the market responds well to its initial move, the pioneer will benefit from a monopoly position (by virtue of being first to market) that enables it to recover its investment costs and make an attractive profit. If the firm's pioneering move gives it a competitive advantage that can be sustained even after other firms enter the market space, its first-mover advantage will be greater still. The extent of this type of advantage, however, will

> **LO 2**
>
> Recognize when being a first mover or a fast follower or a late mover is most advantageous.

depend on whether and how fast follower firms can piggyback on the pioneer's success and either imitate or improve on its move.

The conditions that favor first-mover advantages, then, are those that slow the moves of follower firms or prevent them from imitating the success of the first mover. There are six such conditions in which first-mover advantages are most likely to arise:

1. *When pioneering helps build a firm's reputation with buyers and creates brand loyalty.* A firm's reputation can insulate it from competition when buyer uncertainty about product quality keeps the firm's customers from trying competitors' offerings and when new buyers minimize their risk by choosing on the basis of reputation. Similarly, customer loyalty to an early mover's brand can create a tie that binds, limiting the success of later entrants' attempts to poach from the early mover's customer base and steal market share.

2. *When a first mover's customers will thereafter face significant switching costs.* Switching costs limit the ability of late movers to lure away the customers of early movers by making it expensive for a customer to switch to another company's product or service. Switching costs can arise for a number of reasons. They may be due to the time a consumer invests in learning how to use a specific company's product. They may arise from an investment in complementary products that are also brand-specific. They can also arise from certain types of loyalty programs or long-term contracts that give customers greater incentives to remain with an initial provider.

3. *When property rights protections thwart rapid imitation of the initial move.* In certain types of industries, property rights protections in the form of patents, copyrights, and trademarks prevent the ready imitation of an early mover's initial moves. First-mover advantages in pharmaceuticals, for example, are heavily dependent on patent protections, and patent races in this industry are common. In other industries, however, patents provide limited protection and can frequently be circumvented. Property rights protections also vary among nations, since they are dependent on a country's legal institutions and enforcement mechanisms.

4. *When an early lead enables the first mover to move down the learning curve ahead of rivals.* When there is a steep learning curve and when learning can be kept proprietary, a first mover can benefit from volume-based cost advantages that grow ever larger as its experience accumulates and its scale of operations increases. This type of first-mover advantage is self-reinforcing and, as such, can preserve a first mover's competitive advantage over long periods of time. Honda's advantage in small multiuse motorcycles has been attributed to such an effect, as has the long-lived advantage of Lincoln Electric Company in arc welders, which are used in industries such as construction and shipbuilding.

5. *When a first mover can set the technical standard for the industry.* In many technology-based industries, the market will converge around a single technical standard. By establishing the industry standard, a first mover can gain a powerful advantage that, like experienced-based advantages, builds over time. The greater the importance of technical standards in an industry, the greater the advantage of being the one to set the standard and the more firmly the first mover will be entrenched. The lure of such an advantage, however, can result in standard wars among early movers, as each strives to set the industry standard. The key to winning such wars is to enter early on the

basis of strong fast-cycle product development capabilities, gain the support of key customers and suppliers, employ penetration pricing, and make allies of the producers of complementary products.

To sustain any advantage that may initially accrue to a pioneer, a first mover needs to be a fast learner and continue to move aggressively to capitalize on any initial pioneering advantage. It helps immensely if the first mover has deep financial pockets, important competitive capabilities, and astute managers. What makes being a first mover strategically important is not being the first company to do something but, rather, being the first competitor to put together the precise combination of features, customer value, and sound revenue/cost/profit economics that gives it an edge over rivals in the battle for market leadership.[20] If the marketplace quickly takes to a first mover's innovative product offering, the first mover must have large-scale production, marketing, and distribution capabilities if it is to take full advantage of its market lead. If technology is advancing at a torrid pace, a first mover cannot hope to sustain its lead without having strong capabilities in R&D, design, and new product development, along with the financial strength to fund these activities.

Illustration Capsule 6.1 describes how Amazon.com achieved a first-mover advantage in online retailing.

The Potential for First-Mover Disadvantages or Late-Mover Advantages

There are circumstances when first movers face significant disadvantages and when it is actually better to be an adept follower than a first mover. First-mover disadvantages *(or late-mover advantages)* arise in the following four instances:

1. *When pioneering is more costly than imitating, and only negligible experience or learning-curve benefits accrue to the leader.* Such conditions allow a follower to end up with lower costs than the first mover and either win customers away with lower prices or benefit from more profitable production.

2. *When the products of an innovator are somewhat primitive and do not live up to buyer expectations.* In this situation, a clever follower can study customers' reactions to the pioneer's products and win disenchanted buyers away from the leader with better-performing products. Moreover, the first mover may find itself saddled with a negative reputation that retards its ability to recover from its early missteps.

3. *When rapid market evolution gives fast followers the opening to leapfrog a first mover's products with more attractive next-version products.* Industries characterized by fast-paced changes in either technology or buyer needs and expectations may present opportunities for second movers to improve on the pioneer's products and offer customers a more attractive value proposition as a result.

4. *When market uncertainties make it difficult to ascertain what will eventually succeed.* Under these conditions, first movers are likely to make numerous mistakes that later movers can avoid and learn from. Even if the pioneer manages to please early adopters, it may turn out that the needs of early adopters are very different from mass-market needs. Late movers may find it far more advantageous to wait until these needs are clarified and then focus on satisfying the mass market's demand.

ILLUSTRATION CAPSULE 6.1

Amazon.com's First-Mover Advantage in Online Retailing

Amazon.com's path to becoming the world's largest online retailer began in 1994 when Jeff Bezos, a Manhattan hedge fund analyst at the time, noticed that the number of Internet users was increasing by 2,300 percent annually. Bezos saw the tremendous growth as an opportunity to sell products online that would be demanded by a large number of Internet users and could be easily shipped. Bezos launched the online bookseller Amazon.com in 1995. The start-up's revenues soared to $148 million in 1997, $610 million in 1998, and $1.6 billion in 1999. Bezos' business plan—hatched while on a cross-country trip with his wife in 1994—made him *Time* magazine's Person of the Year in 1999.

The volume-based and reputational benefits of Amazon.com's early entry into online retailing had delivered a first-mover advantage, but between 2000 and 2009 Bezos undertook a series of additional strategic initiatives to solidify the company's number-one ranking in the industry. Bezos undertook a massive building program in the late-1990s that added five new warehouses and fulfillment centers totaling $300 million. The additional warehouse capacity was added years before it was needed, but Bezos wanted to move preemptively against potential rivals and ensure that, as demand continued to grow, the company could continue to offer its customers the best selection, the lowest prices, and the cheapest and most convenient delivery. The company also expanded its product line to include sporting goods, tools, toys, grocery items, electronics, and digital music downloads, giving it another means of maintaining its experience and scale-based advantages. Amazon.com's 2008 revenues of $19.2 billion made it the world's largest Internet retailer; Jeff Bezos' shares in Amazon.com made him the 110th-wealthiest person in the world in 2009, with an estimated net worth of $8.2 billion.

Moving down the learning curve in Internet retailing was not an entirely straightforward process for Amazon.com. Bezos commented in a *Fortune* article profiling the company, "We were investors in every bankrupt, 1999-vintage e-commerce startup. Pets.com, living.com, kozmo.com. We invested in a lot of high-profile flameouts." He went on to specify that although the ventures were a "waste of money," they "didn't take us off our own mission." Bezos also suggested that gaining advantage as a first mover is "taking a million tiny steps—and learning quickly from your missteps."

Sources: Mark Brohan, "The Top 500 Guide," *Internet Retailer,* June 2009 (accessed at www.internetretailer.com on June 17, 2009); Josh Quittner, "How Jeff Bezos Rules the Retail Space," *Fortune,* May 5, 2008, pp. 126–34.

To Be a First Mover or Not

In weighing the pros and cons of being a first mover versus a fast follower versus a late mover, it matters whether the race to market leadership in a particular industry is a marathon or a sprint. In marathons, a slow mover is not unduly penalized—first-mover advantages can be fleeting, and there's ample time for fast followers and sometimes even late movers to play catch-up.[21] Thus the speed at which the pioneering innovation is likely to catch on matters considerably as companies struggle with whether to pursue a particular emerging market opportunity aggressively (as a first mover or fast follower) or cautiously (as a late mover). For instance, it took 18 months for 10 million users to sign up for Hotmail, 5.5 years for worldwide mobile phone use to grow from 10 million to 100 million, and close to 10 years for the number of at-home broadband subscribers to reach 100 million worldwide. The lesson here is that there is a market penetration curve for every emerging opportunity; typically, the curve has an inflection point at which all the pieces of the business model fall into place, buyer demand explodes, and the market takes off. The inflection point can come early on a fast-rising curve (as with use of e-mail) or farther on up a slow-rising curve (as with the use of broadband). Any company that seeks competitive advantage by being a first mover thus needs to ask some hard questions:

- Does market takeoff depend on the development of complementary products or services that currently are not available?
- Is new infrastructure required before buyer demand can surge?
- Will buyers need to learn new skills or adopt new behaviors? Will buyers encounter high switching costs in moving to the newly introduced product or service?
- Are there influential competitors in a position to delay or derail the efforts of a first mover?

When the answers to any of these questions are yes, then a company must be careful not to pour too many resources into getting ahead of the market opportunity—the race is likely going to be more of a 10-year marathon than a 2-year sprint.[22] On the other hand, if the market is a winner-take-all type of market, where powerful first-mover advantages insulate early entrants from competition and prevent later movers from making any headway, then it may be best to move quickly despite the risks.

STRENGTHENING A COMPANY'S MARKET POSITION VIA ITS SCOPE OF OPERATIONS

Apart from considerations of competitive moves and their timing, there is another set of managerial decisions that can affect the strength of a company's market position. These decisions concern the scope of a company's operations—the breadth of its activities and the extent of its market reach. Decisions regarding the **scope of the firm** focus on which activities a firm will perform internally and which it will not. For example, should Spanish fashion retailer Zara design the apparel items it sells in its stores? Should it die its own fabrics and carry out all of its manufacturing needs internally? Should it handle all of its logistics rather than outsource distribution? Scope decisions also concern which segments of the market to serve—decisions that can include geographic market segments as well as product and service segments. Should Zara increase its number of retail locations in North America? Should it make all of its product line available in all stores rather than vary its product assortment by location? Should it expand its product offerings to include accessories, lingerie, and home furnishings?

Decisions such as these, in essence, determine where the boundaries of a firm lie and the degree to which the operations within those boundaries cohere. They also have much to do with the direction and extent of a business's growth. In this

CORE CONCEPT

The **scope of the firm** refers to the range of activities which the firm performs internally, the breadth of its product and service offerings, the extent of its geographic market presence, and its mix of businesses.

CORE CONCEPT

Horizontal scope is the range of product and service segments that a firm serves within its focal market.

CORE CONCEPT

Vertical scope is the extent to which a firm's internal activities encompass one, some, many, or all of the activities that make up an industry's entire value chain system, ranging from raw-material production to final sales and service activities.

chapter, we introduce the topic of company scope and discuss different types of scope decisions in relation to a company's business-level strategy. In the next two chapters, we develop two additional dimensions of a firm's scope. Chapter 7 focuses on international expansion—a matter of extending the company's geographic scope into foreign markets. Chapter 8 takes up the topic of corporate strategy, which concerns diversifying into a mix of different businesses. Scope issues are at the very heart of corporate-level strategy.

Several dimensions of firm scope have relevance for business-level strategy in terms of their capacity to strengthen a company's position in a given market. These include the firm's **horizontal scope,** which is the range of product and service segments that the firm serves within its market. Mergers and acquisitions involving other market participants provide a means for a company to expand its horizontal scope. Expanding the firm's vertical scope by means of vertical integration can also affect the success of its market strategy. **Vertical scope** is the extent to which the firm engages in the various activities that make up the industry's entire value chain system, from initial activities such as raw-material production all the way to retailing and after-sales service activities. Outsourcing decisions concern another dimension of scope since they involve narrowing the firm's boundaries with respect to its participation in value chain activities. We discuss the pros and cons of each of these options in the sections that follow. Since strategic alliances and partnerships provide an alternative to vertical integration and acquisition strategies and are sometimes used to facilitate outsourcing, we conclude this chapter with a discussion of the benefits and challenges associated with cooperative arrangements of this sort.

HORIZONTAL MERGER AND ACQUISITION STRATEGIES

LO 3

Become aware of the strategic benefits and risks of expanding a company's horizontal scope through mergers and acquisitions.

Mergers and acquisitions are much-used strategic options; for example, the total worldwide value of mergers and acquisitions completed in 2008 and 2009 was approximately $5 trillion.[23] A *merger* is the combining of two or more companies into a single corporate entity, with the newly created company often taking on a new name. An *acquisition* is a combination in which one company, the acquirer, purchases and absorbs the operations of another, the acquired. The difference between a merger and an acquisition relates more to the details of ownership, management control, and financial arrangements than to strategy and competitive advantage. The resources and competitive capabilities of the newly created enterprise end up much the same whether the combination is the result of acquisition or merger.

Horizontal mergers and acquisitions, which involve combining the operations of firms within the same general industry, provide an effective means for firms to rapidly increase the scale and horizontal scope of their core business. For example, Microsoft has used an aggressive acquisition strategy to extend its software business into new segments and strengthen its technological capabilities in this domain. Mergers between airlines, such as the 2010 United-Continental merger, have increased their scale of operations and extended their reach geographically. Companies from developing economies are increasingly expanding their businesses through cross-border acquisitions, as we discuss in the following chapter on international strategy.

Combining the operations of two companies, via merger or acquisition, is an attractive strategic option for strengthening the resulting company's competitiveness and opening up avenues of new market opportunity. Increasing a company's horizontal scope can strengthen its business and increase its profitability in five ways: (1) by improving the efficiency of its operations, (2) by heightening its product differentiation, (3) by reducing market rivalry, (3) by increasing the company's bargaining power over suppliers and buyers, and (5) by enhancing its flexibility and dynamic capabilities (discussed in Chapter 4).

To achieve these benefits, horizontal merger and acquisition strategies typically are aimed at any of five outcomes:[24]

1. *Increasing the company's scale of operations and market share.* Many mergers and acquisitions are undertaken with the objective of transforming two or more high-cost companies into one lean competitor with significantly lower costs. When a company acquires another company in the same industry, there's usually enough overlap in operations that less efficient plants can be closed or distribution and sales activities partly combined and downsized. Likewise, it is usually feasible to squeeze out cost savings in administrative activities, again by combining and downsizing such administrative activities as finance and accounting, information technology, human resources, and so on. The combined companies may also be able to reduce supply chain costs because of greater bargaining power over common suppliers and closer collaboration with supply chain partners. By helping to consolidate the industry and remove excess capacity, such combinations can also reduce industry rivalry and improve industry profitability.

2. *Expanding a company's geographic coverage.* One of the best and quickest ways to expand a company's geographic coverage is to acquire rivals with operations in the desired locations. If there is some geographic overlap, then one benefit is being able to reduce costs by eliminating duplicate facilities in those geographic areas where undesirable overlap exists. Since a company's size increases with its geographic scope, another benefit is increased bargaining power with the company's suppliers or buyers. For companies whose business customers require national or international coverage, a broader geographic scope can provide differentiation benefits while also enhancing the company's bargaining power. Food products companies like Nestlé, Kraft, Unilever, and Procter & Gamble have made acquisitions an integral part of their strategies to expand internationally in order to serve key customers such as Walmart on a global basis. Greater geographic coverage can also contribute to product differentiation by enhancing a company's name recognition and brand awareness. Banks like Deutsche Bank and Bank of America have used acquisition strategies to establish a market presence and gain name recognition in an ever-growing number of states and localities.

3. *Extending the company's business into new product categories.* Many times a company has gaps in its product line that need to be filled in order to offer customers a more effective product bundle or the benefits of one-stop-shopping.[25] For example, customers might prefer to acquire a suite of software applications from a single vendor that can offer more integrated solutions to the company's problems. Acquisition can be a quicker and more potent way to broaden a company's product line than going through the exercise of introducing a company's own new product to fill the gap. Expanding

into additional market segments or product categories can offer companies benefits similar to those gained by expanding geographically: greater product differentiation, bargaining power, and efficiencies. It can also reduce rivalry by helping to consolidate an industry. Coca-Cola has increased the effectiveness of the product bundle it provides to retailers by acquiring Minute Maid (juices and juice drinks), Odwalla (juices), Hi-C (ready-to-drink fruit beverages), and Glaceau, the maker of VitaminWater. By entering the low-cost segment of the rental-car industry with its 2010 acquisition of Dollar Thrifty (whose brands include Dollar Rent a Car and Thrifty Rent a Car), Hertz can benefit from greater scale and stronger bargaining power over its suppliers.

4. *Gaining quick access to new technologies or complementary resources and capabilities.* By making acquisitions to bolster a company's technological know-how or to expand its skills and capabilities, a company can bypass a time-consuming and expensive internal effort to build desirable new resources and organizational capabilities. From 2000 through April 2009, Cisco Systems purchased 85 companies to give it more technological reach and product breadth, thereby enhancing its standing as the world's biggest provider of hardware, software, and services for building and operating Internet networks. By acquiring technologies and other resources and capabilities that complement its own set, a company can gain many of the types of benefits available from extending its horizontal scope. Among them is the greater flexibility and dynamic capabilities that spring from greater innovativeness and the ability to compete on the basis of a more effective bundle of resources.

5. *Leading the convergence of industries whose boundaries are being blurred by changing technologies and new market opportunities.* In fast-cycle industries or industries whose boundaries are changing, companies can use acquisition strategies to hedge their bets about the direction that an industry will take, increase their capacity to meet changing demands, and respond flexibly to changing buyer needs and technological demands. Such acquisitions add to a company's dynamic capabilities by bringing together the resources and products of several different companies and enabling the company to establish a strong position in the consolidating markets. Microsoft has made a series of acquisitions that have enabled it to launch Microsoft TV Internet Protocol Television (IPTV). Microsoft TV allows broadband users to use their home computers or Xbox game consoles to watch live programming, see video on demand, view pictures, and listen to music. News Corporation has also prepared for the convergence of media services with the purchase of satellite TV companies that include SKY Italia, British Sky Broadcasting, Sky Deutschland, Asia's TATA SKY, and FOXTEL in Australia and New Zealand to complement its media holdings in TV broadcasting (the Fox network and TV stations in various countries), cable TV (Fox News, Fox Sports, and FX), filmed entertainment (Twentieth Century Fox and Fox studios), newspapers, magazines, and book publishing.

Numerous companies have employed a horizontal acquisition strategy to catapult themselves from the ranks of the unknown into positions of market leadership. In 1998, Wells Fargo & Company became the 10th-largest bank in the United States as a result of the merger between Wells Fargo and Norwest Corporation. Although it was still only a network of small midwestern banks at that time, it continued to grow via acquisition over the next decade, pursuing a business model based on selling a full range of financial services to an ever-larger base of customers.

New opportunity presented itself, however, in the wake of the 2008 financial crisis. By acquiring troubled Wachovia Bank (which operated primarily in the Southeast and parts of the Atlantic Coast), Wells Fargo & Company was able to double its size and transform itself into a nationwide bank with global presence. By 2010, it was the fourth-largest bank in the United States, with $1.2 trillion in assets and over 10,000 branch banks. Moreover, its reputation had grown along with it; it was listed by *Fortune* magazine as the world's 14th "Most Admired Company in 2009," was among *Barron's* "World's 25 Most Respected Companies," and was on *Forbes's* list of the "Top 100 Best Companies in the World."

Illustration Capsule 6.2 describes how Clear Channel Worldwide has used acquisitions to build a leading global position in radio broadcasting.

Why Mergers and Acquisitions Sometimes Fail to Produce Anticipated Results

All too frequently, mergers and acquisitions do not produce the hoped-for outcomes.[26] Cost savings may prove smaller than expected. Gains in competitive capabilities may take substantially longer to realize or, worse, may never materialize at all. Efforts to mesh the corporate cultures can stall due to formidable resistance from organization members. Managers and employees at the acquired company may argue forcefully for continuing to do things the way they were done before the acquisition. Key employees at the acquired company can quickly become disenchanted and leave; the morale of company personnel who remain can drop to disturbingly low levels because they disagree with newly instituted changes. Differences in management styles and operating procedures can prove hard to resolve. The managers appointed to oversee the integration of a newly acquired company can make mistakes in deciding which activities to leave alone and which activities to meld into their own operations and systems.

A number of mergers/acquisitions have been notably unsuccessful. Ford's $2.5 billion acquisition of Jaguar was a failure, as was its $2.5 billion acquisition of Land Rover (both were sold to India's Tata Motors in 2008 for $2.3 billion). Daimler AG, the maker of Mercedes-Benz and Smart cars, entered into a high-profile merger with Chrysler only to dissolve it in 2007, taking a loss of $30 billion. A number of recent mergers and acquisitions have yet to live up to expectations—prominent examples include Oracle's acquisition of Sun Microsystems, the Fiat-Chrysler deal, Bank of America's acquisition of Merrill Lynch, and the merger of Sprint and Nextel in the mobile phone industry. Antitrust concerns on the part of regulatory authorities have prevented the successful conclusion of other mergers and acquisitions. Coca-Cola, for example, failed to win approval in 2009 for its proposed $2.4 billion acquisition of Huiyuan Juice Group under China's new antimonopoly law.

VERTICAL INTEGRATION STRATEGIES

Expanding the firm's vertical scope by means of a vertical integration strategy provides another way to strengthen the company's position in its core market. A **vertically integrated firm** is one that participates in multiple segments or stages of an industry's overall value chain. A good example of a vertically integrated

ILLUSTRATION CAPSULE 6.2

Clear Channel Communications: Using Mergers and Acquisitions to Become a Global Market Leader in Radio Broadcasting

In 2009, Clear Channel Communications was among the worldwide leaders in radio broadcasting. Clear Channel owned and operated more than 1,000 radio stations in the United States and operated an additional 240 radio stations in Australia, New Zealand, and Mexico. The company, which was founded in 1972 by Lowry Mays and Billy Joe McCombs, got its start by acquiring an unprofitable country-music radio station in San Antonio, Texas. Over the next 10 years, Mays learned the radio business and slowly bought other radio stations in a variety of states. Going public in 1984 helped the company raise the equity capital needed to continue acquiring radio stations in additional geographic markets.

By 1998, Clear Channel had used acquisitions to build a leading position in radio stations. Domestically, it owned, programmed, or sold airtime for 69 AM radio stations and 135 FM stations in 48 local markets in 24 states. Clear Channel's big move was to begin expanding internationally by acquiring interests in radio station properties in a variety of countries. In October 1999, Clear Channel made a major acquisition that expanded its horizontal scope significantly: It acquired AM-FM, Inc., and changed its name to Clear Channel Communications. The AM-FM, Inc., acquisition gave Clear Channel operations in 32 countries, including 830 radio stations.

Additional acquisitions were completed during the 2000–2003 period. The emphasis was on buying radio broadcasting properties with operations in many of the same local markets, which made it feasible to (1) cut costs by sharing facilities and staffs, (2) improve programming, and (3) sell advertising to customers in packages that not only helped Clear Channel's advertising clients distribute their messages more effectively but also allowed the company to combine its sales activities, achieving significant cost savings and boosting profit margins. In 2008, Clear Channel sought a buyer for 288 of its 1,005 radio stations that operated in small markets. Its remaining 717 radio stations all operated in the top-100 markets in the United States.

Sources: www.clearchannel.com (accessed May 2008); *BusinessWeek,* October 19, 1999, p. 56.

LO 4

Learn the advantages and disadvantages of extending the company's scope of operations via vertical integration.

firm is Maple Leaf Foods, a major Canadian producer of fresh and processed meats whose best-selling brands include Maple Leaf and Schneiders. Maple Leaf Foods participates in hog and poultry production, with company-owned hog and poultry farms; it has its own meat-processing and -rendering facilities; it packages its products and distributes them from company-owned distribution centers; and it conducts marketing, sales, and customer service activities for its wholesale and retail buyers but does not otherwise participate in the final stage of the meat processing vertical chain—the retailing stage.

A vertical integration strategy can expand the firm's range of activities *backward* into sources of supply and/or *forward* toward end users. When Tiffany & Co, a manufacturer and retailer of fine jewelry, began sourcing, cutting, and polishing its own diamonds, it integrated backward along the diamond supply chain. Mining giant De Beers Group and Canadian miner Aber Diamond integrated forward when they entered the diamond retailing business.

A firm can pursue vertical integration by starting its own operations in other stages of the vertical activity chain, by acquiring a company already performing the activities it wants to bring in-house, or by entering into a strategic alliance or joint venture. Vertical integration strategies can aim at *full integration* (participating in all stages of the vertical chain) or *partial integration* (building positions in selected stages of the vertical chain). Firms can also engage in *tapered integration* strategies, which involve a mix of in-house and outsourced activity in any given stage of the vertical chain. Oil companies, for instance, supply their refineries with oil from their own wells as well as with oil that they purchase from other producers—they engage in tapered backward integration. Since Boston Beer Company, the maker of Samuel Adams, sells most of its beer through distributors but also operates brew-pubs, it practices tapered forward integration.

The Advantages of a Vertical Integration Strategy

Under the right conditions, a vertical integration strategy can add materially to a company's technological capabilities, strengthen the firm's competitive position, and boost its profitability.[27] But it is important to keep in mind that vertical integration has no real payoff strategywise or profitwise unless it produces cost savings and/or differentiation benefits sufficient to justify the extra investment.

Integrating Backward to Achieve Greater Competitiveness

It is harder than one might think to generate cost savings or improve profitability by integrating backward into activities such as parts and components manufacture (which could otherwise be purchased from suppliers with specialized expertise in making these parts and components). For backward integration to be a cost-saving and profitable strategy, a company must be able to (1) achieve the same scale economies as outside suppliers and (2) match or beat suppliers' production efficiency with no drop-off in quality. Neither outcome is a slam dunk. To begin with, a company's in-house requirements are often too small to reach the optimum size for low-cost operation—for instance, if it takes a minimum production volume of 1 million units to achieve mass-production economies and a company's in-house requirements are just 250,000 units, then it falls far short of being able to capture the scale economies of outside suppliers (which may readily find buyers for 1 million or more units). Furthermore, matching the production efficiency of suppliers is fraught with problems when suppliers have considerable production experience of their own, when the technology they employ has elements that are hard to master, and/or when substantial R&D expertise is required to develop next-version parts and components or keep pace with advancing technology in parts/components production.

But that said, there are still occasions when a company can improve its cost position and competitiveness by performing a broader range of vertical chain activities in-house rather than having certain of these activities performed by outside suppliers. When the item being supplied is a major cost component, when there is a sole supplier, or when suppliers have outsized profit margins, vertical integration can lower costs by limiting supplier power. Vertical integration can also lower costs by facilitating the coordination of production flows and avoiding bottleneck problems. Furthermore, when a company has proprietary know-how that it wants to keep from rivals, then in-house performance of value-adding activities related to this know-how is beneficial even if such activities could be performed by outsiders. Apple recently decided to integrate backward

CORE CONCEPT

A **vertically integrated firm** is one that performs value chain activities along several portions or stages of an industry's overall value chain, which begins with the production of raw materials or initial inputs and culminates in final sales and service to the end consumer.

CORE CONCEPT

Backward integration involves performing industry value chain activities previously performed by suppliers or other enterprises engaged in earlier stages of the industry value chain; **forward integration** involves performing industry value chain activities closer to the end user.

into producing its own chips for iPhones, chiefly because chips are a major cost component, they have big profit margins, and in-house production would help coordinate design tasks and protect Apple's proprietary iPhone technology. International Paper Company backward integrates into pulp mills that it sets up nearby its paper mills (outside suppliers are generally unwilling to make a site-specific investment for a buyer) and reaps the benefits of coordinated production flows, energy savings, and transportation economies.

Backward vertical integration can produce a differentiation-based competitive advantage when performing activities internally contributes to a better-quality product/service offering, improves the caliber of customer service, or in other ways enhances the performance of the final product. On occasion, integrating into more stages along the vertical added-value chain can add to a company's differentiation capabilities by allowing it to build or strengthen its core competencies, better master key skills or strategy-critical technologies, or add features that deliver greater customer value. Spanish clothing maker Inditex has backward integrated into fabric making, as well as garment design and manufacture, for its successful Zara brand. By tightly controlling the process and postponing dyeing until later stages, Zara can respond quickly to changes in fashion trends and supply its customers with the hottest items. NewsCorp backward integrated into film studios (Twentieth Century Fox) and TV program production to ensure access to high-quality content for its TV stations (and to limit supplier power).

Integrating Forward to Enhance Competitiveness   Like
backward integration, forward integration can lower costs by increasing efficiency and bargaining power. In addition, it can allow manufacturers to gain better access to end users, strengthen brand awareness, and increase product differentiation. Automakers, for example, have forward integrated into the lending business in order to exercise more control and make auto loans a more attractive part of the car-buying process. Forward integration can also enable companies to make the end users' purchasing experience a differentiating feature. For example, Ducati and Harley motorcycles both have company-owned retail stores that are essentially little museums, filled with iconography, that provide an environment conducive to selling not only motorcycles and gear but memorabilia, clothing, and other items featuring the brand. Insurance companies and brokerages have the ability to make consumers' interactions with local agents and office personnel a differentiating feature by focusing on building relationships.

In many industries, independent sales agents, wholesalers, and retailers handle competing brands of the same product; having no allegiance to any one company's brand, they tend to push whatever earns them the biggest profits. An independent insurance agency, for example, represents a number of different insurance companies and tries to find the best match between a customer's insurance requirements and the policies of alternative insurance companies. Under this arrangement, it's possible for an agent to develop a preference for one company's policies or underwriting practices and neglect other represented insurance companies. An insurance company may conclude, therefore, that it is better off integrating forward and setting up its own local offices. Likewise, some tire manufacturers (such as Goodyear) have integrated forward into tire retailing to exert better control over sales force/customer interactions. A number of consumer-goods manufacturers, like Coach, Ralph Lauren, and Samsonite, have integrated forward into retailing so as to move seconds, overstocked items, and slow-selling merchandise through their own branded factory outlet stores.

Some producers have opted to integrate forward by selling directly to customers at the company's Web site. Bypassing regular wholesale/retail channels in favor of direct sales and Internet retailing can have appeal if it reinforces the brand and enhances consumer satisfaction or if it lowers distribution costs, produces a relative cost advantage over certain rivals, and results in lower selling prices to end users. In addition, sellers are compelled to include the Internet as a retail channel when a sufficiently large number of buyers in an industry prefer to make purchases online. However, a company that is vigorously pursuing online sales to consumers at the same time that it is also heavily promoting sales to consumers through its network of wholesalers and retailers is competing directly against its distribution allies. Such actions constitute *channel conflict* and create a tricky route to negotiate. A company that is actively trying to expand online sales to consumers is signaling *a weak strategic commitment to its dealers* and *a willingness to cannibalize dealers' sales and growth potential.* The likely result is angry dealers and loss of dealer goodwill. Quite possibly, a company may stand to lose more sales by offending its dealers than it gains from its own online sales effort. Consequently, in industries where the strong support and goodwill of dealer networks is essential, companies may conclude that it is important to avoid channel conflict and that their Web sites should be designed to partner with dealers rather than compete against them.

The Disadvantages of a Vertical Integration Strategy

Vertical integration has some substantial drawbacks beyond the potential for channel conflict.[28] The most serious drawbacks to vertical integration include the following concerns:

- Vertical integration raises a firm's capital investment in the industry, *increasing business risk.* What if industry growth and profitability go sour?

- Vertically integrated companies are often *slow to embrace technological advances* or more efficient production methods when they are saddled with older technology or facilities. A company that obtains parts and components from outside suppliers can always shop the market for the latest and best parts and components, whereas a vertically integrated firm that is saddled with older technology or facilities that make items it no longer needs is looking at the high costs of premature abandonment.

- Integrating backward into parts and components manufacture *can impair a company's operating flexibility* when it comes to changing out the use of certain parts and components. It is one thing to design out a component made by a supplier and another to design out a component being made in-house (which can mean laying off employees and writing off the associated investment in equipment and facilities). Most of the world's automakers, despite their expertise in automotive technology and manufacturing, have concluded that purchasing many of their key parts and components from manufacturing specialists results in higher quality, lower costs, and greater design flexibility than does the vertical integration option.

- Vertical integration potentially results in *less flexibility in accommodating shifting buyer preferences* when a new product design doesn't include parts and components that the company makes in-house. Integrating forward or backward locks a firm into relying on its own in-house activities and sources of supply.

- Vertical integration *may not enable a company to realize economies of scale* if its production levels are below the minimum efficient scale. Small companies in particular are likely to suffer a cost disadvantage by producing in-house when suppliers of many small companies can realize scale economies that a small company cannot attain on its own.

- Vertical integration poses all kinds of *capacity matching problems.* In motor vehicle manufacturing, for example, the most efficient scale of operation for making axles is different from the most economic volume for radiators and different yet again for both engines and transmissions. Building the capacity to produce just the right number of axles, radiators, engines, and transmissions in-house—and doing so at the lowest unit costs for each—is much easier said than done. If internal capacity for making transmissions is deficient, the difference has to be bought externally. If internal capacity for radiators proves excessive, customers need to be found for the surplus. And if by-products are generated—as occurs in the processing of many chemical products—they require arrangements for disposal. Consequently, integrating across several production stages in ways that achieve the lowest feasible costs can be a monumental challenge.

- Integration forward or backward often calls for *radical new skills and business capabilities.* Parts and components manufacturing, assembly operations, wholesale distribution and retailing, and direct sales via the Internet represent different kinds of businesses, operating in different types of industries, with different key success factors. Managers of a manufacturing company should consider carefully whether it makes good business sense to invest time and money in developing the expertise and merchandising skills to integrate forward into wholesaling or retailing. Many manufacturers learn the hard way that company-owned wholesale/retail networks present many headaches, fit poorly with what they do best, and don't always add the kind of value to their core business they thought they would.

In today's world of close working relationships with suppliers and efficient supply chain management systems, *very few businesses can make a case for integrating backward into the business of suppliers* to ensure a reliable supply of materials and components or to reduce production costs. The best materials and components suppliers stay abreast of advancing technology and are adept in improving their efficiency and keeping their costs and prices as low as possible. A company that pursues a vertical integration strategy and tries to produce many parts and components in-house is likely to find itself very hard-pressed to keep up with technological advances and cutting-edge production practices for each part and component used in making its product.

Weighing the Pros and Cons of Vertical Integration

All in all, therefore, a strategy of vertical integration can have both important strengths and weaknesses. The tip of the scales depends on (1) whether vertical integration can enhance the performance of strategy-critical activities in ways that lower cost, build expertise, protect proprietary know-how, or increase differentiation; (2) the impact of vertical integration on investment costs, flexibility and response times, and the administrative costs of coordinating operations across more vertical chain activities; and (3) how difficult it will be for the company to acquire the set of skills and capabilities needed to operate in another stage of the vertical chain. *Vertical integration strategies have merit according to which capabilities and value-adding activities truly need to be performed in-house and which can be performed better or cheaper by outsiders.* Without solid benefits, integrating forward or backward is not likely to be an attractive strategy option.

OUTSOURCING STRATEGIES: NARROWING THE SCOPE OF OPERATIONS

In contrast to vertical integration strategies, outsourcing strategies narrow the scope of a business's operations (and the firm's boundaries, in terms of what activities are performed internally). **Outsourcing** involves a conscious decision to forgo attempts to perform certain value chain activities internally and instead to farm them out to outside specialists.[29] Many PC makers, for example, have shifted from assembling units in-house to outsourcing the entire assembly process to manufacturing specialists because enterprises that assemble many brands of PCs are better able to bargain down the prices of PC components (by buying in very large volumes) and because they have greater expertise in performing assembly tasks more cost-effectively. Nike has outsourced most of its manufacturing-related value chain activities so that it can concentrate on marketing and managing its brand.

> **CORE CONCEPT**
>
> **Outsourcing** involves farming out certain value chain activities to outside vendors.

Outsourcing certain value chain activities can be advantageous whenever:

- *An activity can be performed better or more cheaply by outside specialists.* A company should generally *not* perform any value chain activity internally that can be performed more efficiently or effectively by outsiders—the chief exception occurs when a particular activity is strategically crucial and internal control over that activity is deemed essential.

- *The activity is not crucial to the firm's ability to achieve sustainable competitive advantage and won't hollow out its core competencies.* Outsourcing of support activities such as maintenance services, data processing and data storage, fringe-benefit management, and Web site operations has become commonplace. Colgate-Palmolive, for instance, has been able to reduce its information technology operational costs by more than 10 percent per year through an outsourcing agreement with IBM. A number of companies have outsourced their call center operations to foreign-based contractors that have access to lower-cost labor supplies and can employ lower-paid call center personnel to respond to customer inquiries or requests for technical support.

- *It streamlines company operations in ways that improve organizational flexibility and speed time to market.* Outsourcing gives a company the flexibility to switch suppliers in the event that its present supplier falls behind competing suppliers. To the extent that its suppliers can speedily get next-generation parts and components into production, then a company can get its own next-generation product offerings into the marketplace quicker. Moreover, seeking out new suppliers with the needed capabilities already in place is frequently quicker, easier, less risky, and cheaper than hurriedly retooling internal operations to replace obsolete capabilities or trying to install and master new technologies.

> **LO 5**
>
> Become aware of the conditions that favor farming out certain value chain activities to outside parties.

- *It reduces the company's risk exposure to changing technology and/or buyer preferences.* When a company outsources certain parts, components, and services, its suppliers must bear the burden of incorporating state-of-the-art technologies and/or undertaking redesigns and upgrades to accommodate a company's plans to introduce next-generation products. If what a supplier provides falls out of favor with buyers, or is designed out of next-generation products, or rendered unnecessary by technological change, it is the supplier's business that suffers rather than a company's own internal operations.

- *It allows a company to assemble diverse kinds of expertise speedily and efficiently.* A company can nearly always gain quicker access to first-rate capabilities and expertise by employing suppliers who already have them in place than it can by trying to build them from scratch with its own company personnel.

- *It allows a company to concentrate on its core business, leverage its key resources, and do even better what it already does best.* A company is better able to heighten its own competitively valuable capabilities when it concentrates its full resources and energies on performing those activities internally that it can perform better than outsiders and/or that it needs to have under its direct control. Coach, for example, devotes its energy to designing new styles of ladies handbags and leather accessories, opting to outsource handbag production to 40 contract manufacturers in 15 countries. Hewlett-Packard, IBM, and others have sold manufacturing plants to suppliers and then contracted to purchase the output.

The Big Risk of Outsourcing Value Chain Activities

The biggest danger of outsourcing is that a company will farm out too many or the wrong types of activities and thereby hollow out its own capabilities.[30] For example, in recent years, companies anxious to reduce operating costs have opted to outsource such strategically important activities as product development, engineering design, and sophisticated manufacturing tasks—the very capabilities that underpin a company's ability to lead sustained product innovation. While these companies may have been able to lower their operating costs by outsourcing these functions to outsiders that can perform them more cheaply, *their ability to lead the development of innovative new products has been weakened in the process.* For example, nearly every U.S. brand of laptop and cell phone (with the notable exception of Apple) is not only manufactured but designed in Asia.[31] It is strategically dangerous for a company to be dependent on outsiders for competitive capabilities that over the long run determine its market success. Companies like IBM, Dell, American Express, and Bank of America are alert to the danger of farming out the performance of strategy-critical value chain activities and generally only outsource relatively mundane functions: IBM outsources customer support operations, Dell outsources manufacturing, American Express outsources IT functions, and BoA outsources human resource management.

> A company must guard against outsourcing activities that hollow out the resources and capabilities that it needs to be a master of its own destiny.

Another risk of outsourcing comes from the lack of direct control. It may be difficult to monitor, control, and coordinate the activities of outside parties by mean of contracts and arm's-length transactions alone; unanticipated problems may arise that cause delays or cost overruns and become hard to resolve amicably. Moreover, contract-based outsourcing can be problematic because outside parties lack incentives to make investments specific to the needs of the outsourcing company's value chain.

STRATEGIC ALLIANCES AND PARTNERSHIPS

LO 6

Understand when and how strategic alliances can substitute for horizontal mergers and acquisitions or vertical integration and how they can facilitate outsourcing.

Strategic alliances and cooperative partnerships provide one way to gain some of the benefits offered by vertical integration, outsourcing, and horizontal mergers and acquisitions while minimizing the associated problems. Companies frequently engage in cooperative strategies as an alternative to vertical integration or horizontal mergers and acquisitions. Increasingly, companies are also employing strategic alliances and partnerships to extend their scope of operations via international expansion and diversification strategies, as we describe in Chapters 7 and 8. Strategic alliances and cooperative arrangements are now a common means of narrowing a company's scope of operations as well, serving as a useful way to manage outsourcing (in lieu of traditional, purely price-oriented contracts).

For example, oil and gas companies engage in considerable vertical integration—but Shell Oil Company and Pemex (Mexico's state-owned petroleum company) have found that joint ownership of their Deer Park Refinery in Texas lowers their investment costs and risks in comparison to going it alone. The colossal failure of the Daimler-Chrysler merger formed an expensive lesson for Daimler AG about what can go wrong with horizontal mergers and acquisitions; its 2010 strategic alliance with Renault-Nissan may allow the two companies to achieve jointly the global scale required for cost competitiveness in cars and trucks while avoiding the type of problems that so plagued Daimler-Chrysler. Many companies employ strategic alliances to manage the problems that might otherwise occur with outsourcing—Cisco's system of alliances guards against loss of control, protects its proprietary manufacturing expertise, and enables the company to monitor closely the assembly operations of its partners while devoting its energy to designing new generations of the switches, routers, and other Internet-related equipment for which it is known.

Companies in all types of industries and in all parts of the world have elected to form strategic alliances and partnerships to complement their own strategic initiatives and strengthen their competitiveness in domestic and international markets—the very same goals that motivate vertical integration, horizontal mergers and acquisitions, and outsourcing initiatives. This is an about-face from times past, when the vast majority of companies were content to go it alone, confident that they already had or could independently develop whatever resources and know-how were needed to be successful in their markets. But in today's world, large corporations—even those that are successful and financially strong—have concluded that it doesn't always make good strategic and economic sense to be *totally independent* and *self-sufficient* with regard to each and every skill, resource, and capability they may need. When a company needs to strengthen its competitive position, whether through greater differentiation, efficiency improvements, or a stronger bargaining position, the fastest and most effective route may be to partner with other enterprises having similar goals and complementary capabilities; moreover, partnering offers greater flexibility should a company's resource requirements or goals later change.

A **strategic alliance** is a formal agreement between two or more separate companies in which there is strategically relevant collaboration of some sort, joint contribution of resources, shared risk, shared control, and

CORE CONCEPT

A **strategic alliance** is a formal agreement between two or more separate companies in which they agree to work cooperatively toward some common objective.

mutual dependence. Often, alliances involve cooperative marketing, sales or distribution, joint production, design collaboration, or projects to jointly develop new technologies or products. They can vary in terms of their duration and the extent of the collaboration; some are intended as long-term arrangements, involving an extensive set of cooperative activities, while others are designed to accomplish more limited, short-term objectives.

Collaborative arrangements may entail a contractual agreement, but they commonly stop short of formal ownership ties between the partners (although sometimes an alliance member will secure minority ownership of another member). A special type of strategic alliance involving ownership ties is the **joint venture.** A joint venture entails forming a new corporate entity that is jointly owned by two or more companies that agree to share in the revenues, expenses, and control of the newly formed entity. Since joint ventures involve setting up a mutually owned business, they tend to be more durable but also riskier than other arrangements. In other types of strategic alliances, the collaboration between the partners involves a much less rigid structure in which the partners retain their independence from one another. If a strategic alliance is not working out, a partner can choose to simply walk away or reduce its commitment to collaborating at any time.

Five factors make an alliance "strategic," as opposed to just a convenient business arrangement:[32]

1. It helps build, sustain, or enhance a core competence or competitive advantage.
2. It helps block a competitive threat.
3. It increases the bargaining power of alliance members over suppliers or buyers.
4. It helps open up important new market opportunities.
5. It mitigates a significant risk to a company's business.

Strategic cooperation is a much-favored approach in industries where new technological developments are occurring at a furious pace along many different paths and where advances in one technology spill over to affect others (often blurring industry boundaries). Whenever industries are experiencing high-velocity technological advances in many areas simultaneously, firms find it virtually essential to have cooperative relationships with other enterprises to stay on the leading edge of technology and product performance even in their own area of specialization.

It took a $3.2 billion joint venture involving the likes of Sprint-Nextel, Clearwire, Intel, Time Warner Cable, Google, Comcast, and Bright House Networks to roll out next-generation 4G wireless services based on Sprint's and Clearwire's WiMax mobile networks, with the objective of reaching 100 metropolitan areas and 120 million people by the end of 2010. WiMax was an advanced Wi-Fi technology that allowed people to browse the Internet at speeds as great as 10 times faster than other cellular Wi-Fi technologies. The venture was a necessity for Sprint-Nextel and Clearwire since they lacked the financial resources to handle the rollout on their own. The appeal of the partnership for Time Warner, Comcast, and Bright House was the ability to bundle the sale of wireless services to their cable customers, while Intel had the chip sets for WiMax and hoped that WiMax would become the dominant wireless Internet format. Google's interest in the alliance was to strengthen its lead in desktop search on wireless devices.

Clear Channel Communications has entered into a series of partnerships to provide a multiplatform launchpad for artists like Taylor Swift, Phoenix, and Sara Bareilles. In 2008, they launched iHeartRadio on the iPhone, leveraging their relationships with record labels, artists, TV music channels, and media companies to rake in $175 million in digital revenue as compared to $50 million earned by Pandora in the same period. In 2010, they partnered with MySpace, Hulu, and the artist management company 19 Entertainment for "If I Can Dream," an original reality series where unsigned musicians and actors share a "Real World"-style house in Los Angeles and document their attempts at stardom. Clear Channel has helped promote the show by conducting exclusive radio interviews and performances with the talent, which in turn has helped the show become a top-30 weekly program on Hulu.[33]

Since 2003, Samsung Electronics, a global electronics company headquartered in South Korea, has entered into more than 30 major strategic alliances involving such companies as Sony, Nokia, Intel, Microsoft, Dell, Toshiba, Lowe's, IBM, Hewlett-Packard, and Disney Automation; the alliances involved joint investments, technology transfer arrangements, joint R&D projects, and agreements to supply parts and components—all of which facilitated Samsung's strategic efforts to globalize its business and secure its position as a leader in the worldwide electronics industry. Microsoft collaborates very closely with independent software developers to ensure that their programs will run on the next-generation versions of Windows. Genentech, a leader in biotechnology and human genetics, has formed R&D alliances with over 30 companies to boost its prospects for developing new cures for various diseases and ailments. United Airlines, American Airlines, Continental, Delta, and Northwest created an alliance to form Orbitz, an Internet travel site that enabled them to compete head to head against Expedia and Travelocity and, further, gave them more economical access to travelers and vacationers shopping online for airfares, rental cars, lodging, cruises, and vacation packages.

Toyota has forged long-term strategic partnerships with many of its suppliers of automotive parts and components, both to achieve lower costs and to improve the quality and reliability of its vehicles. In 2008, when Chrysler found itself unable to build hybrid SUVs and trucks using its Two Mode technological innovation (because it lacked the economies of scale necessary to produce proprietary components at a reasonable cost), it entered into a strategic alliance with Nissan whereby Nissan would build Chrysler vehicles with the hybrid technology and Chrysler would take over the production of certain Nissan truck models. Daimler AG has been entering a variety of alliances to lower its risks and improve its prospects in electric cars, where it lacks key capabilities. Its equity-based strategic partnership with Tesla Motors, for example, will allow Daimler to use proven technology to bring its electric vehicles to market quickly, while helping Tesla learn how to mass produce its electric cars. Daimler's 2010 joint venture with Chinese car maker BYD is intended to help Daimler make and sell electric cars for the Chinese market.

Studies indicate that large corporations are commonly involved in 30 to 50 alliances and that a number have hundreds of alliances. One study estimated that corporate revenues coming from activities involving strategic alliances have more than doubled since 1995.[34] Another study reported that the typical large corporation relied on alliances for 15 to 20 percent of its revenues, assets, or income.[35] Companies that have formed a host of alliances have a need to manage their alliances like a portfolio—terminating those that no longer serve a useful purpose or that have produced meager results, forming promising new alliances, and restructuring certain existing alliances to correct performance problems and/or redirect the collaborative effort.[36]

Company use of alliances is quite widespread.

Why and How Strategic Alliances Are Advantageous

The most common reasons companies enter into strategic alliances are to expedite the development of promising new technologies or products, to overcome deficits in their own technical and manufacturing expertise, to bring together the personnel and expertise needed to create desirable new skill sets and capabilities, to improve supply chain efficiency, to share the risks of high-stake, risky ventures, to gain economies of scale in production and/or marketing, and to acquire or improve market access through joint marketing agreements.[37] Manufacturers frequently pursue alliances with parts and components suppliers to gain the efficiencies of better supply chain management and to speed new products to market. By joining forces in components production and/or final assembly, companies may be able to realize cost savings not achievable with their own small volumes. Allies can learn much from one another in performing joint research, sharing technological know-how, and collaborating on complementary new technologies and products—sometimes enough to enable them to pursue other new opportunities on their own.[38] In industries where technology is advancing rapidly, alliances are all about fast cycles of learning, staying abreast of the latest developments, gaining quick access to the latest round of technological know-how, and developing dynamic capabilities. In bringing together firms with different skills and knowledge bases, alliances open up learning opportunities that help partner firms better leverage their own resources and capabilities.[39]

> The best alliances are highly selective, focusing on particular value-creating activities, whether within or across industry boundaries, and on obtaining a specific competitive benefit. They enable a firm to build on its strengths and to learn.

There are several other instances in which companies find strategic alliances particularly valuable. As we explain in the next chapter, a company that is racing for *global market leadership* needs alliances to:[40]

- *Get into critical country markets quickly* and accelerate the process of building a potent global market presence.

- *Gain inside knowledge about unfamiliar markets and cultures through alliances with local partners.* For example, U.S., European, and Japanese companies wanting to build market footholds in the fast-growing Chinese market have pursued partnership arrangements with Chinese companies to help get products through the customs process, to help guide them through the maze of government regulations, to supply knowledge of local markets, to provide guidance on adapting their products to better match the buying preferences of Chinese consumers, to set up local manufacturing capabilities, and to assist in distribution, marketing, and promotional activities.

- *Access valuable skills and competencies* that are concentrated in particular geographic locations (such as software design competencies in the United States, fashion design skills in Italy, and efficient manufacturing skills in Japan and China).

A company that is racing to *stake out a strong position in an industry of the future* needs alliances to:[41]

- *Establish a stronger beachhead* for participating in the target industry.
- *Master new technologies and build new expertise and competencies* faster than would be possible through internal efforts.
- *Open up broader opportunities* in the target industry by melding the firm's own capabilities with the expertise and resources of partners.

Capturing the Benefits of Strategic Alliances

The extent to which companies benefit from entering into alliances and partnerships seems to be a function of six factors:[42]

1. *Picking a good partner.* A good partner must bring complementary strengths to the relationship. To the extent that alliance members have nonoverlapping strengths, there is greater potential for synergy and less potential for coordination problems and conflict. In addition, a good partner needs to share the company's vision about the overall purpose of the alliance and to have specific goals that either match or complement those of the company. Strong partnerships also depend on good chemistry among key personnel and compatible views about how the alliance should be structured and managed.

2. *Being sensitive to cultural differences.* Cultural differences among companies can make it difficult for their personnel to work together effectively. Cultural differences can be problematic among companies from the same country, but when the partners have different national origins, the problems are often magnified. Unless there is respect among all the parties for company cultural differences, including those stemming from different local cultures and local business practices, productive working relationships are unlikely to emerge.

3. *Recognizing that the alliance must benefit both sides.* Information must be shared as well as gained, and the relationship must remain forthright and trustful. Many alliances fail because one or both partners grow unhappy with what they are learning. Also, if either partner plays games with information or tries to take advantage of the other, the resulting friction can quickly erode the value of further collaboration. Open, trustworthy behavior on both sides is essential for fruitful collaboration.

4. *Ensuring that both parties live up to their commitments.* Both parties have to deliver on their commitments for the alliance to produce the intended benefits. The division of work has to be perceived as fairly apportioned, and the caliber of the benefits received on both sides has to be perceived as adequate. Such actions are critical for the establishment of trust between the parties; research has shown that trust is an important factor in fostering effective strategic alliances.[43]

5. *Structuring the decision-making process so that actions can be taken swiftly when needed.* In many instances, the fast pace of technological and competitive changes dictates an equally fast decision-making process. If the parties get bogged down in discussions or in gaining internal approval from higher-ups, the alliance can turn into an anchor of delay and inaction.

6. *Managing the learning process and then adjusting the alliance agreement over time to fit new circumstances.* One of the keys to long-lasting success is adapting the nature and structure of the alliance to be responsive to shifting market conditions, emerging technologies, and changing customer requirements. Wise allies are quick to recognize the merit of an evolving collaborative arrangement, where adjustments are made to accommodate changing market conditions and to overcome whatever problems arise in establishing an effective working relationship. Most alliances encounter troubles of some kind within a couple of years—those that are flexible enough to evolve are better able to recover.[44]

Most alliances that aim at sharing technology or providing market access turn out to be temporary, lasting only a few years. This is not necessarily an indicator of failure, however. Strategic alliances can be terminated after a few years simply because they have fulfilled their purpose; indeed, many alliances are intended to be of limited duration, set up to accomplish specific short-term objectives. Longer-lasting collaborative arrangements, however, may provide even greater strategic benefits. Alliances are more likely to be long-lasting when (1) they involve collaboration with partners that do not compete directly, (2) a trusting relationship has been established, and (3) both parties conclude that continued collaboration is in their mutual interest, perhaps because new opportunities for learning are emerging.

The Drawbacks of Strategic Alliances and Partnerships

While strategic alliances provide a way of obtaining the benefits of vertical integration, mergers and acquisitions, and outsourcing, they also suffer from some of the same drawbacks. Culture clash and integration problems due to different management styles and business practices can interfere with the success of an alliance, just as they can with vertical integration or horizontal mergers and acquisitions. Anticipated gains may fail to materialize due to an overly optimistic view of the synergies or a poor fit in terms of the combination of resources and capabilities. When outsourcing is conducted via alliances, there is no less risk of becoming dependent on other companies for essential expertise and capabilities—indeed, this may be the Achilles' heel of such alliances.

Moreover, there are additional pitfalls to collaborative arrangements. The greatest danger is that a partner will gain access to a company's proprietary knowledge base, technologies, or trade secrets, enabling the partner to match the company's core strengths and costing the company its hard-won competitive advantage. This risk is greatest when the alliance is among industry rivals or when the alliance is for the purpose of collaborative R&D, since this type of partnership requires an extensive exchange of closely held information.

The question for managers is when to engage in a strategic alliance and when to choose an alternative means of meeting their objectives. The answer to this question depends on the relative advantages of each method and the circumstances under which each type of organizational arrangement is favored.

The principle advantages of strategic alliances over vertical integration or horizontal mergers/acquisitons are threefold:

1. They lower investment costs and risks for each partner by facilitating resource pooling and risk sharing. This can be particularly important when investment needs and uncertainty are high, such as when a dominant technology standard has not yet emerged.

2. They are more flexible organizational forms and allow for a more adaptive response to changing conditions. Flexibility is key when environmental conditions or technologies are changing rapidly. Moreover, strategic alliances under such circumstances may enable the development of each partner's dynamic capabilities.

3. They are more rapidly deployed—a critical factor when speed is of the essence. Speed is of the essence when there is a winner-take-all type of competitive situation, such as the race for a dominant technological design or a race down a steep experience curve, where there is a large first-mover advantage.

The key advantages of using strategic alliances rather than arm's-length transactions to manage outsourcing are (1) the increased ability to exercise control over the partners' activities and (2) a greater willingness for the partners to make relationship-specific investments. Arm's-length transactions discourage such investments since they imply less commitment and do not build trust.

On the other hand, there are circumstances when other organizational mechanisms are preferable to partnering. Mergers and acquisitions are especially suited for situations in which strategic alliances or partnerships do not go far enough in providing a company with access to needed resources and capabilities.[45] Ownership ties are more permanent than partnership ties, allowing the operations of the merger/acquisition participants to be tightly integrated and creating more in-house control and autonomy. Other organizational mechanisms are also preferable to alliances when there is limited property rights protection for valuable know-how and when companies fear being taken advantage of by opportunistic partners.

While it is important for managers to understand when strategic alliances and partnerships are most likely (and least likely) to prove useful, it is also important to know how to manage them.

How to Make Strategic Alliances Work

A surprisingly large number of alliances never live up to expectations. A recent article reported that even though the number of strategic alliances increases by about 25 percent annually, about 60 to 70 percent of alliances continue to fail each year.[46] The success of an alliance depends on how well the partners work together, their capacity to respond and adapt to changing internal and external conditions, and their willingness to renegotiate the bargain if circumstances so warrant. A successful alliance requires real in-the-trenches collaboration, not merely an arm's-length exchange of ideas. Unless partners place a high value on the skills, resources, and contributions each brings to the alliance and the cooperative arrangement results in valuable win-win outcomes, it is doomed.

While the track record for strategic alliances is poor on average, many companies have learned how to manage strategic alliances successfully and routinely defy these averages. Samsung Group, which includes Samsung Electronics and had worldwide sales of $117.8 billion in 2009, successfully manages an ecosystem of over 1,300 partnerships that enable productive activities from global procurement to local marketing to collaborative R&D. Samsung Group takes a systematic approach to managing its partnerships and devotes considerable resources to this enterprise. In 2008, for example, it established a Partner Collaboration and Enhancement Office under the direct control of its CEO. Samsung Group supports its partners with financial help as well as training and development resources to ensure that its alliance partners' technical, manufacturing, and management capabilities remain globally competitive. As a result, some of its equipment providers have emerged as the leading firms in their industries while contributing to Samsung's competitive advantage in the global TV market.

Companies that have greater success in managing their strategic alliances and partnerships often credit the following factors:

- *They create a system for managing their alliances.* Companies need to manage their alliances in a systematic fashion, just as they manage other functions. This means setting up a process for managing the different aspects of alliance management from partner selection to alliance termination procedures. To ensure that the system is followed on a routine basis by all company managers, many companies create a set of explicit procedures, process templates, manuals, or the like.

- *They build relationships with their partners and establish trust.* Establishing strong interpersonal relationships is a critical factor in making strategic alliances work since they facilitate opening up channels of communication, coordinating activity, aligning interests, and building trust. Cultural sensitivity is a key part of this, particularly for cross-border alliances. Accordingly, many companies include cultural sensitivity training for their managers as a part of their alliance management program.

- *They protect themselves from the threat of opportunism by setting up safeguards.* There are a number of means for preventing a company from being taken advantage of by an untrustworthy partner or unwittingly losing control over key assets. Contractual safeguards, including noncompete clauses, can provide some protection. But if the company's core assets are vulnerable to being appropriated by partners, it may be possible to control their use and strictly limit outside access. Cisco Systems, for example, does not divulge the source code for its designs to its alliance partners, thereby controlling the initiation of all improvements and safeguarding its innovations from imitation.

- *They make commitments to their partners and see that their partners do the same.* When partners make credible commitments to a joint enterprise, they have stronger incentives for making it work and are less likely to "free-ride" on the efforts of other partners. Because of this, equity-based alliances tend to be more successful than nonequity alliances.[47]

- *They make learning a routine part of the management process.* There are always opportunities for learning from a partner, but organizational learning does not take place automatically. Moreover, whatever learning takes place cannot add to a company's knowledge base unless the learning is incorporated into the company's routines and practices. Particularly when the purpose of an alliance is to improve a company's knowledge assets and capabilities, it is important for the company to learn thoroughly and rapidly about its partners' technologies, business practices, and organizational capabilities and then transfer valuable ideas and practices into its own operations promptly.

Finally, managers should realize that alliance management is an organizational capability, much like any other. It develops over time, out of effort, experience, and learning. For this reason, it is wise to begin slowly, with simple alliances, designed to meet limited, short-term objectives. Short-term partnerships that are successful often become the basis for much more extensive collaborative arrangements. Even when strategic alliances are set up with the hope that they will become long-term engagements, they have a better chance of succeeding if they are phased in so that the partners can learn how they can work together most fruitfully.

KEY POINTS

1. Once a company has settled on which of the five generic competitive strategies to employ, attention turns to how strategic choices regarding (1) competitive actions, (2) timing, and (3) scope of operations can complement its competitive approach and maximize the power of its overall strategy.

2. Strategic offensives should, as a general rule, be grounded in a company's strategic assets. The best offensives use a company's resource and capability strengths to attack rivals in the competitive areas where they are comparatively weakest.

3. Companies have a number of offensive strategy options for improving their market positions: using a cost-based advantage to attack competitors on the basis of price or value, leapfrogging competitors with next-generation technologies, pursuing continuous product innovation, adopting and improving the best ideas of others, using hit-and-run tactics to steal sales away from unsuspecting rivals, and launching preemptive strikes. A blue-ocean type of offensive strategy seeks to gain a dramatic and durable competitive advantage by abandoning efforts to beat out competitors in existing markets and, instead, inventing a new industry or distinctive market segment that renders existing competitors largely irrelevant and allows a company to create and capture altogether new demand.

4. The purposes of defensive strategies are to lower the risk of being attacked, weaken the impact of any attack that occurs, and influence challengers to aim their efforts at other rivals. Defensive strategies to protect a company's position usually take one of two forms: (1) actions to block challengers and (2) actions to signal the likelihood of strong retaliation.

5. The timing of strategic moves also has competitive relevance and is especially important when first-mover advantages or disadvantages exist. Company managers are obligated to carefully consider the advantages or disadvantages that attach to being a first mover versus a fast follower versus a wait-and-see late mover.

6. Decisions concerning the scope of a company's operations—which activities a firm will perform internally and which it will not—can also affect the strength of a company's market position. The *scope of the firm* refers to the range of its activities, the breadth of its product and service offerings, the extent of its geographic market presence, and its mix of businesses. Companies can expand their scope horizontally (more broadly within their focal market) or vertically (up or down the chain of value-adding activities that start with raw-material production and end with sales and service to the end consumer). Horizontal mergers and acquisitions (combinations of market rivals) provide a means for a company to expand its horizontal scope. Vertical integration expands a firm's vertical scope.

7. Horizontal mergers and acquisitions can strengthen a firm's competitiveness in five ways: (1) by improving the efficiency of its operations, (2) by heightening its product differentiation, (3) by reducing market rivalry, (3) by increasing the company's bargaining power over suppliers and buyers, and (5) by enhancing its flexibility and dynamic capabilities.

8. Vertical integration, forward or backward, makes strategic sense only if it strengthens a company's position via either cost reduction or creation of a differentiation-based advantage. Otherwise, the drawbacks of vertical integration (increased investment, greater business risk, increased vulnerability to technological changes, less flexibility in making product changes, and the potential for channel conflict) are likely to outweigh any advantages.

9. Outsourcing involves farming out pieces of the value chain formerly performed in-house to outside vendors, thereby narrowing the scope of the firm. Outsourcing can enhance a company's competitiveness whenever (1) an activity can be performed better or more cheaply by outside specialists; (2) having the activity performed by others won't hollow out the outsourcing company's core competencies; (3) it streamlines company operations in ways that improve organizational flexibility, speed decision making, and cut cycle time; (4) it reduces the company's risk exposure; (5) it allows a company to access capabilities more quickly and improves its ability to innovate; and (6) it permits a company to concentrate on its core business and focus on what it does best.

10. Strategic alliances and cooperative partnerships provide one way to gain some of the benefits offered by vertical integration, outsourcing, and horizontal mergers and acquisitions while minimizing the associated problems. They serve as an alternative to vertical integration and mergers and acquisitions; they serve as a supplement to outsourcing, allowing more control relative to outsourcing via arm's-length transactions.

11. Companies that manage their alliances well generally (1) create a system for managing their alliances, (2) build relationships with their partners and establish trust, (3) protect themselves from the threat of opportunism by setting up safeguards, (4) make commitments to their partners and see that their partners do the same, and (5) make learning a routine part of the management process.

ASSURANCE OF LEARNING EXERCISES

LO 2

1. Has Nintendo's timing of strategic moves made it an early-mover or a fast-follower? Could Nintendo's introduction of the Wii be characterized as a Blue Ocean strategy? You may rely on your knowledge of the video game industry and information provided at Nintendo's Investor Relations Web site (www.nintendo.co.jp) to provide justification for your answers to these questions.

LO 4

2. Go to www.bridgstone.co.jp/english/ir, and review information about Bridgestone Corporation's tire and raw-material operations under the About Bridgestone and IR Library links. To what extent is the company vertically integrated? What segments of the vertical chain has the company chosen to enter? What are the benefits and liabilities of Bridgestone's vertical integration strategy?

LO 5, LO 6

3. Go to www.google.com, and do a search on "outsourcing." Identify at least two companies in different industries that have entered into outsourcing agreements with firms with specialized services. In addition, describe what value chain activities the companies have chosen to outsource. Do any of these outsourcing agreements seem likely to threaten any of the companies' competitive capabilities? Are the companies using strategic alliances to manage their outsourcing?

EXERCISES FOR SIMULATION PARTICIPANTS

LO 1

1. What offensive strategy options does your company have? Identify at least two offensive moves that your company should seriously consider to improve the company's market standing and financial performance.

LO 2

2. What options for being a first mover does your company have? Do any of these first-mover options hold competitive advantage potential?

LO 1

3. What defensive strategy moves should your company consider in the upcoming decision round? Identify at least two defensive actions that your company has taken in a past decision round.

LO 3

4. Does your company have the option to merge with or acquire other companies? If so, which rival companies would you like to acquire or merge with?

LO 4

5. Is your company vertically integrated? Explain.

LO 5, LO 6

6. Is your company able to engage in outsourcing? If so, what do you see as the pros and cons of outsourcing? Are strategic alliances involved? Explain.

ENDNOTES

[1] An insightful discussion of aggressive offensive strategies is presented in George Stalk, Jr., and Rob Lachenauer, "Hardball: Five Killer Strategies for Trouncing the Competition," *Harvard Business Review* 82, no. 4 (April 2004), pp. 62–71. For a discussion of offensive strategies to enter attractive markets where existing firms are making above-average profits, see David J. Bryce and Jeffrey H. Dyer, "Strategies to Crack Well-Guarded Markets," *Harvard Business Review* 85, no. 5 (May 2007), pp.

84–92. A discussion of offensive strategies particularly suitable for industry leaders is presented in Richard D'Aveni, "The Empire Strikes Back: Counterrevolutionary Strategies for Industry Leaders," *Harvard Business Review* 80, no. 11 (November 2002), pp. 66–74.
[2] George Stalk, "Playing Hardball: Why Strategy Still Matters," *Ivey Business Journal* 69, no.2 (November–December 2004), pp. 1–2. See K. G. Smith, W. J. Ferrier, and C. M. Grimm, "King of the Hill: Dethroning the

Industry Leader," *Academy of Management Executive* 15, no. 2 (May 2001), pp. 59–70; also see W. J. Ferrier, K. G. Smith, and C. M. Grimm, "The Role of Competitive Action in Market Share Erosion and Industry Dethronement: A Study of Industry Leaders and Challengers," *Academy of Management Journal* 42, no. 4 (August 1999), pp. 372–88.
[3] For a discussion of how to wage offensives against strong rivals, see David B. Yoffie and Mary Kwak, "Mastering Balance: How to Meet and Beat a Stronger Opponent," *California*

Management Review 44, no. 2 (Winter 2002), pp. 8–24.

[4] Stalk, "Playing Hardball," pp. 1–2.

[5] Ian C. MacMillan, Alexander B. van Putten, and Rita Gunther McGrath, "Global Gamesmanship," *Harvard Business Review* 81, no. 5 (May 2003), pp. 66–67; also see Ashkay R. Rao, Mark E. Bergen, and Scott Davis, "How to Fight a Price War," *Harvard Business Review* 78, no. 2 (March–April 2000), pp. 107–16.

[6] D. B. Yoffie and M. A. Cusumano, "Judo Strategy—The Competitive Dynamics of Internet Time," *Harvard Business* Review 77, no. 1 (January–February 1999), pp. 70–81.

[7] Stalk and Lachenauer, "Hardball: Five Killer Strategies," p. 64.

[8] For an interesting study of how small firms can successfully employ guerrilla-style tactics, see Ming-Jer Chen and Donald C. Hambrick, "Speed, Stealth, and Selective Attack: How Small Firms Differ from Large Firms in Competitive Behavior," *Academy of Management Journal* 38, no. 2 (April 1995), pp. 453–82. Other discussions of guerrilla offensives can be found in Ian MacMillan, "How Business Strategists Can Use Guerrilla Warfare Tactics," *Journal of Business Strategy* 1, no. 2 (Fall 1980), pp. 63–65; William E. Rothschild, "Surprise and the Competitive Advantage," *Journal of Business Strategy* 4, no. 3 (Winter 1984), pp. 10–18; Kathryn R. Harrigan, *Strategic Flexibility* (Lexington, MA: Lexington Books, 1985), pp. 30–45; Liam Fahey, "Guerrilla Strategy: The Hit-and-Run Attack," in Liam Fahey (ed.), *The Strategic Management Planning Reader* (Englewood Cliffs, NJ: Prentice Hall, 1989), pp. 194–97.

[9] Yoffie and Cusumano, "Judo Strategy." See also D. B. Yoffie and M. Kwak, "Mastering Balance: How to Meet and Beat a Stronger Opponent," *California Management Review* 44, no. 2 (Winter 2002), pp. 8–24.

[10] The use of preemptive strike offensives is treated comprehensively in Ian MacMillan, "Preemptive Strategies," *Journal of Business Strategy* 14, no. 2 (Fall 1983), pp. 16–26.

[11] Ian C. MacMillan, "How Long Can You Sustain a Competitive Advantage?" in Liam Fahey (ed.), *The Strategic Planning Management Reader* (Englewood Cliffs, NJ: Prentice Hall, 1989), pp. 23–24.

[12] For a discussion of competitors' reactions, see Kevin P. Coyne and John Horn, "Predicting Your Competitor's Reactions," *Harvard Business Review* 87 no. 4 (April 2009), pp. 90–97.

[13] Philip Kotler, *Marketing Management,* 5th ed. (Englewood Cliffs, NJ: Prentice Hall, 1984), p. 400.

[14] Michael E. Porter, *Competitive Advantage* (New York: Free Press, 1985), p. 518.

[15] W. Chan Kim and Renée Mauborgne, "Blue Ocean Strategy," *Harvard Business Review* 82, no. 10 (October 2004), pp. 76–84.

[16] Porter, *Competitive Advantage,* pp. 489–94.

[17] Ibid., pp. 495–97. The list here is selective; Porter offers a greater number of options.

[18] Ibid., pp. 232–33.

[19] For research evidence on the effects of pioneering versus following, see Jeffrey

G. Covin, Dennis P. Slevin, and Michael B. Heeley, "Pioneers and Followers: Competitive Tactics, Environment, and Growth," *Journal of Business Venturing* 15, no. 2 (March 1999), pp. 175–210; Christopher A. Bartlett and Sumantra Ghoshal, "Going Global: Lessons from Late-Movers," *Harvard Business Review* 78, no. 2 (March–April 2000), pp. 132–45.

[20] Gary Hamel, "Smart Mover, Dumb Mover," *Fortune,* September 3, 2001, p. 195.

[21] Ibid., p.192; Costas Markides and Paul A. Geroski, Racing to be 2nd: Conquering the Industries of the Future," *Business Strategy Review* 15, no. 4 (Winter 2004), pp. 25–31.

[22] For a more extensive discussion, see Fernando Suarez and Gianvito Lanzolla, "The Half-Truth of First-Mover Advantage," *Harvard Business Review* 83, no. 4 (April 2005), pp. 121–27.

[23] Henry Gibbon, "Worldwide M&A Declines 28% to US$2trn," *Acquisitions Monthly,* January 2010 (issue 303), pp. 4–11.

[24] For an excellent review of the strategic objectives of various types of mergers and acquisitions and the managerial challenges that different kinds of mergers and acquisitions present, see Joseph L. Bower, "Not All M&As Are Alike—and That Matters," *Harvard Business Review* 79, no. 3 (March 2001), pp. 93–101.

[25] O. Chatain and P. Zemsky, "The Horizontal Scope of the Firm: Organizational Tradeoffs vs. Buyer-Supplier Relationships," *Management Science* 53, no. 4 (April 2007), pp. 550–65.

[26] For a more expansive discussion, see Jeffrey H. Dyer, Prashant Kale, and Harbir Singh, "When to Ally and When to Acquire," *Harvard Business Review* 82, no. 4 (July–August 2004), pp. 109–10.

[27] See Kathryn R. Harrigan, "Matching Vertical Integration Strategies to Competitive Conditions," *Strategic Management Journal* 7, no. 6 (November–December 1986), pp. 535–56; for a more extensive discussion of the advantages and disadvantages of vertical integration, see John Stuckey and David White, "When and When Not to Vertically Integrate," *Sloan Management Review* (Spring 1993), pp. 71–83.

[28] The resilience of vertical integration strategies despite the disadvantages is discussed in Thomas Osegowitsch and Anoop Madhok, "Vertical Integration Is Dead, or Is It?" *Business Horizons* 46, no. 2 (March–April 2003), pp. 25–35.

[29] For a good overview of outsourcing strategies, see Ronan McIvor, "What Is the Right Outsourcing Strategy for Your Process?" *European Management Journal* 26, no. 1 (February 2008), pp. 24–34.

[30] For a good discussion of the problems that can arise from outsourcing, see Gary P. Pisano and Willy C. Shih, "Restoring American Competitiveness," *Harvard Business Review* 87, no. 7–8 (July–August 2009), pp. 114–25; Jérôme Barthélemy, "The Seven Deadly Sins of Outsourcing," *Academy of Management Executive* 17, no. 2 (May 2003), pp. 87–100.

[31] Pisano and Shih, "Restoring American Competitivness," pp. 116–17.

[32] Jason Wakeam, "The Five Factors of a Strategic Alliance," *Ivey Business Journal* 68, no 3 (May–June 2003), pp. 1–4.

[33] *Advertising Age,* May 24, 2010, p. 14.

[34] Salvatore Parise and Lisa Sasson, "Leveraging Knowledge Management across Strategic Alliances," *Ivey Business Journal* 66, no. 4 (March–April 2002), p. 42.

[35] David Ernst and James Bamford, "Your Alliances Are Too Stable," *Harvard Business Review* 83, no. 6 (June 2005), p.133.

[36] An excellent discussion of the portfolio approach to managing multiple alliances and how to restructure a faltering alliance is presented in Ernst and Bamford, "Your Alliances Are Too Stable," pp. 133–41.

[37] Michael E. Porter, *The Competitive Advantage of Nations* (New York: Free Press, 1990), p. 66. For a discussion of how to realize the advantages of strategic partnerships, see Nancy J. Kaplan and Jonathan Hurd, "Realizing the Promise of Partnerships," *Journal of Business Strategy* 23, no. 3 (May–June 2002), pp. 38–42; Parise and Sasson, "Leveraging Knowledge Management across Strategic Alliances," pp. 41-47; Ernst and Bamford, "Your Alliances Are Too Stable," pp. 133–41; and Jonathan Hughes and Jeff Weiss, "Simple Rules for Making Alliances Work," *Harvard Business Review* 85, no. 11 (November 2007), pp. 122–31.

[38] For a discussion of how to raise the chances that a strategic alliance will produce strategically important outcomes, see M. Koza and A. Lewin, "Managing Partnerships and Strategic Alliances: Raising the Odds of Success," *European Management Journal* 18, no. 2 (April 2000), pp. 146–51.

[39] A. Inkpen, "Learning, Knowledge Acquisition, and Strategic Alliances," *European Management Journal* 16, no. 2 (April 1998), pp. 223–29.

[40] Yves L. Doz and Gary Hamel, *Alliance Advantage: The Art of Creating Value through Partnering* (Boston: Harvard Business School Press), chap. 1.

[41] Ibid.

[42] Ibid., chaps. 4–8; Patricia Anslinger and Justin Jenk, "Creating Successful Alliances," *Journal of Business Strategy* 25, no. 2 (2004), pp. 18–23; Rosabeth Moss Kanter, "Collaborative Advantage: The Art of the Alliance," *Harvard Business Review* 72, no. 4 (July–August 1994), pp. 96–108; Joel Bleeke and David Ernst, "The Way to Win in Cross-Border Alliances," *Harvard Business Review* 69, no. 6 (November–December 1991), pp. 127–35; Gary Hamel, Yves L. Doz, and C. K. Prahalad, "Collaborate with Your Competitors—and Win," *Harvard Business Review* 67, no. 1 (January–February 1989), pp. 133–39; Hughes and Weiss, "Simple Rules for Making Alliances Work."

[43] J. B. Cullen, J. L. Johnson, and T. Sakano, "Success through Commitment and Trust: The Soft Side of Strategic Alliance Management," *Journal of World Business* 35, no. 3 (Fall 2000), pp. 223–40; T. K. Das and B. S. Teng, "Between Trust and Control: Developing Confidence in Partner Cooperation in Alliances," *Academy of Management Review* 23, no. 3 (July 1998), pp. 491–512.

[44] K. M. Eisenhardt and C. B. Schoonhoven, "Resource-Based View of Strategic Alliance Formation: Strategic and Social Effects in Entrepreneurial Firms," *Organization Science* 7, no. 2 (March–April 1996), pp. 136–50; M. Zollo, J. J. Reuer, and H. Singh, "Interorganizational Routines and Performance in Strategic Alliances," *Organization Science* 13, no. 6 (November–December 2002), pp. 701–13.

[45] The pros and cons of mergers/acquisitions versus strategic alliances are described in Dyer, Kale, and Singh, "When to Ally and When to Acquire," pp. 109–15.

[46] Hughes and Weiss, "Simple Rules for Making Alliances Work," p. 122.

[47] Y. G. Pan and D. K. Tse, "The Hierarchical Model of Market Entry Modes," *Journal of International Business Studies* 31, no. 4 (2000), pp. 535–54.

CHAPTER 7

STRATEGIES FOR COMPETING IN INTERNATIONAL MARKETS

We're not going global because we want to or because of any megalomania, but because it's really necessary. . . . The costs are so enormous today that you really need to have worldwide revenues to cover them.

—Rupert Murdoch
CEO of the media conglomerate News Corporation

Globalization [provides] a long-lasting competitive advantage. If we build a new gas turbine, in 18 months our

competitors also have one. But building a global company is not so easy to copy.

—Percy Barnevik
Former CEO of the Swiss-Swedish industrial corporation ABB

Capital, technology, and ideas flow these days like quicksilver across national boundaries.

—Robert H. Waterman, Jr.
Internationally recognized expert on management practices

LEARNING OBJECTIVES

LO 1. Develop an understanding of the primary reasons companies choose to compete in international markets.

LO 2. Learn how and why differing market conditions across countries and industries make crafting international strategy a complex undertaking.

LO 3. Learn about the major strategic options for entering and competing in foreign markets.

LO 4. Gain familiarity with the three main strategic approaches for competing internationally.

LO 5. Understand how international companies go about building competitive advantage in foreign markets.

Any company that aspires to industry leadership in the 21st century must think in terms of global, not domestic, market leadership. The world economy is globalizing at an accelerating pace as ambitious growth-minded companies race to build stronger competitive positions in the markets of more and more countries, as countries previously closed to foreign companies open up their markets, as companies in developing countries gain competitive strength, and as advances in information technology and communication shrink the importance of geographic distance. The forces of globalization are changing the competitive landscape in many industries, offering companies attractive new opportunities but at the same time introducing new competitive threats. Companies in industries where these forces are greatest are therefore under considerable pressure to come up with a strategy for competing successfully in foreign markets.

This chapter focuses on strategy options for expanding beyond domestic boundaries and competing in the markets of either a few or a great many countries. In the process of exploring these issues, we will introduce such concepts as multidomestic, global, and transnational strategies; the Porter diamond of national advantage; and cross-country differences in cultural, demographic, and market conditions. The chapter also includes sections on strategy options for entering and competing in foreign markets; the importance of locating value chain operations in the most advantageous countries; and the special circumstances of competing in such developing markets as China, India, Brazil, Russia, and eastern Europe.

WHY COMPANIES DECIDE TO ENTER FOREIGN MARKETS

A company may opt to expand outside its domestic market for any of five major reasons:

1. *To gain access to new customers.* Expanding into foreign markets offers potential for increased revenues, profits, and long-term growth and becomes an especially attractive option when a company's home markets are mature and nearing saturation levels. Companies often expand internationally to extend the life cycle of their products, as Honda has done with its classic 50-cc motorcycle, the Honda cub (which is still selling well in developing markets, more than 50 years after it was first introduced in Japan). A larger target market also offers companies the opportunity to earn a return on large investments more rapidly. This can be particularly important in R&D-intensive industries, where development is fast-paced or competitors imitate innovations rapidly.

2. *To achieve lower costs through economies of scale, experience, and increased purchasing power.* Many companies are driven to sell in more than one country because domestic sales volume alone is not large enough to fully capture economies of scale in product development, manufacturing, or marketing. Similarly, firms expand internationally to increase the rate at which they accumulate experience and move down the learning curve. International expansion can also lower a company's input costs through greater pooled purchasing power. The relatively small size of country markets in Europe and limited domestic volume explains why companies like Michelin, BMW, and Nestlé long ago began selling their products all across Europe and then moved into markets in North America and Latin America.

3. *To further exploit its core competencies.* A company with competitively valuable resources and capabilities can often extend a market-leading position in its home market into a position of regional or global market leadership by leveraging these resources further. Nokia's competencies and capabilities in mobile phones have propelled it to global market leadership in the wireless telecommunications business. Walmart is capitalizing on its considerable expertise in discount retailing to expand into China, Latin America, Japan, South Korea, and the United Kingdom; Walmart executives believe the company has tremendous growth opportunities in China. Companies can often leverage their resources internationally by replicating a successful business model, using it as a basic blueprint for international operations, as Starbucks and McDonald's have done.[1]

4. *To gain access to resources and capabilities located in foreign markets.* An increasingly important motive for entering foreign markets is to acquire resources and capabilities that cannot be accessed as readily in a company's home market. Companies often enter into cross-border alliances or joint ventures, for example, to gain access to resources and capabilities that complement their own or to learn from their partners.[2] Cross-border acquisitions are commonly made for similar reasons.[3] In other cases, companies choose to establish operations in other countries to utilize local distribution networks, employ low-cost human resources, or acquire technical knowledge. In a few

cases, companies in industries based on natural resources (e.g., oil and gas, minerals, rubber, and lumber) find it necessary to operate in the international arena because attractive raw-material supplies are located in many different parts of the world.

5. *To spread its business risk across a wider market base.* A company spreads business risk by operating in many different countries rather than depending entirely on operations in a few countries. Thus, when a company with operations across much of the world encounters economic downturns in certain countries, its performance may be bolstered by buoyant sales elsewhere.

In addition, companies that are the suppliers of other companies often expand internationally when their major customers do so, to meet their needs abroad and retain their position as a key supply chain partner. Automotive parts suppliers, for example, have followed automobile manufacturers abroad, and retail goods suppliers have followed large retailers into foreign markets.

WHY COMPETING ACROSS NATIONAL BORDERS MAKES STRATEGY MAKING MORE COMPLEX

Crafting a strategy to compete in one or more countries of the world is inherently more complex because of (1) factors that affect industry competitiveness that vary from country to country, (2) the potential for location-based advantages in certain countries, (3) different government policies and economic conditions that make the business climate more favorable in some countries than in others, (4) the risks of adverse shifts in currency exchange rates, and (5) cross-country differences in cultural, demographic, and market conditions.

LO 2

Learn how and why differing market conditions across countries and industries make crafting international strategy a complex undertaking.

Cross-Country Variation in Factors That Affect Industry Competitiveness

Certain countries are known for their strengths in particular industries. For example, Chile has competitive strengths in industries such as copper, fruit, fish products, paper and pulp, chemicals, and wine. Japan is known for competitive strength in consumer electronics, automobiles, semiconductors, steel products, and specialty steel. Where industries are more likely to develop competitive strength depends on a set of factors that describe the nature of each country's business environment and vary across countries. Because strong industries are made up of strong firms, the strategies of firms that expand internationally are usually grounded in one or more of these factors. The four major factors are summarized in a framework known as the *Diamond of National Advantage* (see Figure 7.1).[4]

Demand Conditions The demand conditions in an industry's home market include the relative size of the market and the nature of domestic buyers' needs and wants. Industry sectors that are larger and more important in their home market tend to attract more resources and grow faster than others. Demanding domestic buyers for an industry's products spur greater innovativeness and improvements in quality. Such conditions foster the development of stronger

Figure 7.1   **The Diamond of National Advantage**

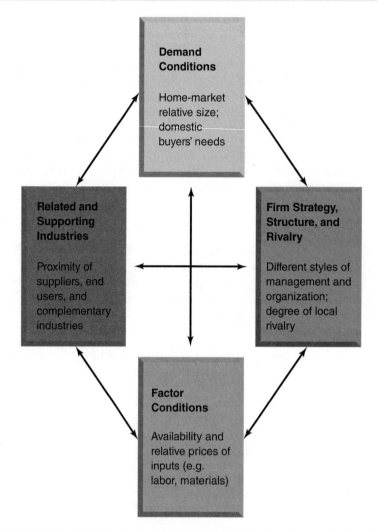

Source: Adapted from M. Porter, "The Competitive Advantage of Nations," *Harvard Business Review,* March–April 1990, pp. 73–93.

industries, with firms that are capable of translating a home-market advantage into a competitive advantage in the international arena.

Factor Conditions   Factor conditions describe the availability, quality, and cost of raw materials and other inputs (called *factors*) that firms in an industry require to produce their products and services. The relevant factors vary from industry to industry but can include different types of labor, technical or managerial knowledge, land, financial capital, and natural resources. Elements of a country's infrastructure may be included as well, such as its transportation, communication, and banking system. For instance, in India there are efficient, well-developed national channels for distributing trucks, scooters, farm equipment, groceries, personal care items, and other packaged products to the country's 3 million retailers, whereas in China distribution is primarily local and there is a limited national network for distributing most products. Competitively strong industries and firms develop where relevant factor conditions are favorable.

Related and Supporting Industries Robust industries often develop as part of a cluster of related industries, including suppliers of components and capital equipment, end users, and the makers of complementary products, including those that are technologically related. The sports car makers Ferrari and Maserati, for example, are located in an area of Italy known as the "engine technological district" that includes other firms involved in racing, such as Ducati Motorcycles, along with hundreds of small suppliers. The advantage to firms that develop as part of a related-industry cluster comes from the close collaboration with key suppliers and the greater knowledge sharing throughout the cluster, resulting in greater efficiency and innovativeness.

Firm Strategy, Structure, and Rivalry Different country environments foster the development of different styles of management, organization, and strategy. For example, strategic alliances are a more common strategy for firms from Asian or Latin American countries, which emphasize trust and cooperation in their organizations, than for firms from North American, where individualism is more influential. In addition, countries vary in terms of the competitiveness of their industries. Fierce competitive conditions in home markets tend to hone domestic firms' competitive capabilities and ready them for competing internationally.

For an industry in a particular country to become competitively strong, all four factors must be favorable for that industry. When they are, the industry is likely to contain firms that are capable of competing successfully in the international arena. Thus the diamond framework can be used to reveal the answers to several questions that are important for competing on an international basis. First, it can help predict where foreign entrants into an industry are most likely to come from. This can help managers prepare to cope with new foreign competitors, since the framework also reveals something about the basis of the new rivals' strengths. Second, it can reveal the countries in which foreign rivals are likely to be weakest and thus help managers decide which foreign markets to enter first. And third, because it focuses on the attributes of a country's business environment that allow firms to flourish, it reveals something about the advantages of conducting particular business activities in that country. Thus the diamond framework is an aid to deciding where to locate different value chain activities most beneficially—a topic that we address next.

Locating Value Chain Activities for Competitive Advantage

Increasingly, companies are locating different value chain activities in different parts of the world to exploit location-based advantages that vary from country to country. This is particularly evident with respect to the location of manufacturing activities. Differences in wage rates, worker productivity, energy costs, environmental regulations, tax rates, inflation rates, and the like, create sizable variations in manufacturing costs from country to country. By locating its plants in certain countries, firms in some industries can reap major manufacturing cost advantages because of lower input costs (especially labor), relaxed government regulations, the proximity of suppliers and technologically related industries, or unique natural resources. In such cases, the low-cost countries become principal production sites, with most of the output being exported to markets in other parts of the world. Companies that build production facilities in low-cost countries (or that source their products from contract manufacturers in these countries) gain a competitive advantage over rivals with plants in countries where costs are higher. The competitive role of low manufacturing costs is most evident in low-wage countries like China, India, Pakistan, Cambodia, Vietnam, Mexico, Brazil, Guatemala, the Philippines, and several countries in Africa and eastern Europe that have become production havens for manufactured goods with high labor content (especially textiles and apparel). Hourly compensation for production workers in 2007 averaged about $0.81 in China versus about $1.10 in the Philippines, $2.92 in Mexico, $5.96 in Brazil, $6.58 in Taiwan, $7.91 in Hungary, $8.27 in Portugal, $19.75 in Japan, $24.59 in the United States, $28.91 in Canada, $37.66 in Germany, and $48.56 in Norway.[5] China is fast becoming the manufacturing capital of the world—virtually all of the world's major manufacturing companies now have facilities in China.

For other types of value chain activities, input quality or availability are more important considerations. Tiffany entered the mining industry in Canada to access diamonds that could be certified as "conflict free" and not associated with either the funding of African wars or unethical mining conditions. Many U.S. companies locate call centers in countries such as India and Ireland, where English is spoken and the workforce is well educated. Other companies locate R&D activities in countries where there are prestigious research institutions and well-trained scientists and engineers. Likewise, concerns about short delivery times and low shipping costs make some countries better locations than others for establishing distribution centers.

The Impact of Government Policies and Economic Conditions in Host Countries

Cross-country variations in government policies and economic conditions affect both the opportunities available to a foreign entrant and the risks of operating within that country. The governments of some countries are anxious to attract foreign investments and go all out to create a business climate that outsiders will view as favorable. A good example is Ireland, which has one of the world's most pro-business environments. Ireland offers companies very low corporate tax rates, has a government that is responsive to the needs of industry, and aggressively recruits high-tech manufacturing facilities and international companies. Ireland's policies were a major factor in Intel's decision to locate a $2.5 billion chip manufacturing plant in Ireland that employs over 4,000 people. Governments anxious to spur economic growth, create more jobs, and raise living standards for their citizens usually enact policies aimed at stimulating business innovation and capital investment. They may provide incentives such as reduced taxes, low-cost loans, site location and site development assistance, and government-sponsored training for workers to encourage companies to construct production and distribution facilities. When new business-related issues or developments arise, pro-business governments make a practice of seeking advice and counsel from business leaders. When tougher business-related regulations are deemed appropriate, they endeavor to make the transition to more costly and stringent regulations somewhat business-friendly rather than adversarial.

On the other hand, governments sometimes enact policies that, from a business perspective, make locating facilities within a country's borders less attractive. For example, the nature of a company's operations may make it particularly costly to achieve compliance with a country's environmental regulations. Some governments, desirous of discouraging foreign imports, provide subsidies and low-interest loans to domestic companies (to enable them to better compete against foreign companies), enact deliberately burdensome procedures and requirements for imported goods to pass customs inspection (to make it harder for imported goods to compete against the products of local businesses), and impose tariffs or quotas on the imports of certain goods (also to help protect local businesses from foreign competition). They may also specify that a certain percentage of the parts and components used in manufacturing a product be obtained from local suppliers, require prior approval of capital spending projects, limit withdrawal of funds from the country, and require minority (sometimes majority) ownership of foreign company operations by local companies or investors. Sometimes foreign companies wanting only to sell their products in a country face a web of regulations regarding technical standards and product certification. Political leaders in some countries may be openly hostile to or suspicious of companies from certain foreign countries operating within their borders. Moreover, there are times when a government may place restrictions on exports to ensure adequate local supplies and regulate the prices of imported and locally produced goods. Such government actions make a country's business climate less attractive and in some cases may be sufficiently onerous as to discourage a company from locating production or distribution facilities in that country or maybe even selling its products in that country.

The decision about whether to enter a particular country must take into account the degree of political and economic risk. **Political risks** stem from government hostility to foreign business, weak governments, and political instability. In industries that a government deems critical to the national welfare, there is sometimes a risk that the government will nationalize the industry and expropriate the assets of foreign companies. In 2010, for example, Ecuador threatened to expropriate the holdings of all foreign oil companies that refused to sign new contracts giving the state control of all production. Other political risks include the loss of investments due to war or political unrest, regulatory changes that create operating uncertainties, security risks due to terrorism, and corruption. **Economic risks** are intertwined with political risks but also stem from factors such as inflation rates and the stability of a country's monetary system. The threat of piracy and lack of protection for intellectual property are important sources of economic risk. Another is fluctuations in the value of different currencies—a factor that we discuss in more detail next.

The Risks of Adverse Exchange Rate Shifts

When companies produce and market their products and services in many different countries, they are subject to the impacts of sometimes favorable and sometimes unfavorable changes in currency exchange rates. The rates of exchange between different currencies can vary by as much as 20 to 40 percent annually, with the changes occurring sometimes gradually and sometimes swiftly. Sizable shifts in exchange rates, which tend to be hard to predict because of the variety of factors involved and the uncertainties surrounding when and by how much these factors will change, shuffle the global cards of which countries represent the low-cost manufacturing locations and which rivals have the upper hand in the marketplace.

To understand the economic risks associated with fluctuating exchange rates, consider the case of a U.S. company that has located manufacturing facilities in Brazil (where the currency is reals—pronounced "ray-alls") and that exports most of the Brazilian-made goods to markets in the European Union (where the currency is euros). To keep the numbers simple, assume that the exchange rate is 4 Brazilian reals for 1 euro and that the product being made in Brazil has a manufacturing cost of 4 Brazilian reals (or 1 euro). Now suppose that for some reason the exchange rate shifts from 4 reals per euro to 5 reals per euro (meaning that the real has declined in value and that the euro is stronger). Making the product in Brazil is now more cost-competitive because a Brazilian good costing 4 reals to produce has fallen to only 0.8 euro at the new exchange rate (4 reals divided by 5 reals per euro = 0.8 euro) and this clearly puts the producer of the Brazilian-made good *in a better position to compete* against the European makers of the same good. On the other hand, should the value of the Brazilian real grow stronger in relation to the euro—resulting in an exchange rate of 3 reals to 1 euro—the same Brazilian-made good formerly costing 4 reals (or 1 euro) to produce now has a cost of 1.33 euros (4 reals divided by 3 reals per euro = 1.33 euros) and this puts the producer of the Brazilian-made good in a weaker competitive position vis-à-vis European producers of the same good. Clearly, the attraction of manufacturing a good in Brazil and selling it in Europe is far greater when the euro is strong (an exchange rate of 1 euro for 5 Brazilian reals) than when the euro is weak and exchanges for only 3 Brazilian reals.

But there is one more piece to the story. When the exchange rate changes from 4 reals per euro to 5 reals per euro, not only is the cost competitiveness of the Brazilian manufacturer stronger relative to European manufacturers of the same item but the Brazilian-made good that formerly cost 1 euro and now costs

only 0.8 euro can also be sold to consumers in the European Union for a lower euro price than before. In other words, the combination of a stronger euro and a weaker real acts to *lower the price of Brazilian-made goods* in all the countries that are members of the European Union, and this is likely to *spur sales of the Brazilian-made good in Europe and boost Brazilian exports to Europe.* Conversely, should the exchange rate shift from 4 reals per euro to 3 reals per euro—which makes the Brazilian manufacturer less cost competitive with European manufacturers of the same item—the Brazilian-made good that formerly cost 1 euro and now costs 1.33 euros will sell for a higher price in euros than before, thus weakening the demand of European consumers for Brazilian-made goods and acting to reduce Brazilian exports to Europe. Thus *Brazilian exporters are likely to experience (1) rising demand for their goods in Europe whenever the Brazilian real grows weaker relative to the euro and (2) falling demand for their goods in Europe whenever the real grows stronger relative to the euro.*

Insofar as U.S.-based manufacturers are concerned, declines in the value of the U.S. dollar against foreign currencies act to reduce or eliminate whatever cost advantage foreign manufacturers might have over U.S. manufacturers and can even prompt foreign companies to establish production plants in the United States. Likewise, a weak euro versus other currencies enhances the cost competitiveness of companies manufacturing goods in Europe for export to foreign markets; a strong euro versus other currencies weakens the cost competitiveness of

European plants that manufacture goods for export. The growing strength of the euro relative to the U.S. dollar has encouraged a number of European manufacturers such as Volkswagen, Fiat, and Airbus to shift production from European factories to new facilities in the United States. Also, the weakening dollar caused Chrysler to discontinue its contract manufacturing agreement with an Austrian firm for assembly of minivans and Jeeps sold in Europe. Beginning in 2008, Chrysler's vehicles sold in Europe were exported from its factories in Illinois and Missouri. The weak dollar was also a factor in Ford's and GM's recent decisions to begin exporting U.S.-made vehicles to China and Latin America.

> Domestic companies facing competitive pressure from lower-cost imports are benefited when their government's currency grows *weaker* in relation to the currencies of the countries where the lower-cost goods are being made.

It is important to note that *currency exchange rates are rather unpredictable,* swinging first one way and then another way, so the competitiveness of any company's facilities in any country is partly dependent on whether exchange rate changes over time have a favorable or unfavorable cost impact. Companies producing goods in one country for export abroad always improve their cost competitiveness when the country's currency grows weaker relative to currencies of the countries where the goods are being exported to, and they find their cost competitiveness eroded when the local currency grow stronger. On the other hand, domestic companies that are under pressure from lower-cost imported goods become more cost competitive when their currency grows weaker in relation to the currencies of the countries where the imported goods are made—in other words, a U.S. manufacturer views a weaker U.S. dollar as a *favorable exchange rate shift* because such shifts help make its costs more competitive than those of foreign rivals.

Cross-Country Differences in Demographic, Cultural, and Market Conditions

Differing population sizes, income levels, and other demographic factors give rise to considerable differences in market size and growth rates from country to country. Less than 20 percent of the populations of Brazil, India, and China have annual purchasing power equivalent to $25,000. Middle-class consumers represent a much smaller portion of the population in these and other developing countries than in North America, Japan, and much of western Europe—China's middle class numbers about 300 million out of a population of 1.35 billion.[6] At the same time, in developing markets like India, China, Brazil, and Malaysia, market growth potential is far higher than it is in the more mature economies of Britain, Denmark, Canada, and Japan. The potential for market growth in automobiles is explosive in China, where 2009 sales of new vehicles amounted to 13.6 million, surpassing U.S. sales of 10 million and making China the world's largest market.[7] Owing to widely differing population demographics and income levels, there is a far bigger market for luxury automobiles in the United States and Germany than in Argentina, India, Mexico, China, and Thailand.

Buyer tastes for a particular product or service sometimes differ substantially from country to country. In France consumers prefer top-loading washing machines, while in most other European countries consumers prefer front-loading machines. Soups that appeal to Swedish consumers are not popular in Malaysia. Italian coffee drinkers prefer espressos, but in North America the preference is for mild-roasted coffees. Sometimes, product designs suitable in one country are inappropriate in another because of differing local standards—for example, in the United States electrical devices run on 110-volt electric systems, but in some

European countries the standard is a 240-volt electric system, necessitating the use of different electrical designs and components. Cultural influences can also affect consumer demand for a product. For instance, in South Korea, many parents are reluctant to purchase PCs even when they can afford them because of concerns that their children will be distracted from their schoolwork by surfing the Web, playing PC-based video games, and becoming Internet "addicts."[8]

Consequently, companies operating in an international marketplace have to wrestle with *whether and how much to customize their offerings in each different country market to match the tastes and preferences of local buyers or whether to pursue a strategy of offering a mostly standardized product worldwide.* While making products that are closely matched to local tastes makes them more appealing to local buyers, customizing a company's products country by country may have the effect of raising production and distribution costs due to the greater variety of designs and components, shorter production runs, and the complications of added inventory handling and distribution logistics. Greater standardization of a multinational company's product offering, on the other hand, can lead to scale economies and learning curve effects, thus contributing to the achievement of a low-cost advantage. *The tension between the market pressures to localize a company's product offerings country by country and the competitive pressures to lower costs is one of the big strategic issues that participants in foreign markets have to resolve.*

THE CONCEPTS OF MULTIDOMESTIC COMPETITION AND GLOBAL COMPETITION

In crafting a strategy to compete on an international basis, it is essential for managers to recognize that the pattern of international competition varies in important ways from industry to industry.[9] At one extreme is **multidomestic competition,** in which there's so much cross-country variation in market conditions and in the companies contending for leadership that the market contest among rivals in one country is localized and not closely connected to the market contests in other countries. The standout features of multidomestic competition are that (1) buyers in different countries are attracted to different product attributes, (2) sellers vary from country to country, and (3) industry conditions and competitive forces in each national market differ in important respects. Take the banking industry in Poland, Mexico, and Australia as an example—the requirements and expectations of banking customers vary among the three countries, the lead banking competitors in Poland differ from those in Mexico or Australia, and the competitive battle going on among the leading banks in Poland is unrelated to the rivalry taking place in Mexico or Australia. Thus, with multidomestic competition, rival firms battle for national championships and winning in one country does not necessarily signal the ability to fare well in other countries. In multidomestic competition, the power of a company's strategy and capabilities in one country has little impact on its competitiveness in other countries where it operates. Moreover, any competitive advantage a company secures in one country is largely confined to that country; the spillover effects to other countries are minimal to nonexistent.

CORE CONCEPT

Multidomestic competition exists when the competition among rivals in each country market is localized and not closely connected to the competition in other country markets—there is no world market, just a collection of self-contained local markets.

Industries characterized by multidomestic competition include radio and TV broadcasting, consumer banking, life insurance, apparel, metals fabrication, many types of food products (coffee, cereals, breads, canned goods, frozen foods), and retailing.

At the other extreme is **global competition,** in which prices and competitive conditions across country markets are strongly linked and the term *global* has true meaning. In a globally competitive industry, much the same group of rival companies competes in many different countries but especially in countries where sales volumes are large and where having a competitive presence is strategically important to building a strong global position in the industry. Thus, a company's competitive position in one country both affects and is affected by its position in other countries. In global competition, a firm's overall competitive advantage grows out of its entire worldwide operations; the competitive advantage it creates at its home base is supplemented by advantages growing out of its operations in other countries (having plants in low-wage countries, being able to transfer expertise from country to country, having the capability to serve customers that also have multinational operations, and having brand-name recognition in many parts of the world). Rival firms in globally competitive industries vie for worldwide leadership. Global competition exists in motor vehicles, television sets, tires, cell phones, personal computers, copiers, watches, digital cameras, bicycles, and commercial aircraft.

> **CORE CONCEPT**
>
> **Global competition** exists when competitive conditions across national markets are linked strongly enough to form a true world market and when leading competitors compete head to head in many different countries.

An industry can have segments that are globally competitive and segments in which competition is country by country.[10] In the hotel/motel industry, for example, the low- and medium-priced segments are characterized by multidomestic competition—competitors mainly serve travelers within the same country. In the business and luxury segments, however, competition is more globalized. Companies like Nikki (owned by Japan Airlines), Marriott, Sheraton, and Hilton have hotels at many international locations, use worldwide reservation systems, and establish common quality and service standards to gain marketing advantages in serving businesspeople and other travelers who make frequent international trips. In lubricants, the marine engine segment is globally competitive—ships move from port to port and require the same oil everywhere they stop. Brand reputations in marine lubricants have a global scope, and successful marine engine lubricant producers (ExxonMobil, BP Amoco, and Shell) operate globally. In automotive motor oil, however, multidomestic competition dominates—countries have different weather conditions and driving patterns, production of motor oil is subject to limited scale economies, shipping costs are high, and retail distribution channels differ markedly from country to country. Thus, domestic firms—like Quaker State and Pennzoil in the United States and Castrol in Great Britain—can be leaders in their home markets without competing globally.

It is also important to recognize that an industry can be in transition from multidomestic competition to global competition. In a number of today's industries—beer and major home appliances are prime examples—leading domestic competitors have begun expanding into more and more foreign markets, often acquiring local companies or brands and integrating them into their operations. As some industry members start to build global brands and a global presence, other industry members find themselves pressured to follow the same strategic path—especially if establishing multinational operations results in important scale economies and a powerhouse brand name. As the industry consolidates to fewer players, such that many of the same companies find themselves in head-to-head competition in more and more country markets, global competition begins to replace multidomestic competition.

At the same time, consumer tastes in a number of important product categories are converging across the world. Less diversity of tastes and preferences opens the way for companies to create global brands and sell essentially the same products in almost all countries of the world. Even in industries where consumer tastes remain fairly diverse, companies are learning to use "custom mass production" to economically create different versions of a product and thereby satisfy the tastes of people in different countries.

In addition to taking the obvious cultural and political differences between countries into account, a company must shape its strategic approach to competing in foreign markets according to whether its industry is characterized by multidomestic competition, global competition, or some combination, depending on differences among industry sectors and on how the industry is evolving.

STRATEGIC OPTIONS FOR ENTERING AND COMPETING IN INTERNATIONAL MARKETS

LO 3

Learn about the major strategic options for entering and competing in foreign markets.

Once a company decides to expand beyond its domestic borders it must consider the question of how to enter foreign markets. There are six primary strategic options for doing so:

1. Maintain a national (one-country) production base and export goods to foreign markets.
2. License foreign firms to produce and distribute the company's products abroad.
3. Employ a franchising strategy.
4. Establish a wholly owned subsidiary in the foreign market by acquiring a foreign company.
5. Create a wholly owned foreign subsidiary from the ground up via a "greenfield" venture.
6. Rely on strategic alliances or joint ventures to partner with foreign companies.

Which option to employ depends on a variety of factors, including the nature of the firm's strategic objectives, whether the firm has the full range of resources and capabilities needed to operate abroad, country-specific factors such as trade barriers, and the transaction costs involved (the costs of contracting with a partner and monitoring its compliance with the terms of the contract, for example). The options vary considerably regarding the level of investment required and the associated risks, but higher levels of investment and risk generally provide the firm with the benefits of greater ownership and control.

Export Strategies

Using domestic plants as a production base for exporting goods to foreign markets is an excellent initial strategy for pursuing international sales. It is a conservative way to test the international waters. The amount of capital needed to begin exporting is often quite minimal; existing production capacity may well be sufficient to make goods for export. With an export strategy, a manufacturer can limit its involvement in foreign markets by contracting with foreign wholesalers experienced in importing to handle the entire distribution and marketing function in their countries or regions of the world. If it is more advantageous to maintain control over these functions, however, a manufacturer can establish its own distribution and sales organizations in some or all of the target foreign markets. Either way, a home-based production and export strategy helps the firm minimize its direct investments in foreign countries. Such strategies have been favored traditionally by Chinese, Korean, and Italian companies—products are designed and manufactured at home and then distributed through local channels in the importing countries; the primary functions performed abroad relate chiefly to establishing a network of distributors and perhaps conducting sales promotion and brand awareness activities.

Whether an export strategy can be pursued successfully over the long run hinges on whether its advantages for the company continue to outweigh its disadvantages. This depends in part on the relative cost competitiveness of the home-country production base. In some industries, firms gain additional scale economies and learning curve benefits from centralizing production in one or several giant plants whose output capability exceeds demand in any one country market; exporting is one obvious way to capture such economies. However, an export strategy is vulnerable when (1) manufacturing costs in the home country are substantially higher than in foreign countries where rivals have plants, (2) the costs of shipping the product to distant foreign markets are relatively high, or (3) adverse shifts occur in currency exchange rates. The disadvantages of export strategies can also swell due to high tariffs and other trade barriers, inadequate control over marketing or distribution, and an inability to tap into location advantages available elsewhere, such as skilled low-cost labor.

Licensing Strategies

Licensing makes sense when a firm with valuable technical know-how, an appealing brand, or a unique patented product has neither the internal organizational capability nor the resources to enter foreign markets. Licensing also has the advantage of avoiding the risks of committing resources to country markets that are unfamiliar, politically volatile, economically unstable, or otherwise risky. By licensing the technology, trademark, or production rights to foreign-based firms, the firm does not have to bear the costs and risks of entering foreign markets on its own, yet it is able to generate income from royalties. The big disadvantage of licensing is the risk of providing valuable technological know-how to foreign companies and thereby losing some degree of control over its use; monitoring licensees and safeguarding the company's proprietary know-how can prove quite difficult in some circumstances. But if the royalty potential is considerable and the companies to whom the licenses are being granted are trustworthy and reputable, then licensing can be a very attractive option. Many software and pharmaceutical companies use licensing strategies.

Franchising Strategies

While licensing works well for manufacturers and owners of proprietary technology, franchising is often better suited to the international expansion efforts of service and retailing enterprises. McDonald's, Yum! Brands (the parent of Pizza Hut,

KFC, and Taco Bell), the UPS Store, Jani-King International (the world's largest commercial cleaning franchisor), Roto-Rooter, 7-Eleven, and Hilton Hotels have all used franchising to build a presence in foreign markets. Franchising has much the same advantages as licensing. The franchisee bears most of the costs and risks of establishing foreign locations; a franchisor has to expend only the resources to recruit, train, support, and monitor franchisees. The big problem a franchisor faces is maintaining quality control; foreign franchisees do not always exhibit strong commitment to consistency and standardization, especially when the local culture does not stress the same kinds of quality concerns. Another problem that can arise is whether to allow foreign franchisees to make modifications in the franchisor's product offering so as to better satisfy the tastes and expectations of local buyers. Should McDonald's allow its franchised units in Japan to modify Big Macs slightly to suit Japanese tastes? Should the franchised Pizza Hut units in China be permitted to substitute spices that appeal to Chinese consumers? Or should the same menu offerings be rigorously and unvaryingly required of all franchisees worldwide?

Acquisition Strategies

Acquisition strategies have the advantages of a high level of control as well as speed, which can be a significant factor when a firm wants to enter a foreign market at a relatively large scale. When a strong presence in the market or local economies of scale are a significant competitive factor in the market, these advantages may make acquiring a large local firm preferable to most other entry modes. Similarly, when entry barriers are high—whether in the form of trade barriers, access to a local distribution network, or building key relationships with local constituents and officials—an acquisition may be the only route to overcoming such hurdles. Acquisition may also be the preferred entry strategy if the strategic objective is to gain access to the core capabilities or well-guarded technologies of a foreign firm.

At the same time, acquisition strategies have their downside as a foreign entry strategy. Acquisition strategies are always costly, since it is necessary to pay a premium over the share-price value of a company in order to acquire control. This can saddle the acquiring company with a good deal of debt, increasing its risk of bankruptcy and limiting its other investment options. Acquiring a foreign firm can be particularly tricky due to the challenge of international negotiations, the burden of foreign legal and regulatory requirements, and the added complexity of postacquisition integration efforts when companies are separated by distance, culture, and language.[11] While the potential benefits of a cross-border acquisition can be high, the risk of failure is high as well.

Greenfield Venture Strategies

A **greenfield venture** strategy is one in which the company creates a subsidiary business in the foreign market by setting up the entire operation (plants, distribution system, etc.) from the ground up. Like acquisition strategies, greenfield ventures have the advantage of high control, but to an even greater degree since starting from scratch allows the company to set up every aspect of the operation to its specifications. Since organizational change is notoriously difficult and hampered by a variety of inertial factors, it is much harder to fine-tune the operations of an acquired firm to this degree—particularly a foreign firm. Entering a foreign market from the ground up provides a firm with another potential advantage: It enables the company to *learn by doing* how to operate in the foreign market and how to best serve local needs, navigate the local politics, and compete most effectively against local rivals. This is not to say, however, that the company needs to acquire all the knowledge and experience needed from the ground up; in building its operation, the company can avail itself of local managerial talent and know-how by simply hiring experienced local managers who understand the local market conditions, local buying habits, local competitors, and local ways of doing business. By assembling a management team that also includes senior managers from the parent company (preferably with considerable international experience), the parent company can transfer technology, business practices, and the corporate culture into the new foreign subsidiary and ensure that there is a conduit for the flow of information between the corporate office and local operations.

Greenfield ventures in foreign markets also pose a number of problems, just as other entry strategies do. They represent a costly capital investment, subject to a high level of risk. They require numerous other company resources as well, diverting them from other uses. They do not work well in countries without strong, well-functioning markets and institutions that protect the rights of foreign investors and provide other legal protections.[12] Moreover, an important disadvantage of greenfield ventures relative to other means of international expansion is that they are the slowest entry route—particularly if the objective is to achieve a sizable market share. On the other hand, successful greenfield ventures may offer higher returns to compensate for their high risk and slower path.

Alliance and Joint Venture Strategies

Collaborative agreements with foreign companies in the form of strategic alliances or joint ventures are widely used as a means of entering foreign markets.[13] Often they are used in conjunction with another entry strategy, such as exporting, franchising, or establishing a greenfield venture. Historically, firms in industrialized nations that wanted to export their products and market them in less developed countries sought alliances with local companies in order to do so—such arrangements were often necessary to win approval for entry from the host country's government. Companies wanting to set up a manufacturing operation abroad often had to do so via a joint venture with a foreign firm. Over the last 20 years, those types of restrictions have been lifted in countries such as India and China, and companies have been able to enter these markets via more direct means.[14]

> Collaborative strategies involving alliances or joint ventures with foreign partners are a popular way for companies to edge their way into the markets of foreign countries.

Today, a more important reason for using strategic alliances and joint ventures as a vehicle for international expansion is that they facilitate resource and risk sharing. When firms need access to complementary resources to succeed abroad, when the venture requires substantial investment, and when the risks are high, the attraction of such strategies grows. A company can benefit immensely from a foreign partner's familiarity with local government regulations, its knowledge of the buying habits and product preferences of consumers, its distribution channel relationships, and so on. Both Japanese and American companies are actively forming alliances with European companies to better compete in the 27-nation European Union and to capitalize on emerging but risky opportunities in the countries of eastern Europe. Similarly, many U.S. and European companies are allying with Asian companies in their efforts to enter markets in China, India, Thailand, Indonesia, and other Asian countries where they lack local knowledge and uncertainties abound. Many foreign companies, of course, are particularly interested in strategic partnerships that will strengthen their ability to gain a foothold in the U.S. market.

Another potential benefit of a collaborative strategy is the learning and added expertise that come from performing joint research, sharing technological know-how, studying one another's manufacturing methods, and understanding how to tailor sales and marketing approaches to fit local cultures and traditions. Indeed, by learning from the skills, technological know-how, and capabilities of alliance partners and implanting the knowledge and know-how of these partners in its own personnel and organization, a company can upgrade its capabilities and become a stronger competitor in its home market. DaimlerChrysler's strategic alliance with Mitsubishi, for example, was motivated by a desire to learn from Mitsubishi's technological strengths in small-size vehicles in order to improve the performance of its loss-making "smart car" division.[15]

> Cross-border alliances enable a growth-minded company to widen its geographic coverage and strengthen its competitiveness in foreign markets; at the same time, they offer flexibility and allow a company to retain some degree of autonomy and operating control.

Many companies believe that cross-border alliances and partnerships are a better strategic means of gaining the above benefits (as compared to acquiring or merging with foreign-based companies to gain much the same benefits) because they allow a company to preserve its independence (which is not the case with a merger), retain veto power over how the alliance operates, and avoid using scarce financial resources to fund acquisitions. Furthermore, an alliance offers the flexibility to readily disengage once its purpose has been served or if the benefits prove elusive, whereas an acquisition is a more permanent sort of arrangement (although the acquired company can, of course, be divested).[16]

Illustration Capsule 7.1 provides four examples of cross-border strategic alliances.

The Risks of Strategic Alliances with Foreign Partners   Alliances and joint ventures with foreign partners have their pitfalls, however. Cross-border allies typically have to overcome language and cultural barriers and figure out how to deal with diverse operating practices. The transaction costs of working out a mutually agreeable arrangement and monitoring partner compliance with the terms of the arrangement can be high. The communication, trust building, and coordination costs are not trivial in terms of management time.[17] Often, partners soon discover they have conflicting objectives and strategies, deep differences of opinion about how to proceed, and/or important differences in corporate values and ethical standards. Tensions build up, working relationships cool, and the hoped-for benefits never materialize.[18] It is not unusual for there to be little personal chemistry among some of the key people on whom success or failure of the alliance depends—the rapport such personnel need to work well together may never emerge. And even if allies are able to develop productive personal relationships, they can still have trouble reaching mutually agreeable ways to deal with key issues or resolve differences. Occasionally, the egos of corporate executives can clash. An alliance between Northwest Airlines and KLM Royal Dutch Airlines resulted in a bitter feud among both companies' top officials (who, according to some reports, refused to speak to each other).[19] Plus there is the thorny problem of getting alliance partners to sort through issues and reach decisions fast enough to stay abreast of rapid advances in technology or fast-changing market conditions.

One worrisome problem with alliances or joint ventures is that a firm may risk losing some of its competitive advantage if an alliance partner is given full access to

ILLUSTRATION CAPSULE 7.1

Four Examples of Cross-Border Strategic Alliances

1. The engine of General Motors' growth strategy in Asia is its three-way joint venture with Wulung, a Chinese producer of mini-commercial vehicles, and SAIC (Shanghai Automotive Industrial Corporation), China's largest automaker. The success of the SAIC-GM-Wulung Automotive Company is also GM's best hope for financial recovery since it emerged from bankruptcy on July 10, 2009. While GM lost $4.8 billion overall before interest and taxes during the last six months of 2009, its international operations (everything except North America and Europe) earned $1.2 billion. Its Chinese joint ventures accounted for approximately one-third of that profit, due in part to the roaring success of the no-frills Wulung Sunshine, a lightweight minivan that has become China's best-selling vehicle. In 2010, General Motors' sales in China topped its U.S. sales—the first time that sales in a foreign market have done so in the 102-year history of the company. GM is now positioning its Chinese joint venture to serve as a springboard for the company's expansion in India, with the possibility of launching a product to rival the Tata Nano there. When GM's president of international operations, Timothy E. Lee, was asked about GM's ability to compete in India, he replied, "When you harvest from your partnerships the collective wisdom of other cultures, it's incredible what you can do."

2. The European Aeronautic Defense and Space Company (EADS) was formed by an alliance of aerospace companies from Britain, Spain, Germany, and France that included British Aerospace, Daimler-Benz Aerospace, and Aerospatiale. The objective of the alliance was to create a European aircraft company capable of competing with U.S.-based Boeing Corp. The alliance has proved highly successful, infusing its commercial airline division, Airbus, with the know-how and resources needed to compete head to head with Boeing for world leadership in large commercial aircraft (those designed for over 100 passengers).

3. Cisco, the worldwide leader in networking components, entered into a strategic alliance with Finnish telecommunications firm Nokia Siemens Networks to develop communications networks capable of transmitting data either across the Internet or by mobile technologies. Nokia Siemens Networks itself was created through a 2006 international joint venture between German-based Siemens AG and the Finnish communications giant Nokia. The Cisco–Nokia Siemens alliance was created to better position both companies for convergence among Internet technologies and wireless communication devices that was expected to dramatically change how both computer networks and wireless telephones would be used.

4. Verio, a subsidiary of Japan-based NTT Communications and one of the leading global providers of Web hosting services and IP data transport, operates with the philosophy that in today's highly competitive and challenging technology market, companies must gain and share skills, information, and technology with technology leaders across the world. Believing that no company can be all things to all customers in the Web hosting industry, Verio executives have developed an alliance-oriented business model that combines the company's core competencies with the skills and products of best-of-breed technology partners. Verio's strategic partners include Accenture, Cisco Systems, Microsoft, Sun Microsystems, Oracle, Arsenal Digital Solutions (a provider of worry-free tape backup, data restore, and data storage services), Internet Security Systems (a provider of firewall and intrusion detection systems), and Mercantec (which develops storefront and shopping cart software). Verio's management believes that its portfolio of strategic alliances allows it to use innovative, best-of-class technologies in providing its customers with fast, efficient, accurate data transport and a complete set of Web hosting services. An independent panel of 12 judges recently selected Verio as the winner of the Best Technology Foresight Award for its efforts in pioneering new technologies.

Developed with Mukund Kulashekaran.

Sources: Company Web sites and press releases; Yves L. Doz and Gary Hamel, *Alliance Advantage: The Art of Creating Value through Partnering* (Boston: Harvard Business School Press, 1998); Joanne Muller, "Can China Save GM?" *Forbes.com,* May 10, 2010, www.forbes.com/forbes/2010/0510/global-2000-10-automobiles-china-detroit-whitacre-save-gm.html; "GM's First-Half China Sales Surge Past the U.S.," *Bloomberg Businessweek,* July 2, 2010, www.businessweek.com/news/2010-07-02/gm-s-first-half-china-sales-surge-past-the-u-s-.html; Nandini Sen Gupta, "General Motors May Drive in Nano Rival with Chinese Help," *Economic Times,* May 31, 2010, http://economictimes.indiatimes.com/articleshow/5992589.cms.

its proprietary technological expertise or other unique and competitively valuable capabilities. There is a natural tendency for allies to struggle to collaborate effectively in competitively sensitive areas, thus spawning suspicions on both sides about forthright exchanges of information and expertise. It requires many meetings of many people working in good faith over a period of time to iron out what is to be shared, what is to remain proprietary, and how the cooperative arrangements will work.

Even if a collaborative arrangement proves to be a win-win proposition for both parties, a company has to guard against becoming overly dependent on foreign partners for essential expertise and competitive capabilities. If a company is aiming for global market leadership and needs to develop capabilities of its own, then at some juncture a cross-border merger or acquisition may have to be substituted for cross-border alliances and joint ventures. One of the lessons about cross-border alliances is that they are more effective in helping a company establish a beachhead of new opportunity in world markets than they are in enabling a company to achieve and sustain global market leadership.

When a Cross-Border Alliance May Be Unnecessary Experienced multinational companies that market in 50 to 100 or more countries across the world find less need for entering into cross-border alliances than do companies in the early stages of globalizing their operations.[20] Multinational companies make it a point to develop senior managers who understand how "the system" works in different countries, plus they can avail themselves of local managerial talent and know-how by simply hiring experienced local managers and thereby detouring the hazards of collaborative alliances with local companies. If a multinational enterprise with considerable experience in entering the markets of different countries wants to detour the hazards of allying with local businesses, it can simply assemble a capable management team consisting of both senior managers with considerable international experience and local managers. The role of its own in-house managers with international business savvy is to transfer technology, business practices, and the corporate culture into the company's operations in the new country market and to serve as conduits for the flow of information between the corporate office and local operations. The role of local managers is to contribute needed understanding of the local market conditions, local buying habits, and local ways of doing business and, often, to head up local operations.

Hence, one cannot automatically presume that a company needs the wisdom and resources of a local partner to guide it through the process of successfully entering the markets of foreign countries. Indeed, experienced multinationals often discover that local partners do not always have adequate local market knowledge—much of the so-called experience of local partners can predate the emergence of current market trends and conditions and sometimes their operating practices can be archaic.[21]

COMPETING INTERNATIONALLY: THE THREE MAIN STRATEGIC APPROACHES

Broadly speaking, a firm's **international strategy** is simply its strategy for competing in two or more countries simultaneously. Typically, a company will start to compete internationally by entering just one or perhaps a select few foreign markets, selling its products or services in countries where there is a ready market for them. But as it expands further internationally, it will have to confront head-on the conflicting pressures of local responsiveness versus efficiency gains from standardizing and integrating operations globally. Moreover, it will have to consider whether the markets abroad are characterized by multidomestic competition, global competition, or some mix. The issue of whether and how to vary the company's competitive approach to fit specific market conditions and buyer preferences in each host country or whether to employ essentially the same strategy in all countries is perhaps the foremost strategic issue that companies must address when they operate in two or more foreign markets.[22] Figure 7.2 shows a company's three options for resolving this issue: a *multidomestic, global,* or *transnational* strategy.

Multidomestic Strategy—Think Local, Act Local

A **multidomestic strategy** is one based on differentiating products and services on a country-by-country or regional basis to meet differing buyer needs and to address divergent local market conditions. It is a good choice for companies that compete primarily in industries characterized by multidomestic competition. This type of strategy involves having plants produce different product versions for different local markets and adapting marketing and distribution to fit local customs, cultures, regulations, and market requirements. Castrol, a specialist in oil lubricants, produces over 3,000 different formulas of lubricants to meet the requirements of different climates, vehicle types and uses, and equipment applications that characterize different country markets. In the food products industry, it is common for companies to vary the ingredients in their products and sell the localized versions under local brand names to cater to country-specific tastes and eating preferences.

In essence, a multidomestic strategy represents a **think-local, act-local** approach to international strategy. A think-local, act-local approach is possible only when decision making is decentralized, giving local managers considerable latitude for crafting and executing strategies for the country markets they are responsible for. Giving local managers decision-making authority allows them to address specific market needs and respond swiftly to local changes in demand. It also enables them to focus their competitive efforts, stake out attractive market positions vis-à-vis local competitors, react to rivals' moves in a timely fashion, and target new opportunities as they emerge.

A think-local, act-local approach to strategy making is most appropriate when the need for local responsiveness is high due to significant cross-country differences in demographic, cultural, and market conditions and when the potential for efficiency gains from standardization is limited, as depicted in Figure 7.2. Consider, for example, the wide variation in refrigerator usage and preference around the world. Northern Europeans want large refrigerators because they tend to shop once a week in supermarkets; southern Europeans prefer small refrigerators because they shop daily. In parts of Asia refrigerators are a status symbol and may be placed in the living room, leading to preferences for stylish designs and

LO 4

Gain familiarity with the three main strategic approaches for competing internationally.

CORE CONCEPT

An **international strategy** is a strategy for competing in two or more countries simultaneously.

CORE CONCEPT

A **multidomestic strategy** is one in which a company varies its product offering and competitive approach from country to country in an effort to be responsive to differing buyer preferences and market conditions. It is a **think-local, act-local** type of international strategy, facilitated by decision making decentralized to the local level.

Figure 7.2   Three Approaches for Competing Internationally

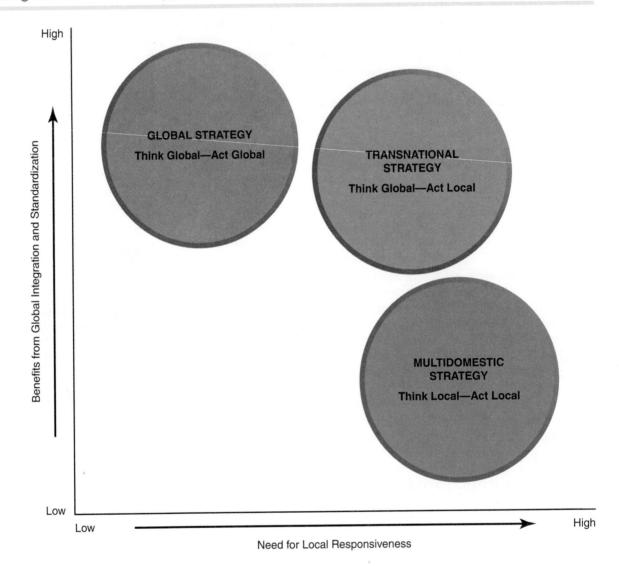

colors—in India bright blue and red are popular colors. In other Asian countries household space is constrained, and many refrigerators are only 4 feet high so that the top can be used for storage. If the minimum efficient scale for producing refrigerators is relatively low, there would be little reason to forgo the benefits of meeting these varying needs precisely in favor of a standardized, one-size-fits-all approach to production.

Despite their obvious benefits, think-local, act-local strategies have three big drawbacks:

1. They hinder transfer of a company's capabilities, knowledge, and other resources across country boundaries, since the company's efforts are not integrated or coordinated across country boundaries. This can make the company less innovative overall.

2. They raise production and distribution costs due to the greater variety of designs and components, shorter production runs for each product version, and complications of added inventory handling and distribution logistics.

3. They are not conducive to building a single, worldwide competitive advantage. When a company's competitive approach and product offering vary from country to country, the nature and size of any resulting competitive edge also tends to vary. At the most, multidomestic strategies are capable of producing a group of local competitive advantages of varying types and degrees of strength.

Global Strategy—Think Global, Act Global

A **global strategy** contrasts sharply with a multidomestic strategy in that it takes a standardized, globally integrated approach to producing, packaging, selling, and delivering the company's products and services worldwide. Companies employing a global strategy sell the same products under the same brand names everywhere, utilize much the same distribution channels in all countries, and compete on the basis of the same capabilities and marketing approaches worldwide. Although the company's strategy or product offering may be adapted in very minor ways to accommodate specific situations in a few host countries, the company's fundamental competitive approach (low cost, differentiation, best cost, or focused) remains very much intact worldwide and local managers stick close to the global strategy.

A **think-global, act-global** strategic theme prompts company managers to integrate and coordinate the company's strategic moves worldwide and to expand into most, if not all, nations where there is significant buyer demand. It puts considerable strategic emphasis on building a *global* brand name and aggressively pursuing opportunities to transfer ideas, new products, and capabilities from one country to another.[23] Global strategies are characterized by relatively centralized value chain activities, such as production and distribution. While there may be more than one manufacturing plant and distribution center to minimize transportation costs, for example, they tend to be few in number. Achieving the efficiency potential of a global strategy requires that resources and best practices be shared, value chain activities be integrated, and capabilities be transferred from one location to another as they are developed. These objectives are best facilitated through centralized decision making and strong headquarters control.

Because a global strategy cannot accommodate varying local needs, it is an appropriate strategic choice when there are pronounced efficiency benefits from standardization and when buyer needs are relatively homogeneous across countries and regions. A globally standardized and integrated approach is especially beneficial when high volumes significantly lower costs due to economies of scale or added experience (moving the company further down a learning curve). It can also be advantageous if it allows the firm to replicate a successful business model on a global basis efficiently or engage in higher levels of R&D by spreading the fixed costs and risks over a higher-volume output. It is a fitting response to industry conditions marked by global competition.

CORE CONCEPT

A **global strategy** is one in which a company employs the same basic competitive approach in all countries where it operates, sells much the same products everywhere, strives to build global brands, and coordinates its actions worldwide with strong headquarters control. It represents a **think-global, act-global** approach.

The drawbacks of global strategies are several: (1) They do not enable firms to address local needs as precisely as locally based rivals can, (2) they are less responsive to changes in local market conditions, either in the form of new opportunities or competitive threats, (3) they raise transportation costs and may involve higher tariffs, and (4) they involve higher coordination costs due to the more complex task of managing a globally integrated enterprise.

Transnational Strategy—Think Global, Act Local

A **transnational strategy** (sometimes called *glocalization*) incorporates elements of both a globalized and a localized approach to strategy making. This type of middle-ground strategy is called for when there are relatively high needs for local responsiveness as well as appreciable benefits to be realized from standardization, as Figure 7.2 suggests. A transnational strategy encourages a company to **think global, act local** to balance these competing objectives.

Often, companies implement a transnational strategy with mass-customization techniques that enable them to address local preferences in an efficient, semi-standardized manner. Both McDonald's and KFC have discovered ways to customize their menu offerings in various countries without compromising costs, product quality, and operating effectiveness. When it first opened Disneyland Paris, Disney learned the hard way that a global approach to its international theme parks would not work; it has since adapted elements of its strategy to accommodate local preferences even though much of its strategy still derives from a globally applied formula. Otis Elevator found that a transnational strategy delivers better results than a global strategy when competing in countries like China where local needs are highly differentiated. In 2000, it switched from its customary single-brand approach to a multibrand strategy aimed at serving different segments of the market. By 2009, it had doubled its market share in China and increased its revenues sixfold.[24]

> **CORE CONCEPT**
>
> A **transnational strategy** is a **think-global, act-local** approach that incorporates elements of both multidomestic and global strategies.

A transnational strategy is far more conducive than other strategies to transferring and leveraging subsidiary skills and capabilities. But, like other approaches to competing internationally, transnational strategies also have significant drawbacks:

1. They are the most difficult of all international strategies to implement due to the added complexity of varying the elements of the strategy to situational conditions.

2. They place large demands on the organization due to the need to pursue conflicting objectives simultaneously.

3. Implementing the strategy is likely to be a costly and time-consuming enterprise, with an uncertain outcome.

Table 7.1 provides a summary of the pluses and minuses of the three approaches to competing internationally.

Table 7.1 Advantages and Disadvantages of Multidomestic, Global, and Transnational Approaches

	Advantages	Disadvantages
Multidomestic (think local, act local)	• Can meet the specific needs of each market more precisely • Can respond more swiftly to localized changes in demand • Can target reactions to the moves of local rivals • Can respond more quickly to local opportunities and threats	• Hinders resource and capability sharing or cross-market transfers • Higher production and distribution costs • Not conducive to a worldwide competitive advantage
Transnational (think global, act local)	• Offers the benefits of both local responsiveness and global integration • Enables the transfer and sharing of resources and capabilities across borders • Provides the benefits of flexible coordination	• More complex and harder to implement • Conflicting goals may be difficult to reconcile and require trade-offs • Implementation more costly and time-consuming
Global (think global, act global)	• Lower costs due to scale and scope economies • Greater efficiencies due to the ability to transfer best practices across markets • More innovation from knowledge sharing and capability transfer • The benefit of a global brand and reputation	• Unable to address local needs precisely • Less responsive to changes in local market conditions • Higher transportation costs and tariffs • Higher coordination and integration costs

THE QUEST FOR COMPETITIVE ADVANTAGE IN THE INTERNATIONAL ARENA

There are three important ways in which a firm can gain competitive advantage (or offset domestic disadvantages) by expanding outside its domestic market.[25] First, it can use location to lower costs or achieve greater product differentiation. Second, it can transfer competitively valuable resources, competencies, and capabilities from one country to another or share them across international borders to extend and deepen its competitive advantages. And third, it can benefit from cross-border coordination in ways that a domestic-only competitor cannot.

LO 5

Understand how international companies go about building competitive advantage in foreign markets.

Using Location to Build Competitive Advantage

To use location to build competitive advantage, a company must consider two issues: (1) whether to concentrate each activity it performs in a few select countries or to disperse performance of the activity to many nations, and (2) in which countries to locate particular activities.[26]

When to Concentrate Activities in a Few Locations   It is advantageous for a company to concentrate its activities in a limited number of locations when:

- *The costs of manufacturing or other activities are significantly lower in some geographic locations than in others.* For example, much of the world's athletic footwear is manufactured in Asia (China and Korea) because of low labor costs; much of the production of circuit boards for PCs is located in Taiwan because of both low costs and the high-caliber technical skills of the Taiwanese labor force.

- *There are significant scale economies in production or distribution.* The presence of significant economies of scale in components production or final assembly means that a company can gain major cost savings from operating a few ultra-efficient plants as opposed to a host of small plants scattered across the world. Achieving low-cost provider status often requires a company to have the largest worldwide manufacturing share (as distinct from brand share or market share), with production centralized in one or a few world-scale plants. Some companies even use such plants to manufacture units sold under the brand names of rivals to further boost production-related scale economies. Makers of digital cameras and LCD TVs located in Japan, South Korea, and Taiwan have used their scale economies to establish a low-cost advantage. Likewise, a company may be able to reduce its distribution costs by capturing scale economies associated with establishing large-scale distribution centers to serve major geographic regions of the world market (for example, North America, Latin America, Europe–Middle East, and Asia-Pacific).

- *There are sizable learning and experience benefits associated with performing an activity in a single location.* In some industries, a manufacturer can lower unit costs, boost quality, or master a new technology more quickly by concentrating production in a few locations. The greater the cumulative volume of production at a plant, the faster the buildup of learning and experience of the plant's workforce, thereby enabling quicker capture of the learning/experience benefits.

- *Certain locations have superior resources, allow better coordination of related activities, or offer other valuable advantages.* A research unit or a sophisticated production facility may be situated in a particular nation because of its pool of technically trained personnel. Samsung became a leader in memory chip technology by establishing a major R&D facility in Silicon Valley and transferring the know-how it gained back to its operations in South Korea. Companies also locate activities to benefit from proximity to a cluster of related and supporting industries, as discussed earlier. Cisco Systems, an international firm that sells networking and communications technology, such as routers, restricts its acquisitions to companies located in one of three well-known clusters of high-tech activity.[27] Where just-in-time inventory practices yield big cost savings and/or where an assembly firm has long-term partnering arrangements with its key suppliers, parts manufacturing plants may be located close to final assembly plants. A customer service center or sales office may be opened in a particular country to help cultivate strong relationships with pivotal customers located nearby.

> Companies that compete internationally can pursue competitive advantage in world markets by locating their value chain activities in whatever nations prove most advantageous.

When to Disperse Activities across Many Locations   There are several instances when dispersing activities is more advantageous than concentrating them. Buyer-related activities—such as distribution to dealers, sales and advertising, and after-sale service—usually must take place close to

buyers. This means physically locating the capability to perform such activities in every country market where a firm has major customers (unless buyers in several adjoining countries can be served quickly from a nearby central location). For example, firms that make mining and oil-drilling equipment maintain operations in many locations around the world to support customers' needs for speedy equipment repair and technical assistance. The four biggest public accounting firms have offices in numerous countries to serve the foreign operations of their international corporate clients. Dispersing activities to many locations is also competitively advantageous when high transportation costs, diseconomies of large size, and trade barriers make it too expensive to operate from a central location. Many companies distribute their products from multiple locations to shorten delivery times to customers. In addition, it is strategically advantageous to disperse activities to hedge against the risks of fluctuating exchange rates, supply interruptions (due to strikes, mechanical failures, and transportation delays), and adverse political developments. Such risks are usually greater when activities are concentrated in a single location.

As discussed earlier, there are a variety of reasons for locating different value chain activities in different countries—all having to do with location-based advantages that vary from country to country. While the classic reason for locating an activity in a particular country is low cost, input quality and availability are also important considerations.[28] Such activities as materials procurement, parts manufacture, finished-goods assembly, technology research, and new product development can frequently be decoupled from buyer locations and performed wherever advantage lies. Components can be made in Mexico; technology research done in Frankfurt; new products developed and tested in Phoenix; and assembly plants located in Spain, Brazil, Taiwan, or South Carolina. Capital can be raised in whatever country it is available on the best terms.

Sharing and Transferring Resources and Capabilities across Borders to Build Competitive Advantage

When a company has competitively valuable resources and capabilities, it may be able to mount a resource-based strategic offensive to enter additional country markets. If a company's resources retain their value in foreign contexts, then entering new markets can extend the company's resource-based competitive advantage over a broader domain. For example, companies have used powerful brand names such as Rolex, Chanel, and Tiffany to extend their differentiation-based competitive advantages into markets far beyond their home-country origins. In each of these cases, the luxury brand name represents a valuable resource that is *shared among all of the company's international operations* and allows the company to command a higher willingness to pay from its customers in each country.

Transferring resources and capabilities across borders provides another means to extend a company's competitive advantage internationally. For example, if a firm learns how to assemble its product more efficiently at its Brazilian plant, the accumulated expertise can be quickly communicated to assembly plants in other world locations. Whirlpool, the leading global manufacturer of home appliances, with 69 manufacturing and technology research centers around the world and sales in nearly every country, uses an online global information technology platform to quickly and effectively transfer key product innovations and improved production techniques both across national borders and across its various appliance brands.

Sharing or transferring resources and capabilities across borders provides a way for a company to leverage its core competencies more fully and extend its competitive advantages into a wider array of geographic markets. Thus a technology-based competitive advantage in one country market may provide a similar basis for advantage in other country markets (depending on local market conditions). But since sharing or transferring valuable resources across borders is a very cost-effective means of extending a company's competitive advantage, these activities can also contribute to a company's competitive advantage on the costs side, giving multinational companies a powerful edge over domestic-only rivals. Since valuable resources and capabilities (such as brands, technologies, and production capabilities) are often developed at very high cost, deploying them abroad spreads the fixed development cost over greater output, thus lowering the company's unit costs. The cost of transferring already developed resources and capabilities is low by comparison. And even if the resources and capabilities need to be fully replicated in the foreign market or adapted to local conditions, this can usually be done at low additional cost relative to the initial investment in capability building.

Consider the case of Walt Disney's theme parks as an example. The success of the theme parks in the United States derives in part from core resources such as the Disney brand name and characters like Mickey Mouse that have universal appeal and worldwide recognition. These resources can be freely shared with new theme parks as Disney expands internationally. Disney can replicate its theme parks in new countries cost-effectively since it has already borne the costs of developing its core resources, park attractions, basic park design, and operating capabilities. The cost of replicating its theme parks abroad should be relatively low, even if they need to be adapted to a variety of local country conditions. By expanding internationally, Disney is able to enhance its competitive advantage over local theme park rivals. It does so by leveraging the differentiation advantage conferred by resources such as the Disney name and the park attractions. And by moving into new foreign markets, it augments its competitive advantage worldwide through the efficiency gains that come from cross border resource sharing and low-cost capability transfer and business model replication.

Sharing and transferring resources and capabilities across country borders may also contribute to the development of broader or deeper competencies and capabilities—ideally helping a company achieve *dominating depth* in some competitively valuable area. For example, an international company that consistently incorporates the same differentiating attributes in its products worldwide has enhanced potential to build a global brand name with significant power in the marketplace. The reputation for quality that Honda established worldwide began in motorcycles but enabled the company to command a position in both automobiles and outdoor power equipment in multiple-country markets. A one-country customer base is often too small to support the resource buildup needed to achieve such depth; this is particularly true when the market is developing or protected and sophisticated resources have not been required. By deploying capabilities across a larger international domain, a company can gain the experience needed to upgrade them to a higher performance standard. And by facing a more challenging set of international competitors, a company may be spurred to develop a stronger set of competitive capabilities. Moreover, by entering international markets, firms may be able to augment their capability set by learning from international rivals, cooperative partners, or acquisition targets.

However, sharing and transferring resources and capabilities across borders cannot provide a guaranteed recipe for competitive success. Because lifestyles and buying habits differ internationally, resources that are valuable in one country may not have value in another. For example, brands that are popular in one country may not transfer well or may lack recognition in the new context and thus offer no advantage against an established local brand. In addition, whether a resource or capability can confer a competitive advantage abroad depends on the conditions of rivalry in each particular market. If the rivals in a foreign country market have superior resources and capabilities, then an entering firm may find itself at a competitive disadvantage even if it has a resource-based advantage domestically and can transfer the resources at low cost.

Using Cross-Border Coordination for Competitive Advantage

Companies that compete on an international basis have another source of competitive advantage relative to their purely domestic rivals: They are able to benefit from coordinating activities across different countries' domains.[29] For example, an international manufacturer can shift production from a plant in one country to a plant in another to take advantage of exchange rate fluctuations, to cope with components shortages, or to profit from changing wage rates or energy costs. Production schedules can be coordinated worldwide; shipments can be diverted from one distribution center to another if sales rise unexpectedly in one place and fall in another. By coordinating their activities, multinational companies may also be able to enhance their leverage with host-country governments or respond adaptively to changes in tariffs and quotas.

Efficiencies can also be achieved by shifting workloads from where they are unusually heavy to locations where personnel are underutilized. Whirlpool's efforts to link its product R&D and manufacturing operations in North America, Latin America, Europe, and Asia allowed it to accelerate the discovery of innovative appliance features, coordinate the introduction of these features in the appliance products marketed in different countries, and create a cost-efficient worldwide supply chain. Whirlpool's conscious efforts to integrate and coordinate its various operations around the world have helped it become a low-cost producer and also speed product innovations to market, thereby giving Whirlpool an edge over rivals worldwide.

PROFIT SANCTUARIES AND CROSS-BORDER STRATEGIC MOVES

Profit sanctuaries are country markets (or geographic regions) in which a company derives substantial profits because of its protected market position or unassailable competitive advantage. Japan, for example, is the chief profit sanctuary for most Japanese companies because trade barriers erected by the Japanese government effectively block foreign companies from competing for a large share of Japanese sales. Protected from the threat of foreign competition in their home market, Japanese companies can safely charge somewhat higher prices to their Japanese customers and thus earn attractively large profits on sales made in Japan. Other profit sanctuaries may be protected because a company has an unassailable market position due to unrivaled and inimitable capabilities. In most cases, a company's biggest and most strategically crucial profit sanctuary is its home market, but multinational companies may also enjoy profit sanctuary status in other nations where they have a strong position based on some type of competitive advantage. Companies that compete worldwide are likely to have more profit sanctuaries than companies that compete in just a few country markets; a domestic-only competitor, of course, can have only one profit sanctuary at most (see Figure 7.3).

Figure 7.3 **Profit Sanctuary Potential of Domestic-only, International, and Global Competitors**

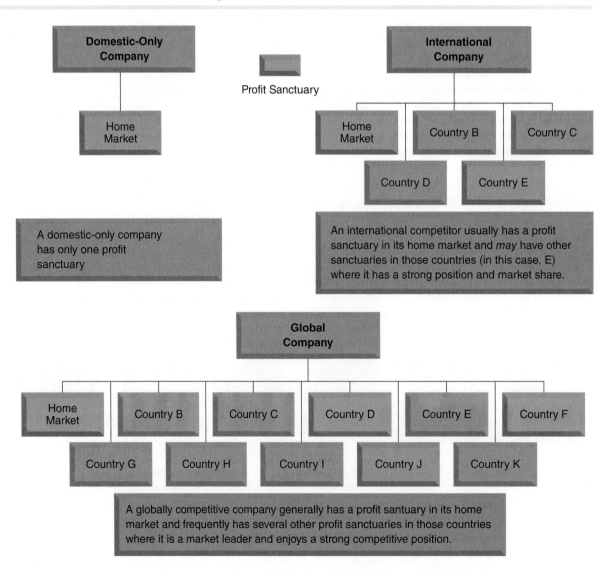

Using Cross-Market Subsidization to Wage a Strategic Offensive

Profit sanctuaries are valuable competitive assets, providing the financial strength to support strategic offensives in selected country markets and fuel a company's race for world-market leadership. The added financial capability afforded by multiple profit sanctuaries gives an international competitor the financial strength to wage a market offensive against a domestic competitor whose only profit sanctuary is its home market. The international company has the flexibility of lowballing its prices or launching high-cost marketing campaigns in the domestic company's home market and grabbing market share at the domestic company's expense. Razor-thin margins or even losses in these markets can be subsidized with the healthy profits earned in its profit sanctuaries—a practice called **cross-market subsidization.** The international company can adjust the depth of its price cutting to move in and capture market share quickly, or it can shave prices slightly to make gradual market inroads (perhaps over a decade or more) so as not to threaten domestic firms precipitously and trigger protectionist government actions. If the domestic company retaliates with matching price cuts or increased marketing expenses, it exposes its entire revenue stream and profit base to erosion; its profits can be squeezed substantially and its competitive strength sapped, even if it is the domestic market leader.

> **CORE CONCEPT**
>
> **Cross-market subsidization**—supporting competitive offensives in one market with resources and profits diverted from operations in another market—can be a powerful competitive weapon.

When taken to the extreme, cut-rate pricing attacks by international competitors may draw charges of unfair dumping. A company is said to be dumping when it sells its goods in foreign markets at prices that are (1) well below the prices at which it normally sells in its home market or (2) well below its full costs per unit. Companies that engage in dumping usually keep their selling prices high enough to cover variable costs per unit, thereby limiting their losses on each unit to some percentage of fixed costs per unit.

Dumping can be a tempting strategy in either of two instances: (1) when selling goods abroad at below-market prices can allow a firm to avoid the high costs of idling plants, and (2) when temporary below-cost pricing can allow a company to make lasting market share gains by driving weak firms from the market. The first may be justified as a legitimate competitive practice, while the latter is usually viewed to be predatory in nature. A charge of unfair dumping is more easily defended when a company with unused production capacity discovers that it is cheaper to keep producing (as long as the selling prices cover average variable costs per unit) than it is to incur the costs associated with idle plant capacity. By keeping its plants operating at or near capacity, not only may a company be able to cover variable costs and earn a contribution to fixed costs, but it also may be able to use its below-market prices to draw price-sensitive customers away from foreign rivals. It is wise for companies pursuing such an approach to court these new customers and retain their business when prices later begin a gradual rise back to normal market levels.

Alternatively, a company may use below-market pricing to drive down the price so far in the targeted country that domestic firms are quickly put in dire financial straits or in danger of being driven out of business. However, using below-market pricing in this way *runs a high risk of host-government retaliation on behalf of the adversely affected domestic companies.* Almost all governments can be expected to retaliate against perceived dumping practices by imposing special tariffs on goods being imported from the countries of the guilty companies.

Indeed, as the trade among nations has mushroomed over the past 10 years, most governments have joined the World Trade Organization (WTO), which promotes fair-trade practices among nations and actively polices dumping. Companies based in France and China were recently found guilty of dumping laminate flooring at unreasonably low prices in Canada to the detriment of Canadian producers.[30] Companies deemed guilty of dumping frequently come under pressure from their government to cease and desist, especially if the tariffs adversely affect innocent companies based in the same country or if the advent of special tariffs raises the specter of an international trade war.

Using Cross-Border Tactics to Defend against International Rivals

Cross-border tactics can also be used as a means of defending against the strategic moves of strong international rivals with multiple profit sanctuaries of their own. If a company finds itself under competitive attack by an international rival in one country market, one way to respond is with a counterattack against one of the rival's key markets in a different country—preferably where the rival is least protected and has the most to lose. This is a possible option when rivals compete against one another in much the same markets around the world.

For companies with at least one profit sanctuary, having a presence in a rival's key markets can be enough to deter the rival from making aggressive attacks. The reason for this is that the combination of some market presence (even at small scale) and a profit sanctuary elsewhere can send a signal to the rival that the company could quickly ramp up production (funded by the profit sanctuary) to mount a competitive attack in that market if the rival attacks one of the company's key markets in another country.

When international rivals compete against one another in multiple-country markets, this type of deterrence effect can restrain them from taking aggressive action against one another due to the fear of a retaliatory response that might escalate the battle into a cross-border competitive war. **Mutual restraint** of this sort tends to stabilize the competitive position of multimarket rivals against one another. And while it may prevent each firm from making any major market share gains at the expense of its rival, it also prevents costly competitive battles that would be likely to erode the profitability of both companies without any compensating gain.

STRATEGIES FOR COMPETING IN THE MARKETS OF DEVELOPING COUNTRIES

Companies racing for global leadership have to consider competing in developing-economy markets like China, India, Brazil, Indonesia, Thailand, Poland, Russia, and Mexico—countries where the business risks are considerable but where the opportunities for growth are huge, especially as their economies develop and living standards climb toward levels in the industrialized world.[31]

With the world now comprising nearly 7 billion people—fully 40 percent of whom live in India and China, and hundreds of millions more live in other, less developed countries in Asia and Latin America—a company that aspires to world market leadership (or to sustained rapid growth) cannot ignore the market opportunities or the base of technical and managerial talent such countries offer. For example, in 2010 China was the world's second-largest economy (behind the United States), as measured by purchasing power. Its population of 1.4 billion people now consumes a quarter of the world's luxury products, due to the rapid growth of a wealthy class.[32] China is also the world's largest consumer of many commodities. China's growth in demand for consumer goods had made it the world's largest market for vehicles by 2009 and put it on track to become the world's largest market for luxury goods by 2014.[33] Thus, no company that aspires to global market leadership can afford to ignore the strategic importance of establishing competitive market positions in China, India, other parts of the Asia-Pacific region, Latin America, and eastern Europe. Illustration Capsule 7.2 describes Yum! Brands' strategy to increase its sales and market share in China.

Tailoring products to fit market conditions in a developing country like China, however, often involves more than making minor product changes and becoming more familiar with local cultures.[34] Ford's attempt to sell a Ford Escort in India at a price of $21,000—a luxury-car price, given that India's best-selling Maruti-Suzuki model sold at the time for $10,000 or less and that fewer than 10 percent of Indian households had an annual purchasing power greater than $20,000—met with a less-than-enthusiastic market response. McDonald's has had to offer vegetable burgers in parts of Asia and to rethink its prices, which are often high by local standards and affordable only by the well-to-do. Kellogg has struggled to introduce its cereals successfully because consumers in many less developed countries do not eat cereal for breakfast and changing habits is difficult and expensive. Single-serving packages of detergents, shampoos, pickles, cough syrup, and cooking oils are very popular in India because they allow buyers to conserve cash by purchasing only what they need immediately. Thus, many companies find that trying to employ a strategy akin to that used in the markets of developed countries is hazardous.[35] Experimenting with some, perhaps many, local twists is usually necessary to find a strategy combination that works.

Strategy Options for Competing in Developing-Country Markets

There are several options for tailoring a company's strategy to fit the sometimes unusual or challenging circumstances presented in developing-country markets:

- *Prepare to compete on the basis of low price.* Consumers in developing markets are often highly focused on price, which can give low-cost local competitors the edge unless a company can find ways to attract buyers with bargain prices as well as better products.[36] For example, when Unilever entered the market for laundry detergents in India, it realized that 80 percent of the population could not afford the brands it was selling to affluent consumers there. To compete against a very low-priced detergent made by a local company, Unilever developed a low-cost detergent (named Wheel), constructed new low-cost production facilities, packaged the detergent in single-use amounts so that it could be sold at a very low unit price, distributed the product to local merchants by handcarts, and crafted an economical marketing campaign that

ILLUSTRATION CAPSULE 7.2

Yum! Brands' Strategy for Becoming the Leading Food Service Brand in China

In 2010, Yum! Brands operated more than 37,000 restaurants in more than 110 countries. Its best-known brands were KFC, Taco Bell, Pizza Hut, A&W, and Long John Silver's. In 2009, its fastest growth in revenues came from its 3,369 restaurants in China, which recorded operating profits of $602 million during the year. KFC was the largest quick-service chain in China, with 2,870 units in 2009, while Pizza Hut was the largest casual-dining chain, with 450 units. Yum! Brands planned to open at least 500 new restaurant locations annually in China, including new Pizza Hut Home delivery units and East Dawning units, which had a menu offering traditional Chinese food. All of Yum! Brands' menu items for China were developed in its R&D facility in Shanghai.

In addition to adapting its menu to local tastes and adding new units at a rapid pace, Yum! Brands also adapted the restaurant ambience and decor to appeal to local consumer preferences and behavior. The company changed its KFC store formats to provide educational displays that supported parents' priorities for their children and to make KFC a fun place for children to visit. The typical KFC outlet in China averaged two birthday parties per day.

In 2009, Yum! Brands operated 60 KFC, Taco Bell, Pizza Hut, A&W, and Long John Silver's restaurants for every 1 million Americans. The company's more than 3,300 units in China represented only 2 restaurants per 1 million Chinese. Yum! Brands management believed that its strategy keyed to continued expansion in the number of units in China and additional menu refinements would allow its operating profits from restaurants located in China to account for 40 percent of system-wide operating profits by 2017.

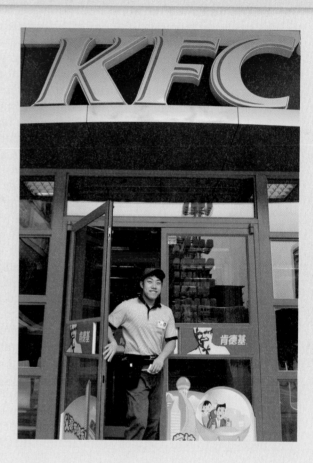

Sources: Yum! Brands 2009 10-K and other information posted at www.yum.com.

included painted signs on buildings and demonstrations near stores. The new brand quickly captured $100 million in sales and was the number-one detergent brand in India in 2008 based on dollar sales. Unilever later replicated the strategy in India with low-priced packets of shampoos and deodorants and in South America with a detergent brand named Ala.

- *Be prepared to modify aspects of the company's business model or strategy to accommodate local circumstances (but not to such an extent that the company loses the advantage of global scale and branding).*[37] For instance, when Dell entered China, it discovered that individuals and businesses were not accustomed to placing orders through the Internet (whereas over 50 percent of Dell's sales in North America were online). To adapt, Dell modified its direct sales model to rely more heavily on phone and fax orders and decided to be patient in getting Chinese customers to place Internet orders. Further, because numerous Chinese government departments and state-owned enterprises insisted that hardware vendors make their bids through distributors and systems integrators (as opposed to dealing directly with Dell salespeople, as did large enterprises in other countries), Dell opted to use third parties in marketing its products to this buyer segment (although it did sell through its own sales force where it could). But Dell was careful not to abandon the parts of its business model that gave it a competitive edge over rivals. Similarly, when McDonald's moved into Russia in the 1990s, it was forced to alter its practice of obtaining needed supplies from outside vendors because capable local suppliers were not available; to supply its Russian outlets and stay true to its core principle of serving consistent-quality fast food, McDonald's set up its own vertically integrated supply chain—cattle were imported from Holland and russet potatoes were imported from the United States. McDonald's management also worked with a select number of Russian bakers for its bread, brought in agricultural specialists from Canada and Europe to improve the management practices of Russian farmers, built its own 100,000-square-foot McComplex to produce hamburgers, French fries, ketchup, mustard, and Big Mac sauce, and set up a trucking fleet to move supplies to restaurants.

- *Try to change the local market to better match the way the company does business elsewhere.*[38] An international company often has enough market clout to drive major changes in the way a local country market operates. When Hong Kong–based STAR launched its first satellite TV channel in 1991, it generated profound impacts on the TV marketplace in India. The Indian government lost its monopoly on TV broadcasts, several other satellite TV channels aimed at Indian audiences quickly emerged, and the excitement of additional TV channels in India triggered a boom in TV manufacturing in India. When Japan's Suzuki entered India, it triggered a quality revolution among Indian auto parts manufacturers. Local component suppliers teamed up with Suzuki's vendors in Japan and worked with Japanese experts to produce higher-quality products. Over the next two decades, Indian companies became proficient in making top-notch components for vehicles, won more prizes for quality than companies in any country other than Japan, and broke into the global market as suppliers to many automakers in Asia and other parts of the world. Mahindra and Mahindra, one of India's premier automobile manufacturers, has been recognized by a number of organizations for its product quality. Among its most noteworthy awards was its number-one ranking by J.D. Power Asia Pacific in 2007 for new vehicle overall quality.

- *Stay away from developing markets where it is impractical or uneconomic to modify the company's business model to accommodate local circumstances.*[39] Home Depot expanded into Mexico in 2001 and China in 2006, but it has avoided entry into other developing countries because its value proposition of good quality, low prices, and attentive customer service relies on (1) good highways and logistical systems to minimize store inventory costs, (2) employee stock ownership to help motivate store personnel to provide good customer service, and (3) high labor costs for housing construction and home repairs that encourage homeowners to engage in do-it-yourself projects. Relying on these factors in the U.S. and Canadian markets has worked spectacularly for

Home Depot, but the company has found that it cannot count on these factors in nearby Latin America.

Company experiences in entering developing markets like China, India, Russia, and Brazil indicate that profitability seldom comes quickly or easily. Building a market for the company's products can often turn into a long-term process that involves re-education of consumers, sizable investments in advertising and promotion to alter tastes and buying habits, and upgrades of the local infrastructure (transportation systems, distribution channels, etc.). In such cases, a company must be patient, work within the system to improve the infrastructure, and lay the foundation for generating sizable revenues and profits once conditions are ripe for market takeoff.

> Profitability in developing markets rarely comes quickly or easily—new entrants have to adapt their business models and strategies to local conditions and be patient in earning a profit.

DEFENDING AGAINST GLOBAL GIANTS: STRATEGIES FOR LOCAL COMPANIES IN DEVELOPING COUNTRIES

If opportunity-seeking, resource-rich multinational companies are looking to enter developing-country markets, what strategy options can local companies use to survive? As it turns out, the prospects for local companies facing global giants are by no means grim. Studies of local companies in developing markets have disclosed five strategies that have proved themselves in defending against globally competitive companies.[40] Illustration Capsule 7.3 discusses how a travel agency in China used a combination of these strategies to become that country's largest travel consolidator and online travel agent.

1. *Develop business models that exploit shortcomings in local distribution networks or infrastructure.* In many instances, the extensive collection of resources possessed by the global giants is of little help in building a presence in developing markets. The lack of well-established wholesaler and distributor networks, telecommunication systems, consumer banking, or media necessary for advertising makes it difficult for large internationals to migrate business models proved in developed markets to developing countries. Such markets sometimes favor local companies whose managers are familiar with the local language and culture and are skilled in selecting large numbers of conscientious employees to carry out labor-intensive tasks. Shanda, a Chinese producer of massively multiplayer online role-playing games (MMORPG), has overcome China's lack of an established credit card network by selling prepaid access cards through local merchants. The company's focus on online games also addresses shortcomings in China's software piracy laws. Emerge Logistics has used its understanding of China's extensive government bureaucracy and fragmented network of delivery services to deliver goods for international companies doing business in China. Many foreign firms have found it difficult to get their goods to market since the average Chinese trucking company owns only one or two trucks. An India-based electronics company has been able to carve out a market niche for itself by developing an all-in-one business machine designed especially for India's 1.2 million small shopkeepers that tolerates the frequent power outages in that country.[41]

ILLUSTRATION CAPSULE 7.3

How Ctrip Successfully Defended against International Rivals to Become China's Largest Online Travel Agency

Ctrip has utilized a business model tailored to the Chinese travel market, its access to low-cost labor, and its unique understanding of customer preferences and buying habits to build scale rapidly and defeat foreign rivals such as Expedia and Travelocity in becoming the largest travel agency in China. The company was founded in 1999 with a focus on business travelers, since corporate travel accounts for the majority of China's travel bookings. The company also placed little emphasis on online transactions, since at the time there was no national ticketing system in China, most hotels did not belong to a national or international chain, and most consumers preferred paper tickets to electronic tickets. To overcome this infrastructure shortcoming, the company established its own central database of 5,600 hotels located throughout China and flight information for all major airlines operating in China. Ctrip set up a call center of 3,000 representatives that could use its proprietary database to provide travel information for up to 100,000 customers per day. Because most of its

transactions were not done over the Internet, the company hired couriers in all major cities in China to ride by bicycle or scooter to collect payments and deliver tickets to Ctrip's corporate customers. Ctrip also initiated a loyalty program that provided gifts and incentives to the administrative personnel who arranged travel for business executives. By 2009, Ctrip.com held 60 percent of China's online travel market and planned to enter the Taiwanese tourism market, having just acquired EzTravel, Taiwan's largest online travel site.* By April 2010, its market cap reached $5.34 billion and was creeping up rapidly on Expedia's market cap of $7.23 billion.**

*"Ctrip.com Acquires ezTravel," *China Hospitality News,* August 11, 2009, www.chinahospitalitynews.com/en/2009/08/11/12859-ctrip-com-acquires-eztravel/. ** Dennis Schaal, "Online Travel Powerhouses—Priceline, Expedia . . . and Ctrip?" *Tnooz.co: Talking Travel Tech,* April 1, 2010, www.tnooz.com/2010/04/01/news/online-travel-powerhouses-priceline-expedia-and-ctrip/.

Source: Based on information in Arindam K. Bhattacharya and David C. Michael, "How Local Companies Keep Multinationals at Bay," *Harvard Business Review 86,* no. 3 (March 2008), pp. 85–95.

2. *Utilize keen understanding of local customer needs and preferences to create customized products or services.* When developing-country markets are largely made up of customers with strong local needs, a good strategy option is to concentrate on customers who prefer a local touch and to accept the loss of the customers attracted to global brands.[42] A local company may be able to astutely exploit its local orientation—its familiarity with local preferences, its expertise in traditional products, its long-standing customer relationships. A small Middle Eastern cell phone manufacturer competes successfully against industry giants Nokia, Samsung, and Motorola by selling a model designed especially for Muslims—it is loaded with the Koran, alerts people at prayer times, and is equipped with a compass that points them toward Mecca. Shenzhen-based Tencent has become the leader in instant messaging in China through its unique understanding of Chinese behavior and culture.

3. *Take advantage of aspects of the local workforce with which large multinational companies may be unfamiliar.* Local companies that lack the technological capabilities of foreign entrants may be able to rely on their better

understanding of the local labor force to offset any disadvantage. Focus Media is China's largest outdoor advertising firm and has relied on low-cost labor to update its 130,000 LCD displays and billboards in 90 cities in a low-tech manner, while multinational companies operating in China use electronically networked screens that allow messages to be changed remotely. Focus uses an army of employees who ride to each display by bicycle to change advertisements with programming contained on a USB flash drive or DVD. Indian information technology firms such as Infosys Technologies and Satyam Computer Services have been able to keep their personnel costs lower than those of international competitors EDS and Accenture because of their familiarity with local labor markets. While the large internationals have focused recruiting efforts in urban centers like Bangalore and Delhi, driving up engineering and computer science salaries in such cities, local companies have shifted recruiting efforts to second-tier cities that are unfamiliar to foreign firms.

4. *Use acquisition and rapid-growth strategies to better defend against expansion-minded internationals.* With the growth potential of developing markets such as China, Indonesia, and Brazil obvious to the world, local companies must attempt to develop scale and upgrade their competitive capabilities as quickly as possible to defend against the stronger international's arsenal of resources. Most successful companies in developing markets have pursued mergers and acquisitions at a rapid-fire pace to build first a nationwide and then an international presence. Hindalco, India's largest aluminum producer, has followed just such a path to achieve its ambitions for global dominance. By acquiring companies in India first, it gained enough experience and confidence to eventually acquire much larger foreign companies with world-class capabilities.[43] When China began to liberalize its foreign trade policies, Lenovo (the Chinese PC maker) realized that its long-held position of market dominance in China could not withstand the onslaught of new international entrants such as Dell and HP. Its acquisition of IBM's PC business allowed Lenovo to gain rapid access to IBM's globally recognized PC brand, its R&D capability, and its existing distribution in developed countries. This has allowed Lenovo not only to hold its own against the incursion of global giants into its home market but to expand into new markets around the world.[44]

5. *Transfer company expertise to cross-border markets and initiate actions to contend on an international level.* When a company from a developing country has resources and capabilities suitable for competing in other country markets, launching initiatives to transfer its expertise to foreign markets becomes a viable strategic option.[45] Televisa, Mexico's largest media company, used its expertise in Spanish culture and linguistics to become the world's most prolific producer of Spanish-language soap operas. Jollibee Foods, a family-owned company with 56 percent of the fast-food business in the Philippines, combated McDonald's entry first by upgrading service and delivery standards and then by using its expertise in seasoning hamburgers with garlic and soy sauce and making noodle and rice meals with fish to open outlets catering to Asian residents in Hong Kong, the Middle East, and California. By continuing to upgrade its capabilities and learn from its experience in foreign markets, a company can sometimes transform itself into one capable of competing on a worldwide basis, as an emerging global giant.[46] Sundaram Fasteners of India began its foray into foreign markets as a supplier of radiator caps to

GM—an opportunity it pursued when GM first decided to outsource the production of this part. As a participant in GM's supplier network, the company learned about emerging technical standards, built its capabilities, and became one of the first Indian companies to achieve QS 9000 quality certification. With the expertise it gained and its recognition for meeting quality standards, Sundaram was then able to pursue opportunities to supply automotive parts in Japan and Europe.

KEY POINTS

1. Competing in international markets allows companies to (1) gain access to new customers, (2) achieve lower costs through greater scale economies, learning curve effects, or purchasing power, (3) leverage core competencies developed domestically in additional country markets, (4) gain access to resources and capabilities located outside a company's domestic market, and (5) spread business risk across a wider market base.

2. Companies electing to expand into international markets must consider five factors when evaluating strategy options: (1) cross-country variation in factors that affect industry competitiveness, (2) location-based drivers regarding where to conduct different value chain activities, (3) varying political and economic risks, (4) potential shifts in exchange rates, and (5) differences in cultural, demographic, and market conditions.

3. The strategies of firms that expand internationally are usually grounded in home-country advantages concerning demand conditions, factor conditions, related and supporting industries, and firm strategy, structure, and rivalry, as described by the Diamond of National Advantage framework.

4. The pattern of international competition varies in important ways from industry to industry. At one extreme is *multidomestic competition,* in which the market contest among rivals in one country is not closely connected to the market contests in other countries—there is no world market, just a collection of self-contained country (or maybe regional) markets. At the other extreme is *global competition,* in which competitive conditions across national markets are linked strongly enough to form a true world market, wherein leading competitors compete head to head in many different countries.

5. There are six strategic options for entering foreign markets. These include (1) maintaining a national (one-country) production base and exporting goods to foreign markets, (2) licensing foreign firms to produce and distribute the company's products abroad, (3) employing a franchising strategy, (4) establishing a wholly owned subsidiary by acquiring a foreign company, (5) creating a wholly owned foreign subsidiary from the ground up via a greenfield venture, and (6) using strategic alliances or other collaborative partnerships to enter a foreign market.

6. A company must choose among three alternative approaches for competing internationally: (1) a *multidomestic strategy,* which is a *think-local, act-local* approach to crafting international strategy; (2) a *global strategy*—a *think-global, act-global* approach; and (3) a combination *think-global, act-local* approach, known as a *transnational strategy.* A think-local, act-local, or multidomestic, strategy is appropriate for industries or companies that must vary

their product offerings and competitive approaches from country to country in order to accommodate different buyer preferences and market conditions. The think-global, act-global approach that characterizes a global strategy works best when there are substantial cost benefits to be gained from taking a standardized and globally integrated approach and little need for local responsiveness. A transnational approach (think global, act local) is called for when there is a high need for local responsiveness as well as substantial benefits from taking a globally integrated approach. While this is the most challenging international strategy to implement, it can be used when it is feasible for a company to employ essentially the same basic competitive strategy in all markets but still customize its product offering and some aspect of its operations to fit local market circumstances.

7. There are three general ways in which a firm can gain competitive advantage (or offset domestic disadvantages) in international markets. One way involves locating various value chain activities among nations in a manner that lowers costs or achieves greater product differentiation. A second way draws on an international competitor's ability to extend or deepen its competitive advantage by cost-effectively sharing, replicating, or transferring its most valuable resources and capabilities across borders. A third concerns benefiting from cross-border coordination in ways that are unavailable to domestic-only competitors.

8. Profit sanctuaries are country markets in which a company derives substantial profits because of its protected market position. They are valuable competitive assets, providing companies with the financial strength to mount strategic offensives in selected country markets or to support defensive moves that can ward off mutually destructive competitive battles. They may be used to wage strategic offenses in international markets through *cross-subsidization*—a practice of supporting competitive offensives in one market with resources and profits diverted from operations in another market. They may be used defensively to encourage *mutual restraint* among competitors when there is international *multimarket competition* by signaling that each company has the financial capability for mounting a strong counterattack if threatened. For companies with at least one profit sanctuary, having a presence in a rival's key markets can be enough to deter the rival from making aggressive attacks.

9. Companies racing for global leadership have to consider competing in developing markets like China, India, Brazil, Indonesia, and Mexico—countries where the business risks are considerable but the opportunities for growth are huge. To succeed in these markets, companies often have to (1) compete on the basis of low price, (2) be prepared to modify aspects of the company's business model or strategy to accommodate local circumstances (but not so much that the company loses the advantage of global scale and global branding), and/or (3) try to change the local market to better match the way the company does business elsewhere. Profitability is unlikely to come quickly or easily in developing markets, typically because of the investments needed to alter buying habits and tastes, the increased political and economic risk, and/or the need for infrastructure upgrades. And there may be times when a company should simply stay away from certain developing markets until conditions for entry are better suited to its business model and strategy.

10. Local companies in developing-country markets can seek to compete against large multinational companies by (1) developing business models that exploit shortcomings in local distribution networks or infrastructure, (2) utilizing superior understanding of local customer needs and preferences or local relationships, (3) taking advantage of competitively important qualities of the local workforce with which large multinational companies may be unfamiliar, (4) using acquisition strategies and rapid-growth strategies to better defend against expansion-minded multinational companies, or (5) transferring company expertise to cross-border markets and initiating actions to compete on a global level.

ASSURANCE OF LEARNING EXERCISES

LO 2, LO 3, LO 4

1. Chile's largest producer of wine, Concha y Toro, chooses to compete in Europe, North America, the Caribbean, and Asia using an export strategy. Go to the Investor Relations section of the company's Web site (http://www.conchaytoro.com/the-company/investor-relations/) to review the company's press releases, annual reports, and presentations. Why does it seem that the company has avoided developing vineyards and wineries in wine growing regions outside of South America?

LO 3, LO 5

2. The Hero Group is among the 10 largest corporations in India, with 20 business segments and annual revenues of $3.2 billion in fiscal 2006. Many of the corporation's business units have utilized strategic alliances with foreign partners to compete in new product and geographic markets. Review the company's statements concerning its alliances and international business operations at www.herogroup.com/alliance.htm, and prepare a two-page report that outlines the group's successful use of international strategic alliances.

LO 2, LO 4, LO 5

3. Assume you are in charge of developing the strategy for an international company selling products in 50 different countries around the world. One of the issues you face is whether to employ a multidomestic strategy, a global strategy, or a transnational strategy.

    a. If your company's product is mobile phones, do you think it would make better strategic sense to employ a multidomestic strategy, a global strategy, or a transnational strategy? Why?

    b. If your company's product is dry soup mixes and canned soups, would a multidomestic strategy seem to be more advisable than a global strategy? Why?

    c. If your company's product is large home appliances such as washing machines, ranges, ovens, and refrigerators, would it seem to make more sense to pursue a multidomestic strategy, a global strategy, or a transnational strategy? Why?

    d. If your company's product is apparel and footwear, would a multidomestic strategy, a global strategy, or a transnational strategy seem to have more appeal? Why?

EXERCISES FOR SIMULATION PARTICIPANTS

The questions below are for simulation participants whose companies operate in an international market arena. If your company competes only in a single country, then skip the questions in this section.

LO 2

1. Does your company compete in a world-market arena characterized by multi-domestic competition or global competition? Explain why.

LO 3, LO 4, LO 5

2. Which one of the following best describes the strategic approach your company is taking in trying to compete successfully on an international basis?

   • Think local, act local
   • Think global, act local
   • Think global, act global

   Explain your answer, and indicate two or three chief elements of your company's strategic approach to competing in two or more different geographic regions.

LO 2

3. To what extent, if any, have you and your co-managers adapted your company's strategy to take shifting exchange rates into account? In other words, have you undertaken any actions to try to minimize the impact of adverse shifts in exchange rates?

LO 2

4. To what extent, if any, have you and your co-managers adapted your company's strategy to take geographic differences in import tariffs or import duties into account?

ENDNOTES

[1] Sidney G. Winter and Gabriel Szulanski, "Replication as Strategy," *Organization Science* 12, no. 6 (November–December 2001), pp. 730–43; Sidney G. Winter and Gabriel Szulanski, "Getting It Right the Second Time," *Harvard Business Review* 80, no. 1 (January 2002), pp. 62–69.

[2] A. C. Inkpen and A. Dinur, "Knowledge Management Processes and International Joint Ventures," *Organization Science* 9, no. 4 (July–August 1998), pp. 454–68; P. Dussauge, B. Garrette, and W. Mitchell, "Learning from Competing Partners: Outcomes and Durations of Scale and Link Alliances in Europe, North America and Asia," *Strategic Management Journal* 21, no. 2 (February 2000), pp. 99–126; C. Dhanaraj, M. A. Lyles, H. K. Steensma et al., "Managing Tacit and Explicit Knowledge Transfer in IJVs: The Role of Relational Embeddedness and the Impact on

Performance," *Journal of International Business Studies* 35, no. 5 (September 2004), pp. 428–42; K. W. Glaister and P. J. Buckley, "Strategic Motives for International Alliance Formation," *Journal of Management Studies* 33, no. 3 (May 1996), pp. 301–32.

[3] J. Anand and B. Kogut, "Technological Capabilities of Countries, Firm Rivalry and Foreign Direct Investment," *Journal of International Business Studies* 28, no. 3 (1997), pp. 445–65; J. Anand and A. Delios, "Absolute and Relative Resources as Determinants of International Acquisitions," *Strategic Management Journal* 23, no. 2 (February 2002), pp. 119–35; A. Seth, K. Song, and A. Pettit, "Value Creation and Destruction in Cross-Border Acquisitions: An Empirical Analysis of Foreign Acquisitions of U.S. Firms," *Strategic Management Journal* 23, no. 10 (October 2002), pp. 921–40; J. Anand, L. Capron, and W. Mitchell, "Using

Acquisitions to Access Multinational Diversity: Thinking beyond the Domestic versus Cross-Border M&A Comparison," *Industrial & Corporate Change* 14, no. 2 (April 2005), pp. 191–224.

[4] M. Porter, "The Competitive Advantage of Nations," *Harvard Business Review,* March–April 1990, pp. 73–93.

[5] U.S. Department of Labor, "International Comparisons of Hourly Compensation Costs in Manufacturing in 2007," *Bureau of Labor Statistics Newsletter,* March 26, 2009, p. 8.

[6] "China's Middle Class Found Wanting for Happiness," *The Independent,* March 19, 2010, www.independent.co.uk/life-style/house-and-home/chinas-middle-class-found-wanting-for-happiness-1924180.html.

[7] "China Car Sales 'Overtook the US' in 2009," *BBC News,* January 11, 2010, http://news.bbc.co.uk/2/hi/8451887.stm.

[8] Sangwon Yoon, "South Korea Targets Internet Addicts; 2 Million Hooked," *Valley News,* April 25, 2010, p. C2.

[9] Michael E. Porter, *The Competitive Advantage of Nations* (New York: Free Press, 1990), pp. 53–54.

[10] Ibid., p. 61.

[11] K.E. Meyer, M. Wright, and S. Pruthi, "Institutions, Resources, and Entry Strategies in Emerging Economies," *Strategic Management Journal* 30, no. 5 (2009), pp. 61–80; E. Pablo, "Determinants of Cross-Border M&As in Latin America," *Journal of Business Research* 62, no. 9 (2009), pp. 861–67; R. Olie, "Shades of Culture and Institutions in International Mergers," *Organization Studies* 15, no. 3 (1994), pp. 381–406.

[12] Meyer et al., "Institutions, Resources, and Entry Strategies in Emerging Economies."

[13] See Yves L. Doz and Gary Hamel, *Alliance Advantage* (Boston: Harvard Business School Press, 1998), especially chaps. 2–4; Joel Bleeke and David Ernst, "The Way to Win in Cross-Border Alliances," *Harvard Business Review* 69, no. 6 (November –December 1991), pp. 127–33; Gary Hamel, Yves L. Doz, and C. K. Prahalad, "Collaborate with Your Competitors—and Win," *Harvard Business Review* 67, no. 1 (January–February 1989), pp. 134–35; Porter, *The Competitive Advantage of Nations,* p. 66.

[14] N. Kumar and A. Chadha, "India's Outward Foreign Direct Investments in Steel Industry in a Chinese Comparative Perspective," *Industrial and Corporate Change* 18, no. 2 (2009), pp. 249–67; R. Chittoor, S. Ray, P. Aulakh, and M. B. Sarkar, "Strategic Responses to Institutional Changes: 'Indigenous Growth' Model of the Indian Pharmaceutical Industry," *Journal of International Management* 14 (2008), pp. 252–69.

[15] F. Froese and L. Goeritz, "Integration Management of Western Acquisitions in Japan," *Asian Business and Management* 6 (2007) pp. 95–114.

[16] For a discussion of the pros and cons of alliances versus acquisitions, see Jeffrey H. Dyer, Prashant Kale, and Harbir Singh, "When to Ally and When to Acquire," *Harvard Business Review* 82, no. 7–8 (July–August 2004), pp. 109–15.

[17] For additional discussion of company experiences with alliances and partnerships, see Doz and Hamel, *Alliance Advantage,* chaps. 2–7; and Rosabeth Moss Kanter, "Collaborative Advantage: The Art of the Alliance," *Harvard Business Review* 72, no. 4 (July–August 1994), pp. 96–108.

[18] Jeremy Main, "Making Global Alliances Work," *Fortune,* December 19, 1990, p. 125.

[19] Details are reported in Shawn Tully, "The Alliance from Hell," *Fortune,* June 24, 1996, pp. 64–72.

[20] C. K. Prahalad and K. Lieberthal, "The End of Corporate Imperialism," *Harvard Business Review,* 81, no. 8 (August 2003), pp.109–117.

[21] Ibid.

[22] For an in-depth discussion of the challenges of crafting strategies suitable for a world in which both production and markets are globalizing, see Pankaj Ghemawat, "Managing Differences: The Central Challenge of Global Strategy," *Harvard Business Review* 85, no. 3 (March 2007), pp. 59–68.

[23] For more details on the merits of and opportunities for cross-border transfer of successful strategy experiments, see C. A. Bartlett and S. Ghoshal, *Managing across Borders: The Transnational Solution,* 2nd ed. (Boston: Harvard Business School Press, 1998), pp. 79–80 and chap. 9. Also see Pankaj Ghemawat, "Managing Differences: The Central Challenge of Global Strategy," *Harvard Business Review* 85, no. 3 (March 2007), pp. 58–68.

[24] Lynn S. Paine, "The China Rules," *Harvard Business Review* 88, no. 6 (June 2010) pp. 103–8.

[25] Porter, *The Competitive Advantage of Nations,* pp. 53–55.

[26] Ibid., pp. 55–58.

[27] A. Inkpen, A. Sundaram, and K. Rockwood, "Cross-Border Acquisitions of U.S. Technology Assets," *California Management Review* 42, no. 3 (Spring 2000), pp. 50–71.

[28] Porter, *The Competitive Advantage of Nations,* p. 57.

[29] C. K. Prahalad and Yves L. Doz, *The Multinational Mission* (New York: Free Press, 1987), pp. 58–60; Ghemawat, "Managing Differences," pp. 58–68.

[30] Canadian International Trade Tribunal, findings issued June 16, 2005, and posted at www.citt-tcce.gc.ca (accessed September 28, 2005).

[31] This point is discussed at greater length in Prahalad and Lieberthal, "The End of Corporate Imperialism," pp. 68–79; also see David J. Arnold and John A. Quelch, "New Strategies in Emerging Markets," *Sloan Management Review* 40, no. 1 (Fall 1998), pp. 7–20. For a more extensive discussion of strategy in emerging markets, see C. K. Prahalad, *The Fortune at the Bottom of the Pyramid: Eradicating Poverty through Profits* (Upper Saddle River, NJ: Wharton, 2005), especially chaps. 1–3.

[32] "Is a Luxury Good Consumption Tax Useful?" *Beijing Review.com.cn,* June 18, 2010, www.bjreview.com.cn/print/txt/2010-06/18/content_280191.htm; "GM's First-Half China Sales Surge Past the U.S.," *Bloomberg Businessweek,* July 2, 2010, http://businessweek.com/news/2010-07-02/gm-s-first-half-china-sales-surge-past-the-u-s-.html.

[33] Joanne Muller, "Can China Save GM?" *Forbes.com,* May 10, 2010, www.forbes.com/forbes/2010/0510/global-2000-10-automobiles-china-detroit-whitacre-save-gm.html; "Is a Luxury Good Consumption Tax Useful?"

[34] Prahalad and Lieberthal, "The End of Corporate Imperialism," pp. 72–73.

[35] Tarun Khanna, Krishna G. Palepu, and Jayant Sinha, "Strategies That Fit Emerging Markets," *Harvard Business Review* 83, no. 6 (June 2005), p. 63; Arindam K. Bhattacharya and David C. Michael, "How Local Companies Keep Multinationals at Bay," *Harvard Business Review* 86, no. 3 (March 2008), pp. 94–95.

[36] Prahalad and Lieberthal, "The End of Corporate Imperialism," p. 72.

[37] Khanna, Palepu, and Sinha, "Strategies That Fit Emerging Markets," pp. 73–74.

[38] Ibid., p. 74.

[39] Ibid., p. 76.

[40] The results and conclusions from a study of 134 local companies in 10 emerging markets are presented in Tarun Khanna and Krishna G. Palepu, "Emerging Giants: Building World-Class Companies in Developing Countries," *Harvard Business Review* 84, no. 10 (October 2006), pp. 60–69; also, an examination of strategies used by 50 local companies in emerging markets is discussed in Arindam K. Bhattacharya and David C. Michael, "How Local Companies Keep Multinationals at Bay," pp. 85–95.

[41] Steve Hamm, "Tech's Future," *BusinessWeek,* September 27, 2004, p. 88.

[42] Niroj Dawar and Tony Frost, "Competing with Giants: Survival Strategies for Local Companies in Emerging Markets," *Harvard Business Review* 77, no. 1 (January–February 1999), p. 122; see also Guitz Ger, "Localizing in the Global Village: Local Firms Competing in Global Markets," *California Management Review* 41, no. 4 (Summer 1999), pp. 64–84; Khanna and Palepu, "Emerging Giants," pp. 63–66.

[43] N. Kumar, "How Emerging Giants Are Rewriting the Rules of M&A," *Harvard Business Review,* May 2009, pp. 115–21.

[44] H. Rui and G. Yip, "Foreign Acquisitions by Chinese Firms: A Strategic Intent Perspective," *Journal of World Business* 43 (2008), pp. 213–26.

[45] Dawar and Frost, "Competing with Giants," p. 124.

[46] Ibid., p. 126; Khanna and Palepu, "Emerging Giants," pp. 60–69.

CHAPTER 8

CORPORATE STRATEGY

Diversification and the Multibusiness Company

> Fit between a parent and its businesses is a two-edged sword: A good fit can create value; a bad one can destroy it.
>
> —**Andrew Campbell,**
> *Michael Gould, and Marcus Alexander*

> We are quite pragmatic. If a business does not contribute to our overall vision, it has to go.
>
> —**Richard Wambold**
> *CEO, Pactiv*

> Make winners out of every business in your company. Don't carry losers.
>
> —**Jack Welch**
> *Former CEO, General Electric*

> I think our biggest achievement to date has been bringing back to life an inherent Disney synergy that enables each part of our business to draw from, build upon, and bolster the others.
>
> —**Michael Eisner**
> *Former CEO, Walt Disney Company*

LEARNING OBJECTIVES

LO 1. Understand when and how business diversification can enhance shareholder value.

LO 2. Gain an understanding of how related diversification strategies can produce cross-business strategic fit capable of delivering competitive advantage.

LO 3. Become aware of the merits and risks of corporate strategies keyed to unrelated diversification.

LO 4. Gain command of the analytical tools for evaluating a company's diversification strategy.

LO 5. Understand a diversified company's four main corporate strategy options for solidifying its diversification strategy and improving company performance.

I n this chapter, we move up one level in the strategy-making hierarchy, from strategy making in a single-business enterprise to strategy making in a diversified enterprise. Because a diversified company is a collection of individual businesses, the strategy-making task is more complicated. In a one-business company, managers have to come up with a plan for competing successfully in only a single industry environment—the result is what we labeled in Chapter 2 as *business strategy* (or *business-level strategy*). But in a diversified company, the strategy-making challenge involves assessing multiple industry environments and developing a *set* of business strategies, one for each industry arena in which the diversified company operates. And top executives at a diversified company must still go one step further and devise a companywide or *corporate strategy* for improving the attractiveness and performance of the company's overall business lineup and for making a rational whole out of its diversified collection of individual businesses.

In most diversified companies, corporate-level executives delegate considerable strategy-making authority to the heads of each business, usually giving them the latitude to craft a business strategy suited to their particular industry and competitive circumstances and holding them accountable for producing good results. But the task of crafting a diversified company's overall or corporate strategy falls squarely in the lap of top-level executives and involves four distinct facets:

1. *Picking new industries to enter and deciding on the mode of entry.* The first concerns in diversifying are what new industries to get into and whether to enter by starting a new business from the ground up, acquiring a company already in the target industry, or forming a joint venture or strategic alliance with another company.

2. *Pursuing opportunities to leverage cross-business value chain relationships and strategic fit into competitive advantage.* A company that diversifies into businesses with competitively important value chain matchups (pertaining to common technology, supply chain logistics, production, distribution channels, and/or customers) gains competitive advantage potential not open to a company that diversifies into businesses whose value chains are totally unrelated and that require totally different resources and capabilities. Capturing this competitive advantage potential requires capitalizing on such cross-business opportunities as transferring skills or technology from one business to another, reducing costs via sharing common facilities and resources, utilizing the company's well-known brand names and distribution muscle to increase the sales of newly acquired products, and encouraging knowledge-sharing and collaborative activity among the businesses.

3. *Establishing investment priorities and steering corporate resources into the most attractive*

business units. A diversified company's different businesses are usually not equally attractive from the standpoint of investing additional funds. It is incumbent on corporate management to (a) decide on the priorities for investing capital in the company's different businesses, (b) channel resources into areas where earnings potentials are higher and away from areas where they are lower, and (c) divest business units that are chronically poor performers or are in an increasingly unattractive industry. Divesting poor performers and businesses in unattractive industries frees up unproductive investments either for redeployment to promising business units or for financing attractive new acquisitions.

4. *Initiating actions to boost the combined performance of the corporation's collection of businesses.* Corporate strategists must craft moves to improve the overall performance of the corporation's business lineup and sustain increases in shareholder value. Strategic options for diversified corporations include (a) sticking closely with the existing business lineup and pursuing opportunities presented by these businesses, (b) broadening the scope of diversification by entering additional industries, (c) divesting some businesses and retrenching to a narrower collection of diversified businesses with better overall performance prospects, and (d) restructuring the entire company by divesting some businesses and acquiring others so as to put a whole new face on the company's business lineup.

The demanding and time-consuming nature of these four tasks explains why corporate executives generally refrain from becoming immersed in the details of crafting and executing business-level strategies, preferring instead to delegate lead responsibility for business strategy and business-level operations to the heads of each business unit.

In the first portion of this chapter we describe the various means a company can use to become diversified, and we explore the pros and cons of related versus unrelated diversification strategies. The second part of the chapter looks at how to evaluate the attractiveness of a diversified company's business lineup, decide whether the company has a good diversification strategy, and identify ways to improve its future performance. In the chapter's concluding section, we survey the strategic options open to already diversified companies.

WHEN TO DIVERSIFY

As long as a company has its hands full trying to capitalize on profitable growth opportunities in its present industry, there is no urgency to pursue diversification. But the opportunities for profitable growth are often limited in mature industries and declining markets. A company may also encounter diminishing market opportunities and stagnating sales if its industry becomes competitively unattractive and unprofitable. A company's growth prospects may dim quickly if demand for the industry's product is eroded by the appearance of alternative technologies, substitute products, or fast-shifting buyer preferences. Consider, for example, how digital cameras have virtually destroyed the business of companies dependent on making camera film and doing film processing, how iPods and other brands of digital music players (as well as online music stores) have affected the revenues of retailers of music CDs, and how the mushrooming use of cell phones and Internet-based voice communication have diminished demand for landline-based telecommunication services and eroded the revenues of such once-dominant long-distance providers as AT&T, British Telecommunications, and NTT in Japan. Under conditions such as these, diversification into new industries always merits strong consideration—particularly if the resources and capabilities of a company can be employed more fruitfully in other industries.[1]

A company becomes a prime candidate for diversifying under the following four circumstances:[2]

1. When it spots opportunities for expanding into industries whose technologies and products complement its present business.

2. When it can leverage its collection of resources and capabilities by expanding into businesses where these resources and capabilities are valuable competitive assets.

3. When diversifying into additional businesses opens new avenues for reducing costs via cross-business sharing or transfer of competitively valuable resources and capabilities.

4. When it has a powerful and well-known brand name that can be transferred to the products of other businesses and thereby used as a lever for driving up the sales and profits of such businesses.

BUILDING SHAREHOLDER VALUE: THE ULTIMATE JUSTIFICATION FOR DIVERSIFYING

Diversification must do more for a company than simply spread its business risk across various industries. In principle, diversification cannot be considered a success unless it results in *added long-term economic value for shareholders*—value that shareholders cannot capture on their own by purchasing stock in companies in different industries or investing in mutual funds so as to spread their investments across several industries.

For there to be reasonable expectations of producing added long-term shareholder value, a move to diversify into a new business must pass three tests:[3]

1. *The industry attractiveness test.* The industry to be entered must be attractive enough to yield consistently good returns on investment. Whether an industry is attractive depends chiefly on the presence of industry and competitive conditions that are conducive to earning as-good or better profits and return on investment than the company is earning in its present business(es). It is hard to justify diversifying into an industry where profit expectations are *lower* than those in the company's present businesses.

2. *The cost-of-entry test.* The cost of entering the target industry must not be so high as to erode the potential for good profitability. Industry attractiveness is not a sufficient reason for a firm to diversify into an industry. In fact, the more attractive an industry's prospects are for growth and long-term profitability, the more expensive the industry can be to get into. Entry barriers for start-up companies are likely to be high in attractive industries; were barriers

LO 1

Understand when and how business diversification can enhance shareholder value.

low, a rush of new entrants would soon erode the potential for high profitability. And buying a well-positioned company in an appealing industry often entails a high acquisition cost that makes passing the cost-of-entry test less likely. Since the owners of a successful and growing company usually demand a price that reflects their business's profit prospects, it's easy for such an acquisition to fail the cost-of-entry test.

3. *The better-off test.* Diversifying into a new business must offer potential for the company's existing businesses and the new business to perform better together under a single corporate umbrella than they would perform operating as independent, stand-alone businesses—an effect known as **synergy.** For example, let's say that company A diversifies by purchasing company B in another industry. If A and B's consolidated profits in the years to come prove no greater than what each could have earned on its own, then A's diversification won't provide its shareholders with added value. Company A's shareholders could have achieved the same $1 + 1 = 2$ result by merely purchasing stock in company B. Diversification does not result in added long-term value for shareholders unless it produces a $1 + 1 = 3$ effect where the businesses *perform better together* as part of the same firm than they could have performed as independent companies.

> **CORE CONCEPT**
>
> Creating added value for shareholders via diversification requires building a multibusiness company where the whole is greater than the sum of its parts—an outcome known as **synergy.**

Diversification moves must satisfy all three tests to grow shareholder value over the long term. Diversification moves that can pass only one or two tests are suspect.

STRATEGIES FOR ENTERING NEW BUSINESSES

The means of entering new businesses can take any of three forms: acquisition, internal start-up, or joint ventures with other companies.

Acquisition of an Existing Business

Acquisition is a popular means of diversifying into another industry. Not only is it quicker than trying to launch a brand-new operation, but it also offers an effective way to hurdle such entry barriers as acquiring technological know-how, establishing supplier relationships, becoming big enough to match rivals' unit costs, having to spend large sums on introductory advertising and promotions, and securing adequate distribution. Acquisitions are also commonly employed to access resources and capabilities that are complementary to those of the acquiring firm and that cannot be developed readily internally. Buying an ongoing operation allows the acquirer to move directly to the task of building a strong market position in the target industry, rather than getting bogged down in trying to develop the knowledge, experience, scale of operation, and market reputation necessary for a start-up entrant to become an effective competitor.

However, acquiring an existing business can prove quite expensive. The costs of acquiring another business include not only the acquisition price but also the costs of negotiating and completing the purchase transaction and the costs of integrating the business into the diversified company's portfolio. If the company to be acquired is a successful company, the acquisition price will include a hefty *premium* over the preacquisition value of the company. For example, the $5.8 billion that Xerox paid to acquire Affiliated Computer Services in 2010 included a 38 percent premium over the service company's market value.[4] Premiums are paid in order to convince the shareholders and managers of the target company that it is in their financial interests to approve the deal. The average premium in deals between U.S. companies rose to 56 percent in 2009, but it is more often in the 30 to 40 percent range.[5]

> **CORE CONCEPT**
>
> An **acquisition premium** is the amount by which the price offered exceeds the preacquisition market value of the target company.

The big dilemma an acquisition-minded firm faces is whether to pay a premium price for a successful company or to buy a struggling company at a bargain price.[6] If the buying firm has little knowledge of the industry but ample capital, it is often better off purchasing a capable, strongly positioned firm—even if its current owners demand a premium price. However, when the acquirer sees promising ways to transform a weak firm into a strong one and has the resources, the know-how, and the patience to do it, a struggling company can be the better long-term investment.

While acquisitions offer an enticing means for entering a new business, many fail to deliver on their promise.[7] Realizing the potential gains from an acquisition requires a successful integration of the acquired company into the culture, systems, and structure of the acquiring firm. This can be a costly and time-consuming operation. Acquisitions can also fail to deliver long-term shareholder value if the acquirer overestimates the potential gains and pays a premium in excess of the realized gains. High integration costs and excessive price premiums are two reasons that an acquisition might fail the cost-of-entry test. Firms with significant experience in making acquisitions are better able to avoid these types of problems.[8]

Internal Development

Internal development of new businesses has become an increasingly important means for companies to diversify and is often referred to as **corporate venturing** or *new venture development*. It involves building a new business from scratch. Although building a new business from the ground up is generally a time-consuming and uncertain process, it avoids the pitfalls associated with entry via acquisition and may allow the firm to realize greater profits in the end. It may offer a viable means of entering a new or emerging industry where there are no good acquisition candidates.

> **CORE CONCEPT**
>
> **Corporate venturing** (or *new venture development*) is the process of developing new businesses as an outgrowth of a company's established business operations. It is also referred to as *corporate entrepreneurship* or *intrapreneurship* since it requires entrepreneurial-like qualities within a larger enterprise.

Entering a new business via internal development also poses some significant hurdles. An internal new venture not only has to overcome industry entry barriers but also has to invest in new production capacity, develop sources of supply, hire and train employees, build channels of distribution, grow a customer base, and so on. The risks associated with internal start-ups are substantial, and the likelihood of failure is often high. Moreover, the culture, structures, and organizational systems of some companies may impede innovation and make it difficult for corporate entrepreneurship to flourish.

Generally, internal development of a new business has appeal only when (1) the parent company already has in-house most or all of the skills and resources it needs to piece together a new business and compete effectively; (2) there is ample time to launch the business; (3) the internal cost of entry is lower than the cost of entry via acquisition; (4) the targeted industry is populated with many relatively small firms such that the new start-up does not have to compete head to head against larger, more powerful rivals; (5) adding new production capacity will not adversely impact the supply-demand balance in the industry; and (6) incumbent firms are likely to be slow or ineffective in responding to a new entrant's efforts to crack the market.[9]

Joint Ventures

Joint ventures entail forming a new business that is owned jointly by two or more companies. Entering a new business via joint venture can be useful in at least three types of situations.[10] First, a joint venture is a good vehicle for pursuing an opportunity that is too complex, uneconomical, or risky for one company to pursue alone. Second, joint ventures make sense when the opportunities in a new industry require a broader range of competencies and know-how than a company can marshal. Many of the opportunities in satellite-based telecommunications, biotechnology, and network-based systems that blend hardware, software, and services call for the coordinated development of complementary innovations and the tackling of an intricate web of financial, technical, political, and regulatory factors simultaneously. In such cases, pooling the resources and competencies of two or more companies is a wiser and less risky way to proceed. Third, companies sometimes use joint ventures to diversify into a new industry when the diversification move entails having operations in a foreign country—several governments require foreign companies operating within their borders to have a local partner that has minority, if not majority, ownership in the local operations. Aside from fulfilling host-government ownership requirements, companies usually seek out a local partner with expertise and other resources that will aid the success of the newly established local operation.

However, as discussed in Chapters 6 and 7, partnering with another company—in the form of either a joint venture or a collaborative alliance—has significant drawbacks due to the potential for conflicting objectives, disagreements over how to best operate the venture, culture clashes, and so on. Joint ventures are generally the least durable of the entry options, usually lasting only until the partners decide to go their own ways.

Choosing a Mode of Entry

The choice of how best to enter a new business—whether through internal development, acquisition, or joint venture—depends on the answers to four important questions:

- Does the company have all of the resources and capabilities it requires to enter the business through internal development or is it lacking some critical resources?
- Are there entry barriers to overcome?
- Is speed an important factor in the firm's chances for successful entry?
- Which is the least costly mode of entry, given the company's objectives?

The Question of Critical Resources and Capabilities   If a firm has all the resources it needs to start up a new business or will be able to easily purchase or lease any missing resources, it may choose to enter the business via internal development. However, if missing critical resources cannot be easily purchased or leased, a firm wishing to enter a new business must obtain these missing resources through either acquisition or joint venture. Bank of America acquired Merrill Lynch in 2008 to obtain critical investment banking resources and capabilities that it lacked. The acquisition of these additional capabilities complemented Bank of America's strengths in corporate banking and opened up new business opportunities for Bank of America. Firms often acquire other companies as a way to enter foreign markets where they lack local marketing knowledge, distribution capabilities, and relationships with local suppliers or customers. McDonald's acquisition of Burghy, Italy's only national hamburger chain, offers an example.[11] If there are no good acquisition opportunities or if the firm wants to avoid the high cost of acquiring and integrating another firm, it may choose to enter via joint venture. This type of entry mode has the added advantage of spreading the risk of entering a new business, which is particularly attractive when uncertainty is high. DeBeers's joint venture with the luxury goods company LVMH provided DeBeers with the complementary marketing capabilities it needed to enter the diamond retailing business, as well as partner to share the risk.

The Question of Entry Barriers   The second question to ask is whether entry barriers would prevent a new entrant from gaining a foothold and succeeding in the industry. If entry barriers are low and the industry is populated by small firms, internal development may be the preferred mode of entry. If entry barriers are high, the company may still be able to enter with ease if it has the requisite resources and capabilities for overcoming high barriers. For example, entry barriers due to reputational advantages may be surmounted by a diversified company with a widely known and trusted corporate name. But if the entry barriers cannot be overcome readily, then the only feasible entry route may be through acquisition of a well-established company. While entry barriers may also be overcome with a strong complementary joint venture, this mode is the more uncertain choice due to the lack of industry experience.

The Question of Speed   Speed is another determining factor in deciding how to go about entering a new business. Acquisition is a favored mode of entry when speed is of the essence, as is the case in rapidly changing industries where fast movers can secure long-term positioning advantages. Speed is important in industries where early movers gain experience-based advantages that grow ever larger over time as they move down the learning curve and in technology-based industries where there is a race to establish an industry standard or leading technological platform. But in other cases it can be better to enter a market after the uncertainties about technology or consumer preferences have been resolved and learn from the missteps of early entrants. In these cases, joint venture or internal development may be preferred.

The Question of Comparative Cost   The question of which mode of entry is most cost-effective is a critical one, given the need for a diversification strategy to pass the cost-of-entry test. Acquisition can be a high-cost mode of entry due to the need to pay a premium over the share price of the target company. When the premium is high, the price of the deal will exceed the worth of the acquired company as a stand-alone business by a substantial amount. Moreover, the true cost of an acquisition must include the *transaction costs* of identifying and evaluating potential targets, negotiating a price, and completing other aspects of deal making. In addition, the true cost must take into account the costs of integrating the acquired company into the parent company's portfolio of businesses.

Strategic alliances and other types of partnerships may provide a way to conserve on such entry costs. But even here, there are organizational coordination costs and transaction costs that must be considered, including settling on the terms of the arrangement. If the partnership doesn't proceed smoothly and is not founded on trust, these costs may be significant. In making the choice about how to proceed, the firm should also consider the possibility of even simpler arrangements. If the objective is simply to leverage a brand name and company logo, for example, a strategic alliance centered on licensing may be the lowest-cost alternative. Licensing is particularly attractive if the company lacks other resources and capabilities that are needed for an entry move. Harley-Davidson, for example, has chosen to license its brand name to makers of apparel as an alternative to entering the apparel industry, for which it is ill suited.

CHOOSING THE DIVERSIFICATION PATH: RELATED VERSUS UNRELATED BUSINESSES

Once a company decides to diversify, it faces the choice of whether to diversify into **related businesses, unrelated businesses,** or some mix of both. Businesses are said to be *related* when their value chains exhibit competitively important cross-business relationships. By this, we mean that there is a close correspondence between the businesses in terms of how they perform *key* value chain activities and the resources and capabilities each needs to perform those activities. The big appeal of related diversification is to build shareholder value by leveraging these cross-business relationships into competitive advantages, thus allowing the company as a whole to perform better than just the sum of its individual businesses. Businesses are said to be *unrelated* when the resource requirements and key value chain activities are so dissimilar that no competitively important cross-business relationships exist.

The next two sections explore the ins and outs of related and unrelated diversification.

STRATEGIC FIT AND DIVERSIFICATION INTO RELATED BUSINESSES

A related diversification strategy involves building the company around businesses where there is *strategic fit with respect to key value chain activities and competitive assets.* **Strategic fit** exists whenever one or more activities constituting the value chains of different businesses are sufficiently similar as to present opportunities for cross-business sharing or transferring of the resources and capabilities that enable these activities.[12] Prime examples of such opportunities include:

LO 2

Gain an understanding of how related diversification strategies can produce cross-business strategic fit capable of delivering competitive advantage.

- *Transferring specialized expertise, technological know-how, or other competitively valuable capabilities from one business's value chain to another's.*
- *Combining the related value chain activities of separate businesses into a single operation to achieve lower costs.* For instance, it is often feasible to manufacture the products of different businesses in a single plant, use the same warehouses for shipping and distribution, or have a single sales force for the products of different businesses (because they are marketed to the same types of customers).
- *Exploiting common use of a well-known brand name that connotes excellence in a certain type of product range.* For example, Yamaha's name in motorcycles gave the company instant credibility and recognition in entering the personal-watercraft business, allowing it to achieve a significant market share without spending large sums on advertising to establish a brand identity for the WaveRunner. Sony's name in consumer electronics made it easier for Sony to enter the market for video games with its PlayStation console and lineup of PlayStation video games. Apple's well-known and highly popular iPods gave the firm instant credibility and name recognition in launching its iPhones and iPads.
- *Sharing other resources that support corresponding value chain activities of the businesses, such as relationships with suppliers or a dealer network.* After acquiring Marvel Comics in 2009, the Walt Disney Company saw to it that Marvel's iconic characters, such as Spiderman, Iron Man, and the Black Widow, were shared with many of the other Disney businesses, including its theme parks, retail stores, and video game business. (Disney's characters, starting with Mickey Mouse, have always been among the most valuable of its resources.)
- *Engaging in cross-business collaboration and knowledge sharing to create new competitively valuable resources and capabilities.*

CORE CONCEPT

Strategic fit exists when the value chains of different businesses present opportunities for cross-business resource transfer, lower costs through combining the performance of related value chain activities or resource sharing, cross-business use of a potent brand name, and cross-business collaboration to build stronger competitive capabilities.

Related diversification is based on value chain matchups with respect to *key* value chain activities—those that play a central role in each business's strategy and that link to its industry's key success factors. Such matchups facilitate the sharing or transfer of the competitively important resources and capabilities that enable the performance of these activities and underlie each business's quest for competitive advantage. By facilitating the sharing or transferring of such important competitive assets, related diversification can boost each business's prospects for competitive success.

The resources and capabilities that are leveraged in related diversification are *specialized resources and capabilities.* By this, we mean that they have very *specific* applications; their use is restricted to a limited range of business contexts in which these applications are competitively relevant. Because they are adapted for particular applications, specialized resources and capabilities must be utilized by certain kinds of businesses operating in specific types of industries to have value; they have limited utility outside this specific range of industry and business applications. This is in contrast to *generalized resources and capabilities* (such as general management capabilities, human resource management capabilities, and general accounting services), which can be applied usefully across a wide range of industry and business types.

L'Oréal is the world's largest beauty products company, with more than $25 billion in revenues and a successful strategy of related diversification built upon leveraging a highly specialized set of resources and capabilities. These include 18 dermatologic and cosmetic research centers, R&D capabilities and scientific knowledge concerning skin and hair care, patents and secret formulas for hair and skin care products, and robotic applications developed specifically for testing the safety of hair and skin care products. These resources and capabilities are highly valuable for businesses focused on products for human skin and hair—they are *specialized* to such applications, and, in consequence, they are of little or no value beyond this restricted range of applications. To leverage these resources in a way that maximizes their potential value, L'Oréal has diversified into cosmetics, hair care products, skin care products, and fragrances (but not food, transportation, industrial services, or any application area far from the narrow domain in which its specialized resources are competitively relevant). L'Oréal's businesses are related to one another on the basis of its value-generating specialized resources and capabilities and the cross-business linkages among the value chain activities that they enable.

Corning's most competitively valuable resources and capabilities are specialized to applications concerning fiber optics and specialty glass and ceramics. Over the course of its 150-year history, it has developed an unmatched understanding of fundamental glass science and related technologies in the field of optics. Its capabilities now span a variety of sophisticated technologies and include expertise in domains such as custom glass composition, specialty glass melting and forming, precision optics, high-end transmissive coatings, and opto-mechanical materials. Corning has leveraged these specialized capabilities into a position of global leadership in five related market segments: display technologies based on glass substrates, environmental technologies using ceramic substrates and filters, optical fibers and cables for telecommunications, optical biosensors for drug discovery, and specialty materials employing advanced optics and specialty glass solutions. The market segments into which Corning has diversified are all related by their reliance on Corning's specialized capability set and by the many value chain activities that they have in common as a result.

General Mills has diversified into a closely related set of food businesses on the basis of its capabilities in the realm of "kitchen chemistry" and food production technologies. Its businesses include General Mills cereals, Pillsbury and Betty Crocker baking products, yogurts, organic foods, dinner mixes, canned goods, and snacks. Earlier it had diversified into restaurant businesses on the mistaken notion that all food businesses were related. As a result of exiting these businesses in the mid-1990s, the company was able to improve its overall profitability and strengthen its position in its remaining businesses. The lesson from its experience—and a takeaway for the managers of any diversified company—is that it is not product relatedness that defines a well-crafted related diversification strategy. Rather, the businesses must be related in terms of their key value chain activities and the specialized resources and capabilities that enable these activities.[13] An example is Citizen Holdings Company, whose products appear to be different (watches, miniature card calculators, handheld televisions) but are related in terms of their common reliance on miniaturization know-how and advanced precision technologies.[14]

While companies pursuing related diversification strategies may also have opportunities to share or transfer their *generalized* resources and capabilities (e.g. information systems; human resource management practices; accounting and tax services; budgeting, planning, and financial reporting systems; expertise in legal and regulatory affairs; and fringe-benefit management systems), the most competitively valuable opportunities for resource sharing or transfer always come from leveraging their specialized resources and capabilities. The reason for this is that specialized resources and capabilities drive the key value-creating activities that both connect the businesses (at points where there is strategic fit) and link to the key success factors in the markets where they are competitively relevant. Figure 8.1 illustrates the range of opportunities to share and/or transfer specialized resources and capabilities among the value chain activities of related businesses. It is important to recognize that even though generalized resources and capabilities may be shared by multiple business units, such resource sharing alone cannot form the backbone of a strategy keyed to related diversification.

CORE CONCEPT

Related diversification involves sharing or transferring *specialized* resources and capabilities. **Specialized resources and capabilities** have very specific applications and their use is limited to a restricted range of industry and business types, in contrast to **generalized resources and capabilities** that can be widely applied and can be deployed across a broad range of industry and business types.

Figure 8.1   Related Businesses Provide Opportunities to Benefit from Competitively Valuable Strategic Fit

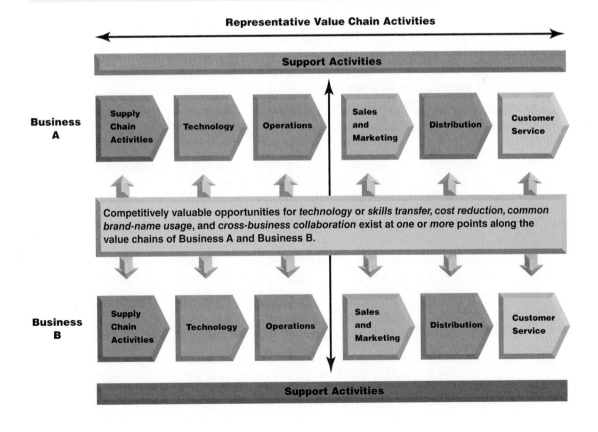

Identifying Cross-Business Strategic Fit along the Value Chain

Cross-business strategic fit can exist anywhere along the value chain—in R&D and technology activities, in supply chain activities and relationships with suppliers, in manufacturing, in sales and marketing, in distribution activities, or in customer service activities.[15]

Strategic Fit in Supply Chain Activities Businesses that have strategic fit with respect to supply chain activities can perform better together because of the potential for skills transfer in procuring materials, the sharing of capabilities in logistics, the benefits of added collaboration with common supply chain partners, and/or added leverage with shippers in securing volume discounts on incoming parts and components. Dell Computer's strategic partnerships with leading suppliers of microprocessors, circuit boards, disk drives, memory chips, flat-panel displays, wireless capabilities, long-life batteries, and other PC-related components have been an important element of the company's strategy to diversify into servers, data storage devices, networking components, and LCD TVs—products that include many components common to PCs and that can be sourced from the same strategic partners that provide Dell with PC components.

Strategic Fit in R&D and Technology Activities Businesses with technology-sharing benefits can perform better together than apart because of potential cost savings in R&D, potentially shorter times in getting new products to market, and more innovative products or processes. Moreover, technological advances in one business can lead to increased sales for both. Technological innovations have been the driver behind the efforts of cable TV companies to diversify into high-speed Internet access (via the use of cable modems) and, further, to explore providing local and long-distance telephone service to residential and commercial customers either through a single wire or by means of VoIP (voice over Internet protocol) technology.

Manufacturing-Related Strategic Fit Cross-business strategic fit in manufacturing-related activities can represent an important source of competitive advantage in situations where a diversifier's expertise in quality manufacture and cost-efficient production methods can be transferred to another business. When Emerson Electric diversified into the chain-saw business, it transferred its expertise in low-cost manufacture to its newly acquired Beaird-Poulan business division; the transfer drove Beaird-Poulan's new strategy—to be the low-cost provider of chain-saw products—and fundamentally changed the way Beaird-Poulan chain saws were designed and manufactured. Another benefit of production-related value chain matchups is the ability to consolidate production into a smaller number of plants and significantly reduce overall production costs. When snowmobile maker Bombardier diversified into motorcycles, it was able to set up motorcycle assembly lines in the same manufacturing facility where it was assembling snowmobiles. When Smucker's acquired Procter & Gamble's Jif peanut butter business, it was able to combine the manufacture of its own Smucker's peanut butter products with those of Jif, plus it gained greater leverage with vendors in purchasing its peanut supplies.

Strategic Fit in Sales and Marketing Activities Various cost-saving opportunities spring from diversifying into businesses with closely related sales and marketing activities. When the products are sold directly to the same customers, sales costs can often be reduced by using a single sales force and avoiding having two different salespeople call on the same customer. The products of related businesses can be promoted at the same Web site and included in the same media ads and sales brochures. After-sale service and repair organizations for the products of closely related businesses can often be consolidated into a single operation. There may be opportunities to reduce costs by consolidating order processing and billing and using common promotional tie-ins. When global power-tool maker Black & Decker acquired Vector Products, it was able to use its own global sales force and distribution facilities to sell and distribute the newly acquired Vector power inverters, vehicle battery chargers, and rechargeable spotlights because the types of customers that carried its power tools (discounters like Walmart and Target, home centers, and hardware stores) also stocked the types of products produced by Vector.

A second category of benefits arises when different businesses use similar sales and marketing approaches; in such cases, there may be competitively valuable opportunities to transfer selling, merchandising, advertising, and product differentiation skills from one business to another. Procter & Gamble's product lineup includes Folgers coffee, Tide laundry detergent, Crest toothpaste, Ivory soap, Charmin toilet tissue, Gillette razors and blades, Duracell batteries, Oral-B toothbrushes, and Head & Shoulders shampoo. All of these have different competitors and different supply chain and production requirements, but they all move through the same wholesale distribution systems, are sold in common retail settings to the same shoppers, are advertised and promoted in much the same ways, and require the same marketing and merchandising skills.

Distribution-Related Strategic Fit   Businesses with closely related distribution activities can perform better together than apart because of potential cost savings in sharing the same distribution facilities or using many of the same wholesale distributors and retail dealers to access customers. When Conair Corporation acquired Allegro Manufacturing's travel bag and travel accessory business in 2007, it was able to consolidate its own distribution centers for hair dryers and curling irons with those of Allegro, thereby generating cost savings for both businesses. Likewise, since Conair products and Allegro's neck rests, ear plugs, luggage tags, and toiletry kits were sold by the same types of retailers (discount stores, supermarket chains, and drugstore chains), Conair was able to convince many of the retailers not carrying Allegro products to take on the line.

Strategic Fit in Customer Service Activities   Opportunities for cost savings from sharing resources or for greater differentiation through skills transfer can come from strategic fit with respect to customer service activities, just as they do along other points of the value chain. For example, cost savings may come from consolidating after-sale service and repair organizations for the products of closely related businesses into a single operation. Likewise, different businesses can often use the same customer service infrastructure. For instance, an electric utility that diversifies into natural gas, water, appliance sales and repair services, and home security services can use the same customer data network, the same customer call centers and local offices, the same billing and customer accounting systems, and the same customer service infrastructure to support all of its products and services. Through the transfer of best practices in customer service across a set of related businesses or through sharing resources such as proprietary information about customer preferences, a multibusiness company can create a differentiation advantage through higher-quality customer service.

Strategic Fit, Economies of Scope, and Competitive Advantage

What makes related diversification an attractive strategy is the opportunity to convert cross-business strategic fit into a competitive advantage over business rivals whose operations do not offer comparable strategic-fit benefits. The greater the relatedness among a diversified company's businesses, the bigger a company's window for converting strategic fit into competitive advantage via (1) transferring skills or knowledge, (2) combining related value chain activities to achieve lower costs, (3) leveraging the use of a well-respected brand name or other differentiation-enhancing resources, and (4) using cross-business collaboration and knowledge sharing to create new resources and capabilities and drive innovation.

The Path to Competitive Advantage and Economies of Scope

Sharing or transferring valuable specialized assets among the company's businesses can help each business perform its value chain activities more proficiently. This translates into competitive advantage for the businesses in one or two basic ways: (1) The businesses can contribute to greater efficiency and lower costs relative to their competitors, and/or (2) they can provide a basis for differentiation so that customers are willing to pay relatively more for the businesses' goods and services. In either or both of these ways, a firm with a well-executed related diversification strategy can boost the chances of its businesses attaining a competitive advantage.

> **CORE CONCEPT**
>
> **Economies of scope** are cost reductions that flow from operating in multiple businesses (a *larger scope* of operation), whereas *economies of scale* accrue from a *larger-size* operation.

Related businesses often present opportunities to eliminate or reduce the costs of performing certain value chain activities; such cost savings are termed **economies of scope**—a concept distinct from *economies of scale*. Economies of *scale* are cost savings that accrue directly from a larger-size operation; for example, unit costs may be lower in a large plant than in a small plant, lower in a large distribution center than in a small one, lower for large-volume purchases of network advertising than for small-volume purchases. Economies of *scope*, however, stem directly from resource sharing, facilitated by strategic fit along the value chains of related businesses. Such economies are open only to a multibusiness enterprise that enables its businesses to share technology, perform R&D together, use common manufacturing or distribution facilities, share a common sales force or distributor-dealer network, use the same established brand name, and/or share other commonly employed resources and capabilities. *The greater the cross-business economies associated with resource sharing and strategic fit, the greater the potential for a related diversification strategy to yield a competitive advantage based on lower costs than those of rivals.*

From Competitive Advantage to Added Profitability and Gains in Shareholder Value

The competitive advantage potential that flows from economies of scope and the capture of other strategic-fit benefits is what enables a company pursuing related diversification to achieve $1 + 1 = 3$ financial performance and the hoped-for gains in shareholder value. The strategic and business logic is compelling: Capturing the benefits of strategic fit along the value chains of its related businesses gives a diversified company a clear path to achieving competitive advantage over undiversified competitors and competitors whose own diversification efforts don't offer equivalent strategic-fit benefits.[16] Such competitive advantage potential provides a company with a dependable basis for earning profits and a return on investment that exceeds what the company's businesses could earn as stand-alone enterprises. Converting the competitive advantage potential into greater profitability is what fuels $1 + 1 = 3$ gains in shareholder value—the necessary outcome for satisfying the better-off test and proving the business merit of a company's diversification effort.

There are four things to bear in mind here:

1. Capturing cross-business strategic-fit benefits via a strategy of related diversification builds shareholder value in ways that shareholders cannot undertake by simply owning a portfolio of stocks of companies in different industries.
2. The capture of cross-business strategic-fit benefits is possible only via a strategy of related diversification.
3. The benefits of cross-business strategic fit come from the transferring or sharing of competitively valuable resources and capabilities among the businesses—resources and capabilities that are *specialized* to certain applications and have value only in specific types of industries and businesses.
4. The benefits of cross-business strategic fit are not automatically realized when a company diversifies into related businesses; *the benefits materialize only after management has successfully pursued internal actions to capture them.*

> Diversifying into related businesses where competitively valuable strategic-fit benefits can be captured puts a company's businesses in position to perform better financially as part of the company than they could have performed as independent enterprises, thus providing a clear avenue for boosting shareholder value.

DIVERSIFICATION INTO UNRELATED BUSINESSES

An unrelated diversification strategy discounts the merits of pursuing cross-business strategic fit and, instead, focuses squarely on entering and operating businesses in industries that allow the company as a whole to increase its earnings. Companies that pursue a strategy of unrelated diversification generally exhibit a willingness to diversify into *any industry* where senior managers see an opportunity to realize consistently good financial results. Such companies are frequently labeled *conglomerates* because their business interests range broadly across diverse industries. Companies that pursue unrelated diversification nearly always enter new businesses by acquiring an established company rather than by forming a start-up subsidiary within their own corporate structures or participating in joint ventures.

With a strategy of unrelated diversification, the emphasis is on satisfying the attractiveness and cost-of-entry tests and each business's prospects for good financial performance. Thus, with an unrelated diversification strategy, company managers spend much time and effort screening acquisition candidates and evaluating the pros and cons of keeping or divesting existing businesses, using such criteria as:

- Whether the business can meet corporate targets for profitability and return on investment.
- Whether the business is in an industry with attractive growth potential.
- Whether the business is big enough to contribute *significantly* to the parent firm's bottom line.

> **LO 3**
>
> Become aware of the merits and risks of corporate strategies keyed to unrelated diversification.

But the key to successful unrelated diversification is to go beyond these considerations and ensure that the strategy passes the better-off test as well. This test requires more than just growth in revenues; it requires *growth in profits*—beyond what could be achieved by a mutual fund or a holding company that owns the businesses without adding any value. Unless the different businesses are more profitable together under the corporate umbrella than they are apart as independent businesses, *the strategy cannot create economic value for shareholders.* And unless it does so, there is *no real justification for unrelated diversification,* since top executives have a fiduciary responsibility to maximize long-term shareholder value.

Building Shareholder Value via Unrelated Diversification

Given the absence of cross-business strategic fit with which to create competitive advantages, building economic shareholder value via unrelated diversification ultimately hinges on the ability of the parent company to improve its businesses via other means. Critical to this endeavor is the role that the parent company plays *as a corporate parent.* To the extent that a company has strong *parenting capabilities*—capabilities that involve nurturing, guiding, grooming, and governing constituent businesses—a corporate parent can propel its businesses forward and help them gain ground over their market rivals. Corporate parents also contribute to the competitiveness of their unrelated businesses by sharing or transferring *generalized resources and capabilities* across the businesses—competitive assets that have utility in any type of industry and that can be leveraged across a wide range of business types as a result. Examples of the kinds of generalized resources that a corporate parent leverages in unrelated diversification include the corporation's reputation, credit rating, and access to financial markets; governance mechanisms; a corporate ethics program; a central data and communications center; shared administrative resources such as public relations and legal services; and common systems for functions such as budgeting, financial reporting, and quality control.

The three principal ways in which a parent company can further the prospects of its unrelated businesses and increase long-term economic shareholder value are discussed below.

Astute Corporate Parenting   An effective way for a diversified company to improve the performance of its otherwise unrelated businesses is through astute corporate parenting. *Corporate parenting* refers to the role that a diversified corporation plays in nurturing its component businesses through the provision of top management expertise, disciplined control, financial resources, and other types of generalized resources and capabilities such as long-term planning systems, business development skills, management development processes, and incentive systems.[17]

One of the most important ways that corporate parents contribute to the success of their businesses is by offering high-level oversight and guidance.[18] The top executives of a large diversified corporation have among them many years of accumulated experience in a variety of business settings and can often contribute expert problem-solving skills, creative strategy suggestions, and first-rate advice and guidance on how to improve competitiveness and financial performance to the heads of the company's various business subsidiaries; this is especially true in the case of newly acquired businesses. Particularly astute high-level guidance from corporate executives can help the subsidiaries perform better than they would otherwise be able to do through the efforts of the business-unit heads alone.[19]

The outstanding leadership of Royal Little, the founder of Textron, was a major reason that the company became an exemplar of the unrelated diversification strategy while he was CEO. Little's bold moves transformed the company from its origins as a small textile manufacturer into a global powerhouse known for its Bell helicopters, Cessna aircraft, and host of other strong brands in a wide array of industries. Norm Wesley, CEO of the conglomerate Fortune Brands from 1999 to 2007, is similarly credited with driving the sharp rise in the company's stock price while he was at the helm. Fortune Brands is now the $7 billion maker of products ranging from spirits (e.g., Jim Beam bourbon and rye, Gilbey's gin and vodka, Courvoisier cognac) to golf products (e.g., Titleist golf balls and clubs, FootJoy golf shoes and apparel, Scotty Cameron putters) to hardware (e.g., Moen faucets, American Lock security devices, Therma-Tru doors).

Corporate parents can also create added value for their businesses by providing them with other types of generalized or parenting resources that lower the operating costs of the individual businesses or that enhance their operating effectiveness. The administrative resources located at a company's corporate headquarters are a prime example. They typically include legal services, accounting expertise and tax services, and other elements of the administrative infrastructure, such as risk management capabilities, information technology resources, and resources concerning public relations and corporate communications. Providing individual business with such types of generalized and support resources and capabilities creates value by lowering companywide overhead costs, since each business would otherwise have to duplicate the centralized activities.

Corporate brands that do not connote any specific type of product are another type of generalized corporate resource that can be shared among unrelated businesses. GE's brand is an example, having been applied to businesses as diverse as financial services (GE Capital), medical imaging (GE medical diagnostics), and lighting (GE lightbulbs). Corporate brands that are applied in this fashion are sometimes called *umbrella brands*. Utilizing a well-known corporate name (GE) in a diversified company's individual businesses has potential not only to lower costs (by spreading the fixed cost of developing and maintaining the brand over many businesses) but also to enhance each business's customer value proposition by linking its products to a name that consumers trust. In similar fashion, a corporation's reputation for well-crafted products, for product reliability, or for trustworthiness can lead to greater customer willingness to purchase the products of a wider range of a diversified company's businesses. Incentive systems, financial control systems, and a company's culture are other types of generalized corporate resources that may prove useful in enhancing the daily operations of a diverse set of businesses.

Judicious Cross-Business Allocation of Financial Resources

Widely diversified firms may also be able to create added value by serving as an internal capital market and allocating surplus cash flows from some businesses to fund the capital requirements of other businesses. This can be particularly important when interest rates are high or credit is unusually tight (such as in the wake of the worldwide banking crisis that began in 2008) or in economies with less well developed capital markets. Under these conditions, an unrelated diversifier with strong financial resources can add value by shifting funds from business units generating excess cash (more than they need to fund their own operating requirements and new capital investment opportunities) to other, cash-short businesses with appealing growth prospects. A parent company's ability to function as its own internal capital market enhances overall corporate performance and boosts shareholder value to the extent that its top managers have better access to information about investment opportunities internal to the firm than do external financiers and can avoid the costs of external borrowing.

Acquiring and Restructuring Undervalued Companies

One way for parent companies to add value to unrelated businesses is by acquiring weakly performing companies at a bargain price and then *restructuring* their operations (and perhaps their strategies) in ways that produce sometimes dramatic increases in profitability. **Restructuring** refers to overhauling and streamlining the operations of a business—combining plants with excess capacity, selling off redundant or underutilized assets, reducing unnecessary expenses, revamping its product offerings, instituting new sales and marketing approaches, consolidating administrative functions to reduce overhead costs, instituting new financial controls and accounting systems, and otherwise improving the operating efficiency and profitability of a company. Restructuring sometimes involves transferring seasoned managers to the newly acquired business, either to replace the top layers of management or to step in temporarily until the business is returned to profitability or is well on its way to becoming a major market contender.

> **CORE CONCEPT**
>
> **Restructuring** refers to overhauling and streamlining the activities of a business—combining plants with excess capacity, selling off underutilized assets, reducing unnecessary expenses, and otherwise improving the productivity and profitability of a company.

Restructuring is often undertaken when a diversified company acquires a new business that is performing well below levels that the corporate parent believes are achievable. Diversified companies that have capabilities in restructuring (sometimes called *turnaround capabilities*) are often able to significantly boost the performance of weak businesses in a relatively wide range of industries. Newell Rubbermaid (whose diverse product line includes Sharpie pens, Levolor window treatments, Bernzomatic propane torches, Goody hair accessories, Aprica strollers and car seats, Calphalon cookware, and Lenox power and hand tools) developed such a strong set of turnaround capabilities that the company was said to "Newellize" the businesses it acquired.

Successful unrelated diversification strategies based on restructuring require the parent company to have considerable expertise in identifying underperforming target companies and in negotiating attractive acquisition prices so that each acquisition passes the cost-of-entry test. The capabilities in this regard of Lords James Hanson and Gordon White, who headed up the storied British conglomerate Hanson Trust, played a large part in Hanson's impressive record of profitability through the early 1990s.

The Path to Greater Shareholder Value through Unrelated Diversification

For a strategy of unrelated diversification to produce companywide financial results above and beyond what the businesses could generate operating as standalone entities, corporate executives must:

- Do a superior job of diversifying into new businesses that can produce consistently good earnings and returns on investment (to satisfy the attractiveness test).
- Do an excellent job of negotiating favorable acquisition prices (to satisfy the cost-of-entry test).
- Do a superior job of corporate parenting via high-level managerial oversight and resource sharing, financial resource allocation and portfolio management, or restructuring underperforming businesses (to satisfy the better-off test).

The best corporate parents understand the nature and value of the kinds of resources at their command and know how to leverage them effectively across their businesses. Those that are able to create more value in their businesses than other diversified companies have what is called a **parenting advantage**.[20] When a corporation has a parenting advantage, its top executives have the best chance of being able to craft and execute an unrelated diversification strategy that can satisfy all three tests and truly enhance long-term economic shareholder value.

The Drawbacks of Unrelated Diversification

Unrelated diversification strategies have two important negatives that undercut the pluses: very demanding managerial requirements and limited competitive advantage potential.

Demanding Managerial Requirements Successfully managing a set of fundamentally different businesses operating in fundamentally different industry and competitive environments is a very challenging and exceptionally difficult proposition.[21] Consider, for example, that corporations like General Electric and Berkshire Hathaway have dozens of business subsidiaries making hundreds and sometimes thousands of products. While headquarters executives can glean information about the industry from third-party sources, ask lots of questions when making occasional visits to the operations of the different businesses, and do their best to learn about the company's different businesses, they still remain heavily dependent on briefings from business-unit heads and on "managing by the numbers"—that is, keeping a close track on the financial and operating results of each subsidiary. Managing by the numbers works well enough when business conditions are normal and the heads of the various business units are capable of consistently meeting their numbers. But the problem comes when things start to go awry in a business due to exceptional circumstances and corporate management has to get deeply involved in the problems of a business it does not know all that much about. Because every business tends to encounter rough sledding at some juncture, unrelated diversification is thus a somewhat risky strategy from a managerial perspective.[22] Just one or two unforeseen problems or big strategic mistakes (like misjudging the importance of certain competitive forces, not recognizing that a newly acquired business has some serious resource deficiencies and/or competitive shortcomings, or being too optimistic about turning around a struggling subsidiary) can cause a precipitous drop in corporate earnings and crash the parent company's stock price.

Hence, competently overseeing a set of widely diverse businesses can turn out to be much harder than it sounds. In practice, comparatively few companies have proved that they have top management capabilities that are up to the task. There are far more companies whose corporate executives have failed at delivering consistently good financial results with an unrelated diversification strategy than there are companies with corporate executives who have been successful.[23] Unless a company truly has a parenting advantage, the odds are that the result of unrelated diversification will be $1 + 1 = 2$ or less.

Limited Competitive Advantage Potential The second big negative is that *unrelated diversification offers a limited potential for competitive advantage beyond what each individual business can generate on its own.* Unlike

Relying solely on the expertise of corporate executives to wisely manage a set of unrelated businesses is *a much weaker foundation for enhancing shareholder value* than is a strategy of related diversification.

a related diversification strategy, unrelated diversification provides no cross-business strategic-fit benefits that allow each business to perform its key value chain activities in a more efficient and effective manner. A cash-rich corporate parent pursuing unrelated diversification can provide its subsidiaries with much-needed capital, may achieve economies of scope in activities relying on generalized corporate resources, and may even offer some managerial know-how to help resolve problems in particular business units, but otherwise it has little to offer in the way of enhancing the competitive strength of its individual business units. In comparison to the highly specialized resources that facilitate related diversification, the generalized resources that support unrelated diversification tend to be relatively low value, for the simple reason that they are more common. Unless they are of exceptionally high quality (such as GE's world-renowned general management capabilities), resources and capabilities that are generalized in nature are less likely to provide a source of competitive advantage for diversified companies. *Without the competitive advantage potential of strategic fit in strategically important value chain activities, consolidated performance of an unrelated group of businesses stands to be little more than the sum of what the individual business units could achieve if they were independent, in most circumstances.*

Inadequate Reasons for Pursuing Unrelated Diversification

When firms pursue an unrelated diversification strategy for the wrong reasons, the odds are that the result will be 1 + 1 = 2 or less. Rationales for unrelated diversification that are not likely to increase shareholder value include the following:

- *Risk reduction.* Managers sometimes pursue unrelated diversification in order to reduce risk by spreading the company's investments over a set of truly diverse industries whose technologies and markets are largely disconnected. But this cannot create long-term shareholder value since the company's shareholders can more flexibly (and more efficiently) reduce their exposure to risk by investing in a diversified portfolio of stocks and bonds.

- *Growth.* While unrelated diversification may enable a company to achieve rapid or continuous growth, firms that pursue growth for growth's sake are unlikely to maximize shareholder value. While growth can bring more attention and prestige to a firm from greater visibility and higher industry rankings, only profitable growth—the kind that comes from creating added value for shareholders—can justify a strategy of unrelated diversification.

- *Stabilization.* In a broadly diversified company, there's a chance that market downtrends in some of the company's businesses will be partially offset by cyclical upswings in its other businesses, thus producing somewhat less earnings volatility. In actual practice, however, there's no convincing evidence that the consolidated profits of firms with unrelated diversification strategies are more stable or less subject to reversal in periods of recession and economic stress than the profits of firms with related diversification strategies.

- *Managerial motives.* Unrelated diversification can provide benefits to managers such as higher compensation (which tends to increase with firm size and degree of diversification) and reduced employment risk. Diversification for these reasons is far more likely to reduce shareholder value than to increase it.

Because unrelated diversification strategies *at their best* have only a limited potential for creating long-term economic value for shareholders, it is essential that managers not compound this problem by taking a misguided approach toward unrelated diversification, in pursuit of objectives that are more likely to destroy shareholder value than create it.

COMBINATION RELATED-UNRELATED DIVERSIFICATION STRATEGIES

There's nothing to preclude a company from diversifying into both related and unrelated businesses. Indeed, in actual practice the business makeup of diversified companies varies considerably. Some diversified companies are really *dominant-business enterprises*—one major "core" business accounts for 50 to 80 percent of total revenues and a collection of small related or unrelated businesses accounts for the remainder. Some diversified companies are *narrowly diversified* around a few (two to five) related or unrelated businesses. Others are *broadly diversified* around a wide-ranging collection of related businesses, unrelated businesses, or a mixture of both. And a number of multibusiness enterprises have diversified into unrelated areas but have a collection of related businesses within each area—thus giving them a business portfolio consisting of *several unrelated groups of related businesses.* There's ample room for companies to customize their diversification strategies to incorporate elements of both related and unrelated diversification, as may suit their own competitive asset profile and strategic vision. *Combination related-unrelated diversification strategies have particular appeal for companies with a mix of valuable competitive assets, covering the spectrum from generalized to specialized resources and capabilities.*

Figure 8.2 shows the range of alternatives for companies pursuing diversification.

EVALUATING THE STRATEGY OF A DIVERSIFIED COMPANY

Strategic analysis of diversified companies builds on the concepts and methods used for single-business companies. But there are some additional aspects to consider and a couple of new analytical tools to master. The procedure for evaluating the pluses and minuses of a diversified company's strategy and deciding what actions to take to improve the company's performance involves six steps:

LO 4

Gain command of the analytical tools for evaluating a company's diversification strategy.

1. Assessing the attractiveness of the industries the company has diversified into, both individually and as a group.
2. Assessing the competitive strength of the company's business units and determining which are strong contenders in their respective industries.

Figure 8.2   Strategy Alternatives for a Company Pursuing Diversification

3. Checking the competitive advantage potential of cross-business strategic fit among the company's various business units.

4. Checking whether the firm's resources fit the requirements of its present business lineup.

5. Ranking the performance prospects of the businesses from best to worst and determining what the corporate parent's priority should be in allocating resources to its various businesses.

6. Crafting new strategic moves to improve overall corporate performance.

The core concepts and analytical techniques underlying each of these steps merit further discussion.

Step 1: Evaluating Industry Attractiveness

A principal consideration in evaluating a diversified company's business makeup and the caliber of its strategy is the attractiveness of the industries in which it has business operations. Answers to several questions are required:

1. *Does each industry the company has diversified into represent a good market for the company to be in?* Ideally, each industry in which the firm operates will pass the attractiveness test.

2. *Which of the company's industries are most attractive, and which are least attractive?* Comparing the attractiveness of the industries and ranking them

from most to least attractive is a prerequisite to wise allocation of corporate resources across the various businesses.

3. *How appealing is the whole group of industries in which the company has invested?* The answer to this question points to whether the group of industries holds promise for attractive growth and profitability. A company whose revenues and profits come chiefly from businesses in relatively unattractive industries probably needs to look at divesting businesses in unattractive industries and entering industries that qualify as highly attractive.

The more attractive the industries (both individually and as a group) a diversified company is in, the better its prospects for good long-term performance.

Calculating Industry Attractiveness Scores for Each Industry into Which the Company Has Diversified

A simple and reliable analytical tool involves calculating quantitative industry attractiveness scores, which can then be used to gauge each industry's attractiveness, rank the industries from most to least attractive, and make judgments about the attractiveness of all the industries as a group.

Assessing industry attractiveness involves a consideration of the conditions of each business's macro-environment as well as its competitive environment—the very same factors that are used to evaluate the strategy of a single-business company, as discussed in Chapter 3. Key indicators of industry attractiveness thus include:

- Social, political, regulatory, and environmental factors
- Seasonal and cyclical factors
- Industry uncertainty and business risk
- Market size and projected growth rate
- Industry profitability
- The intensity of competition (five forces)
- Emerging opportunities and threats

In addition, it is critically important to consider those aspects of industry attractiveness that pertain *specifically* to a company's diversification strategy. This involves looking at all the industries in which the company has invested to assess their resource requirements and to consider whether there is good cross-industry strategic fit. The following measures are typically used to gauge industry attractiveness from this multibusiness perspective:

- *The presence of cross-industry strategic fit.* The more an industry's value chain and resource requirements match up well with the value chain activities of other industries in which the company has operations, the more attractive the industry is to a firm pursuing related diversification.
- *Resource requirements.* Industries having resource requirements that match those of the parent company or are otherwise within the company's reach are more attractive than industries in which capital and other resource requirements could strain corporate financial resources and organizational capabilities.

After a set of attractiveness measures that suit a diversified company's circumstances has been identified, each attractiveness measure is assigned a weight reflecting its relative importance in determining an industry's attractiveness—it is weak methodology to assume that the various attractiveness measures are equally important. The intensity of competition in an industry should nearly always carry a high weight (say, 0.20 to 0.30). Strategic-fit considerations should be assigned a high weight in the case of companies with related diversification strategies; but for companies with an unrelated diversification strategy, strategic fit with other industries may be dropped from the list of attractiveness measures altogether. The importance weights must add up to 1.

Next, each industry is rated on each of the chosen industry attractiveness measures, using a rating scale of 1 to 10 (where a *high* rating signifies *high* attractiveness and a *low* rating signifies *low* attractiveness). *Keep in mind here that the more intensely competitive an industry is, the lower the attractiveness rating for that industry.* Likewise, the more the resource requirements associated with being in a particular industry are beyond the parent company's reach, the lower the attractiveness rating. On the other hand, the presence of good cross-industry strategic fit should be given a very high attractiveness rating, since there is good potential for competitive advantage and added shareholder value. Weighted attractiveness scores are then calculated by multiplying the industry's rating on each measure by the corresponding weight. For example, a rating of 8 times a weight of 0.25 gives a weighted attractiveness score of 2.00. The sum of the weighted scores for all the attractiveness measures provides an overall industry attractiveness score. This procedure is illustrated in Table 8.1.

Interpreting the Industry Attractiveness Scores
Industries with a score much below 5 probably do not pass the attractiveness test. If a company's industry attractiveness scores are all above 5, it is probably fair to conclude that the group of industries the company operates in is attractive as a whole. But the group of industries takes on a decidedly lower degree of attractiveness as the number of industries with scores below 5 increases, especially if industries with low scores account for a sizable fraction of the company's revenues.

Table 8.1 Calculating Weighted Industry Attractiveness Scores*

Industry Attractiveness Measure	Importance Weight	Industry A Rating/ Score	Industry B Rating/ Score	Industry C Rating/ Score	Industry D Rating/ Score
Market size and projected growth rate	0.10	8/0.80	5/0.50	7/0.70	3/0.30
Intensity of competition	0.25	8/2.00	7/1.75	3/0.75	2/0.50
Emerging opportunities and threats	0.10	2/0.20	9/0.90	4/0.40	5/0.50
Cross-industry strategic fit	0.20	8/1.60	4/0.80	8/1.60	2/0.40
Resource requirements	0.10	9/0.90	7/0.70	10/1.00	5/0.50
Seasonal and cyclical influences	0.05	9/0.45	8/0.40	10/0.50	5/0.25
Societal, political, regulatory, and environmental factors	0.05	10/0.50	7/0.35	7/0.35	3/0.15
Industry profitability	0.10	5/0.50	10/1.00	3/0.30	3/0.30
Industry uncertainty and business risk	0.05	5/0.25	7/0.35	10/0.50	1/0.05
Sum of the assigned weights	1.00				
Overall weighted industry attractiveness scores		**7.20**	**6.75**	**5.10**	**2.95**

*Rating scale: 1 = very unattractive to company; 10 = very attractive to company.

For a diversified company to be a strong performer, a substantial portion of its revenues and profits must come from business units with relatively high attractiveness scores. It is particularly important that a diversified company's principal businesses be in industries with a good outlook for growth and above-average profitability. Having a big fraction of the company's revenues and profits come from industries with slow growth, low profitability, or intense competition tends to drag overall company performance down. Business units in the least attractive industries are potential candidates for divestiture, unless they are positioned strongly enough to overcome the unattractive aspects of their industry environments or they are a strategically important component of the company's business makeup.

The Difficulties of Calculating Industry Attractiveness Scores   There are two hurdles to using this method of evaluating industry attractiveness. One is deciding on appropriate weights for the industry attractiveness measures, since they have a subjective component; different analysts may have different views about which weights are appropriate for the different attractiveness measures. The second hurdle is gaining sufficient command of the industry to assign more accurate and objective ratings. Generally, a company can come up with the statistical data needed to compare its industries on such factors as market size, growth rate, seasonal and cyclical influences, and industry profitability. Cross-industry fit and resource requirements are also fairly easy to judge. But the attractiveness measure on which judgment weighs most heavily is intensity of competition. It is not always easy to conclude whether competition in one industry is stronger or weaker than in another industry because of the different types of competitive influences that prevail and the differences in their relative importance. In the event that the available information is too skimpy to confidently assign a rating value to an industry on a particular attractiveness measure, then it is usually best to use a score of 5, which avoids biasing the overall attractiveness score either up or down.

But despite the hurdles, calculating industry attractiveness scores is a systematic and reasonably reliable method for ranking a diversified company's industries from most to least attractive—numbers like those shown for the four industries in Table 8.1 help pin down the basis for judging which industries are more attractive and to what degree.

Step 2: Evaluating Business-Unit Competitive Strength

The second step in evaluating a diversified company is to appraise how strongly positioned each of its business units is in its respective industry. Doing an appraisal of each business unit's strength and competitive position in its industry not only reveals its chances for industry success but also provides a basis for ranking the units from competitively strongest to competitively weakest and sizing up the competitive strength of all the business units as a group.

Calculating Competitive Strength Scores for Each Business Unit   Quantitative measures of each business unit's competitive strength can be calculated using a procedure similar to that for measuring industry attractiveness.

The following factors are used in quantifying the competitive strengths of a diversified company's business subsidiaries:

- *Relative market share.* A business unit's *relative market share* is defined as the ratio of its market share to the market share held by the largest rival firm in the industry, with market share measured in unit volume, not dollars. A 10 percent market share, for example, does not signal much competitive strength if the leader's share is 50 percent (a 0.20 relative market share), but a 10 percent share is actually quite strong if the leader's share is only 12 percent (a 0.83 relative market share)—this why a company's relative market share is a better measure of competitive strength than a company's market share based on either dollars or unit volume.
- Costs relative to competitors' costs.
- Ability to match or beat rivals on key product attributes.
- Brand image and reputation.
- Other competitively valuable resources and capabilities.
- Ability to benefit from strategic fit with the company's other businesses.
- Ability to exercise bargaining leverage with key suppliers or customers.
- Caliber of alliances and collaborative partnerships with suppliers and/or buyers.
- Profitability relative to competitors. Above-average profitability is a signal of competitive advantage, while below-average profitability usually denotes competitive disadvantage.

After settling on a set of competitive strength measures that are well matched to the circumstances of the various business units, weights indicating each measure's importance need to be assigned. A *case can be made for using different weights* for different business units whenever the importance of the strength measures differs significantly from business to business, but otherwise it is simpler just to go with a single set of weights and avoid the added complication of multiple weights. As before, the importance weights must add up to 1. Each business unit is then rated on each of the chosen strength measures, using a rating scale of 1 to 10 (where a *high* rating signifies competitive *strength* and a *low* rating signifies competitive *weakness*). In the event that the available information is too skimpy to confidently assign a rating value to a business unit on a particular strength measure, then it is usually best to use a score of 5, which avoids biasing the overall score either up or down. Weighted strength ratings are calculated by multiplying the business unit's rating on each strength measure by the assigned weight. For example, a strength score of 6 times a weight of 0.15 gives a weighted strength rating of 0.90. The sum of the weighted ratings across all the strength measures provides a quantitative measure of a business unit's overall market strength and competitive standing. Table 8.2 provides sample calculations of competitive strength ratings for four businesses.

Interpreting the Competitive Strength Scores

Business units with competitive strength ratings above 6.7 (on a scale of 1 to 10) are strong market contenders in their industries. Businesses with ratings in the 3.3-to-6.7 range have moderate competitive strength vis-à-vis rivals. Businesses with ratings below 3.3 are in competitively weak market positions. If a diversified company's business units all have competitive strength scores above 5, it is fair to conclude that its business units are all fairly strong market contenders in their respective industries.

Table 8.2   Calculating Weighted Competitive Strength Scores for a Diversified Company's Business Units*

Competitive Strength Measure	Importance Weight	Business A in Industry A Rating/ Score	Business B in Industry B Rating/ Score	Business C in Industry C Rating/ Score	Business D in Industry D Rating/ Score
Relative market share	0.15	10/1.50	1/0.15	6/0.90	2/0.30
Costs relative to competitors' costs	0.20	7/1.40	2/0.40	5/1.00	3/0.60
Ability to match or beat rivals on key product attributes	0.05	9/0.45	4/0.20	8/0.40	4/0.20
Ability to benefit from strategic fit with company's other businesses	0.20	8/1.60	4/0.80	8/0.80	2/0.60
Bargaining leverage with suppliers/ buyers; caliber of alliances	0.05	9/0.45	3/0.15	6/0.30	2/0.10
Brand image and reputation	0.10	9/0.90	2/0.20	7/0.70	5/0.50
Competitively valuable capabilities	0.15	7/1.05	2/0.30	5/0.75	3/0.45
Profitability relative to competitors	0.10	5/0.50	1/0.10	4/0.40	4/0.40
Sum of the assigned weights	1.00				
Overall weighted competitive strength scores		**7.85**	**2.30**	**5.25**	**3.15**

*Rating scale: 1 = very weak; 10 = very strong.

But as the number of business units with scores below 5 increases, there's reason to question whether the company can perform well with so many businesses in relatively weak competitive positions. This concern takes on even more importance when business units with low scores account for a sizable fraction of the company's revenues.

Using a Nine-Cell Matrix to Simultaneously Portray Industry Attractiveness and Competitive Strength The industry attractiveness and business strength scores can be used to portray the strategic positions of each business in a diversified company. Industry attractiveness is plotted on the vertical axis and competitive strength on the horizontal axis. A nine-cell grid emerges from dividing the vertical axis into three regions (high, medium, and low attractiveness) and the horizontal axis into three regions (strong, average, and weak competitive strength). As shown in Figure 8.3, high attractiveness is associated with scores of 6.7 or greater on a rating scale of 1 to 10, medium attractiveness to scores of 3.3 to 6.7, and low attractiveness to scores below 3.3. Likewise, high competitive strength is defined as scores greater than 6.7, average strength as scores of 3.3 to 6.7, and low strength as scores below 3.3. *Each business unit is plotted on the nine-cell matrix according to its overall attractiveness score and strength score, and then it is shown as a "bubble."* The size of each bubble is scaled to the percentage of revenues the business generates relative to total corporate revenues. The bubbles in Figure 8.3 were located on the grid using the four industry attractiveness scores from Table 8.1 and the strength scores for the four business units in Table 8.2.

The locations of the business units on the attractiveness-strength matrix provide valuable guidance in deploying corporate resources to the various business units. In general, *a diversified company's prospects for good overall performance are*

Figure 8.3   A Nine-Cell Industry Attractiveness–Competitive Strength Matrix

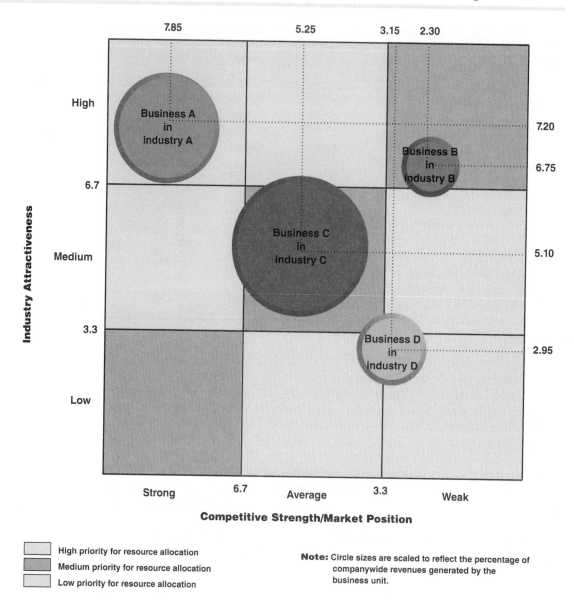

High priority for resource allocation
Medium priority for resource allocation
Low priority for resource allocation

Note: Circle sizes are scaled to reflect the percentage of companywide revenues generated by the business unit.

enhanced by concentrating corporate resources and strategic attention on those business units having the greatest competitive strength and positioned in highly attractive industries—specifically, businesses in the three cells in the upper left portion of the attractiveness-strength matrix, where industry attractiveness and competitive strength/market position are both favorable. The general strategic prescription for businesses falling in these three cells (for instance, business A in Figure 8.3) is "grow and build," with businesses in the high-strong cell standing first in line for resource allocations by the corporate parent.

Next in priority come businesses positioned in the three diagonal cells stretching from the lower left to the upper right (businesses B and C in Figure 8.3). Such businesses usually merit medium or intermediate priority in the parent's resource allocation ranking. However, some businesses in the medium-priority diagonal cells may have brighter or dimmer prospects than others. For example, a small business in the upper right cell of the matrix (like business B), despite being in a highly attractive industry, may occupy too weak a competitive position in its industry to justify the investment and resources needed to turn it into a strong market contender and shift its position leftward in the matrix over time. If, however, a business in the upper right cell has attractive opportunities for rapid growth and a good potential for winning a much stronger market position over time, it may merit a high claim on the corporate parent's resource allocation ranking and be given the capital it needs to pursue a grow-and-build strategy—the strategic objective here would be to move the business leftward in the attractiveness-strength matrix over time.

Businesses in the three cells in the lower right corner of the matrix (like business D in Figure 8.3) typically are weak performers and have the lowest claim on corporate resources. Most such businesses are good candidates for being divested (sold to other companies) or else managed in a manner calculated to squeeze out the maximum cash flows from operations—the cash flows from low-performing/low-potential businesses can then be diverted to financing expansion of business units with greater market opportunities. In exceptional cases where a business located in the three lower right cells is nonetheless fairly profitable (which it might be if it is in the low-average cell) or has the potential for good earnings and return on investment, the business merits retention and the allocation of sufficient resources to achieve better performance.

The nine-cell attractiveness-strength matrix provides clear, strong logic for why a diversified company needs to consider both industry attractiveness and business strength in allocating resources and investment capital to its different businesses. A good case can be made for concentrating resources in those businesses that enjoy higher degrees of attractiveness and competitive strength, being very selective in making investments in businesses with intermediate positions on the grid, and withdrawing resources from businesses that are lower in attractiveness and strength unless they offer exceptional profit or cash flow potential.

Step 3: Checking the Competitive Advantage Potential of Cross-Business Strategic Fit

While this step can be bypassed for diversified companies whose businesses are all unrelated (since, by design, strategic fit is lacking), a high potential for converting strategic fit into competitive advantage is central to concluding just how good a company's related diversification strategy is. Checking the competitive advantage potential of cross-business strategic fit involves searching for and evaluating how much benefit a diversified company can gain from cross-business resource and value chain matchups.

But more than just strategic-fit identification is needed. The real test is what competitive value can be generated from strategic fit. To what extent can cost savings be realized? How much competitive value will come from cross-business transfer of skills, technology, or intellectual capital? Will transferring a potent brand name to the products of other businesses increase sales significantly? Will cross-business collaboration to create or strengthen competitive capabilities lead to significant gains in the marketplace or in financial performance? Without significant strategic fit and

> The greater the value of cross-business strategic fit in enhancing a company's performance in the marketplace or on the bottom line, the more competitively powerful is its strategy of related diversification.

Figure 8.4   **Identifying the Competitive Advantage Potential of Cross-Business Strategic Fit**

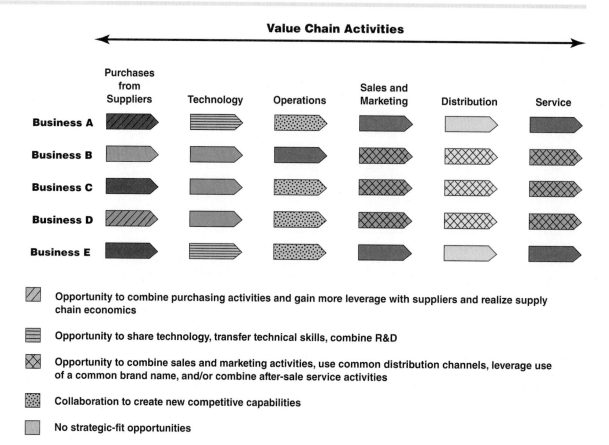

Opportunity to combine purchasing activities and gain more leverage with suppliers and realize supply chain economics

Opportunity to share technology, transfer technical skills, combine R&D

Opportunity to combine sales and marketing activities, use common distribution channels, leverage use of a common brand name, and/or combine after-sale service activities

Collaboration to create new competitive capabilities

No strategic-fit opportunities

dedicated company efforts to capture the benefits, one has to be skeptical about the potential for a diversified company's businesses to perform better together than apart.

Figure 8.4 illustrates the process of comparing the value chains of a company's businesses and identifying opportunities to exploit competitively valuable cross-business strategic fit.

Step 4: Checking for Resource Fit

A diversified company exhibits **resource fit** when its businesses add to a company's overall resource strengths and have matching resource requirements and/or when the parent company has adequate corporate resources to support its businesses' needs and add value.

The businesses in a diversified company's lineup need to exhibit good **resource fit.** In firms with a related diversification strategy, resource fit exists when the firm's businesses strengthen its overall mix of resources and capabilities and when the businesses have matching resource requirements at points along their value chains that are critical for the businesses' market success. In companies pursuing unrelated diversification, resource fit exists when the parent company has capabilities *as a corporate parent* of unrelated businesses, resources of a general nature that it can share or transfer to its component businesses, and corporate resources sufficient to support its entire group of businesses without being spread too thin. Resource fit in terms of a sufficiency of corporate resources to manage and support the entire enterprise is also relevant for related diversifiers and companies pursuing a mixed diversification strategy; Firms pursuing related diversification can also benefit from leveraging the resources of the corporate parent.

Financial Resource Fit One dimension of resource fit concerns whether a diversified company can generate the internal cash flows sufficient to fund the capital requirements of its businesses, pay its dividends, meet its debt obligations, and otherwise remain financially healthy. While additional capital can usually be raised in financial markets, it is important for a diversified firm to have a healthy **internal capital market** that can support the financial requirements of its business lineup. The greater the extent to which a diversified company is able to fund investment in its businesses through internally generated cash flows rather than from equity issues or borrowing, the more powerful its financial resource fit and the less dependent the firm is on external financial resources. This can provide an important competitive advantage over single business rivals when credit market conditions are tight, as they have been in the United States and abroad in recent years.

A *portfolio approach* to ensuring financial fit among a firm's businesses is based on the fact that different businesses have different cash flow and investment characteristics. For example, business units in rapidly growing industries are often **cash hogs**—so labeled because the cash flows they are able to generate from internal operations aren't big enough to fund their expansion. To keep pace with rising buyer demand, rapid-growth businesses frequently need sizable annual capital investments—for new facilities and equipment, for new product development or technology improvements, and for additional working capital to support inventory expansion and a larger base of operations. A business in a fast-growing industry becomes an even bigger cash hog when it has a relatively low market share and is pursuing a strategy to become an industry leader.

In contrast, business units with leading market positions in mature industries may be **cash cows**—businesses that generate substantial cash surpluses over what is needed to adequately fund their operations. Market leaders in slow-growth industries often generate sizable positive cash flows *over and above what is needed for growth and reinvestment* because their industry-leading positions tend to enable them to earn attractive profits and because the slow-growth nature of their industry often entails relatively modest annual investment requirements. Cash cows, although not always attractive from a growth standpoint, are valuable businesses from a financial resource perspective. The surplus cash flows they generate can be used to pay corporate dividends, finance acquisitions, and provide funds for investing in the company's promising cash hogs.

Viewing a diversified group of businesses as a collection of cash flows and cash requirements (present and future) is a major step forward in understanding what the financial ramifications of diversification are and why having businesses with good financial resource fit can be important. For instance, *a diversified company's businesses exhibit good financial resource fit when the excess cash generated by its cash cow businesses is sufficient to fund the investment requirements of*

CORE CONCEPT

A strong **internal capital market** allows a diversified company to add value by shifting capital from business units generating *free cash flow* to those needing additional capital to expand and realize their growth potential.

CORE CONCEPT

A **cash hog** business generates cash flows that are too small to fully fund its operations and growth and requires cash infusions to provide additional working capital and finance new capital investment.

CORE CONCEPT

A **cash cow** business generates cash flows over and above its internal requirements, thus providing a corporate parent with funds for investing in cash hog businesses, financing new acquisitions, or paying dividends.

promising cash hog businesses. Ideally, investing in promising cash hog businesses over time results in growing the hogs into self-supporting *star businesses* that have strong or market-leading competitive positions in attractive, high-growth markets and high levels of profitability. Star businesses are often the cash cows of the future—when the markets of star businesses begin to mature and their growth slows, their competitive strength should produce self-generated cash flows more than sufficient to cover their investment needs. The "success sequence" is thus cash hog to young star (but perhaps still a cash hog) to self-supporting star to cash cow. While the practice of viewing a diversified company in terms of cash cows and cash hogs has declined in popularity, it illustrates one approach to analyzing financial resource fit and allocating financial resources across a portfolio of different businesses.

Aside from cash flow considerations, there are two other factors to consider in assessing whether a diversified company's businesses exhibit good financial fit:

- *Does the company have adequate financial strength to fund its different businesses and maintain a healthy credit rating?* A diversified company's strategy fails the resource-fit test when the company's financial resources are stretched across so many businesses that its credit rating is impaired. Severe financial strain sometimes occurs when a company borrows so heavily to finance new acquisitions that it has to trim way back on capital expenditures for existing businesses and use the big majority of its financial resources to meet interest obligations and to pay down debt. Many of the world's largest banks (e.g., Royal Bank of Scotland, Citigroup, HSBC) recently found themselves so undercapitalized and financially overextended that they were forced to sell off some of their business assets to meet regulatory requirements and restore public confidence in their solvency.

- *Do any of the company's individual businesses not contribute adequately to achieving companywide performance targets?* A business exhibits poor financial fit with the company if it soaks up a disproportionate share of the company's financial resources, makes subpar bottom-line contributions, is too small to make a material earnings contribution, or is unduly risky (such that the financial well-being of the whole company could be jeopardized in the event it falls on hard times).

Nonfinancial Resource Fit   Just as a diversified company must have adequate financial resources to support its various individual businesses, it must also have a big-enough and deep-enough pool of managerial, administrative, and competitive capabilities to support all of its different businesses. The following two questions help reveal whether a diversified company has sufficient nonfinancial resources:

- *Does the company have (or can it develop) the specific resources and capabilities needed to be successful in each of its businesses?*[24] Sometimes a diversified company's resources and capabilities are poorly matched to the resource requirements of one or more businesses it has diversified into. For instance, BTR, a multibusiness company in Great Britain, discovered that the company's resources and managerial skills were quite well suited for parenting its industrial manufacturing businesses but not for parenting its distribution businesses (National Tyre Services and Texas-based Summers Group). As a result, BTR decided to divest its distribution businesses and focus exclusively on diversifying around small industrial manufacturing.[25] For companies pursuing related diversification strategies, a mismatch between the company's competitive assets and the key success factors of an industry can be serious enough to warrant divesting businesses in that industry or not acquiring a new business. In contrast, when a company's resources and capabilities are a good match with the key success factors of industries it is not presently in, it makes sense to take a hard look at acquiring companies in these industries and expanding the company's business lineup.

- *Are the company's resources being stretched too thinly by the resource requirements of one or more of its businesses?* A diversified company must guard against overtaxing its resources and capabilities, a condition that can arise when (1) it goes on an acquisition spree and management is called on to assimilate and oversee many new businesses very quickly or (2) it lacks sufficient resource depth to do a creditable job of transferring skills and competencies from one of its businesses to another. The broader the diversification, the greater the concern about whether the company has sufficient managerial depth to cope with the diverse range of operating problems its wide business lineup presents. Plus, the more a company's diversification strategy is tied to transferring its existing know-how or technologies to new businesses, the more it has to develop a big-enough and deep-enough resource pool to supply these businesses with sufficient capability to create competitive advantage.[26] Otherwise, its competitive assets end up being thinly spread across many businesses, and the opportunity for competitive advantage slips through the cracks.

Step 5: Ranking the Performance Prospects of Business Units and Assigning a Priority for Resource Allocation

Once a diversified company's strategy has been evaluated from the perspective of industry attractiveness, competitive strength, strategic fit, and resource fit, the next step is to rank the performance prospects of the businesses from best to worst and determine which businesses merit top priority for resource support and new capital investments by the corporate parent.

The most important considerations in judging business-unit performance are sales growth, profit growth, contribution to company earnings, and return on capital invested in the business. Sometimes, cash flow is a big consideration. As a rule, the prior analyses, taken together, signal which business units are likely to be strong performers on the road ahead and which are likely to be laggards. And it is a short step from ranking the prospects of business units to drawing conclusions about whether the company as a whole is capable of strong, mediocre, or weak performance in upcoming years.

The rankings of future performance generally determine what priority the corporate parent should give to each business in terms of resource allocation. *Business subsidiaries with the brightest profit and growth prospects and solid strategic and resource fit generally should head the list for corporate resource support.* More specifically, corporate executives must be diligent in steering resources out of low-opportunity areas into high-opportunity areas. Divesting marginal businesses is one of the best ways of freeing unproductive assets for redeployment. Surplus funds from cash cows also can be used to finance the range of chief strategic and financial options shown in Figure 8.5. Ideally, a company will have enough funds to do what is needed, both strategically and financially. If not,

Figure 8.5   The Chief Strategic and Financial Options for Allocating a Diversified Company's Financial Resources

strategic uses of corporate resources should usually take precedence unless there is a compelling reason to strengthen the firm's balance sheet or divert financial resources to pacify shareholders.

Step 6: Crafting New Strategic Moves to Improve Overall Corporate Performance

LO 5

Understand a diversified company's four main corporate strategy options for solidifying its diversification strategy and improving company performance.

The diagnosis and conclusions flowing from the five preceding analytical steps set the agenda for crafting strategic moves to improve a diversified company's overall performance. Corporate strategy options once a company has diversified boil down to four broad categories of actions (see Figure 8.6):

1. Sticking closely with the existing business lineup and pursuing the opportunities these businesses present.
2. Broadening the company's business scope by making new acquisitions in new industries.
3. Divesting some businesses and retrenching to a narrower base of business operations.
4. Restructuring the company's business lineup with a combination of divestitures and new acquisitions to put a whole new face on the company's business makeup.

Sticking Closely with the Existing Business Lineup   The option of sticking with the current business lineup makes sense when the company's present businesses offer attractive growth opportunities and can be counted on to create economic value for shareholders. As long as the company's set of existing businesses puts it in good position for the future and these businesses

Figure 8.6   A Company's Four Main Strategic Alternatives After It Diversifies

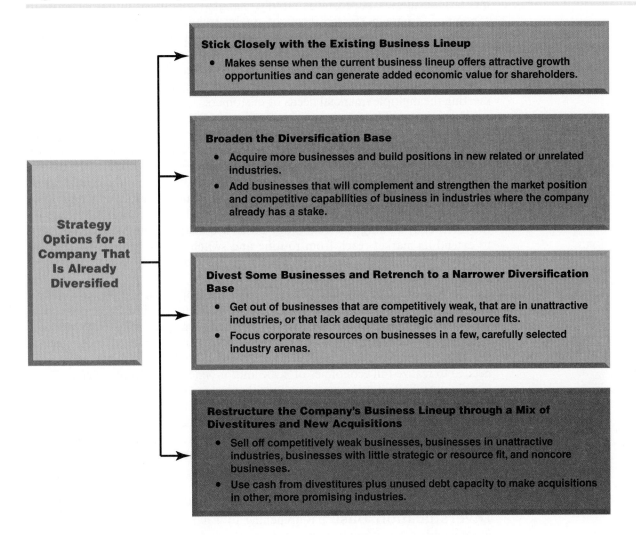

have good strategic and resource fit, then rocking the boat with major changes in the company's business mix is unnecessary. Corporate executives can concentrate their attention on getting the best performance from each of the businesses, steering corporate resources into areas of greatest potential and profitability. The specifics of "what to do" to wring better performance from the present business lineup have to be dictated by each business's circumstances and the preceding analysis of the corporate parent's diversification strategy.

However, in the event that corporate executives are not entirely satisfied with the opportunities they see in the company's present set of businesses and conclude that changes in the company's direction and business makeup are in order, they can opt for any of the three other strategic alternatives that follow.

Broadening a Diversified Company's Business Base   Diversified companies sometimes find it desirable to build positions in new industries, whether related or unrelated. There are several motivating factors. One is the potential for transferring resources and capabilities to other related or complementary businesses. A second is rapidly changing conditions in one or more of a company's core businesses brought on by technological, legislative, or new product innovations that alter buyer preferences and resource requirements. For instance, the passage of legislation in the United States allowing banks, insurance companies, and stock brokerages to enter each other's businesses spurred a raft of acquisitions and mergers to create full-service financial enterprises capable of meeting the multiple financial needs of customers.

A third, and often very important, motivating factor for adding new businesses is to complement and strengthen the market position and competitive capabilities of one or more of the company's present businesses. Procter & Gamble's acquisition of Gillette strengthened and extended P&G's reach into personal care and household products—Gillette's businesses included Oral-B toothbrushes, Gillette razors and razor blades, Duracell batteries, and Braun shavers and small appliances. Cisco Systems built itself into a worldwide leader in networking systems for the Internet by making 130 technology-based acquisitions between 1993 and 2008 to extend its market reach from routing and switching into IP telephony, home networking, wireless LAN, storage networking, network security, broadband, and optical and broadband systems.

Another important avenue for expanding the scope of a diversified company is to grow by extending the operations of existing businesses into additional country markets. Expanding a company's geographic scope may offer an exceptional competitive advantage potential by facilitating the full capture of economies of scale and learning/experience curve effects. In some businesses, the volume of sales needed to realize full economies of scale and/or benefit fully from experience and learning curve effects exceeds the volume that can be achieved by operating within the boundaries of just one or several country markets, especially small ones.

Illustration Capsule 8.1 describes how Johnson & Johnson has used acquisitions to diversify far beyond its well-known Band-Aid and baby care businesses and become a major player in pharmaceuticals, medical devices, and medical diagnostics.

Divesting Some Businesses and Retrenching to a Narrower Diversification Base   Retrenching to a narrower diversification base is usually undertaken when top management concludes that its diversification strategy has ranged too far afield and that the company can improve long-term performance by concentrating on building stronger positions in a smaller number of core businesses and industries. Hewlett-Packard spun off its testing and measurement businesses into a stand-alone company called Agilent Technologies so that it could better concentrate on its PC, workstation, server, printer and peripherals, and electronics businesses.

But there are other important reasons for divesting one or more of a company's present businesses. Sometimes divesting a business has to be considered because market conditions in a once-attractive industry have badly deteriorated. A business can become a prime candidate for divestiture because it lacks adequate strategic or resource fit, because it is a cash hog with questionable long-term potential, or because it is weakly positioned in its industry with little prospect the corporate parent can realize a decent return on its investment in the business. Sometimes a company acquires businesses that, down the road, just do not work out as expected even though management has tried all it can think of to make them profitable. Subpar performance by some business units is bound to occur,

ILLUSTRATION CAPSULE 8.1

Managing Diversification at Johnson & Johnson: The Benefits of Cross-Business Strategic Fit

Johnson & Johnson (J&J), once a consumer products company known for its Band-Aid line and its baby care products, has evolved into a $61 billion diversified enterprise consisting of some 250-plus operating companies organized into three divisions: pharmaceuticals, medical devices and diagnostics, and consumer health care products. Over the past decade J&J has made acquisitions totaling more than $50 billion; about 10 to 15 percent of J&J's annual growth in revenues has come from acquisitions. Much of the company's recent growth has been in the pharmaceutical division, which in 2009 accounted for 36 percent of J&J's revenues and 41 percent of its operating profits.

While each of J&J's business units sets its own strategies and operates with its own finance and human resource departments, corporate management strongly encourages cross-business cooperation and collaboration, believing that many of the advances in 21st-century medicine will come from applying advances in one discipline to another. J&J's drug-coated stent grew out of a discussion between a drug researcher and a researcher in the company's stent business. The innovative product helps prevent infection after cardiac procedures. (When stents are inserted to prop open arteries following angioplasty, the drug coating helps prevent infection.) A gene technology database compiled by the company's gene research lab was shared with personnel from the diagnostics division, who developed a test that the drug researchers used to predict which patients would most benefit from an experimental cancer therapy. J&J's liquid Band-Aid product (a liquid coating applied to hard-to-cover places like fingers and knuckles) is based on a material used in a wound-closing product sold by the company's hospital products company. Scientists from three separate business units worked collaboratively toward the development of an absorbable patch that would stop bleeding on contact. The development of the instant clotting patch was expected to save the lives of thousands of accident victims since uncontrolled bleeding was the number-one cause of death due to injury.

J&J's corporate management maintains that close collaboration among people in its diagnostics, medical devices, and pharmaceutical businesses—where numerous examples of cross-business strategic fit exist—gives J&J an edge on competitors, most of whom cannot match the company's breadth and depth of expertise.

Sources: Amy Barrett, "Staying on Top," *BusinessWeek,* May 5, 2003, pp. 60–68; Johnson & Johnson 2007 Annual Report; www. jnj.com (accessed July 29, 2010).

thereby raising questions of whether to divest them or keep them and attempt a turnaround. Other business units, despite adequate financial performance, may not mesh as well with the rest of the firm as was originally thought. For instance, PepsiCo divested its group of fast-food restaurant businesses to focus its resources on its core soft-drink and snack-food businesses, where their resources and capabilities could add more value.

On occasion, a diversification move that seems sensible from a strategic-fit standpoint turns out to be a poor *cultural fit.*[27] Several pharmaceutical companies had just this experience. When they diversified into cosmetics and perfume, they discovered their personnel had little respect for the "frivolous" nature of such products compared to the far nobler task of developing miracle drugs to cure the ill. The absence of shared values and cultural compatibility between the medical research and chemical-compounding expertise of the pharmaceutical companies and the fashion/marketing orientation of the cosmetics business was the undoing of what otherwise was diversification into businesses with technology-sharing potential, product-development fit, and some overlap in distribution channels.

There's evidence indicating that pruning businesses and narrowing a firm's diversification base improves corporate performance.[28] A useful guide to determine whether or when to divest a business subsidiary is to ask, "If we were not in this business today, would we want to get into it now?"[29] When the answer is no or probably not, divestiture should be considered. Another signal that a business should become a divestiture candidate is whether it is worth more to another company than to the present parent; in such cases, shareholders would be well served if the company sells the business and collects a premium price from the buyer for whom the business is a valuable fit.[30]

Selling a business outright to another company is far and away the most frequently used option for divesting a business. But sometimes a business selected for divestiture has ample resources and capabilities to compete successfully on its own. In such cases, a corporate parent may elect to spin the unwanted business off as a financially and managerially independent company, either by selling shares to the investing public via an initial public offering or by distributing shares in the new company to existing shareholders of the corporate parent.

Restructuring a Diversified Company's Business Lineup through a Mix of Divestitures and New Acquisitions

If there is a serious mismatch between the company's resources and the type of diversification it has pursued, then a **companywide restructuring** effort may be called for. Restructuring a diversified company on a companywide basis *(corporate restructuring)* involves divesting some businesses and acquiring others so as to put a whole new face on the company's business lineup.[31] Performing radical surgery on a company's group of businesses may also be an appealing strategy alternative when its financial performance is being squeezed or eroded by:

CORE CONCEPT

Companywide restructuring *(corporate restructuring)* involves divesting some businesses and acquiring others so as to put a whole new face on the company's business lineup.

- Too many businesses in slow-growth, declining, low-margin, or otherwise unattractive industries (a condition indicated by the number and size of businesses with industry attractiveness ratings below 5 and located on the bottom half of the attractiveness-strength matrix—see Figure 8.3).
- Too many competitively weak businesses (a condition indicated by the number and size of businesses with competitive strength ratings below 5 and located on the right half of the attractiveness-strength matrix).
- Ongoing declines in the market shares of one or more major business units that are falling prey to more market-savvy competitors.
- An excessive debt burden with interest costs that eat deeply into profitability.
- Ill-chosen acquisitions that haven't lived up to expectations.

Companywide restructuring can also be mandated by the emergence of new technologies that threaten the survival of one or more of a diversified company's important businesses. On occasion, corporate restructuring can be prompted by special circumstances—such as when a firm has a unique opportunity to make an acquisition so big and important that it has to sell several existing business units to finance the new acquisition or when a company needs to sell off some businesses in order to raise the cash for entering a potentially big industry with wave-of-the-future technologies or products.

Candidates for divestiture in a corporate restructuring effort typically include not only weak performers or those in unattractive industries but also business units that lack strategic fit with the businesses to be retained, businesses that are cash hogs or that lack other types of resource fit, and businesses incompatible with the company's revised diversification strategy (even though they may be profitable or in an attractive industry). As businesses are divested, corporate restructuring generally involves aligning the remaining business units into groups with the best strategic fit and then redeploying the cash flows from the divested business to either pay down debt or make new acquisitions to strengthen the parent company's business position in the industries it has chosen to emphasize.[32]

Over the past decade, corporate restructuring has become a popular strategy at many diversified companies, especially those that had diversified broadly into many different industries and lines of business. In 2008, GE's CEO Jeffrey Immelt announced that GE would spin off its industrial division, which included GE appliances, lighting, and various industrial businesses. Earlier, he had led GE's withdrawal from the insurance business by divesting several companies and spinning off others. He further restructured GE's business lineup with two other major initiatives: (1) spending $10 billion to acquire British-based Amersham and extend GE's Medical Systems business into diagnostic pharmaceuticals and biosciences, thereby creating a $15 billion business designated as GE Healthcare, and (2) acquiring the entertainment assets of debt-ridden French media conglomerate Vivendi Universal Entertainment and integrating its operations into GE's NBC division, thereby creating a broad-based $13 billion media business positioned to compete against Walt Disney, Time Warner, Fox, and Viacom.

KEY POINTS

1. The purpose of diversification is to build shareholder value. Diversification builds shareholder value when a diversified group of businesses can perform better under the auspices of a single corporate parent than they would as independent, stand-alone businesses—the goal is to achieve not just a 1 + 1 = 2 result but, rather, to realize important 1 + 1 = 3 performance benefits. Whether getting into a new business has potential to enhance shareholder value hinges on whether a company's entry into that business can pass the attractiveness test, the cost-of-entry test, and the better-off test.

2. Entry into new businesses can take any of three forms: acquisition, internal start-up, or joint venture/strategic partnership. The choice of which is best depends on the firm's resources and capabilities, the industry's entry barriers, the importance of speed, and the relative costs.

3. There are two fundamental approaches to diversification—into related businesses and into unrelated businesses. The rationale for *related* diversification is to benefit from *strategic fit:* Diversify into businesses with matchups along their respective value chains, and then capitalize on the strategic fit by sharing or transferring the resources and capabilities that enable the matching value chain activities in order to gain competitive advantage.

4. *Unrelated* diversification strategies surrender the competitive advantage potential of strategic fit at the value chain level in return for the potential that can be realized from superior corporate parenting. An outstanding corporate parent can benefit its businesses through (1) providing high-level oversight and making available other corporate resources, (2) allocating financial resources across the business portfolio, and (3) restructuring underperforming acquisitions.

5. Related diversification provides a stronger foundation for creating shareholder value than unrelated diversification, since the *specialized resources and capabilities* that are leveraged in related diversification tend to be more valuable competitive assets than the *generalized resources and capabilities* underlying unrelated diversification, which in most cases are relatively common and easier to imitate.

6. Analyzing how good a company's diversification strategy is consists of a six-step process:

    Step 1: *Evaluate the long-term attractiveness of the industries into which the firm has diversified.* Industry attractiveness needs to be evaluated from three angles: the attractiveness of each industry on its own, the attractiveness of each industry relative to the others, and the attractiveness of all the industries as a group.

    Step 2: *Evaluate the relative competitive strength of each of the company's business units.* The purpose of rating the competitive strength of each business is to gain a clear understanding of which businesses are strong contenders in their industries, which are weak contenders, and the underlying reasons for their strength or weakness. The conclusions about industry attractiveness can be joined with the conclusions about competitive strength by drawing an industry attractiveness–competitive strength matrix that helps identify the prospects of each business and what priority each business should be given in allocating corporate resources and investment capital.

    Step 3: *Check for cross-business strategic fit.* A business is more attractive strategically when it has value chain relationships with the company's other business units that offer potential to (1) realize economies of scope or cost-saving efficiencies, (2) transfer technology, skills, know-how, or other resource capabilities from one business to another, (3) leverage use of a trusted brand name or other resources that enhance differentiation, and (4) build new resources and competitive capabilities via cross-business collaboration. Cross-business strategic fit represents a significant avenue for producing competitive advantage beyond what any one business can achieve on its own.

    Step 4: *Check whether the firm's resource mix fits the resource requirements of its present business lineup.* In firms with a related diversification strategy, resource fit exists when the company's businesses add to its overall resource position and when they have matching resource requirements at the value chain level. In companies pursuing unrelated diversification, resource fit exists when the parent company has generalized resources that can add value to its component businesses and when it has corporate resources sufficient to support its entire group of businesses without spreading itself too thin. When there is financial resource fit among the businesses of any type of diversified company, the company can generate internal cash flows sufficient to fund the capital requirements of its businesses, pay its dividends, meet its debt obligations, and otherwise remain financially healthy.

Step 5: *Rank the performance prospects of the businesses from best to worst, and determine what the corporate parent's priority should be in allocating resources to its various businesses.* The most important considerations in judging business-unit performance are sales growth, profit growth, contribution to company earnings, and the return on capital invested in the business. Normally, strong business units in attractive industries have significantly better performance prospects than weak businesses or businesses in unattractive industries. Business subsidiaries with the brightest profit and growth prospects and solid strategic and resource fit generally should head the list for corporate resource support.

Step 6: *Crafting new strategic moves to improve overall corporate performance.* This step entails using the results of the preceding analysis as the basis for devising actions to strengthen existing businesses, make new acquisitions, divest weak-performing and unattractive businesses, restructure the company's business lineup, expand the scope of the company's geographic reach into new markets around the world, and otherwise steer corporate resources into the areas of greatest opportunity.

7. Once a company has diversified, corporate management's task is to manage the collection of businesses for maximum long-term performance. There are four different strategic paths for improving a diversified company's performance: (1) sticking with the existing business lineup, (2) broadening the firm's business base by diversifying into additional businesses or geographic markets, (3) retrenching to a narrower diversification base by divesting some of its present businesses, and (4) restructuring the company's business lineup with a combination of divestitures and new acquisitions to put a whole new face on the company's business makeup.

ASSURANCE OF LEARNING EXERCISES

LO 1, LO 2

1. See if you can identify the value chain relationships that make the businesses of the following companies related in competitively relevant ways. In particular, you should consider whether there are cross-business opportunities for (1) transferring skills/technology, (2) combining related value chain activities to achieve economies of scope, and/or (3) leveraging the use of a well-respected brand name or other resources that enhance differentiation.

OSI Restaurant Partners

- Outback Steakhouse
- Carrabba's Italian Grill

- Roy's Restaurant (Hawaiian fusion cuisine)
- Bonefish Grill (market-fresh fine seafood)
- Fleming's Prime Steakhouse & Wine Bar

L'Oréal

- Maybelline, Lancôme, Helena Rubinstein, Kiehl's, Garner, and Shu Uemura cosmetics
- L'Oréal and Soft Sheen/Carson hair care products
- Redken, Matrix, L'Oréal Professional, and Kerastase Paris professional hair care and skin care products
- Ralph Lauren and Giorgio Armani fragrances
- Biotherm skincare products
- La Roche–Posay and Vichy Laboratories dermocosmetics

Johnson & Johnson

- Baby products (powder, shampoo, oil, lotion)
- Band-Aids and other first-aid products
- Women's health and personal care products (Stayfree, Carefree, Sure & Natural)
- Neutrogena and Aveeno skin care products
- Nonprescription drugs (Tylenol, Motrin, Pepcid AC, Mylanta, Monistat)
- Prescription drugs
- Prosthetic and other medical devices
- Surgical and hospital products
- Acuvue contact lenses

LO 2, LO 3

2. Peruse the business group listings for United Technologies shown below and listed at its Web site (www.utc.com). How would you characterize the company's corporate strategy? related diversification, unrelated diversification, or a combination related-unrelated diversification strategy? Explain your answer.

   - Carrier—the world's largest provider of air-conditioning, heating, and refrigeration solutions.
   - Hamilton Sundstrand—technologically advanced aerospace and industrial products.
   - Otis—the world's leading manufacturer, installer and maintainer of elevators, escalators and moving walkways.
   - Pratt & Whitney—designs, manufactures, services and supports aircraft engines, industrial gas turbines and space propulsion systems.
   - Sikorsky—a world leader in helicopter design, manufacture and service.
   - UTC Fire & Security—fire and security systems developed for commercial, industrial and residential customers.
   - UTC Power—a full-service provider of environmentally advanced power solutions.

LO 1, LO 2, LO 3

3. The Walt Disney Company is in the following businesses:

    *   Theme parks
    *   Disney Cruise Line
    *   Resort properties
    *   Movie, video, and theatrical productions (for both children and adults)
    *   Television broadcasting (ABC, Disney Channel, Toon Disney, Classic Sports Network, ESPN and ESPN2, E!, Lifetime, and A&E networks)
    *   Radio broadcasting (Disney Radio)
    *   Musical recordings and sales of animation art
    *   Anaheim Mighty Ducks NHL franchise
    *   Anaheim Angels major-league baseball franchise (25 percent ownership)
    *   Books and magazine publishing
    *   Interactive software and Internet sites
    *   The Disney Store retail shops

    Based on the above listing, would you say that Walt Disney's business lineup reflects a strategy of related diversification, unrelated diversification, or a combination of related and unrelated diversification? Be prepared to justify and explain your answer in terms of the nature of Disney's shared or transferred resources and capabilities and the extent to which the value chains of Disney's different businesses seem to have competitively valuable cross-business relationships.

    If need be, visit the company's Web site (http://corporate.disney.go.com/index.html?ppLink=pp_wdig) to obtain additional information about its business lineup and strategy.

EXERCISES FOR SIMULATION PARTICIPANTS

LO 1, LO 2, LO 3

1. In the event that your company had the opportunity to diversify into other products or businesses of your choosing, would you opt to pursue related diversification, unrelated diversification, or a combination of both? Explain why.

LO 1, LO 2

2. What specific resources and capabilities does your company possess that would make diversifying into related businesses attractive? Indicate what kinds of strategic-fit benefits could be captured by transferring these resources and competitive capabilities to newly acquired related businesses.

LO 1, LO 2

3. If your company opted to pursue a strategy of related diversification, what industries or product categories could it diversify into that would allow it to achieve economies of scope? Name at least two or three such industries or product categories, and indicate the specific kinds of cost savings that might accrue from entry into each.

LO 1, LO 2

4. If your company opted to pursue a strategy of related diversification, what industries or product categories could it diversify into that would allow it to capitalize on using its present brand name and corporate image to good advantage in the newly entered businesses or product categories? Name at least two or three such industries or product categories, and indicate *the specific benefits* that might be captured by transferring your company's brand name to each.

ENDNOTES

[1] For a more detailed discussion of when diversification makes good strategic sense, see Constantinos C. Markides, "To Diversify or Not to Diversify," *Harvard Business Review* 75, no. 6 (November–December 1997), pp. 93–99.

[2] For a discussion of how hidden opportunities within a corporation's existing asset base may offer growth to corporations with declining core businesses, see Chris Zook, "Finding Your Next Core Business," *Harvard Business Review* 85, no. 4 (April 2007), pp. 66–75.

[3] Michael E. Porter, "From Competitive Advantage to Corporate Strategy," *Harvard Business Review* 45, no. 3 (May–June 1987), pp. 46–49.

[4] Rita Nazareth, "CEOs Paying 56% M&A Premium Shows Stocks May Be Cheap (Update3)," *Bloomberg.com,* December 21, 2009, www.bloomberg.com/apps/news?pid=20603037&sid=ahPolYY.zgQ.

[5] Ibid.

[6] Michael E. Porter, *Competitive Strategy: Techniques for Analyzing Industries and Competitors* (New York: Free Press, 1980), pp. 354–55.

[7] A. Shleifer and R. Vishny, "Takeovers in the 60s and the 80s—Evidence and Implications," *Strategic Management Journal* 12 (Winter 1991), pp. 51–59; T. Brush, "Predicted Change in Operational Synergy and Post-Acquisition Performance of Acquired Businesses," *Strategic Management Journal* 17, no. 1(1996), pp. 1–24; J. P. Walsh, "Top Management Turnover Following Mergers and Acquisitions," *Strategic Management Journal* 9, no. 2 (1988), pp. 173–83; A. Cannella and D. Hambrick, "Effects of Executive Departures on the Performance of Acquired Firms," *Strategic Management Journal* 14 (Summer 1993), pp.137–52; R. Roll, "The Hubris Hypothesis of Corporate Takeovers," *Journal of Business* 59, no. 2 (1986), pp. 197–216; P. Haspeslagh and D. Jemison, *Managing Acquisitions* (New York: Free Press, 1991).

[8] M. L. A. Hayward, "When Do Firms Learn from Their Acquisition Experience? Evidence from 1990–1995," *Strategic Management Journal* 23, no. 1 (2002), pp. 21–29; G. Ahuja and R. Katila, "Technological Acquisitions and the Innovation Performance of Acquiring Firms: A Longitudinal Study," *Strategic Management Journal* 22, no. 3 (2001), pp. 197–220; H. Barkema and F. Vermeulen,

"International Expansion through Start-Up or Acquisition: A Learning Perspective," *Academy of Management Journal* 41, no. 1 (1998), pp. 7–26.

[9] Haspeslagh and Jemison, *Managing Acquisitions,* pp. 344–45.

[10] Yves L. Doz and Gary Hamel, *Alliance Advantage: The Art of Creating Value through Partnering* (Boston: Harvard Business School Press, 1998), chaps. 1 and 2.

[11] J. Glover, "The Guardian," March 23, 1996, www.mcspotlight.org/media/press/guardpizza_23mar96.html.

[12] Michael E. Porter, *Competitive Advantage* (New York: Free Press, 1985), pp. 318–19 and pp. 337–53; Porter, "From Competitive Advantage to Corporate Strategy," pp. 53–57. For an empirical study supporting the notion that strategic fit enhances performance (provided the resulting combination is competitively valuable and difficult to duplicate by rivals), see Constantinos C. Markides and Peter J. Williamson, "Corporate Diversification and Organization Structure: A Resource-Based View," *Academy of Management Journal* 39, no. 2 (April 1996), pp. 340–67.

[13] David J. Collis and Cynthia A. Montgomery, "Creating Corporate Advantage," *Harvard Business Review* 76, no. 3 (May–June 1998), pp. 72–80; Markides and Williamson, "Corporate Diversification and Organization Structure."

[14] Markides and Williamson, "Corporate Diversification and Organization Structure."

[15] For a discussion of the strategic significance of cross-business coordination of value chain activities and insight into how the process works, see Jeanne M. Liedtka, "Collaboration across Lines of Business for Competitive Advantage," *Academy of Management Executive* 10, no. 2 (May 1996), pp. 20–34.

[16] For a discussion of what is involved in actually capturing strategic-fit benefits, see Kathleen M. Eisenhardt and D. Charles Galunic, "Coevolving: At Last, a Way to Make Synergies Work," *Harvard Business Review* 78, no. 1 (January–February 2000), pp. 91–101; Constantinos C. Markides and Peter J. Williamson, "Related Diversification, Core Competences and Corporate Performance," *Strategic Management Journal* 15 (Summer 1994), pp. 149–65.

[17] A. Campbell, M. Goold, and M. Alexander, "Corporate Strategy: The Quest for Parenting Advantage," *Harvard Business Review* 73, no. 2 (March–April 1995), pp. 120–32.

[18] C. Montgomery and B. Wernerfelt, "Diversification, Ricardian Rents, and Tobin-Q," *RAND Journal of Economics* 19, no. 4 (1988), pp. 623–32.

[19] Ibid.

[20] Ibid.

[21] For a review of the experiences of companies that have pursued unrelated diversification successfully, see Patricia L. Anslinger and Thomas E. Copeland, "Growth through Acquisitions: A Fresh Look," *Harvard Business Review* 74, no. 1 (January–February 1996), pp. 126–35.

[22] Of course, management may be willing to assume the risk that trouble will not strike before it has had time to learn the business well enough to bail it out of almost any difficulty. But there is research that shows this is very risky from a financial perspective; see, for example, M. Lubatkin and S. Chatterjee, "Extending Modern Portfolio Theory," *Academy of Management Journal* 37, no.1(February 1994), pp. 109–36.

[23] For research evidence of the failure of broad diversification and trend of companies to focus their diversification efforts more narrowly, see Lawrence G. Franko, "The Death of Diversification? The Focusing of the World's Industrial Firms, 1980–2000," *Business Horizons* 47, no. 4 (July–August 2004), pp. 41–50.

[24] For an excellent discussion of what to look for in assessing this type of strategic fit, see Campbell, Goold, and Alexander, "Corporate Strategy: The Quest for Parenting Advantage."

[25] Ibid., p. 128.

[26] A good discussion of the importance of having adequate resources, as well as upgrading corporate resources and capabilities, can be found in David J. Collis and Cynthia A. Montgomery, "Competing on Resources: Strategy in the 90s," *Harvard Business Review* 73, no. 4 (July–August 1995), pp. 118–28.

[27] Peter F. Drucker, *Management: Tasks, Responsibilities, Practices,* (New York: Harper & Row, 1974), p. 709.

[28] See, for example, Constantinos C. Markides, "Diversification, Restructuring, and Economic Performance," *Strategic*

Management Journal 16 (February 1995), pp. 101–18.

[29] Drucker, *Management: Tasks, Responsibilities, Practices,* p. 94.

[30] Collis and Montgomery, "Creating Corporate Advantage."

[31] For a discussion of why divestiture needs to be a standard part of any company's diversification strategy, see Lee Dranikoff, Tim Koller, and Anton Schneider, "Divestiture: Strategy's Missing Link," *Harvard Business Review* 80, no. 5 (May 2002), pp. 74–83.

[32] Evidence that restructuring strategies tend to result in higher levels of performance is contained in Markides, "Diversification, Restructuring, and Economic Performance."

CHAPTER 9

ETHICS, CORPORATE SOCIAL RESPONSIBILITY, ENVIRONMENTAL SUSTAINABILITY, AND STRATEGY

> Business is the most important engine for social change in our society.
>
> **—Lawrence Perlman**
> *Former CEO of Ceridian Corporation*

> It takes many good deeds to build a good reputation and only one bad one to lose it.
>
> **—Benjamin Franklin**
> *American Statesman, Inventor, and Philosopher*

> Corporations are economic entities, to be sure, but they are also social institutions that must justify their existence by their overall contribution to society.
>
> **—Henry Mintzberg, Robert Simons, and Kunal Basu**
> *Professors*

> Companies have to be socially responsible or shareholders pay eventually.
>
> **—Warren Shaw**
> *Former CEO of LGT Asset Management*

LEARNING OBJECTIVES

LO 1. Understand how the standards of ethical behavior in business relate to the ethical standards and norms of the larger society and culture in which a company operates.

LO 2. Recognize conditions that can give rise to unethical business strategies and behavior.

LO 3. Gain an understanding of the costs of business ethics failures.

LO 4. Gain an understanding of the concepts of corporate social responsibility and environmental sustainability and of how companies balance these duties with economic responsibilities to shareholders.

Clearly, a company has a responsibility to make a profit and grow the business—in capitalistic or market economies, management's fiduciary duty to create value for shareholders is not a matter for serious debate. Just as clearly, a company and its personnel also have a duty to obey the law and play by the rules of fair competition. But does a company have a duty to go beyond legal requirements and operate according to the ethical norms of the societies in which it operates—should all company personnel be held to some standard of ethical conduct? And does a company have a duty or obligation to contribute to the betterment of society independent of the needs and preferences of the customers it serves? Should a company display a social conscience and devote a portion of its resources to bettering soci-

ety? How far should a company go in protecting the environment, conserving natural resources for use by future generations, and ensuring that its operations do not ultimately endanger the planet?

The focus of this chapter is to examine what link, if any, there should be between a company's efforts to craft and execute a winning strategy and its duties to (1) conduct its activities in an ethical manner, (2) demonstrate socially responsible behavior by being a committed corporate citizen and directing corporate resources to the betterment of employees, the communities in which it operates, and society as a whole, and (3) adopt business practices that conserve natural resources, protect the interests of future generations, and preserve the well-being of the planet.

WHAT DO WE MEAN BY *BUSINESS ETHICS*?

Ethics concerns principles of right or wrong conduct. **Business ethics** is the application of ethical principles and standards to the actions and decisions of business organizations and the conduct of their personnel.[1] Ethical principles in business are not materially different from ethical principles in general because business actions have to be judged in the context of society's standards of right and wrong. There is not a special set of ethical standards applicable only to business situations. If dishonesty is considered unethical and immoral, then dishonest behavior in business—whether it relates to customers, suppliers, employees, shareholders, competitors, government, or society—qualifies as equally unethical and immoral. If being ethical entails not deliberately harming others, then

CORE CONCEPT

Business ethics is the application of general ethical principles to the actions and decisions of businesses and the conduct of their personnel.

recalling a defective or unsafe product is ethically necessary. If society deems bribery unethical, then it is unethical for company personnel to make payoffs to government officials or bestow gifts and other favors on prospective customers to win or retain business. In short, ethical behavior in business situations requires adhering to generally accepted norms about right or wrong conduct. As a consequence, company managers have an obligation—indeed, a duty—to observe ethical norms when crafting and executing strategy.

WHERE DO ETHICAL STANDARDS COME FROM—ARE THEY UNIVERSAL OR DEPENDENT ON LOCAL NORMS?

LO 1

Understand how the standards of ethical behavior in business relate to the ethical standards and norms of the larger society and culture in which a company operates.

Notions of right and wrong, fair and unfair, ethical and unethical are present in all societies and cultures. But there are three distinct schools of thought about the extent to which ethical standards travel across cultures and whether multinational companies can apply the same set of ethical standards in any and all locations where they operate. Illustration Capsule 9.1 describes the difficulties Apple has faced in trying to enforce a common set of ethical standards across its vast global supplier network.

The School of Ethical Universalism

According to the school of **ethical universalism,** the most important concepts of what is right and what is wrong are *universal* and transcend culture, society, and religion.[2] For instance, being truthful (or not being deliberately deceitful) strikes a chord of what's right in the peoples of all nations. Likewise, demonstrating integrity of character, not cheating, and treating people with courtesy and respect are concepts that resonate with people of virtually all cultures and religions. In most societies, people would concur that it is unethical for companies to knowingly expose workers to toxic chemicals and hazardous materials or to sell products known to be unsafe or harmful to the users.

CORE CONCEPT

The school of **ethical universalism** holds that common understandings across multiple cultures and countries about what constitutes right and wrong give rise to universal ethical standards that apply to members of all societies, all companies, and all businesspeople.

Common moral agreement about right and wrong actions and behaviors across multiple cultures and countries gives rise to universal ethical standards that apply to members of all societies, all companies, and all businesspeople. These universal ethical principles set forth the traits and behaviors that are considered virtuous and that a good person is supposed to believe in and to display. Thus, adherents of the school of ethical universalism maintain it is entirely appropriate to expect all businesspeople to conform to these universal ethical standards.[3]

The strength of ethical universalism is that it draws on the collective views of multiple societies and cultures to put some clear boundaries on what constitutes ethical business behavior and what constitutes unethical business behavior regardless of the country or culture in which a company's personnel are conducting activities. This means that in those instances where basic moral standards really do not vary significantly according to local cultural beliefs, traditions, or religious convictions, a multinational company can develop a code

ILLUSTRATION CAPSULE 9.1

Many of Apple's Suppliers Flunk the Ethics Test

Apple requires its suppliers to comply with the company's Supplier Code of Conduct as a condition of being awarded contracts. To ensure compliance, Apple has a supplier monitoring program that includes audits of supplier factories, corrective action plans, and verification measures. In the company's 24-page 2010 Progress Report on Supplier Responsibility, Apple reported that in 2009 it conducted 102 audits of supplier facilities in such countries as China, the Czech Republic, Malaysia, the Philippines, Singapore, South Korea, Taiwan, Thailand, and the United States; 80 of these audits were first-time audits and 22 were repeat audits.

Apple distinguishes among the seriousness of infractions, designating "core violations" as those that go directly against the core principles of its Supplier Code of Conduct and must be remedied immediately. During the 2009 audits, 17 such violations were discovered, including 3 cases of underage labor, 8 cases involving excessive recruitment fees, 3 cases of improper hazardous waste disposal, and 3 cases of deliberately falsified audit records. Apple responded by ensuring that immediate corrective actions were taken, placing violators on probation, and planning to audit them again in a year's time.

While all six of Apple's final assembly manufacturers had high compliance scores—on average, registering well above 90 percent compliance on all issues—other suppliers did not fare so well on the 2009 audits. At 60 of the audited facilities, workers were required to work more than 60 hours per week more than 50 percent of the time—Apple sets a maximum of 60 hours per week (except in unusual or emergency circumstances). In 65 of the audited facilities, workers were found to have been required to work more than six consecutive days a week at least once per month—Apple requires at least one day of rest per seven days of work (except in unusual or emergency circumstances).

At 48 facilities, Apple found that overtime wages had been calculated improperly, resulting in underpayment of overtime compensation. Apple

auditors discovered that at 24 facilities workers were being paid less than the specified minimum wage and that at 45 facilities wage deductions were used to discipline employees. At 57 of the audited facilities, worker benefits (for such things as retirement, sick leave, or maternity leave) were below the legally required amounts.

Apple requires suppliers to provide a safe working environment and to eliminate physical hazards to employees where possible. But the 2009 audits revealed that workers were not wearing appropriate protective personal equipment at 49 facilities. Violations were found at 70 facilities where workers were improperly trained, where unlicensed workers were operating equipment, and where required inspections of equipment were not being conducted. Apple auditors found that 44 facilities had failed to conduct environmental impact assessments, 11 facilities did not have permits for air emissions, and 4 facilities did not meet the conditions specified in their emission permits. Moreover, the audits revealed that 55 supplier facilities did not have any personnel assigned to ensuring compliance with Apple's Supplier Code of Conduct.

For Apple, the audits represent a starting point for bringing its suppliers into compliance, through greater scrutiny, education and training of suppliers' personnel, and incentives. Apple collects quarterly data to hold its suppliers accountable for their actions and makes procurement decisions based, in part, on these numbers. Suppliers that are unable to meet Apple's high standards of conduct ultimately end up losing Apple's business.

Sources: Apple's 2010 Progress Report on Supplier Responsibility; Dan Moren, "Apple Releases 2010 Report on Supplier Responsibility," *Macworld.com,* February 23, 2010, www.macworld.com/article/146653/2010/02/suppliers_2010.htm (accessed July 1, 2010); Andrew Morse and Nick Wingfield, "Apple Audits Labor Practices: Company Says Suppliers Hired Underage Workers, Violated Other Core Policies," *Wall Street Journal Online,* March 1, 2010, http://online.wsj.com/article/SB10001424 052748704231304575091920704104154.html (accessed July 1, 2010); Nicholas Kolakowski, "Apple Finds Violations during 2009 Supplier and Manufacturer Audit," *eWeek.com,* March 1, 2010, www.eweek.com/c/a/Mobile-and-Wireless/Apple-Finds-Violations-During-2009-Supplier-and-Manufacturer-Audit-522622/ (accessed July 1, 2010).

of ethics that it applies more or less evenly across its worldwide operations.[4] It can avoid the slippery slope that comes from having different ethical standards for different company personnel depending on where in the world they are working.

The School of Ethical Relativism

Apart from a select set of universal moral prescriptions—like being truthful and trustworthy—that apply in every society and business circumstance, there are meaningful variations in the ethical standards by which different societies judge the conduct of business activities. Indeed, differing religious beliefs, social customs, traditions, and behavioral norms frequently give rise to different standards about what is fair or unfair, moral or immoral, and ethically right or wrong. The school of **ethical relativism** holds that when there are cross-country or cross-cultural differences in what is deemed ethical or unethical in business situations, it is appropriate for local moral standards to take precedence over what the ethical standards may be in a company's home market. The thesis is that what constitutes ethical or unethical behavior on the part of local businesspeople is properly governed by local ethical standards rather than the standards that prevail in other locations.[5] Consider the following examples.

The Use of Underage Labor   In industrialized nations, the use of underage workers is considered taboo. Social activists are adamant that child labor is unethical and that companies should neither employ children under the age of 18 as full-time employees nor source any products from foreign suppliers that employ underage workers. Many countries have passed legislation forbidding the use of underage labor or, at a minimum, regulating the employment of people under the age of 18. However, in India, Bangladesh, Botswana, Sri Lanka, Ghana, Somalia, and more than 100 other countries, it is customary to view children as potential, even necessary, workers.[6] Many poverty-stricken families cannot subsist without the income earned by young family members; sending their children to school instead of having them work is not a realistic option. In 2006, the International Labor Organization estimated that 191 million children ages 5 to 14 were working around the world.[7] If such children are not permitted to work—due to pressures imposed by activist groups in industrialized nations—they may be forced to go out on the streets begging or to seek work in parts of the "underground" economy such as drug trafficking and prostitution.[8] So if all businesses in countries where employing underage workers is common succumb to the pressures of activist groups and government organizations to stop employing underage labor, then have they served the best interests of the underage workers, their families, and society in general?

The Payment of Bribes and Kickbacks   A particularly thorny area facing multinational companies is the degree of cross-country variability in paying bribes.[9] In many countries in eastern Europe, Africa, Latin America, and Asia, it is customary to pay bribes to government officials in order to win a government contract, obtain a license or permit, or facilitate an administrative ruling.[10] Likewise, in many countries it is normal to make payments to prospective customers in order to win or retain their business. In some developing nations, it is difficult for any company, foreign or domestic, to move goods through customs without paying off low-level officials.[11] A *Wall Street Journal* article reported that

30 to 60 percent of all business transactions in eastern Europe involved paying bribes and the costs of bribe payments averaged 2 to 8 percent of revenues.[12] Some people stretch to justify the payment of bribes and kickbacks on grounds that bribing government officials to get goods through customs or giving kickbacks to customers to retain their business or win new orders is simply a payment for services rendered, in the same way that people tip for service at restaurants.[13] But while this is a clever rationalization, it rests on moral quicksand.

Companies that forbid the payment of bribes and kickbacks in their codes of ethical conduct and that are serious about enforcing this prohibition face a particularly vexing problem in countries where bribery and kickback payments are an entrenched local custom.[14] Refusing to pay bribes or kickbacks in these countries (so as to comply with the company's code of ethical conduct) is very often tantamount to losing business to competitors willing to make such payments—an outcome that penalizes ethical companies and ethical company personnel (who may suffer lost sales commissions or bonuses). On the other hand, the payment of bribes or kickbacks not only undercuts the company's code of ethics but also risks breaking the law. U.S. companies are prohibited by the Foreign Corrupt Practices Act (FCPA) from paying bribes to government officials, political parties, political candidates, or others in all countries where they do business. The Organization for Economic Cooperation and Development (OECD) has antibribery standards that criminalize the bribery of foreign public officials in international business transactions—as of 2009, the 30 OECD members and 8 nonmember countries had adopted these standards.[15] In 2008, Siemens, one of the world's largest corporations and headquartered in Munich, Germany, was fined $1.6 billion by the U.S. and German governments for bribing foreign officials to help it secure huge public works contracts around the world. Investigations revealed that Siemens created secret offshore bank accounts and used middlemen posing as consultants to deliver suitcases filled with cash, paying an estimated $1.4 billion to over 4,000 well-placed government officials in Asia, Africa, Europe, the Middle East, and Latin America between 2001 and 2007. An estimated 300 Siemens sales employees, executives, and board members were being investigated in 2009 for their roles in the scheme. The evidence gathered indicated that such bribes were a core element of Siemens' strategy and business model.

Penalizing companies for overseas bribes is becoming more widespread internationally. The Serious Fraud Office (SFO) in London held a landmark investigation in December 2009 of DePuy International, a subsidiary of Johnson & Johnson, for bribing Greek officials to purchase products. This comes after DePuy was fined over $311 million by the U.S. government for kickbacks to U.S. surgeons in 2007.[16]

Ethical Relativism Equates to Multiple Sets of Ethical Standards   The existence of varying ethical norms such as those cited above explains why the adherents of ethical relativism maintain that there are few absolutes when it comes to business ethics and thus few ethical absolutes for consistently judging a company's conduct in various countries and markets. Indeed, ethical relativists argue that while there are some general moral prescriptions that apply regardless of the business circumstance, there are plenty of situations where ethical norms must be contoured to fit the local customs, traditions, and notions of fairness shared by the parties involved. They argue that a "one-size-fits-all" template for judging the ethical appropriateness of business actions and the behaviors of company personnel simply does not exist—in other

> Under ethical relativism, there can be no one-size-fits-all set of authentic ethical norms against which to gauge the conduct of company personnel.

words, ethical problems in business cannot be fully resolved without appealing to the shared convictions of the parties in question.[17] While European and American managers may want to impose standards of business conduct that give heavy weight to such core human rights as personal freedom, individual security, political participation, and the ownership of property, managers in China may have a much weaker commitment to these kinds of human rights. Japanese managers may prefer ethical standards that show respect for the collective good of society. Muslim managers may wish to apply ethical standards compatible with the teachings of Mohammed. Clearly, there is some merit in the school of ethical relativism's view that what is deemed right or wrong, fair or unfair, moral or immoral, ethical or unethical in business situations depends partly on the context of each country's local customs, religious traditions, and societal norms. Hence, there is a kernel of truth in the argument that businesses need some room to tailor their ethical standards to fit local situations. A company has to be very cautious about exporting its home-country values and ethics to foreign countries where it operates—"photocopying" ethics is disrespectful of other cultures and neglects the important role of moral free space (in which there is room to accommodate local ethical standards).

Pushed to the Extreme, Ethical Relativism Breaks Down

While the ethical relativism rule of "When in Rome, do as the Romans do" appears reasonable, it nonetheless presents a big problem—when the envelope starts to be pushed, as will inevitably be the case, *it is tantamount to rudderless ethical standards.* Consider, for instance, the following example: In 1992, the owners of the *SS United States,* an aging luxury ocean liner constructed with asbestos in the 1940s, had the liner towed to Turkey, where a contractor had agreed to remove the asbestos for $2 million (versus a far higher cost in the United States, where asbestos removal safety standards were much more stringent).[18] When Turkish officials blocked the asbestos removal because of the dangers to workers of contracting cancer, the owners had the liner towed to the Black Sea port of Sevastopol, in the Crimean Republic, where the asbestos removal standards were quite lax and where a contractor had agreed to remove more than 500,000 square feet of carcinogenic asbestos for less than $2 million. There are no moral grounds for arguing that exposing workers to carcinogenic asbestos is ethically correct, regardless of what a country's law allows or the value the country places on worker safety.

A company that adopts the principle of ethical relativism and holds company personnel to local ethical standards necessarily assumes that what prevails as local morality is an adequate guide to ethical behavior. This can be ethically dangerous—it leads to the conclusion that if a country's culture is accepting of bribery or environmental degradation or exposing workers to dangerous conditions (toxic chemicals or bodily harm), then so much the worse for honest people and environmental protection and safe working conditions. Such a position is morally unacceptable. Even though bribery of government officials in China is a common practice, when Lucent Technologies found that managers in its Chinese operations had bribed government officials, it fired the entire senior management team.[19]

Moreover, from a global markets perspective, ethical relativism results in a maze of conflicting ethical standards for multinational companies wanting to address the very real issue of which ethical standards to enforce companywide. It is a slippery slope indeed to resolve such ethical diversity without any kind of higher-order moral compass. Imagine, for example, that a multinational company (in the name of ethical relativism) permits company personnel to pay bribes and kickbacks in countries where such payments are customary but forbids them to make such payments in countries where bribes and kickbacks are considered unethical or illegal. Or that the company says it is appropriate to use child labor in its plants in countries where underage labor is acceptable but inappropriate to employ child labor at the remainder of its plants. Having thus adopted conflicting ethical standards for operating in different countries, company managers have little moral basis for enforcing any ethical standards companywide—rather, the clear message to employees would be that the company has no ethical standards or principles of its own. This is scarcely strong moral ground to stand on.

> Codes of conduct based on ethical relativism can be *ethically dangerous* for multinational companies by creating a maze of conflicting ethical standards.

Ethics and Integrative Social Contracts Theory

Social contract theory provides a middle position between the opposing views of universalism (that the same set of ethical standards should apply everywhere) and relativism (that ethical standards vary according to local custom).[20] According to **integrated social contracts theory,** universal ethical principles or norms based on the collective views of multiple cultures and societies combine to form a "social contract" that all individuals, groups, organizations and businesses in all situations have a duty to observe. *Within the boundaries of this social contract,* local cultures or groups can specify what other actions may or may not be ethically permissible. While this system leaves some "moral free space" for the people in a particular country (or local culture or even a company) to make specific interpretations of what other actions may or may not be permissible, universal ethical norms always take precedence. Thus, local ethical standards can be *more* stringent than the universal ethical standards, but never less so.

> **CORE CONCEPT**
>
> According to **integrated social contracts theory,** universal ethical principles based on the collective views of multiple societies form a "social contract" that all individuals and organizations have a duty to observe in all situations. *Within the boundaries of this social contract,* local cultures or groups can specify what additional actions may or may not be ethically permissible.

Hence, while firms, industries, professional associations, and other business-relevant groups are "contractually obligated" to society to observe universal ethical norms, they have the discretion to go beyond these universal norms and specify other behaviors that are out of bounds and place further limitations on what is considered ethical. For example, both the legal and medical professions have standards regarding what kinds of advertising are ethically permissible that extend beyond the universal norm that advertising not be false or misleading. Similarly, food products companies are beginning to establish ethical guidelines for judging what is and is not appropriate advertising for food products that are inherently unhealthy and may cause dietary or obesity problems for people who eat them regularly or consume them in large quantities.

The strength of integrated social contracts theory is that it accommodates the best parts of ethical universalism and ethical relativism. It is indisputable that cultural differences impact how business is conducted in various parts of the world and that these cultural differences sometimes give rise to different ethical norms. But it is just as indisputable that some ethical norms are more authentic or universally applicable than others, meaning that in many instances of cross-country differences one side may be more "ethically correct" than another. In such instances, resolving cross-cultural differences over what is ethically permissible entails applying the rule that *universal or "first-order" ethical norms override the local or "second-order" ethical norms.* A good example is the payment of bribes and kickbacks. Yes, bribes and kickbacks seem to be common in some countries, but does this justify paying them? Just because bribery flourishes in a country does not mean it is an authentic or legitimate ethical norm. Virtually all of the world's major religions (e.g., Buddhism, Christianity, Confucianism, Hinduism, Islam, Judaism, Sikhism, and Taoism) and all moral schools of thought condemn bribery and corruption.[21] Therefore, a multinational company might reasonably conclude that the right ethical standard is one of refusing to condone bribery and kickbacks on the part of company personnel no matter what the local custom is and no matter what the sales consequences are.

Granting an automatic preference to local-country ethical norms presents vexing problems to multinational company managers when the ethical standards followed in a foreign country are lower than those in its home country or are in conflict with the company's code of ethics. Sometimes—as with bribery and kickbacks—there can be no compromise on what is ethically permissible and what is not. *This is precisely what integrated social contracts theory maintains—adherence to universal or "first-order" ethical norms should always take precedence over local or "second-order" norms.* Consequently, integrated social contracts theory offers managers in multinational companies clear guidance in resolving cross-country ethical differences: Those parts of the company's code of ethics that involve universal ethical norms must be enforced worldwide, but *within* these boundaries there is room for ethical diversity and opportunity for host-country cultures to exert *some* influence in setting their own moral and ethical standards. Such an approach avoids the discomforting case of a self-righteous multinational company trying to operate as the standard bearer of moral truth and imposing its interpretation of its code of ethics worldwide no matter what. And it avoids the equally disturbing case for a company's ethical conduct to be no higher than local ethical norms in situations where local ethical norms permit practices that are generally considered immoral or when local norms clearly conflict with a company's code of ethical conduct.

> According to integrated social contracts theory, adherence to universal or "first-order" ethical norms should always take precedence over local or "second-order" norms.

HOW AND WHY ETHICAL STANDARDS IMPACT THE TASKS OF CRAFTING AND EXECUTING STRATEGY

Many companies have acknowledged their ethical obligations in official codes of ethical conduct and statements of company values. In the United States, for example, the Sarbanes-Oxley Act, passed in 2002, requires that companies whose stock is publicly traded have a code of ethics or else explain in writing to the Securities and Exchange Commission (SEC) why they do not. But there's a big difference between having a code of ethics that serves merely as public window dressing and having ethical standards that truly paint the white lines for a company's actual strategy and business conduct.[22] *The litmus test of whether a company's code of ethics is cosmetic is the extent to which it is embraced in crafting strategy and in operating the business day to day.*

It is up to senior executives to walk the talk and make a point of considering three sets of questions whenever a new strategic initiative is under review:

- Is what we are proposing to do fully compliant with our code of ethical conduct? Are there any areas of ambiguity that may be of concern?
- Is it apparent that this proposed action is in harmony with our core values? Are any conflicts or potential problems evident?
- Is there anything in the proposed action that could be considered ethically objectionable? Would our stakeholders, our competitors, the SEC, or the media view this action as ethically objectionable?

Unless questions of this nature are posed—either in open discussion or by force of habit in the minds of strategy makers—there's room for strategic initiatives to become disconnected from the company's code of ethics and stated core values. If a company's executives believe strongly in living up to the company's ethical standards, they will unhesitatingly reject strategic initiatives and operating approaches that don't measure up. However, in companies with a cosmetic approach to ethics, any strategy-ethics-values linkage stems mainly from a desire to avoid the risk of embarrassment and possible disciplinary action should strategy makers be held accountable for approving a strategic initiative that is deemed by society to be unethical and perhaps illegal.

While most company managers are careful to ensure that a company's strategy is within the bounds of what is legal, evidence indicates they are not always so careful to ensure that all elements of their strategies and operating activities are within the bounds of what is considered ethical. In recent years, there have been revelations of ethical misconduct on the part of managers at such companies as Enron, Tyco International, HealthSouth, Adelphia, Royal Dutch/Shell, Parmalat (an Italy-based food products company), Rite Aid, Mexican oil giant Pemex, AIG, Citigroup, several leading brokerage houses, mutual fund companies, investment banking firms, and a host of mortgage lenders. Much of the crisis in residential real estate that emerged in the United States in 2007–2008 stemmed from consciously unethical strategies at certain banks and mortgage companies to boost the fees they earned on processing home mortgage applications by deliberately lowering lending standards and finding ways to secure mortgage approvals for home buyers who lacked sufficient income to make their monthly mortgage payments. Once these lenders earned their fees on the so-called subprime loans (a term used for high-risk mortgage loans to home buyers with dubious qualifications to repay the loans), they secured the assistance of investment banking firms to bundle those and other mortgages into collateralized debt obligations (CDOs), found means of having the CDOs assigned triple-A bond ratings, and auctioned them to unsuspecting investors, who later suffered huge losses when the high-risk borrowers began to default on their loan payments (government authorities later forced some of the firms that auctioned off these CDOs to repurchase them at the auction price and bear the losses themselves).

The consequences of crafting strategies that cannot pass the test of moral scrutiny are manifested in sizable fines, devastating public relations hits, sharp drops in stock prices that cost shareholders billions of dollars, and criminal indictments and convictions of company executives. The fallout from all these scandals has resulted in heightened management attention to legal and ethical considerations in crafting strategy.

WHAT ARE THE DRIVERS OF UNETHICAL STRATEGIES AND BUSINESS BEHAVIOR?

LO 2

Recognize conditions that can give rise to unethical business strategies and behavior.

Confusion over conflicting ethical standards may suggest one reason for the lack of an effective moral compass in business dealings and why certain elements of a company's strategy may be unethical. But apart from this, three main drivers of unethical business behavior stand out:[23]

- Faulty oversight that implicitly allows the overzealous pursuit of personal gain, wealth, and self-interest.
- Heavy pressures on company managers to meet or beat short-term performance targets.
- A company culture that puts profitability and business performance ahead of ethical behavior.

Faulty Oversight and the Overzealous Pursuit of Personal Gain, Wealth, and Self-Interest   People who are obsessed with wealth accumulation, greed, power, status, and their own self-interest often push ethical principles aside in their quest for personal gain. Driven by their ambitions, they exhibit few qualms in skirting the rules or doing whatever is necessary to achieve their goals. A general disregard for business ethics can prompt all kinds of unethical strategic maneuvers and behaviors at companies. According to a civil complaint filed by the Securities and Exchange Commission, the chief executive officer (CEO) of Tyco International, a well-known $35.6 billion manufacturing and services company, conspired with the company's chief financial officer (CFO) to steal more than $170 million, including a company-paid $2 million birthday party for the CEO's wife held on an island off the coast of Italy, a $7 million Park Avenue apartment for his wife, and secret interest-free loans to finance personal investments and purchase lavish artwork, yachts, estate jewelry, and vacation homes. Tyco's CEO and CFO were further charged with conspiring to reap more than $430 million from sales of stock, using questionable accounting to hide their actions, and engaging in deceptive accounting practices to distort the company's financial condition from 1995 to 2002. In 2005, both Tyco executives were convicted on multiple counts of looting the company and sent to jail.

Responsible corporate governance and oversight by the company's corporate board is necessary to guard against self-dealing and the manipulation of information to disguise such actions by a company's managers. **Self-dealing** occurs when managers take advantage of their position to further their own private interests rather than those of the firm. As discussed in Chapter 2, the duty of the corporate board (and its compensation and audit committees in particular) is to guard against such actions. A strong, independent board is necessary to have proper oversight of the company's financial practices and to hold top managers accountable for their actions.

A particularly egregious example of the lack of proper oversight is the case of Enron Corporation, a former diversified energy company that has become a symbol of corporate corruption and fraud. Andrew Fastow, Enron's chief financial officer (CFO), set himself up as the manager of one of Enron's off-the-books partnerships and as the part-owner of another, allegedly earning extra compensation of $30 million for his owner-manager roles in the two partnerships; Enron's board of directors agreed to suspend the company's conflict-of-interest rules designed to protect the company from this very kind of executive self-dealing. Although *Fortune* magazine had named Enron "America's Most Innovative Company" for six years running, in the end it turned out that Enron's real creativity was in its accounting practices. Enron's eventual downfall resulted not only in the company's bankruptcy in 2001 but also in the dissolution of its auditor, Arthur Andersen, which was one of the top-five accounting firms at the time.

> **CORE CONCEPT**
>
> **Self-dealing** occurs when managers take advantage of their position to further their own private interests rather than those of the firm.

Illustration Capsule 9.2 discusses the more recent multibillion-dollar Ponzi schemes perpetrated at Bernard L. Madoff Investment Securities and alleged at Stanford Financial Group.

Heavy Pressures on Company Managers to Meet or Beat Short-Term Earnings Targets

Performance expectations of Wall Street analysts and investors create enormous pressure on management to do whatever it takes to deliver good financial results each and every quarter. Executives at high-performing companies know that investors will see the slightest sign of a slowdown in earnings growth as a red flag and drive down the company's stock price. In addition, slowing growth or declining profits could lead to a downgrade of the company's credit rating if it has used lots of debt to finance its growth. The pressure to "never miss a quarter"—so as not to upset the expectations of analysts, investors, and creditors—prompts nearsighted managers to engage in short-term maneuvers to make the numbers, regardless of whether these moves are really in the best long-term interests of the company. Sometimes the pressure induces company personnel to continue to stretch the rules until the limits of ethical conduct are overlooked.[24] Once ethical boundaries are crossed in efforts to "meet or beat their numbers," the threshold for making more extreme ethical compromises becomes lower.

Several top executives at the former telecommunications company WorldCom were convicted of concocting a fraudulent $11 billion accounting scheme to hide costs and inflate revenues and profit over several years; the scheme was said to have helped the company keep its stock price propped up high enough to make additional acquisitions, support its nearly $30 billion debt load, and allow executives to cash in on their lucrative stock options. HealthSouth's chief financial managers were convicted of overstating the company's earnings by $1.4 billion between 1996 and 2002 in an attempt to hide the company's slowing growth from investors. A 2007 internal investigation at Dell Computer found that executives had engaged in a scheme to manipulate the company's accounting data to meet investors' quarterly earnings expectations. The fraudulent accounting practices inflated the company's earnings by $150 million between 2002 and 2006. The executives were terminated by Dell Computer in 2007.

Company executives often feel pressured to hit financial performance targets because their compensation depends heavily on the company's performance. During the late 1990s, it became fashionable for boards of directors to grant lavish bonuses, stock option awards, and other compensation benefits to executives for meeting specified performance targets. So outlandishly large were these rewards that executives had strong personal incentives to bend the rules and engage in behaviors that allowed the targets to be met. Much of the accounting manipulation at the root of recent corporate scandals has entailed situations in which executives benefited enormously from misleading accounting or other shady activities that

Investment Fraud at Bernard L. Madoff Investment Securities and Stanford Financial Group

Bernard Madoff engineered the largest investment scam in history to accumulate a net worth of more than $800 million and build a reputation as one of Wall Street's most savvy investors—he was appointed to various Securities and Exchange Commission panels, invited to testify before Congress on investment matters, made chairman of Nasdaq, and befriended by some of the world's most influential people. Madoff deceived Wall Street and investors with a simple Ponzi scheme that promised investors returns that would beat the market by 400 to 500 percent. The hedge funds, banks, and wealthy individuals that sent Bernard L. Madoff Investment Securities billions to invest on their behalf were quite pleased when their statements arrived showing annual returns as high as 45 percent. But, in fact, the portfolio gains shown on these statements were fictitious. Funds placed with Bernard Madoff were seldom, if ever, actually invested in any type of security—the money went to cover losses in his legitimate stock-trading business, fund periodic withdrawals of investors' funds, and support Madoff's lifestyle (including three vacation homes, a $7 million Manhattan condominium, yachts, and luxury cars).

For decades, the Ponzi scheme was never in danger of collapse because most Madoff investors were so impressed with the reported returns that they seldom made withdrawals from their accounts, and when they did withdraw funds Madoff used the monies being deposited by new investors to cover the payments. Madoff's deception came to an end in late 2008 when the dramatic drop in world stock prices caused so many of Madoff's investors to request withdrawals of their balances that there was not nearly enough new money coming in to cover the amounts being withdrawn. As with any Ponzi scheme, the first investors to ask Madoff for their funds were paid, but those asking later were left empty-handed. All told, more than 1,300 account holders lost about $65 billion when Bernard Madoff admitted to the scam in December 2008. As of late October 2009, investigators had located assets of only about $1.4 billion to return to Madoff account holders. Madoff was sentenced to 150 years in prison for his crimes.

Increased oversight at the Securities and Exchange Commission after the December 2008

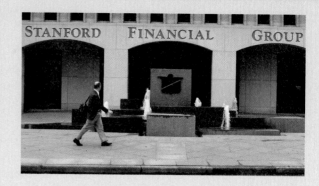

Madoff confession led to the June 2009 indictment of R. Allen Stanford and five others who were accused of running an investment scheme similar to that perpetrated by Bernard Madoff. Stanford was alleged to have defrauded more than 30,000 Stanford Financial Group account holders out of $7 billion through the sale of spurious certificates of deposit (CDs). The CDs marketed by Stanford Financial Group were issued by the company's Antiguan subsidiary, Stanford International Bank, and carried rates that were as much as three to four times greater than the CD rates offered by other financial institutions. Stanford claimed that the Stanford International Bank was able to provide such exceptional yields because of its investment in a globally diversified portfolio of stocks, bonds, commodities, and alternative investments and because of the tax advantages provided by the bank's location in Antigua. All the investments made by Stanford International Bank were said to be safe and liquid financial instruments monitored by more than 20 analysts and audited by Antiguan regulators. In fact, the deposits were invested in much riskier private equity placements and real estate investments and were subject to severe fluctuations in value. The statements provided to CD holders were alleged by prosecutors to be based on fabricated performance and phony financial statements.

Federal prosecutors also alleged that deposits of at least $1.6 billion were diverted into undisclosed personal loans to Allen Stanford. At the time of Stanford's indictment, he ranked 605th on *Forbes* magazine's list of the world's wealthiest persons, with an estimated net worth of

$2.2 billion. Stanford was a notable sports enthusiast and philanthropist—he supported a cricket league in Antigua and professional golf tournaments in the United States and contributed millions to the St. Jude Children's Research Hospital and museums in Houston and Miami.

Stanford also pledged $100 million to support programs aimed at slowing global warming. In May 2009, Stanford Investment Bank disclosed that it owed $7.2 billion to about 28,000 account holders. Its total assets at the time stood at $1 billion, including $46 million in cash.

Developed with C. David Morgan.

Sources: James Bandler, Nicholas Varchaver, and Doris Burke, "How Bernie Did It," *Fortune Online,* April 30, 2009 (accessed July 7, 2009); Duncan Greenberg, "Billionaire Responds to SEC Probe," *Forbes Online,* February 13, 2009 (accessed July 9, 2009); Katie Benner, "Stanford Scandal Sets Antigua on Edge," *Fortune Online,* February 25, 2009 (accessed July 9, 2009); Alyssa Abkowitz, "The Investment Scam-Artist's Playbook," *Fortune Online,* February 25, 2009 (accessed July 9, 2009); Kathryn Glass, "Stanford Bank Assets Insufficient to Repay Depositors," *Fox Business.com,* May 15, 2009 (accessed July 9, 2009); Bill McQuillen, Justin Blum, and Laurel Brubaker Calkins, "Allen Stanford Indicted by U.S. in $7 Billion Scam," *Bloomberg.com,* June 19, 2009 (accessed July 9, 2009); Jane J. Kim, "The Madoff Fraud: SIPC Sets Payouts in Madoff Scandal," *Wall Street Journal* (Eastern Edition), October 29, 2009, p. C4.

allowed them to hit the numbers and receive incentive awards ranging from $10 million to $100 million.

The fundamental problem with **short-termism**—the tendency for managers to focus excessive attention on short-term performance objectives—is that it doesn't create value for customers or improve the firm's competitiveness in the marketplace; that is, it sacrifices the activities that are the most reliable drivers of higher profits and added shareholder value in the long run. Cutting ethical corners in the name of profits carries exceptionally high risk for shareholders—the steep stock price decline and tarnished brand image that accompany the discovery of scurrilous behavior leave shareholders with a company worth much less than before—and the rebuilding task can be arduous, taking both considerable time and resources.

> **CORE CONCEPT**
>
> **Short-termism** is the tendency for managers to focus excessively on short-term performance objectives at the expense of longer-term strategic objectives. It has negative implications for the likelihood of ethical lapses as well as company performance in the longer run.

A Company Culture That Puts Profitability and Business Performance Ahead of Ethical Behavior
When a company's culture spawns an ethically corrupt or amoral work climate, people have a company-approved license to ignore "what's right" and engage in any behavior or employ any strategy they think they can get away with.[25] At such companies, unethical people are given free reign, and otherwise honorable people may succumb to the many opportunities around them to engage in unethical practices. A perfect example of a company culture gone awry on ethics is Enron.[26]

Enron's leaders encouraged company personnel to focus on the current bottom line and to be innovative and aggressive in figuring out how to grow current earnings—regardless of the methods. Enron's annual "rank and yank" performance evaluation process, in which the lowest-ranking 15 to 20 percent of employees were let go, made it abundantly clear that bottom-line results were what mattered most. The name of the game at Enron became devising clever ways to boost revenues and earnings, even if this sometimes meant operating outside established policies. In fact, outside-the-lines behavior was celebrated if it generated profitable new business.

A high-performance/high-rewards climate came to pervade the Enron culture, as the best workers (determined by who produced the best bottom-line results) received impressively large incentives and bonuses (amounting to as much as

$1 million for traders and even more for senior executives). On Car Day at Enron, an array of luxury sports cars arrived for presentation to the most successful employees. Understandably, employees wanted to be seen as part of Enron's star team and partake in the benefits granted to Enron's best and brightest employees. The high monetary rewards, the ambitious and hard-driving people whom the company hired and promoted, and the competitive, results-oriented culture combined to give Enron a reputation not only for trampling competitors at every opportunity but also for internal ruthlessness. The company's super-aggressiveness and win-at-all-costs mindset nurtured a culture that gradually and then more rapidly fostered the erosion of ethical standards, eventually making a mockery of the company's stated values of integrity and respect. When it became evident in fall 2001 that Enron was a house of cards propped up by deceitful accounting and a myriad of unsavory practices, the company imploded in a matter of weeks—one of the biggest bankruptcies of all time, costing investors $64 billion in losses.

More recently, a team investigating an ethical scandal at oil giant Royal Dutch/Shell Group that resulted in the payment of $150 million in fines found that an ethically flawed culture was a major contributor to why managers made rosy forecasts that they couldn't meet and why top executives engaged in maneuvers to mislead investors by overstating Shell's oil and gas reserves by 25 percent (equal to 4.5 billion barrels of oil). The investigation revealed that top Shell executives knew that a variety of internal practices, together with unrealistic and unsupportable estimates submitted by overzealous, bonus-conscious managers in Shell's exploration and production group, were being used to overstate reserves. An e-mail written by Shell's top executive for exploration and production (who was caught up in the ethical misdeeds and later forced to resign) said, "I am becoming sick and tired of lying about the extent of our reserves issues and the downward revisions that need to be done because of our far too aggressive/optimistic bookings."[27]

In contrast, when high ethical principles are deeply ingrained in the corporate culture of a company, culture can function as a powerful mechanism for communicating ethical behavioral norms and gaining employee buy-in to the company's moral standards, business principles, and corporate values. In such cases, the ethical principles embraced in the company's code of ethics and/or in its statement of corporate values are seen as integral to the company's identity, self-image, and ways of operating. Stories of former and current moral heroes are kept in circulation, and the deeds of company personnel who display ethical values and are dedicated to walking the talk are celebrated at internal company events. The message that ethics matters—and matters a lot—resounds loudly and clearly throughout the organization and in its strategy and decisions. Illustration Capsule 9.3 discusses GE's approach to building a culture that combines demands for high performance with expectations for ethical conduct.

WHY SHOULD COMPANY STRATEGIES BE ETHICAL?

There are two reasons why a company's strategy should be ethical: (1) because a strategy that is unethical is morally wrong and reflects badly on the character of the company personnel and (2) because an ethical strategy can be good business and serve the self-interest of shareholders.

How General Electric's Top Management Built a Culture That Fuses High Performance with High Integrity

GE's CEO, Jeffrey Immelt, has made it a priority to foster a culture built on high ethical standards. The company's heavy reliance on financial controls and performance-based reward systems—which are necessary because of GE's broad multinational diversification—could easily tempt managers at all levels to cut corners, engage in unethical sales tactics, inaccurately record revenues or expenses, or participate in corrupt practices prevalent in the many emerging markets where GE competes. Immelt and GE's other top managers clearly recognize that without a strong ethical culture, there would be little to deter the company's thousands of managers across the globe from pursuing the many types of unethical behavior that would, on the surface, boost performance.

The first step in establishing an ethical culture at GE was for its top management to forcefully communicate the company's principles that should guide decision making. Jeffrey Immelt begins and ends each annual meeting of the company's 220 officers and 600 senior managers with a recitation of the company's fundamental ethical principles. Immelt and GE's other managers are careful to not violate these principles themselves or give implied consent for others to skirt these principles, since human nature makes subordinates at all levels ever vigilant for the signs of hypocrisy in the actions of higher-ups. The importance of walking the talk justifies GE's "one strike and you're out" standard for its top management. For example, a high-level manager in an emerging market was terminated for failing to conduct required diligence on a third-party vendor known for its shady business practices, including the payment of bribes to local officials. Another executive was fired from GE for agreeing to a large and important Asian customer's request to falsify supplier documents that were used by regulatory agencies.

With so many ethical standards prevailing in the more than 100 countries where GE operates, the company has turned to global ethical standards rather than allowing local cultures to shape business behavior. The company's global standards cover such topics as how to best evaluate suppliers' environmental records

and working conditions in its manufacturing businesses and how to avoid money-laundering schemes or aiding and abetting financial services customers engaged in tax evasion or accounting fraud. Operating-level managers are formally responsible for ensuring ethical compliance in their divisions and are required to submit quarterly tracking reports to GE's corporate offices on key indicators such as spills, accident rates, and violation notices. Managers of operating units falling in the bottom quartile on the quarterly assessments are required to submit plans for improving the ethical shortcomings. GE also evaluates the ethical performance of its 4,000 managers who are responsible for profit centers or are key contributors on business teams.

GE's approach to culture building also includes instilling such principles into the behavior of the company's 300,000-plus employees with no managerial responsibility. Employees are provided training to help them understand the company's ethical principles and how those principles can help them make decisions in the ethical gray areas that arise while making everyday decisions. In Immelt's words, "At a time when many people are more cynical than ever about business, GE must seek to earn this high level of trust every day, employee by employee."* GE also allows employees to lodge anonymous complaints about ethics compliance; the complaints are evaluated by more than 500 employees around the world with either full-time or part-time ombudsperson capacity. About 20 percent of the

(Continued)

1,500 concerns lodged annually lead to serious discipline. Hourly employees are also included in annual assessments of ethical performance and are rewarded through bonuses, promotions, or recognition for identifying or resolving ethical issues at the operating level.

* *General Electric*, "The Spirit and the Letter," January 2008, www.ge.com/citizenship/reporting/spirit_and_letter.jsp.

Developed with C. David Morgan.

Source: Based on the discussion of GE's culture-building process by the company's former legal counsel in Ben W. Heineman, Jr., "Avoiding Integrity Land Mines," *Harvard Business Review* 85, no. 4 (April 2007), pp. 100–8.

The Moral Case for an Ethical Strategy

Managers do not dispassionately assess what strategic course to steer. Ethical strategy making generally begins with managers who themselves have strong moral character (i.e., who are trustworthy, have integrity, and truly care about conducting the company's business in an honorable manner). Managers with high ethical principles are usually advocates of a corporate code of ethics and strong ethics compliance, and they are genuinely committed to upholding corporate values and ethical business principles. They demonstrate their commitment by displaying the company's stated values and living up to its business principles and ethical standards. They understand there's a big difference between adopting value statements and codes of ethics and ensuring that they are followed strictly in a company's actual strategy and business conduct. As a consequence, ethically strong managers consciously opt for strategic actions that can pass the strictest moral scrutiny—they display no tolerance for strategies with ethically controversial components.

LO 3

Gain an understanding of the costs of business ethics failures.

The Business Case for Ethical Strategies

In addition to the moral reasons for adopting ethical strategies, there may be solid business reasons. Pursuing unethical strategies and tolerating unethical conduct not only damages a company's reputation but also may result in a wide-ranging set of other costly consequences. Figure 9.1 shows the types of costs a company can incur when unethical behavior on its part is discovered, the wrongdoings of company personnel are headlined in the media, and it is forced to make amends for its behavior. The more egregious are a company's ethical violations, the higher the costs and the bigger the damage to its reputation (and to the reputations of the company personnel involved). In high-profile instances, the costs of ethical misconduct can easily run into the hundreds of millions and even billions of dollars, especially if they provoke widespread public outrage and many people were harmed. The penalties levied on executives caught in wrongdoing can skyrocket as well, as the 150-year prison term sentence of financier Bernie Madoff illustrates.

The fallout of ethical misconduct on the part of a company goes well beyond the costs of making amends for the misdeeds. Rehabilitating a company's shattered reputation is time-consuming and costly. Customers shun companies known for their shady behavior. Companies known to have engaged in unethical conduct have difficulty in recruiting and retaining talented employees; indeed, many people take a company's ethical reputation into account when deciding whether to accept a job

Conducting business in an ethical fashion is not only morally right—it is in a company's enlightened self-interest.

Figure 9.1   The Costs Companies Incur When Ethical Wrongdoing Is Found Out

Visible Costs	Internal Administrative Costs	Intangible or Less Visible Costs
• Government fines and penalties • Civil penalties arising from class-action lawsuits and other litigation aimed at punishing the company for its offense and the harm done to others • The costs to shareholders in the form of a lower stock price (and possibly lower dividends)	• Legal and investigative costs incurred by the company • The costs of providing remedial education and ethics training to company personnel • Costs of taking corrective actions • Administrative costs associated with ensuring future compliance	• Customer defections • Loss of reputation • Lost employee morale and higher degrees of employee cynicism • Higher employee turnover • Higher recruiting costs and difficulty in attracting talented employees • Adverse effects on employee productivity • The costs of complying with often harsher government regulations

Source: Adapted from Terry Thomas, John R. Schermerhorn, and John W. Dienhart, "Strategic Leadership of Ethical Behavior," *Academy of Management Executive* 18, no. 2 (May 2004), p. 58.

offer.[28] Most ethically upstanding people are repulsed by a work environment where unethical behavior is condoned; they don't want to get entrapped in a compromising situation, nor do they want their personal reputations tarnished by the actions of an unsavory employer. Creditors are usually unnerved by the unethical actions of a borrower because of the potential business fallout and subsequent risk of default on loans.

All told, a company's unethical behavior risks doing considerable damage to shareholders in the form of lost revenues, higher costs, lower profits, lower stock prices, and a diminished business reputation. To a significant degree, therefore, ethical strategies and ethical conduct are *good business.* Most companies understand the value of operating in a manner that wins the approval of suppliers, employees, investors, and society at large. Most businesspeople recognize the risks and adverse fallout attached to the discovery of unethical behavior. Hence, companies have an incentive to employ strategies that can pass the test of being ethical. Even if a company's managers are not of strong moral character and personally committed to high ethical standards, they have good reason to operate within ethical bounds, if only to (1) avoid the risk of embarrassment, scandal, and possible disciplinary action for unethical conduct on their part and (2) escape being held accountable for unethical behavior by personnel under their supervision and their own lax enforcement of ethical standards.

> Shareholders suffer major damage when a company's unethical behavior is discovered. Making amends for unethical business conduct is costly, and it takes years to rehabilitate a tarnished company reputation.

STRATEGY, CORPORATE SOCIAL RESPONSIBILITY, AND ENVIRONMENTAL SUSTAINABILITY

LO 4

Gain an understanding of the concepts of corporate social responsibility and environmental sustainability and of how companies balance these duties with economic responsibilities to shareholders.

The idea that businesses have an obligation to foster social betterment, a much-debated topic in the past 50 years, took root in the 19th century when progressive companies in the aftermath of the industrial revolution began to provide workers with housing and other amenities. The notion that corporate executives should balance the interests of all stakeholders—shareholders, employees, customers, suppliers, the communities in which they operated, and society at large—began to blossom in the 1960s. Some years later, a group of chief executives of America's 200 largest corporations, calling themselves the Business Roundtable, came out in strong support of the concept of **corporate social responsibility:**[29]

> Balancing the shareholder's expectations of maximum return against other priorities is one of the fundamental problems confronting corporate management. The shareholder must receive a good return but the legitimate concerns of other constituencies (customers, employees, communities, suppliers and society at large) also must have the appropriate attention. . . . [Leading managers] believe that by giving enlightened consideration to balancing the legitimate claims of all its constituents, a corporation will best serve the interest of its shareholders.

Today, corporate social responsibility (CSR) is a concept that resonates in western Europe, the United States, Canada, and such developing nations as Brazil and India.

What Do We Mean by *Corporate Social Responsibility?*

CORE CONCEPT

Corporate social responsibility (CSR) refers to a company's *duty* to operate in an honorable manner, provide good working conditions for employees, encourage workforce diversity, be a good steward of the environment, and actively work to better the quality of life in the local communities where it operates and in society at large.

The essence of socially responsible business behavior is that a company should balance strategic actions to benefit shareholders against the *duty* to be a good corporate citizen. The underlying thesis is that company managers should display a *social conscience* in operating the business and specifically take into account how management decisions and company actions affect the well-being of employees, local communities, the environment, and society at large.[30] Acting in a socially responsible manner thus encompasses more than just participating in community service projects and donating monies to charities and other worthy social causes. Demonstrating social responsibility also entails undertaking actions that earn trust and respect from all stakeholders—operating in an honorable and ethical manner, striving to make the company a great place to work, demonstrating genuine respect for the environment, and trying to make a difference in bettering society. As depicted in Figure 9.2, corporate responsibility programs commonly include the following elements:

- *Making efforts to employ an ethical strategy and observe ethical principles in operating the business.* A sincere commitment to observing ethical principles is a necessary component of a CSR strategy simply because unethical conduct is incompatible with the concept of good corporate citizenship and socially responsible business behavior.

Figure 9.2   **The Five Components of a Corporate Social Responsibility Strategy**

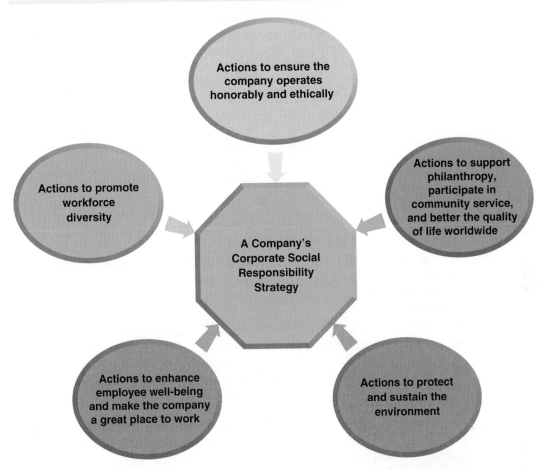

Source: Adapted from material in Ronald Paul Hill, Debra Stephens, and Iain Smith, "Corporate Social Responsibility: An Examination of Individual Firm Behavior," *Business and Society Review* 108, no. 3 (September 2003), p. 348.

- *Making charitable contributions, supporting community service endeavors, engaging in broader philanthropic initiatives, and reaching out to make a difference in the lives of the disadvantaged.* Some companies fulfill their philanthropic obligations by spreading their efforts over a multitude of charitable and community activities—for instance, Microsoft and Johnson & Johnson support a broad variety of community, art, and social welfare programs. Others prefer to focus their energies more narrowly. McDonald's, for example, concentrates on sponsoring the Ronald McDonald House program (which provides a home away from home for the families of seriously ill children receiving treatment at nearby hospitals). British Telecom gives 1 percent of its profits directly to communities, largely for education—teacher training, in-school workshops, and digital technology. Leading prescription drug maker GlaxoSmithKline and other pharmaceutical companies either donate or heavily discount medicines for distribution in the least developed nations. Companies frequently reinforce their philanthropic efforts by encouraging employees to support charitable causes and participate in community affairs, often through programs that match employee contributions.

- *Taking actions to protect the environment and, in particular, to minimize or eliminate any adverse impact on the environment stemming from the company's own business activities.* Social responsibility as it applies to environmental protection entails actively striving to be a good steward of the environment. This means using the best available science and technology to reduce environmentally harmful aspects of the company's operations *below the levels required by prevailing environmental regulations.* It also means putting time and money into improving the environment in ways that extend past a company's own industry boundaries—such as participating in recycling projects, adopting energy conservation practices, and supporting efforts to clean up local water supplies. Retailers like Walmart and Home Depot in the United States and B&Q in the United Kingdom have pressured their suppliers to adopt stronger environmental protection practices in order to lower the carbon footprint of their entire supply chains.[31]

- *Taking actions to create a work environment that enhances the quality of life for employees.* Numerous companies exert extra effort to enhance the quality of life for their employees, both at work and at home. This can include on-site day care, flexible work schedules, workplace exercise facilities, special leaves for employees to care for sick family members, work-at-home opportunities, career development programs and education opportunities, special safety programs, and the like.

- *Taking actions to build a workforce that is diverse with respect to gender, race, national origin, and other aspects that different people bring to the workplace.* Most large companies in the United States have established workforce diversity programs, and some go the extra mile to ensure that their workplaces are attractive to ethnic minorities and inclusive of all groups and perspectives. At some companies, the diversity initiative extends to suppliers—sourcing items from small businesses owned by women or ethnic minorities, for example. The pursuit of workforce diversity can be good business. At Coca-Cola, where strategic success depends on getting people all over the world to become loyal consumers of the company's beverages, efforts to build a public persona of inclusiveness for people of all races, religions, nationalities, interests, and talents have considerable strategic value.

The particular combination of socially responsible endeavors a company elects to pursue defines its **corporate social responsibility (CSR) strategy.** Illustration Capsule 9.4 describes John Deere's approach to corporate social responsibility—an approach that corresponds closely to the description in Figure 9.2. But the specific components emphasized in a CSR strategy vary from company to company and are typically linked to a company's core values. General Mills, for example, builds its CSR strategy around the theme of "nourishing lives" to emphasize its commitment to good nutrition as well as philanthropy, community building, and environmental protection.[32] Starbucks' CSR strategy includes four main elements (ethical sourcing, community service, environmental stewardship, and farmer support), all of which have touch points with the way that the company procures its coffee—a key aspect of its product differentiation strategy.[33] Some companies use other terms, such as *corporate citizenship, corporate responsibility,* or *sustainable responsible business (SRB)* to characterize their CSR initiatives.

CORE CONCEPT

A company's **CSR strategy** is defined by the specific combination of socially beneficial activities the company opts to support with its contributions of time, money, and other resources.

John Deere's Approach to Corporate Social Responsibility

Principal Components of John Deere's Corporate Social Responsibility Strategy	Specific Actions to Execute the Strategy
Adhering to the core values of integrity, quality commitment, and innovation *Integrity* means telling the truth, keeping our word, and treating others with fairness and respect. *Quality* means delivering the value customers, employees, shareholders, and other business partners expect every day. *Commitment* means doing our best to meet expectations over the long run. *Innovation* means inventing, designing, and developing breakthrough products and services that customers want to buy from John Deere.	• Committing to ethical behavior and fair dealing in all relationships • Providing Business Conduct Guidelines that show employees how they are expected to carry out company business • Creating an Office of Corporate Compliance to ensure ethical and fair business practices are maintained throughout global operations • Instituting a 24-hour hotline for confidential anonymous reporting of ethical violations • Offering employees professional guidance when they feel they are operating in complicated or ambiguous business and cultural situations
Engaging in philanthropy and community betterment	• Supporting agricultural development in resource-poor countries • Providing increased access to financing for the rural poor in Africa (in partnership with Opportunity International) • Helping start *BackPack* programs in the U.S. to supply supplemental food for school-age children • Supporting a variety of higher educational programs and such programs as Junior Achievement, FFA, and the National 4-H Council • Instituting an employee matching gift program
Conserving resources and sustaining the environment	• Establishing ambitious greenhouse-gas reduction goals to be achieved over the next 5 to 10 years • Mandating the use of recycling and waste reduction practices across all company operations • Implementing a worldwide Environmental Management System geared to ISO14001 standards • Helping to develop long-term comprehensive climate change strategies through EPS's Climate Leaders Program • Designing products to conserve water, encourage biofuel development, and support sustainable agriculture
Supporting and enhancing the workforce	• Maintaining effective workplace safety programs—more than 1,000 awards from the U.S. National Safety Council • Providing programs to promote employee health and wellness and work-life balance • Establishing global occupational health programs keyed to local health issues and infrastructure

(Continued)

Principal Components of John Deere's Corporate Social Responsibility Strategy	Specific Actions to Execute the Strategy
	• Helping employees with career development through mentoring, coaching, and a programmatic approach • Creating a continuous learning environment with extensive training opportunities and a tuition reimbursement program
Promoting diversity and inclusiveness	• Creating an inclusive culture in which employees of all backgrounds can develop their leadership potential • Providing training and tools designed to make work teams more diverse, productive, and effective • Sponsoring employee networks that bring together people from around the world with shared interests, gender, ethnicity, or skills • Encouraging diversity within the company's dealer and supplier base • Supporting minority education programs and collegiate diversity initiatives

Source: Information posted at www.deere.com (accessed July 8, 2010).

Although there is wide variation in how companies devise and implement a CSR strategy, communities of companies concerned with corporate social responsibility (such as CSR Europe) have emerged to help companies share best CSR practices. Moreover, a number of reporting standards have been developed, including ISO 26000—a new internationally recognized standard for social responsibility produced by the International Standards Organization (ISO).[34] Companies that exhibit a strong commitment to corporate social responsibility are often recognized by being included on lists such as *Corporate Responsibility* magazine's "100 Best Corporate Citizens" or *Corporate Knights* magazine's "Global 100 Most Sustainable Corporations."

Corporate Social Responsibility and the Triple Bottom Line CSR initiatives undertaken by companies are frequently directed at improving the company's "triple bottom line"—a reference to three types of performance metrics: *economic, social, environmental.* The goal is for a company to succeed simultaneously in all three dimensions, as illustrated in Figure 9.3.[35] The three dimensions of performance are often referred to in terms of the "three pillars" of "people, planet, and profit." The term *people* refers to the various social initiatives that make up CSR strategies, such as corporate giving, community involvement, and company efforts to improve the lives of its internal and external stakeholders. *Planet* refers to a firm's ecological impact and environmental practices. The term *profit* has a broader meaning with respect to the triple bottom line than it does otherwise. It encompasses not only the profit a firm earns for its shareholders but also the economic impact that the company has on society more generally, in terms of the overall value that it creates and the overall costs that it imposes on society. For example, Procter & Gamble's Swiffer cleaning system, one of the company's best-selling products, not only offers an earth-friendly design but also outperforms less ecologically friendly alternatives in terms of its broader economic impact: It

Figure 9.3   The Triple Bottom Line: Excelling on Three Measures of Company Performance

Source: Developed with help from Amy E. Florentino.

reduces demands on municipal water sources, saves electricity that would be needed to heat mop water, and doesn't add to the amount of detergent making its way into waterways and waste treatment facilities. Nike sees itself as bringing people, planet, and profits into balance by producing innovative new products in a more sustainable way, recognizing that sustainability is key to its future profitability.

Many companies now make a point of citing the beneficial outcomes of their CSR strategies in press releases and issue special reports for consumers and investors to review. Staples, the world's largest office products company, makes reporting an important part of its commitment to corporate responsibility; the company posts a "Staples Soul Report" on its Web site that describes its initiatives and accomplishments in the areas of diversity, environment, community, and ethics. Triple-bottom-line (TBL) reporting is emerging as an increasingly important way for companies to make the results of their CSR strategies apparent to stakeholders and for stakeholders to hold companies accountable for their impact on society. The use of standard reporting frameworks and metrics, such as those developed by the Global Reporting Initiative, promotes greater transparency and facilitates benchmarking CSR efforts across firms and industries.

Investment firms have created mutual funds comprising companies that are excelling on the basis of the triple bottom line in order to attract funds from environmentally and socially aware investors. The Dow Jones Sustainability World Index is made up of the top 10 percent of the 2,500 companies listed in the Dow Jones World Index in terms of economic performance, environmental performance, and social performance. Companies are evaluated in these three performance areas, using indicators such as corporate governance, climate change mitigation, and labor practices. Table 9.1 shows a sampling of the companies selected for the Dow Jones Sustainability World Index in 2009 and 2010.

Table 9.1 **A Selection of Companies Recognized for Their Triple Bottom Line Performance in 2009 and 2010**

Name	Market Sector	Country
Johnson & Johnson	Health care and pharmaceuticals	United States
PepsiCo	Food and beverages	United States
adidas	Athletic footwear, apparel, and equipment	Germany
Intel	Technology	United States
Unilever	Food and beverages	Netherlands
Samsung	Electronics	Korea
Nokia	Technology	Finland
Caterpillar	Machinery and equipment	United States
Roche AG	Health care	Switzerland
Air France–KLM	Travel and leisure	France
3M	Adhesives and abrasives	United States
Procter & Gamble	Consumer goods	United States
Sony	Electronics	Japan
BMW	Automobiles and parts	Germany
Novartis	Health care	Switzerland
IBM	Technology	United States
CEMIG	Utilities	Brazil
Cisco Systems	Technology	United States
General Electric	Technology	United States
Coca-Cola	Beverages	United States

Sources: Dow Jones indexes, STOXX Limited, and SAM Group, www.sustainability-indexes.com/07_htmle/indexes/djsiworld_supersectorleaders.html, www.sustainability-indexes.com/07_htmle/publications/factsheets.html (accessed July 5, 2010).

What Do We Mean by *Sustainability* and *Sustainable Business Practices?*

The term *sustainability* is used in a variety of ways. In many firms, it is synonymous with corporate social responsibility; it is seen by some as a term that is gradually replacing CSR in the business lexicon. Indeed, sustainability reporting and TBL reporting are often one and the same, as illustrated by the Dow Jones Sustainability Index, which tracks the same three types of performance measures that constitute the triple bottom line.

More often, however, the term takes on a more focused meaning, concerned with the relationship of a company to its *environment* and its use of *natural resources,* including land, water, air, plants, animals, minerals, fossil fuels, and biodiversity. It is widely recognized that the world's natural resources are finite and are being consumed and degraded at rates that threaten their capacity for renewal. Since corporations are the biggest users of natural resources, managing and maintaining these resources is critical for the long-term economic interests of corporations.

For some companies, this issue has direct and obvious implications for the continued viability of their business model and strategy. Pacific Gas and Electric has begun measuring the full carbon footprint of its supply chain to become not only "greener" but a more efficient energy producer.[36] Beverage companies such as Coca-Cola and PepsiCo are having to rethink their business models because of the prospect of future worldwide water shortages. For other companies, the connection is less direct, but all companies are part of a business ecosystem whose economic health depends on the availability of natural resources. In response, most major companies have begun to change *how* they do business, emphasizing the use of **sustainable business practices,** defined as those capable of meeting the needs of the present without compromising the ability to meet the needs of the future.[37] Many have also begun to incorporate a consideration of environmental sustainability into their strategy-making activities.

> **CORE CONCEPT**
>
> **Sustainable business practices** are those that meet the needs of the present without compromising the ability to meet the needs of the future.

Environmental sustainability strategies entail deliberate and concerted actions to operate businesses in a manner that protects natural resources and ecological support systems, guards against outcomes that will ultimately endanger the planet, and is therefore sustainable for centuries.[38] One aspect of environmental sustainability is keeping use of the Earth's natural resources within levels that can be replenished via the use of sustainable business practices. In the case of some resources (like crude oil, fresh water, and the harvesting of edible fish from the oceans), scientists say that use levels either are already unsustainable or will be soon, given the world's growing population and propensity to consume additional resources as incomes and living standards rise. Another aspect of sustainability concerns containing the adverse effects of greenhouse gases and other forms of air pollution so as to reduce global warming and other undesirable climate and atmospheric changes. Other aspects of sustainability include greater reliance on sustainable energy sources, greater use of recyclable materials, the use of sustainable methods of growing foods (so as to reduce topsoil depletion and the use of pesticides, herbicides, fertilizers, and other chemicals that may be harmful to human health or ecological systems), habitat protection, environmentally sound waste management practices, and increased attempts to decouple environmental degradation and economic growth (according to many scientists, economic growth has historically been accompanied by declines in the well-being of the environment).

> **CORE CONCEPT**
>
> A company's **environmental sustainability strategy** consists of its deliberate actions to protect the environment, provide for the longevity of natural resources, maintain ecological support systems for future generations, and guard against ultimate endangerment of the planet.

Unilever, a diversified producer of processed foods, personal care, and home cleaning products, is among the many committed corporations pursuing sustainable business practices. The company tracks 11 sustainable agricultural indicators in its processed-foods business and has launched a variety of programs to improve the environmental performance of its suppliers. Examples of such programs include special low-rate financing for tomato suppliers choosing to switch to water-conserving irrigation systems and training programs in India that have allowed contract cucumber growers to reduce pesticide use by 90 percent while improving yields by 78 percent. Unilever has also reengineered many internal processes to improve the company's overall performance on sustainability measures. For example, the company's factories have reduced water usage by 63 percent and total waste by 67 percent since 1995 through the implementation of sustainability initiatives. Unilever has also redesigned packaging for many of its products to conserve natural resources and reduce the volume of consumer waste. For example, the company's Suave shampoo bottles were reshaped to save almost 150 tons of plastic resin per year, which is the equivalent of 15 million fewer empty bottles making it to landfills annually. As the producer of Lipton Tea, Unilever is the world's largest purchaser of tea leaves; the company has committed to sourcing all of its tea from Rainforest Alliance Certified farms by 2015, due to their comprehensive triple-bottom-line approach toward sustainable farm management.

Crafting Corporate Social Responsibility and Sustainability Strategies

While CSR and environmental sustainability strategies take many forms, those that both provide valuable social benefits *and* fulfill customer needs in a superior fashion may also contribute to a company's competitive advantage.[39] For example, while carbon emissions may be of some concern for financial institutions such as Wells Fargo, Toyota's sustainability strategy for reducing carbon emissions has produced both competitive advantage and environmental benefits. Its Prius hybrid electric- and gasoline-powered automobile is not only among the least polluting automobiles but is also the best-selling hybrid vehicle in the United States; it has earned the company the loyalty of fuel-conscious buyers and given Toyota a green image. Green Mountain Coffee Roasters' commitment to protect the welfare of coffee growers and their families (in particular, making sure they receive a fair price) also meets its customers' wants and needs. In its dealings with suppliers at small farmer cooperatives in Peru, Mexico, and Sumatra, Green Mountain pays "fair-trade" prices for coffee beans (in 2009, the fair-trade prices were a minimum of $1.26 per pound for conventional coffee versus market prices of $0.65 per pound). Green Mountain also purchases about 29 percent of its coffee directly from farmers so as to cut out intermediaries and see that farmers realize a higher price for their efforts—coffee is the world's second most heavily traded commodity after oil, requiring the labor of some 20 million people, most of whom live at the poverty level.[40] Its consumers are aware of these efforts and purchase Green Mountain coffee, in part, to encourage such practices.

CSR strategies and environmental sustainability strategies are more likely to contribute to a company's competitive advantage if they are linked to a company's competitively important resources and capabilities or value chain activities. Thus, it is common for companies engaged in natural resource extraction, electric power production, forestry and paper products, motor vehicles, and chemical production to place more emphasis on addressing environmental concerns than, say, software and electronics firms or apparel manufacturers. Companies whose business success is heavily dependent on high employee morale or attracting and retaining the best and brightest employees are somewhat more prone to stress the well-being of their employees and foster a positive, high-energy workplace environment that elicits the dedication and enthusiastic commitment of employees, thus putting real meaning behind the claim "Our people are our greatest asset." Ernst & Young, one of the four largest global accounting firms, stresses its "People First" workforce diversity strategy that is all about respecting differences, fostering individuality, and promoting inclusiveness so that its more than 144,000 employees in 140 countries

> CSR strategies and environmental sustainability strategies that both provide valuable social benefits *and* fulfill customer needs in a superior fashion can lead to competitive advantage. Corporate social agendas that address only social issues may help boost a company's reputation for corporate citizenship but are unlikely to improve its competitive strength in the marketplace.

can feel valued, engaged, and empowered in developing creative ways to serve the firm's clients. As a service business, Marriot's most competitively important resource is also people. Thus its social agenda includes providing 180 hours of paid classroom and on-the-job training to the chronically unemployed. Ninety percent of the graduates from the job training program take jobs with Marriott, and about two-thirds of those remain with Marriott for more than a year. At Whole Foods Market, an $8 billion supermarket chain specializing in organic and natural foods, its environmental sustainability strategy is evident in almost every segment of its company value chain and is a big part of its differentiation strategy. The company's procurement policies encourage stores to purchase fresh fruits and vegetables from local farmers and screen processed-food items for more than 400 common ingredients that the company considers unhealthy or environmentally unsound. Spoiled food items are sent to regional composting centers rather than landfills, and all cleaning products used in its stores are biodegradable. The company also has created the Animal Compassion Foundation to develop natural and humane ways of raising farm animals and has converted all of its vehicles to run on biofuels.

Not all companies choose to link their corporate environmental or social agendas to their value chain, their business model, or their industry. For example, Chick-Fil-A, an Atlanta-based fast-food chain with over 1,400 outlets in 38 states, has a charitable foundation that funds two scholarship programs and supports 12 foster homes as well as a summer camp for some 1,900 campers.[41] However, unless a company's social responsibility initiatives become part of the way it operates its business every day, the initiatives are unlikely to catch fire and be fully effective. As an executive at Royal Dutch/Shell put it, corporate social responsibility "is not a cosmetic; it must be rooted in our values. It must make a difference to the way we do business."[42] The same is true for environmental sustainability initiatives.

The Moral Case for Corporate Social Responsibility and Environmentally Sustainable Business Practices

The moral case for why businesses should act in a manner that benefits all of the company's stakeholders—not just shareholders—boils down to "It's the right thing to do." Ordinary decency, civic-mindedness, and contributions to the well-being of society should be expected of any business.[43] In today's social and political climate, most business leaders can be expected to acknowledge that socially responsible actions are important and that businesses have a duty to be good corporate citizens. But there is a complementary school of thought that business operates on the basis of an implied social contract with the members of society. According to this contract, society grants a business the right to conduct its business affairs and agrees not to unreasonably restrain its pursuit of a fair profit for the goods or services it sells. In return for this "license to operate," a business is obligated to act as a responsible citizen, do its fair share to promote the general welfare, and avoid doing any harm. Such a view clearly puts a moral burden on a company to take corporate citizenship into consideration and do what's best for shareholders within the confines of discharging its duties to operate honorably, provide good working conditions to employees, be a good environmental steward, and display good corporate citizenship.

> Every action a company takes can be interpreted as a statement of what it stands for.

The Business Case for Corporate Social Responsibility and Environmentally Sustainable Business Practices

Whatever the moral arguments for socially responsible business behavior and environmentally sustainable business practices, it has long been recognized that it is in the enlightened self-interest of companies to be good citizens and devote some of their energies and resources to the betterment of employees, the communities in which they operate, and society in general. In short, there are reasons why the exercise of social and environmental responsibility may be good business:

- *Such actions can lead to increased buyer patronage.* A strong visible social responsibility or environmental sustainability strategy may give a company an edge in differentiating itself from rivals and in appealing to consumers who prefer to do business with companies that are good corporate citizens. The Body Shop, Puma, Ben & Jerry's, and Patagonia have definitely expanded their customer bases because of their visible and well-publicized activities as socially conscious companies. More and more companies are also recognizing the cash register payoff of social responsibility strategies that reach out to people of all cultures and demographics (women, retirees, and ethnic groups).

- *A strong commitment to socially responsible behavior reduces the risk of reputation-damaging incidents.* Companies that place little importance on operating in a socially responsible manner are more prone to scandal and embarrassment. Consumer, environmental, and human rights activist groups are quick to criticize businesses whose behavior they consider to be out of line, and they are adept at getting their message into the media and onto the Internet. Pressure groups can generate widespread adverse publicity, promote boycotts, and influence like-minded or sympathetic buyers to avoid an offender's products. Research has shown that product boycott announcements are associated with a decline in a company's stock price.[44] When a major oil company suffered damage to its reputation on environmental and social grounds, the CEO repeatedly said that the most negative impact the company suffered—and the one that made him fear for the future of the company—was that bright young graduates were no longer attracted to working for the company.[45] For many years, Nike received stinging criticism for not policing sweatshop conditions in the Asian factories that produced Nike footwear, causing Nike cofounder and former CEO Phil Knight to observe that "Nike has become synonymous with slave wages, forced overtime, and arbitrary abuse."[46] In 1997, Nike began an extensive effort to monitor conditions in the 800 factories of the contract manufacturers that produced Nike shoes. As Knight said, "Good shoes come from good factories and good factories have good labor relations." Nonetheless, Nike has continually been plagued by complaints from human rights activists that its monitoring procedures are flawed and that it is not doing enough to correct the plight of factory workers. As this suggests, a damaged reputation is not easily repaired.

- *Socially responsible actions and sustainable business practices can lower costs and enhance employee recruiting and workforce retention.* Companies with

> The higher the public profile of a company or its brand, the greater the scrutiny of its activities and the higher the potential for it to become a target for pressure group action.

deservedly good reputations for social responsibility and sustainable business practices are better able to attract and retain employees, compared to companies with tarnished reputations. Some employees just feel better about working for a company committed to improving society.[47] This can contribute to lower turnover, better worker productivity, and lower costs for staff recruitment and training. For example, Starbucks is said to enjoy much lower rates of employee turnover because of the company's socially responsible practices as well as superior employee benefits and management efforts to make Starbucks a great place to work. Making a company a great place to work pays dividends in recruitment of talented workers, more creativity and energy on the part of workers, higher worker productivity, and greater employee commitment to the company's business mission/vision and success in the marketplace. Sustainable business practices are often concomitant with greater operational efficiencies. For example, when a U.S. manufacturer of recycled paper, taking eco-efficiency to heart, discovered how to increase its fiber recovery rate, it saved the equivalent of 20,000 tons of waste paper—a factor that helped the company become the industry's lowest-cost producer.[48]

- *Opportunities for revenue enhancement may also come from CSR and environmental sustainability strategies.* The drive for sustainability and social responsibility can spur innovative efforts that in turn lead to new products and opportunities for revenue enhancement. Electric cars such as the Chevy Volt and the Tesler Roadster are one example. In many cases, the revenue opportunities are tied to a company's core products. PepsiCo and Coca-Cola, for example, have expanded into the juice business to offer a healthier alternative to their carbonated beverages. GE has created a profitable new business in wind turbines. In other cases, revenue enhancement opportunities come from innovative ways to reduce waste and use the by-products of a company's production. Tyson Foods now produces jet fuel for B52 bombers from the vast amount of animal waste resulting from its meat product business. Staples has become one of the largest nonutility corporate producers of renewable energy in the United States due to its installation of solar power panels in all of its outlets (and sale of what it does not consume in renewable energy credit markets).

- *Well-conceived CSR strategies and sustainable business practices are in the best long-term interest of shareholders.* Social responsibility strategies and strategies to promote environmental sustainability can work to the advantage of shareholders in several ways. They help avoid or preempt legal and regulatory actions that could prove costly and otherwise burdensome. In addition, when CSR and sustainability strategies increase buyer patronage, offer revenue-enhancing opportunities, lower costs, increase productivity, and reduce the risk of reputation-damaging incidents, they contribute to the total value created by a company and improve its profitability. In this manner, well-conceived socially and environmentally responsible strategies can enhance shareholder value even as they address the needs of other company stakeholders. While some question whether addressing social needs is truly in the interest of a company's shareholders, the answer depends on how well such strategies are crafted and whether they contribute to the success of the company's business model. A review of 135 studies indicated there is a positive, but small, correlation between good corporate behavior and good financial

> Socially responsible strategies that create value for customers and lower costs can improve company profits and shareholder value at the same time that they address other stakeholder interests.

performance; only 2 percent of the studies showed that dedicating corporate resources to social responsibility harmed the interests of shareholders.[49] Another indicator is the performance of mutual funds dedicated to socially responsible investments (SRIs) relative to other types of funds. The longest-running SRI index, the Domini 400, has continued to perform competitively, slightly outperforming the S&P 500 (the top-500 firms in the Standard and Poor's Index).[50] Similarly, the Dow Jones Sustainability Index has performed comparably to the Dow Jones Large Cap and Total Market Indexes.[51]

In sum, companies that take social responsibility and environmental sustainability seriously can improve their business reputations and operational efficiency while also reducing their risk exposure and encouraging loyalty and innovation. Overall, companies that take special pains to protect the environment (beyond what is required by law), are active in community affairs, and are generous supporters of charitable causes and projects that benefit society are more likely to be seen as good investments and as good companies to work for or do business with. Shareholders are likely to view the business case for social responsibility as a strong one, particularly when it results in the creation of more customer value, greater productivity, lower operating costs, and lower business risk—all of which should increase firm profitability and enhance shareholder value even as the company's actions address broader stakeholder interests.

> There's little hard evidence indicating shareholders are disadvantaged in any meaningful way by a company's actions to be socially responsible.

Companies are, of course, sometimes rewarded for bad behavior—a company that is able to shift environmental and other social costs associated with its activities onto society as a whole can reap large short-term profits. The major cigarette producers for many years were able to earn greatly inflated profits by shifting the health-related costs of smoking onto others and escaping any responsibility for the harm their products caused to consumers and the general public. Only recently have they been facing the prospect of having to pay high punitive damages for their actions. Unfortunately, the cigarette makers are not alone in trying to evade paying for the social harms of their operations for as long as they can. Calling a halt to such actions usually hinges on (1) the effectiveness of activist social groups in publicizing the adverse consequences of a company's social irresponsibility and marshaling public opinion for something to be done, (2) the enactment of legislation or regulations to correct the inequity, and (3) widespread actions on the part of socially conscious buyers to take their business elsewhere.

KEY POINTS

1. Ethics concerns standards of right and wrong. Business ethics concerns the application of ethical principles and standards to the actions and decisions of business organizations and the conduct of their personnel. Ethical principles in business are not materially different from ethical principles in general.

2. There are three schools of thought about ethical standards for companies with international operations:

   - According to the *school of ethical universalism,* common understandings across multiple cultures and countries about what constitutes right and wrong behaviors give rise to universal ethical standards that apply to members of all societies, all companies, and all businesspeople.

- According to the *school of ethical relativism*, different societal cultures and customs have divergent values and standards of right and wrong. Thus, what is ethical or unethical must be judged in the light of local customs and social mores and can vary from one culture or nation to another.

- According to the *integrated social contracts theory*, universal ethical principles or norms based on the collective views of multiple cultures and societies combine to form a "social contract" that all individuals in all situations have a duty to observe. Within the boundaries of this social contract, local cultures or groups can specify what additional actions are not ethically permissible. However, when local ethical norms are more permissive than the universal norms, universal norms always take precedence.

3. Confusion over conflicting ethical standards may provide one reason why some company personnel engage in unethical strategic behavior. But three other factors prompt unethical business behavior: (1) faulty oversight that implicitly sanctions the overzealous pursuit of wealth and personal gain, (2) heavy pressures on company managers to meet or beat short-term earnings targets, and (3) a company culture that puts profitability and good business performance ahead of ethical behavior. In contrast, culture can function as a powerful mechanism for promoting ethical business conduct when high ethical principles are deeply ingrained in the corporate culture of a company.

4. Business ethics failures can result in three types of costs: (1) visible costs, such as fines, penalties, and lower stock prices, (2) internal administrative costs, such as legal costs and costs of taking corrective action, and (3) intangible costs, such as customer defections and damage to the company's reputation.

5. The term *corporate social responsibility* concerns a company's *duty* to operate in an honorable manner, provide good working conditions for employees, encourage workforce diversity, be a good steward of the environment, and support philanthropic endeavors in local communities where it operates and in society at large. The particular combination of socially responsible endeavors a company elects to pursue defines its corporate social responsibility (CSR) strategy.

6. The triple bottom line refers to company performance in three realms: economic, social, environmental. Increasingly, companies are reporting their performance with respect to all three performance dimensions.

7. *Sustainability* is a term that is used in various ways, but most often it concerns a firm's relationship to the environment and its use of natural resources. Sustainable business practices are those capable of meeting the needs of the present without compromising the world's ability to meet future needs. A company's environmental sustainability strategy consists of its deliberate actions to protect the environment, provide for the longevity of natural resources, maintain ecological support systems for future generations, and guard against ultimate endangerment of the planet.

8. CSR strategies and environmental sustainability strategies that both provide valuable social benefits *and* fulfill customer needs in a superior fashion can lead to competitive advantage.

9. The moral case for social responsibility boils down to a simple concept: It's the right thing to do. There are also solid reasons why CSR and environmental sustainability strategies may be good business—they can be conducive to greater buyer patronage, reduce the risk of reputation-damaging incidents, provide opportunities for revenue enhancement, and lower costs. Well-crafted CSR and environmental sustainability strategies are in the best long-term interest of shareholders, for the reasons above and because they can avoid or preempt costly legal or regulatory actions.

ASSURANCE OF LEARNING EXERCISES

LO 1, LO 4

1. Ikea is widely known for its commitment to business ethics and environmental sustainability. After reviewing the About Ikea section of its Web site (http://www.ikea.com/ms/en_US/about_ikea/index.html), prepare a list of 10 specific policies and programs that help the company achieve its vision of creating a better everyday life for people around the world.

LO 4

2. Review Microsoft's statements about its corporate citizenship programs at www.microsoft.com/about/corporatecitizenship. How does the company's commitment to global citizenship provide positive benefits for its stakeholders? How does Microsoft plan to improve social and economic empowerment in developing countries through its Unlimited Potential program? Why is this important to Microsoft shareholders?

LO4

3. Go to www.nestle.com, and read the company's latest sustainability report. What are Nestlé's key sustainable environmental policies? How is the company addressing social needs? How do these initiatives relate to the company's principles, values, and culture and its approach to competing in the food industry?

EXERCISES FOR SIMULATION PARTICIPANTS

LO 1

1. Is your company's strategy ethical? Why or why not? Is there anything that your company has done or is now doing that could legitimately be considered "shady" by your competitiors?

LO 4

2. In what ways, if any, is your company exercising corporate social responsibility and good corporate citizenship? What are the elements of your company's CSR strategy? Are there any changes to this strategy that you would suggest?

LO 3, LO 4

3. If some shareholders complained that you and your co-managers have been spending too little or too much on corporate social responsibility, what would you tell them?

LO 4

4. Is your company striving to conduct its business in an environmentally sustainable manner? What specific *additional* actions could your company take that would make an even greater contribution to environmental sustainability?

LO4

5. In what ways is your company's environmental sustainability strategy in the best long-term interest of shareholders? Does it contribute to your company's competitive advantage or profitability?

ENDNOTES

[1] James E. Post, Anne T. Lawrence, and James Weber, *Business and Society: Corporate Strategy, Public Policy, Ethics,* 10th ed. (Burr Ridge, IL: McGraw-Hill Irwin, 2002), p. 103.

[2] For research on what are the universal moral values (six are identified—trustworthiness, respect, responsibility, fairness, caring, and citizenship), see Mark S. Schwartz, "Universal Moral Values for Corporate Codes of Ethics," *Journal of Business Ethics* 59, no. 1 (June 2005), pp. 27–44.

[3] See Mark. S. Schwartz, "A Code of Ethics for Corporate Codes of Ethics," *Journal of Business Ethics* 41, nos. 1–2 (November–December 2002), pp. 27–43.

[4] Ibid., pp. 29–30.

[5] T. L. Beauchamp and N. E. Bowie, *Ethical Theory and Business* (Upper Saddle River, NJ: Prentice-Hall, 2001), p. 8.

[6] Based on information in U.S. Department of Labor, "The Department of Labor's 2002 Findings on the Worst Forms of Child Labor," 2003, accessible at www.dol.gov/ILAB/media/reports.

[7] U.S. Department of Labor, "The Department of Labor's 2006 Findings on the Worst Forms of Child Labor," 2006, www.dol.gov/ilab/programs/ocft/PDF/2006OCFTreport.pdf; ibid., p. 17.

[8] W. M. Greenfield, "In the Name of Corporate Social Responsibility," *Business Horizons* 47, no. 1 (January–February 2004), p. 22.

[9] For a study of why such factors as low per-capita income, lower disparities in income distribution, and various cultural factors are often associated with a higher incidence of bribery, see Rajib Sanyal, "Determinants of Bribery in International Business: The Cultural and Economic Factors," *Journal of Business Ethics* 59, no. 1 (June 2005), pp. 139–45.

[10] For data relating to bribe-paying frequency in 30 countries, see Transparency International, *2007 Global Corruption Report,* p. 332, and *2008 Global Corruption Report,* p. 306, www.globalcorruptionreport.org.

[11] Thomas Donaldson and Thomas W. Dunfee, "When Ethics Travel: The Promise and Peril of Global Business Ethics," *California Management Review* 41, no. 4 (Summer 1999), p. 53.

[12] John Reed and Erik Portanger, "Bribery, Corruption Are Rampant in Eastern Europe, Survey Finds," *Wall Street Journal,* November 9, 1999, p. A21.

[13] For a study of "facilitating" payments to obtain a favor (such as expediting an administrative process, obtaining a permit or license, or avoiding an abuse of authority), which are sometimes condoned as unavoidable or are excused on grounds of low wages and lack of professionalism among public officials, see Antonio Argandoña, "Corruption and Companies: The Use of Facilitating Payments," *Journal of Business Ethics* 60, no. 3 (September 2005), pp. 251–64.

[14] Donaldson and Dundee, "When Ethics Travel," p. 59.

[15] See "OECD Convention on Combating Bribery of Foreign Public Officials in International Business Transactions," www.oecd.org/document/21/0,3343, en_2649_34859_2017813_1_1_1_1,00.html (accessed May 22, 2009).

[16] Michael Peel, "Landmark Bribery Case Goes to Trial," *Financial Times,* December 2, 2009, p. 4 (retrieved December 27, 2009, from ABI/INFORM Global, document ID:1913325051).

[17] Thomas Donaldson and Thomas W. Dunfee, *Ties That Bind: A Social Contracts Approach to Business Ethics* (Boston: Harvard Business School Press, 1999), pp. 35 and 83.

[18] Based on a report in M. J. Satchell, "Deadly Trade in Toxics," *U.S. News & World Report,* March 7, 1994, p. 64, and cited in Donaldson and Dunfee, "When Ethics Travel," p. 46.

[19] R. Chen and C. Chen, "Chinese Professional Managers and the Issue of Ethical Behavior," *Ivey Business Journal* 69, no. 5 (May/June 2005), pp. 1–5.

[20] Two of the definitive treatments of integrated social contracts theory as applied to ethics are Thomas Donaldson and Thomas W. Dunfee, "Towards a Unified Conception of Business Ethics: Integrative Social Contracts Theory," *Academy of Management Review* 19, no. 2 (April 1994), pp. 252–84, and Donaldson and Dunfee, *Ties That Bind,* especially chaps. 3, 4, and 6. See also Andrew Spicer, Thomas W. Dunfee, and Wendy J. Bailey, "Does National

Context Matter in Ethical Decision Making? An Empirical Test of Integrative Social Contracts Theory," *Academy of Management Journal* 47, no. 4 (August 2004), p. 610.

[21] P. M. Nichols, "Outlawing Transnational Bribery through the World Trade Organization," *Law and Policy in International Business* 28, no. 2 (1997), pp. 321–22.

[22] For an overview of widely endorsed guidelines for creating codes of conduct, see Lynn Paine, Rohit Deshpandé, Joshua D. Margolis, and Kim Eric Bettcher, "Up to Code: Does Your Company's Conduct Meet World-Class Standards?" *Harvard Business Review* 83, no. 12 (December 2005), pp. 122–33.

[23] For survey data on what managers say about why they sometimes behave unethically, see John F. Veiga, Timothy D. Golden, and Kathleen Dechant, "Why Managers Bend Company Rules," *Academy of Management Executive* 18, no. 2 (May 2004), pp. 84–89.

[24] For more details, see Ronald R. Sims and Johannes Brinkmann, "Enron Ethics (Or: Culture Matters More than Codes)," *Journal of Business Ethics* 45, no. 3 (July 2003), pp. 244–46.

[25] Veiga, Golden, and Dechant, "Why Managers Bend Company Rules," p. 36.

[26] The following account is based largely on the discussion and analysis in Sims and Brinkmann, "Enron Ethics," pp. 245–52. Perhaps the definitive book-length account of the corrupt Enron culture is Kurt Eichenwald, *Conspiracy of Fools: A True Story* (New York: Broadway Books, 2005).

[27] Chip Cummins and Almar Latour, "How Shell's Move to Revamp Culture Ended in Scandal," *Wall Street Journal,* November 2, 2004, p. A14.

[28] Archie B. Carroll, "The Four Faces of Corporate Citizenship," *Business and Society Review* 100/101 (September 1998), p. 6.

[29] Business Roundtable, "Statement on Corporate Responsibility," October 1981, p. 9.

[30] For an argument that the concept of corporate social responsibility is not viable because of the inherently conflicted nature of a corporation, see Timothy M. Devinney, "Is the Socially Responsible Corporation a Myth? The Good, the Bad, and the Ugly of Corporate Social Responsibility," *Academy*

of Management Perspectives 23, no. 2 (May 2009), pp. 44–56.

[31] Sarah Roberts, Justin Keeble, and David Brown, "The Business Case for Corporate Citizenship" (study conducted by Arthur D. Little for the World Economic Forum), p. 3, www.afic.am (accessed June 9, 2009). A revised and more wide-ranging version of this study can be found at www.bitc.org.uk/document.rm?id = 5253.

[32] "General Mills' 2010 Corporate Social Responsibility Report Highlights New and Longstanding Achievements in the Areas of Health, Community, and Environment" (CSR press release), *CSRwire*, April 15, 2010, www.csrwire.com/press_releases/29347-General-Mills-2010- Corporate-Social-Responsibility-report-now-available.html.

[33] Arthur A. Thompson and Amit J. Shah, "Starbucks' Strategy and Internal Initiatives to Return to Profitable Growth," a case study appearing in the Cases section of this text.

[34] Adrian Henriques, "ISO 26000: A New Standard for Human Rights?" Institute for Human Rights and Business, March 23, 2010, www.institutehrb.org/blogs/guest/iso_26000_a_new_standard_for_human_rights.html?gclid = CJih7NjN2alCFVs65Qo-drVOdyQ (accessed July 7, 2010).

[35] Gerald I. J. M. Zetsloot and Marcel N. A. van Marrewijk, "From Quality to Sustainability," *Journal of Business Ethics* 55 (2004), pp. 79–82.

[36] Tilde Herrera, "PG&E Claims Industry First with Supply Chain Footprint Project," *GreenBiz.com,* June 30, 2010, www.greenbiz.com/news/2010/06/30/pge-claims-industry-first-supply-chain-carbon-footprint-project.

[37] This definition is based on the Brundtland Commission's report, which described sustainable development in a like manner: United Nations General Assembly, "Report of the World Commission on Environment and Development: Our Common Future," 1987, www.un-documents.net/wced-ocf.htm, transmitted to the General Assembly as an annex to document A/42/427—"Development and International Co-operation: Environment" (retrieved February 15, 2009).

[38] See, for example, Robert Goodland, "The Concept of Environmental Sustainability," *Annual Review of Ecology and Systematics* 26 (1995), pp. 1–25; J. G. Speth, *The Bridge at the End of the World: Capitalism, the Environment, and Crossing from Crisis to Sustainability* (New Haven, CT: Yale University Press, 2008).

[39] For an excellent discussion of crafting corporate social responsibility strategies capable of contributing to a company's competitive advantage, see Michael E. Porter and Mark R. Kramer, "Strategy & Society: The Link between Competitive Advantage and Corporate Social Responsibility," *Harvard Business Review* 84, no. 12 (December 2006), pp. 78–92.

[40] World Business Council for Sustainable Development, "Corporate Social Responsibility: Making Good Business Sense," January 2000, p. 7, www.wbscd.ch (accessed October 10, 2003). For a discussion of how companies are connecting social initiatives to their core values, see David Hess, Nikolai Rogovsky, and Thomas W. Dunfee, "The Next Wave of Corporate Community Involvement: Corporate Social Initiatives," *California Management Review* 44, no. 2 (Winter 2002), pp. 110–25. See also Susan Ariel Aaronson, "Corporate Responsibility in the Global Village: The British Role Model and the American Laggard," *Business and Society Review* 108, no. 3 (September 2003), p. 323.

[41] www.chick-fil-a.com (accessed June 1, 2009).

[42] N. Craig Smith, "Corporate Responsibility: Whether and How," *California Management Review* 45, no. 4 (Summer 2003), p. 63.

[43] For an excellent discussion of the social responsibilities that corporations have in emerging countries where many people live in poverty, see Jeb Brugmann and C. K. Pralahad, "Cocreating Business's New Social Compact," *Harvard Business Review* 85, no. 2 (February 2007), pp. 80–90.

[44] Wallace N. Davidson, Abuzar El-Jelly, and Dan L. Worrell, "Influencing Managers to Change Unpopular Corporate Behavior

through Boycotts and Divestitures: A Stock Market Test," *Business and Society* 34, no. 2 (1995), pp. 171–96.

[45] Ibid., p. 3.

[46] Tom McCawley, "Racing to Improve Its Reputation: Nike Has Fought to Shed Its Image as an Exploiter of Third-World Labor Yet It Is Still a Target of Activists," *Financial Times,* December 2000, p. 14; Smith, "Corporate Responsibility," p. 61.

[47] Smith, "Corporate Responsibility," p. 63; see also World Economic Forum, "Findings of a Survey on Global Corporate Leadership," www.weforum.org/corporatecitizenship (accessed October 11, 2003).

[48] Roberts, Keeble, and Brown, "The Business Case for Corporate Citizenship," p. 6.

[49] Joshua D. Margolis and Hillary A. Elfenbein, "Doing Well by Doing Good: Don't Count on It," *Harvard Business Review* 86, no. 1 (January 2008), pp. 19–20. Of some 80 studies that examined whether a company's social performance is a good predictor of its financial performance, 42 concluded yes, 4 concluded no, and the remainder reported mixed or inconclusive findings. See Smith, "Corporate Responsibility," p. 65; Lee E. Preston and Douglas P. O'Bannon, "The Corporate Social-Financial Performance Relationship," *Business and Society* 36, no. 4 (December 1997), pp. 419–29; Ronald M. Roman, Sefa Hayibor, and Bradley R. Agle, "The Relationship between Social and Financial Performance: Repainting a Portrait," *Business and Society* 38, no. 1 (March 1999), pp. 109–25; Joshua D. Margolis and James P. Walsh, *People and Profits* (Mahwah, NJ: Lawrence Erlbaum, 2001).

[50] "Performance and Socially Responsible Investments," *The Social Investment Forum,* 2009, www.socialinvest.org/resources/performance.cfm (accessed November 15, 2009).

[51] Glenn Cheney, "Sustainability Looms as a Bigger Issue," *Accounting Today,* May 18, 2009, www.accessmylibrary.com/article-1G1-199972817/sustainability-looms-bigger-issue.html (accessed November 15, 2009).

CHAPTER 10

BUILDING AN ORGANIZATION CAPABLE OF GOOD STRATEGY EXECUTION

People, Capabilities, and Structure

> Strategies most often fail because they aren't executed well.
>
> **—Larry Bossidy and Ram Charan**
> *CEO Honeywell International, author and consultant*

> People are not your most important asset. The right people are.
>
> **—Jim Collins**
> *Professor and author*

> Of all the things I've done, the most vital is coordinating the talents of those who work for us and pointing them toward a certain goal.
>
> **—Walt Disney**
> *Founder of the Disney Company*

LEARNING OBJECTIVES

LO 1. Gain an understanding of what managers must do to execute strategy successfully.

LO 2. Learn why hiring, training, and retaining the right people constitute a key component of the strategy execution process.

LO 3. Understand that good strategy execution requires continuously building and upgrading the organization's resources and capabilities.

LO 4. Gain command of what issues to consider in establishing a strategy-supportive organizational structure and organizing the work effort.

LO 5. Become aware of the pros and cons of centralized and decentralized decision making in implementing the chosen strategy.

Once managers have decided on a strategy, the emphasis turns to converting it into actions and good results. Putting the strategy into place and getting the organization to execute it well call for different sets of managerial skills. Whereas crafting strategy is largely a market-driven and resource-driven activity, executing strategy is an operations-driven activity revolving around the management of people and business processes. Whereas successful strategy making depends on strategic vision, solid industry and competitive analysis, and shrewd market positioning, successful strategy execution depends on doing a good job of working with and through others; allocating resources; building and strengthening competitive capabilities; creating an appropriate organizational structure; instituting strategy-supportive policies, processes, and systems; motivating and rewarding people; and instilling a discipline of getting things done. Executing strategy is an action-oriented, make-things-happen task that tests a manager's ability to direct organizational change, achieve continuous improvement in operations and business processes, create and nurture a strategy-supportive culture, and consistently meet or beat performance targets.

Experienced managers are emphatic in declaring that it is a whole lot easier to develop a sound strategic plan than it is to execute the plan and achieve the desired outcomes. According to one executive, "It's been rather easy for us to decide where we wanted to go. The hard part is to get the organization to act on the new priorities."[1] In a recent study of 1,000 companies, government agencies, and not-for-profit organizations in over 50 countries, 60 percent of employees rated their organizations poor in terms of strategy implementation.[2] *Just because senior managers announce a new strategy doesn't mean that organization members will embrace it and move forward enthusiastically to implement it.* Senior executives cannot simply direct immediate subordinates to abandon old ways and take up new ways, and they certainly cannot expect the needed actions and changes to occur in rapid-fire fashion and still lead to the desired outcomes. Some managers and employees may be skeptical about the merits of the strategy, seeing it as contrary to the organization's best interests, unlikely to succeed, or threatening to their departments or careers. Moreover, employees may have misconceptions about the new strategy or have different ideas about what internal changes are needed to execute it. Long-standing attitudes, vested interests, inertia, and ingrained organizational practices don't melt away when managers decide on a new strategy and begin efforts to implement it—especially if only a few people have been involved in crafting the strategy or if the rationale for strategic change requires quite a bit of salesmanship. It takes adept managerial leadership to convincingly communicate a new strategy and the reasons for it, overcome pockets of doubt and disagreement, secure the commitment and enthusiasm of key personnel, gain agreement on how to implement the strategy, and move forward to get all the pieces into place. Company personnel must understand—in their heads and hearts—why a new strategic direction is necessary and where the new strategy is taking them.[3] Instituting change is, of course, easier when the problems with the old strategy have become obvious and/or the company has spiraled into a financial crisis.

But the challenge of successfully implementing new strategic initiatives goes well beyond managerial adeptness in overcoming resistance to change. What really makes executing strategy a tougher, more time-consuming management challenge than crafting strategy are the wide array of managerial activities that must be attended to and the number of bedeviling issues that must be worked out. It takes first-rate "managerial smarts" to zero in on what exactly needs to be done to put new strategic initiatives in place and, further, how best to get these things done in a timely manner that yields good results. Demanding people-management skills and perseverance are required to get a variety of initiatives launched and moving and to integrate the efforts of many different work groups into a smoothly functioning whole. Depending on how much consensus building and organizational change is involved, the process of implementing strategy changes can take several months to several years. To achieve *real proficiency* in executing the strategy can take even longer.

Like crafting strategy, *executing strategy is a job for a company's whole management team, not just a few senior managers.* While the chief executive officer and the heads of major units (business divisions, functional departments, and key operating units) are ultimately responsible for seeing that strategy is executed successfully, the process typically affects every part of the firm—all value chain activities and all work groups. Top-level managers must rely on the active support and cooperation of middle and lower managers to institute whatever new operating practices are needed in the various functional areas and operating units to achieve proficient strategy execution. It is middle and lower-level managers who ultimately must ensure that work groups and frontline employees do a good job of performing strategy-critical value chain activities and produce operating results that allow companywide performance targets to be met. In consequence, strategy execution requires every manager to think through the answer to the question: *"What does my area have to do to implement its part of the strategic plan, and what should I do to get these things accomplished efficiently and effectively?"*

CORE CONCEPT

Good strategy execution requires a *team effort.* All managers have strategy-executing responsibility in their areas of authority, and all employees are active participants in the strategy execution process.

A FRAMEWORK FOR EXECUTING STRATEGY

LO 1

Gain an understanding of what managers must do to execute strategy successfully.

Executing strategy entails figuring out the specific techniques, actions, and behaviors that are needed for a smooth strategy-supportive operation—and then following through to get things done and deliver results. The idea is to make things happen and make them happen right. The first step in implementing strategic change is for management to communicate the case for organizational change so clearly and persuasively to organization members that a determined commitment takes hold throughout the ranks to find ways to put the strategy into place, make it work, and meet performance targets. The ideal condition is for managers to arouse enough enthusiasm for the strategy to turn the implementation process into a companywide crusade. Management's handling of the strategy implementation process can be considered successful if and when the company achieves the targeted strategic and financial performance and shows good progress in making its strategic vision a reality.

The specifics of how to execute a strategy—the exact items that need to be placed on management's action agenda—always need to be customized to fit the particulars of a company's situation. The hot buttons for successfully executing a low-cost provider strategy are different from those for executing a high-end differentiation strategy. Implementing a new strategy for a struggling company in the midst of a financial crisis is a different job from that of making minor improvements to strategy execution in a company that is doing relatively well. Moreover, some managers are more adept than others at using particular approaches to achieving the desired kinds of organizational changes. Hence, there's no definitive managerial recipe for successful strategy execution that cuts across all company situations and all types of strategies or that works for all types of managers. Rather, the specific actions required to implement a strategy—the "to-do list" that constitutes management's action agenda—always represent management's judgment about how best to proceed in light of prevailing circumstances.

The Principal Components of the Strategy Execution Process

Despite the need to tailor a company's strategy-executing approaches to the particulars of its situation, certain managerial bases must be covered no matter what the circumstances. Ten basic managerial tasks crop up repeatedly in company efforts to execute strategy (see Figure 10.1):

1. Staff the organization with managers and employees capable of executing the strategy well.
2. Build the organizational capabilities required for successful strategy execution.
3. Create a strategy-supportive organizational structure.
4. Allocate sufficient budgetary (and other) resources to the strategy execution effort.
5. Institute policies and procedures that facilitate strategy execution.
6. Adopt best practices and business processes that drive continuous improvement in strategy execution activities.
7. Install information and operating systems that enable company personnel to carry out their strategic roles proficiently.
8. Tie rewards and incentives directly to the achievement of strategic and financial targets.
9. Instill a corporate culture that promotes good strategy execution.
10. Exercise the internal leadership needed to propel strategy implementation forward.

How well managers perform these 10 tasks has a decisive impact on whether the outcome of the strategy execution effort is a spectacular success, a colossal failure, or something in between.

Figure 10.1   The 10 Basic Tasks of the Strategy Execution Process

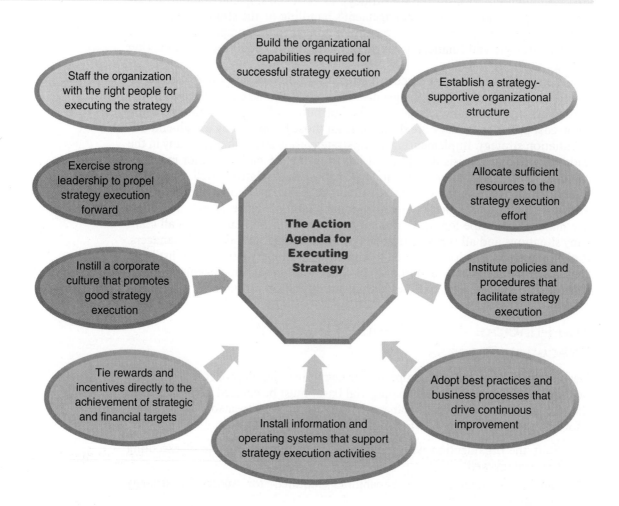

When strategies fail, it is often because of poor execution. Strategy execution is therefore a critical managerial endeavor.

In devising an action agenda for executing strategy, the way for managers to start is with *a probing assessment of what the organization must do differently to carry out the strategy successfully.* They should then consider *precisely how to make the necessary internal changes* as rapidly as possible. Successful strategy implementers have a knack for diagnosing what their organizations need to do to execute the chosen strategy well and figuring out how to get things done cost-efficiently and with all deliberate speed. They are masters in promoting results-oriented behaviors on the part of company personnel and following through on making the right things happen in a timely fashion.[4]

In big organizations with geographically scattered operating units, the action agenda of senior executives mostly involves communicating the case for change, building consensus for how to proceed, installing strong managers to move the process forward in key organizational units, directing resources to the right places, establishing deadlines and measures of progress, rewarding those who achieve implementation milestones, and personally leading the strategic change process. Thus, the bigger the organization, the more that successful strategy execution depends on the cooperation and implementing skills of operating managers who can promote needed changes at the lowest organizational levels and deliver results. In small organizations, top managers can deal directly with frontline managers and employees, personally orchestrating the action steps and implementation sequence, observing firsthand how implementation is progressing, and deciding how hard and how fast to push the process along. Regardless of the organization's size and whether implementation involves sweeping or minor changes, the most important leadership trait is a strong, confident sense of what to do and how to do it. Having a strong grip on these two things comes from understanding the circumstances of the organization and the requirements for effective strategy execution. Then it remains for company personnel in strategy-critical areas to step up to the plate and produce the desired results.

> The two best signs of good strategy execution are whether a company is meeting or beating its performance targets and performing value chain activities in a manner that is conducive to company-wide operating excellence.

What's Covered in Chapters 10, 11, and 12

In the remainder of this chapter and the next two chapters, we will discuss what is involved in performing the 10 key managerial tasks that shape the process of executing strategy. This chapter explores the first three of these tasks (highlighted in blue in Figure 10.1): (1) staffing the organization with people capable of executing the strategy well, (2) building the organizational capabilities needed for successful strategy execution, and (3) creating an organizational structure supportive of the strategy execution process. Chapter 11 concerns the tasks of allocating resources, instituting strategy-facilitating policies and procedures, employing business process management tools and best practices, installing operating and information systems, and tying rewards to the achievement of good results (highlighted in green in Figure 10.1). Chapter 12 deals with the two remaining tasks: creating a strategy-supportive corporate culture and exercising the leadership needed to drive the execution process forward (highlighted in purple in Figure 10.1).

BUILDING AN ORGANIZATION CAPABLE OF GOOD STRATEGY EXECUTION: WHERE TO BEGIN

Building an organization capable of good strategy execution depends foremost on ensuring that the resources and capabilities that are the basis for the strategy are in place, ready to be deployed. Recall from Chapter 4 that these include the skills, talents, experience, and knowledge of the company's human resources (managerial and otherwise). Proficient strategy execution depends heavily on competent personnel of all types, but because of the many managerial tasks involved and the role of leadership in strategy execution, assembling a strong management team is especially important.

If the strategy being implemented is a new strategy, the company may need to add to its resource and capability mix in other respects as well. But renewing, upgrading, and revising the organization's resources and capabilities is a part of the strategy execution process even if the strategy is fundamentally the same, since resources depreciate and conditions are always changing. Thus, augmenting and strengthening the firm's core competencies and seeing that they are suited to the current strategy are also top priorities.

Figure 10.2   **Building an Organization Capable of Proficient Strategy Execution: Three Types of Paramount Actions**

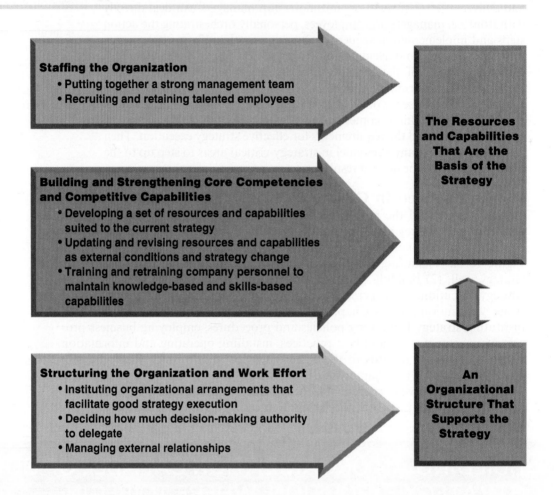

Structuring the organization and work effort is another critical aspect of building an organization capable of good strategy execution. An organization structure that is well matched to the strategy can help facilitate its implementation; one that is not well suited can lead to higher bureaucratic costs and communication or coordination breakdowns. As shown in Figure 10.2, three types of organization-building actions are paramount:

- *Staffing the organization:* putting together a strong management team, and recruiting and retaining employees with the needed experience, technical skills, and intellectual capital.

- *Building and strengthening core competencies and competitive capabilities:* developing proficiencies in performing strategy-critical value chain activities and updating them to match changing market conditions and customer expectations.

- *Structuring the organization and work effort:* organizing value chain activities and business processes, establishing lines of authority and reporting relationships, deciding how much decision-making authority to delegate to lower-level managers and frontline employees, and managing external relationships.

STAFFING THE ORGANIZATION

No company can hope to perform the activities required for successful strategy execution without attracting and retaining talented managers and employees with suitable skills and intellectual capital.

Putting Together a Strong Management Team

Assembling a capable management team is a cornerstone of the organization-building task.[5] While different strategies and company circumstances sometimes call for different mixes of backgrounds, experiences, management styles, and know-how, *the most important consideration is to fill key managerial slots with smart people who are clear thinkers, capable of figuring out what needs to be done, good at managing people, and skilled in delivering good results.*[6] The task of implementing challenging strategic initiatives must be assigned to executives who have the skills and talents to turn their decisions into results that meet or beat the established performance targets. Without a smart, capable, results-oriented management team, the implementation process is likely to be hampered by missed deadlines, misdirected or wasteful efforts, and managerial ineptness.[7] Weak executives are serious impediments to getting optimal results because they are unable to differentiate between ideas that have merit and those that are misguided—the caliber of work done under their supervision usually suffers accordingly.[8] In contrast, managers with strong strategy-implementing capabilities have a talent for asking tough, incisive questions; they know enough about the details of the business to be able to ensure the soundness of the decisions of the people around them, and they can discern whether the resources people are asking for to put the strategy in place make sense. They are good at getting things done through others, partly by making sure they have the right people under them and that these people are put in the right jobs.[9] They consistently follow through on issues, monitor progress carefully, make adjustments when needed, and keep important details from slipping through the cracks. In short, they understand how to drive organizational change, and they have the managerial skills and discipline requisite for first-rate strategy execution.

Putting together a talented management team with the right mix of experiences, skills, and abilities to get things done is one of the first strategy-implementing steps.

Sometimes a company's existing management team is up to the task; at other times it may need to be strengthened or expanded by promoting qualified people from within or by bringing in outsiders whose experiences, talents, and leadership styles better suit the situation. In turnaround and rapid-growth situations, and in instances when a company doesn't have insiders with the requisite know-how, filling key management slots from the outside is a fairly standard organization-building approach. In addition, it is important to ferret out and replace managers who, for whatever reasons, either do not buy into the case for making organizational changes or do not see ways to make things better.[10] For a management team to be truly effective at strategy execution, it must be composed of managers who recognize that organizational changes are needed and who are ready to get on with the process. Weak executives and die-hard resisters have to be replaced or sidelined, perhaps by shifting them to areas where they cannot hamper new strategy execution initiatives.

The overriding aim in building a management team should be to assemble a *critical mass* of talented managers who can function as agents of change and further the cause of first-rate strategy execution. Every manager's success is enhanced (or limited) by the quality of his or her managerial colleagues and the degree to which they freely exchange ideas, debate ways to make operating improvements, and join forces to tackle issues and solve problems.[11] When a first-rate manager enjoys the help and support of other first-rate managers, it's possible to create a managerial whole that is greater than the sum of individual efforts—talented managers who work well together as a team can produce organizational results that are dramatically better than what one or two star managers acting individually can achieve.[12]

Illustration Capsule 10.1 describes General Electric's widely acclaimed approach to developing a top-caliber management team.

Recruiting, Training, and Retaining Capable Employees

Assembling a capable management team is not enough. Staffing the organization with the right kinds of people must go much deeper than managerial jobs in order for strategy-critical value chain activities to be performed competently. *The quality of an organization's people is always an essential ingredient of successful strategy execution—knowledgeable, engaged employees are a company's best source of creative ideas for the nuts-and-bolts operating improvements that lead to operating excellence.* Companies like Google, Microsoft, McKinsey & Company, Cisco Systems, Amazon.com, Procter & Gamble, PepsiCo, Nike, Electronic Data Systems (EDS), Goldman Sachs, and Intel make a concerted effort to recruit the best and brightest people they can find and then retain them with excellent compensation packages, opportunities for rapid advancement and professional growth, and interesting assignments. Having a pool of "A players" with strong skill sets and lots of brainpower is essential to their business.

In many industries, adding to a company's talent base and building intellectual capital are more important to good strategy execution than additional investments in capital projects.

Microsoft makes a point of hiring the very brightest and most talented programmers it can find and motivating them with both good monetary incentives and the challenge of working on cutting-edge software design projects. McKinsey & Company, one of the world's premier management consulting firms, recruits only cream-of-the-crop MBAs at the nation's top-10 business schools; such talent is essential to McKinsey's strategy of performing high-level consulting for the world's top corporations. The leading global accounting firms screen candidates not only on the basis of their accounting expertise but also on whether they possess the people skills needed to relate well with clients and colleagues. Southwest Airlines goes to considerable lengths to hire people who can have fun and be fun on the job; it uses special interviewing and screening methods to gauge whether applicants for customer-contact jobs have outgoing personality traits that match its strategy of creating a high-spirited, fun-loving, in-flight atmosphere for passengers. Southwest Airlines is so selective that only about 3 percent of the people who apply are offered jobs.

In high-tech companies, the challenge is to staff work groups with gifted, imaginative, and energetic people who can bring life to new ideas quickly and inject into the organization what one Dell executive calls "hum."[13] The saying "People are our most important asset" may seem trite, but it fits high-technology companies precisely. Besides checking closely for functional and technical skills, Dell tests

General Electric (GE) is widely considered to be one of the best-managed companies in the world, partly because of its concerted effort to develop outstanding managers. It ranked number one among the best companies for leadership in the most recent global survey conducted by the Hay Group. For starters, GE strives to hire talented people with high potential for executive leadership; it then goes to great lengths to expand the leadership, business, and decision-making capabilities of all its managers. The company spends about $1 billion annually on training and education programs. In 2009, all of its 191 most-senior executives had spent at least 12 months in training and professional development during their first 15 years at GE.

Four key elements undergird GE's efforts to build a talent-rich stable of managers:

1. GE makes a practice of transferring managers across divisional, business, or functional lines for sustained periods of time. Such transfers allow managers to develop relationships with colleagues in other parts of the company, help break down insular thinking in business "silos," promote the sharing of cross-business ideas and best practices, and build a mindset open and adaptive to international markets. There is an enormous emphasis at GE on transferring ideas and best practices from business to business and making GE a "boundaryless" company.

2. In selecting executives for key positions, GE is strongly disposed to candidates who exhibit what are called the four E's—enormous personal *energy,* the ability to *energize* others, *edge* (a GE code word for instinctive competitiveness and the ability to make tough decisions in a timely fashion—saying yes or no, and not maybe), and *execution* (the ability to carry things through to fruition). Considerable attention is also paid to problem-solving ability, experience in multiple functions or businesses, and experience in driving business growth (as indicated by good market instincts, in-depth knowledge of particular markets, customer touch, and technical understanding).

3. All managers are expected to be proficient at what GE calls *workout*—a process in which managers and employees come together to confront issues as soon as they come up, pinpoint the root cause of the issues, and bring about quick resolutions so that the business can move forward. Workout is GE's way of training its managers to diagnose what to do and how to do it.

4. Each year GE sends about 10,000 newly hired and longtime managers to its John F. Welch Leadership Development Center (generally regarded as one of the best corporate training centers in the world) for a three-week course on the company's Six Sigma quality initiative. GE's Leadership Development Center also offers advanced courses for senior managers that may focus on a single management topic for a month. All classes involve managers from different GE businesses and different parts of the world. Some of the most valuable learning comes between formal class sessions when GE managers from different businesses trade ideas about how to improve processes and better serve the customer. This knowledge sharing not only spreads best practices throughout the organization but also improves each GE manager's knowledge.

One of the keys to the success of the management development process at GE is its ability to be adapted to a changing environment: "It's a constant evolution," according to Chief Learning Officer Susan Peters.* Under the leadership of Jack Welch, GE's CEO from 1980 to 2001, training activities were

(Continued)

focused around cost cutting, efficiency, and deal making. His successor, Jeffrey Immelt, adapted the focus of development programs to drive toward new goals of risk taking, innovation, and customer focus. Recently, GE has tackled the ascendancy of emerging markets by increased focus on global capability development, including the development of the China Learning Center in Shanghai. This has had a visible impact on the organization: In the last seven years the proportion of non-U.S. executives has doubled, from 15 percent to more than 30.

As a key part of talent development, talent assessment and feedback are approached with characteristic GE energy. Each of GE's 85,000 managers and professionals is graded in an annual process that divides them into five tiers: the top 10 percent, the next 15 percent, the middle 50 percent, the next 15 percent, and the bottom 10 percent. Everyone in the top tier gets stock awards, nobody in the fourth tier gets shares of stock, and most of those in the fifth tier become candidates for being weeded out. Business heads are pressured to wean out "C" players. CEO Jeffrey Immelt personally reviews the performance reviews of the top-600 employees each year, as part of GE's intensive, months-long performance review process.

* D. Brady, "Can GE Still Manage?" *Bloomberg BusinessWeek,* April 25, 2010, pp. 26–32.

Developed with Jeffrey L. Boyink.

Sources: GE Web site (accessed June 2010); Hewitt Associates, "Managing Leadership in Turbulent Times—Why and How the Global Top Companies for Leaders Optimize Leadership Talent in Emerging Markets" (White Paper), www.hewittassociates.com/_MetaBasicCMAssetCache_/Assets/Articles/2009/Managing_Leadership_Turbulent_Times_033009.pdf; D. Brady, "Can GE Still Manage?" *Bloomberg BusinessWeek,* April 25, 2010, pp. 26–32; "Hay Group Study Identifies Best Companies for Leadership," *Bloomberg BusinessWeek.com,* February 18, 2010, www.greatleadershipbydan.com/2010/02/bloomberg-businessweekcomhay-group.html.

> The best companies make a point of recruiting and retaining talented employees—the objective is to make the company's entire workforce (managers and rank-and-file employees) a genuine competitive asset.

applicants for their tolerance of ambiguity and change, their capacity to work in teams, and their ability to learn on the fly. Companies like Amazon. com, Google, and Cisco Systems have broken new ground in recruiting, hiring, cultivating, developing, and retaining talented employees—almost all of whom are in their 20s and 30s. Cisco goes after the top 10 percent, raiding other companies and endeavoring to retain key people at the companies it acquires. Cisco executives believe that a cadre of star engineers, programmers, managers, salespeople, and support personnel is the backbone of the company's efforts to execute its strategy and remain the world's leading provider of Internet infrastructure products and technology.

The practices listed below are common among companies dedicated to recruiting, training, and retaining the most capable people they can find:

1. Spending considerable effort on screening and evaluating job applicants—selecting only those with suitable skill sets, energy, initiative, judgment, aptitude for learning, and personality traits that mesh well with the company's work environment and culture.

2. Putting employees through training programs that continue throughout their careers.

3. Providing promising employees with challenging, interesting, and skill-stretching assignments.

4. Rotating people through jobs that span functional and geographic boundaries. Providing people with opportunities to gain experience in a variety of international settings is increasingly considered an essential part of career development in multinational or global companies.

5. Making the work environment stimulating and engaging so that employees will consider the company a great place to work. Progressive companies work hard at creating an environment in which employees are made to feel that their views and suggestions count.

6. Striving to retain talented, high-performing employees via promotions, salary increases, performance bonuses, stock options and equity ownership, fringe-benefit packages, and other perks.

7. Coaching average performers to improve their skills and capabilities, while weeding out underperformers and benchwarmers.

BUILDING AND STRENGTHENING CORE COMPETENCIES AND COMPETITIVE CAPABILITIES

High among the organization-building priorities in the strategy execution process is the need to build and strengthen competitively valuable core competences and capabilities. As explained in Chapter 4, a company's ability to perform the value-creating activities that express its strategy derives from its resources and capabilities. In the course of crafting strategy, managers identify the resources and capabilities that will enable the firm's strategy. In executing the strategy, managers deploy those resources and capabilities in the form of value-creating activities. But the first step is to ensure that the necessary resources and capabilities are in place and that they are renewed, upgraded, or augmented, as needed.

If the strategy being implemented is new, company managers may have to acquire new resources, significantly broaden or deepen certain capabilities, or even add entirely new competencies in order to put the strategic initiatives in place and execute them proficiently. But even if the strategy has not changed materially, good strategy execution involves refreshing and strengthening the firm's resources and capabilities to keep them in top form. Moreover, it involves augmenting and modifying them to keep pace with evolving market needs and competitive conditions.

> **LO 3**
>
> Understand that good strategy execution requires continuously building and upgrading the organization's resources and capabilities.

Three Approaches to Building and Strengthening Capabilities

Building core competencies and competitive capabilities is a time-consuming, managerially challenging exercise. While some assistance can be gotten from discovering how best-in-industry or best-in-world companies perform a particular activity, trying to replicate and then improve on the competencies and capabilities of others is, however, much easier said than done—for the same reasons that one is unlikely to ever become a good golfer just by studying what Tiger Woods does.

> Building new competencies and capabilities is a multistage process that occurs over a period of months and years. It is not something that is accomplished overnight.

With deliberate effort, well-orchestrated organizational actions, and continued practice, however, it is possible for a firm to become proficient at capability building despite the difficulty. Indeed, by making capability-building activities a routine part of their strategy execution endeavors, some firms are able to develop *dynamic capabilities* that assist them in managing resource and capability change, as discussed in Chapter 4. The most common approaches to capability building include (1) internal development, (2) acquiring capabilities through mergers and acquisitions, and (3) accessing capabilities via collaborative partnerships.[14]

Developing Capabilities Internally   Capabilities develop incrementally along an evolutionary development path as organizations search for solutions to their problems. The process is a complex one, since capabilities are the product of bundles of skills and know-how that are integrated into organizational routines and deployed within activity systems through the combined efforts of teams and work groups that are often cross-functional in nature, spanning a variety of departments and locations. For instance, the capability of speeding new products to market involves the collaborative efforts of personnel in R&D, engineering and design, purchasing, production, marketing, and distribution. Similarly, the capability to provide superior customer service is a team effort among people in customer call centers (where orders are taken and inquiries are answered), shipping and delivery, billing and accounts receivable, and after-sale support. The process of building a capability begins when managers set an objective of developing a particular capability and organize activity around that objective.[15] Managers can ignite the process by having high aspirations and setting "stretch goals" for the organization.[16]

Because the process is incremental, the first step is to develop the *ability* to do something, however imperfectly or inefficiently. This entails selecting people with the requisite skills and experience, upgrading or expanding individual abilities as needed, and then molding the efforts of individuals into a collaborative effort to create an organizational ability. At this stage, progress can be fitful since it depends on experimentation, active search for alternative solutions, and learning through trial and error.[17]

As experience grows and company personnel learn how to perform the activities consistently well and at an acceptable cost, the ability evolves into a tried-and-true competence or capability. Getting to this point requires a continual investment of resources and systematic efforts to improve processes and solve problems creatively as they arise. Improvements in the functioning of a capability come from task repetition and the resulting learning by doing of individuals and teams.[18] But the process can be accelerated by making learning a more deliberate endeavor and providing the incentives that will motivate company personnel to achieve the desired ends.[19] This can be critical to successful strategy execution when market conditions are changing rapidly.

> A company's capabilities must be continually refreshed and renewed to remain aligned with changing customer expectations, altered competitive conditions, and new strategic initiatives.

It is generally much easier and less time-consuming to update and remodel a company's existing capabilities as external conditions and company strategy change than it is to create them from scratch. Maintaining capabilities in top form may simply require exercising them continually and fine-tuning them as necessary. Refreshing and updating capabilities require only a limited set of modifications to a set of routines that is otherwise in place. Phasing out an existing capability takes significantly less effort than adding a brand-new one. Replicating a company capability, while not an easy process, still begins with an established template.[20] Even the process of augmenting a capability may require less effort if it involves the recombination of well-established company capabilities and draws on existing company resources.[21] Companies like Cray in large computers and Honda in gasoline engines, for example, have leveraged the expertise of their talent pool by frequently re-forming high-intensity teams and reusing key people on special projects designed to augment their capabilities. Canon combined miniaturization capabilities that it developed in producing calculators with its existing capabilities in precision optics to revolutionize the 35-mm camera market.[22] Toyota, en route to overtaking General Motors as the global leader in motor vehicles, has aggressively upgraded its capabilities in fuel-efficient hybrid engine technology and constantly fine-tuned its famed Toyota Production System to enhance its already proficient capabilities in manufacturing top-quality vehicles at relatively low costs—see Illustration Capsule 10.2.

The heart of Toyota's strategy in motor vehicles is to outcompete rivals by manufacturing world-class, quality vehicles at lower costs and selling them at competitive price levels. Executing this strategy requires top-notch manufacturing capability and super-efficient management of people, equipment, and materials. Toyota began conscious efforts to improve its manufacturing competence over 50 years ago. Through tireless trial and error, the company gradually took what started as a loose collection of techniques and practices and integrated them into a full-fledged process that has come to be known as the Toyota Production System (TPS). The TPS drives all plant operations and the company's supply chain management practices. TPS is grounded in the following principles, practices, and techniques:

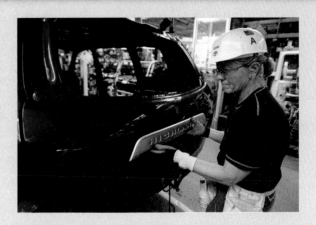

- *Use just-in-time delivery of parts and components to the point of vehicle assembly.* The idea here is to cut out all the bits and pieces of transferring materials from place to place and to discontinue all activities on the part of workers that don't add value (particularly activities where nothing ends up being made or assembled).

- *Develop people who can come up with unique ideas for production improvements.* Toyota encourages employees at all levels to question existing ways of doing things—even if this means challenging a boss on the soundness of a directive. Former Toyota president Katsuaki Watanabe encouraged the company's employees to "pick a friendly fight." Also, Toyota doesn't fire its employees who, at first, have little judgment for improving work flows; instead, the company gives them extensive training to become better problem solvers.

- *Emphasize continuous improvement.* Workers are expected to use their heads and develop better ways of doing things, rather than mechanically follow instructions. Toyota managers tout messages such as "Never be satisfied" and "There's got to be a better way." Another mantra at Toyota is that the *T* in TPS also stands for "Thinking." The thesis is that a work environment where people have to think generates the wisdom to spot opportunities for making tasks simpler and easier to perform, increasing the speed and efficiency with which activities are performed, and constantly improving product quality.

- *Empower workers to stop the assembly line when there's a problem or a defect is spotted.* Toyota views worker efforts to purge defects and sort out the problem immediately as critical to the whole concept of building quality into the production process. According to TPS, "If the line doesn't stop, useless defective items will move on to the next stage. If you don't know where the problem occurred, you can't do anything to fix it."

- *Deal with defects only when they occur.* TPS philosophy holds that when things are running smoothly, they should not be subject to control; if attention is directed to fixing problems that are found, quality control along the assembly line can be handled with fewer personnel.

- *Ask yourself "Why?" five times.* While errors need to be fixed whenever they occur, the value of asking "Why?" five times enables identifying the root cause of the error and correcting it so that the error won't recur.

- *Organize all jobs around human motion to create a production/assembly system with no wasted effort.* Work organized in this fashion is called "standardized work" and people are trained to observe standardized work procedures (which include supplying parts to each process on the

(Continued)

assembly line at the proper time, sequencing the work in an optimal manner, and allowing workers to do their jobs continuously in a set sequence of subprocesses).

- *Find where a part is made cheaply, and use that price as a benchmark.*

The TPS utilizes a unique vocabulary of terms (such as *kanban, takt-time, jikoda, kaizen, heijunka, mono-zukuri, poka yoke,* and *muda*) that facilitates precise discussion of specific TPS elements. In 2003, Toyota established its Global Production Center to efficiently train large numbers of shop-floor experts in the latest TPS methods and better operate an increasing number of production sites worldwide. Since then, additional upgrades and refinements have been introduced, some in response to the large number of defects in Toyota vehicles that surfaced in 2009–2010.

There's widespread agreement that Toyota's ongoing effort to refine and improve on its renowned TPS gives it important manufacturing capabilities that are the envy of other motor vehicle manufacturers. Not only have such auto manufacturers as Ford, Daimler, Volkswagen, and General Motors attempted to emulate key elements of TPS, but elements of Toyota's production philosophy have been adopted by hospitals and postal services.

Sources: Information posted at www.toyotageorgetown.com; Hirotaka Takeuchi, Emi Osono, and Norihiko Shimizu, "The Contradictions That Drive Toyota's Success," *Harvard Business Review* 86, no. 6 (June 2008), pp. 96–104; Taiichi Ohno, *Toyota Production System: Beyond Large-Scale Production* (New York: Sheridan, 1988).

Managerial actions to develop core competencies and competitive capabilities generally take one of two forms: either strengthening the company's base of skills, knowledge, and intellect or coordinating and integrating the efforts of the various work groups and departments. Actions of the first sort can be undertaken at all managerial levels, but actions of the second sort are best orchestrated by senior managers who not only appreciate the strategy-executing significance of strong capabilities but also have the clout to enforce the necessary cooperation and coordination among individuals, groups, departments, and external allies.[23]

Acquiring Capabilities through Mergers and Acquisitions

Sometimes a company can refresh and strengthen its competencies by acquiring another company with attractive resources and capabilities.[24] An acquisition aimed at building a stronger portfolio of competencies and capabilities can be every bit as valuable as an acquisition aimed at adding new products or services to the company's lineup of offerings. The advantage of this mode of acquiring new capabilities is primarily one of speed, since developing new capabilities internally can take many years of effort. Capabilities-motivated acquisitions are essential (1) when a market opportunity can slip by faster than a needed capability can be created internally and (2) when industry conditions, technology, or competitors are moving at such a rapid clip that time is of the essence.

At the same time, acquiring capabilities in this way is not without difficulty. Capabilities involve tacit knowledge and complex routines that cannot be transferred readily from one organizational unit to another. This may limit the extent to which the new capability can be utilized. For example, the Newell Company acquired Rubbermaid in part for its famed product innovation capabilities. Transferring these capabilities to other parts of the Newell organization proved easier said than done, however, contributing to a slump in the firm's stock prices that lasted for some time. Integrating the capabilities of two firms involved in a merger or acquisition may pose an additional challenge, particularly if there are underlying incompatibilities in their supporting systems or processes. Moreover, since internal fit is important, there is always the risk that under new management the acquired capabilities may not be as productive as they had been. In a worst-case scenario, the acquisition process may end up damaging or destroying the very capabilities that were the object of the acquisition in the first place.

Accessing Capabilities through Collaborative Partnerships

Another method of acquiring capabilities from an external source is to access them via collaborative partnerships with suppliers, competitors, or other companies having the cutting-edge expertise. There are three basic ways to pursue this course of action:

1. *Outsource the function requiring the capabilities to a key supplier or another provider.* Whether this is a wise move depends on what can be safely delegated to outside suppliers or allies versus what internal capabilities are key to the company's long-term success. As discussed in Chapter 6, outsourcing has the advantage of conserving resources so that the firm can focus its energies on those activities most central to its strategy. It may be a good choice for firms that are too small and resource-constrained to execute all the parts of their strategy internally.

2. *Collaborate with a firm that has complementary resources and capabilities in a joint venture, strategic alliance, or other type of partnership established for the purpose of achieving a shared strategic objective.* This requires launching initiatives to identify the most attractive potential partners and to establish collaborative working relationships. Since the success of the venture will depend on how well the partners work together, potential partners should be selected as much for their management style, culture, and goals as for their resources and capabilities.

3. *Engage in a collaborative partnership for the purpose of learning how the partner does things, internalizing its methods and thereby acquiring its capabilities.* Since this method involves an abuse of trust, it not only puts the cooperative venture at risk but also encourages the firm's partner to treat the firm similarly or refuse further dealings with the firm.

Upgrading Employee Skills and Knowledge Resources

Good strategy execution also requires that employees have the skills and knowledge resources they will need to perform their tasks well. Employee training thus plays an important role in the strategy execution process. Training and retraining are important when a company shifts to a strategy requiring different skills, competitive capabilities, and operating methods. Training is also strategically important in organizational efforts to build skills-based competencies. And it is a key activity in businesses where technical know-how is changing so rapidly that a company loses its ability to compete unless its employees have cutting-edge knowledge and expertise. Successful strategy implementers see to it that the training function is both adequately funded and effective. If the chosen strategy calls for new skills, deeper technological capability, or the building and using of new capabilities, training should be placed near the top of the action agenda.

The strategic importance of training has not gone unnoticed. Over 600 companies have established internal "universities" to lead the training effort, facilitate continuous organizational learning, and help upgrade company capabilities. Many companies conduct orientation sessions for new employees, fund an assortment of competence-building training programs, and reimburse employees for tuition and other expenses associated with obtaining additional college education, attending professional development courses, and earning professional certification of one kind or another. A number of companies offer online, just-in-time training courses to employees around the clock. Increasingly, employees at all levels are expected to take an active role in their own professional development and assume responsibility for keeping their skills up to date and in sync with the company's needs.

Strategy Execution Capabilities and Competitive Advantage

As firms get better at executing their strategies, they develop capabilities in the domain of strategy execution much as they build other organizational capabilities. Superior strategy execution capabilities allow companies to get the most from their organizational resources and competitive capabilities. In this way they contribute to the success of a firm's business model. But excellence in strategy execution can also be a more direct source of competitive advantage, since more efficient and effective strategy execution can lower costs and permit firms to deliver more value to customers. Superior strategy execution capabilities may also enable a company to react more quickly to market changes and beat other firms to the market with new products and services. This can allow a company to profit from a period of uncontested market dominance.

> Superior strategy execution capabilities are the only source of sustainable competitive advantage when strategies are easy for rivals to copy.

Because strategy execution capabilities are socially complex capabilities that develop with experience over long periods of time, they are hard to imitate. And there is no substitute for good strategy execution. (Recall the tests of resource advantage from Chapter 4.) As such, they may be as important a source of sustained competitive advantage as the capabilities that drive a firm's strategies. Indeed, they may be a far more important avenue for securing a competitive edge over rivals in situations where it is relatively easy for rivals to copy promising strategies. In such cases, the only way for firms to achieve lasting competitive advantage is to outexecute their competitors.

ORGANIZING THE WORK EFFORT WITH A SUPPORTIVE ORGANIZATIONAL STRUCTURE

LO 4

Gain command of what issues to consider in establishing a strategy-supportive organizational structure and organizing the work effort.

There are few hard-and-fast rules for organizing the work effort to support good strategy execution. Every firm's organization chart is partly a product of its particular situation, reflecting prior organizational patterns, varying internal circumstances, executive judgments about reporting relationships, and the politics of who gets which assignments. Moreover, every strategy is grounded in its own set of organizational capabilities and value chain activities. But some considerations in organizing the work effort are common to all companies. These are summarized in Figure 10.3 and discussed in the following sections.

Figure 10.3   Structuring the Work Effort to Promote Successful Strategy Execution

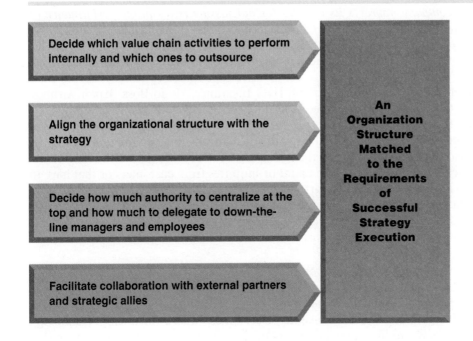

Deciding Which Value Chain Activities to Perform Internally and Which to Outsource

The advantages of a company's having an outsourcing component in its strategy were discussed in Chapter 6, but there is also a need to consider the role of outsourcing in executing the strategy. Aside from the fact that another company (because of its experience, scale of operations, and specialized know-how) may be able to perform certain value chain activities better or cheaper than a company can perform them internally, outsourcing can also sometimes make a positive contribution to better strategy execution. Managers too often spend inordinate amounts of time, mental energy, and resources haggling with functional support groups or other internal bureaucracies over needed services, leaving less time for them to devote to performing strategy-critical activities in the most proficient manner.

One way to reduce such distractions is to outsource the performance of assorted administrative support functions and perhaps even selected primary value chain activities to outside vendors, thereby enabling the company to concentrate its full energies on performing the value chain activities that are at the core of its strategy, where it can create unique value. For example, E. & J. Gallo Winery outsources 95 percent of its grape production, letting farmers take on weather-related and other grape-growing risks while it concentrates its efforts on wine production and sales.[25] Broadcom, a global leader in chips for broadband communication systems, outsources the manufacture of its chips to Taiwan Semiconductor, thus freeing company personnel to focus their full energies on R&D, new chip design, and marketing. Nike concentrates on design, marketing, and distribution while outsourcing virtually all production of its shoes and sporting apparel.

> Wisely choosing which activities to perform internally and which to outsource can lead to several strategy-executing advantages—lower costs, heightened strategic focus, less internal bureaucracy, speedier decision making, and a better arsenal of organizational capabilities.

Such heightened focus on performing strategy-critical activities can yield three important execution-related benefits:

- *The company improves its chances for outclassing rivals in the performance of strategy-critical activities and turning a core competence into a distinctive competence.* At the very least, the heightened focus on performing a select few value chain activities should promote more effective performance of those activities. This could materially enhance competitive capabilities by either lowering costs or improving quality. Whirlpool, ING Insurance, Hugo Boss, Japan Airlines, and Chevron have outsourced their data processing activities to computer service firms, believing that outside specialists can perform the needed services at lower costs and equal or better quality. A relatively large number of companies outsource the operation of their Web sites to Web design and hosting enterprises. Many business that get a lot of inquiries from customers or that have to provide 24/7 technical support to users of their products across the world have found that it is considerably less expensive to outsource these functions to specialists (often located in foreign countries where skilled personnel are readily available and worker compensation costs are much lower) than to operate their own call centers.

- *The streamlining of internal operations that flows from outsourcing often serves to decrease internal bureaucracies, flatten the organizational structure, speed internal decision making, and shorten the time it takes to respond to changing market conditions.*[26] In consumer electronics, where advancing technology drives new product innovation, organizing the work effort in a manner that expedites getting next-generation products to market ahead of rivals is a critical competitive capability. The world's motor vehicle manufacturers have found that they can shorten the cycle time for new models by outsourcing the large majority of their parts and components from independent suppliers and then working closely with their vendors to swiftly incorporate new technology and better integrate individual parts and components to form engine cooling systems, transmission systems, and electrical systems.

- *Partnerships can add to a company's arsenal of capabilities and contribute to better strategy execution.* By building, continually improving, and then leveraging partnerships, a company enhances its overall organizational capabilities and strengthens its competitive assets—assets that deliver more value to customers and consequently pave the way for competitive success. Soft-drink and beer manufacturers cultivate their relationships with their bottlers and distributors to strengthen access to local markets and build loyalty, support, and commitment for corporate marketing programs, without which their own sales and growth are weakened. Similarly, fast-food enterprises like McDonald's and KFC find it essential to work hand in hand with franchisees on outlet cleanliness, consistency of product quality, in-store ambience, courtesy and friendliness of store personnel, and other aspects of store operations. Unless franchisees continuously deliver sufficient customer satisfaction to attract repeat business, a fast-food chain's sales and competitive standing will suffer quickly. Companies like Boeing, Aerospatiale, Vodafone, and Dell have learned that their central R&D groups cannot begin to match the innovative capabilities of a well-managed network of supply chain partners.[27]

However, as was emphasized in Chapter 6, a company must guard against going overboard on outsourcing and becoming overly dependent on outside suppliers.

A company cannot be the master of its own destiny unless it maintains expertise and resource depth in performing those value chain activities that underpin its long-term competitive success.[28] As a general rule, therefore, it is the strategically less important activities—like handling customer inquiries and providing technical support, doing the payroll, administering employee benefit programs, providing corporate security, managing stockholder relations, maintaining fleet vehicles, operating the company's Web site, conducting employee training, and managing an assortment of information and data processing functions—for which outsourcing makes the most strategic sense.

Aligning the Firm's Organizational Structure with Its Strategy

The design of the firm's **organizational structure** is a critical aspect of the strategy execution process. The organizational structure comprises the formal and informal arrangement of tasks, responsibilities, and lines of authority and communication by which the firm is administered.[29] It specifies the linkages among parts of the organization, the reporting relationships, the direction of information flows, and the decision-making processes. It is a key factor in strategy implementation since it exerts a strong influence on how well managers can coordinate and control the complex set of activities involved.[30]

> **CORE CONCEPT**
>
> A firm's **organizational structure** comprises the formal and informal arrangement of tasks, responsibilities, lines of authority, and reporting relationships by which the firm is administered.

A well-designed organizational structure is one in which the various parts (e.g., decision-making rights, communication patterns) are aligned with one another and also matched to the requirements of the strategy. With the right structure in place, managers can orchestrate the various aspects of the implementation process with an even hand and a light touch. Without a supportive structure, strategy execution is more likely to become bogged down by administrative confusion, political maneuvering, and bureaucratic waste.

Good organizational design may even contribute to the firm's ability to create value for customers and realize a profit. By enabling lower bureaucratic costs and facilitating operational efficiency, it can lower a firm's operating costs. By facilitating the coordination of activities within the firm, it can improve the capability-building process, leading to greater differentiation and/or lower costs. Moreover, by improving the speed with which information is communicated and activities are coordinated, it can enable the firm to beat rivals to the market and profit from a period of unrivaled advantage.

Making Strategy-Critical Activities the Main Building Blocks of the Organizational Structure
In any business, some activities in the value chain are always more critical to successful strategy execution than others. For instance, a ski apparel manufacturer must be good at styling and design, low-cost manufacturing, distribution (convincing an attractively large number of retailers to stock and promote the company's brand), and marketing and advertising (building a brand image that generates buzz and appeal among ski enthusiasts). In discount stock brokerage, the strategy-critical activities are fast access to information, accurate order execution, efficient record keeping and transactions processing, and good customer service. In specialty chemicals, the critical activities are R&D, product innovation, getting new products onto the market quickly, effective marketing, and expertise in assisting customers.

Where such is the case, it is important for management to build its organizational structure around proficient performance of these activities, making them the centerpieces or main building blocks in the enterprise's organizational structure.

The rationale for making strategy-critical activities the main building blocks in structuring a business is compelling: If activities crucial to strategic success are to have the resources, decision-making influence, and organizational impact they need, they have to be centerpieces in the organizational scheme. Making them the focus of structuring efforts will also facilitate their coordination and promote good internal fit—an essential attribute of a winning strategy, as summarized in Chapter 1. To the extent that implementing a new strategy entails new or altered key activities or capabilities, different organizational arrangements may be required.[31]

Matching Type of Organizational Structure to Strategy Execution Requirements

Organizational structures can be classified into a limited number of standard types. The type that is most suitable for a given firm will depend on the firm's size and complexity as well as its strategy. As firms grow and their needs for structure evolve, their structural form is likely to evolve from one type to another. The four basic types are the *simple structure,* the *functional structure,* the *multidivisional structure,* and the *matrix structure,* as described below.

1. Simple Structure   A **simple structure** is one in which a central executive (often the owner-manager) handles all major decisions and oversees the operations of the organization with the help of a small staff.[32] Simple structures are also known as *line-and-staff structures,* since a central administrative staff supervises line employees who conduct the operations of the firm, or *flat structures,* since there are few levels of hierarchy.[33] It is characterized by limited task specialization; few rules; informal relationships; minimal use of training, planning, and liaison devices; and a lack of sophisticated support systems. It has all the advantages of simplicity, including low administrative costs, ease of coordination, flexibility, quick decision making, adaptability, and responsiveness to change.[34] Its informality and lack of rules may foster creativity and heightened individual responsibility.

Simple organizational structures are typically employed by small firms and entrepreneurial start-ups. The simple structure is the most common type of organizational structure since small firms are the most prevalent type of business. As an organization grows, however, this structural form becomes inadequate to the demands that come with size and complexity. In response, growing firms tend to alter their organizational structure from a simple structure to a functional structure.

2. Functional Structure   A **functional structure** is one that is organized along functional lines, where a function represents a major step in the firm's value chain, such as R&D, engineering and design, manufacturing, sales and marketing, logistics, and customer service. Each functional unit is supervised by functional line managers who report to the chief executive officer and a corporate staff. This arrangement allows functional managers to focus on their area of responsibility, leaving it to the CEO and headquarters to provide direction and ensure that their activities are coordinated and integrated. Functional structures are also known as *departmental structures,* since the functional units are commonly called departments, and *unitary structures* or *U-forms,* since a single unit is responsible for each function.

In large organizations, functional structures lighten the load on top management, relative to simple structures, and make for a more efficient use of managerial resources. Their primary advantage, however, is due to greater task specialization, which promotes learning, enables the realization of scale economies, and offers productivity advantages not otherwise available. Their disadvantage is that the departmental boundaries can inhibit the flow of information and limit the opportunities for cross-functional cooperation and coordination.

It is generally agreed that some type of functional structure is the best organizational arrangement when a company is in just one particular business (regardless of which of the five generic competitive strategies it opts to pursue). For instance, a technical instruments manufacturer may be organized around research and development, engineering, supply chain management, assembly, quality control, marketing, and technical services. A discount retailer, such as Metro, Walmart, and Tesco, may organize around such functional units as purchasing, warehousing and distribution, store operations, advertising and sales, merchandising, and customer service. Functional structures can also be appropriate for firms with high-volume production, products that are closely related, and a limited degree of vertical integration. For example, General Motors now manages all of its brands (e.g., Cadillac, Oldsmobile, Chevrolet, Buick) under a common functional structure designed to promote technical transfer and capture economies of scale.[35]

> Functional structures are also called *departmental* structures, *unitary* structures, or *U-forms.*

As firms continue to grow, they often become more diversified and complex, placing a greater burden on top management. At some point, the centralized control that characterizes the functional structure becomes a liability, and the advantages of functional specialization begin to break down. To resolve these problems and address a growing need for coordination across functions, firms generally turn to the multidivisional structure.

3. *Multidivisional Structure*

A **multidivisional structure** is a decentralized structure consisting of a set of operating divisions organized along market, customer, product, or geographic lines, and a central corporate headquarters, which monitors divisional activities, allocates resources, performs assorted support functions, and exercises overall control. Since each division is essentially a business, the divisions typically operate as independent profit centers (i.e., with profit/loss responsibility) and are organized internally along functional lines.[36] Division managers oversee day-to-day operations and the development of business-level strategy, while corporate executives attend to overall performance and corporate strategy, the elements of which were described in Chapter 8. Multidivisional structures are also called *divisional structures* or *M-forms,* in contrast with the U-form (functional) structure.

> **CORE CONCEPT**
>
> A **multidivisional structure** is a decentralized structure consisting of a set of operating divisions organized along business, product, customer group, or geographic lines, and a central corporate headquarters that allocates resources, provides support functions, and monitors divisional activities.

Multidivisional structures are common among companies pursuing some form of diversification strategy or global strategy, with operations in a number of businesses or countries. When the strategy is one of unrelated diversification, as in a conglomerate or holding company, the divisions generally represent separate industries. When the strategy is based on related diversification, the divisions may be organized according to markets, customer groups, product lines, geographic regions, or technologies. In this arrangement, the decision about where to draw the divisional lines depends foremost on the nature of the relatedness and the strategy-critical building blocks, in terms of which businesses have key value chain activities in common. For example, a company selling closely related products to business customers as well as two types of end consumers—online buyers and in-store buyers— may organize its divisions according to customer groups since the value chains involved in serving the three groups differ. Another company may organize by product line due to commonalities in product development and production within each product line. Multidivisional structures are also common among vertically integrated firms. There the major building blocks are often divisional units performing one or more of the major processing steps along the value chain (e.g., raw-material production, components manufacture, assembly, wholesale distribution, retail store operations).

Multidivisional structures offer significant advantages over functional structures in terms of facilitating the management of a complex and diverse set of operations.[37] Putting business-level strategy in the hands of division managers while leaving corporate strategy to top executives reduces the potential for information overload and improves the quality of decision making in each domain. This also minimizes the costs of coordinating divisionwide activities while enhancing top management's ability to control a diverse and complex operation. Moreover, multidivisional structures can help align individual incentives with the goals of the corporation and spur productivity by encouraging competition for resources among the different divisions.

But a divisional business-unit structure can also present some problems to a company pursuing related diversification, because having independent business units—each running its own business in its own way—inhibits cross-business collaboration and the capture of cross-business synergies. To solve this type of problem, firms turn to more complex structures, such as the matrix structure.

4. Matrix Structure   A **matrix structure** is a combination structure in which the organization is organized along two or more dimensions at once (e.g., business, geographic area, value chain function) for the purpose of enhancing cross-unit communication, collaboration, and coordination. In essence, it overlays one type of structure onto another type. Matrix structures are managed through multiple reporting relationships, so a middle manager may report to several bosses. For instance, in a matrix structure based on product line, region, and function, a sales manager for plastic containers in Georgia might report to the manager of the plastics division, the head of the southeast sales region, and the head of marketing.

Matrix organizational structures have evolved from the complex, overformalized structures that were popular in the 60s, 70s and 80s but often produced inefficient, unwieldy bureaucracies. The modern incarnation of the matrix structure is generally a more flexible arrangement, with a single primary reporting relationship that can be overlaid with a temporary secondary reporting relationship as need arises. For example, a software company that is organized into functional departments (software design, quality control, customer relations) may assign employees from those departments to different projects on a temporary basis, so an employee reports to a project manager as well as to his or her primary boss (the functional department head) for the duration of a project.

Matrix structures are also called *composite structures* or *combination structures*. They are often used for project-based, process-based, or team-based management.

Such approaches are common in businesses involving projects of limited duration, such as consulting, architecture, and engineering services. The type of close cross-unit collaboration that a flexible matrix structure supports is also needed to build competitive capabilities in strategically important activities, such as speeding new products to market, that involve employees scattered across several organizational units.[38] Capabilities-based matrix structures that combine process departments (like new product development) with more traditional functional departments provide a solution.

An advantage of matrix structures is that they facilitate the sharing of plant and equipment, specialized knowledge, and other key resources—they lower costs by enabling the realization of economies of scope. They also have the advantage of flexibility in form and may allow for better oversight since supervision is provided from more than one perspective. A disadvantage is that they add an additional layer of management, thereby increasing bureaucratic costs and decreasing response time to new situations.[39] In addition, there is a potential for confusion among employees due to dual reporting relationships and divided loyalties. While there is some controversy over the utility of matrix structures, the modern approach to matrix structures does much to minimize their disadvantages.[40]

> Matrix structures are also called *composite* structures or *combination* structures.

Determining How Much Authority to Delegate

On average, larger companies with more complex organizational structures are more decentralized in their decision making than smaller firms with simple structures—by necessity and by design. Under any organizational structure, however, there is still room for considerable variation in how much authority top managers retain and how much is delegated to down-the-line managers and employees. In executing strategy, then, companies must decide how much authority to delegate to the managers of each organizational unit—especially the heads of divisions, functional departments, and other operating units—and how much decision-making latitude to give individual employees in performing their jobs. The two extremes are to *centralize decision making* at the top (the CEO and a few close lieutenants) or to *decentralize decision making* by giving managers and employees considerable decision-making latitude in their areas of responsibility. As shown in Table 10.1, the two approaches are based on sharply different underlying principles and beliefs, with each having its pros and cons.

> **LO 5**
>
> Become aware of the pros and cons of centralized and decentralized decision making in implementing the chosen strategy.

Centralized Decision Making: Pros and Cons *In a highly centralized organizational structure, top executives retain authority for most strategic and operating decisions and keep a tight rein on business-unit heads, department heads, and the managers of key operating units; comparatively little discretionary authority is granted to frontline supervisors and rank-and-file employees.* The command-and-control paradigm of centralized structures is based on the underlying assumptions that frontline personnel have neither the time nor the inclination to direct and properly control the work they are performing and that they lack the knowledge and judgment to make wise decisions about how best to do it—hence the need for managerially prescribed policies and procedures, close supervision, and tight control. The thesis underlying authoritarian structures is that strict enforcement of detailed procedures backed by rigorous managerial oversight is the most reliable way to keep the daily execution of strategy on track.

One advantage of an authoritarian structure is tight control by the manager in charge—it is easy to know who is accountable when things do not go well.

Table 10.1   **Advantages and Disadvantages of Centralized versus Decentralized Decision Making**

Centralized Organizational Structures	Decentralized Organizational Structures
Basic Tenets • Decisions on most matters of importance should be in the hands of top-level managers who have the experience, expertise, and judgment to decide what is the best course of action. • Lower-level personnel have neither the knowledge, the time, nor the inclination to properly manage the tasks they are performing. • Strong control from the top is a more effective means for coordinating company actions.	**Basic Tenets** • Decision-making authority should be put in the hands of the people closest to, and most familiar with, the situation. • Those with decision-making authority should be trained to exercise good judgment. • A company that draws on the combined intellectual capital of all its employees can outperform a command-and-control company.
Chief Advantages • Fixes accountability through tight control from the top. • Eliminates goal conflict among those with differing perspectives or interests. • Allows for quick decision making and strong leadership under crisis situations.	**Chief Advantages** • Encourages company employees to exercise initiative and act responsibly. • Promotes greater motivation and involvement in the business on the part of more company personnel. • Spurs new ideas and creative thinking. • Allows fast response to market change. • May entail fewer layers of management.
Primary Disadvantages • Lengthens response times by those closest to the market conditions because they must seek approval for their actions. • Does not encourage responsibility among lower-level managers and rank-and-file employees. • Discourages lower-level managers and rank-and-file employees from exercising any initiative.	**Primary Disadvantages** • Top management lacks "full control"—higher-level managers may be unaware of actions taken by empowered personnel under their supervision. • Puts the organization at risk if empowered employees happen to make "bad" decisions. • Can impair cross-unit collaboration.

This structure can also reduce goal conflict among managers from different parts of the organization who may have different perspectives, incentives, and objectives. For example, a manager in charge of an engineering department may be more interested in pursuing a new technology than is a marketing manager who doubts that customers will value the technology as highly. Another advantage of a command-and-control structure is that it can enable a more uniform and swift response to a crisis situation that affects the organization as a whole.

But there are some serious disadvantages as well. Hierarchical command-and-control structures make a large organization with a complex structure sluggish in responding to changing market conditions because of the time it takes for the review/approval process to run up all the layers of the management bureaucracy. Furthermore, to work well, centralized decision making requires top-level managers to gather and process whatever information is relevant to the decision. When the relevant knowledge resides at lower organizational levels (or is technical, detailed, or hard to express in words), it is difficult and time-consuming to get all the facts and nuances in front of a high-level executive located far from the scene of the action—full understanding of the situation cannot be readily copied from one mind to another. Hence, centralized decision making is often impractical—the larger the company and the more scattered its operations, the more that decision-making authority must be delegated to managers closer to the scene of the action.

Decentralized Decision Making: Pros and Cons   *In a highly decentralized organization, decision-making authority is pushed down to the lowest organizational level capable of making timely, informed, competent decisions.* The objective is to put adequate decision-making authority in the hands of the people closest to and most familiar with the situation and train them to weigh all the factors and exercise good judgment. Decentralized decision making means, for example, that employees with customer contact are empowered to do what it takes to please customers. At Starbucks, for example, employees are encouraged to exercise initiative in promoting customer satisfaction—there's the oft-repeated story of a store employee who, when the computerized cash register system went offline, enthusiastically offered free coffee to waiting customers.[41]

> The ultimate goal of decentralized decision making is to put authority in the hands of those persons or teams closest to and most knowledgeable about the situation.

The case for empowering down-the-line managers and employees to make decisions regarding daily operations and strategy execution is based on the belief that a company that draws on the combined intellectual capital of all its employees can outperform a command-and-control company.[42] The challenge in a decentralized system is in maintaining adequate control. With decentralized decision making, top management maintains control by determining the limits to authority for each type of position, installing companywide strategic control systems, holding people accountable for their decisions, instituting compensation incentives that reward people for doing their jobs in a manner that contributes to good company performance, and creating a corporate culture where there's strong peer pressure on individuals to act responsibly.[43]

Decentralized organization structures have much to recommend them. Pushing decision-making authority down to subordinate managers, work teams, and individual employees shortens organizational response times and spurs new ideas, creative thinking, innovation, and greater involvement on the part of all company personnel. Moreover, in worker-empowered structures, jobs can be defined more broadly, several tasks can be integrated into a single job, and people can direct their own work. Fewer layers of managers are needed because deciding how to do things becomes part of each person's or team's job. Today's online communication systems and smart phones make it easy and relatively inexpensive for people at all organizational levels to have direct access to data, other employees, managers, suppliers, and customers. They can access information quickly (via the Internet or company network), readily check with superiors or whomever else as needed, and take responsible action. Typically, there are genuine gains in morale and productivity when people are provided with the tools and information they need to operate in a self-directed way.

But decentralization also has some disadvantages. Top managers lose an element of control over what goes on (since empowered subordinates have authority to act on their own) and may thus be unaware of actions being taken by personnel under their supervision. Such lack of control can put a company at risk in the event that empowered employees make unwise decisions. Moreover, because decentralization gives organizational units the authority to act independently, there is risk of too little collaboration and coordination between different organizational units.

Many companies have concluded that the advantages of decentralization outweigh the disadvantages. Over the past 15 to 20 years, there's been a decided shift from authoritarian multilayered hierarchical structures to flatter, more decentralized structures that stress employee empowerment. This shift reflects a strong and growing consensus that authoritarian, hierarchical organizational structures are not well suited to implementing and executing strategies in an era when extensive information and instant communication are the norm and when a big fraction of the organization's most valuable assets consists of intellectual capital and resides in the knowledge and capabilities of its employees.

Capturing Cross-Business Strategic Fit in a Decentralized Structure

Diversified companies striving to capture the benefits of synergy between separate businesses have to beware of giving business-unit heads full rein to operate independently. Cross-business strategic fit typically has to be captured either by enforcing close cross-business collaboration or by centralizing performance of functions requiring close coordination at the corporate level.[44] For example, if businesses with overlapping process and product technologies have their own independent R&D departments—each pursuing its own priorities, projects, and strategic agendas—it's hard for the corporate parent to prevent duplication of effort, capture either economies of scale or economies of scope, or encourage more collaborative R&D efforts. Where the potential for cross-business R&D synergies exist, the best solution is usually to centralize the R&D function and have a coordinated corporate R&D effort that serves the interests of both the individual businesses and the company as a whole. Likewise, centralizing the related activities of separate businesses makes sense when there are opportunities to share a common sales force, use common distribution channels, rely on a common field service organization, use common e-commerce systems, and so on.

> Efforts to decentralize decision making and give company personnel some leeway in conducting operations must be tempered with the need to maintain adequate control and cross-unit coordination.

Facilitating Collaboration with External Partners and Strategic Allies

Organizational mechanisms—whether formal or informal—are also required to ensure effective working relationships with each major outside constituency involved in strategy execution. Strategic alliances, outsourcing arrangements, joint ventures, and cooperative partnerships present immediate opportunities and open the door to future possibilities, but little of value can be realized without active management of the relationship. Unless top management sees that constructive organizational bridge building with strategic partners occurs and that productive working relationships emerge, the value of cooperative relationships is lost and the company's power to execute its strategy is weakened. If close working relationships with suppliers are crucial, then supply chain management must enter into considerations regarding how to create an effective organizational structure. If distributor/dealer/franchisee relationships are important, someone must be assigned the task of nurturing the relationships with forward channel allies. If working in parallel with providers of complementary products and services contributes to enhanced organizational capability, then cooperative organizational arrangements have to be put in place and managed to good effect.

Building organizational bridges with external allies can be accomplished by appointing "relationship managers" with responsibility for making particular strategic partnerships or alliances generate the intended benefits. Relationship managers have many roles and functions: getting the right people together, promoting good rapport, seeing that plans for specific activities are developed and carried out, helping adjust internal organizational procedures and communication systems, ironing out operating dissimilarities, and nurturing interpersonal cooperation. Multiple cross-organization ties have to be established and kept open to ensure proper communication and coordination.[45] There has to be enough information sharing to make the relationship work and periodic frank discussions of conflicts, trouble spots, and changing situations.

Organizing and managing a network structure provides another mechanism for encouraging more effective collaboration and cooperation among external partners. A **network structure** is the arrangement linking a number of independent organizations involved in some common undertaking. A well-managed network structure typically includes one firm in a more central role, with the responsibility of ensuring that the right partners are included and the activities across the network are coordinated. The high-end Italian motorcycle company Ducati operates in this manner, assembling its motorcycles from parts obtained from a hand-picked integrated network of parts suppliers.

> **CORE CONCEPT**
>
> A **network structure** is the arrangement linking a number of independent organizations involved in some common undertaking.

Further Perspectives on Structuring the Work Effort

All organization designs have their strategy-related strengths and weaknesses. To do a good job of matching structure to strategy, strategy implementers first have to pick a basic design and modify it as needed to fit the company's particular business lineup. They must then (1) supplement the design with appropriate coordinating mechanisms (cross-functional task forces, special project teams, self-contained work teams, and so on) and (2) institute whatever networking and communications arrangements it takes to support effective execution of the firm's strategy. Some companies may avoid setting up "ideal" organizational arrangements because they do not want to disturb existing reporting relationships or because they need to accommodate other situational idiosyncrasies, yet they must still work toward the goal of building a competitively capable organization.

The ways and means of developing stronger core competencies and organizational capabilities (or creating altogether new ones) have to fit a company's own circumstances. Not only do different companies and executives tackle the capabilities-building challenge in different ways, but the task of building different capabilities requires different organizing techniques. Thus, generalizing about how to build capabilities has to be done cautiously. What can be said unequivocally is that building a capable organization entails a process of consciously knitting together the efforts of individuals and groups. Organizational capabilities emerge from establishing and nurturing cooperative working relationships among people and groups to perform activities in a more efficient, value-creating fashion. While an appropriate organizational structure can facilitate this, organization building is a task in which senior management must be deeply involved. Indeed, effectively managing both internal organization processes and external collaboration to create and develop competitively valuable organizational capabilities remains a top challenge for senior executives in today's companies.

KEY POINTS

1. Executing strategy is an action-oriented, operations-driven activity revolving around the management of people and business processes. The way for managers to start in implementing a new strategy is with *a probing assessment of what the organization must do differently to carry out the strategy successfully.* They should then consider *precisely how to make the necessary internal changes* as rapidly as possible.

2. Good strategy execution requires a *team effort.* All managers have strategy-executing responsibility in their areas of authority, and all employees are active participants in the strategy execution process.

3. Ten managerial tasks crop up repeatedly in company efforts to execute strategy: (1) staffing the organization well, (2) building the necessary organizational capabilities, (3) creating a supportive organizational structure, (4) allocating sufficient resources, (5) instituting supportive policies and procedures, (6) adopting processes for continuous improvement, (7) installing systems that enable proficient company operations, (8) tying incentives to the achievement of desired targets, (9) instilling the right corporate culture, and (10) exercising internal leadership.

4. The two best signs of good strategy execution are whether a company is meeting or beating its performance targets and performing value chain activities in a manner that is conducive to companywide operating excellence. *Shortfalls in performance signal weak strategy, weak execution, or both.*

5. Building an organization capable of good strategy execution entails three types of organization-building actions: (1) *staffing the organization*—assembling a talented management team, and recruiting and retaining employees with the needed experience, technical skills, and intellectual capital; (2) *building and strengthening core competencies and competitive capabilities*—developing proficiencies in performing strategy-critical value chain activities and updating them to match changing market conditions and customer expectations; and (3) *structuring the organization and work effort*—instituting organizational arrangements that facilitate good strategy execution, deciding how much decision-making authority to delegate, and managing external relationships.

6. Building core competencies and competitive capabilities is a time-consuming, managerially challenging exercise that can be approached in three ways: (1) developing capabilities internally, (2) acquiring capabilities through mergers and acquisitions, and (3) accessing capabilities via collaborative partnerships.

7. In building capabilities internally, the first step is to develop the *ability* to do something, through experimentation, active search for alternative solutions, and learning by trial and error. As experience grows and company personnel learn how to perform the activities consistently well and at an acceptable cost, the ability evolves into a tried-and-true capability. The process can be accelerated by making learning a more deliberate endeavor and providing the incentives that will motivate company personnel to achieve the desired ends.

8. As firms get better at executing their strategies, they develop capabilities in the domain of strategy execution. Superior strategy execution capabilities allow companies to get the most from their organizational resources and competitive capabilities. But excellence in strategy execution can also be a more direct source of competitive advantage, since more efficient and effective strategy execution can lower costs and permit firms to deliver more value to customers. Superior

strategy execution capabilities are hard to imitate and have no good substitutes. As such, they can be an important source of *sustainable* competitive advantage. Any time rivals can readily duplicate successful strategies, making it impossible to *outstrategize* rivals, the chief way to achieve lasting competitive advantage is to *outexecute* them.

9. Structuring the organization and organizing the work effort in a strategy-supportive fashion has four aspects: (1) deciding which value chain activities to perform internally and which ones to outsource; (2) aligning the firm's organizational structure with its strategy; (3) deciding how much authority to centralize at the top and how much to delegate to down-the-line managers and employees; and (4) facilitating the necessary collaboration and coordination with external partners and strategic allies.

10. To align the firm's organizational structure with its strategy, it is important to make strategy-critical activities the main building blocks. There are four basic types of organizational structures: the simple structure, the functional structure, the multidivisional structure, and the matrix structure. Which is most appropriate depends on the firm's size, complexity, and strategy.

ASSURANCE OF LEARNING EXERCISES

LO 2, LO 3

1. Review the Careers link on L'Oréal's worldwide corporate Web site (go to www.loreal.com and click on the company's worldwide corporate Web site option). The section provides extensive information about personal development, international learning opportunities, integration of new hires into existing teams, and other areas of management development. How do the programs discussed help L'Oréal to hire good people and build core competencies and competitive capabilities? Please use the chapter's discussions of recruiting, training, and retaining capable employees and building core competencies and competitive capabilities as a guide for preparing your answer.

LO 3

2. Using Google or your university library's access to EBSCO, InfoTrac, or other online databases, search for FedEx's February 2011 acquisition of India's AFL Pvt. Ltd. and its affiliate, Unifreight India Pvt. How does the acquisition help build and strengthen FedEx's competencies and competitive capabilities? What specific capabilities gained through the acquisition will make FedEx a stronger competitor in India?

LO 5

3. Using Google Scholar or your university library's access to EBSCO, InfoTrac, or other online databases, do a search for recent writings on decentralized decision making and employee empowerment. According to the articles you find in the various management journals, what are the conditions under which decision making should be pushed down to lower levels of management?

EXERCISES FOR SIMULATION PARTICIPANTS

LO 5

1. How would you describe the organization of your company's top management team? Is some decision making decentralized and delegated to individual managers? If so, explain how the decentralization works. Or are decisions made more by consensus, with all co-managers having input? What do you see as the advantages and disadvantages of the decision-making approach your company is employing?

LO 3

2. What specific actions have you and your co-managers taken to develop core competencies or competitive capabilities that can contribute to good strategy execution and potential competitive advantage? If no actions have been taken, explain your rationale for doing nothing.

LO 1, LO 4

3. What value chain activities are most crucial to good execution of your company's strategy? Does your company have the ability to outsource any value chain activities? If so, have you and your co-managers opted to engage in outsourcing? Why or why not?

ENDNOTES

[1] As quoted in Steven W. Floyd and Bill Wooldridge, "Managing Strategic Consensus: The Foundation of Effective Implementation," *Academy of Management Executive* 6, no. 4 (November 1992), p. 27.

[2] As cited in Gary L. Neilson, Karla L. Martin, and Elizabeth Powers, "The Secrets of Successful Strategy Execution," *Harvard Business Review* 86, no. 6 (June 2008), pp. 61–62.

[3] Jack Welch with Suzy Welch, *Winning* (New York: HarperBusiness, 2005), p. 135.

[4] For an excellent and very pragmatic discussion of this point, see Larry Bossidy and Ram Charan, *Execution: The Discipline of Getting Things Done* (New York: Crown Business, 2002), chap. 1.

[5] For an insightful discussion of how important staffing an organization with the right people is, see Christopher A. Bartlett and Sumantra Ghoshal, "Building Competitive Advantage through People," *MIT Sloan Management Review* 43, no. 2 (Winter 2002), pp. 34–41.

[6] The importance of assembling an executive team that has an exceptional ability to gauge what needs to be done and an instinctive talent for figuring out how to get it done is discussed in Justin Menkes, "Hiring for Smarts," *Harvard Business Review* 83, no. 11 (November 2005), pp. 100–9, and Justin Menkes, *Executive Intelligence* (New York: HarperCollins, 2005), especially chaps. 1 to 4.

[7] See Bossidy and Charan, *Execution: The Discipline of Getting Things Done,* chap. 1.

[8] Menkes, *Executive Intelligence,* pp. 68, 76.

[9] Bossidy and Charan, *Execution: The Discipline of Getting Things Done,* chap. 5.

[10] Welch with Welch, *Winning,* pp. 141–42.

[11] Menkes, *Executive Intelligence,* pp. 65–71.

[12] Jim Collins, *Good to Great* (New York: HarperBusiness, 2001), p. 44.

[13] John Byrne, "The Search for the Young and Gifted," *BusinessWeek,* October 4, 1999, p. 108.

[14] See chapters 5 and 6 in Helfat et al., *Dynamic Capabilities: Understanding Strategic Change in Organizations* (Malden, MA: Blackwell, 2007); R. Grant, *Contemporary Strategy Analysis,* 6th ed. (Malden, MA: Blackwell, 2008).

[15] C. Helfat and M. Peteraf, "The Dynamic Resource-Based View: Capability Lifecycles," *Strategic Management Journal,* 24, no. 10 (October 2003), pp. 997–1010.

[16] G. Hamel and C. K. Prahalad, "Strategy as Stretch and Leverage," *Harvard Business Review* 71, no. 2 (March/April 1993), pp. 75–84.

[17] G. Dosi, R. Nelson, and S. Winter (eds.), *The Nature and Dynamics of Organizational Capabilities* (Oxford, England: Oxford University Press, 2001).

[18] C. Helfat and M. Peteraf, "The Dynamic Resource-Based View: Capability Lifecycles."

[19] S. Winter, "The Satisficing Principle in Capability Learning," *Strategic Management Journal* 21, nos. 10/11 (October/November 2000), pp. 981–96; M. Zollo and S. Winter, "Deliberate Learning and the Evolution of Dynamic Capa-

bilities," *Organization Science* 13, no. 3 (May/June 2002), pp. 339–51.

[20] G. Szulanski and S. Winter, "Getting It Right the Second Time," *Harvard Business Review* 80 (January 2002), pp. 62–69; S. Winter and G. Szulanski, "Replication as Strategy," *Organization Science* 12, no. 6 (November/December 2001), pp. 730–43.

[21] B. Kogut and U. Zander, "Knowledge of the Firm, Combinative Capabilities, and the Replication of Technology," *Organization Science* 3, no. 3 (August 1992), pp. 383–97.

[22] C. Helfat and R. Raubitschek, "Product Sequencing: Co-Evolution of Knowledge, Capabilities and Products," *Strategic Management Journal* 21, nos. 10/11 (October/November 2000), pp. 961–80.

[23] Robert H. Hayes, Gary P. Pisano, and David M. Upton, *Strategic Operations: Competing through Capabilities* (New York: Free Press, 1996), pp. 503–7. Also see Jonas Ridderstråle, "Cashing In on Corporate Competencies," *Business Strategy Review* 14, no. 1 (Spring 2003), pp. 27–38; Danny Miller, Russell Eisenstat, and Nathaniel Foote, "Strategy from the Inside Out: Building Capability-Creating Organizations," *California Management Review* 44, no. 3 (Spring 2002), pp. 37–55.

[24] S. Karim and W. Mitchell, "Path-Dependent and Path-Breaking Change: Reconfiguring Business Resources Following Business," *Strategic Management Journal* 21, nos. 10/11 (October/November 2000), pp. 1061–82; L. Capron, P. Dussague, and W. Mitchell,

"Resource Redeployment Following Horizontal Acquisitions in Europe and North America, 1988–1992," *Strategic Management Journal* 19, no. 7 (July 1998), pp. 631–62.

[25] J. B. Quinn, *Intelligent Enterprise* (New York: Free Press, 1992), p. 43.

[26] Ibid., pp. 33 and 89; J. B. Quinn and F. Hilmer, "Strategic Outsourcing," *McKinsey Quarterly* 1 (1995), pp. 48–70; Jussi Heikkilä and Carlos Cordon, "Outsourcing: A Core or Non-core Strategic Management Decision," *Strategic Change* 11, no. 3 (June–July 2002), pp. 183–93; and J. B. Quinn, "Strategic Outsourcing: Leveraging Knowledge Capabilities," *Sloan Management Review* 40, no. 4 (Summer 1999), pp. 9–21. A strong case for outsourcing is presented in C. K. Pralahad, "The Art of Outsourcing," *Wall Street Journal*, June 8, 2005, p. A13. For a discussion of why outsourcing initiatives fall short of expectations, see Jérôme Barthélemy, "The Seven Deadly Sins of Outsourcing," *Academy of Management Executive* 17, no. 2 (May 2003), pp. 87–98.

[27] Quinn, "Strategic Outsourcing: Leveraging Knowledge Capabilities," p. 17.

[28] Quinn, *Intelligent Enterprise,* pp. 39–40; also see Gary P. Pisano and Willy C. Shih, "Restoring American Competitiveness," *Harvard Business Review* 87, nos. 7–8 (July–August 2009), pp. 114–25; Barthélemy, "The Seven Deadly Sins of Outsourcing."

[29] A. Chandler, *Strategy and Structure* (Cambridge, MA: MIT Press, 1962).

[30] E. Olsen, S. Slater, and G. Hult, "The Importance of Structure and Process to Strategy Implementation," *Business Horizons* 48, no. 1 (2005), pp. 47–54; H. Barkema, J. Baum, and E. Mannix, "Management Challenges in a New Time", *Academy of Management Journal* 45, no. 5 (October 2002), pp. 916–30.

[31] The importance of matching organization design and structure to the particular requirements for good strategy execution was first brought to the forefront in a landmark study of 70 large corporations conducted by Professor Alfred Chandler of Harvard University. Chandler's research revealed that changes in an organization's strategy bring about new administrative problems that, in turn, require a new or refashioned structure for the new strategy to be successfully implemented and executed. He found that structure tends to follow the growth strategy of the firm—but often not until inefficiency and internal operating problems provoke a structural adjustment. The experiences of these firms followed a consistent sequential pattern: new strategy creation, emergence of new administrative problems, a decline in profitability and performance, a shift to a more appropriate organizational structure, and then recovery to more profitable levels and improved strategy execution. See Chandler, *Strategy and Structure.*

[32] H. Mintzberg, *The Structuring of Organizations* (Englewood Cliffs, NJ: Prentice Hall, 1979); C. Levicki, *The Interactive Strategy Workout,* 2nd ed. (London: Prentice Hall, 1999).

[33] Chandler, *Strategy and Structure.*

[34] Mintzberg, *The Structuring of Organizations.*

[35] Grant, *Contemporary Strategy Analysis.*

[36] Chandler, *Strategy and Structure.*

[37] O. Williamson, *Market and Hierarchies* (New York: Free Press, 1975); R. M. Burton and B. Obel, "A Computer Simulation Test of the M-Form Hypothesis," *Administrative Science Quarterly* 25 (1980), pp. 457–76.

[38] J. Baum and S. Wally, "Strategic Decision Speed and Firm Performance," *Strategic Management Journal* 24 (2003), pp. 1107–29.

[39] C. Bartlett and S. Ghoshal, "Matrix Management: Not a Structure, a Frame of Mind," *Harvard Business Review,* July–August 1990, pp. 138–45.

[40] M. Goold and A. Campbell, "Structured Networks: Towards the Well Designed Matrix," *Long Range Planning* 36, no. 5 (2003), pp. 427–39.

[41] Iain Somerville and John Edward Mroz, "New Competencies for a New World," in Frances Hesselbein, Marshall Goldsmith, and Richard Beckard (eds.), *The Organization of the Future* (San Francisco: Jossey-Bass, 1997), p. 70.

[42] The importance of empowering workers in executing strategy and the value of creating a great working environment are discussed in Stanley E. Fawcett, Gary K. Rhoads, and Phillip Burnah, "People as the Bridge to Competitiveness: Benchmarking the 'ABCs' of an Empowered Workforce," *Benchmarking: An International Journal* 11, no. 4 (2004), pp. 346–60.

[43] A discussion of the problems of maintaining adequate control over empowered employees and possible solutions is presented in Robert Simons, "Control in an Age of Empowerment," *Harvard Business Review* 73 (March–April 1995), pp. 80–88.

[44] For a discussion of the importance of cross-business coordination, see Jeanne M. Liedtka, "Collaboration across Lines of Business for Competitive Advantage," *Academy of Management Executive* 10, no. 2 (May 1996), pp. 20–34.

[45] Rosabeth Moss Kanter, "Collaborative Advantage: The Art of the Alliance," *Harvard Business Review* 72, no. 4 (July–August 1994), pp. 105–6.

CHAPTER 11

MANAGING INTERNAL OPERATIONS

Actions That Promote Good Strategy Execution

> True motivation comes from achievement, personal development, job satisfaction, and recognition.
>
> **—Frederick Herzberg**
> *Expert on motivation*

> Leadership almost always involves cooperative and collaborative activity that can occur only in a conducive context.
>
> **—Lt. General William G. Pagonis**
> *Retired U.S. Army officer and author*

> Note to salary setters: Pay your people the least possible and you'll get the same from them.
>
> **—Malcolm Forbes**
> *Late publisher of Forbes Magazine*

LEARNING OBJECTIVES

LO 1. Learn why resource allocation should always be based on strategic priorities.

LO 2. Understand how well-designed policies and procedures can facilitate good strategy execution.

LO 3. Learn how process management tools that drive continuous improvement in the performance of value chain activities can help an organization achieve superior strategy execution.

LO 4. Recognize the role of information and operating systems in enabling company personnel to carry out their strategic roles proficiently.

LO 5. Appreciate how and why the use of well-designed incentives and rewards can be management's single most powerful tool for promoting adept strategy execution and operating excellence.

In Chapter 10, we emphasized the importance of building organization capabilities and structuring the work effort so as to perform execution-critical value chain activities in a coordinated and competent manner. In this chapter, we discuss five additional managerial actions that promote good strategy execution:

- Allocating resources to the drive for good strategy execution.
- Instituting policies and procedures that facilitate strategy execution.
- Using process management tools to drive continuous improvement in how value chain activities are performed.
- Installing information and operating systems that enable company personnel to carry out their strategic roles proficiently.
- Using rewards and incentives to promote better strategy execution and the achievement of strategic and financial targets.

ALLOCATING RESOURCES TO THE STRATEGY EXECUTION EFFORT

Early in the process of implementing a new strategy, managers need to determine what resources (in terms of funding, people, etc.) will be required for good strategy execution and how they should be distributed across the various organizational units involved. A company's ability to marshal the resources needed to support new strategic initiatives has a major impact on the strategy execution process. Too little funding slows progress and impedes the efforts of organizational units to execute their pieces of the strategic plan proficiently. Too much funding wastes organizational resources and reduces financial performance. Both outcomes argue for managers to be deeply involved in reviewing budget proposals and directing the proper amounts of resources to strategy-critical organizational units. This includes carefully screening requests for more people and new facilities and equipment, approving those that hold promise for making a contribution to strategy execution and turning down those that don't. Should internal cash flows prove insufficient to fund the planned strategic initiatives, then management must raise additional funds through borrowing or selling additional shares of stock to willing investors.

A change in strategy nearly always calls for budget reallocations and resource shifting. Previously important units having a lesser role in the new strategy may need downsizing. Units that now have a bigger strategic role may need more people, new equipment, additional facilities, and above-average increases in their operating budgets. Implementing a new strategy requires managers to take an active and sometimes forceful role in shifting resources, downsizing some functions and upsizing others, not only to amply fund activities with a critical role in the new strategy but also to avoid inefficiency and achieve profit projections. It requires putting enough resources behind new strategic initiatives to fuel their success and making the tough decisions to kill projects and activities that are no longer justified. Honda's strong support of R&D activities allowed it to develop the first motorcycle airbag, the first low-polluting four-stroke outboard marine engine, a wide range of ultra-low-emission cars, the first hybrid car (Honda Insight) in the U.S. market, and the first hydrogen fuel cell car (Honda Clarity). However, Honda managers had no trouble stopping production of the Honda Insight in 2006 when its sales failed to take off and then shifting resources to the development and manufacture of other promising hybrid models, including a totally redesigned Insight that was launched in the United States in 2009.

Visible actions to reallocate operating funds and move people into new organizational units signal a determined commitment to strategic change and frequently are needed to catalyze the implementation process and give it credibility. Microsoft has made a practice of regularly shifting hundreds of programmers to new high-priority programming initiatives within a matter of weeks or even days. At Harris Corporation, where the strategy was to diffuse research ideas into areas that were commercially viable, top management regularly moved groups of engineers out of low-opportunity activities into its most promising new commercial venture divisions. Fast-moving developments in many markets are prompting companies to abandon traditional annual or semiannual budgeting and resource allocation cycles in favor of resource allocation processes supportive of more rapid adjustments in strategy.

The bigger the change in strategy (or the more obstacles that lie in the path of good strategy execution), the bigger the resource shifts that will likely be required. Merely fine-tuning the execution of a company's existing strategy seldom requires big movements of people and money from one area to another. The desired improvements can usually be accomplished through above-average budget increases to organizational units launching new initiatives and below-average increases (or even small budget cuts) for the remaining organizational units. However, there are times when strategy changes or new execution initiatives need to be made without adding to total company expenses. In such circumstances, managers have to work their way through the existing budget line by line and activity by activity, looking for ways to trim costs and shift resources to higher-priority activities where new execution initiatives are needed. In the event that a company needs to make significant cost cuts during the course of launching new strategic initiatives, then managers have to be especially creative in finding ways to do more with less and execute the strategy more efficiently. Indeed, it is not unusual for strategy changes and the drive for good strategy execution to be conducted in a manner that entails achieving considerably higher levels of operating efficiency and, at the same time, making sure key activities are performed as effectively as possible.

Figure 11.1 How Policies and Procedures Facilitate Good Strategy Execution

Policies and Procedures

Provide top-down guidance about how certain things need to be done:
- Channel individual efforts along a strategy-supportive path
- Align the actions and behavior of company personnel with the requirements for good strategy execution
- Place limits on independent action and help overcome resistance to change

Help ensure consistency in how strategy-critical activities are performed:
- Improve the quality and reliability of strategy execution
- Help align and coordinate the strategy execution efforts of individuals and groups throughout the organization

Promote the creation of a work climate that facilitates good strategy execution

INSTITUTING POLICIES AND PROCEDURES THAT FACILITATE STRATEGY EXECUTION

A company's policies and procedures can either support or obstruct good strategy execution. Any time a company moves to put new strategy elements in place or improve its strategy execution capabilities, some changes in work practices and the behavior of company personnel are usually required. Managers are thus well advised to examine whether existing policies and procedures support such changes and to proactively revise or discard those that are out of sync.

As shown in Figure 11.1, well-conceived policies and operating procedures facilitate strategy execution in three ways:

- *They provide top-down guidance regarding how things need to be done.* Policies and procedures provide company personnel with a set of guidelines for how to perform organizational activities, conduct various aspects of operations, solve problems as they arise, and accomplish particular tasks. In essence, they represent a store of organizational or managerial knowledge about efficient and effective ways of doing things. They clarify uncertainty about how to proceed in executing strategy and align the actions and behavior of company personnel

LO 2

Understand how well-designed policies and procedures can facilitate good strategy execution.

Well-conceived policies and procedures aid strategy execution; out-of-sync ones hinder effective execution.

with the requirements for good strategy execution. Moreover, they place limits on ineffective independent action. When they are well matched with the requirements of the strategy implementation plan, they channel the efforts of individuals along a path that supports the plan and facilitates good strategy execution. When existing ways of doing things are misaligned with strategy execution initiatives, actions and behaviors have to be changed. Under these conditions, the managerial role is to establish and enforce new policies and operating practices that are more conducive to executing the strategy appropriately. Policies are a particularly useful way to counteract tendencies for some people to resist change. People generally refrain from violating company policy or going against recommended practices and procedures without gaining clearance and having strong justification.

- *They help ensure consistency in how execution-critical activities are performed.* Policies and procedures serve to standardize the way that activities are performed and encourage strict conformity to the standardized approach. This is important for ensuring the quality and reliability of the strategy execution process. It helps align and coordinate the strategy execution efforts of individuals and groups throughout the organization—a feature that is particularly beneficial when there are geographically scattered operating units. For example, eliminating significant differences in the operating practices of different plants, sales regions, customer service centers, or the individual outlets in a chain operation helps a company deliver consistent product quality and service to customers. Good strategy execution nearly always entails an ability to replicate product quality and the caliber of customer service at every location where the company does business—anything less blurs the company's image and lowers customer satisfaction.

- *They promote the creation of a work climate that facilitates good strategy execution.* A company's policies and procedures help to set the tone of a company's work climate and contribute to a common understanding of "how we do things around here." Because discarding old policies and procedures in favor of new ones invariably alters the internal work climate, managers can use the policy-changing process as a powerful lever for changing the corporate culture in ways that produce a stronger fit with the new strategy. The trick here, obviously, is to come up with new policies or procedures that catch the immediate attention of company personnel, quickly shift their actions and behavior, and then become embedded in how things are done.

To ensure consistency in product quality and service behavior patterns, McDonald's policy manual spells out detailed procedures that personnel in each McDonald's unit are expected to observe. For example, "Cooks must turn, never flip, hamburgers. If they haven't been purchased, Big Macs must be discarded in 10 minutes after being cooked and French fries in 7 minutes. Cashiers must make eye contact with and smile at every customer." The upscale U.S. department store chain Nordstrom has a company policy of promoting only those people whose personnel records contain evidence of "heroic acts" to please customers—especially customers who may have made "unreasonable requests" that require special efforts. This induces store personnel to dedicate themselves to outstanding customer service, consistent with the requirements of executing a strategy based on exceptionally high service quality. To ensure that its R&D activities are responsive to customer needs and expectations, Hewlett-Packard requires its R&D people to make regular visits to customers to learn about their problems and learn their reactions to HP's latest new products.

One of the big policy-making issues concerns what activities need to be rigidly prescribed and what activities ought to allow room for independent action on the part of empowered personnel. Few companies need thick policy manuals to direct the strategy execution process or prescribe exactly how daily operations are to be conducted. Too much policy can be as much of a hindrance as wrong policy and as confusing as no policy. There is wisdom in a middle approach: *Prescribe enough policies to give organization members clear direction and to place reasonable boundaries on their actions; then empower them to act within these boundaries in whatever way they think makes sense.* Allowing company personnel to act with some degree of freedom is especially appropriate when individual creativity and initiative are more essential to good strategy execution than standardization and strict conformity. Instituting policies that facilitate strategy execution can therefore mean more policies, fewer policies, or different policies. It can mean policies that require things be done according to a strictly defined standard or policies that give employees substantial leeway to do activities the way they think best.

USING PROCESS MANAGEMENT TOOLS TO STRIVE FOR CONTINUOUS IMPROVEMENT

Company managers can significantly advance the cause of superior strategy execution by using various process management tools to drive continuous improvement in how internal operations are conducted. One of the most widely used and effective tools for gauging how well a company is executing pieces of its strategy entails benchmarking the company's performance of particular activities and business processes against "best-in-industry" and "best-in-world" performers.[1] It can also be useful to look at "best-in-company" performers of an activity if a company has a number of different organizational units performing much the same function at different locations. Identifying, analyzing, and understanding how top-performing companies or organizational units conduct particular value chain activities and business processes provides useful yardsticks for judging the effectiveness and efficiency of internal operations and setting performance standards for organizational units to meet or beat.

> **LO 3**
>
> Learn how process management tools that drive continuous improvement in the performance of value chain activities can help an organization achieve superior strategy execution.

How the Process of Identifying and Incorporating Best Practices Works

A **best practice** is a technique for performing an activity or business process that has been shown to consistently deliver superior results compared to other methods.[2] To qualify as a legitimate best practice, the technique must have a proven record in significantly lowering costs, improving quality or performance, shortening time requirements, enhancing safety, or delivering some other highly positive operating outcome. Best practices thus identify a path to operating excellence. For a best practice to be valuable and transferable, it must demonstrate success over time, deliver quantifiable and highly positive results, and be repeatable.

> **CORE CONCEPT**
>
> A **best practice** is a method of performing an activity that has been shown to consistently deliver superior results compared to other methods.

Figure 11.2   From Benchmarking and Best-Practice Implementation to Operating Excellence

As discussed in Chapter 4, *benchmarking* is the backbone of the process of identifying, studying, and implementing best practices. A company's benchmarking effort looks outward to find best practices and then proceeds to develop the data for measuring how well a company's own performance of an activity stacks up against the best-practice standard. For individual managers, benchmarking involves being humble enough to admit that others have come up with world-class ways to perform particular activities yet wise enough to try to learn how to match, and even surpass, them. But, as shown in Figure 11.2, the payoff of benchmarking comes from adapting the top-notch approaches pioneered by other companies to the company's own operation and thereby boosting, perhaps dramatically, the proficiency with which strategy-critical value chain tasks are performed.

However, benchmarking is more complicated than simply identifying which companies are the best performers of an activity and then trying to imitate their approaches—especially if these companies are in other industries. Normally, the outstanding practices of other organizations have to be *adapted* to fit the specific circumstances of a company's own business, strategy, and operating requirements. Since each organization is unique, the telling part of any best-practice initiative is how well the company puts its own version of the best practice into place and makes it work.

Indeed, a best practice remains little more than another company's interesting success story unless company personnel buy into the task of translating what can be learned from other companies into real action and results. The agents of change must be frontline employees who are convinced of the need to abandon the old ways of doing things and switch to a best-practice mindset. *The more that organizational units use best practices in performing their work, the closer a company moves toward performing its value chain activities as effectively and efficiently as possible.* This is what excellent strategy execution is all about.

Legions of companies across the world now engage in benchmarking to improve their strategy execution efforts. Scores of trade associations and special-interest organizations have undertaken efforts to collect best-practice data relevant to a particular industry or business function and make their databases available online to members. Good examples include The Benchmarking Exchange (www.benchnet.com); Best Practices, LLC

> The more that organizational units use best practices in performing their work, the closer a company comes to achieving effective and efficient strategy execution.

(www.best-in-class.com); and the American Productivity and Quality Center (www.apqc.org). Benchmarking and best-practice implementation have clearly emerged as legitimate and valuable managerial tools for promoting operational excellence and enhancing strategy execution.

Business Process Reengineering, Total Quality Management, and Six Sigma Quality Programs: Tools for Promoting Operating Excellence

In striving for operating excellence, many companies have also come to rely on three other potent process management tools: business process reengineering, total quality management (TQM), and Six Sigma quality control techniques. Indeed, these three tools have become globally pervasive techniques for implementing strategies keyed to cost reduction, defect-free manufacture, superior product quality, superior customer service, and total customer satisfaction. The following sections describe how business process reengineering, TQM, and Six Sigma programs can contribute to top-notch strategy execution and operating excellence.

Business Process Reengineering Companies scouring for ways to improve their operations have sometimes discovered that the execution of strategy-critical activities is hindered by an organizational arrangement where pieces of the activity are performed in several different functional departments, with no one manager or group being accountable for optimal performance of the entire activity. This can easily occur in such inherently cross-functional activities as customer service (which can involve personnel in order filling, warehousing and shipping, invoicing, accounts receivable, after-sale repair, and technical support), new product development (which typically involves personnel in R&D, design and engineering, purchasing, manufacturing, and sales and marketing), and supply chain management (which cuts across such areas as purchasing, inventory management, manufacturing and assembly, warehousing, and shipping).

To address the suboptimal performance problems that can arise from this type of situation, many companies have opted to *reengineer the work effort,* pulling the pieces of strategy-critical activities out of different departments and creating a single department or work group to take charge of the whole process and perform it in a better, cheaper, and more strategy-supportive fashion. The use of cross-functional teams has been popularized by the practice of **business process reengineering,** which involves radically redesigning and streamlining the workflow (often enabled by cutting-edge use of online technology and information systems), with the goal of achieving quantum gains in performance of the activity.[3]

> **CORE CONCEPT**
>
> **Business process reengineering** involves radically redesigning and streamlining how an activity is performed, with the intent of achieving dramatic improvements in performance.

When done properly, business process reengineering can produce dramatic operating benefits. Hallmark reengineered its process for developing new greeting cards, creating teams of mixed-occupation personnel (artists, writers, lithographers, merchandisers, and administrators) to work on a single holiday or greeting card theme; the reengineered process speeded development times for new lines of greeting cards by up to 24 months, was more cost-efficient, and increased customer satisfaction.[4] In the order-processing section of General Electric's circuit breaker division, elapsed time from order receipt to delivery was cut from three weeks to three days by consolidating six production units into one, reducing a variety of former inventory and handling steps, automating the design system to replace a human custom-design process, and cutting the organizational layers between managers and workers from three to one. Productivity rose 20 percent in one year, and unit manufacturing costs dropped 30 percent. Northwest Water, a British utility, used process reengineering to eliminate 45 work depots that served as home bases to crews who installed and repaired water and sewage lines and equipment. Under the reengineered arrangement, crews worked directly from their vehicles, receiving assignments and reporting work completion from computer terminals in their trucks. Crew members became contractors to Northwest Water rather than employees, a move that not only eliminated the need for the work depots but also allowed Northwest Water to eliminate a big percentage of the bureaucratic personnel and supervisory organization that managed the crews.[5]

Reengineering of value chain activities has been undertaken at many companies in many industries all over the world, with excellent results at some firms.[6] At companies where it has produced only modest results, this is usually because of ineptness and/or lack of wholehearted commitment from the top. While business process reengineering has been criticized for its use by some companies as an excuse for downsizing, it has nonetheless proved itself as a useful tool for streamlining a company's work effort and moving closer to operational excellence. It has also inspired more technologically based approaches to integrating and streamlining business processes, such as *Enterprise Resource Planning,* a software-based system implemented with the help of consulting companies such as SAP (the leading provider of business software).

Total Quality Management Programs

Total quality management (TQM) is a philosophy of managing a set of business practices that emphasizes continuous improvement in all phases of operations, 100 percent accuracy in performing tasks, involvement and empowerment of employees at all levels, team-based work design, benchmarking, and total customer satisfaction.[7]

While TQM concentrates on producing quality goods and fully satisfying customer expectations, it achieves its biggest successes when it is extended to employee efforts in *all departments*—for example, human resources, billing, accounting, and information systems—that may lack pressing, customer-driven incentives to improve. It involves reforming the corporate culture and shifting to a total quality/continuous improvement business philosophy that permeates every facet of the organization.[8] TQM aims at instilling enthusiasm and commitment to doing things right from the top to the bottom of the organization. Management's job is to kindle an organizationwide search for ways to improve, a search that involves all company personnel exercising initiative and using their ingenuity. TQM doctrine preaches that there's no such thing as "good enough" and that everyone has a responsibility to participate in continuous improvement. TQM is thus a race without a finish. Success comes from making little steps forward each day, a process that the Japanese call *kaizen.*

TQM takes a fairly long time to show significant results—very little benefit emerges within the first six months. The long-term payoff of TQM, if it comes, depends heavily on management's success in implanting a culture within which the TQM philosophy and practices can thrive. TQM is a managerial tool that has attracted numerous users and advocates over several decades, and it can deliver good results when used properly.

Six Sigma Quality Programs   Six Sigma programs offer another way to drive continuous improvement in quality and strategy execution. This approach entails the use of advanced statistical methods to identify and remove the causes of defects (errors) and variability in performing an activity or business process. When performance of an activity or process reaches "Six Sigma quality," there are *no more than 3.4 defects per million iterations* (equal to 99.9997 percent accuracy).[9]

There are two important types of Six Sigma programs. DMAIC (define, measure, analyze, improve, and control) is an improvement system for existing processes falling below specification and needing incremental improvement. The DMADV process of define, measure, analyze, design, and verify is used to develop *new* processes or products at Six Sigma quality levels. DMADV is sometimes referred to as a Design for Six Sigma, or DFSS. Both Six Sigma programs are overseen by personnel who have completed Six Sigma "master black belt" training and are executed by personnel who have earned Six Sigma "green belts" and Six Sigma "black belts." According to the Six Sigma Academy, personnel with black belts can save companies approximately $230,000 per project and can complete four to six projects a year.[10]

The statistical thinking underlying Six Sigma is based on the following three principles: All work is a process, all processes have variability, and all processes create data that explain variability.[11] To illustrate how these three principles drive the metrics of DMAIC, consider the case of a hypothetical janitorial company that wants to improve the caliber of work done by its cleaning crews and thereby improve customer satisfaction. The janitorial company's Six Sigma team can pursue quality enhancement and continuous improvement via the DMAIC process as follows:

- *Define.* Because Six Sigma is aimed at reducing defects, the first step is to define what constitutes a defect. Six Sigma team members might decide that leaving streaks on windows is a defect because it is a source of customer dissatisfaction.
- *Measure.* The next step is to collect data to find out why, how, and how often this defect occurs. This might include creating a process flow map of the specific ways that cleaning crews go about the task of cleaning a commercial customer's windows. Other metrics may include recording what tools and cleaning products the crews use to clean windows.
- *Analyze.* After the data are gathered and the statistics analyzed, the company's Six Sigma team may discover that the tools and window-cleaning techniques of certain employees are better than those of other employees because their tools and procedures leave no streaked windows—a "best practice" for avoiding window streaking is thus identified and documented.
- *Improve.* The Six Sigma team implements the documented best practice as a standard way of cleaning windows.
- *Control.* The company teaches new and existing employees the best-practice technique for window cleaning. Over time, there is significant improvement in customer satisfaction and increased business.

Six Sigma's DMAIC process is a particularly good vehicle for improving performance when there are *wide variations* in how well an activity is performed.[12] For instance, airlines striving to improve the on-time performance of their flights have more to gain from actions to curtail the number of flights that are late by more than 30 minutes than from actions to reduce the number of flights that are late by less than 5 minutes. Likewise, FedEx might have a 16-hour average delivery time for its overnight package service operation, but if the actual delivery time varies around the 16-hour average from a low of 12 hours to a high of 26 hours, such that 10 percent of its packages are delivered over 6 hours late, then it has a huge reliability problem of the sort that Six Sigma programs are well suited to address.

Since the mid-1990s, thousands of companies and nonprofit organizations around the world have used Six Sigma programs to promote operating excellence. Such manufacturers as Motorola, Caterpillar, DuPont, Xerox, Alcan Aluminum, BMW, Volkswagen, Nokia, Owens Corning, Boeing, and Emerson Electric have employed Six Sigma techniques to improve their strategy execution and increase production quality. General Electric (GE), one of the most successful companies implementing Six Sigma training and pursuing Six Sigma perfection across the company's entire operations, estimated benefits on the order of $10 billion during the first five years of implementation; its Lighting division, for example, cut invoice defects and disputes by 98 percent, while GE Capital Mortgage improved the chances of a caller reaching a "live" GE person from 76 to 99 percent.[13] Illustration Capsule 11.1 describes Whirlpool's use of Six Sigma in its appliance business.

Six Sigma is, however, not just a quality-enhancing tool for manufacturers. At one company, product sales personnel typically wined and dined customers to close their deals, but the costs of such entertaining were viewed as excessively high.[14] A Six Sigma project that examined sales data found that although face time with customers was important, wining, dining, and other types of entertainment were not. The data showed that regular face time helped close sales, but that time could be spent over a cup of coffee instead of golfing at a resort or taking clients to expensive restaurants. In addition, analysis showed that too much face time with customers was counterproductive. A regularly scheduled customer picnic was found to be detrimental to closing sales because it was held at a busy time of year, when customers preferred not to be away from their offices. Changing the manner in which prospective customers were wooed resulted in a 10 percent increase in sales. Six Sigma has also been used to improve processes in health care. A Milwaukee, Wisconsin, hospital used Six Sigma to improve the accuracy of administering the proper drug doses to patients. DMAIC analysis of the three-stage process by which prescriptions were written by doctors, filled by the hospital pharmacy, and then administered to patients by nurses revealed that most mistakes came from misreading the doctors' handwriting.[15] The hospital implemented a program requiring doctors to enter the prescription on the hospital's computers, which slashed the number of errors dramatically. Bank of America, Credit Suisse, Amazon.com, Philips, and Siemens also have reportedly used Six Sigma techniques successfully in their operations.

While many enterprises have used Six Sigma methods to improve the quality with which activities are performed, there is evidence that Six Sigma techniques can stifle innovation and creativity.[16] The essence of Six Sigma is to reduce variability in processes, but creative processes, by nature, include quite a bit of variability. In many instances, breakthrough innovations occur only after thousands of ideas have been abandoned and promising ideas have gone through multiple iterations and extensive prototyping. Google CEO Eric Schmidt has commented

ILLUSTRATION CAPSULE 11.1

Whirlpool's Use of Six Sigma to Promote Operating Excellence

Top management at Whirlpool Corporation (with 67 manufacturing and technology centers around the globe and sales in some 170 countries totaling $17 billion in 2009) has a vision of Whirlpool appliances in "Every Home . . . Everywhere with Pride, Passion, and Performance." One of management's chief objectives in pursuing this vision is to build unmatched customer loyalty to the Whirlpool brand. Whirlpool's strategy to win the hearts and minds of appliance buyers the world over has been to produce and market appliances with top-notch quality and innovative features that users will find appealing. In addition, Whirlpool's strategy has been to offer a wide selection of models (recognizing that buyer tastes and needs differ) and to strive for low-cost production efficiency, thereby enabling Whirlpool to price its products very competitively. Executing this strategy at Whirlpool's operations in North America (where it is the market leader), Latin America (where it is also the market leader), Europe (where it ranks third), and Asia (where it is number one in India and has a foothold with huge growth opportunities elsewhere) has involved a strong focus on continuous improvement, lean manufacturing capabilities, and a drive for operating excellence. To marshal the efforts of its 67,000 employees in executing the strategy successfully, management developed a comprehensive Operational Excellence program with Six Sigma as one of the centerpieces.

The Operational Excellence initiative, which began in the 1990s, incorporated Six Sigma techniques to improve the quality of Whirlpool products and, at the same time, lower costs and trim the time it took to get product innovations into the marketplace. The Six Sigma program helped Whirlpool save $175 million in manufacturing costs in its first three years.

To sustain the productivity gains and cost savings, Whirlpool embedded Six Sigma practices within each of its manufacturing facilities worldwide and instilled a culture based on Six Sigma and lean manufacturing skills and capabilities. In 2002, each of Whirlpool's operating units began taking the Six Sigma initiative to a higher level by first placing the needs of the customer at the center of every function—R&D, technology, manufacturing, marketing, and administrative support—and then striving to consistently improve quality levels while eliminating all unnecessary costs. The company systematically went through every aspect of its business with the view that company personnel should perform every activity at every level in a manner that delivers value to the customer and leads to continuous improvement on how things are done.

Whirlpool management believes that the company's Operational Excellence process has been a major contributor in sustaining the company's position as the leading global manufacturer and marketer of home appliances.

Source: www.whirlpool.com, accessed September 25, 2003, November 15, 2005, August 16, 2008, and July 9, 2010; Lexis-Nexis -Edgar Online, exhibit type: exhibit 99 - additional exhibits, filing date: June 21, 2010.

that the innovation process is "anti-Six Sigma" and that applying Six Sigma principles to those performing creative work at Google would choke off innovation at the company.[17]

James McNerney, a GE executive schooled in the constructive use of Six Sigma, became CEO at 3M Corporation and proceeded to institute a series of Six Sigma–based principles. McNerney's dedication to Six Sigma and his elimination of 8 percent of the company's workforce did cause 3M's profits to jump shortly after his arrival, but the application of Six Sigma in 3M's R&D and new product development activities soon proved to stifle innovation and new product introductions, undermining the company's long-standing reputation for innovation. 3M's researchers complained that the innovation process did not lend itself well to the extensive data collection and analysis required under Six Sigma and that too much time was spent completing reports that outlined the market potential and possible manufacturing concerns for projects in all stages of the R&D pipeline. Six Sigma rigidity and a freeze on 3M's R&D budget from McNerney's first year as CEO through 2005 was blamed for the company's drop from first to seventh place on the Boston Consulting Group's Most Innovative Companies list.[18]

A blended approach to Six Sigma implementation that is gaining in popularity pursues incremental improvements in operating efficiency, while R&D and other processes that allow the company to develop new ways of offering value to customers are given freer rein. Managers of these *ambidextrous organizations* are adept at employing continuous improvement in operating processes but allowing R&D to operate under a set of rules that allows for the development of breakthrough innovations. However, the two distinctly different approaches to managing employees must be carried out by tightly integrated senior managers to ensure that the separate and diversely oriented units operate with a common purpose. Ciba Vision, a global leader in contact lenses, has dramatically reduced operating expenses through the use of continuous improvement programs, while simultaneously and harmoniously developing new series of contact lens products that have allowed its revenues to increase by 300 percent over a 10-year period.[19] An enterprise that systematically and wisely applies Six Sigma methods to its value chain, activity by activity, can make major strides in improving the proficiency with which its strategy is executed without sacrificing innovation. As is the case with TQM, obtaining managerial commitment, establishing a quality culture, and fully involving employees are all of critical importance to the successful implementation of Six Sigma quality programs.[20]

The Difference between Business Process Reengineering and Continuous Improvement Programs like Six Sigma and TQM

Business process reengineering and continuous improvement efforts like TQM and Six Sigma both aim at improved productivity and reduced costs, better product quality, and greater customer satisfaction. The essential difference between business process reengineering and continuous improvement programs is that reengineering aims at *quantum gains* on the order of 30 to 50 percent or more, whereas programs like TQM and Six Sigma stress *incremental progress,* striving for inch-by-inch gains again and again in a never-ending stream. The two approaches to improved performance of value chain activities and operating excellence are not mutually exclusive; it makes sense to use them in tandem. Reengineering can be used first to produce a good basic design that yields quick, dramatic improvements in performing a business process. Total quality programs can then be used as a follow-on to reengineering and/or best-practice implementation, delivering gradual improvements over a longer period of time. Such a two-pronged approach to implementing operational excellence is like a marathon race in which you run the first 4 miles as fast as you can and then gradually pick up speed the remainder of the way.

Business process reengineering aims at one-time quantum improvement, while continuous improvement programs like TQM and Six Sigma aim at ongoing incremental improvements.

Capturing the Benefits of Initiatives to Improve Operations

The biggest beneficiaries of benchmarking and best-practice initiatives, reengineering, TQM, and Six Sigma are companies that view such programs not as ends in themselves but as tools for implementing company strategy more effectively. The skimpiest payoffs occur when company managers seize on them as something worth trying—novel ideas that could improve things. In most such instances, they result in strategy-blind efforts to simply manage better.

There's an important lesson here. Business process management tools all need to be linked to a company's strategic priorities to contribute effectively to improving the strategy's execution. Only strategy can point to which value chain activities matter and what performance targets make the most sense. Without a strategic framework, managers lack the context in which to fix things that really matter to business-unit performance and competitive success.

To get the most from initiatives to execute strategy more proficiently, managers must have a clear idea of what specific outcomes really matter. Is it high on-time delivery, lower overall costs, fewer customer complaints, shorter cycle times, a higher percentage of revenues coming from recently introduced products, or what? Benchmarking best-in-industry and best-in-world performance of most or all value chain activities provides a realistic basis for setting internal performance milestones and longer-range targets.

Once initiatives to improve operations are linked to the company's strategic priorities, then comes the managerial task of building a total quality culture that is genuinely committed to achieving the performance outcomes that strategic success requires.[21] Managers can take the following action steps to realize full value from TQM or Six Sigma initiatives and promote a culture of operating excellence:[22]

1. Visible, unequivocal, and unyielding commitment to total quality and continuous improvement, including a vision concerned with quality and specific, measurable objectives for increasing quality and making continuous improvement.

2. Nudging people toward quality-supportive behaviors by:
   a. Screening job applicants rigorously and hiring only those with attitudes and aptitudes right for quality-based performance.
   b. Providing quality training for most employees.
   c. Using teams and team-building exercises to reinforce and nurture individual effort (the creation of a quality culture is facilitated when teams become more cross-functional, multitask-oriented, and increasingly self-managed).
   d. Recognizing and rewarding individual and team efforts to improve quality regularly and systematically.
   e. Stressing prevention (doing it right the first time), not inspection (instituting ways to correct mistakes).

3. Empowering employees so that authority for delivering great service or improving products is in the hands of the doers rather than the overseers—*improving quality has to be seen as part of everyone's job.*

4. Using online systems to provide all relevant parties with the latest best practices, thereby speeding the diffusion and adoption of best practices throughout the organization. Online systems can also allow company personnel to exchange data and opinions about how to upgrade the prevailing best practices.

5. Emphasizing that performance can, and must, be improved because competitors are not resting on their laurels and customers are always looking for something better.

If the quality initiatives are linked to the strategic objectives and if all organization members buy into a supporting culture of operating excellence, then a company's continuous improvement practices become decidedly more conducive to proficient strategy execution.

> The purpose of using benchmarking, best practices, business process reengineering, TQM, and Six Sigma programs is to improve the performance of strategy-critical activities and thereby enhance strategy execution.

In sum, benchmarking, the adoption of best practices, business process reengineering, TQM, and Six Sigma techniques all need to be seen and used as part of a bigger-picture effort to execute strategy proficiently. Used properly, all of these tools are capable of improving the proficiency with which an organization performs its value chain activities. Not only do improvements from such initiatives add up over time and strengthen organizational capabilities, but they also help build a culture of operating excellence. All this lays the groundwork for gaining a competitive advantage.[23] While it is relatively easy for rivals to also implement process management tools, it is much more difficult and time-consuming for them to instill a deeply ingrained culture of operating excellence (as occurs when such techniques are religiously employed and top management exhibits lasting commitment to operational excellence throughout the organization).

INSTALLING INFORMATION AND OPERATING SYSTEMS

> **LO 4**
>
> Recognize the role of information and operating systems in enabling company personnel to carry out their strategic roles proficiently.

Company strategies can't be executed well without a number of internal systems for business operations. Southwest Airlines, Singapore Airlines, Lufthansa, British Airways, and other successful airlines cannot hope to provide passenger-pleasing service without a user-friendly online reservation system, an accurate and speedy baggage handling system, and a strict aircraft maintenance program that minimizes problems requiring at-the-gate service that delay departures. FedEx has internal communication systems that allow it to coordinate its over 80,000 vehicles in handling an average of 8.0 million packages a day. Its leading-edge flight operations systems allow a single controller to direct as many as 200 of FedEx's 664 aircraft simultaneously, overriding their flight plans should weather problems or other special circumstances arise. In addition, FedEx has created a series of e-business tools for customers that allow them to ship and track packages online, create address books, review shipping history, generate custom reports, simplify customer billing, reduce internal warehousing and inventory management costs, purchase goods and services from suppliers, and respond to quickly changing customer demands. All of FedEx's systems support the company's strategy of providing businesses and individuals with a broad array of package delivery services (from premium next-day to economical five-day deliveries) and enhancing its competitiveness against UPS and DHL.

Otis Elevator, the world's largest manufacturer of elevators, with some 2.3 million elevators and escalators installed worldwide, has a 24-hour remote electronic monitoring system that can detect when an elevator or escalator installed on a customer's site has any of 325 problems.[24] If the monitoring system detects a problem, it analyzes and diagnoses the cause and location, then makes the service call to an Otis mechanic at the nearest location, and helps the mechanic (who is equipped with a Web-enabled cell phone) identify the component causing the problem. The company's maintenance system helps keep outage times under three hours. All trouble-call data are relayed to design and manufacturing personnel, allowing them to quickly alter design specifications or manufacturing procedures when needed to correct recurring problems. All customers have online access to performance data on each of their Otis elevators and escalators.

Amazon.com ships customer orders of books, CDs, toys, and myriad other items from fully computerized warehouses with a capacity of over 17½ million square feet in 2010. The warehouses are so technologically sophisticated that they require about as many lines of code to run as Amazon's Web site does. Using complex picking algorithms, computers initiate the order-picking process by sending signals to workers' wireless receivers, telling them which items to pick off the shelves in which order. Computers also generate data on misboxed items, chute backup times, line speed, worker productivity, and shipping weights on orders. Systems are upgraded regularly, and productivity improvements are aggressively pursued. In 2003 Amazon turned their inventory over 20 times annually in an industry whose average was 15 turns; by 2009 its industry turnover had decreased to an unprecedented 12. Amazon's warehouse efficiency and cost per order filled was so low that one of the fastest-growing and most profitable parts of Amazon's business was using its warehouses to run the e-commerce operations of large retail chains such as Target.

Most telephone companies, electric utilities, and TV broadcasting systems have online monitoring systems to spot transmission problems within seconds and increase the reliability of their services. At eBay, there are systems for real-time monitoring of new listings, bidding activity, Web site traffic, and page views. Kaiser Permanente spent $3 billion to digitize the medical records of its 8.2 million members so that it could manage patient care more efficiently.[25] IBM makes extensive use of social software applications such as Lotus Connections to support its 1,796 online communities, having discovered that many of its employees depend on these tools to do their work.[26] In businesses such as public accounting and management consulting, where large numbers of professional staff need cutting-edge technical know-how, companies have developed systems that identify when it is time for certain employees to attend training programs to update their skills and know-how. Many companies have cataloged best-practice information on their intranets to promote faster transfer and implementation organizationwide.[27]

Well-conceived state-of-the-art operating systems not only enable better strategy execution but also strengthen organizational capabilities—sometimes enough to provide a competitive edge over rivals. For example, a company with a differentiation strategy based on superior quality has added capability if it has systems for training personnel in quality techniques, tracking product quality at each production step, and ensuring that all goods shipped meet quality standards. If the systems it employs are advanced systems that have not yet been adopted by rivals, the systems may provide the company with a competitive advantage as long as the costs of deploying the systems do not outweigh their benefits. Similarly, a company striving to be a low-cost provider is competitively stronger if it has an unrivaled benchmarking system that identifies opportunities to implement best practices and drive costs out of the business. Fast-growing companies get an important assist from having capabilities in place to recruit and train new employees in large numbers and from investing in infrastructure that gives them the capability to handle rapid growth as it occurs. It is nearly always better to put infrastructure and support systems in place before they are actually needed than to have to scramble to catch up to customer demand.

Instituting Adequate Information Systems, Performance Tracking, and Controls

Accurate and timely information about daily operations is essential if managers are to gauge how well the strategy execution process is proceeding. Information systems need to cover five broad areas: (1) customer data, (2) operations data, (3) employee data, (4) supplier/partner/collaborative ally data, and (5) financial performance data. All key strategic performance indicators must be tracked and reported in real time where possible. Long the norm, monthly profit-and-loss statements and monthly statistical summaries are fast being replaced with daily statistical updates and even up-to-the-minute performance monitoring, made possible by online technology. Most retail companies have automated online systems that generate daily sales reports for each store and maintain up-to-the-minute inventory and sales records on each item. Manufacturing plants typically generate daily production reports and track labor productivity on every shift. Many retailers and manufacturers have online data systems connecting them with their suppliers that monitor the status of inventories, track shipments and deliveries, and measure defect rates.

Real-time information systems permit company managers to stay on top of implementation initiatives and daily operations and to intervene if things seem to be drifting off course. Tracking key performance indicators, gathering information from operating personnel, quickly identifying and diagnosing problems, and taking corrective actions are all integral pieces of the process of managing strategy implementation and exercising adequate control over operations. A number of companies have recently begun creating "electronic scorecards" for senior managers that gather daily or weekly statistics from different databases about inventory, sales, costs, and sales trends; such information enables these managers to easily stay abreast of what's happening and make better on-the-spot decisions.[28] Telephone companies have elaborate information systems to measure signal quality, connection times, interrupts, wrong connections, billing errors, and other measures of reliability that affect customer service and satisfaction. British Petroleum (BP) has outfitted rail cars carrying hazardous materials with sensors and global-positioning systems (GPS) so that it can track the status, location, and other information about these shipments via satellite and relay the data to its corporate intranet. Companies that rely on empowered customer-contact personnel to act promptly and creatively in pleasing customers have installed online information systems that make essential customer data accessible to such personnel through a few keystrokes; this enables them to respond more effectively to customer inquiries and deliver personalized customer service.

Statistical information gives managers a feel for the numbers; briefings and meetings provide a feel for the latest developments and emerging issues; and personal contacts add a feel for the people dimension. All are good barometers.

> Having state-of-the-art operating systems, information systems, and real-time data is integral to superior strategy execution and operating excellence.

Managers must identify problem areas and deviations from plans before they can take action to get the organization back on course, by either improving the approaches to strategy execution or fine-tuning the strategy. Jeff Bezos, Amazon's CEO, is an ardent proponent of managing by the numbers. As he puts it, "Math-based decisions always trump opinion and judgment. The trouble with most corporations is that they make judgment-based decisions when data-based decisions could be made."[29]

Monitoring Employee Performance Information systems also provide managers with a means for monitoring the performance of empowered workers to see that they are acting within the specified limits.[30] Leaving empowered employees to their own devices in meeting performance standards without appropriate checks and balances can expose an organization to excessive risk.[31] Instances abound of employees' decisions or behavior having gone awry, sometimes costing a company huge sums or producing lawsuits aside from just generating embarrassing publicity.

Scrutinizing daily and weekly operating statistics is one of the important ways in which managers can monitor the results that flow from the actions of empowered subordinates without resorting to constant over-the-shoulder supervision; if the operating results flowing from the actions of empowered employees look good, then it is reasonable to assume that empowerment is working. But close monitoring of operating performance is only one of the control tools at management's disposal. Another valuable lever of control in companies that rely on empowered employees, especially in those that use self-managed work groups or other such teams, is peer-based control. Because peer evaluation is such a powerful control device, companies organized into teams can remove some layers of the management hierarchy and rely on strong peer pressure to keep team members operating between the white lines. This is especially true when a company has the information systems capability to monitor team performance daily or in real time.

TYING REWARDS AND INCENTIVES TO STRATEGY EXECUTION

It is essential that company personnel be enthusiastically committed to executing strategy successfully and achieving performance targets. Company managers typically use an assortment of motivational techniques and rewards to enlist organizationwide commitment to executing the strategic plan. Indeed, a properly designed reward structure is management's most powerful tool for mobilizing organizational commitment to successful strategy execution. But incentives and rewards do more than just strengthen the resolve of company personnel to succeed—they also focus their attention on the accomplishment of specific strategy execution objectives. Not only do they spur the efforts of individuals to achieve those aims, but they also help to coordinate the activities of individuals throughout the organization by aligning their personal motives with the goals of the organization. In this manner, reward systems serve as an indirect type of control mechanism that conserves on the more costly control mechanism of supervisory oversight.

LO 5

Appreciate how and why the use of well-designed incentives and rewards can be management's single most powerful tool for promoting adept strategy execution and operating excellence.

> A properly designed reward structure is management's most powerful tool for mobilizing organizational commitment to successful strategy execution and aligning efforts throughout the organization with strategic priorities.

To win employees' sustained, energetic commitment to the strategy execution process, management must be resourceful in designing and using motivational incentives—both monetary and nonmonetary. The more a manager understands what motivates subordinates and the more he or she relies on motivational incentives as a tool for achieving the targeted strategic and financial results, the greater will be employees' commitment to good day-in, day-out strategy execution and achievement of performance targets.[32]

Incentives and Motivational Practices That Facilitate Good Strategy Execution

> **CORE CONCEPT**
>
> Financial rewards provide **high-powered incentives** when rewards are tied to specific outcome objectives.

Financial incentives generally head the list of motivating tools for gaining wholehearted employee commitment to good strategy execution and focusing attention on strategic priorities. They provide *high-powered* motivation for individuals to increase their efforts when rewards are tied to specific outcome objectives. A company's package of monetary rewards typically includes some combination of base-pay increases, performance bonuses, profit-sharing plans, stock awards, company contributions to employee 401(k) or retirement plans, and piecework incentives (in the case of production workers). But most successful companies and managers also make extensive use of nonmonetary incentives. Some of the most important nonmonetary approaches companies can use to enhance motivation are listed below:[33]

- *Provide attractive perks and fringe benefits.* The various options include full coverage of health insurance premiums, college tuition reimbursement, generous paid vacation time, on-site child care, on-site fitness centers, getaway opportunities at company-owned recreational facilities, personal concierge services, subsidized cafeterias and free lunches, casual dress every day, personal travel services, paid sabbaticals, maternity and paternity leaves, paid leaves to care for ill family members, telecommuting, compressed workweeks (four 10-hour days instead of five 8-hour days), flextime (variable work schedules that accommodate individual needs), college scholarships for children, and relocation services.

- *Give awards and other forms of public recognition to high performers, and celebrate the achievement of organizational goals.* Many companies hold award ceremonies to honor top-performing individuals, teams, and organizational units and to showcase company successes. This can help create healthy competition among units and teams within the company, but it can also create a positive esprit de corps among the organization as a whole. Other examples include special recognition at informal company gatherings or in the company newsletter, tangible tokens of appreciation for jobs well done, and frequent words of praise.

- *Rely on promotion from within whenever possible.* The practice of promoting from within helps bind workers to their employer, and employers to their workers, providing strong incentives for good performance. Moreover, promoting from within helps ensure that people in positions of responsibility have knowledge specific to the business, technology, and operations they are managing.

- *Invite and act on ideas and suggestions from employees.* Many companies find that their best ideas for nuts-and-bolts operating improvements come from the suggestions of employees. Moreover, research indicates that the moves of many companies to push decision making down the line and empower employees increases employees' motivation and satisfaction as well as their productivity. The use of self-managed teams has much the same effect.

- *Create a work atmosphere in which there is genuine caring and mutual respect among workers and between management and employees.* A "family" work environment where people are on a first-name basis and there is strong camaraderie promotes teamwork and cross-unit collaboration.

- *State the strategic vision in inspirational terms so that employees feel they are a part of something very worthwhile in a larger social sense.* There's strong motivating power associated with giving people a chance to be part of something exciting and personally satisfying. Jobs with noble purpose tend to inspire employees to give their all. As described in Chapter 9, this not only increases productivity but reduces turnover and lowers costs for staff recruitment and training as well.

- *Share information with employees about financial performance, strategy, operational measures, market conditions, and competitors' actions.* Broad disclosure and prompt communication send the message that managers trust their workers and regard them as valued partners in the enterprise. Keeping employees in the dark denies them information useful to performing their jobs, prevents them from being intellectually engaged, saps their motivation, and detracts from performance.

- *Maintain attractive office space and facilities.* A workplace environment that is attractive and comfortable usually has decidedly positive effects on employee morale and productivity. An appealing work environment is particularly important when workers are expected to spend long hours at work.

For specific examples of the motivational tactics employed by several prominent companies (many of which appear on *Fortune*'s list of the 100 best companies to work for in America), see Illustration Capsule 11.2.

Striking the Right Balance between Rewards and Punishment

Decisions on salary increases, incentive compensation, promotions, key assignments, and the ways and means of awarding praise and recognition are potent attention-getting, commitment-generating devices. Such decisions seldom escape the closest employee scrutiny, thus saying more about what is expected and who is considered to be doing a good job than virtually any other factor. While most approaches to motivation, compensation, and people management accentuate the positive, companies also combine positive rewards with the risk of punishment. At General Electric, McKinsey & Company, several global public accounting firms, and other companies that look for and expect top-notch individual performance, there's an "up-or-out" policy—managers and professionals whose performance is not good enough to warrant promotion are first denied bonuses and stock awards and eventually weeded out. A number of companies deliberately give employees heavy workloads and tight deadlines—personnel are pushed hard to achieve "stretch" objectives and are expected to put in long hours (nights and weekends if need be). At most companies, senior executives and key personnel in underperforming units are pressured to raise performance to acceptable levels and keep it there or risk being replaced.

Companies have come up with an impressive variety of motivational and reward practices to help create a work environment that energizes employees and promotes better strategy execution. Here's a sampling of what companies are doing:

- Google has a sprawling 20-building headquarters complex known as the Googleplex where its several thousand employees have access to 19 cafes and 60 snack centers, unlimited ice cream, four gyms, heated swimming pools, ping-pong and pool tables, and community bicycles to go from building to building. Management built the Googleplex to be "a dream workplace" and a showcase for environmentally correct building design and construction.

- Lincoln Electric, widely known for its piecework pay scheme and incentive bonus plan, rewards individual productivity by paying workers for each nondefective piece produced. Workers have to correct quality problems on their own time—defects in products used by customers can be traced back to the worker who caused them. Lincoln's piecework plan motivates workers to pay attention to both quality and volume produced. In addition, the company sets aside a substantial portion of its profits above a specified base for worker bonuses. To determine bonus size, Lincoln Electric rates each worker on four equally important performance measures: (1) dependability, (2) quality, (3) output, and (4) ideas and cooperation. The higher a worker's merit rating, the higher the incentive bonus earned; the highest-rated workers in good profit years receive bonuses of as much as 110 percent of their piecework compensation.

- At JM Family Enterprises, a Toyota distributor in Florida, employees get attractive lease options on new Toyotas and enjoy on-site amenities such as a heated lap pool, a fitness center, a free nail salon, free prescriptions delivered by a "pharmacy concierge," and professionally made take-home dinners. Exceptionally high performers are flown to the Bahamas for cruises on the 172-foot company yacht.

- Wegmans, a family-owned grocer with 75 stores on the East Coast of the United States, provides employees with flexible schedules and benefits that include onsite fitness centers. The company's approach to managing people allows it to provide a very high level of customer service not found in other grocery chains. Employees ranging from cashiers to butchers to store managers are all treated equally and viewed as experts in their jobs. Employees receive 50 hours of formal training per year and are allowed to make decisions that they believe are appropriate for their jobs. The company's 2009 annual turnover rate is only 7 percent, which is less than one-half the 19 percent average turnover rate in the U.S. supermarket industry.

- Nordstrom, widely regarded for its superior in-house customer service experience, typically pays its retail salespeople an hourly wage higher than the prevailing rates paid by other department store chains plus a commission on each sale. Spurred by a culture that encourages salespeople to go all out to satisfy customers and to seek out and promote new fashion ideas, Nordstrom salespeople earn nearly 65 percent more than the average sales employee at competing stores. The typical Nordstrom salesperson earns nearly $38,900 per year, but top performers can earn salaries in the six figures.[34] Nordstrom's rules for employees are simple: "Rule #1: Use your good judgment in all situations. There will be no additional rules."

- At W. L. Gore (the maker of GORE-TEX), employees get to choose what project/team they work on, and each team member's compensation is based on other team members' rankings of his or her contribution to the enterprise.
- At Ukrop's Super Markets, a family-owned chain in Virginia, stores stay closed on Sunday; the company pays out 20 percent of pretax profits to employees in the form of quarterly bonuses; and the company picks up the membership tab for employees if they visit their health club 30 times a quarter.
- At biotech leader Amgen, employees get 16 paid holidays, generous vacation time, tuition reimbursements up to $10,000, on-site massages, discounted car-wash services, and the convenience of shopping at on-site farmers' markets.

Sources: Fortune's lists of the 100 best companies to work for in America, 2002, 2004, 2005, 2008, 2009, and 2010; Jefferson Graham, "The Search Engine That Could," *USA Today,* August 26, 2003, p. B3; company Web sites (accessed June 2010).

As a general rule, it is unwise to take off the pressure for good individual and group performance or play down the adverse consequences of shortfalls in performance. There is no evidence that a no-pressure/no-adverse-consequences work environment leads to superior strategy execution or operating excellence. As the CEO of a major bank put it, "There's a deliberate policy here to create a level of anxiety. Winners usually play like they're one touchdown behind."[35] High-performing organizations nearly always have a cadre of ambitious people who relish the opportunity to climb the ladder of success, love a challenge, thrive in a performance-oriented environment, and find some competition and pressure useful to satisfy their own drives for personal recognition, accomplishment, and self-satisfaction.

However, if an organization's motivational approaches and reward structure induce too much stress, internal competitiveness, job insecurity, and fear of unpleasant consequences, the impact on workforce morale and strategy execution can be counterproductive. Evidence shows that managerial initiatives to improve strategy execution should incorporate more positive than negative motivational elements because when cooperation is positively enlisted and rewarded, rather than coerced by orders and threats (implicit or explicit), people tend to respond with more enthusiasm, dedication, creativity, and initiative.[36]

Linking Rewards to Strategically Relevant Performance Outcomes

To create a strategy-supportive system of rewards and incentives, a company must reward people for accomplishing results, not for just dutifully performing assigned tasks. To make the work environment results-oriented, managers need to focus jobholders' attention and energy on what to *achieve* as opposed to what to *do*. It is flawed management to tie incentives and rewards to satisfactory performance of duties and activities instead of desired business outcomes and company achievements.[37] In any job, performing assigned tasks is not equivalent to achieving intended outcomes. Diligently showing up for work and attending to one's job assignment does not, by itself, guarantee results. Employee productivity among employees at Best Buy's corporate headquarters rose by 35 percent after the company began to focus on the results of each employee's work rather than on employees' willingness to come to work early and stay late.

> Incentives must be based on accomplishing the right results, not on dutifully performing assigned tasks.

The key to creating a reward system that promotes good strategy execution is to make measures of good business performance and good strategy execution the *dominating basis* for designing incentives, evaluating individual and group efforts, and handing out rewards.

Ideally, performance targets should be set for every organizational unit, every manager, every team or work group, and perhaps every employee—targets that measure whether strategy execution is progressing satisfactorily. If the company's strategy is to be a low-cost provider, the incentive system must reward actions and achievements that result in lower costs. If the company has a differentiation strategy based on superior quality and service, the incentive system must reward such outcomes as Six Sigma defect rates, infrequent need for product repair, low numbers of customer complaints, speedy order processing and delivery, and high levels of customer satisfaction. If a company's growth is predicated on a strategy of new product innovation, incentives should be tied to factors such as the percentages of revenues and profits coming from newly introduced products.

Incentive compensation for top executives is typically tied to such financial measures as revenue and earnings growth, stock price performance, return on investment, and creditworthiness or to strategic measures such as market share growth. However, incentives for department heads, teams, and individual workers may be tied to performance outcomes more closely related to their strategic area of responsibility. In manufacturing, incentive compensation may be tied to unit manufacturing costs, on-time production and shipping, defect rates, the number and extent of work stoppages due to equipment breakdowns, and so on. In sales and marketing, there may be incentives for achieving dollar sales or unit volume targets, market share, sales penetration of each target customer group, the fate of newly introduced products, the frequency of customer complaints, the number of new accounts acquired, and customer satisfaction. Which performance measures to base incentive compensation on depends on the situation—the priority placed on various financial and strategic objectives, the requirements for strategic and competitive success, and what specific results are needed in different facets of the business to keep strategy execution on track.

Illustration Capsule 11.3 provides a vivid example of how one company has designed incentives linked directly to outcomes reflecting good execution.

Guidelines for Designing Effective Incentive Compensation Systems   As explained above, the first principle in designing an effective incentive compensation system is to tie rewards to performance outcomes directly linked to good strategy execution and targeted strategic and financial objectives. But for a company's reward system to truly motivate organization members, inspire their best efforts, and sustain high levels of productivity, it is equally important to observe the following additional guidelines in designing and administering the reward system:

- *Make the financial incentives a major, not minor, piece of the total compensation package.* Performance payoffs must be at least 10 to 12 percent of base salary to have much impact. Incentives that amount to 20 percent or more of total compensation are big attention-getters, likely to really drive individual or team efforts. Incentives amounting to less than 5 percent of total compensation have a comparatively weak motivational impact. Moreover, the payoff for high-performing individuals and teams must be meaningfully greater than the payoff for average performers, and the payoff for average performers meaningfully bigger than that for below-average performers.

- *Have incentives that extend to all managers and all workers, not just top management.* Lower-level managers and employees are just as likely as senior executives to be motivated by the possibility of lucrative rewards.

ILLUSTRATION CAPSULE 11.3

Nucor Corporation: Tying Incentives Directly to Strategy Execution

The strategy at Nucor Corporation, one of the three largest steel producers in the United States, is to be *the* low-cost producer of steel products. Because labor costs are a significant fraction of total cost in the steel business, successful implementation of Nucor's low-cost leadership strategy entails achieving lower labor costs per ton of steel than competitors' costs. Nucor management uses an incentive system to promote high worker productivity and drive labor costs per ton below rivals'. Each plant's workforce is organized into production teams (each assigned to perform particular functions), and weekly production targets are established for each team. Base-pay scales are set at levels comparable to wages for similar manufacturing jobs in the local areas where Nucor has plants, but workers can earn a 1 percent bonus for each 1 percent that their output exceeds target levels. If a production team exceeds its weekly production target by 10 percent, team members receive a 10 percent bonus in their next paycheck; if a team exceeds its quota by 20 percent, team members earn a 20 percent bonus. Bonuses, paid every two weeks, are based on the prior two weeks' actual production levels measured against the targets.

Nucor's piece-rate incentive plan has produced impressive results. The production teams put forth exceptional effort; it is not uncommon for most teams to beat their weekly production targets anywhere from 20 to 50 percent. When added to their base pay, the bonuses earned by Nucor workers make Nucor's work force among the highest-paid in the U.S. steel industry. From a management perspective, the incentive system has resulted

in Nucor having labor productivity levels 10 to 20 percent above the average of the unionized workforces at several of its largest rivals, which in turn has given Nucor a significant labor cost advantage over most rivals.

After years of record-setting profits, Nucor struggled in the economic downturn of 2008–2010, along with the manufacturers and builders who buy its steel. But while bonuses have dwindled, Nucor showed remarkable loyalty to its production workers, avoiding layoffs by having employees get ahead on maintenance, perform work formerly done by contractors, and search for cost savings. Morale at the company has remained high and Nucor's CEO Daniel DiMicco has received thank-you notes from grateful employees by the basketful. As industry growth resumes, Nucor will have a well-trained workforce still in place, more committed than ever to achieving the kind of productivity for which Nucor is justifiably famous. When the turnaround comes, DiMicco has good reason to expect Nucor to be "first out of the box."

Sources: Company Web site (accessed July 2010); N. Byrnes, "Pain, but No Layoffs at Nucor," *Bloomberg Businessweek,* March 26, 2009.

- *Administer the reward system with scrupulous objectivity and fairness.* If performance standards are set unrealistically high or if individual/group performance evaluations are not accurate and well documented, dissatisfaction with the system will overcome any positive benefits.

- *Ensure that the performance targets each individual or team is expected to achieve involve outcomes that the individual or team can personally affect.* The role of incentives is to enhance individual commitment and channel behavior in beneficial directions. This role is not well served when the performance measures by which company personnel are judged are outside their arena of influence.

- *Keep the time between achieving the targeted performance outcome and the payment of the reward as short as possible.* Companies like Nucor Steel and Continental Airlines have discovered that weekly or monthly payments for good performance work much better than annual payments. Nucor pays weekly bonuses based on prior-week production levels, while Continental pays employees a bonus whenever actual on-time flight performance meets or beats the monthly on-time target. Annual bonus payouts work best for higher-level managers and for situations where the outcome target relates to overall company profitability or stock price performance.

- *Avoid rewarding effort rather than results.* While it is tempting to reward people who have tried hard yet fallen short of achieving performance targets because of circumstances beyond their control, it is ill advised. The problem with making exceptions for unknowable, uncontrollable, or unforeseeable circumstances is that once "good excuses" start to creep into justifying rewards for subpar results, the door is open for all kinds of reasons why actual performance has failed to match targeted performance. A "no excuses" standard is more even-handed, easier to administer, and more conducive to creating a results-oriented work climate.

> The unwavering standard for judging whether individuals, teams, and organizational units have done a good job must be whether they meet or beat performance targets that reflect good strategy execution.

Once an organization's incentive plan is designed, it must be communicated and explained. Everybody needs to understand how his or her incentive compensation is calculated and how individual/group performance targets contribute to organizational performance targets. The pressure to continuously improve strategy execution and achieve performance objectives should be unrelenting, with no loopholes for rewarding shortfalls in performance. People at all levels must be held accountable for carrying out their assigned parts of the strategic plan, and they must understand that their rewards are based on the caliber of results achieved. But with the pressure to perform should come meaningful rewards. Without an ample payoff, the system breaks down, and managers are left with the less workable options of issuing orders, trying to enforce compliance, and depending on the goodwill of employees.

KEY POINTS

1. Implementing and executing a new or different strategy calls for managers to identify the resource requirements of each new strategic initiative and then consider whether the current pattern of resource allocation and the budgets of the various subunits are suitable.

2. Company policies and procedures facilitate strategy execution when they are designed to fit the strategy and its objectives. Anytime a company alters its strategy, managers should review existing policies and operating procedures and replace those that are out of sync. Well conceived policies and procedures aid the task of strategy execution by (1) providing top-down guidance to company personnel regarding how certain things need to be done and

what the boundaries are on independent actions and decisions, (2) enforcing consistency in the performance of strategy-critical activities, thereby improving the quality of the strategy execution effort and aligning the actions of company personnel, however widely dispersed, and (3) promoting the creation of a work climate conducive to good strategy execution.

3. Competent strategy execution entails visible unyielding managerial commitment to best practices and continuous improvement. Benchmarking, best-practice adoption, business process reengineering, total quality management (TQM), and Six Sigma programs are important process management tools for promoting better strategy execution.

4. Company strategies can't be implemented or executed well without a number of support systems to carry on business operations. Real-time information systems and control systems further aid the cause of good strategy execution.

5. Strategy-supportive motivational practices and reward systems are powerful management tools for gaining employee commitment and focusing their attention on the strategy execution goals. The key to creating a reward system that promotes good strategy execution is to make measures of good business performance and good strategy execution the *dominating basis* for designing incentives, evaluating individual and group efforts, and handing out rewards. Positive motivational practices generally work better than negative ones, but there is a place for both. While financial rewards provide high-powered incentives, there's also place for nonmonetary incentives. For an incentive compensation system to work well, (1) the monetary payoff should be a major percentage of the compensation package, (2) the use of incentives should extend to all managers and workers, (3) the system should be administered with care and fairness, (4) each individual's performance targets should involve outcomes the person can personally affect, (5) rewards should promptly follow the determination of good performance, and (6) rewards should be given for results and not just effort.

ASSURANCE OF LEARNING EXERCISES

LO 3

1. Read some of the recent Six Sigma articles posted at isixsigma.com. Prepare a one-page report to your instructor detailing how Six Sigma is being used in various companies and what benefits these companies are reaping from Six Sigma implementation.

LO 3

2. Review the profiles and applications of the latest Malcolm Baldrige National Quality Award recipients at www.baldrige.nist.gov. What are the standout features of the companies' approaches to managing operations? What do you find impressive about the companies' policies and procedures, use of best practices, emphasis on continuous improvement, and use of rewards and incentives?

LO 4

3. Using Google or your university library's access to online business periodicals, search for articles discussing radio frequency identification (RFID) technology. Prepare a 1–2 page report that discusses how information systems that incorporate RFID technology provide more accurate and timely supplier data and have improved strategy execution at various companies.

LO 5

4. Consult the issue of *Fortune* containing the latest annual "100 Best Companies to Work For" (usually a late-January or early-February issue), or else go to www.fortune.com to access the list, and identify at least five compensation incentives and work practices that these companies use to enhance employee motivation and reward them for good strategic and financial performance. You should identify compensation methods and work practices that are different from those cited in Illustration Capsule 11.2.

EXERCISES FOR SIMULATION PARTICIPANTS

LO 1

1. Have you and your co-managers allocated ample resources to strategy-critical areas? If so, explain how these investments have contributed to good strategy execution and improved company performance.

LO 3

2. Is benchmarking data available in the simulation exercise in which you are participating? If so, do you and your co-managers regularly study the benchmarking data to see how well your company is doing? Do you consider the benchmarking information provided to be valuable? Why or why not? Cite three recent instances in which your examination of the benchmarking statistics has caused you and your co-managers to take corrective actions to boost company performance.

LO 2, LO 3, LO 4

3. What actions, if any, is your company taking to pursue continuous improvement in how it performs certain value chain activities?

LO 5

4. Does your company have opportunities to use incentive compensation techniques? If so, explain your company's approach to incentive compensation. Is there any hard evidence you can cite that indicates your company's use of incentive compensation techniques has worked? For example, have your company's compensation incentives actually increased productivity? Can you cite evidence indicating that the productivity gains have resulted in lower labor

costs? If the productivity gains have *not* translated into lower labor costs, is it fair to say that your company's use of incentive compensation is a failure?

LO 2, LO 3, LO 4

5. Are you and your co-managers consciously trying to achieve "operating excellence"? What are the indicators of operating excellence at your company? Based on these indicators, how well does your company measure up?

LO 3

6. What hard evidence can you cite that indicates your company's management team is doing a *better* or *worse* job of achieving operating excellence and executing your strategy than are the management teams at rival companies?

ENDNOTES

[1] For a discussion of the value of benchmarking in implementing and executing strategy, see Christopher E. Bogan and Michael J. English, *Benchmarking for Best Practices: Winning through Innovative Adaptation* (New York: McGraw-Hill, 1994) chaps. 2 and 6; Mustafa Ungan, "Factors Affecting the Adoption of Manufacturing Best Practices," *Benchmarking: An International Journal* 11, no. 5 (2004), pp. 504–20; Paul Hyland and Ron Beckett, "Learning to Compete: The Value of Internal Benchmarking," *Benchmarking: An International Journal* 9, no. 3 (2002), pp. 293–304; Yoshinobu Ohinata, "Benchmarking: The Japanese Experience," *Long-Range Planning* 27, no. 4 (August 1994), pp. 48–53.

[2] www.businessdictionary.com/definition/best-practice.html (accessed December 2, 2009).

[3] M. Hammer and J. Champy, *Reengineering the Corporation: A Manifesto for Business Revolution* (New York: Harper Collins Publishers, 1993), pp. 26–27.

[4] Information on the greeting card industry is posted at www.answers.com (accessed July 8, 2009), and "Reengineering: Beyond the Buzzword," *BusinessWeek,* May 24, 1993, www.businessweek.com (accessed July 8, 2009).

[5] Gene Hall, Jim Rosenthal, and Judy Wade, "How to Make Reengineering Really Work," *Harvard Business Review* 71, no. 6 (November–December 1993), pp. 119–31.

[6] For more information on business process reengineering and how well it has worked in various companies, see James Brian Quinn, *Intelligent Enterprise* (New York: Free Press, 1992), p. 162; Ann Majchrzak and Qianwei Wang, "Breaking the Functional Mind-Set in Process Organizations," *Harvard Business Review* 74, no. 5 (September–October 1996), pp. 93–99; Stephen L. Walston, Lawton. R. Burns, and John R. Kimberly, "Does Reengineering Really Work? An Examination of the Context and Outcomes of Hospital Reengineering Initiatives," *Health*

Services Research 34, no. 6 (February 2000), pp. 1363–88; Allessio Ascari, Melinda Rock, and Soumitra Dutta, "Reengineering and Organizational Change: Lessons from a Comparative Analysis of Company Experiences," *European Management Journal* 13, no. 1 (March 1995), pp. 1–13. For a review of why some company personnel embrace process reengineering and some don't, see Ronald J. Burke, "Process Reengineering: Who Embraces It and Why?" *TQM Magazine* 16, no. 2 (2004), pp. 114–19.

[7] For some of the seminal discussions of what TQM is and how it works, written by ardent enthusiasts of the technique, see M. Walton, *The Deming Management Method* (New York: Pedigree, 1986); J. Juran, *Juran on Quality by Design* (New York: Free Press, 1992); Philip Crosby, *Quality Is Free: The Act of Making Quality Certain* (New York: McGraw-Hill, 1979); S. George, *The Baldrige Quality System* (New York: Wiley, 1992). For a critique of TQM, see Mark J. Zbaracki, "The Rhetoric and Reality of Total Quality Management," *Administrative Science Quarterly* 43, no 3 (September 1998), pp. 602–36.

[8] For a discussion of the shift in work environment and culture that TQM entails, see Robert T. Amsden, Thomas W. Ferratt, and Davida M. Amsden, "TQM: Core Paradigm Changes," *Business Horizons* 39, no. 6 (November–December 1996), pp. 6–14.

[9] For easy-to-understand overviews of what Six Sigma is all about, see Peter S. Pande and Larry Holpp, *What Is Six Sigma?* (New York: McGraw-Hill, 2002); Jiju Antony, "Some Pros and Cons of Six Sigma: An Academic Perspective," *TQM Magazine* 16, no. 4 (2004), pp. 303–6; Peter S. Pande, Robert P. Neuman, and Roland R. Cavanagh, *The Six Sigma Way: How GE, Motorola and Other Top Companies Are Honing Their Performance* (New York: McGraw-Hill, 2000); Joseph Gordon and M. Joseph Gordon, Jr., *Six Sigma Quality for Business and Manufacture* (New York: Elsevier, 2002). For how Six Sigma can be

used in smaller companies, see Godecke Wessel and Peter Burcher, "Six Sigma for Small and Medium-Sized Enterprises," *TQM Magazine* 16, no. 4 (2004), pp. 264–72.

[10] Based on information posted at www.isixsigma.com (accessed November 4, 2002).

[11] Kennedy Smith, "Six Sigma for the Service Sector," *Quality Digest Magazine,* May 2003, www.qualitydigest.com (accessed September 28, 2003).

[12] Del Jones, "Taking the Six Sigma Approach," *USA Today,* October 31, 2002, p. 5B.

[13] Pande, Neuman, and Cavanagh, *The Six Sigma Way,* pp. 5–6.

[14] Smith, "Six Sigma for the Service Sector."

[15] Jones, "Taking the Six Sigma Approach," p. 5B.

[16] See, for example, "A Dark Art No More," *Economist* 385, no. 8550 (October 13, 2007), p. 10; Brian Hindo, "At 3M, a Struggle between Efficiency and Creativity," *BusinessWeek,* June 11, 2007, pp. 8–16.

[17] As quoted in "A Dark Art No More."

[18] Hindo, "At 3M, a Struggle between Efficiency and Creativity."

[19] For a discussion of approaches to pursuing radical or disruptive innovations while also seeking incremental gains in efficiency, see Charles A. O'Reilly and Michael L. Tushman, "The Ambidextrous Organization," *Harvard Business Review* 82, no. 4 (April 2004), pp. 74–81.

[20] Terry Nels Lee, Stanley E. Fawcett, and Jason Briscoe, "Benchmarking the Challenge to Quality Program Implementation," *Benchmarking: An International Journal* 9, no. 4 (2002), pp. 374–87.

[21] For a recent study documenting the imperatives of establishing a supportive culture, see Milan Ambrož, "Total Quality System as a Product of the Empowered Corporate Culture," *TQM Magazine* 16, no. 2 (2004), pp. 93–104. Research confirming the factors that are important in making TQM programs successful in both Europe and the United States is

presented in Nick A. Dayton, "The Demise of Total Quality Management," *TQM Magazine* 15, no. 6 (2003), pp. 391–96.

[22] Judy D. Olian and Sara L. Rynes, "Making Total Quality Work: Aligning Organizational Processes, Performance Measures, and Stakeholders," *Human Resource Management* 30, no. 3 (Fall 1991), pp. 310–11; Paul S. Goodman and Eric D. Darr, "Exchanging Best Practices Information through Computer-Aided Systems," *Academy of Management Executive* 10, no. 2 (May 1996), p. 7.

[23] Thomas C. Powell, "Total Quality Management as Competitive Advantage," *Strategic Management Journal* 16 (1995), pp. 15–37. See also Richard M. Hodgetts, "Quality Lessons from America's Baldrige Winners," *Business Horizons* 37, no. 4 (July–August 1994), pp. 74–79; Richard Reed, David J. Lemak, and Joseph C. Montgomery, "Beyond Process: TQM Content and Firm Performance," *Academy of Management Review* 21, no. 1 (January 1996), pp. 173–202.

[24] Based on information at www.otiselevator.com (accessed July 9, 2009).

[25] "The Web Smart 50," *BusinessWeek*, November 21, 2005, pp. 87–88.

[26] Aishah Mustapha, "Net Value: Social Software a New Way to Work," *The Edge Malaysia (Weekly)*, February 16, 2009.

[27] Such systems speed organizational learning by providing fast, efficient communication, creating an organizational memory for collecting and retaining best-practice information, and permitting people all across the organization to exchange information and updated solutions. See Goodman and Darr, "Exchanging Best Practices Information through Computer-Aided Systems," pp. 7–17.

[28] "The Web Smart 50," pp. 85–90.

[29] Fred Vogelstein, "Winning the Amazon Way," *Fortune* 147, no. 10 (May 26, 2003), pp. 60–69.

[30] For a discussion of the need for putting appropriate boundaries on the actions of empowered employees and possible control and monitoring systems that can be used, see Robert Simons, "Control in an Age of Empowerment," *Harvard Business Review* 73 (March–April 1995), pp. 80–88.

[31] Ibid. Also see David C. Band and Gerald Scanlan, "Strategic Control through Core Competencies," *Long Range Planning* 28, no. 2 (April 1995), pp. 102–14.

[32] The importance of motivating and empowering workers so as to create a working environment that is highly conducive to good strategy execution is discussed in Stanley E. Fawcett, Gary K. Rhoads, and Phillip Burnah, "People as the Bridge to Competitiveness: Benchmarking the 'ABCs' of an Empowered Workforce," *Benchmarking: An International Journal* 11 no. 4 (2004), pp. 346–60.

[33] Jeffrey Pfeffer and John F. Veiga, "Putting People First for Organizational Success," *Academy of Management Executive* 13, no. 2 (May 1999), pp. 37–45; Linda K. Stroh and Paula M. Caliguiri, "Increasing Global Competitiveness through Effective People Management," *Journal of World Business* 33, no. 1 (Spring 1998), pp. 1–16; articles in *Fortune* on the 100 best companies to work for (various issues).

[34] Jenni Mintz, "Nordstrom Opening in Three Weeks: Company Plans 'Tailgate Party for Women' and Other Events," *Ventura County Star* (California), *McClatchy-Tribune Regional News*, August 12, 2008.

[35] As quoted in John P. Kotter and James L. Heskett, *Corporate Culture and Performance* (New York: Free Press, 1992), p. 91.

[36] Clayton M. Christensen, Matt Marx, and Howard Stevenson, "The Tools of Cooperation and Change," *Harvard Business Review* 84, no. 10 (October 2006), pp. 73–80.

[37] See Steven Kerr, "On the Folly of Rewarding A While Hoping for B," *Academy of Management Executive* 9, no. 1 (February 1995), pp. 7–14; S. Kerr and E. Davies, "Risky Business: The New Pay Game," *Fortune* 134, no. 2 (July 22, 1996) pp. 94–96; and Doran Twer, "Linking Pay to Business Objectives," *Journal of Business Strategy* 15, no. 4 (July–August 1994), pp. 15–18.

CHAPTER 12

CORPORATE CULTURE AND LEADERSHIP

Keys to Good Strategy Execution

> The biggest levers you've got to change a company are strategy, structure, and culture. If I could pick two, I'd pick strategy and culture.
>
> **—Wayne Leonard**
> *Chairman and CEO, Entergy Corporation*

> Success goes to those with a corporate culture that assures the ability to anticipate and meet customer demand.
>
> **—Tadashi Okamura**
> *Former Chairman and CEO of Toshiba Corporation*

> The soft stuff is always harder than the hard stuff.
>
> **—Roger Enrico**
> *Former CEO of PepsiCo*

LEARNING OBJECTIVES

LO 1. Be able to identify the key features of a company's corporate culture and appreciate the role of a company's core values and ethical standards in building corporate culture.

LO 2. Gain an understanding of how and why a company's culture can aid the drive for proficient strategy execution and operating excellence.

LO 3. Learn the kinds of actions management can take to change a problem corporate culture.

LO 4. Understand what constitutes effective managerial leadership in achieving superior strategy execution.

In the previous two chapters, we examined six of the managerial tasks that drive good strategy execution: building a capable organization, marshaling the needed resources and steering them to strategy-critical operating units, establishing appropriate policies and procedures, driving continuous improvement in value chain activities, creating the necessary operating systems, and providing the incentives needed to ensure employee commitment to the strategy execution process. In this chapter, we explore the two remaining managerial tasks that contribute to good strategy execution: creating a strategy-supportive corporate culture and exerting the internal leadership needed to drive the implementation of strategic initiatives forward and achieve higher plateaus of operating excellence.

INSTILLING A CORPORATE CULTURE THAT PROMOTES GOOD STRATEGY EXECUTION

Every company has its own unique culture. The character of a company's culture or work climate is a product of the core values and business principles that executives espouse, the standards of what is ethically acceptable and what is not, the work practices and norms of behavior that define "how we do things around here," the approach to people management and style of operating, the "chemistry" and the "personality" that permeates the work environment, and the stories that get told over and over to illustrate and reinforce the company's values, business practices, and traditions. The meshing together of shared values, beliefs, business principles, and traditions into a style of operating, behavioral norms, ingrained attitudes, and work atmosphere defines a company's **corporate culture.**[1] A company's culture is important because it influences the organization's actions and approaches to conducting business—in a very real sense, the culture is the company's automatic, self-replicating "operating system"—it can be thought of as the organizational DNA.[2] As we learned in Chapter 4, a superior corporate culture can also be a source of sustainable competitive advantage under some circumstances.

Corporate cultures vary widely. For instance, the bedrock of Walmart's culture is dedication to zealous pursuit of low costs and frugal operating practices, a strong work ethic, ritualistic headquarters meetings to exchange ideas and review problems, and company executives' commitment to visiting stores, listening to customers, and soliciting suggestions from employees. General Electric's culture is founded on a hard-driving, results-oriented atmosphere; extensive cross-business sharing of ideas, best practices, and learning; reliance on "workout sessions" to identify, debate, and resolve burning issues; a commitment to Six Sigma quality; and a globalized approach to operations. At U.S. upscale department store chain, Nordstrom, the corporate culture is centered on delivering exceptional service to customers—the company's motto is "Respond to unreasonable customer requests," and each out-of-the-ordinary request is seen as an opportunity for a "heroic" act by an employee that can further the company's reputation for unparalleled customer service. Nordstrom makes a point of promoting employees noted for their heroic acts and dedication to outstanding service; the company motivates its salespeople with a commission-based compensation system that enables Nordstrom's best salespeople to earn more than double what other department stores pay. Illustration Capsule 12.1 relates how Google and Albert-Culver describe their corporate cultures.

Identifying the Key Features of a Company's Corporate Culture

A company's corporate culture is mirrored in the character or "personality" of its work environment—the factors that underlie how the company tries to conduct its business and the behaviors that are held in high esteem. Some of these factors are readily apparent, and others operate quite subtly. The chief things to look for include the following:

- The values, business principles, and ethical standards that management preaches and *practices*—these are the key to a company's culture, but actions speak much louder than words here.
- The company's approach to people management and the official policies, procedures, and operating practices that provide guidelines for the behavior of company personnel.
- The atmosphere and spirit that pervades the work climate. Is the workplace vibrant and fun? Methodical and all business? Tense and harried? Highly competitive and politicized? Are people excited about their work and emotionally connected to the company's business, or are they just there to draw a paycheck? Is there an emphasis on empowered worker creativity, or do people have little discretion in how jobs are done?
- The way managers and employees interact and relate to one another—the reliance on teamwork and open communication, the extent to which there is good camaraderie, whether people are called by their first names, whether co-workers spend little or lots of time together outside the workplace, and what the dress codes are (the accepted styles of attire and whether there are casual days).
- The strength of peer pressure to do things in particular ways and conform to expected norms—what actions and behaviors are encouraged on a peer-to-peer basis?

Founded in 1998 by Larry Page and Sergey Brin, two Ph.D. students in computer science at Stanford University, Google has become world-renowned for its search engine technology. Google.com was the most frequently visited Internet site in 2009, attracting over 844 million unique visitors monthly from around the world. Google has some unique ways of operating, and its culture is also rather quirky. The company describes its culture as follows:

Though growing rapidly, Google still maintains a small company feel. At lunchtime, almost everyone eats in the office café, sitting at whatever table has an opening and enjoying conversations with Googlers from different teams. Our commitment to innovation depends on everyone being comfortable sharing ideas and opinions. Every employee is a hands-on contributor, and everyone wears several hats. Because we believe that each Googler is an equally important part of our success, no one hesitates to pose questions directly to Larry or Sergey in our weekly all-hands ("TGIF") meetings—or spike a volleyball across the net at a corporate officer.

We are aggressively inclusive in our hiring, and we favor ability over experience. We have offices around the world and dozens of languages are spoken by Google staffers, from Turkish to Telugu. The result is a team that reflects the global audience Google serves. When not at work, Googlers pursue interests from cross-country cycling to wine tasting, from flying to frisbee.

As we continue to grow, we are always looking for those who share a commitment to creating search perfection and having a great time doing it.

Our corporate headquarters, fondly nicknamed the Googleplex, is located in Mountain View, California. Today it's one of our many offices around the globe. While our offices are not identical, they tend to share some essential elements. Here are a few things you might see in a Google workspace:

- *Local expressions of each location, from a mural in Buenos Aires to ski gondolas in Zurich, showcasing each office's region and personality.*
- *Bicycles or scooters for efficient travel between meetings; dogs; lava lamps; massage chairs; large inflatable balls.*
- *Googlers sharing cubes, yurts and huddle rooms—and very few solo offices.*
- *Laptops everywhere—standard issue for mobile coding, email on the go and note-taking.*
- *Foosball, pool tables, volleyball courts, assorted video games, pianos, ping pong tables, and gyms that offer yoga and dance classes.*
- *Grassroots employee groups for all interests, like meditation, film, wine tasting and salsa dancing.*
- *Healthy lunches and dinners for all staff at a variety of cafés.*
- *Break rooms packed with a variety of snacks and drinks to keep Googlers going.*

The Alberto-Culver Company, with fiscal 2009 revenues of more than $1.4 billion, is the producer and marketer of Alberto VO5, TRESemmé, Motions, Soft & Beautiful, Just for Me, and Nexxus hair care products; St. Ives skin care products; and such brands as Molly McButter, Mrs. Dash, Sugar Twin, and Static Guard. Alberto-Culver brands are sold in more than 120 countries.

At the careers section of its Web site, the company described its culture in the following words:

Building careers is as important to us as building brands. We believe that passionate people create powerful growth. We believe in a workplace built on values and believe our best people display those same values in their families and their communities. We believe in recognizing and rewarding accomplishment and celebrating our victories.

We believe the best ideas work their way—quickly—up an organization, not down. We believe that we should take advantage of every ounce of your talent on teams and cross-functional activities, not just assign you to a box.

We believe in open communication. We believe that you can improve what you measure, so we survey and spot check all the time. For that same reason, everyone has specific goals so that their expectations are in line with their managers' and the company's.

We believe that victory is a team accomplishment. We believe in personal development. We believe if you talk with us you will catch our enthusiasm and want to be a part of the Alberto-Culver team.

Sources: Information posted at www.google.com and www.alberto.com (accessed June 30, 2010); S. McClellan, "Alberto Culver Launches Global Search: The Client's Annual U.S. Ad Spending Alone Touches $100 Mil.," *Adweek*, January 29, 2010, www.adweek.com/aw/content_display/news/account-activity/e3i68e64a3cf2727350dd0013083626e8ae.

- The actions and behaviors that are explicitly encouraged and rewarded by management in the form of compensation and promotion.
- The company's revered traditions and oft-repeated stories about "heroic acts" and "how we do things around here."
- The manner in which the company deals with external stakeholders (particularly vendors and local communities where it has operations)—whether it treats suppliers as business partners or prefers hard-nosed, arm's-length business arrangements, and the strength and genuineness of the commitment to corporate citizenship and environmental sustainability.

The values, beliefs, and practices that undergird a company's culture can come from anywhere in the organizational hierarchy, most often representing the business philosophy and managerial style of influential executives but also resulting from exemplary actions on the part of company personnel and consensus agreement about appropriate norms of behavior.[3] Typically, key elements of the culture originate with a founder or certain strong leaders who articulated them as a set of business principles, company policies, operating approaches, and ways of dealing with employees, customers, vendors, shareholders, and local communities where the company has operations. Over time, these cultural underpinnings take root, become embedded in how the company conducts its business, come to be accepted by company managers and employees alike, and then persist as new employees are encouraged to embrace the company values and adopt the implied attitudes, behaviors, and work practices.

The Role of Core Values and Ethics

The foundation of a company's corporate culture nearly always resides in its dedication to certain core values and the bar it sets for ethical behavior. The culture-shaping significance of core values and ethical behaviors accounts for one reason why so many companies have developed a formal values statement and a code of ethics. Many executives want the work climate at their companies to mirror certain values and ethical standards, partly because they are personally committed to these values and ethical standards but also because they are convinced that adherence to such values and ethical principles will promote better strategy execution, make the company a better performer, and improve its image.[4] And, not incidentally, strongly ingrained values and ethical standards reduce the likelihood of lapses in ethical and socially approved behavior that mar a company's reputation and put its financial performance and market standing at risk, as discussed in Chapter 9.

> A company's culture is grounded in and shaped by its core values and ethical standards.

As depicted in Figure 12.1, a company's stated core values and ethical principles have two roles in the culture-building process. First, a company that works hard at putting its stated core values and ethical principles into practice fosters a work climate in which company personnel share strongly held convictions about how the company's business is to be conducted. Second, the stated values and ethical principles provide company personnel with guidance about the manner in which they are to do their jobs—which behaviors and ways of doing things are approved (and expected) and which are out-of-bounds. These values-based and ethics-based cultural norms serve as yardsticks for gauging the appropriateness of particular actions, decisions, and behaviors, thus helping steer company personnel toward both doing things right and doing the right thing.

Figure 12.1   **The Two Culture-Building Roles of a Company's Core Values and Ethical Standards**

Transforming Core Values and Ethical Standards into Cultural Norms

Once values and ethical standards have been formally adopted, they must be institutionalized in the company's policies and practices and embedded in the conduct of company personnel. This can be done in a number of different ways.[5] Tradition-steeped companies with a rich folklore rely heavily on word-of-mouth indoctrination and the power of tradition to instill values and enforce ethical conduct. But most companies employ a variety of techniques, drawing on some or all of the following:

> A company's values statement and code of ethics communicate expectations of how employees should conduct themselves in the workplace.

1. Giving explicit attention to values and ethics in recruiting and hiring to screen out applicants who do not exhibit compatible character traits.

2. Incorporating the statement of values and the code of ethics into orientation programs for new employees and training courses for managers and employees.

3. Having senior executives frequently reiterate the importance and role of company values and ethical principles at company events and in internal communications to employees.

4. Using values statements and codes of ethical conduct as benchmarks for judging the appropriateness of company policies and operating practices.

5. Making the display of core values and ethical principles a big factor in evaluating each person's job performance—there's no better way to win the attention and commitment of company personnel than by using the degree to which individuals observe core values and ethical standards as a basis for compensation increases and promotion.

6. Making sure that managers, from the CEO down to frontline supervisors, are diligent in stressing the importance of ethical conduct and observance of core values. Line managers at all levels must give serious and continuous attention to the task of explaining how the values and ethical code apply in their areas.

7. Encouraging everyone to use his or her influence in helping enforce observance of core values and ethical standards—strong peer pressure to exhibit core values and ethical standards is a deterrent to wayward behavior.

8. Periodically having ceremonial occasions to recognize individuals and groups who display the company values and ethical principles.

9. Instituting ethics enforcement procedures.

To deeply ingrain the stated core values and high ethical standards, companies must turn them into *strictly enforced cultural norms.* They must put a stake in the ground, making it unequivocally clear that living up to the company's values and ethical standards has to be "a way of life" at the company and that there will be little toleration of errant behavior.

The Role of Stories   Frequently, a significant part of a company's culture is captured in the stories that get told over and over again to illustrate to newcomers the importance of certain values and the depth of commitment that various company personnel have displayed. One of the folktales at FedEx, world renowned for the reliability of its next-day package delivery guarantee, is about a deliveryman who had been given the wrong key to a FedEx drop box. Rather than leave the packages in the drop box until the next day when the right key was available, the deliveryman unbolted the drop box from its base, loaded it into the truck, and took it back to the station. There, the box was pried open and the contents removed and sped on their way to their destination the next day. Nordstrom keeps a scrapbook commemorating the heroic acts of its employees and uses it as a regular reminder of the above-and-beyond-the-call-of-duty behaviors that employees are encouraged to display. When a customer was unable to find a shoe she was looking for at Nordstrom, a salesman found the shoe at a competing store and had it shipped to her, at Nordstrom's expense.[6] At Frito-Lay, there are dozens of stories about truck drivers who went to extraordinary lengths in overcoming adverse weather conditions in order to make scheduled deliveries to retail customers and keep store shelves stocked with Frito-Lay products. At Microsoft, there are stories of the long hours programmers put in, the emotional peaks and valleys in encountering and overcoming coding problems, the exhilaration of completing a complex program on schedule, the satisfaction of working on cutting-edge projects, the rewards of being part of a team responsible for a popular new software program, and the tradition of competing aggressively. Such stories serve the valuable purpose of illustrating the kinds of behavior the company reveres and inspiring company personnel to perform similarly. Moreover, each retelling of a legendary story puts a bit more peer pressure on company personnel to display core values and do their part in keeping the company's traditions alive.

Perpetuating the Culture   Once established, company cultures are perpetuated in six important ways: (1) by screening and selecting new employees that will mesh well with the culture, (2) by systematic indoctrination of new members in the culture's fundamentals, (3) by the efforts of senior managers to reiterate core values in daily conversations and pronouncements, (4) by the telling and retelling of company legends, (5) by regular ceremonies honoring employees who display desired cultural behaviors, and (6) by visibly rewarding those who display cultural norms and penalizing those who don't.[7] *The more new employees a company is hiring, the more important it becomes to screen job applicants every bit as much for how well their values, beliefs, and personalities match up with the* *culture as for their technical skills and experience.* For example, a company that stresses operating with integrity and fairness has to hire people who themselves have integrity and place a high value on fair play. A company whose culture revolves around creativity, product innovation, and leading change has to screen new hires for their ability to think outside the box, generate new ideas, and thrive in a climate of rapid change and ambiguity. Southwest Airlines—whose two core values, "LUV" and fun, permeate the work environment and whose objective is to ensure that passengers have a positive and enjoyable flying experience—goes to considerable lengths to hire flight attendants and gate personnel who are witty, cheery, and outgoing and who display "whistle while you work" attitudes. Fast-growing companies risk creating a culture by chance rather than by design if they rush to hire employees mainly for their talents and credentials and neglect to screen out candidates whose values, philosophies, and personalities aren't a good fit with the organizational character, vision, and strategy being articulated by the company's senior executives.

As a rule, companies are careful to hire people who they believe will fit in and embrace the prevailing culture. And, usually, job seekers lean toward accepting jobs at companies where they feel comfortable with the atmosphere and the people they will be working with. Employees who don't fit in well at a company tend to leave quickly, while employees who thrive and are pleased with the work environment stay on, eventually moving up the ranks to positions of greater responsibility. The longer people stay at an organization, the more that they come to embrace and mirror the corporate culture—their values and beliefs tend to be molded by mentors, co-workers, company training programs, and the reward structure. Normally, employees who have worked at a company for a long time play a major role in indoctrinating new employees into the culture.

Forces That Cause a Company's Culture to Evolve   However, cultures aren't static—just like strategy and organization structure, they evolve. New challenges in the marketplace, revolutionary technologies, and shifting internal conditions—especially eroding business prospects, an internal crisis, or top executive turnover—tend to breed new ways of doing things and, in turn, drive cultural evolution. An incoming CEO who decides to shake up the existing business and take it in new directions often triggers a cultural shift, perhaps one of major proportions. Likewise, diversification into new businesses, expansion into foreign countries, rapid growth that brings an influx of new employees, and merger with or acquisition of another company can all precipitate significant cultural change.

Company Cultures Can Be Strongly or Weakly Embedded

Company cultures vary widely in strength and influence. Some are strongly embedded and have a big influence on a company's operating practices and the behavior of company personnel. Others are weakly ingrained and have little effect on behaviors and how company activities are conducted.

Strong-Culture Companies   The hallmark of a **strong-culture company** is the dominating presence of certain deeply rooted values, behavioral norms, and operating approaches that are widely shared and "regulate" the conduct of a company's business and the climate of its workplace.[8] Strong cultures emerge over a period of years (sometimes decades) and are never an overnight phenomenon. In strong-culture companies, senior managers make a point of reiterating the company's principles and values to organization members and explaining how they relate to its business environment. But, more importantly, the managers make a conscious effort to display these principles in their own actions and behavior—they walk the talk and *insist* that *company values and business principles be reflected in the decisions and actions taken by all company personnel.* An unequivocal expectation that company personnel will act and behave in accordance with the adopted values and ways of doing business leads to two important outcomes: (1) Over time, the values come to be widely shared by rank-and-file employees—people who dislike the culture tend to leave—and (2) individuals encounter strong peer pressure from co-workers to observe the culturally approved norms and behaviors. Hence, a strongly implanted corporate culture ends up having a powerful influence on behavior because so many company personnel are accepting of cultural traditions and because this acceptance is reinforced by both management expectations and co-worker peer pressure to conform to cultural norms.

Two factors contribute to the development of strong cultures: (1) a founder or strong leader who established core values, principles, and practices that are viewed as having contributed to the success of the company, and (2) a sincere, long-standing company commitment to operating the business according to these established traditions and values, thereby creating an internal environment that supports decision making based on cultural norms. Continuity of leadership, low workforce turnover, geographic concentration, and considerable organizational success all contribute to the emergence and sustainability of a strong culture.[9]

In strong-culture companies, values and behavioral norms are so ingrained that they can endure leadership changes at the top—although their strength can erode over time if new CEOs cease to nurture them or move aggressively to institute cultural adjustments. The cultural norms in a strong-culture company typically do not change much as strategy evolves, either because the culture constrains the choice of new strategies or because the dominant traits of the culture are somewhat strategy-neutral and compatible with evolving versions of the company's strategy.

Weak-Culture Companies In direct contrast to strong-culture companies, weak-culture companies lack values and principles that are consistently preached or widely shared (sometimes because the company has had a series of CEOs with differing values and differing views about how the company's business ought to be conducted). As a consequence, few widely revered traditions and few culture-induced norms are evident in employee behavior or operating practices. Because top executives at a weak-culture company don't repeatedly espouse any particular business philosophy or exhibit long-standing commitment to particular values or behavioral norms, individuals encounter little pressure to do things in particular ways. A weak company culture breeds no strong employee allegiance to what the company stands for or to operating the business in well-defined ways. While individual employees may well have some bonds of identification with and loyalty toward their department, their colleagues, their union, or their immediate boss, there's neither passion about the company nor emotional commitment to what it is trying to accomplish—a condition that often results in many employees viewing their company as just a place to work and their job as just a way to make a living.

As a consequence, *weak cultures provide little or no assistance in executing strategy* because there are no traditions, beliefs, values, common bonds, or behavioral norms that management can use as levers to mobilize commitment to executing the chosen strategy. The only plus of a weak culture is that it does not usually pose a strong barrier to strategy execution, but the negative of not providing any support means that culture building has to be high on management's action agenda. Without a work climate that channels organizational energy in the direction of good strategy execution, managers are left with the options of either using compensation incentives and other motivational devices to mobilize employee commitment, supervising and monitoring employee actions more closely, or trying to establish cultural roots that will in time start to nurture the strategy execution process.

Why Corporate Cultures Matter to the Strategy Execution Process

Unlike weak cultures, strong cultures can have a powerful effect on the strategy execution process. This effect may be *positive or negative* since a company's present culture and work climate may or may not be compatible with what is needed for effective implementation and execution of the chosen strategy. When a company's present culture promotes attitudes, behaviors, and ways of doing things that are conducive to first-rate strategy execution, the culture functions as a valuable ally in the strategy execution process.

For example, a corporate culture characterized by frugality and thrift nurtures employee actions to identify cost-saving opportunities—the very behavior needed for successful execution of a low-cost leadership strategy. A culture built around such business principles as outstanding customer satisfaction, operating excellence, and employee empowerment promotes employee behaviors and an esprit de corps that facilitate execution of strategies keyed to high product quality and superior customer service. A culture in which taking initiative, exhibiting creativity, taking risks, and embracing change are the behavioral norms is conducive to successful execution of product innovation and technological leadership strategies.[10]

A culture that is grounded in actions, behaviors, and work practices that are conducive to good strategy implementation assists the strategy execution effort in three ways:[11]

1. *A culture that is well matched to the requirements of the strategy execution effort focuses the attention of employees on what is most important to this effort.* Moreover, it directs their behavior and serves as a guide to their decision making. In this manner, it can align the efforts and decisions of employees throughout the firm and minimize the need for direct supervision.

2. *Culture-induced peer pressure further induces company personnel to do things in a manner that aids the cause of good strategy execution.* The stronger the culture (the more widely shared and deeply held the values), the more effective peer pressure is in shaping and supporting the strategy execution effort. Research has shown that strong group norms can shape employee behavior even more powerfully than can financial incentives.[12]

3. *A company culture that is consistent with the requirements for good strategy execution can energize employees, deepen their commitment to execute the*

LO 2

Gain an understanding of how and why a company's culture can aid the drive for proficient strategy execution and operating excellence.

A strong culture that encourages actions, behaviors, and work practices conducive to good strategy execution adds significantly to the power and effectiveness of a company's strategy execution effort.

strategy flawlessly, and enhance worker productivity in the process. When a company's culture is grounded in many of the needed strategy-executing behaviors, employees feel genuinely better about their jobs, the company they work for, and the merits of what the company is trying to accomplish. As a consequence, greater numbers of company personnel exhibit passion in their work and exert their best efforts to execute the strategy and achieve performance targets.

In sharp contrast, when a culture is in conflict with what is required to execute the company's strategy well, a strong culture becomes a hindrance to the success of the implementation effort.[13] Some of the very behaviors needed to execute the strategy successfully run contrary to the attitudes, behaviors, and operating practices embedded in the prevailing culture. Such a clash poses a real dilemma for company personnel. Should they be loyal to the culture and company traditions (to which they are likely to be emotionally attached) and thus resist or be indifferent to actions that will promote better strategy execution—a choice that will certainly weaken the drive for good strategy execution? Alternatively, should they go along with the strategy execution effort and engage in actions that run counter to the culture—a choice that will likely impair morale and lead to a less-than-wholehearted commitment to management's strategy execution efforts? Neither choice leads to desirable outcomes. Culture-bred resistance to the actions and behaviors needed for good strategy execution, particularly if strong and widespread, poses a formidable hurdle that must be cleared for a strategy's execution to get very far.

> It is in management's best interest to dedicate considerable effort to establishing a corporate culture that encourages behaviors and work practices conducive to good strategy execution.

This says something important about the task of managing the strategy execution process: *Closely aligning corporate culture with the requirements for proficient strategy execution merits the full attention of senior executives.* The culture-building objective is to create a work climate and style of operating that mobilize the energy and behavior of company personnel squarely behind efforts to execute strategy competently. The more deeply that management can embed execution-supportive ways of doing things, the more that management can rely on the culture to automatically steer company personnel toward behaviors and work practices that aid good strategy execution and veer from doing things that impede it. Moreover, culturally astute managers understand that nourishing the right cultural environment not only adds power to their push for proficient strategy execution but also promotes strong employee identification with and commitment to the company's vision, performance targets, and strategy.

Healthy Cultures That Aid Good Strategy Execution

A strong culture, provided it embraces execution-supportive attitudes, behaviors, and work practices, is definitely a healthy culture. Two other types of cultures exist that tend to be healthy and largely supportive of good strategy execution: high-performance cultures and adaptive cultures.

High-Performance Cultures   Some companies have so-called high-performance cultures where the standout traits are a "can-do" spirit, pride in doing things right, no-excuses accountability, and a pervasive results-oriented work climate in which people go all out to meet or beat stretch objectives.[14] In high-performance cultures, there's a strong sense of involvement on the part of company personnel and emphasis on individual initiative and effort. Performance expectations are clearly delineated for the company as a whole, for each organizational unit, and for each individual. Issues and problems are promptly addressed; there's a razor-sharp focus on what needs to be done. The clear and unyielding expectation is that all company personnel, from senior executives to frontline employees, will display high-performance behaviors and a passion for making the company successful. Such a culture—supported by constructive pressure to achieve good results—is a valuable contributor to good strategy execution and operating excellence. Results-oriented cultures are permeated with a spirit of achievement and have a good track record in meeting or beating performance targets.[15]

The challenge in creating a high-performance culture is to inspire high loyalty and dedication on the part of employees, such that they are energized to put forth their very best efforts to do things right and be unusually productive. Managers have to take pains to reinforce constructive behavior, reward top performers, and purge habits and behaviors that stand in the way of high productivity and good results. They must work at knowing the strengths and weaknesses of their subordinates, so as to better match talent with task and enable people to make meaningful contributions by doing what they do best.[16] They have to stress learning from mistakes and building on strengths and must put an unrelenting emphasis on moving forward and making good progress—in effect, there has to be a disciplined, performance-focused approach to managing the organization.

Adaptive Cultures   The hallmark of adaptive corporate cultures is willingness on the part of organization members to accept change and take on the challenge of introducing and executing new strategies.[17] Company personnel share a feeling of confidence that the organization can deal with whatever threats and opportunities arise; they are receptive to risk taking, experimentation, innovation, and changing strategies and practices. The work climate is supportive of managers and employees at all ranks who propose or initiate useful change. Internal entrepreneurship on the part of individuals and groups is encouraged and rewarded. Senior executives seek out, support, and promote individuals who exercise initiative, spot opportunities for improvement, and display the skills to implement them. Managers openly evaluate ideas and suggestions, fund initiatives to develop new or better products, and take prudent risks to pursue emerging market opportunities. As in high-performance cultures, the company exhibits a proactive approach to identifying issues, evaluating the implications and options, and moving ahead quickly with workable solutions. Strategies and traditional operating practices are modified as needed to adjust to or take advantage of changes in the business environment.

But why is change so willingly embraced in an adaptive culture? Why are organization members not fearful of how change will affect them? Why does an adaptive culture not break down from the force of ongoing changes in strategy, operating practices, and approaches to strategy execution? The answers lie in two distinctive and dominant traits of an adaptive culture: (1) Any changes in operating practices and behaviors must *not* compromise core values and long-standing business principles (since they are at the root of the culture), and (2) the changes that are instituted must satisfy the legitimate interests of stakeholders—customers, employees, shareowners, suppliers, and the communities where the company operates.[18] In other words, what sustains an adaptive culture is that organization members

> As a company's strategy evolves, an adaptive culture is a definite ally in the strategy-implementing, strategy-executing process as compared to cultures that are resistant to change.

perceive the changes that management is trying to institute as *legitimate* and in keeping with the core values and business principles that form the heart and soul of the culture.[19] Not surprisingly, company personnel are usually more receptive to change when their employment security is not threatened and when they view new duties or job assignments as part of the process of adapting to new conditions. Should workforce downsizing be necessary, it is important that layoffs be handled humanely and employee departures be made as painless as possible.

Technology companies, software companies, and Internet-based companies are good illustrations of organizations with adaptive cultures. Such companies thrive on change—driving it, leading it, and capitalizing on it. Companies like Google, Intel, Cisco Systems, eBay, Amazon.com, and Apple cultivate the capability to act and react rapidly. They are avid practitioners of entrepreneurship and innovation, with a demonstrated willingness to take bold risks to create altogether new products, new businesses, and new industries. To create and nurture a culture that can adapt rapidly to shifting business conditions, they make a point of staffing their organizations with people who are flexible, who rise to the challenge of change, and who have an aptitude for adapting well to new circumstances.

In fast-changing business environments, a corporate culture that is receptive to altering organizational practices and behaviors is a virtual necessity. However, adaptive cultures work to the advantage of all companies, not just those in rapid-change environments. Every company operates in a market and business climate that is changing to one degree or another and that, in turn, requires internal operating responses and new behaviors on the part of organization members.

Unhealthy Cultures That Impede Good Strategy Execution

The distinctive characteristic of an unhealthy corporate culture is the presence of counterproductive cultural traits that adversely impact the work climate and company performance.[20] Five particularly unhealthy cultural traits are hostility to change, heavily politicized decision making, insular thinking, behaviors that are driven by greed and a disregard for ethical standards, and the presence of incompatible, clashing subcultures.

Change-Resistant Cultures   In contrast to adaptive cultures, change-resistant cultures—where skepticism about the importance of new developments and a fear of change are the norm—place a premium on not making mistakes, prompting managers to lean toward safe, conservative options intended to maintain the status quo, protect their power base, and guard the interests of their immediate work groups. When such companies encounter business environments with accelerating change, going slow on altering traditional ways of doing things can be a serious liability. Under these conditions, change-resistant cultures encourage a number of undesirable or unhealthy behaviors—viewing circumstances myopically, avoiding risks, not capitalizing on emerging opportunities, taking a lax approach to both product innovation and continuous improvement in performing value chain activities, and responding more slowly than is warranted to market change. In change-resistant cultures, word quickly gets around that proposals to do things differently face an uphill battle and that people who champion them may be seen as something of a nuisance. Executives who don't value managers or employees with initiative and new ideas put a damper on product innovation, experimentation, and efforts to improve. At the same time, change-resistant companies have little appetite for being first movers or fast followers, believing that being in the forefront of change is too risky and that acting too quickly increases vulnerability to costly mistakes. Hostility to change is most often found in companies with multilayered management bureaucracies that have enjoyed considerable market success in years past and that are wedded to the "We have done it this way for years" syndrome. Before filing bankruptcy in 2009, General Motors was a classic example of a company whose change-resistant bureaucracy was slow to adapt to fundamental changes in its markets, preferring to cling to the traditions, operating practices, and business approaches that had at one time made it the global industry leader.

Politicized Cultures   What makes a politicized internal environment so unhealthy is that political infighting consumes a great deal of organizational energy, often with the result that what's best for the company takes a backseat to political maneuvering. In companies where internal politics pervades the work climate, empire-building managers jealously guard their decision-making prerogatives. They have their own agendas and operate the work units under their supervision as autonomous "fiefdoms"; the positions they take on issues are usually aimed at protecting or expanding their own turf. Collaboration with other organizational units is viewed with suspicion, and cross-unit cooperation occurs grudgingly. The support or opposition of politically influential executives and/or coalitions among departments with vested interests in a particular outcome tends to shape what actions the company takes. All this political maneuvering takes away from efforts to execute strategy with real proficiency and frustrates company personnel who are less political and more inclined to do what is in the company's best interests.

Insular, Inwardly Focused Cultures   Sometimes a company reigns as an industry leader or enjoys great market success for so long that its personnel start to believe they have all the answers or can develop them on their own. There is a strong tendency to neglect what customers are saying and how their needs and expectations are changing. Such confidence in the correctness of its approach to business and an unflinching belief in the company's competitive superiority breeds arrogance, prompting company personnel to discount the merits of what outsiders are doing and the payoff from studying best-in-class performers. Insular thinking, internally driven solutions, and a must-be-invented-here mindset come to permeate the corporate culture. An inwardly focused corporate culture gives rise to managerial inbreeding and a failure to recruit people who can offer fresh thinking and outside perspectives. The big risk of insular cultural thinking is that the company can underestimate the capabilities and accomplishments of rival companies and overestimate its own progress—until its loss of market position makes the realities obvious.

Unethical and Greed-Driven Cultures   Companies that have little regard for ethical standards or that are run by executives driven by greed and ego gratification are scandals waiting to happen, as discussed in Chapter 9. Executives exude the negatives of arrogance, ego, greed, and an "ends-justify-the-means" mentality in pursuing stretch revenue and profitability targets.[21] Senior managers wink at unethical behavior and may cross over the line to unethical (and sometimes criminal) behavior themselves. They are prone to adopt accounting principles that make financial performance look better than it really is. Legions of companies have fallen prey to unethical behavior and greed, most notably WorldCom, Enron, Quest, HealthSouth, Adelphia, Tyco, Parmalat, Rite Aid, Hollinger International, Refco, Marsh & McLennan, Siemens, Countrywide Financial, and Stanford Financial Group, with executives being indicted and/or convicted of criminal behavior.

Incompatible Subcultures   Although it is common to speak about corporate culture in the singular, it is not unusual for companies to have multiple cultures (or subcultures).[22] Values, beliefs, and practices within a company sometimes vary significantly by department, geographic location, division, or business unit. As long as the subcultures are compatible with the overarching corporate culture and are supportive of the strategy execution efforts, this is not problematic. Multiple cultures pose an unhealthy situation when they are composed of incompatible subcultures that embrace conflicting business philosophies, support inconsistent approaches to strategy execution, and encourage incompatible methods of people management. Clashing subcultures can prevent a company from coordinating its efforts to craft and execute strategy and can distract company personnel from the business of business. When incompatible subcultures encourage the emergence of warring factions within the company, they are not just unhealthy—they are downright poisonous.

Incompatible subcultures arise most commonly because of important cultural differences between a company's culture and that of a recently acquired company or because of a merger between companies with cultural differences. Companies with M&A experience are quite alert to the importance of cultural compatibility in making acquisitions and the need to integrate the cultures of newly acquired companies—cultural due diligence is often as important as financial due diligence in deciding whether to go forward on an acquisition or merger. On a number of occasions, companies decided to pass on acquiring particular companies because of culture conflicts they believed would be hard to resolve.

Changing a Problem Culture: The Role of Leadership

LO 3

Learn the kinds of actions management can take to change a problem corporate culture.

When a strong culture is unhealthy or otherwise out of sync with the actions and behaviors needed to execute the strategy successfully, the culture must be changed as rapidly as can be managed. While correcting a strategy-culture conflict can occasionally mean revamping a company's approach to strategy execution to better fit the company's culture, more usually it means altering aspects of the mismatched culture to better enable first-rate strategy execution. The more entrenched the mismatched or unhealthy aspects of a company culture, the more likely the culture will impede strategy execution and the greater the need for change.

Changing a problem culture is among the toughest management tasks because of the heavy anchor of ingrained behaviors and attitudes. It is natural for company personnel to cling to familiar practices and to be wary, if not hostile, to new approaches of how things are to be done. Consequently, it takes concerted management action over a period of time to root out unconstructive behaviors and replace them with new ways of doing things deemed more conducive to executing the strategy.

The single most visible factor that distinguishes successful culture-change efforts from failed attempts is competent leadership at the top. Great power is needed to force major cultural change and overcome the "springback" resistance of entrenched cultures—and great power is possessed only by the most senior executives, especially the CEO. However, while top management must be out front leading the effort, marshaling support for a new culture and instilling the desired cultural behaviors is a job for the whole management team. Middle managers and frontline supervisors play a key role in implementing the new work practices and operating approaches, helping win rank-and-file acceptance of and support for the desired behavioral norms.

As shown in Figure 12.2, the first step in fixing a problem culture is for top management to identify those facets of the present culture that are dysfunctional and pose obstacles to executing new strategic initiatives and meeting company performance targets. Second, managers must clearly define the desired new behaviors and features of the culture they want to create. Third, managers have to convince company personnel of why the present culture poses problems and why and how new behaviors and operating approaches will improve company performance—the case for cultural reform has to be persuasive. Fourth, and most important, all the talk about remodeling the present culture has to be followed swiftly by visible, forceful actions to promote the desired new behaviors and work practices—actions that company personnel will interpret as a determined top management commitment to bringing about a different work climate and new ways of operating.

Making a Compelling Case for Culture Change   The way for management to begin a major remodeling of the corporate culture is by selling company personnel on the need for new-style behaviors and work practices. This means making a compelling case for why the culture-remodeling efforts are in the organization's best interests and why company personnel should wholeheartedly join the effort to doing things somewhat differently. Skeptics and opinion leaders have to be convinced that all is not well with the status quo. This can be done by:

- Explaining why and how certain behavioral norms and work practices in the current culture pose obstacles to good execution of strategic initiatives.
- Explaining how new behaviors and work practices will be more advantageous and produce better results. Effective culture-change leaders are good at telling stories to describe the new values and desired behaviors and connect them to everyday practices.
- Citing reasons why the current strategy has to be modified, if the need for cultural change is due to a change in strategy. This includes explaining why the new strategic initiatives will bolster the company's competitiveness and performance and how a change in culture can help in executing the new strategy.

It is essential for the CEO and other top executives to talk personally to company personnel all across the company about the reasons for modifying work practices and culture-related behaviors. Senior officers and department heads have to play a lead role in explaining the need for a change in behavioral norms to those they manage—and the explanations will likely have to be repeated many times. For the culture-change effort to be successful, frontline supervisors and employee opinion leaders must be won over to the cause, which means convincing them of the merits of *practicing* and *enforcing* cultural norms at every level of the organization, from the highest to the lowest. Arguments for new ways of doing things and new work practices tend to be embraced more readily if employees understand how they will benefit company stakeholders (particularly customers, employees, and shareholders).

Figure 12.2   **Steps to Take in Changing a Problem Culture**

Until a large majority of employees accept the need for a new culture and agree that different work practices and behaviors are called for, there's more work to be done in selling company personnel on the whys and wherefores of culture change. Building widespread organizational support requires taking every opportunity to repeat the message of why the new work practices, operating approaches, and behaviors are good for company stakeholders.

Management's efforts to make a persuasive case for changing what is deemed to be a problem culture must be *followed quickly* by forceful, high-profile actions across several fronts. The actions to implant the new culture must be both substantive and symbolic.

Substantive Culture-Changing Actions   No culture change effort can get very far with just talk about the need for different actions, behaviors, and work practices. Company executives must give the culture-change effort some teeth by initiating *a series of actions* that company personnel will see as credible and unmistakably indicative of the seriousness of management's commitment to cultural change. The strongest signs that management is truly committed to instilling a new culture include:

- Replacing key executives who are stonewalling needed organizational and cultural changes.
- Promoting individuals who have stepped forward to advocate the shift to a different culture and who can serve as role models for the desired cultural behavior.
- Appointing outsiders with the desired cultural attributes to high-profile positions—bringing in new-breed managers sends an unmistakable message that a new era is dawning.
- Screening all candidates for new positions carefully, hiring only those who appear to fit in with the new culture.

- Mandating that all company personnel attend culture-training programs to learn more about the new work practices and to better understand the culture-related actions and behaviors that are expected.

- Designing compensation incentives that boost the pay of teams and individuals who display the desired cultural behaviors. Company personnel are much more inclined to exhibit the desired kinds of actions and behaviors when it is in their financial best interest to do so.

- Revising policies and procedures in ways that will help drive cultural change.

Executives must take care to launch enough companywide culture-change actions at the outset so as to leave no room for doubt that management is dead serious about changing the present culture and that a cultural transformation is inevitable. The series of actions initiated by top management must create lots of hallway talk across the whole company, get the change process off to a fast start, and be followed by unrelenting efforts to firmly establish the new work practices, desired behaviors, and style of operating as "standard."

Symbolic Culture-Changing Actions   There's also an important place for symbolic managerial actions to alter a problem culture and tighten the strategy-culture fit. The most important symbolic actions are those that top executives take to *lead by example.* For instance, if the organization's strategy involves a drive to become the industry's low-cost producer, senior managers must display frugality in their own actions and decisions: inexpensive decorations in the executive suite, conservative expense accounts and entertainment allowances, a lean staff in the corporate office, scrutiny of budget requests, few executive perks, and so on. At Walmart, all the executive offices are simply decorated; executives are habitually frugal in their own actions, and they are zealous in their efforts to control costs and promote greater efficiency. At Nucor, one of the world's low-cost producers of steel products, executives fly coach class and use taxis at airports rather than limousines. If the culture-change imperative is to be more responsive to customers' needs and to pleasing customers, the CEO can instill greater customer awareness by requiring all officers and executives to spend a significant portion of each week talking with customers about their needs. Top executives must be alert to the fact that company personnel will be watching their actions and decisions to see if their actions match their rhetoric. Hence, they need to make sure their current decisions and behaviors will be construed as consistent with the new-culture values and norms.[23]

Another category of symbolic actions includes holding ceremonial events to single out and honor people whose actions and performance exemplify what is called for in the new culture. A point is made of holding events to celebrate each culture-change success (and any other outcome that management would like to see happen again). Executives sensitive to their role in promoting strategy-culture fit make a habit of appearing at ceremonial functions to praise individuals and groups that exemplify the desired behaviors. They show up at employee training programs to stress strategic priorities, values, ethical principles, and cultural norms. Every group gathering is seen as an opportunity to repeat and ingrain values, praise good deeds, expound on the merits of the new culture, and cite instances of how the new work practices and operating approaches have worked to good advantage.

The use of symbols in culture building is widespread. Many universities give outstanding teacher awards each year to symbolize their commitment to good teaching and their esteem for instructors who display exceptional classroom talents. Numerous businesses have employee-of-the-month awards. The military has a long-standing custom of awarding ribbons and medals for exemplary actions. Avon awards an array of prizes ceremoniously to its beauty consultants for reaching various sales plateaus.

How Long Does It Take to Change a Problem Culture?   Planting and growing the seeds of a new culture require a determined effort by the chief executive and other senior managers. A sustained and persistent effort to reinforce the culture at every opportunity through both word and deed is required. Changing a problem culture is never a short-term exercise. It takes time for a new culture to emerge and prevail; overnight transformations simply don't occur. And it takes even longer for a new culture to become deeply embedded. The bigger the organization and the greater the cultural shift needed to produce an execution-supportive fit, the longer it takes. In large companies, fixing a problem culture and instilling a new set of attitudes and behaviors can take two to five years. In fact, it is usually tougher to reform an entrenched problematic culture than it is to instill a strategy-supportive culture from scratch in a brand new organization.

LEADING THE STRATEGY EXECUTION PROCESS

LO 4

Understand what constitutes effective managerial leadership in achieving superior strategy execution.

For an enterprise to execute its strategy in truly proficient fashion and approach operating excellence, top executives have to take the lead in the implementation/execution process and personally drive the pace of progress. The have to be out in the field, seeing for themselves how well operations are going, gathering information firsthand, and gauging the progress being made. Proficient strategy execution requires company managers to be diligent and adept in spotting problems, learning what obstacles lie in the path of good execution, and then clearing the way for progress—the goal must be to produce better results speedily and productively. There has to be constructive, but unrelenting, pressure on organizational units to (1) demonstrate excellence in all dimensions of strategy execution and (2) do so on a consistent basis—ultimately, that's what will enable a well-crafted strategy to achieve the desired performance results.

The strategy execution process must be driven by mandates to get things on the right track and show good results. The specifics of how to implement a strategy and deliver the intended results must start with understanding the requirements for good strategy execution. Afterward comes a diagnosis of the organization's preparedness to execute the strategic initiatives and decisions as to which of several ways to proceed to move forward and achieve the targeted results.[24] In general, leading the drive for good strategy execution and operating excellence calls for three actions on the part of the manager in charge:

- Staying on top of what is happening and closely monitoring progress.
- Putting constructive pressure on the organization to execute the strategy well and achieve operating excellence.
- Initiating corrective actions to improve strategy execution and achieve the targeted performance results.

Staying on Top of How Well Things Are Going

To stay on top of how well the strategy execution process is going, senior executives have to tap into information from a wide range of sources. In addition to talking with key subordinates and reviewing the latest operating results, watching the competitive reactions of rival firms, and visiting with key customers and suppliers to get their perspectives, they usually make regular visits to various company facilities and talk with many different company personnel at many different organization levels—a technique often labeled **managing by walking around (MBWA)**. Most managers attach great importance to spending time with people at company facilities, asking questions, listening to their opinions and concerns, and gathering firsthand information about how well aspects of the strategy execution process are going. Facilities tours and face-to-face contacts with operating-level employees give executives a good grasp of what progress is being made, what problems are being encountered, and whether additional resources or different approaches may be needed. Just as important, MBWA provides opportunities to give encouragement, lift spirits, shift attention from the old to the new priorities, and create some excitement—all of which can boost strategy execution efforts.

> **CORE CONCEPT**
>
> **Management by walking around (MBWA)** is one of the techniques that effective leaders use to stay informed about how well the strategy execution process is progressing.

Jeff Bezos, Amazon.com's CEO, is noted for his practice of MBWA, firing off a battery of questions when he tours facilities and insisting that Amazon managers spend time in the trenches with their people to prevent getting disconnected from the reality of what's happening.[25] Walmart executives have had a long-standing practice of spending two to three days every week visiting Walmart's stores and talking with store managers and employees. Sam Walton, Walmart's founder, insisted, "The key is to get out into the store and listen to what the associates have to say." Jack Welch, the highly effective CEO of General Electric (GE) from 1980 to 2001, not only spent several days each month personally visiting GE operations and talking with major customers but also arranged his schedule so that he could spend time exchanging information and ideas with GE managers from all over the world who were attending classes at the company's leadership development center near GE's headquarters.

Many manufacturing executives make a point of strolling the factory floor to talk with workers and meeting regularly with union officials. Some managers operate out of open cubicles in big spaces populated with open cubicles for other personnel so that they can interact easily and frequently with co-workers. Managers at some companies host weekly get-togethers (often on Friday afternoons) to create a regular opportunity for information to flow freely between down-the-line employees and executives.

Putting Constructive Pressure on Organizational Units to Execute the Strategy Well and Achieve Operating Excellence

Managers have to be out front in mobilizing organizational energy behind the drive for good strategy execution and operating excellence. Part of the leadership task entails nurturing a results-oriented work climate, where performance standards are high and a spirit of achievement is pervasive. Successfully leading the effort to foster a results-oriented, high-performance culture generally entails such leadership actions and managerial practices as:

- *Treating employees as valued partners in the drive for operating excellence and good business performance.* Some companies symbolize the value of individual employees and the importance of their contributions by referring to them as cast members (Disney), crew members (McDonald's), partners (Starbucks), or associates (Walmart, W. L. Gore, and Marriott International). Very often, there is a strong company commitment to providing thorough training, offering attractive compensation and career opportunities, emphasizing promotion from within, providing a high degree of job security, and otherwise making employees feel well treated and valued.

- *Fostering an esprit de corps that energizes organization members.* The task here is to skillfully use people-management practices calculated to build morale, foster pride in doing things right, promote teamwork, create a strong sense of involvement on the part of company personnel, win their emotional commitment, and inspire them to do their best.[26]

- *Using empowerment to help create a fully engaged workforce.* Top executives must seek to engage the full organization in the strategy execution effort. A fully engaged workforce, one where individuals bring their best to work every day, is necessary to produce great results.[27] So is having a group of dedicated managers committed to making a difference in their organization. The two best things top-level executives can do to create a fully engaged organization are (1) delegate authority to middle and lower-level managers to get the implementation/execution process moving and (2) empower rank-and-file employees to act on their own initiative. Operating excellence requires that everybody contribute ideas, exercise initiative and creativity in performing his or her work, and have a desire to do things in the best possible manner.

- *Making champions out of the people who spearhead new ideas and/or turn in winning performances.* The best champions and change agents are persistent, competitive, tenacious, committed, and fanatical about seeing their ideas through to success. It is particularly important that people who champion an unsuccessful idea not be punished or sidelined but, rather, be encouraged to try again. Encouraging lots of "tries" is important, since many ideas won't pan out.

- *Setting stretch objectives and clearly communicating an expectation that company personnel are to give their best in achieving performance targets.* Stretch objectives—those beyond an organization's current capacities—can sometimes spur organization members to increase their resolve and redouble their efforts to execute the strategy flawlessly and ultimately reach the stretch objectives. When stretch objectives are met, the satisfaction of achievement and boost to employee morale can result in an even higher level of organizational drive.

- *Using the tools of benchmarking best practices, business process reengineering, TQM, and Six Sigma to focus attention on continuous improvement.* These are proven approaches to getting better operating results and facilitating better strategy execution.

- *Using the full range of motivational techniques and compensation incentives to inspire company personnel, nurture a results-oriented work climate, and enforce high-performance standards.* Managers cannot mandate innovative improvements by simply exhorting people to "be creative," nor can they make continuous progress toward operating excellence with directives to "try harder." Rather, they must foster a culture where innovative ideas and experimentation with new ways of doing things can blossom and thrive. Individuals and groups should be strongly encouraged to brainstorm, let their imaginations fly in all directions, and come up with proposals for improving how things are done. This means giving company personnel enough autonomy to stand out, excel, and contribute. And it means that the rewards for successful champions of new ideas and operating improvements should be large and visible.

- *Celebrating individual, group, and company successes.* Top management should miss no opportunity to express respect for individual employees and appreciation of extraordinary individual and group effort.[28] Companies like Avon, Tupperware, and McDonald's actively seek out reasons and opportunities to give pins, ribbons, buttons, badges, and medals for good showings by average performers—the idea being to express appreciation and give a motivational boost to people who stand out in doing ordinary jobs. General Electric and 3M Corporation make a point of ceremoniously honoring individuals who believe so strongly in their ideas that they take it on themselves to hurdle the bureaucracy, maneuver their projects through the system, and turn them into improved services, new products, or even new businesses.

While leadership efforts to instill a results-oriented, high-performance culture usually accentuate the positive, negative reinforcers abound too. Managers whose units consistently perform poorly must be replaced. Low-performing workers and people who reject the results-oriented cultural emphasis must be weeded out or at least employed differently. Average performers should be candidly counseled that they have limited career potential unless they show more progress in the form of additional effort, better skills, and improved ability to execute the strategy well and deliver good results.

Leading the Process of Making Corrective Adjustments

Since strategy execution takes place amid changing environmental and organizational circumstances, there is often a need for corrective adjustments. The process of making corrective adjustments in strategy execution varies according to the situation. In a crisis, taking remedial action fairly quickly is of the essence. But it still takes time to review the situation, examine the available data, identify and evaluate options (crunching whatever numbers may be appropriate to determine which options are likely to generate the best outcomes), and decide what to do. When the situation allows managers to proceed more deliberately in deciding when to make changes and what changes to make, most managers seem to prefer a process of incrementally solidifying commitment to a particular course of action.[29] The process that managers go through in deciding on corrective adjustments is essentially the same for both proactive and reactive changes: They sense needs, gather information, broaden and deepen their understanding of the situation, develop options and explore their pros and cons, put forth action proposals, strive for a consensus, and finally formally adopt an agreed-on course of action.[30] The time frame for deciding what corrective changes to initiate can be a few hours, a few days, a few weeks, or even a few months if the situation is particularly complicated.

Success in making corrective actions hinges on (1) a thorough analysis of the situation, (2) the exercise of good business judgment in deciding what actions to take, and (3) good implementation of the corrective actions that are initiated. Successful managers are skilled in getting an organization back on track rather quickly. They (and their staffs) are good at discerning what actions to take and in bringing them to a successful conclusion. Managers who struggle to show measurable progress in implementing corrective actions in a timely fashion are often candidates for being replaced.

The challenges of making the right corrective adjustments and leading a successful strategy execution effort are, without question, substantial.[31] Because each instance of executing strategy occurs under different organizational circumstances, the managerial agenda for executing strategy always needs to be situation-specific—there's no generic procedure to follow. But the job is definitely doable. Although there is no prescriptive answer to the question of exactly what to do, any of several courses of action may produce good results. And, as we said at the beginning of Chapter 10, executing strategy is an action-oriented, make-the-right-things-happen task that challenges a manager's ability to lead and direct organizational change, create or reinvent business processes, manage and motivate people, and achieve performance targets.

A FINAL WORD ON LEADING THE PROCESS OF CRAFTING AND EXECUTING STRATEGY

In practice, it is hard to separate leading the process of executing strategy from leading the other pieces of the strategy process. As we emphasized in Chapter 2, the job of crafting, implementing, and executing strategy consists of five interrelated and linked stages, with much looping and recycling to fine-tune and adjust the strategic vision, objectives, strategy, and implementation/execution approaches to fit one another and to fit changing circumstances. The process is continuous, and the conceptually separate acts of crafting and executing strategy blur together in real-world situations. The best tests of good strategic leadership are whether the company has a good strategy and business model, whether the strategy is being competently executed, and whether the enterprise is meeting or beating its performance targets. If these three conditions exist, then there is every reason to conclude that the company has good strategic leadership and is a well managed enterprise.

KEY POINTS

1. Corporate culture is the character of a company's internal work climate—as shaped by a system of *shared* values, beliefs, ethical standards, and traditions that in turn define behavioral norms, ingrained attitudes, accepted work practices, and styles of operating. A company's culture is important because it influences the organization's actions and approaches

to conducting business. In a very real sense, the culture is the company's organizational DNA.

2. The key features of a company's culture include the company's values and ethical standards, its approach to people management, its work atmosphere and company spirit, how its personnel interact, the behaviors awarded through incentives (both financial and symbolic), the traditions and oft-repeated "myths," and its manner of dealing with stakeholders.

3. A company's culture is grounded in and shaped by its core values and ethical standards. Core values and ethical principles serve two roles in the culture-building process: (1) They foster a work climate in which employees share common and strongly held convictions about how company business is to be conducted, and (2) they serve as yardsticks for gauging the appropriateness of particular actions, decisions, and behaviors, thus helping steer company personnel toward both doing things right and doing the right thing.

4. Company cultures vary widely in strength and influence. Some are strongly embedded and have a big impact on a company's practices and behavioral norms. Others are weak and have comparatively little influence on company operations.

5. Strong company cultures can have either positive or negative effects on strategy execution. When they are well matched to the behavioral requirements of the company's strategy implementation plan, they can be a powerful aid to strategy execution. A culture that is grounded in the types of actions and behaviors that are conducive to good strategy execution assists the effort in three ways:

   - By focusing employee attention on the actions that are most important in the strategy execution effort.
   - Through culture-induced peer pressure for employees to contribute to the success of the strategy execution effort.
   - By energizing employees, deepening their commitment to the strategy execution effort, and increasing the productivity of their efforts

6. It is thus in management's best interest to dedicate considerable effort to establishing a strongly implanted corporate culture that encourages behaviors and work practices conducive to good strategy execution.

7. Strong corporate cultures that are conducive to good strategy execution are healthy cultures. So are high-performance cultures and adaptive cultures. The latter are particularly important in dynamic environments. Strong cultures can also be unhealthy. The five types of unhealthy cultures are (1) those that are change-resistant, (2) those that are characterized by heavily politicized decision making, (3) those that are insular and inwardly focused, (4) those that are ethically unprincipled and infused with greed, and (5) those that are composed of incompatible subcultures. All five impede good strategy execution.

8. Changing a company's culture, especially a strong one with traits that don't fit a new strategy's requirements, is a tough and often time-consuming challenge. Changing a culture requires competent leadership at the top. It requires making a compelling case for cultural change and employing both symbolic actions and substantive actions that unmistakably indicate serious commitment on the part of top management. The more that culture-driven

actions and behaviors fit what's needed for good strategy execution, the less managers must depend on policies, rules, procedures, and supervision to enforce what people should and should not do.

9. Leading the drive for good strategy execution and operating excellence calls for three actions on the part of the manager in charge:

    •   Staying on top of what is happening and closely monitoring progress. This is often accomplished through managing by walking around (MBWA).

    •   Putting constructive pressure on the organization to execute the strategy well and achieve operating excellence.

    •   Initiating corrective actions to improve strategy execution and achieve the targeted performance results.

ASSURANCE OF LEARNING EXERCISES

LO 1, LO 2

1. Go to www.google.com. Click on the About Google link and then on the Corporate Info link. Under the Culture link, read what Google has to say about its culture. Also, in the "Our Philosophy" section, read "Ten things Google has found to be true." How do the "ten things" and Google's culture aid in management's attempts to execute the company's strategy?

LO 1, LO 2

2. Go to the Jobs section at www.intel.com, and see what Intel has to say about its culture under the links for Careers, Diversity, and The Workplace. Does what's on this Web site appear to be just recruiting propaganda, or does it convey the type of work climate that management is actually trying to create? Explain your answer.

LO 1, LO 2

3. Go to www.jnj.com, the Web site of Johnson & Johnson, and read the J&J Credo, which sets forth the company's responsibilities to customers, employees, the community, and shareholders. Then read the "Our Company" section. Why do you think the credo has resulted in numerous awards and accolades that recognize the company as a good corporate citizen?

LO 4

4. In the last couple of years, Liz Claiborne, Inc., has been engaged in efforts to turn around its faltering Mexx chain. Use your favorite browser to search for information on the turnaround plan at Mexx, and read at least two articles or reports on this subject. Describe in 1 to 2 pages the approach being taken to turn around the Mexx chain. In your opinion, have the managers involved been demonstrating the kind of internal leadership needed for superior strategy execution at Mexx? Explain your answer.

EXERCISES FOR SIMULATION PARTICIPANTS

LO 1, LO 2

1. If you were making a speech to company personnel, what would you tell them about the kind of corporate culture you would like to have at your company? What specific cultural traits would you like your company to exhibit? Explain.

LO 1

2. What core values would you want to ingrain in your company's culture? Why?

LO 3, LO 4

3. Following each decision round, do you and your co-managers make corrective adjustments in either your company's strategy or how well the strategy is being executed? List at least three such adjustments you made in the most recent decision round. What hard evidence (in the form of results relating to your company's performance in the most recent year) can you cite that indicates the various corrective adjustments you made either succeeded or failed to improve your company's performance?

LO 4

4. What would happen to your company's performance if you and your co-managers stick with the status quo and fail to make any corrective adjustments after each decision round?

ENDNOTES

[1] Jennifer A. Chatham and Sandra E. Cha, "Leading by Leveraging Culture," *California Management Review* 45, no. 4 (Summer 2003), pp. 20–34.

[2] Joanne Reid and Victoria Hubbell, "Creating a Performance Culture," *Ivey Business Journal* 69, no. 4 (March–April 2005), p. 1.

[3] John P. Kotter and James L. Heskett, *Corporate Culture and Performance* (New York: Free Press, 1992), p. 7. See also Robert Goffee and Gareth Jones, *The Character of a Corporation* (New York: HarperCollins, 1998).

[4] For several perspectives on the role and importance of core values and ethical behavior, see Joseph L. Badaracco, *Defining Moments: When Managers Must Choose between Right and Wrong* (Boston: Harvard Business School Press, 1997); Joe Badaracco and Allen P. Webb. "Business Ethics: A View from the Trenches," *California Management Review* 37, no. 2 (Winter 1995), pp. 8–28; Patrick E. Murphy, "Corporate Ethics Statements: Current Status and Future Prospects," *Journal of Business Ethics* 14 (1995), pp. 727–40; and Lynn Sharp Paine, "Managing for Organizational Integrity," *Harvard Business Review* 72, no. 2 (March–April 1994), pp. 106–17.

[5] For a study of the status of formal codes of ethics in large corporations, see Emily F. Carasco and Jang B. Singh, "The Content and Focus of the Codes of Ethics of the World's Largest Transnational Corporations," *Business and Society Review* 108, no. 1 (January 2003), pp. 71–94, and Patrick E. Murphy, "Corporate Ethics Statements: Current Status and Future Prospects," *Journal of Business Ethics* 14 (1995), pp. 727–40. For a discussion of the strategic benefits of formal statements of corporate values, see John Humble, David Jackson, and Alan Thomson, "The Strategic Power of Corporate Values," *Long Range Planning* 27, no. 6 (December 1994), pp. 28–42. An excellent discussion of whether one should assume that company codes of ethics are always ethical is presented in Mark S. Schwartz, "A Code of Ethics for Corporate Codes of Ethics," *Journal of Business Ethics* 41, nos. 1–2 (November–December 2002), pp. 27–43.

[6] Chatham and Cha, "Leading by Leveraging Culture."

[7] Kotter and Heskett, *Corporate Culture and Performance*, pp. 7–8.

[8] Terrence E. Deal and Allen A. Kennedy, *Corporate Cultures* (Reading, MA: Addison-Wesley, 1982), p. 22. See also Terrence E. Deal and Allen A. Kennedy, *The New Corporate Cultures: Revitalizing the Workplace after Downsizing, Mergers, and Reengineering* (Cambridge, MA: Perseus Publishing, 1999); Chatham and Cha, "Leading by Leveraging Culture."

[9] Vijay Sathe, *Culture and Related Corporate Realities* (Homewood, IL: Irwin, 1985).

[10] Avan R. Jassawalla and Hemant C. Sashittal, "Cultures That Support Product-Innovation Processes," *Academy of Management Executive* 16, no. 3 (August 2002), pp. 42–54.

[11] Kotter and Heskett, *Corporate Culture and Performance*, pp. 15–16. Also see Chatham and Cha, "Leading by Leveraging Culture."

[12] Chatham and Cha, "Leading by Leveraging Culture."

[13] Kotter and Heskett, *Corporate Culture and Performance*, p. 5.

[14] For a discussion of how to build a high-performance culture, see Reid and Hubbell, "Creating a Performance Culture," pp. 1–5.

[15] A strategy-supportive, high-performance culture can contribute to competitive advantage; see Jay B. Barney and Delwyn N. Clark, *Resource-Based Theory: Creating and Sustaining Competitive Advantage* (New York: Oxford University Press, 2007), chap. 4.

[16] Reid and Hubbell, "Creating a Performance Culture," pp. 2 and 5.

[17] This section draws heavily on the discussion of Kotter and Heskett, *Corporate Culture and Performance,* chap. 4.

[18] There's no inherent reason why new strategic initiatives should conflict with core values and business principles. While conflict is always possible, most strategy makers lean toward choosing strategic initiatives that are compatible with the company's character and culture and that don't go against ingrained values and beliefs. After all, the company's culture is usually something that strategy makers have had a hand in building and perpetuating, so they are not often anxious to undermine core values and business principles without serious soul-searching and compelling business reasons.

[19] For a more in-depth discussion of using values as legitimate boundaries, see Rosabeth Moss Kanter, "Transforming Giants," *Harvard Business Review* 86, no. 1 (January 2008), pp. 43–52.

[20] Ibid., chap. 6.

[21] See Kurt Eichenwald, *Conspiracy of Fools: A True Story* (New York: Broadway Books, 2005).

[22] Ibid., p. 5.

[23] Judy D. Olian and Sara L. Rynes, "Making Total Quality Work: Aligning Organizational Processes, Performance Measures, and Stakeholders," *Human Resource Management* 30, no. 3 (Fall 1991), p. 324.

[24] For excellent discussions of the problems and pitfalls in leading the transition to a new strategy and to fundamentally new ways of doing business, see Larry Bossidy and Ram Charan, *Confronting Reality: Doing What Matters to Get Things Right* (New York: Crown Business, 2004); Larry Bossidy and Ram Charan, *Execution: The Discipline of Getting Things Done* (New York: Crown Business, 2002), especially chaps. 3 and 5; John P. Kotter, "Leading Change: Why Transformation Efforts Fail," *Harvard Business Review* 73, no. 2 (March–April 1995), pp. 59–67; Thomas M. Hout and John C. Carter, "Getting It Done: New Roles for Senior Executives," *Harvard Business Review* 73, no. 6 (November–December 1995), pp. 133–45; Sumantra Ghoshal and Christopher A. Bartlett, "Changing the Role of Top Management: Beyond Structure to Processes," *Harvard Business Review* 73, no. 1 (January–February 1995), pp. 86–96.

[25] Fred Vogelstein, "Winning the Amazon Way," *Fortune,* May 26, 2003, p. 64.

[26] For a more in-depth discussion of the leader's role in creating a results-oriented culture that nurtures success, see Benjamin Schneider, Sarah K. Gunnarson, and Kathryn Niles-Jolly, "Creating the Climate and Culture of Success," *Organizational Dynamics,* Summer 1994, pp. 17–29.

[27] Michael T. Kanazawa and Robert H. Miles, *Big Ideas to Big Results* (Upper Saddle River, NJ: FT Press, 2008), p. 96.

[28] Jeffrey Pfeffer, "Producing Sustainable Competitive Advantage through the Effective Management of People," *Academy of Management Executive* 9, no.1 (February 1995), pp. 55–69.

[29] James Brian Quinn, *Strategies for Change: Logical Incrementalism* (Homewood, IL: Richard D. Irwin, 1980), pp. 20–22.

[30] Ibid., p. 146.

[31] For a good discussion of the challenges, see Daniel Goleman, "What Makes a Leader," *Harvard Business Review* 76, no. 6 (November–December 1998), pp. 92–102; Ronald A. Heifetz and Donald L. Laurie, "The Work of Leadership," *Harvard Business Review* 75, no. 1 (January–February 1997), pp. 124–34; Charles M. Farkas and Suzy Wetlaufer, "The Ways Chief Executive Officers Lead," *Harvard Business Review* 74, no. 3 (May–June 1996), pp. 110–22. See also Michael E. Porter, Jay W. Lorsch, and Nitin Nohria, "Seven Surprises for New CEOs," *Harvard Business Review* 82, no. 10 (October 2004), pp. 62–72.

PART 2

Readings in Crafting and Executing Strategy

New Business Models in Emerging Markets

Matthew J. Eyring, Innosight
Mark W. Johnson, Innosight

Hari Nair, Innosight Venture Partner

Right now more than 20,000 multinationals are operating in emerging economies. According to the *Economist*, Western multinationals expect to find 70% of their future growth there—40% of it in China and India alone. But if the opportunity is huge, so are the obstacles to seizing it. On its 2010 Ease of Doing Business Index, the World Bank ranked China 89th, Brazil 129th, and India 133rd out of 183 countries. Summarizing the bank's conclusions, the *Economist* wrote, "The only way that companies can prosper in these markets is to cut costs relentlessly and accept profit margins close to zero."

Yes, the challenges are significant. But we couldn't disagree more with that opinion. We have seen the opportunities of the future on a street corner in Bangalore, in a small city in central India, in a village in Kenya—and they don't require companies to forgo profits. On the surface, nothing could be more prosaic: a laundry, a compact fridge, a money-transfer service. But look closely at the businesses behind these offerings and you will find the frontiers of business model innovation. These novel ventures reveal a way to help companies escape stagnant demand at home, create new and profitable revenue streams, and find competitive advantage.

That may sound overly optimistic, given the difficulty Western companies have had entering emerging markets to date. But we believe they've struggled not because they can't create viable offerings but because they get their business models wrong. Many multinationals simply import their domestic models into emerging markets. They may tinker at the edges, lowering prices—perhaps by selling smaller sizes or by using lower-cost labor, materials, or other resources. Sometimes they even design and manufacture their products locally and hire local country managers. But their fundamental profit formulas and operating models remain unchanged, consigning these companies to selling largely in the highest income tiers, which in most emerging markets aren't big enough to generate sufficient returns.

What's often missing from even the savviest of these efforts is a systematic process for reconceiving the business model. For more than a decade, through research and our work in both mature and emerging markets, we have been developing our business model innovation and implementation process (see "Reinventing Your Business Model," HBR December 2008, and "Beating the Odds When You Launch a New Venture," HBR May 2010). At its most basic level, the process consists of three steps: *Identify an important unmet job* a target customer needs done; *blueprint a model* that can accomplish that job profitably for a price the customer is willing to pay; and carefully *implement and evolve the model* by testing essential assumptions and adjusting as you learn.

START IN THE MIDDLE

Established companies entering emerging markets should take a page from the strategy of start-ups, for which all markets are new: Instead of looking for additional outlets for existing offerings, they should identify unmet needs—"the jobs to be done" in our terminology—that can be fulfilled at a profit. Emerging markets teem with such jobs. Even the basic needs of their large populations may not yet have been met. In fact, the challenge lies less in finding jobs than in settling on the ones most appropriate for your company to tackle.

Many companies have already been lured by the promise of profits from selling low-end products and services in high volume to the very poor in emerging markets. And high-end products and services are widely available in these markets for the very few who can afford them: You can buy a Mercedes or a washing machine, or stay at a nice hotel, almost anywhere in the world. Our experience suggests a far more promising place to begin: between these two extremes, in the vast middle market. Consumers there are defined not so much by any particular income band as by a common circumstance: Their needs are being met very poorly by existing low-end solutions, because they cannot afford even the cheapest of the high-end alternatives. Companies that devise new business models and offerings to better meet those consumers' needs affordably will discover enormous opportunities for growth.

Take, for example, the Indian consumer durables company Godrej & Boyce. Founded in 1897 to sell locks, Godrej is today a diversified manufacturer of everything from safes to hair dye to refrigerators and washing machines. In workshops we conducted with key managers in the appliances division, refrigerators emerged as a high-potential area: Because of the cost both to buy and to operate them, traditional compressor-driven refrigerators had penetrated only 18% of the market.

The first thing these managers wanted to know, naturally enough, was "Could Godrej provide a cheaper, stripped-down version of our higher-end refrigerator?" We asked them to consider instead the key needs of those with poor or no refrigeration. Did they know what those consumers really wanted? In a word, no. A small team was assigned to conduct detailed observations, open-ended interviews, and video ethnography to illuminate the job to be done for that untapped market.

The semiurban and rural people the team observed typically earned 5,000 to 8,000 rupees (about $125 to $200) a month, lived in single-room dwellings with four or five family members, and changed residences frequently. Unable to afford conventional refrigerators in their own homes, they were making do with communal, usually secondhand ones.

The shared fridges weren't meeting these people's needs very well, but not for the reasons one might expect. The observers found that they almost invariably contained only a few items. Their users tended to shop daily and buy small quantities of vegetables and milk. Electricity was unreliable, putting even the little food they did want to preserve at risk. What's more, although they wanted to cool their drinking water, making ice wasn't a job for which these people would "hire" a refrigerator.

The team concluded that what this group needed to do was to stretch one meal into two by preserving leftovers and to keep drinks cooler than room temperature—a job markedly different from the one higher-end refrigerators do, which is to keep a large supply of perishables on hand, cold or frozen. Clearly, there was no reason to spend a month's salary on a conventional refrigerator and pay steep electricity prices to get the simpler job done. And just as clearly, the solution wasn't a cheaper conventional fridge. Here was an opportunity to create a fundamentally new product for the underserved middle market.

Targeting this market has two great advantages. First, it's easier to upgrade the solution to a job people are already trying to do than to create sufficient customer demand where none yet exists—as would-be vendors of purified water and other seemingly essential offerings have found to their dismay. Second, it's easier to reach people who are already spending money to get their jobs done. That's essentially what Ratan Tata did with the $2,500 Nano. He didn't ask, "How can I get people who've never bought any form of transportation to buy a car?" He asked, "How can I produce a better alternative for people who hire motor scooters to transport their families?" The goal is to redirect existing demand by offering a clear path from an unsatisfactory solution to a better one.

OFFER UNIQUE BENEFITS FOR LESS

To redirect demand, your customer value proposition (CVP) must solve a problem more effectively,

Idea in Brief

Multinationals are looking to emerging markets for future growth. But in trying to transplant their domestic business models, they end up slashing margins or confining themselves to the higher-income tiers, which aren't big enough to generate sufficient returns.

They are overlooking a vast opportunity: the underserved "middle market" of people who struggle to meet basic needs such as refrigeration and clothes washing with low-end options because high-end alternatives are beyond their reach.

To exploit this market, companies must identify important unsatisfied needs, devise fundamentally new business models that can meet them profitably and affordably, and carefully implement and evolve the models by continually testing assumptions and adjusting them.

---

simply, accessibly, or affordably than the alternatives. In developing markets, we have found, the components of a CVP that matter most are affordability and access. Let's look at each in turn.

Affordability. Western companies know that they need to come up with lower-cost offerings in emerging markets, but they too often limit themselves to providing less for less. In 2001, for instance, a 300 ml bottle of Coke cost 10 rupees—a day's wages, on average, and a luxury the company estimated only 4% of the population could afford. To reach the other 96%, it introduced a 200 ml bottle and cut the price in half, shaving margins to make Coke more competitive with common alternatives such as lemonade and tea.

In our experience, though, a far more robust approach to creating an affordable emerging market offering is to trade off expensive features and functions that people don't need for less-expensive ones they do need. To get that right requires a clear understanding of the context in which the offering will be sold—which calls for further fieldwork, preferably of a collaborative rather than a merely observational kind. This is good product-development advice in any market. In fact, it applies to indigenous players operating close to home, like Godrej, as well as to Western companies confronting the unfamiliar.

Godrej's team designed and built a prototype cooling unit from the ground up and tested it in the field with consumers. Then, in February 2008, more than 600 women in Osmanabad, a city in India's Marathwada region, gathered to participate in a co-creation event. Working with the original prototypes and several others that had

followed, they collaborated with Godrej on every aspect of the product's design. They helped plan the interior arrangements, made suggestions for the lid, and provided insights on color (eventually settling on candy red).

The result was the ChotuKool ("little cool"), a top-opening unit that, at 1.5×2 feet and with a capacity of 43 liters, has enough room for the few items users want to keep fresh for a day or two. With only 20 (rather than the usual 200) parts, it has no compressor, cooling tubes, or refrigerant. Instead it uses a chip that cools when a current is applied and a fan like those that prevent desktop computers from overheating. Its top-opening design keeps most of the cold air inside when the lid is opened. It uses less than half the energy of a conventional refrigerator and can run on a battery during the power outages that are common in rural villages. At just 7.8 kilograms, it's highly portable, and at $69, it costs half what the most basic refrigerator does. Because it's the right size for the job, easier to move, and more reliable in a power outage than a conventional fridge, it surpasses the higher-end offering on the performance measures that matter most to these consumers.

Access. It's not surprising that portability is important to potential ChotuKool customers, given that they move frequently. And because populations in emerging markets tend to be dispersed, obtaining goods and services can be more difficult than in the West. This creates opportunities for companies that solve challenges of access.

In Kenya, for example, banking services are scarce and transferring money is complicated and expensive. Without access to traditional services, many people must use unsafe alternatives such as *hawala*—an unregulated network of brokers operating on the honor system—or transport cash by bus. The UK-based Vodafone solved this problem by developing a secure, low-cost mobile money-transfer service. Called M-PESA (*M* for "mobile" and *PESA* from the Swahili word for "money"), the system is operated by Safaricom, Kenya's leading mobile network.

Customers register free with an authorized M-PESA agent—typically a Safaricom dealer, but sometimes a gas station, food market, or other local shop. Once registered, they can deposit or withdraw cash at the agent or transfer money electronically to any mobile phone user, even if the recipient is not a Safaricom subscriber. They can also buy Safaricom airtime for themselves or other subscribers. Customers pay a flat fee of about US 40 cents for person-to-person transfers, 33 cents for withdrawals under $33, and 1.3 cents for balance inquiries. Vodafone (which owns a significant stake in Safaricom) manages individual customer accounts on its server, and Safaricom deposits its customers' balances in pooled accounts in two regulated banks, so their full value is backed by highly liquid assets.

Since its launch, in March 2007, the service has acquired more than 9 million customers—40% of Kenya's adult population. As of June 2010, the *Economist* reported, M-PESA customers could conduct transactions at some 17,900 retail outlets, more than half of them in rural areas. That figure dwarfs the total number of bank branches, post offices, and Post Banks—which is only about 840 nationwide.

Spurred by the success of its original offerings, the service has expanded to include bill payment, business-to-customer payments such as paychecks and microfinance loan disbursements, delivery of humanitarian aid, and international money transfers. After just three years M-PESA accounted for 9% of Safaricom's total revenue. More important, it has become the engine driving the company's profits, which have shifted dramatically from voice to data traffic. Vodafone has launched similar services in Tanzania, Afghanistan, and South Africa and plans to introduce them in Egypt, Fiji, and Qatar as well.

Failure to address the access challenge is an important reason that so many companies have little success adapting their current models to emerging markets. Time and again, the increased volume they hope will offset slimmer profit margins doesn't in fact result in profits, because the costs of serving far-flung customers in infrastructure-poor developing countries are just too high. But companies that, like Vodafone, devise novel approaches may find them to be widely applicable in many markets.

INTEGRATE THE ELEMENTS

Business models can be conceived in a variety of ways. Our approach focuses on the basics and also on factors that make it difficult to move from an existing model to a new one—margin requirements, overhead, and "resource velocity" (the capacity to generate a given volume of business within a specific time frame). It has four parts: the customer value proposition, a profit formula, key processes, and key resources the company must use to deliver the CVP repeatedly and at scale. Creating competitive advantage lies in integrating these elements to produce value for both the customer and the company. That's easy to say but devilishly hard to do. Mapping the traditional functions of your company to these broad categories will show you how much you'd have to change to integrate those functions into a new business model (see the exhibit "Building a New Model").

Once you've devised a CVP for your proposed offering, consider the basis on which you compete—differentiation or price. Offerings that compete on differentiation require that you ask, "What do I have to do to produce this?" which leads you counter-clockwise around the model, looking first at what resources and processes are needed, the cost of which (both fixed and variable) will determine what price can deliver the desired profit margin. That's what Whole Foods did when it created a new market for organic foods. Costs drove prices.

For offerings that compete on the basis of price, you move clockwise around the model, again starting with the CVP, but next setting the price, devising a rough cost structure, and then determining what processes and resources (often radically different from those in your current model) are needed to meet your price requirements. Because affordability is so critical in emerging markets, the decision journey is almost

Building a New Model

Business models must integrate four elements: the customer value proposition(CVP), the profit formula, key processes, and key resources. Developing new business models always begins with devising a new CVP. Models designed to compete on differentiation next establish the resources and processes needed to deliver the CVP, the cost of which determines the price required in the profit formula. Models designed to compete on price proceed in the opposite way, establishing first the offering's price, then the cost structure, and finally the processes and resources required.

invariably clockwise. Innovators start with a revenue model—"We think we can sell this offering to X number of people at price Y"—and then devise the cost structure required to deliver a certain unit margin. Becoming profitable at that margin means operating at a certain resource velocity, which in turn drives decisions about how to organize operations, what materials to use, and other questions.

More often than not, this exercise reveals that a company can't meet its profit goals in emerging markets merely by reducing variable costs in its current profit formula and that a viable model will require changes to fixed costs or overhead as well. That's what Ratan Tata discovered when he set out to produce his $2,500 car. He couldn't just send the car down the production line and somehow spend less to make it. He needed to reduce fixed costs by designing a car with far fewer parts and changing assembly methods and

other key processes. Implementing models that require changes in overhead, margins, or resource velocity tends to be problematic for incumbent companies, which is why it's not surprising that start-ups so often have the edge in bringing to market offerings that require new ways to turn a profit. An open mind is perhaps the most important asset anyone can bring to emerging markets. We learned that lesson when we set out to solve a basic but knotty cleaning problem for a vast group of frustrated consumers.

Village Laundry Service—which was founded by our company and uses the Chamak brand—was aimed squarely at the emerging middle market. In India people who can't afford a washing machine but want an alternative to laborious washing by hand after a long day's work have unappealing choices: They can patronize a *dhobi* (a traditional washing person), or they can take their clothes to a neighborhood laundry or dry-cleaning establishment. The dhobis are cheap, but they use any available water, which can be unhygienic. They slap the clothes against rocks to clean them, which wears down the fabrics, and they don't compensate customers for damage. Turnaround time is five to seven days. A laundry or dry cleaner can do the job in four or five days, generally returns the clothes in good shape, and makes amends if something goes wrong. A laundry may or may not use clean water, however, and both are far more expensive than a dhobi.

In early 2009 we ventured into several parts of India, from urban slums to rural villages, conducting interviews and immersing ourselves in the lives of the people who faced this frustrating choice. What, exactly, was the job to be done? What sort of laundry service would these customers hire? We discovered several things: The job wasn't to make it affordable for them to clean their clothes the way rich people did; it was to replicate the advantage of a home washer and dryer at a price they could afford. It wouldn't be sufficient to get the clothes back in four days—they'd have to be ready within 24 hours, and at a price well below the laundry's or dry cleaner's. And they'd have to be easy to pick up at a nearby location.

With those requirements clearly in mind, we examined all parts of the business model to come up with an inventive way of extending access while keeping costs low. We immediately realized that it would be hard to create a profitable business that placed many traditional self-service laundries across a town, because demand was unpredictable and up-front capital investment and rental deposits would be high. Our solution: Portable seven-foot-square kiosks, each holding an efficient front-loading washer and a dryer, which can be placed wherever there is heavy foot traffic. Customers drop off their clothes to be washed, dried, and ironed, all within 24 hours. The kiosk's small footprint minimizes rents, and its independent water supply, delivered through a fixed contract, is both less expensive and more reliable than the public utility connection. Covered with ads for the Chamak brand, the kiosks also serve as bill-boards, reducing the need for paid advertising. We keep transaction costs low through an innovative point-of-sale system, made up of a cell phone linked to a Bluetooth printer and report server, which prints receipts, tracks orders, and captures data on business volume.

After much experimentation, we developed standard procedures for staffing and running the kiosks, including tests to gauge potential operators' aptitude and commitment; simple picture-based operating instructions (much like those used in fast-food restaurants) to ensure consistent service; and a score-card for traffic level, customer satisfaction, marketing effectiveness, and other variables, allowing us to predict the chances of success at each location and to make operations replicable and scalable.

It is this innovative marriage of a novel solution with all the other elements of the business model that makes Chamak's services affordable and profitable. The model allows the company to charge 40 rupees (about $1) per kilogram of clothing—little more than what dhobis charge and significantly less than what professional laundries and dry cleaners do (sometimes 90 rupees per garment). Village Laundry Service currently has 5,000 customers patronizing some 20 booths in Mumbai, Bangalore, and Mysore. The company expects to reach breakeven in late 2011. Of course, as with any new business, how Village Laundry Service performs over the long term will depend on a number of hard-to-predict factors.

FROM BLUEPRINT TO OPERATING BUSINESS

Testing and implementing the business model blueprint in emerging markets is as much an art as a science. Having a cadre of global "experts" study the market for months and create a plan that is then handed over to the local team for execution simply doesn't work. Quick adjustments based on early lessons learned on the ground trump the best and most detailed strategic plan developed before the fact.

M-PESA succeeded in part because Kenya's banking regulator permitted Safaricom to test various business models from the very beginning. Safaricom made the most of the opportunity. It started in 2004 by experimenting with 500 customers and a system designed to allow them to repay microloans. As the company market-tested this concept, it discovered a more-compelling value proposition—namely, a way for urban workers to transfer funds to friends and family members in rural areas. That fundamental insight was the basis on which subsequent services were built, and since M-PESA's commercial launch, its simple but powerful branding message has been "Send money home."

This doesn't mean that expertise is unimportant when launching a new business in an emerging market. But we've found that agile functional expertise is the most critical kind, because the uncertainties in emerging markets are so great. A broad network of resources—including responsive advertising agencies, companies that can produce prototypes on demand, financial service advisers who understand local regulatory guidelines, and a healthy bench of local entrepreneurs to execute the plan—is essential.

The ability to conduct rapid experiments inexpensively and use what you learn from them to hone the business model is essential to success. It allows you to make course corrections before you commit to major operational or strategic investments. Recently a company we incubated was looking to launch a men's grooming business but was uncertain about demand. Rather than commission an expensive 10-city quantitative research study, we rented a small air-conditioned truck and created a mini hair salon on wheels, outfitted with a barber's chair, scissors and other implements, and a mirror. For two weeks we drove the truck around the streets of Bangalore to gauge demand and test various pricing scenarios at various locations. The experiment, which cost all of $3,000, provided essential answers that no survey could have and demonstrated the business potential for an affordable and convenient Supercuts-like business for men. The company changed from a roving barbershop model to a kiosk-based model and is considering offering additional services, such as facials and skin lightening, that many customers desire.

Ultimately, the potential for such business model innovations, as for many other disruptive innovations, may extend far beyond the markets for which they were created. G. Sunderraman, the vice president of corporate development at Godrej, sees the ChotuKool as a new growth platform. Unit sales are projected to reach 10,000 in the first year and 100,000 by the end of the second. If Godrej considered the ChotuKool to be simply a no-frills refrigerator for the middle market, it might be content with a moderate penetration rate. But the company's managers regard it as a new product category, based on new technology, that has the potential to perform jobs for people at many income levels. In areas with frequent power outages, the owners of conventional refrigerators might want an inexpensive and reliable backup. Small shops, offices, and manufacturing sites might use it to maintain a supply of cool drinks. Higher-income customers—perhaps in developed economies as well—might use it in their bedrooms, their cars, or their boats. When the technology improves, Godrej believes, it can enter mainstream markets as ChotuKool changes consumers' expectations about refrigerator prices and performance and addresses a need that previously went unmet.

Many companies view emerging markets as one large foothold market, and in this they are right. Classic disruptive innovation theory holds that, ideally, innovations should first be introduced in markets where the alternatives fall short on some dimension (typically price) or are utterly unavailable. Emerging markets fit that bill in spades. They are excellent arenas for trying out product innovations far from competitors' prying eyes. But we are convinced that a much greater opportunity lies in viewing these markets not as one vast lab for *product* R&D but as unique environments filled with poorly done jobs that could be creatively addressed with *business model* R&D. Creating new business models will give your company a more enduring competitive advantage.

Four Ways to Uncover Unmet Needs

Study what your customers are doing with your product. Be aware that, as Peter Drucker famously said, "The customer rarely buys what the business thinks it sells him."

Look at the alternatives to your offerings that consumers buy. Investigate a wide range of substitutes for your products, not just what your competitors make.

Watch for compensating behaviors. Discover what jobs people are satisfying poorly.

Search for explanations. Uncover the root causes of consumers' behavior by asking what people are trying to accomplish with the goods and services they use.

The Power of Vision: Statements That Resonate

Sooksan Kantabutra
Madihol University, Bangkok, Thailand

Gayle C. Avery
Macquarie University, Sydney, Australia

In a fast-changing world, the question for many senior managers is: "What leadership strategy is needed for my organization to stay competitive and to thrive?" To many academics and consultants, visionary leadership or leadership with vision as a core component is the answer. Although scholars, corporate trainers, and management consultants often emphasize the importance of espousing a vision and even suggest characteristics of an effective vision, no one really knows what such a vision looks like (Avery, 2004). In today's corporate world, we can observe that vision statements appear with a wide variety of characteristics, as these examples demonstrate:

> Year after year, Westin and its people will be regarded as the best and most sought after hotel and resort management group in North America. (Westin Hotels & Resorts)

> FirstEnergy will be a leading regional energy provider, recognized for operational excellence, customer service and its commitment to safety; the choice for long-term growth, investment value and financial strength; and a company driven by the leadership, skills, diversity and character of its employees. (FirstEnergy)

> Macy's, Inc., is a premier national retailer with brands that reflect the spirit of America. The timeless values that made our nation strong are the same values that make our company strong:
>
> - A belief in the promise of the future with the energy and determination to get us there.
> - A belief that our heritage mirrors the optimism, inclusion and integrity that provide for both stability and growth.
> - A belief that taking advantage of the right opportunities will continue to lead us to success in all that we do. (Macy's, Inc.)

Adding to the confusion is when practitioners and consultants have great difficulty in differentiating vision from other related terms of mission, values, beliefs, principles, and strategy. This is illustrated in Sage Software's "Corporate Vision and Strategy" as follows:

> As Sage Software has grown, we've been guided by a simple statement of purpose: to help make it easier for our customers to manage their business processes. Standing behind that purpose are our principles for operating the business—with a focus on agility, innovation, trust and integrity, and simplicity—all of which keep us closely connected with our customers. . . .
>
> We are confident in achieving those successes for our customers and have developed a strategy to guide our efforts. With the support of our customers, and through the dedication of our employees and partners, we invite you to share in that vision.

Some organizations already have a vision, but how effective is it? How should senior managers go about developing an effective vision? We know that vision is the starting point of any organizational transformation process and should

Reprinted from "The Power of Vision: Statements that Resonate," by Sooksan Kantabutra and Gayle C. Avery, *Journal of Business Strategy* 31, no. 1 (2010), pp. 37–45. Copyright © Emerald Group Publishing Limited.

underpin business strategy. But senior managers have often been developing vision statements unaware of what the empirical evidence tells us about constructing an effective vision. According to many leadership scholars, senior managers need to distinguish between "strong" and "weak" visions (Rafferty and Griffin, 2004), as well as "positive" and "negative" (Senge, 1990) visions to ensure their vision is effective. This is particularly important in geographically dispersed organizations where people down the line must share the same vision. Given that senior managers want to develop a "right" vision, knowing about the latest research findings about vision is critical.

We first investigated this issue among retailers in Sydney, the most populous city of Australia (Kantabutra and Avery, 2007), and then their counterparts in Thailand's Bangkok, one of Asia's most populous cities (Kantabutra, 2008a). Our findings reveal that powerful visions that make a significant impact on customer and employee satisfaction—the bottom line of any business—possess certain characteristics: conciseness, clarity, abstractness, challenge, future orientation, stability, and desirability or the ability to inspire. We found similar results by examining the vision statements of *Fortune*'s "Best Companies to Work For," a set of high-performing organizations from a wide range of industries in the USA (Levering and Moskowitz, 2002). Our research has led us to believe that these findings about the characteristics of powerful visions have important implications for leaders working across a wide range of industries, and possibly across different cultures.

Even if one already accepts that vision is critical to organizational performance, our research has identified a few practical guidelines for creating effective visions. In this article, we analyze and describe characteristics of effective visions, and offer practical tips for leaders.

VISIONS THAT WORK

For almost three decades, scholars have argued that vision is important to leadership, strategy implementation, and change. Kenneth Leithwood and colleagues (Leithwood et al., 1996) even point out that vision building is intended to create a fundamental, ambitious sense of purpose, one

to be pursued over many years. Despite its clear importance in the management literature, vision is still not defined in a generally agreed-upon manner (Kantabutra and Avery, 2002). This is a critical issue because how we define *vision* affects how it is espoused by practicing managers and studied by scholars. Indeed, a survey of practicing managers found little agreement as to what they thought *vision* is (Baetz and Bart, 1996), and in the corporate world today there is no commonly agreed definition for a vision.

Avoiding the definitional issue altogether, Robert Baum and his colleagues (Baum et al., 1998) chose not to define vision in advance, but to accept the term as each *individual leader defines it*. They argued that it is the leader's actual vision that guides his or her choices and actions. This approach makes sense to us for three reasons. First, each leader develops a vision in his or her own way, sometimes rationally and objectively, often intuitively and subjectively. Second, visionary leadership often varies from leader to leader on important dimensions. For example, vision has been found to differ based on the leader's style, the content of the vision, and the context in which it takes root. Third, every leader induces his/her followers to act on the vision by using a range of techniques, such as legitimate authority, modeling, intellectual stimulation, goal setting, rewarding and punishing, organizational restructuring, and team building.

Adopting the definition based upon what individual leaders regard as a vision offers a pragmatic way around the definitional confusion in the vision literature. This approach was adopted by Robert Baum and colleagues (Baum et al., 1998) in their study of American start-up firms. They found that vision—based upon the definition espoused by each individual leader—had a statistically significant and positive impact on venture growth. Therefore, we adopted this vision definition for both our Sydney and Bangkok studies.

WHAT DO "POWERFUL" VISIONS LOOK LIKE?

Although business strategy and leadership writers have proposed different characteristics that a vision should have, some commonly shared characteristics can be identified (Kantabutra, 2008b). These include:

1. Conciseness.
2. Clarity.
3. Future orientation.
4. Stability.
5. Challenge.
6. Abstractness.
7. Desirability or ability to inspire.

These seven vision characteristics hold varying degrees of empirical support in the research literature, as well as face validity among managers. Nonetheless, few if any studies have incorporated all of them into a single vision construct for thorough empirical testing. This is the approach that we followed in our research.

Both our retail store studies used the above framework to explore the relationship between vision characteristics and organizational performance, as measured by customer and employee satisfaction. Both these measures are regarded as leading indicators of financial performance.

In the real world, many factors potentially affect organizational performance, and need to be taken into account by researchers. These are known as vision "realization factors." In our research, we included the following factors that previous research indicated were likely to affect realizing a vision:

- Communicating the vision.
- Aligning organizational processes and systems to suit the vision.
- Empowering others to act to achieve the vision.
- Motivating staff.

We hypothesized that rating higher on these factors would demonstrate the existence of a more powerful vision. We further predicted that more powerful visions would be associated with stronger organizational performance.

THE SAMPLES

The samples were drawn from apparel stores in Sydney and in Bangkok that sell brand-new, finished clothing products for individual use, excluding shoes and accessories. Both independent stores and those belonging to a parent company were sampled. All were located in a shopping mall and had their own identity, being in a clearly defined walled area.

A total of 19 of Sydney's major shopping centers were selected and all qualifying stores approached. Of these, 111 stores (70 percent) agreed to participate, with 48 stores (30 percent) declining. From the participating stores, store managers and up to three staff and three customers were interviewed. Store managers refer to those full-time store employees who manage their own stores and are stationed there daily. The latter criterion is important because we were interested in the effects of one manager's vision only. Staff includes full-time, part-time, and casual employees working under the store managers. Customers comprise individuals who were observed buying a product during our visit. If no customer was observed buying during our visit, we returned later until three customers agreed to participate or three visits were made to the store. One hundred and forty-eight staff members and 214 customers participated in our Sydney study.

A total of 12 malls in major Bangkok shopping areas were selected. All qualifying stores in each center were approached. Of these, 126 stores (88.7 percent) agreed to participate, with 16 stores (11.3 percent) declining. From the participating shops, store managers and up to half of each store's total staff members were asked to respond to store manager and staff questionnaires. Based on the number of staff determined for each store, the same number of customers for each respective store was also asked to respond to a customer questionnaire. If no customer was observed buying during our visit, we returned later until the determined number of customers agreed to participate or three visits were made to the store. Store managers, staff, and customers were defined in the same way as those of the Sydney samples. A total of 251 staff members and 258 customers were surveyed in Bangkok.

The store managers were asked to answer questions concerning their vision and organizational alignment, while staff members were asked about vision communication, motivation, and empowerment, as well as their level of job satisfaction. Customers responded to questions concerning their level of customer satisfaction with the store.

DOES VISION MAKE A DIFFERENCE?

From our results, we confirmed prior findings that powerful business visions possess all seven characteristics—conciseness, clarity, abstractness, challenge, future orientation, stability, and desirability or inspiration. Robert Baum and colleagues (Baum et al., 1998) were among the first who found positive relationships between vision characteristics of brevity, challenge, future orientation, aspiring, abstractness, clarity, stability and vision content, and organizational performance in entrepreneurial firms. They surveyed CEOs of architectural woodwork firms, and found that vision characteristics and vision content were directly related to venture growth, as measured by sales, profits, employment, and net worth in these entrepreneurial firms. These vision characteristics were strongly related to venture growth through their effects on vision communication. In our Australian study, we discovered that when one or more of the seven characteristics were missing from a vision, there was no significant effect on either staff or customer satisfaction. Visions with the seven characteristics also impacted the satisfaction of both customers and staff in Bangkok retail stores in significant, positive ways. How each characteristic combines with the other six characteristics to create this effect is explained next.

A vision's conciseness is indicated by whether the vision statement is brief; effective visions contain between 11 and 22 words, rendering them easy to communicate and remember. This was the case in both retail studies where concise visions were indeed frequently communicated.

Clear visions directly point at a prime goal. They can be understood without extended presentation and discussion, often in five minutes. The following is an example of a store manager vision that rates highly on both conciseness and clarity: "to be known as the most interesting store in Sydney."

At the same time, however, powerful visions certainly do not consist of a one-time, specific goal or productivity target (e.g., sales or profit) that can be met and then discarded. They are also abstract, such as the example above. After all, a vision is meant to act as a guide for a wide range of business activities over a long period of time. More critically, abstract visions suggest a longer-term goal that also allows for individual interpretations. This characteristic provides a basis for achieving support from a broader base of stakeholders. This abstractness also allows staff members to apply their own creativity within the framework of their store manager's vision as they carry out daily store operations. An example of a vision rated highly on abstractness is: "to be the market leader in fashionability." This abstract vision allows staff members from all store functions (e.g., designers, front officers, and even support officers) to interpret the vision in their own creative ways as they carry out daily store operations for their store to become "the market leader in fashionability."

In addition, effective visions are challenging—being challenged motivates staff members to try their best to achieve desired outcomes. Challenging visions possess a high but achievable degree of difficulty enabling staff members to enhance their self-esteem as they seek to achieve the store's vision. In our studies, challenging visions usually aim at achieving a national or international status for the store and/or its brand, such as "to be the best retailer in Australia."

Powerful visions clearly indicate the long-term perspective of the business, and the future environment in which it functions. This is because a vision has no power to inspire staff members or attract their commitment unless it offers a view of a clearly better future.

In addition, powerful visions are *stable.* They do not shift in response to short-term trends, technology changes, or market changes, although they must be flexible enough to weather fluctuations. An example of an effective vision with these two characteristics is: "to be the best retailer in New South Wales." This vision statement indicates the long-term perspective of the business (to be the best retailer) and the future environment in which it functions (New South Wales). It is also stable, because no matter how far it is projected into the future, being the best retailer will still be meaningful, despite any change in markets or technology.

Since the hallmark of management is achieving results through others, the ability to motivate staff is central to leadership. As a consequence, powerful visions must be highly desirable and inspiring. They state a goal that directly inspires staff.

An especially strong vision statement in our studies incorporating the seven characteristics is "to be the number one retailer in Australia." This vision statement is brief, pointing directly at a prime goal. Aiming to be the number one retailer in Australia makes this vision statement very challenging and inspiring. Unlikely to be affected by technology or market changes, it also indicates the long-term perspective of the organization and the future environment in which it functions. This vision statement is abstract, inclusive to all organizational interests. Anyone in the organization can use this vision to guide his/her daily operations. Some other powerful visions in our studies include:

> To remain the flagship store of the company by excellent customer service, having the best product and a beautiful store.

> To be the number one choice for youth in surfwear, streetwear and to also do this at the best quality yet the cheapest price.

> To bring the store to its full potential, giving it recognition as one of the best in the company.

HOW DOES VISION MAKE A DIFFERENCE?

Since the literature so consistently emphasizes the importance of vision sharing between leader and followers, we investigated this relationship further in the Sydney retail stores (Kantabutra and Avery, 2005). More specifically, we examined the relationships between vision components shared between store managers and their staff, the way store managers motivate and empower staff to achieve and sustain the shared vision, staff enactment of the vision, and both customer and staff satisfaction.

Instead of investigating the seven vision characteristics alone, these analyses also took into account vision content. It makes more sense to investigate both characteristics and content when it comes to understanding how vision is shared between the leader and followers. Vision content examined in our study focused on images relating to customer and staff satisfaction in the vision statement—because both staff and customer satisfaction are critical to organizational performance.

Our analysis reveals that the shared vision characteristics and content have positive, direct effects on both customer and staff satisfaction. Moreover, staff use of the shared vision to guide their daily operations; and employee motivation and empowerment are critical to staff satisfaction. The most surprising discovery, perhaps a convincing endorsement for the essence of shared vision, is that sharing both vision characteristics and vision content is especially important to customer and staff satisfaction. Simply sharing a vision is even more important than either the leader's efforts at motivation and empowerment, or employees actually using the shared vision to guide their daily activities.

In the Sydney study, in addition to shared vision being important, empowering staff directly improved customer satisfaction, while motivation and empowerment of staff directly predicted improvements in staff satisfaction. Organizational alignment and vision communication predicted improvements in staff satisfaction, but only indirectly.

The vision realization factors appear to operate differently in Bangkok retail stores. Motivation of staff is the only direct predictor of enhanced staff satisfaction, while empowerment of staff, organizational alignment, and vision communication indirectly predicted improvements in staff satisfaction. On the other hand, vision, vision communication, empowerment of staff, motivation of staff, and staff satisfaction indirectly predicted improvements in customer satisfaction.

DO THESE FINDINGS APPLY MORE BROADLY?

Of course, we must be careful about overstating the results of a few studies, even when they are built upon a foundation of earlier research. Thus, it is natural to ask, "Are these findings about vision specific to the retail industry?" In response to this question, we followed up the earlier studies with additional research aimed at determining whether these findings could apply in other industries.

To begin to answer this question, we analyzed 41 available vision statements from the 2002 *Fortune*'s "Best Companies to Work For." This sample comprised high-performing U.S.

companies from a wide range of industries. These organizations claim that their vision statements guide their strategic behaviors, strategies and plans.

Our analysis suggests that the vision statements used by these *Fortune* best companies also reflect the seven characteristics found in the Sydney and Bangkok research. Judged against the seven vision characteristics, the most powerful vision statement from our *Fortune* best companies sample is: "to be recognized as the best professional services firm in the world" (Deloitte Touche Tohmatsu). This vision statement is concise, pointing directly at a prime goal. It is unlikely to be affected by technology or market changes. Very challenging and desirable, this vision statement indicates the long-term perspective of the organization and the future environment in which it functions. No matter how large or dispersed the organization, everyone can use the vision to guide his or her daily operations because it is abstract. Other visions from the *Fortune* sample that strongly conform with the seven attributes are shown as follows:

> To provide the most useful and ethical financial services in the world. (Charles Schwab Corporation)
> To be a world-class provider of food and services. (Ukrop's Food Group)

This research leads us to believe that the seven characteristics of powerful visions found among Sydney and Bangkok apparel retailers, and previously among U.S. start-up firms, could apply across different industries and even cultures.

LINKING VISION AND RESULTS

At first glance, one may question what is so new and original about the samples of effective vision statements from both the Sydney and Bangkok retailers and the *Fortune* best companies. These sample vision statements may not appear to contain innovative ideas. In some cases, they highlight simple, known ideas. However, simplicity and banality do not limit the value of powerful visions.

Kotter (1999) found in his research that successful visions do not have to be brilliantly innovative; in fact, some of the best ones are not.

Effective business visions can even have an almost mundane quality, often consisting of fundamental ideas that are already well known. We believe this is because a vision is used to guide organizational members, and therefore needs to encompass all organizational interests. That is, the more inclusive a vision, the more mundane. Although this quality seems obvious, Daft (2005) found in his research of business organizations that many visions fail to adequately involve employees. The more specific, unique, and innovative a vision statement, the less likely it will appeal to a wide range of organizational interests and stakeholders.

In addition, we found that the retail store managers' visions enhanced staff satisfaction in both Sydney and Bangkok. This applies especially to those managers who actively communicate their visions, model their visions through their own actions, and motivate and empower their staff to act on the visions. Furthermore, where store managers align store management systems to match their visions, staff satisfaction is enhanced. In such settings, visions displaying the seven characteristics also positively affected the satisfaction of both customers and staff. This is important because customer and staff satisfaction are frequently correlated with financial and other performance measures.

HOW DIFFERENTLY SHOULD MANAGERS NOW DEVELOP A VISION?

Clearly, more research is still needed into characteristics of powerful visions and vision realization factors. However, our studies, building on prior research, suggest several interesting practical implications. An organizational vision should be shared by organizational members. Vision sharing can be developed when each manager first develops a vision and then communicates it to organizational members or when all organizational members derive a vision. In particular, research suggests that visions that are concise, clear, future-oriented, stable, challenging, abstract, and inspiring are likely to bring about better performance outcomes than visions without these characteristics. Appropriate realization factors should also be put in place. For example, the vision should be aligned with the strategy, and the people empowered.

Some specific guidelines for developing a vision are provided below. A leader should espouse a vision that:

- Is brief (so that it can be remembered and repeated easily).
- Contains a prime goal to be achieved.
- Can encompass all organizational interests.
- Is not a one-time, specific goal that can be met and then discarded.
- Provides a source of motivation for employees to do their best by including a degree of difficulty or stretch (e.g., to achieve a national/international status).
- Offers a long-term perspective for the organization and indicates the future environment in which it will function.

- Is unlikely to be changed by market or technology changes.
- Is viewed as desirable by employees.

Visions containing these characteristics are expected to bring about higher performance outcomes, initially through employee and customer satisfaction, than those without.

Simply having a vision that meets the above criteria is not enough. To maximize performance outcomes, managers should also communicate the vision, motivate and empower employees to act on the vision, and align organizational systems to support the vision. As for employees, the research suggests that they too benefit when managers are able to create and shape a vision meeting the attributes described here. This enables followers to work more effectively, and leads to higher job satisfaction. Therefore, managers who work effectively with a powerful vision could benefit from being aware of these characteristics and realization factors.

REFERENCES

Avery, G. C. (2004), *Understanding Leadership,* Sage Publications, London.

Baetz, M. C. and Bart, C. K. (1996), "Developing mission statements which work," *Long Range Planning,* Vol. 29 No. 4, pp. 524–31.

Baum, J. R., Locke, E. A. and Kirkpatrick, S. A. (1998), "A longitudinal study of the relation of vision and vision communication to venture growth in entrepreneurial firms," *Journal of Applied Psychology,* Vol. 83, pp. 43–54.

Daft, R. L. (2005), *The Leadership Experience,* Thomson South-Western, Mason, OH.

Kantabutra, S. (2008a), "Vision effects in Thai retail stores: practical implications," *International Journal of Retail & Distribution Management,* Vol. 36 No. 4, pp. 323–42.

Kantabutra, S. (2008b), "What do we know about vision?" *Journal of Applied Business Research,* Vol. 24 No. 2, pp. 127–38.

Kantabutra, S. and Avery, G. C. (2002), "Proposed model for investigating relationships between vision components and business unit performance," *Journal of Management and Organization,* Vol. 8 No. 2, pp. 22–39.

Kantabutra, S. and Avery, G. C. (2005), "Essence of shared vision: empirical investigation," *New Zealand Journal of Human Resources Management,* Vol. 5, pp. 1–28.

Kantabutra, S. and Avery, G. C. (2007), "Vision effects in customer and staff satisfaction: an empirical investigation," *Leadership & Organization Development Journal,* Vol. 28 No. 3, pp. 209–29.

Kotter, J. P. (1999), *What Do Leaders Really Do?* Harvard Business School Press, Boston, MA.

Leithwood, K., Tomlinson, D. and Genge, M. (1996), "Transformational school leadership," in Leithwood, K., Chapman, J., Corson, D., Hallinger, Ph. and Hart, A. (Eds.), *International Handbook of Educational Leadership and Administration,* Kluwer, Dordrecht.

Levering, R. and Moskowitz, M. (2002), "Best companies to work for: the best in the worst of times," *Fortune,* Vol. 145 No. 3, pp. 148–68.

Rafferty, A. E. and Griffin, M. A. (2004), "Dimensions of transformational leadership: conceptual and empirical extensions," *The Leadership Quarterly,* Vol. 15 No. 3, pp. 329–54.

Senge, P. M. (1990), *The Fifth Discipline: The Art and Practice of the Learning Organization,* Currency Doubleday, New York, NY.

Getting into Your Competitor's Head

Hugh Courtney
University of Maryland

John T. Horn
McKinsey & Company

Jayanti Kar
McKinsey & Company

The global financial crisis that erupted in 2008 shows, with painful clarity, that we live in an interdependent business world. In bleak times and fair, the success of a company's strategy often depends greatly on the strategies of its competitors. In periods of financial turmoil, for instance, the prospects—and even survival—of a bank often depend on the near-term M&A of its rivals. Similarly, the ultimate success of Boeing's new commercial jet, the 787 Dreamliner, will depend on the way Airbus positions, markets, and sells its new and competing A380 and A350. Pfizer's ability to sustain market share and profitability in the market for cholesterol-lowering treatments will depend on the moves of the company's branded and generic pharmaceutical competitors, to say nothing of biotech and medical-product companies developing alternative treatments.

This strategic interdependence implies that the ability to anticipate your competitors' strategies is essential. Yet a recent survey of business executives found that the actions and reactions of potential rivals almost never play a role in, for example, decisions to introduce and price new products.[1] An important reason for this neglect, we believe, is that strategic-planning tools, such as game theory and scenario planning, are of limited use unless a company can correctly define the key elements of the strategic game, especially the strategic options and objectives of competitors. This is no easy task. Rare is the company that truly understands what its competitors and their decision makers care about most, how they perceive their assets and capabilities, and what all this means for their strategies. A company with such insights could reverse-engineer the moves of competitors and predict what they were likely to do. In a credit crunch, for instance, such a company would be well positioned to buy financial and nonfinancial assets at attractive prices if it knew that poorly capitalized competitors would avoid new risk and therefore not bid for these assets.

Getting inside your competitor's head is difficult because companies (and their decision makers) usually are not alike. At any time, a company has assets, resources, market positions, and capabilities it must protect, leverage, and build upon. Different endowments imply different strategies even in the same general market environment. What's more, even a competitor with similar endowments may pursue different strategies if its owners, stakeholders, and decision makers have a different objective.

So if you want to anticipate rather than react to strategic moves, you must analyze a competitor at two levels: organizational and individual. At the organizational level, you have to think like a strategist of your competitor by searching for the perfect strategic fit between its endowments and its changing market environment. At the

Reprinted from *McKinsey Quarterly* Issue 1 (2009), pp. 128–37.
This article was originally published in McKinsey Quarterly, www.mckinseyquarterly.com. Copyright © 2009 McKinsey & Company. All rights reserved. Reprinted by permission.

individual level, you have to think like the decision makers of the competitor, identifying who among them makes which decisions and the influences and incentives guiding their choices. This approach moves you beyond the data-gathering efforts of most competitive-intelligence functions, toward a thought process that helps turn competitive intelligence into competitive insights. While our approach won't eliminate surprises, it will help you better understand your competitors and their likely moves and eliminate some of the guesswork that undermines the development of strategies in an increasingly interdependent business world.

THINK LIKE YOUR COMPETITOR'S STRATEGIST

When your competitor resembles you, chances are it will pursue similar strategies—what we call symmetric competition. When companies have different assets, resources, capabilities, and market positions, they will probably react to the same market opportunities and threats in different ways—what we call asymmetric competition. One of the keys to predicting a competitor's future strategies is to understand how much or little it resembles your company.

In the fast-food industry, for example, two leading players, McDonald's and Burger King, face the same market trends but have responded in markedly different ways to the obesity backlash. McDonald's has rolled out a variety of foods it promotes as healthy. Burger King has introduced high-fat, high-calorie sandwiches supported by in-your-face, politically incorrect ads. As the dominant player, McDonald's is the lightning rod for the consumer and government backlash on obesity. It can't afford to thumb its nose at these concerns. Smaller players like Burger King, realizing this, see an opportunity to cherry-pick share in the less health-conscious fast-food segment. Burger King competes asymmetrically.

Companies can determine whether they face symmetric or asymmetric competition by using the resource-based view of strategy: the idea that they should protect, leverage, extend, build, or acquire resources and capabilities that are valuable, rare, and

inimitable and that can be successfully exploited. Resources come in three categories: tangible assets (for example, physical, technological, financial, and human resources), intangible assets (brands, reputation, and knowledge), and current market positions (access to customers, economies of scale and scope, and experience). Capabilities come in two categories: the ability both to identify and to exploit opportunities better than others do.

In the video-game-console business, the strategies of Microsoft and Sony, which are attempting to dominate next-generation systems, are largely predictable—based on each company's tangible and intangible assets and current market position. Although the core businesses of the two competitors will be affected by video game consoles differently, both sides see them as potential digital hubs replacing some current stand-alone consumer electronic devices, such as DVD players, and interconnecting with high-definition televisions, personal computers, MP3 players, digital cameras, and so forth.

For Sony, which has valuable businesses in consumer electronics and in audio and video content, it is important to establish the PlayStation as the living-room hub, so that any cannibalization of the company's consumer electronics businesses comes from within. After the recent victory of Sony's Blu-ray standard over Toshiba's HD-DVD, Sony stands to realize a huge payoff in future licensing revenues. The PlayStation, which plays only Blu-ray disks, is thus one of the company's most important vehicles in driving demand for Blu-ray gaming, video, and audio content.

Microsoft has limited hardware and content businesses but dominates personal computers and network software. Establishing the Xbox as the living-room hub would therefore help to protect and extend its software businesses. For Microsoft, it is crucial that the "digital living room" of the future should run on Microsoft software. If an Apple product became the hub of future "iHome" living rooms, Microsoft's software business might suffer.

Sony and Microsoft therefore have different motives for fighting this console battle. Yet the current market positions (existing businesses and economies of scope), tangible assets (patents, cash), and intangible assets (knowledge, brands) of both companies suggest that they will compete aggressively to win. It was predictable that they would produce consoles which, so far, have been far superior technologically to previous systems and interconnect seamlessly with the Internet, computers, and a wide variety of consumer electronics devices. It was also predictable that both companies would price their consoles below cost to establish an installed base in the world's living rooms quickly. The competition to win exclusive access to the best third-party developers' games, as well as consumer mind-share, will also probably continue to be waged more aggressively than it was in previous console generations. For Microsoft and Sony, the resource-based view of strategy helps us to understand that this battle is about far more than dominance in the video game industry and thus to identify the aggressive strategies both are likely to follow.

Nintendo, in contrast, is largely a pure-play video game company and thus an asymmetric competitor to Microsoft and Sony. The resource-based view of strategy explains why Nintendo's latest console, the Wii, focuses primarily on the game-playing experience and isn't positioned as a digital hub for living rooms. The Wii's most innovative feature is therefore a new, easy-to-use controller appealing to new and hardcore gamers alike. The Wii has few of the expensive digital-hub features built into the rival consoles and thus made its debut with a lower retail price.

Applying the resource-based view of strategy to competitors in a rigorous, systematic, and fact-based way can help you identify the options they will probably consider for any strategic issue. But if you want to gain better insight into which of those options your competitors are likeliest to choose, you have to move beyond a general analysis of their communications, behavior, assets, and capabilities and also think about the personal perceptions and incentives of their decision makers.

THINK LIKE YOUR COMPETITOR'S DECISION MAKERS

Since the objectives of corporate decision makers rarely align completely with corporate objectives, companies often act in ways that seem inconsistent with their stated strategic intentions or with the unbiased assessments of outsiders about the best paths for them to follow. So if you want to predict the next moves of a competitor, you must often consider the preferences and incentives of its decision makers.

The key to getting inside the head of a competitor making any decision is first identifying who is most likely to make it and then figuring out how the objectives and incentives of that person or group may influence the competitor's actions. In most companies, owners and top managers make divestment decisions, for example. Strategic pricing and service decisions are often made, within broad corporate guidelines, by frontline sales personnel and managers.

Owners and Other Important Stakeholders

The objectives of the person or group with a controlling interest in your competitor probably have a major influence on its strategy. Sometimes, personal preferences are particularly relevant: it's likely that Virgin's pioneering foray into the commercial space travel industry partially reflects the adventurous tastes of its charismatic founder, Sir Richard Branson. For family-owned or -controlled businesses—public or private—family values, history, and relationships may drive strategy. A competitor owned by a private-equity firm is likely to focus on near-term performance improvements to generate cash and make the company more attractive to buyers. While every private-equity firm is different, you can often forecast the tactics any given one will take by studying its history, since many such firms often repeat their successful strategies.

Other stakeholders may also profoundly influence a company's strategy, so it often pays to get inside their heads as well. You can't evaluate any large strategic moves GM or Ford might make without considering the interests of the United Auto Workers and how those interests might check or facilitate such moves. The importance of nonowner stakeholders in driving a company's strategy varies by country of origin too. If you compete with a Chinese company, the Chinese government is often a critical stakeholder. In Europe, environmental organizations and other nongovernmental stakeholders exert more power over corporate decision making than they do in the United States.

Top-Level Management

Since the owners of companies hire top-level management to pursue the owners' strategic objectives, a Martian might think that management's decisions reflect those interests. Earthlings know that this may or may not be true. That's why you must study your competitor's top team.

First, that analysis provides another source of insight into the objectives of the company's owners. When James McNerney arrived at 3M in 2001, for instance, he brought along his belief in GE's "operating system," a centralized change-management methodology that inspired GE's successful approach to Six Sigma, globalization, and e-Business. If you were a 3M competitor, McNerney's history suggested that he would try to turn 3M, which had traditionally favored a fairly loose style of experimentation, into a more operationally accountable company. His hiring signaled the 3M board's intention to focus more aggressively than before on costs and quality. It surely came as no surprise to 3M's board or to the company's competitors that one of McNerney's first strategic moves was to launch a corporate Six Sigma program.

And of course, senior executives aren't always perfect "agents" for a company's owners, whose personal interests and incentives may differ from theirs. Such agency problems quite commonly bedevil even companies with the best governance practices, so it often pays to focus on the objectives of senior leaders as well.

General Managers and Frontline Employees

Competitors of a decentralized company must focus not only on the objectives of its owner and corporate leaders but also on those of business unit leaders, middle management, and even frontline staff. Until recently, for example, Ford was decentralized, with each geographic region run almost independently. Automotive competitors that wished to predict Ford's behavior would have needed to focus on the statements and actions of each regional and brand manager, because the company's objectives could vary from location

to location and across divisions. But since Alan Mullaly took over as CEO in 2006, he has moved to coordinate some decisions and platforms across divisions and regions. Competitors must now understand what is still decided by regional managers and what by Detroit.

For certain decisions, frontline employees and managers are also important, especially if they make pricing, marketing, service, and operational decisions that significantly influence a company's competitive advantage. Even if decision making is more centralized, the incentives of frontline employees may be misaligned with the objectives of a company's owners or senior leaders. Agency problems may inspire the front line to undercut these objectives.

Suppose, for example, that the head of a division at one of your competitors wants its commissioned sales force to promote a new product. If the sales force is enjoying strong sales from established products, reps may hesitate to risk their compensation to promote the new one. A knowledge of such agency problems—which can often be detected through the chatter between your frontline sales force and the customers you share with competitors—can have great strategic importance for your company. In this case, agency problems will probably delay the point when the new product wins significant sales. You could exploit that time lag to fortify your own presence in the market and possibly to preempt the competitor's new offering.

REACH A POINT OF VIEW

What happens once you have a better sense of the options your competitors may consider and the way they may evaluate those options?

Let's say that your company's market environment is relatively stable and that you have much useful information about your main competitors and their decision makers. You can then apply game theory to determine, with considerable confidence, the strategies your competitors will probably follow to maximize their objectives, as well as the way your own choices may influence those strategies. Suppose, however, that even your best efforts don't give you a clear picture of the resources of your competitors or their decision makers' objectives. Then it is often best to avoid trying to predict the competition's exact behavior and instead to use scenario planning to test your company's strategic possibilities.

In a financial crisis, for example, even the best competitive-intelligence efforts may provide incomplete, excessively complex, or inconsistent information on the competition's strategies and thus fail to support game theory or scenario planning. We have found that one way of generating a point of view in such situations is to conduct "war games." In these exercises, each team, representing a specific competitor, receives a fact pack about that company and its decision makers. The teams then make key strategic decisions for the companies they represent. Through several rounds of competition, every team can act on its own strategies and react to the moves of other teams. The war game forces the players to combine incomplete, and perhaps inconsistent, information on competitors to develop a point of view about which moves make the most and least sense for them and are therefore the most and least likely moves for them to make.

No matter how thorough and insightful your analysis may be, two things are almost sure to happen: your competitor will make some moves you considered unlikely, and some of your data will quickly become obsolete. When a competitor acts in unexpected ways, your company has a crucial learning opportunity. Why were you wrong? Did you, say, miss an important agency problem that undermined the execution of the strategy you thought the competitor would follow? Did the market environment change, creating new threats and opportunities for the competitor? Did it bring in a new chairman or CEO? You must diagnose your mistakes, learn from them, and ensure that you use the latest data to develop your point of view.

Learning from your mistakes means managing these competitive-insight activities as an ongoing process for real-time strategic planning and decision making, not as an annual or biannual event in a bureaucratic planning process. Particularly in dynamic markets, where companies have to make decisions constantly, information about competitors must be updated as soon as possible (see Exhibit 1).

One key to making this ongoing process more insightful is tapping into the latest competitive intelligence dispersed throughout the frontline workforce. An e-mail address, a blog, or a shared database could let sales reps report on the latest pricing, promotion, negotiation, and sales tactics that competitors use with key customers or customer segments. Engineers might

Exhibit 1   The Competitor-Insight Loop

The competitor-insight loop

4 Synthesize, learn, and repeat
- Synthesize information to a point of view about which moves make the most and least sense for your competitor
- Learn from ongoing indicators and monitoring
- Repeat

1 Listen to your competitor
- Gather basic competitive intelligence—what are your competitors saying?
- Use pattern recognition—do recent moves and countermoves reveal strategy?

3 Think like the decision makers for your competitor
- Who is the likely decision maker?
- Are the decision makers' interests aligned with those of the company's owners?

2 Think like a strategist for your competitor
- What are its assets, capabilities, market positions?
- How might it protect, extend, and leverage them?

use such facilities to report the latest product pipeline rumors from professional conferences. When possible, companies should also establish appropriate information-sharing arrangements with key partners; suppliers, for example, may provide the latest intelligence on future input prices. As Ken McGee argues in *Heads Up,* most of the information needed for sound business strategy decisions is already available. You just have to create a process to capture and synthesize it meaningfully.

Particularly today, no company is an island. Those that most accurately perceive the competitive landscape as it is and is likely to be in the future have a distinct competitive advantage. Our process—focusing on changes in the resources, decision-making structures, and compensation systems of competitors—moves beyond the usual updates on key market trends and uncertainties. Its rewards are huge: fewer surprises from competitors and more opportunities to shape markets to your own advantage.

ENDNOTE

[1] David Montgomery, Marian Chapman Moore, and Joel Urbany, "Reasoning about competitive reactions: Evidence from executives," *Marketing Science,* 2005, Volume 24, Number 1, pp. 138–49.

Operational Capabilities: Hidden in Plain View

Barbara B. Flynn
Indiana University

Sarah Jinhui Wu
Fordham University

Steven Melnyk
Michigan State University

OPERATIONAL CAPABILITIES 101

Operational capabilities are a lot like love: we know them when we see them, but it can be difficult to articulate precisely what they are. There has been much discussion about the importance of operational capabilities to the competitive success of U.S. businesses. However, it is difficult to develop and nurture operational capabilities when we do not have a good handle on how to recognize them.

Furthermore, there is a tendency to throw around terms like "capabilities," "resources," and "best practices" as though they are interchangeable; they are, in fact, very different. Each is important in its own way, but effective operations strategy requires understanding the differences between them and deploying each in the most effective way.

In this article, we focus primarily on operational capabilities, developing the concept in a way that is easy to understand and visualize. We then briefly differentiate between operational capabilities and other closely related concepts, focusing on implications for managers.

Reprinted from *Business Horizons*, Vol. 53, No. 3 (May 2010), pp. 247–256, by Barbara B. Flynn, Sarah Jinhui Wu, and Steven Melnyk, "Operational Capabilities: Hidden in Plain View," with permission from Elsevier.

WADING IN

What are capabilities? In attempting to answer this question, it is helpful to look to the strategic management literature, which has studied the concept of capability—in general—for many years. By understanding the broader concept of capabilities, we can isolate their key features and apply them in an operations context. Although strategic management researchers use various terms to define capabilities, there seems to be consensus that a capability is not the same as a resource, but rather that it represents a distinctive and superior way of allocating, coordinating, and deploying resources (Amit & Schoemaker, 1993; Schreyogg & Kliesch-Eberl, 2007).

Examining how capabilities are developed better illustrates their essential attributes. Strategic management scholars argue that capabilities can be purposely built by focusing on the complex interactions between a firm's resources (Amit & Schoemaker, 1993; Dierickx & Cool, 1989), deeply rooted within its idiosyncratic social structure (Schreyogg & Kliesch-Eberl, 2007) and spanning functions and hierarchical levels (Grant, 1996; Zeitz, Mittal, & McCauly, 1999). As such, capabilities become embedded into the fabric of a firm through managers' deliberate decisions over time (Grewal & Slotegraaf, 2007). Specifically, capabilities are embedded in organizational processes that are focused on coordination, learning, and transformation (Harreld, O'Reilly, & Tushman,

2007). They are distinct behavioral patterns that are unique to a firm, because each firm's organizational units are unique and different from those of every other firm (Teece, Pisano, & Shuen, 1997). Capabilities are tacit social processes, which means that they emerge gradually over time—so gradually that participants may not even be aware of their existence and may ultimately take them for granted (Leonard-Barton, 1992).

As social processes, capabilities are path dependent, influenced by factors such as firm history (Teece et al., 1997); the actions of decision makers at the individual, group, and firm levels (Rothaermel & Hess, 2007); and the firm's learning process (Schreyogg & Kliesch-Eberl, 2007). They provide a way for the firm to make sense of its environment (Schreyogg & Kliesch-Eberl, 2007), giving it a means of configuring its resources at various levels (Lee & Kelley, 2008). Capabilities facilitate problem-solving decision making under conditions of uncertainty (Dosi, Hobday, & Marengo, 2003), allowing managers to deal with ambiguous and ill-structured tasks (Schreyogg & Kliesch-Eberl, 2007). Thus, they are validated through experience, by a process of identifying problems, applying the embedded skill sets, and verifying that the desired results have been attained. To summarize, according to the strategic management literature:

- Capabilities are *firm-specific.*
- Capabilities *emerge gradually* over time.
- Capabilities are *tacit*; participants may be unaware of their existence.
- Capabilities are *path dependent*, influenced by a firm's history and the actions of its decision makers.
- Capabilities are *empirically validated*, through their application to problems faced by a firm.

WHAT ARE OPERATIONAL CAPABILITIES?

How does this apply in an operations context? Synthesizing the research on capabilities and applying it in the operations context, we offer the following definition of operational capabilities:

Operational capabilities are firm-specific sets of skills, processes, and routines, developed within the operations management system, that are regularly used in solving the problems faced by a unit and which provide that unit—and, ultimately, the firm—with the means of configuring the resources of the operations management system to meet the firm's distinctive needs and challenges.

In order to better clarify the boundaries of operational capabilities, it is crucial to differentiate them from interrelated constructs; particularly, resources and operational practices. Resources form a firm's foundation, consisting of the firm's capacity and all of its stocks (Wang & Ahmed, 2007). In contrast, operational practices are fairly standardized activities, programs, or procedures that have been developed to address the attainment of certain specific operational goals or objectives (Flynn, Sakakibara, & Schroeder, 1995). For instance, while just-in-time (JIT) strives to reduce and eliminate all forms of waste, the goal of total productive maintenance (TPM) is to maximize equipment effectiveness (Cua, McKone, & Schroeder, 2001). Operational capabilities, then, provide unity, integration, and direction to resources and operational practices. Operational capabilities encapsulate both explicit elements—for example, resources and operational practices—and tacit elements that are less visible—such as know-how, skill sets, and leadership—for handling a variety of problems or dealing with uncertainty. That is, operational capabilities draw on resources and operational practices to generate outcomes consistent with desired results. Operational capabilities help the firm generate solutions that "make sense."

AN EXAMPLE FROM THE KITCHEN

While what we've discussed may seem to make sense in the abstract, it is vital to develop a working picture of operational capabilities and how they are different from resources and operational practices. To this end, consider the illustrative metaphor of a restaurant kitchen. A kitchen's resources include assets, such as stoves (number, size, type); the size of the kitchen; the pantry (size, types of ingredients); its layout; and the kitchen staff (size, skill level, knowledge, experience). These resources determine how much food can be prepared and the bounds of what can and cannot be done in the kitchen, just as an organization's resources determine the boundaries of what the firm can do. However, resources—in and of themselves—only define potential, because they are passive and reactive. They are like a stick of dynamite: nothing happens to the dynamite until it is lit, when it reacts to the flame and explodes. Similarly, a stove can't prepare a meal. Like all resources, a stove is passive and has potential, but it can't do anything on its own.

What about operational practices? Operational practices are essentially recipes. They provide generic instructions on how the various resources (e.g., ingredients, stoves) can be combined to make a meal. Once the ingredients and process have been documented as a recipe, the recipe becomes a standard solution that can be applied every time we want to make the same meal, much like the way that best practices are followed in a factory. However, although many kitchens may use the same chocolate mousse recipe, there is no guarantee that the resulting mousses will all look and taste the same. In fact, it wouldn't be surprising to find that the sweetness or creaminess of the ensuing mousses are different, because the recipe provides only basic guidance about how to combine resources; it does not capture the impact of less tangible and explicit factors, such as the freshness and quality of the ingredients, the chef's skill in setting the stove's flame at the proper height, or precise measurements of ingredients.

So, how does this relate to operational capabilities? A restaurant kitchen's capability is more than a stove, a chef, and/or a recipe; it is the capacity to leverage the chef's skill sets to deploy the kitchen's resources and recipes to create dishes that reflect the restaurant's history, style of cooking, and the preferences of its customers.

The traits of operational capabilities that we listed are evident in many ways in a restaurant kitchen. First, although the chef is a critical resource, she needs to extend her standard training from cooking school and customize it to her kitchen's specific context; for example, its menu, affordability, acceptable ingredients, cuisine history, and customers' needs. The restaurant itself has a history that has shaped its character, including the type of chef that was hired and whether she was hired through internal promotion, from a similar restaurant, or from a restaurant that this establishment wanted to emulate. This history makes the restaurant unique. Therefore, a kitchen's operational capabilities are *firm specific*, and a chef would be unable to take them with her if she moved to the kitchen of a different restaurant.

Second, restaurants often use apprenticeships, whereby a chef learns how to cook and prepare meals, as well as mastering the rules that govern how the various ingredients can and cannot be combined. Although the chef already learned how to cook during her formal culinary training, it probably took years for the chef to complete her apprenticeship. Graduating from a well-known cooking school may get a new chef in the door, but she still needs to master the subtleties which make her kitchen unique, observing interactions between kitchen staff and picking up clues from the context of the kitchen. It is in this way that the kitchen's operational capabilities are passed on to future generations of chefs, illustrating *path dependence*.

Third, a kitchen's operational capabilities are formed in a system whereby various resources—such as the chef's skill, supplier relationships, kitchen equipment, and chef/staff relationships—interact in a harmonious way, which takes time to develop. Thus, operational capabilities *emerge gradually over time*.

Fourth, if one wants to learn about a specific main course—say, roast duck—the chef could easily write down the recipe and perhaps emphasize a few key points. However, the chef cannot articulate all the subtleties of making roast duck, since she has taken many things (e.g., relationships with staff and suppliers) for granted over the years and they seem like second nature to her. However, these are the necessary, but intangible, elements associated with the kitchen's operational capabilities. Thus, the operational capabilities of the kitchen are *tacit* and deeply embedded, and are not easily observed, even by those who work in the kitchen.

Lastly, the existence of operational capabilities is reflected in the kitchen's ability to solve its primary strategic problem. The famous Quan-JuDe (全聚德) in Beijing has long been regarded as the most authentic Peking Duck restaurant in the world. The uniqueness of its roast duck comes from an overall cooking process that integrates explicit resources, practices, and tacit elements (e.g., know-how, skill sets, leadership) which have become institutionalized over time. Over the 100-year history of QuanJuDe, neither the ingredients nor the recipe for roast duck have changed much. Yet, today's customers live in a fast-paced world, where they cannot afford to spend hours waiting for a meal to be prepared. Therefore, QuanJuDe had to update its process to more quickly prepare its roast duck, while retaining the original flavor. Thus, the restaurant's operational capabilities were *empirically validated* through diners' reactions to traditional roast duck prepared using updated methods.

It is the chef—more properly known as the "chef de cuisine"—and staff (the executive chef, sous chef, expediter, pastry chef, chef de garde, and various line cooks) that determine how the kitchen's resources are used in addressing the various problems it faces; for example, whether the kitchen's resources are used to prepare Italian meals or Chinese meals, and whether the kitchen prepares unique meals for a small clientele or standard meals for a large volume of diners. The specific problem to be solved is critical, since it determines which types of "solutions" are acceptable and which are not. It also affects how the chef interacts with the staff and the nature of their relationship (whether they work collaboratively or are tightly controlled). In solving these problems, the chef and her staff are themselves the product of a process, ultimately shaping the types of meals prepared, the types of customers targeted, and the restaurant's ability to innovate by creating new and unique dishes that reflect the inimitable characteristics of the restaurant, its style of cooking, or the region in which the restaurant is located. They may not be able to articulate the subtleties of making roast duck or chocolate mousse, because it seems like second nature to them. Thus, the operational capabilities of a restaurant are tacit and deeply embedded.

To summarize, while resources are passive and reactive—like dynamite or a stove—both operational practices and operational capabilities are active and proactive. While resources are readily observable and operational practices combine resources in a relatively explicit and observable way, operational capabilities are tacit and difficult to articulate. Because they are intertwined with resources, operational practices, and even organizational culture, operational capabilities are very difficult to see or identify.

Resources like stoves can be directly purchased from factory markets. That means they can be easily transferred across firms. Similarly, operational practices can be learned from competitors through benchmarking, making them relatively easy to transfer across firms. However, it is the elusive nature of operational capabilities that makes them key to competitive advantage. Because they evolve within a firm and are time and path dependent, it is very difficult to transfer operational capabilities between firms. They are institutionalized within a particular firm, making operational capabilities a powerful competitive weapon.

EMERGENT OPERATIONAL CAPABILITIES

Based on our definition of operational capabilities, we searched through the literature for potentially critical operational capabilities. Our starting point was research conducted by Swink and Hegarty (1998), which proposed seven capabilities relevant in an operations context: improvement, innovation, integration, acuity, control, agility, and responsiveness. Although this work provides a solid foundation, several of these capabilities require further refinement in terms of their dimensionality and uniqueness. Thus, we introduced perspectives drawn from other literature on operational capabilities.

Schroeder, Bates, and Junttila (2002) empirically demonstrated that the operational capabilities inherent in firm-specific, path-dependent learning resulted in the development of proprietary production processes that confer competitive advantage. Although there are many different firm-specific practices associated with the development of proprietary production processes, each reflects an underlying ability to customize a process to meet the unique needs of a firm's products and target markets. It is this commonality that reflects an operational capability. Consequently, we included operational customization as an additional operational capability.

Teece et al. (1997) argued that the ability to sense the need to reconfigure a firm's asset structure, and accomplish the necessary internal and external transformation, is valuable when a firm is faced with a rapidly changing external environment. This construct overlaps somewhat with the operational capability that Swink and Hegarty (1998) termed agility. In many studies (e.g., Christopher, 2000; Fliedner & Vokurka, 1997; Swink & Hegarty, 1998), agility is operationalized by flexibility's two dimensions: volume and variety. However, agility is a higher level construct than flexibility (Aitken, Christopher, & Towill, 2002; Sharifi & Zhang, 2001; Zhang & Sharifi, 2007), because it includes the ability to sense unexpected demand, maintain flexible responses, and implement synchronized operations. This draws on two other operational capabilities: process responsiveness and the ability to reconfigure resources. Thus, we define operational reconfiguration as the ability of a firm in a dynamic environment to reconfigure its asset structure and accomplish the necessary internal and external transformations.

Swink and Hegarty (1998) defined integration in a relatively narrow way, only considering the integration between the operations function and the product/process design function. Considering the need for integration/coordination with other internal functions and external supply chain partners (Escrig-Tena & Bou-Llusar, 2005; Teece et al., 1997), we expanded Swink and Hegarty's definition to emphasize the cooperation skills needed to achieve this broad integration. We renamed this *operational cooperation,* in order to suggest an operational capability that is manifested both internally and externally. Furthermore, acuity—which Swink and Hegarty defined as the ability to understand customers' needs, and convey valuable information and insights regarding products and processes—largely relies on effective cooperation between marketing and operations. We view this as subsumed by the broader operational capability of operational cooperation.

FOCUS GROUP

To verify our proposed set of operational capabilities, we utilized a focus group of eight middle-level managers who worked primarily in the operations area of a single firm that produced household appliances. Asked to compare our suggested operational capabilities with those they experienced on the job, these participants had worked in operations and supply chain management for 14.75 years, with a minimum of 8 years and a maximum of 25 years. Five worked at the plant level, while three were employed at the division level. The number of plants/divisions they had worked for varied from 1 to 6, with a mean of 2.25. Thus, each participant was knowledgeable about his or her firm and its operational capabilities.

The participants were first introduced to the concept of operational capabilities, and then were asked to develop a list of what they believed to be key operational capabilities, listing a total of 15 items (see Table 1). Of this number, 11 of the 15 items listed mapped well to the operational capabilities that we had identified based on the literature. Thus, there was substantial agreement between the focus group and our list of operational capabilities. The four items that did not correspond to items on our list of operational capabilities were carefully assessed, in order to determine whether they should be added to our list.

Our analysis revealed that one item actually represented an outcome, while the other three reflected organizational—rather than operational—capabilities; thus, the original set of operational capabilities was retained. "Dependability and reliability" is a process outcome rather than an operational capability, because it focuses on process performance, not on the way in which process performance is achieved. "Control of the supply chain" goes beyond the domain of operational capabilities, since having control of the supply chain can be related to factors such as brand name, unique technology, and order size. While this may reflect a capability of an organization, it is not an operational capability because it cuts across functions. Similarly, "value creation for core customers" focuses on creating value for customers, which is an organizational—rather than an operational—capability. Finally, "new product testing facility" is also an organizational capability because it reflects the ability to quickly change both the design of new products and reduce new product introduction lead time.

Table 1 **Operational Capabilities Identified from the Literature and by the Focus Group**

Focus Group	Literature
• Collaboration and trust with partners	Operational cooperation
• Intellectual property and know-how (specialized tooling, technology, equipment)	Operational customization
• Specialization (service experts)	
• Process customization	
• Responsiveness	Operational responsiveness
• Sense of urgency to meet short lead time	
• Fulfillment of customers' orders	
• Process improvement to make price competitive	Operational improvement
• Process standardization	
• Radical process innovation	Operational innovation
• Change management	Operational reconfiguration
• New product testing facility	Others
• Control of the supply chain	
• Value creation for core customers	
• Dependability and reliability	

KEY OPERATIONAL CAPABILITIES

Through our review of the literature and discussion with focus group participants, we developed a list of six key operational capabilities. Each is described next.

Operational Improvement

Operational improvement is based on the concept that Swink and Hegarty (1998) called "improvement." It consists of differentiated skills, processes, and routines for incrementally refining and reinforcing existing operations processes. By "differentiated," we mean that these skills, processes, and routines were developed in a way that was unique to the organization. For example, over time, a restaurant kitchen may develop efficient approaches for preparing its specialties. This might include assigning tasks to those with the most appropriate skills, developing shortcuts that do not affect the taste of a dish, learning which dishes can go into the oven at the same time, learning which parts of the dish can be prepared ahead of time, and so forth. Similarly, an organization may develop the ability to complete its routine work in the most

efficient way possible, through assigning various tasks to those who are most qualified to complete them; developing shortcuts that do not affect the end product; developing approaches for multiprocessing; learning which parts of a job can be done in advance and held in inventory, and which must be completed at the last minute; and so forth. This ability develops over time and is empirically validated as the organization experiments with different approaches for completing the task, and learns about the skills and abilities of the employees who are involved. An organization with an operational improvement capability will have the ability to continuously adapt the process as new employees are added and as particular features of the job at hand change over time. Furthermore, the ability to improve processes will be transferred to the organization's other processes. Thus, operational improvement capability is embedded in the organization, not in particular people. Similarly, even if a chef leaves a restaurant for other employment, the process and the ability to incrementally refine it remain.

Operational Innovation

While operational improvement is based on incremental change, operational innovation focuses on radical change. Operational innovation is centered on what Swink and Hegarty (1998) term "improvement" capability. It represents the differentiated skills, processes, and routines for radically improving existing operations processes or for creating and implementing new and unique manufacturing processes. A chef borrows from different recipes and uses her experiences and knowledge to create a few specialties for her restaurant. For example, Brennan's in New Orleans is widely acknowledged as having the best bananas Foster. Brennan's has been around since 1946, and the original chef who created this recipe is long gone. The restaurant's recipe for bananas Foster is publically available via the Brennan's website, so it is clearly something beyond the recipe that causes Brennan's to have the best bananas Foster. The unique process for making bananas Foster—which at Brennan's involves a tableside cart cooking arrangement, complete with flaming liqueur—was an operational innovation when it was developed, and it remains difficult to precisely imitate. Similarly, a restaurant may develop recipes that capitalize on the unique skills of its staff and the specific assets in the kitchen. For example, a restaurant with a skilled pastry chef and confectionery oven may develop innovative pastry-based entrees like Beef Wellington, to present a course in a manner unique from other establishments.

Operational Customization

While operational improvement focuses on incremental change and operational innovation focuses on radical change, operational customization has at its core the creation of something unique. Operational customization is based on the notion put forth by Schroeder et al. (2002) regarding "proprietary process and equipment." It consists of differentiated skills, processes, and routines for the creation of knowledge through extending and customizing operations processes and systems. A kitchen skilled in operational customization has the ability to create something completely unique. Consider a mother whose college-aged child returns home after a long absence. Mom will prepare whatever the child wants for dinner; this could entail shopping for unusual ingredients, scanning the Internet for special recipe ideas, and perhaps even purchasing additional resources such as a donut fryer or ice cream freezer.

Similar operational innovations can be seen on the television program *Iron Chef*, which features competitions between chefs that focus on the novel use of a particular ingredient during each episode—for example, artichokes one week and sea bass the next—to create uniquely specialized dishes. Likewise, a manufacturer that is strong in operational customization will have the ability to produce exactly what a customer desires. This requires having flexible equipment, access to a wide variety of materials, and employees who are skilled and experienced at interpreting vaguely articulated client desires, using general purpose equipment to translate them into products that meet the customers' needs.

Operational Cooperation

Operational cooperation builds upon the concepts of "skills for cooperation" (Escrig-Tena & Bou-Llusar, 2005) and Swink and Hegarty's (1998) "integration" and "acuity." It is defined as differentiated skills, processes, and routines for creating healthy and stable relationships with people from various internal functional areas, as well as external supply chain partners. In a restaurant setting, the purchasing staff works closely with the chef, in order to buy the best-quality ingredients in a timely manner. For example, in a Thai restaurant, papaya is commonly used in both hot and cold dishes. Because the freshness of the papaya greatly influences the flavor of the dishes, the effectiveness of the purchasing staff to work with both the chef and suppliers is crucial for obtaining the best papayas. Although individual members of the purchasing staff may form relationships with particular suppliers, operational cooperation moves beyond personal relationships to institutional relationships that transcend the particular individuals.

Operational Responsiveness

Operational responsiveness is based on the "responsiveness" construct put forth by Swink and Hegarty (1998). At its core is the ability to quickly modify a standard product to meet the unique needs of an individual customer. Operational responsiveness is defined as differentiated skills, processes, and routines for reacting quickly and easily to changes in inputs or output requirements.

For example, a restaurant may be known for its ability to customize its dishes for vegetarians, patrons with gluten or peanut allergies, or patrons with religious dietary restrictions. Because this customization involves removing ingredients that may contribute significantly to the taste of a particular dish, operational responsiveness capability is important in responding to customer needs by developing dishes that have the same taste without a particular ingredient.

Operational Reconfiguration

Operational reconfiguration is based on "reconfiguration" as articulated by Teece et al. (1997), and "agility" as offered by Swink and Hegarty (1998). Because a strategic mismatch between an organization's operations strategy and its market environment can be devastating, the ability to sense subtle points about the market environment and react appropriately can be a potent competitive weapon. Operational reconfiguration is the differentiated skills, processes, and routines for accomplishing any transformations needed to reestablish the fit between operations strategy and the market environment, if their equilibrium has been disturbed. For example, a chef may replace ingredients in a standard recipe in order to cater to the tastes of customers in a particular environment. Many Chinese restaurants in the United States replace traditional Chinese green vegetables, which are unfamiliar to U.S. customers, with the more familiar broccoli. The taste of the dishes remains the same, but U.S. customers view them as less exotic than dishes which include unfamiliar Chinese green vegetables. Similarly, there are many anecdotes about mistakes made by U.S. businesses as they marketed their products in a different culture without being savvy to the nuances of that culture.

HIDDEN IN PLAIN VIEW

This study provided a rationale for viewing operational capabilities as critical to success at both the operations and corporate levels. We suggest operational capabilities are much like a "secret ingredient" because, as with the purloined letter of Edgar Allan Poe (1845), operational capabilities are essentially hidden in plain view. That is, operational capabilities are present but overlooked both by the managers who work with them and by researchers. They are taken for granted. They fail to generate attention because they do not seem unusual. This is due to the very nature of operational capabilities: they are tightly embedded in the organizational fabric of the operations management system. This embeddedness is the result of three factors: (1) the interconnectedness of operational capabilities with resources and operational practices, (2) linkages between operations capabilities and the social network, and (3) the fit with the primary problems that the firm and its operations management address. This embeddedness makes operational capabilities tacit in nature and path dependent. These traits, in turn, create a barrier to imitation (Grewal & Slotegraaf, 2007). As a result, operational capabilities are crucial in understanding and explaining performance variability. Thus, while resources and operational practices are critical, they are not sufficient.

Operational capabilities are the secret ingredient that is hidden in plain view for several reasons. First, operational capabilities are not as obvious and tangible as operational practices and resources. When trying to explain success, managers tend to focus on factors that are readily perceived and relatively easy to duplicate and implement. This is what Spear and Bowen (1999) and Spear (2004) observed when describing how others viewed the success of Toyota. While observers saw Toyota using general purpose equipment, statistical process control, and cross-functional employees, what they did not as readily observe was how Toyota had extended and customized all of these elements to address its specific problems. In sum, they did not see Toyota's "DNA" (Spear & Bowen, 1999). A critical element of this DNA is Toyota's operational capabilities. Employing this perspective, it is evident why even the most detailed and precise duplication efforts by mimicking companies could not achieve the same level of performance. The resources and practices that work so well at Toyota might not fit the implementing organization's culture or history, or may not even be consistent with the problem that the firm is interested in solving; these elements are central attributes of operational capabilities. This observation is also supported by research conducted by Westphal, Gulati, and Shortell (1997). When studying corporate experiences with total quality management (TQM), they found that the factors which explained high performers could not adequately explain low performers. The high performers understood, expanded, and tailored TQM and its specific practices to their unique needs, resource profiles, and interfirm relationships. In contrast, the lower performers blindly imitated techniques and tools without any modification or adjustment. While the former group developed operational capabilities and subsequently improved performance, the latter group did not. A similar explanation is provided by the four stages of Hayes and Wheelwright (1984). Stage II firms (externally neutral) strive to improve through extensive and indiscriminant imitation of competitors. In contrast, Stage III firms are more successful in their improvement efforts by screening potential new resources and practices for consistency with operations strategy.

Second, operational capabilities are closely linked to resources and operational practices. This interconnectedness makes operational capabilities difficult to identify separately; consequently, their existence may be overlooked. There is a tendency for both managers and researchers to confuse resource and operational practices with operational capabilities. For example, Eisenhardt and Martin (2000) and Lee and Kelley (2008) have noted that "best practices" can be viewed as a type of capability. Yet, Teece (2007) disagreed with this position, stating that, under certain conditions, best practices are not capabilities, nor does their use lead to a sustainable competitive advantage. This position was repeated by Hayes, Pisano, Upton, and Wheelwright (2005). Such confusion is not surprising given the close linkages that exist between operational capabilities, resources, and operational practices.

Third, the development of operational capabilities is associated with the culture and history of a particular firm and the specific problems that it is striving to solve. There are two types of fit related to operational capabilities: fit with organizational culture and history, and fit with the specific problem being addressed (e.g., cost reduction vs. radical product innovation). Both types of fit tend to be overlooked in cross-sectional/benchmarking analysis. For example, Toyota's operational capabilities were built to solve the company's primary problem: given its production lines, how could it be flexible enough to change the product mix to accommodate changing demand (Womack, Jones, & Roos, 1990)? While General Motors (GM) spent a great deal of time and money studying Toyota's success, its management did not appreciate that GM and Toyota were solving fundamentally different problems. To GM, the central issue was that of reducing cost, producing the most with a given level of resources. In contrast, Toyota was more interested in improving flexibility, minimizing the level of resources needed to satisfy a given level of demand.

This may be one of the reasons why the best practices construct cannot be applied universally: they must be developed to fit the specific problem being solved and the specific environment in which they will be deployed, and they must be extended—that is, improved upon in unique ways—so that they help the system offer customers better solutions (Westphal et al., 1997). Managers from one firm, when studying another, tend to view activities through a lens built on the assumption that the firm being studied is solving the same type of problem, or problems, that the observers are. This myopia prevents them from seeing and assessing operational capabilities.

CLOSING COMMENTS

The goal of operations strategy is to help managers develop, position, and align managerial policies and resources in a way that is consistent with the organization's overall business strategy. This level of planning and decision making focuses on developing operations into a source of sustainable competitive advantage. In addressing this objective, managers must speak to the dynamic tension that exists between the two critical elements of strategy: efficiency and effectiveness. Efficiency is concerned with issues related to reducing cost for a given level of demand or increasing output for a given level of resources. In contrast, effectiveness deals with how well the operations process internally supports the overall corporate strategy and externally supports the organization in meeting or exceeding the needs of critical customers, relative to its competitors.

The tension between efficiency and effectiveness is evidenced in the historical competition between Kmart and Walmart. During the late 1970s, Kmart enjoyed an enormous size advantage, which translated into substantial efficiencies in purchasing, distribution, and marketing. At the time, Walmart was only a small niche player. Within a decade, however, Walmart transformed itself into a giant in the discount retail industry and has continued growing. The secret of Walmart's success lies in its effectiveness in satisfying customer needs; Walmart uses cross-docking in replenishing its inventory, which makes goods available when and where customers want them, without the need to hold a lot of costly inventory.

One strategy for improving operations efficiency is to study other organizations and apply those practices and tools that have been successfully used by them. By focusing on operations practices such as JIT and TQM, managers deal with activities that are highly observable, easy to articulate, and well defined. In applying best practices from other firms and benchmarking leading firms, though, it must be recognized that we are introducing a force for homogenization and standardization of practices. When everyone implements best practices, they become the norm. While the adoption of such practices can improve operations and corporate performance to a certain extent, it cannot help a firm develop and maintain a sustainable competitive advantage. This approach also runs counter to the central concept of strategic management: that is, the need to differentiate a firm and its capabilities from those offered by its competitors.

In the context of operations strategy, we can argue that while efficiency comes from operational practices, effectiveness is based on operational capabilities. Yet, for many managers, operations practices and operational capabilities remain a source of major confusion. In part, this confusion reflects the fact that these two concepts have not been clearly articulated and delineated with sufficient precision. Operational capabilities need to be clearly defined and systematically identified, because operations performance is the result of operational capabilities. How a manufacturer can change or shape its operations performance depends on how it invests in operations capabilities.

We have proposed a conceptual definition of operational capabilities and a metaphor which captures their essential traits. These traits help us differentiate operational capabilities from operational practices and resources, and understand the process by which competitive advantage is developed. In addition, we provided a comprehensive framework of operational capabilities that covers six salient dimensions. This concept of operational capabilities forms a foundation for improved understanding of dynamic capabilities and their development process, which is imperative in today's turbulent environment.

REFERENCES

Aitken, J., Christopher, M., & Towill, D. (2002). Understanding, implementing, and exploiting agility and leanness. *International Journal of Logistics: Research and Applications, 5*(1), 59–74.

Amit, R., & Schoemaker, P. J. H. (1993). Strategic assets and organizational rent. *Strategic Management Journal, 14*(1), 33–46.

Christopher, M. (2000). The agile supply chain, competing in volatile markets. *Industrial Marketing Management, 29*(1), 37–44.

Cua, K. O., McKone, K. E., & Schroeder, R. G. (2001). Relationship between implementation of TQM, JIT, and TPM, and manufacturing performance. *Journal of Operations Management, 19*(6), 675–694.

Dierickx, I., & Cool, K. (1989). Asset stock accumulation and sustainability of competitive advantage. *Management Science, 35*(12), 1504–1511.

Dosi, G., Hobday, M., & Marengo, L. (2003). Problem-solving behavior, organizational forms and the complexity of tasks. In C. E. Helfat (Ed.), *The SMS Blackwell handbook of organizational capabilities* (pp. 167–192). Malden, MA: Blackwell.

Eisenhardt, K. M., & Martin, J. A. (2000). Dynamic capabilities: What are they? *Strategic Management Journal, 21*(10–11), 1105–1121.

Escrig-Tena, A. B., & Bou-Llusar, J. C. (2005). A model for evaluating organizational competencies: An application in the context of a quality management initiative. *Decision Sciences, 36*(2), 221–257.

Fliedner, D., & Vokurka, R. J. (1997). Agility: Competitive weapon of the 1990s and beyond? *Production and Inventory Management Journal, 38*(3), 19–24.

Flynn, B. B., Sakakibara, S., & Schroeder, R. G. (1995). Relationship between JIT and TQM: Practices and performance. *Academy of Management Journal, 38*(5), 1325–1360.

Grant, R. (1996). Toward a knowledge-based theory of the firm. *Strategic Management Journal, 17*(SI Winter), 109–122.

Grewal, R., & Slotegraaf, R. J. (2007). Embeddedness of organizational capabilities. *Decision Sciences, 38*(3), 451–488.

Harreld, J. B., O'Reilly, C. A., & Tushman, M. L. (2007). Dynamic capabilities at IBM: Driving strategy into action. *California Management Review, 49*(4), 21–43.

Hayes, R. H., Pisano, G. P., Upton, D. M., & Wheelwright, S. C. (2005). *Operations, strategy, and technology: Pursuing the competitive edge.* Hoboken, NJ: Wiley Higher Education.

Hayes, R. H., & Wheelwright, S. C. (1984). *Restoring our competitive edge: Competing through manufacturing.* New York: John Wiley.

Lee, H., & Kelley, D. (2008). Building dynamic capabilities for innovation: An exploratory study of key management practices. *R&D Management, 38*(2), 155–168.

Leonard-Barton, D. (1992). Core capabilities and core rigidities: A paradox in managing new product development. *Strategic Management Journal, 13*(2), 111–125.

Poe, E. A. (1845). *The purloined letter.* Retrieved from http://xroads.virginia.edu/HYPER/POE/purloine.html.

Rothaermel, F. T., & Hess, A. M. (2007). Building dynamic capabilities: Innovation driven by individual-, firm-, and network-level effects. *Organizational Science, 18*(6), 898–921.

Schreyogg, G., & Kliesch-Eberl, M. (2007). How dynamic can organizational capabilities be? Towards a dual-process model of capability dynamization. *Strategic Management Journal, 28*(9), 913–933.

Schroeder, R. G., Bates, K. A., & Junttila, M. A. (2002). A resource-based view of manufacturing strategy and the relationship to manufacturing performance. *Strategic Management Journal, 23*(2), 105–117.

Sharifi, H., & Zhang, Z. (2001). Agile manufacturing in practice: Application of a methodology. *International Journal of Operations and Production Management, 21*(5/6), 772–794.

Spear, S. J. (2004). Learning to lead at Toyota. *Harvard Business Review, 82*(5), 78–86.

Spear, S. J., & Bowen, H. K. (1999). Decoding the DNA of the Toyota production system. *Harvard Business Review, 77*(5), 96–106.

Swink, M., & Hegarty, W. H. (1998). Core manufacturing capabilities and their links to product differentiation. *International Journal of Operations and Production Management, 18*(4), 374–396.

Teece, D. (2007). Explicating dynamic capabilities: The nature and microfoundations of (sustainable) enterprise performance. *Strategic Management Journal, 28*(13), 1319–1350.

Teece, D. J., Pisano, G., & Shuen, A. (1997). Dynamic capabilities and strategic management. *Strategic Management Journal, 18*(7), 509–533.

Wang, C. L., & Ahmed, P. K. (2007). Dynamic capabilities: A review and research agenda. *International Journal of Management Reviews, 9*(1), 31–51.

Westphal, J. D., Gulati, R., & Shortell, S. M. (1997). Customization or conformity? An institutional and network perspective on the content and consequences of TQM adoption. *Administrative Science Quarterly, 42*(2), 366–394.

Womack, J. P., Jones, D. T., & Roos, D. (1990). *The machine that changed the world.* New York: Rowson Associates.

Zeitz, G., Mittal, V., & McCauly, B. (1999). Distinguishing adoption and entrenchment of management practices: A framework for analysis. *Organization Studies, 20*(5), 741–776.

Zhang, Z., & Sharifi, H. (2007). Towards theory building in agile manufacturing strategy: A taxonomical approach. *IEEE Transactions on Engineering Management, 54*(2), 351–370.

Orchestrating the New Dynamic Capabilities

Amy Shuen
CEIBS (China Europe International
Business School)

Sandra Sieber
IESE Business School
University of Navarra, Spain

EXECUTIVE SUMMARY

Over a decade ago, "dynamic capabilities" were introduced to the business world as a way for companies to get ahead in times of rapid technological change through orchestration, recombination and transformative collaboration. Now, with the advent of Web 2.0 and the opportunities that presents, dynamic capabilities achieve a new relevance. The emerging technological landscape enables firms to put dynamic capabilities into practice easier than ever before, since it allows for ongoing collaboration and interaction between companies and users, hence fostering new types of innovation. In this article, the authors outline the principles behind Web 2.0-empowered business models, giving managers numerous ideas they can try out immediately, at low cost, and with potentially much higher ROI than could ever be achieved with a non-Web-enabled business. Why not put your own dynamic capabilities to the test? You're only a click away.

When Skype first burst onto the scene, everyone predicted the familiar story of disruptive innovation in the telecom industry, where the new destroys the old way of doing business in a spiraling zero-sum game. Fast-forward to the present: Apple's iPhone has shown a new win–win path to success using collaborative innovation on the Web. The iPhone brought together thousands of handset makers, operators, and software developers, giving them a considerable share of a market already worth $2 billion a year, and reinvented several industries in the process.

In a similar fashion, diverse companies—from Google and Amazon, to IBM, Cisco, and Intuit—are continuing to innovate their business models and grow, despite the economic crisis, with revenue and success widely shared. Many industry leaders are wondering if the core principles of strategic management and competitive advantage have changed. The answer, we argue, is a resounding yes.

Here's why: The Web has changed the economics of business and collaboration. Companies can no longer conceive of their capabilities in isolation, but must learn to co-create them within a broader, dynamic and non-zero-sum ecosystem of external partners. The new "managed" but open ecosystems range from "orchestrated" standards-based networks of developers, to communities and "crowds" of lead users and bloggers, to e-commerce affiliates, to complementary businesses that cross industry divides.

A highly cited *Strategic Management Journal* article from 1997 once defined "dynamic capabilities" as a company's strategic ability to combine inside and outside competences to address volatile environments and periods of rapid change. *Orchestration* was lauded over positioning, *management innovation* and *combinations* over structure, and *transformative collaboration* over traditional strategizing as the means of gaining competitive advantage.

Reprinted from "Orchestrating the New Dynamic Capabilities," by Amy Shuen and Sandra Sieber, *IESE Insight*, Issue 3 (2009), pp. 58–65. Reprinted with permission.

Sophie Mancuso contributed to this article.

Few could have predicted when that article was written the widespread social transformation that the Web, broadband, and mobile technologies would trigger, nor the exponential growth of Google, Facebook, Twitter, Amazon, and Apple—businesses that rely on the economics of network effects, social influence, viral distribution, and Web-enabled business models. Now, thanks to Web 2.0 business models and platforms, collective user value, along with ways to more productively monetize and enhance the "wisdom of the crowd," has become commonplace. It's the modern version of the old fable "Stone Soup," in which hungry villagers each contribute whatever they can spare—a carrot here, a potato there, some leftover scraps of meat. In the end, everyone enjoys a hearty, collectively co-created soup. The Web is today's soup pot, taking individual contributions, remixing them, and redistributing them as something new across many networks with almost zero costs.

This year, Berkeley's Oliver Williamson won the Nobel Memorial Prize in Economic Sciences for his research on the transaction costs underlying industrial structure and organizational boundaries. These are the very same transaction and coordination costs that Web-enabled business models are transforming substantially. Little wonder that "collaborative innovation" and the new "dynamic capabilities" of orchestrating knowledge, ecosystems, partnerships, and collective user value across multiple industrial and geographic boundaries have become top strategic priorities for the Fortune 500 agenda.

THE NEW COLLABORATIVE MATRIX

Web 2.0 has changed the rules of business. But it isn't simply about building Web-based businesses to put the old-style ones out of the picture. It's about using a company's own "dynamic capabilities" to orchestrate and recombine the best of what the online world has to offer while multiplying the value of existing networks of users and partners. New-style click-and-mortar, online-offline network partnerships focus on bridging and building new networks so that everyone gains, and potential competitors become potential partners. Figure 1 shows at least three ways to combine users with company capabilities profitably and speedily. The New Collaborative Matrix has its roots in traditional innovation theory, but wouldn't be as profitable or as successful without the help of digital-plus-network economics.

Democratized Innovation

The lower left-hand corner of the innovation matrix reminds us that many peer-to-peer, or user-to-user, innovations produce positive network effects, but the benefits become public goods or consumer surplus. Wikipedia is an example of positive network externalities in which many benefit from the widespread sharing and distribution of digital knowledge or music. However, the founders did not capture or internalize the pecuniary value of these network effects. In contrast, the other three boxes show that collective network effects can be successfully monetized and create new business value.

Crowdsourcing

How many users of Google, YouTube, Flickr, Amazon, or Trip Advisor realize that their usage, clicks, tags, photos, videos, reviews, comments, and participation in online contests and polls are being turned into positive network effects by *crowdsourcing,* which makes the site better for everyone? The main difference between user-to-company and user-to-user innovation is that a company is able to capture tangible, monetary benefits of the user in exchange for continued innovation and improvement. There are numerous well-known examples: IBM, which identified and developed several fast-growing, high-potential new businesses via its global Innovation Jams; and Google's PageRank and AdWords algorithms, which both improve the relevance of search results for users while pricing advertising according to relevant clicks. But it doesn't stop there: Threadless.com harnesses the power of the online community to design funky T-shirts; and the mining company Gold-corp mobilizes prospectors to find gold for them.

Figure 1   **The New Collaborative Matrix**

Source: Based on concepts originally published in *Web 2.0: A Strategy Guide* by Amy Shuen (O'Reilly Media, 2008).

Platform Innovation

Company-to-user innovation is when a company provides the platform for users and developers to distribute their software, applications, or digital goods, such as music or games, to their social or professional networks, or simply to the market-place at large. IBM, Apple, and Facebook spring to mind, but Neopets and South Korea's Cyworld also stand out in this regard.

Recombinant Innovation

Perhaps the best-known example of company-to-company innovation is Apple. Before the iTunes store, it had already teamed up with Gracenote to give the names of the tracks to consumers ripping CDs. But rather than working against the record companies by encouraging consumers to download music illegally, Apple wanted to legitimize the sale of music online, so it worked with record companies, convincing them to collaborate and sell music digitally. The result was a win–win situation, with all parties dependent on each other for success.

As we can see from these examples, you don't have to invent the wheel to have a successful project. By simply working with other companies, you can make something highly valuable for a specific group of consumers and users. The biggest challenge for companies innovating in these areas is to convert from an ingrained culture of competition to collaboration. It's not easy to turn around and preach "give to get" and "let's revenue-share," but the payoffs are worth it.

HOW TO MULTIPLY YOUR DYNAMIC CAPABILITIES

Build on Collective User Value

The first and critical step is to start thinking exponentially rather than incrementally. The Web makes it 10 times faster for any company with an existing network of relationships to orchestrate 10 times the users and 10 times the partners to connect and combine for new value creation. And you don't have to be a Fortune 500 company, or an online store, to benefit. Governments, public agencies, and nonprofits are relatively lacking in capital, assets, and resources, but they have managed to achieve great things simply by leveraging their rich social capital. Barack Obama's use of Web 2.0 during his bid for the White House serves as an excellent example (see Figure 2).

This same comparison of the ROI and cash flow curves of Web 2.0, Web 1.0, and traditional approaches characterizes many other cases. A great example of a company that built itself on collective user value is the photo-sharing site Flickr. It initially offered users free online space to store and organize photos with features to comment and tag. Of course, word soon spread, and as people contributed to Flickr, they made it better and better. When the site had a critical mass of users, popularity, and information, it offered a premium service to those willing to pay for more benefits. With virtually zero marketing costs and low-cost online distribution and capital investment, Flickr managed to create a number of positive revenue streams quickly to cover the cost of the free services it offered.

Nevertheless, coming up with a viable business model based on collective user value is not without its challenges. First, you need to start from a blank slate and honestly look at your business from the customers' point of view: What are their real needs? How do you propose to address them? This is crucial, as in order for your effort to be effective, the collaboration and cooperation must be conceived in ways that users consider helpful and valuable to them.

Once people get engaged, you need to clarify the different types of value that are created by their contributions, and then decide on the revenue model. This normally implies a cost structure that allows the top contributors to be rewarded in some way, for collective user value to be incentivized, and then monetizing this value.

An interesting example in this vein is that of professional online networks, of which there are currently several vying for dominance in Europe. The initial leader—the German company Xing—has managed to develop a business model that relies heavily on its community, which

Figure 2   The Multiplied Advantages of Web 2.0

A traditional brick-and-mortar business spends a lot at the outset before seeing any profit. Think of the traditional pavement-pounding, knocking-on-doors approach to drumming up sales, or getting out the vote.

A typical Web 1.0 method is "robocalling" – automated dialing of phone lists using a prerecorded message. This requires an expensive initial outlay, which will only see returns over time. It also risks alienating potential supporters who don't like being interrupted at meal times. Besides, would you rather receive a call from an old friend or an impersonal machine?

In the 2008 U.S. presidential election, Barack Obama used Web 2.0 innovation: The initial cost of his iPhone downloads was much lower, and the payback was enormous almost immediately. There were about 5,000 downloads the first day, and within minutes people had a powerful tool that enabled them to call their "first degree of separation" friends and associates in key battleground states using their iPhone contact lists. What's

more, they received up-to-the-minute coverage and position statements on key campaign talking points. This generated half a million phone calls in the run-up to the election. One simple application turned supporters nationwide into a powerful, targeted, evangelistic telesales force. The rest is history.

Now, imagine getting that kind of multiplied response from marketing your own product or service. Every business could use a similar customized sales and customer relationship management tool on their company cell phones.

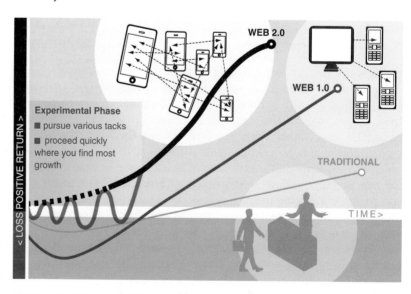

Source: Based on concepts originally published in *Web 2.0: A Strategy Guide* by Amy Shuen (O'Reilly Media, 2008).

numbered some 8 million in August 2009. Apart from the usual staying-in-touch with colleagues and job contacts, Xing facilitates over 30,000 specialized groups and 90,000 live networking events a year, organized by members for members. So far, users have acknowledged the value of these services, and the site currently counts around 700,000 paying Premium Members. In the midst of the crisis, Xing announced a 35 percent increase in total revenues to 21.54 million euros for the first six months of 2009, largely driven by Premium Membership revenues, which were up by 41 percent in 2009 over 2008. The international leader, LinkedIn, which is aggressively entering the European market, has adopted a different approach by building a large user base that only gets limited services, while some lead users—headhunters and recruiters—pay a significant sum for the possibility of browsing the huge database that LinkedIn has, and afterward contacting individual profiles.

Tactical Questions to Consider:
- Do you allow users to participate on your site with their own ideas?
- How do you support your most active community members?

Activate Network Effects

For most of us, traffic has negative connotations. But in the digital world, it's good news for business. Why? Because under certain conditions online traffic may be made up of network effects, which, put simply, are the effect each user has on the value of a product or service. They are very often at the heart of the new Web business models. If strong network effects exist, this may have a potentially huge effect on the overall profitability of a company.

Activating network effects, however, is tricky, since one has to understand that there are different kinds of effects, and that a misunderstanding of the effect has vast implications on the overall viability of the envisioned strategy. The five different kinds of network effects are direct, indirect, demand-side, cross-network and social.

A classic example of a *direct network effect* is the telephone. An individual telephone was useless but as people bought them, their value increased. *Indirect network effects* are when the popularity of a product or service spawns the production of increasingly valuable complementary goods—for example, the iPod and its accessories. *Demand-side*

effects are, as we saw with Flickr, when willingness to pay for a service increases as more and more people use it. *Cross-network effects* are when a rise in usage by one group of users increases the value of a complementary product or service to another distinct group of users, such as readerwriter software pairs. Lastly, *social or local network effects,* such as instant messaging, are when a user is influenced directly by the decisions of other consumers.

Network effects are the results of users jumping on the bandwagon. For this reason, they can mean the difference between your company having the lion's share or the leftovers of a competitive market. If two companies are locked in battle and one is slightly ahead of the other, network effects can tip the scales in favor of one of the competitors. Positive feedback can amplify the stronger company so that it gets stronger while the reverse is true of the weaker. In such tippy markets, network effects are so powerful that they can ultimately determine the rise or fall of entire companies.

In order to make network effects work, you need to figure out what yours are and how you can measure their value. Find out which groups could generate positive network effects for you and how you can get them to do so. Free or highly subsidized services, such as Google's search engine, are usually the answer. In addition, figure out a way to monetize the business model by finding a group of users that has a positive willingness to pay. Google gets almost all of its revenue from advertising, by placing ads (that then need to be clicked on) on either its own or third-party pages. Don't forget that network effects accumulate exponentially, and once you have activated them, the sky's the limit, because one network effect gives birth to more, which in turn give birth to even more and so on.

Tactical Questions to Consider:
- As users visit your site, do you learn from their activities, or just present information to them?
- If you are in a competitive race, how do your users see your offerings versus your competitor's?

Work Through Social Networks

While people might think of social networking as a particular kind of Web 2.0 application, it can enrich projects even when it isn't the central focus. The communities built by social networks can serve to strengthen the appeal of an endeavor.

Members of a community naturally influence each other, so positive network effects can be triggered left, right, and center. As in the physical world, once key influencers are talking about a product or service, everybody will be, but the pace of this picks up online.

Again, the extreme power law of the Web means that once a network has a critical mass, more and more want to join, and the number of members grows exponentially. As we see with websites such as Facebook, Flickr, and MySpace, social networks acquire customers fast. They can attract tens of millions of new, active, and frequently engaged customers in a short amount of time, bringing with them valuable storehouses of openly uploaded, digital, personal and social content. This content can be turned into cash through charging certain users. But the value of this base can also be immediately monetized through target revenue advertising. Just think, while Google can offer advertisers the relevance of a keyword, Facebook gives them a personalized view of the consumers they want to reach.

Facebook isn't just a great audience for advertisers, though; developers are able to distribute their applications on the site. Consider possibilities within your own organization. Very often, IT projects have to be pushed back because of a lack of programming resources available internally. Outsourcing may be a solution. But traditional outsourcing only partially overcomes the resourcing problem, since the solution will be restricted to available capacity. What if we try to organize the idle capacity of IT programmers from virtually any country on earth, and go for crowdsourcing?

"What could you accomplish with a team of 225,534?" poses TopCoder.com, citing the number of developers in 200 countries that it counts among its software development community—and that number is constantly rising. TopCoder proposes a novel method of building and delivering software. TopCoder receives a project from a corporate client, and breaks it down into manageable pieces, which are then put out for competition online. Programmers in the community write the pieces that are put together according to the client's requirements and time frame. The client only pays the prize money for the chosen result, not for the hours of time the developers may have spent coming up with various solutions. Since several teams are competing for the same project, the quality of the winning solution is usually quite high. With this business model, TopCoder has turned an age-old labor problem into a business proposition.

Tactical Questions to Consider:
- Do you provide mechanisms for your users to communicate among themselves?
- Could user information, like profiles, create advertising value for you?

Multiply Your Partners Through Syndication

In the online world, almost anything can be syndicated, because everything is in digital bits that can be copied at no extra cost. But the online syndication of competences takes it to a whole new level. When a company has the dynamic capabilities to change its initial business model and embrace syndication, it can find itself in a different league.

Originally an online bookseller, Amazon soon wised up to the fact that a lead in the market would be difficult to maintain when competitors were a click away. So, in 2001, it decided to sell shelf space, or zShops, to rivals. Sales increased by 34 percent in 2003 and at the end of that year Amazon posted its first profit after operating at a loss for a decade. Today, zShops have morphed into Amazon Marketplace, and Amazon has become the online platform for a broad range of online retailers, providing them back-office services, such as its shopping cart or payment system, which they never would have had the resources to build on their own. Paradoxically, Amazon gained competitive advantage by openly selling company secrets to potential rivals, and then turning them into a new set of partners and affiliates. Again, like Apple, IBM, and other network-savvy corporations, Amazon preferred to take advantage of a small segment of businesses in the long tail, and then expanding that market sliver exponentially, while sharing revenue with others.

The online phenomenon of mashups also sees companies working with each other. Mash-ups are digital open remixing of information from different sources. For example, HousingMaps.com combined the rentals on Craigslist with Google maps so that viewers could instantly see where addresses were. Two formerly unrelated sites were remixed to produce something that was more useful than its parts to a certain group of users. Web 2.0 competence syndication can turn competitors, ecosystem partners, and a broad range of small and medium enterprises into loyal, revenue-generating, revenue-sharing users, while increasing economies of scale and scope. This is a long way from the game theory of business strategy in the 80s, which saw keeping rivals on their toes as the key to success.

Tactical Questions to Consider:
- Are there aspects of your business that you could sell or syndicate as services?
- Could you work with businesses that might feel threatened by your projects?
- Do you have a product or service that could complement an existing Web service?

NO EXCUSES

Though many examples of the new high-tech business models are Web-based, traditional businesses have no excuse for failing to take full advantage of these opportunities as well. Let's look at some who have done just that.

Webkinz

This stuffed-toy company used dynamic capabilities and Web 2.0 to meet the demands of the Noughties child who likes teddy bears and computer games. The plush toys are no different from any others in the physical sense, but each comes with a secret code that enables its owner to enter the online Webkinz World, a virtual play area with its own economy. Every time you buy a pet, play a game, answer questions, or do activities, you get KinzCash to be spent in the online store. In addition, you interact with other pet owners through Webkinz chat. However, accounts expire within a year, unless another Webkinz animal is purchased, so kids have to keep buying if they want to remain part of the world.

The Webkinz business model has a big element of recombinant innovation, where a company took a classic product and mixed it with new technology to make something more valuable than the sum of its parts. The Webkinz World exploits a range of network effects including: direct—the experience of being part of the world gets better as more people join; indirect—the stuffed toys encourage complementary products in the shop; and social—the online chat room connects fellow pet owners who influence each other.

Zopa

In the current economy, access to credit is increasingly difficult for consumers and enterprises alike. But money hasn't vanished. Part of the difficulty arises from a lack of trust in the system. This is precisely where social financiers such as Zopa.com come in. These platforms want to cut out the traditional middleman—the bank—and connect lenders and borrowers directly. So, if someone has some spare money to lend, he or she can check out the lending options, and then proceed directly to the description of a potential borrower and the motives of his or her financial need. The lender sets the lending rate that suits him or her, and the loan enters an online auction. Thus, social lending is putting risk assessment, rates, and returns back in the hands of individual lenders and borrowers themselves, and eschewing the overheads and money-making schemes employed by banks, which many regard with cynicism in the wake of the crisis.

GE/Google Smart Grid

GE provides consumers with wireless "smart meters" and Google makes the detailed energy data available to users via their laptops. In a pilot project involving Oklahoma G&E, even teenagers got in on the act, unplugging the toaster after breakfast when they knew down to the cent the value of doing so, as their minute-by-minute energy use was being calculated and fed to them via the Web. GE has recombined an old product (metering) with information technologies, and used aspects of Web 2.0 in its business model. Vitally, this innovation has an energy-saving motive at its core, which these days gives any project an added edge.

Lego

The Danish company Lego allows customers to design their own Lego sets through its "Design byME" initiative. This program, launched in

October 2009 as a continuation of its Lego Factory customization program, allows users to create their own Lego product, from beginning to end, providing all the necessary information and tools to get the job done. Customers download digital design software provided by Lego at no charge. They custom-design their own dream Lego models on computer, right down to the box and building guide. Then the product can be ordered online and shipped to their door.

Maybe some of these ideas inspire you. Try them out. The low cost and high connectivity of the Web means you can experiment easily—indeed, experimentation is key to finding out what works and what doesn't. Once you've seen the difference it makes, you can build in the directions that you find the most growth.

WEB 3.0 AND BEYOND

Like backseat passengers on a road trip, we tend to ignore the amazing scenery whizzing past us as we impatiently ask the driver, "Are we at Web 3.0 yet?" If we date the start of the first generation of the Web to Netscape going public in 1995, then it took us a full decade to reach the "crossover point" in 2005—the year when more bits, bytes, and digital goods were being uploaded and shared on the Web than were being downloaded. So, if it took 10 years to go from Web 1.0 to Web 2.0—from static to dynamic, from passive users to active contributors—and we are nearly halfway through the second decade of the Web, what's next on the horizon?

Part of our impatience is due to the instant gratification we have come to expect from the Web, and we're disappointed that the Web at work doesn't look that much different from the Web at home. This, in itself, says a lot about how we've changed.

John Chambers, CEO of Cisco, speaking at an O'Reilly Media Web 2.0 Summit, pointed out that the new Web paradigm has reversed the usual sequence of technology and business innovation. In the past, disruptive high-tech innovations, such as semiconductor chips, began life in big industry labs, and then trickled down to the mass market in simplified versions, after proving their commercial worth in the professional world. Customers had to be educated by companies on how to use these new products and services, with a small group of early adopters and lead users acting as pioneers before opening up the path to mainstream acceptance.

Those days are fast disappearing. We're witnessing a quantum social shift that has business implications for both digital and traditional industries. All around us, we see industry transformations and network convergence—in media, entertainment, music, telecom, financial services, energy, life sciences, health care, consumer electronics, precious metals. Even everyday branded products like Heinz Ketchup and Doritos are bringing new collaborative innovation and dynamic capabilities to the forefront. In the United States, Europe, and Asia, whole new ecosystems and networks of small businesses are forming around these leaders.

The next Web crossover point will be when the world puts the Web to work in jumping the digital divide and bringing local entrepreneurs and users at the bottom of the pyramid into the networked, digital knowledge economy. A few promising and influential innovators in this area include Kiva, the world's first online microlending platform connecting lenders to entrepreneurs across the globe.

Another example is the pharmaceutical distributor McKesson, which has been an IT innovator in providing preventive and emergency services to homeless people in partnership with state health and hospital agencies. In return for a free cell phone and monthly minutes, previously hard-to-reach but at-risk groups such as homeless people can be monitored and receive health care and medical advice to reduce the likelihood of high-cost emergency room and acute-care cases down the road.

Such initiatives are pursuing collaborative innovation on a large scale, connecting digital, financial, and knowledge-based capabilities and resources with external networks of local partners and government agencies. The Web of the future, we believe, will see more "feet on the street," featuring even greater transparency, visibility, localization, and distribution to global participants at the bottom of the pyramid.

The Battle of the Value Chains: New Specialized versus Old Hybrids

Gillis Jonk
A. T. Kearney

Martin Handschuh
A. T. Kearney

Sandra Niewiem
A. T. Kearney

Imagine taking a week's vacation in a tiny rural village, with only one store to supply your needs—from food and drink to clothes, hardware, and entertainment. Such temporary simplicity has its attractions—yet sooner or later most of us would happily return to civilization, where we can buy exactly what we want at our favorite niche outlets, on the Internet, or at the mall. Goodbye, simple life; hello, specialization.

This metaphor of the Village Store versus the Internet illustrates how customers have embraced this trend of commercial specialization, demanding and rewarding constantly multiplying permutations of choice. Increasingly, specialized offerings are within almost everyone's reach, and the village store, where it still survives, is an artifact of an earlier era. In fact, the shift toward specialization—driven by globalization, buying via the Internet, modular value chains, and the growth of low-wage economies—is playing out faster than some big companies can adapt. Especially at risk are companies that continue to view their customers in terms of unique buying segments, instead of realizing that today the same customer may demand different varieties of a product or service at different times.

To illustrate this trend we have identified examples of the challenges posed to established firms in various industries as new fronts of specialization emerge. To counter these threats we propose that they adopt a practical approach for discovering where they are likely to be effectively attacked by emerging rivals, and for developing both preemptive first strikes and successful counterattacks. Our recommendation is that established players compete by first considering and then creating a number of specialized value chains. This suggestion contradicts the conventional wisdom that established firms are more competitive if they continue to adjust and augment a single value chain.

WHO IS AT RISK?

As the following examples show, it's not the small, fast-growing focused companies that are at risk; they're often the ones exploiting the opportunity to specialize. Those in danger are well-established leaders, in particular those that cling to old assumptions. Behaviors to watch out for include:

- Serving your customers just as you always have, not realizing these customers are changing their expectations—for example, by wanting newer, faster, and better services and products at the high end, while expecting to get better quality than once might have been expected, and for lower prices, on the low end.

- Attempting to fight back via business process improvement alone, since this is always easier than implementing radical structural changes. Such business process improvement

Reprinted from *Strategy & Leadership* 36, no. 2 (2008), pp. 24–29.

efforts treat the symptoms, not the disease, and they offer no guarantee of success. You may find yourself making continuous process improvements with little to show for it, even as you lose more and more of your business to focused players.

• Not recognizing that things are likely to get worse. Even if today you can cope, tomorrow you may find that focused competitors have poached parts of your business so successfully you lack the resources to fight back.

Here are some typical examples of challenges in various industries that show why competition has gained a foothold and why large existing players find it so difficult to respond.

INFRASTRUCTURE MADE EASY: RETAIL COMPUTER

Once upon a time IBM happily sold laptops and PCs through a class-leading network of retailers; its strength in this channel made competition difficult for new entrants. Then Dell discovered it could bypass the reseller channel altogether by selling online, and in the process allow customers to customize the features of their computer and thus control the price. IBM found itself in a quandary as to how to respond. If it followed Dell down the direct channel route, it would instantly cannibalize its existing reseller channel. However, it couldn't compete using only its resellers because they couldn't afford to configure customized computers and sell them at competitive prices. Such dilemmas are one of several signs that specialization will soon make a competitive challenge and must be addressed.

GLOBALIZATION AND LOW-COST PLAYERS: LIGHT BULBS, AUTOS

In several industries, low-cost players have taken advantage of globalization, new ways to find customers, and specialization. An example is the lighting industry, particularly the lamps market. Until a decade ago, this market was dominated by large and sophisticated players such as General Electric, Osram, and Philips Electronics. These companies built their dominance in part on the strength of being able to supply every conceivable light source to meet every possible lighting need—from basic incandescent lamps in all shapes and wattages to specialty lamps of all kinds, including sophisticated energy-saving lamps.

But as lamps became more sophisticated, they also became more expensive. A high-end energy-saving lamp, for example, can cost 30 times more than a basic incandescent lamp, making transportation costs a smaller fraction of the price tag. New players in China seized this opening to begin exporting halogen and energy-saving lamps to Europe and North America. These entrants focused on producing only the most popular models, avoiding the costs of a more varied line. They also found consumers would accept slightly inferior products at lower prices—for example, cheaper energy-saving lamps that don't come on instantly, but flicker for a few moments before burning at full brightness.

The large do-it-yourself chains and furniture chains such as IKEA happily sell these low-cost lights, while still keeping the full range of lights made by the market leaders on their shelves to satisfy every consumer demand.

The global auto industry provides a dramatic example. In India, the Tata conglomerate is working on the Rs 1-lakh car, which is being designed to cost about $2,275. Sales are anticipated to be millions of cars per model. Clearly this offering will require a specialized value chain not only to engineer, source, produce, and assemble the cars but also to sell and service them.

Initially such a car will compete primarily in India and other emerging world markets—but other low-cost cars are already penetrating the developed world. We can see this from the success of Dacia, with its Logan and MPV car model—attractively priced basic cars sold in Western Europe, with a waiting list longer than many if not all mainstream brand cars.

Can the big automakers serve this low-cost need simply by stripping goodies from cars and selling them with as little service as possible? No, for it is impossible by mere tinkering to compete against a setup that is not only entirely specialized but has huge and appropriate scale just for the low-cost market. This is an example of why specialization is such a potential risk to leading players in industries everywhere; the big players may lead in overall market share, but that doesn't mean they're scaled right to compete in multiple specialized theaters.

MODULARIZATION: SPECIALTY MINERAL WATERS AND NON-ALCOHOLIC BEVERAGES

Modular value chains are another factor in specialization; they help smaller companies overcome their scale disadvantage by tapping into scaled-up parts of the value chains of other companies.

This frequently happens in the consumer goods market segment. Many new and highly differentiated premium products are brought to market—often by relatively small companies. The high-concept mineral waters and non-alcoholic beverages such as Fuji, POM, and VitaminWater are good examples. The companies behind these products have taken advantage of plug 'n play value chains to reduce their scale disadvantage

and efficiently bring their products into today's consolidated retail market.

Innovation based on this sort of partnering isn't easy for established fast-moving consumer goods (FMCG) leaders to duplicate—an indication of this is Coca-Cola's $4.1 billion purchase of VitaminWater in the spring of 2007. Yet some are finding ways to do so just the same. Procter & Gamble, for example, has made it a goal to adopt the entrepreneurial and modular approach toward innovation: its Connect + Develop Web sites reach out to tens of thousands of outside developers and scientists, indicating P&G's willingness to partner when such arrangements are mutually beneficial.

HYBRID VERSUS SPECIALIZED VALUE CHAINS

The difference between a hybrid value chain and a specialized value chain is that a hybrid focuses on the full breadth of the needs of specific customer segments, whereas the specialized value chain focuses on segments of specific customer needs (see Figures 1, 2, and 3).

How do you know when your hybrid value chain can't compete effectively against specialized competitors? How do you know when there

Figure 1   Hybrid versus Specialized Value Chains

Figure 2   Moving from Hybrid to Specialized Value Chains

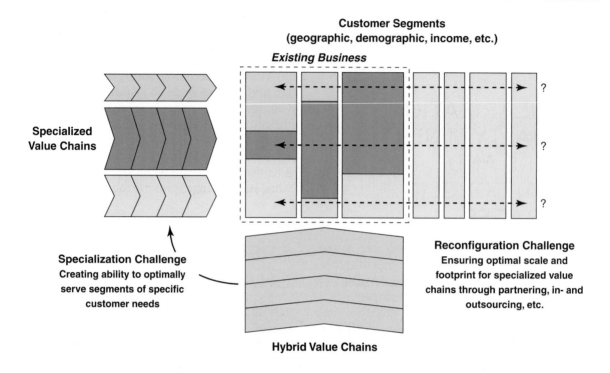

Figure 3   Hybrid versus Specialized Value Chains

is sufficient potential to warrant the effort of creating multiple specialized chains? Here are some telltale signs:

- Your business segment is having a hard time finding growth, yet focused competitors are gaining ground.

- Internal complexity is rising; customer satisfaction isn't.

- The potential for horizontal synergies between units can no longer be ignored.

- You need to find external partners, but find more obstacles than opportunities.

- Channel conflicts and price cannibalizations are increasing.
- Customers are being cherry-picked, their loyalty is eroding, and competitive requests for proposals (RFPs) and tender situations are on the rise.

If you're experiencing such symptoms, you may nonetheless be tempted to stay with your hybrid chain, rather than take on the seemingly high-effort exercise of developing specialized chains. Such a shift would require new, often non-traditional organization and governance structures, a thorough analysis of scale versus scope strategies, the pursuit of new customers for the newly specialized chains, and many more interfaces and alliances to manage. Yet it's important to remember that customer expectations are likely to diverge more, rather than less, and that once specialized competitors reach scale, they will be very hard to compete against if your firm is still using its hybrid value chain.

REDEFINING CUSTOMER FOCUS; ORCHESTRATING CANNIBALIZATION

For well-established companies with a long history of success, two aspects of specialization pose particular challenges.

First, customer focus has to be redefined. Instead of trying to figure out how to better serve existing customer segments, the focus shifts. Now it becomes a hunt to uncover segments of specific customer needs that benefit from being served by a more specialized value chain, especially those segments of customer needs that are underserved by the current hybrid value chains. Consider the market entry strategy of the low-cost air carriers. Companies such as EasyJet, Ryan Air, and Southwest didn't look for customers around specific hubs—instead, they targeted attractive routes, and made their offering available to anybody and everybody who wanted no-frills transportation on these routes. For a network carrier, such a switch would represent a radical departure from the decades of building customer bases around hubs and improving connections and services.

This brings us to the second challenge: if a network airline carrier does decide to set up a low-cost operation, it must inevitably cannibalize its existing network operations to make the new unit a success. Mergers and acquisitions can help provide the scale needed for specialization, an example of this being the merger that created Air France–KLM a few years ago.

THE VALUE CHAIN SPECIALIZATION ASSESSMENT

Given the highly strategic nature of specializing value chains, there's obviously a need for assessing where and when parts of the value chain might have to be specialized. This will help evaluate opportunities against other strategic opportunities and threats. To do so requires managers to develop two insights:

> Understanding which different segments of specific customer needs would potentially benefit from increased value chain specialization.

> Creating strategic business plans for such specialization opportunities that address customer needs, market offerings, competition, and resources. The plans should assess both the impact on the current business and the reconfiguration requirements.

In our experience, evaluating which segments of specific customer needs would gain from value chain specialization requires comprehensive analysis. Typical dimensions to consider are:

- High-end versus midrange versus low-end products and pricing.
- Standard versus semi-standard versus customized.
- Products versus service versus solutions.
- Emerging markets versus developed markets.
- Old technology versus contemporary technology versus new technology.
- Single channel versus multichannel distribution.

Another important approach is to assess the competitive playing field, looking for instances where focused players are gaining market share;

One reason companies stick with traditional business optimization in the face of focused competition is that one of the key tools for understanding the market—customer segmentation—is no longer as helpful as it used to be.

Most air travelers, for example, don't limit themselves to charter flights, or network flights, or low-cost flights; they treat air travel as a smorgasbord and choose based on their present needs. Likewise, people buying books and CDs from Amazon are also likely to frequent Waterstone's or Barnes & Noble, where they can actually handle books and CDs and also get together with friends for a Starbucks coffee and muffin—that is, a complete shopping and leisure experience.

In such cases, to continue thinking in terms of customer segments can only cloud our thinking about real customer needs. We will mistakenly continue to believe that our value chains should be responsive, agile, and lean and mean, all at the same time—rather than realizing that value chain specialization and scale reconsideration would be far more effective.

The answer is simple: give up the old assumptions, and start segmenting in terms of customer needs, not individual customers. Then the dialog on value chain specialization can begin in earnest.

they are likely doing something you can learn from. It's also important to search for emerging needs; it may be that a specialized value chain to cater to them effectively doesn't yet exist.

Once opportunities for value chain specialization have been identified, they will have to be strategically evaluated during the regular strategic decision-making processes—for example, by developing business plans.

THE END OF THE VILLAGE STORE

Aligning the segments of present or future customer needs, on the one hand, and the company's degree of value chain specialization, on the other, can represent an important source of growth and value for established firms and new entrants alike.

Customers, who have learned how to rapidly value new offerings, are the main drivers of the trend toward specialized value chains. To return to the metaphor we began with, if our customers have said goodbye to the village store, then so must we.

Low-Cost Strategy through Product Architecture: Lessons from China

Hua Wang
Euromed Management Ecole
de Marseille, France

Chris Kimble
Euromed Management Ecole
de Marseille, France

INTRODUCTION

The global financial downturn that began in 2008 has pushed much of the world's car industry into crisis; carmakers serving the U.S. market, including strong performers like Toyota and Honda, have experienced double-digit declines in their sales. The Chinese car industry, on the other hand, is booming. It overtook the U.S. industry in 2008 to become the second largest in the world, producing 9.4 million vehicles.

Foreign carmakers located in China have played their part, but local players such as Geely, Chery, and BYD have also had a role in the expansion. This article will argue that the rapid growth of indigenous Chinese carmakers is driven not by low labor costs, but by innovations in product architecture that have enabled Chinese carmakers to follow a low-cost strategy while still producing products that are broadly equivalent to their foreign counterparts. By changing the product design, local carmakers with less than 15 years' experience have managed to produce cars in the same product category as their Western competitors but at a significantly lower price.

We begin by briefly highlighting the link between breakthrough strategies and product design. We follow this with a discussion of product architecture and identify a form of transitional product architecture created by Chinese carmakers known as a quasi-open modular architecture. We then present a case study of a Chinese carmaker, Geely, which illustrates the nature of the car industry in China and shows the impact that this transitional architecture can have. Finally, we address the possible implications of this approach for car production by the mainstream U.S. and European car industry.

BREAKTHROUGH STRATEGIES AND PRODUCT DESIGN

Breakthrough Strategies

The notion of breakthrough strategy has its own literature and is dealt with elsewhere (e.g., Markides, 2000). Our aim here is not to enter into a discussion of these ideas but to outline the key concepts. Although there is disagreement on points of detail, there is broad agreement on the key features:

- A breakthrough strategy involves a radical or fundamental shift in the way in which things are done.
- A breakthrough strategy is not about playing the existing game better but about changing the rules of the game.
- A breakthrough strategy involves a complete reconceptualization or reconfiguration of an existing business model.

For the purposes of this paper, we will simply define a breakthrough strategy as the successful

Reprinted from "Low-Cost Strategy Through Product Architecture: Lessons From China," by Hua Wang and Chris Kimble, *Journal of Business Strategy*, Vol. 31, No. 3 (2010), pp. 12–20. Copyright © Emerald Group Publishing Limited. All rights reserved.

introduction of a radical change in the way a business operates that creates an entirely new way of doing business. Success, in this context, is defined in terms of the company's ability to outperform its competitors significantly.

Examples of companies that achieve this sort of breakthrough are often drawn from the high-tech sector. For example, eBay based its business operations on the same principles as long-established auction houses such as Christie's and Sotheby's, but achieved a breakthrough by the dematerialization of the auction process, coupled with the creation of PayPal, which both makes payment easier and generates additional revenue for eBay. Although most of the recent literature on breakthrough strategies tends to focus on the alignment of IT and business strategy, other approaches can be followed.

Product Design

Fraser (2007) describes how companies can achieve strategic breakthroughs by applying the principles of design to business strategy. She describes this as consisting of three interacting gears. The first gear is user understanding; being able to reframe the business through the eyes of the customer. She describes this as "more than marketing 101" (Fraser, 2007, p. 68), as it involves a deep and profound understanding of the customer's needs.

The second gear is concept visualization, where an abstract understanding of users' needs becomes a concrete expression of what the product should be and how it will serve the customer's needs. Finally, the third gear, what Fraser calls strategic business design, involves applying abductive reasoning—making the conceptual leap to think, "If feature X were possible, all of our ideas about what we want to do with the product would follow naturally" (Figure 1).

The following section will present an approach that makes such a link between strategy and design. To do this, we will need to narrow the field of design to a subcategory known as product architecture.

PRODUCT ARCHITECTURE: THE MISSING LINK IN BREAKTHROUGH STRATEGY?

Product architecture is a conceptual representation of the physical components that go to make up a product, together with any interactions between them that affect the functioning of that product. Takahiro Fujimoto argues that a fit between

Figure 1   The Three Gears of Design

Source: Adapted from Fraser (2007).

capabilities in manufacturing and product architecture can create an advantage for a particular industry in a particular country or region and identifies product architecture as one of the most important sources of a country's comparative advantage (Fujimoto, 2007).

Fujimoto defines product architecture in terms of an approach that links the functional and structural design of a product. He divides product architecture along two dimensions: modular-integral and open-closed. The modular-integral dimension refers to the level of integration of the components in a product. Products with a high degree of component integration have many-to-many links between their components, meaning that the product has to be produced as a single integrated unit. A low level of component integration means that components have a simple one-to-one correspondence and can be treated as discrete modules. The open-closed dimension refers to the level of standardization. An open architecture implies the existence of industry-level standards for components; a closed architecture means that standardization exists only within the boundaries of a single firm.

By combining these two dimensions, Fujimoto identifies three possible forms of product architecture: open-modular, closed-modular, and closed-integral. According to Fujimoto, the fourth

category, open-integral, is a logical contradiction and a practical impossibility (Figure 2).

Fujimoto's classification of product architecture provides us with a useful way to think about the links between the design of products and the strategic positioning of a company. For example, the often-repeated story of IBM (Baldwin and Clark, 1997) can be recast in terms architectural evolution.

Viewed in this way, IBM's story is as follows. In the 1950s, computers were specialized, custom-built machines created to perform specific tasks, clearly corresponding to the closed-integral cell in Fujimoto's model. At that time, IBM was the market leader in the manufacture of custom-built data-processing machines such as the IBM 704. However, in response to growing demand in the 1960s, IBM began to introduce new products such as the IBM System 360 range that shared the same hardware and software. This moved IBM into the closed-modular cell in the model. In the late 1970s and early 1980s, a new market for desktop computing began to emerge in which Apple was the market leader. IBM launched its own desktop PC in 1981 and, in order to cut costs and speed up development time, outsourced heavily (Figure 3). This effectively moved the desktop into the third open-modular cell of Fujimoto's model, which in turn created the conditions for companies such

Figure 2   Fujimoto's Taxonomy of Product Architecture

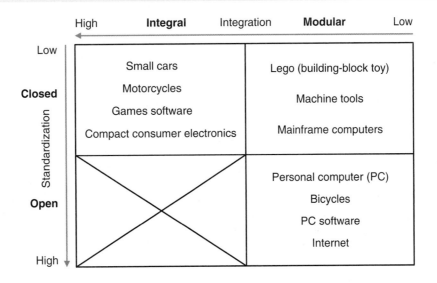

Figure 3   The IBM Story in Terms of an Evolution in Product Architecture

as Intel and Microsoft to make a strategic break-through and become the new market leaders.

Although there is no single pattern to architectural evolution, according to Baldwin and Clark (1997), the general trend is a movement from closed-integral to open-modular architectures, a trajectory that can also be seen in the production of complex mechanical products such as cars.

For example, according to Langlois (2002), the 1930s marked the transition from craftsman-built, open-modular car production to a mass-production closed-integral model. This model remained dominant until the 1990s, when, driven by competitive pressures, a number of leading European carmakers began to move to a closed-modular type production, for example, platform sharing between Citroën and Peugeot cars in the PSA group, or Volkswagen, Audi, Skoda, and Seat in the Volkswagen group. However, this modularity has remained at the company, rather than the industrial, level; consequently, the change from closed to open product architectures that we can see in the PC industry is not present in the U.S. or European car industry.

In China, however, carmakers and their suppliers have begun to move toward a more open, modular form of production based on what is termed a quasi-open modular product architecture. Fujimoto describes this development in the following way:

> Imitation-turned-versatile parts are being gathered and assembled by numerous companies and this is different from a full-fledged open architecture based on a carefully worked-out plan as seen in various digital products made by American companies. (Fujimoto, 2002, p. 35)

In China, best-selling foreign cars are routinely imitated through reverse engineering. Major components from those foreign cars, such as engines and chassis, have, through repetitive remodeling, become defacto generic components that can be used by indigenous manufacturers. By mixing and matching remodeled components from existing cars, Chinese manufacturers are able to produce completely new cars more quickly and at a much lower price than their foreign counterparts are able to achieve (Figure 4). Although this approach is a radical departure from Western practices, it remains only a quasi-open modular architecture, as the modularity of the remodeled components has not yet reached the industry level.

The analysis of the case study that follows provides a concrete illustration of how this quasi-open

Figure 4 The Emerging Chinese Automobile Industry

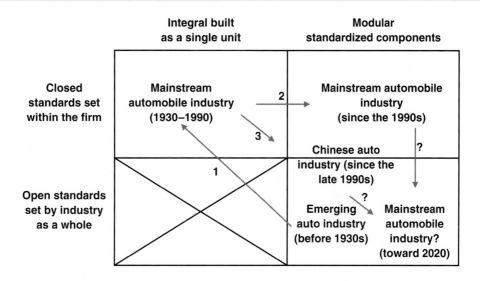

CASE STUDY—CHINA GEELY AUTOMOBILE CO. LTD

Method

The methodology used to produce this case study was an in-depth, longitudinal case history (Yin, 2003). The study was undertaken over a period of five years and was divided into three stages. The first stage was a preliminary field study that took place over a period of a year in 2002; the second stage was an in-depth investigation conducted between January and April 2006; the final stage involved onsite interviews and was carried out between March and May 2007. The majority of interviewees for this final stage were middle- or senior-level managers who had at least 15 years' experience as carmakers. This approach afforded a broader understanding of the Chinese market and moved beyond the experiences of a single firm. The full details of the case study have been published elsewhere (Wang, 2008).

modular architecture works in practice and additionally illustrates some of the unique features of the Chinese car industry that contributed to its emergence.

Findings and Analysis

In 1998, a successful private manufacturer of refrigerators and motorcycles in China named Geely made what might have appeared to be a surprising decision and expanded into the production to motorcars. At the time, there were already around 120 carmakers in China and the central government was actively promoting a car industry based around a small number of state-owned companies. The approval process for any new projects was extremely severe. Geely had little credibility as a car manufacturer and was compelled to resort to some rather creative and unorthodox practices, such as listing their first cars in the less-regulated bus category.

Despite such an inauspicious start, in December 2001, Geely was registered officially as a carmaker and became the first privately owned car manufacturer in China. In less than 10 years, it has become the ninth-largest carmaker in China. It sold 230,000 units in 2008, a year-on-year increase of 11.6 percent, and succeeded in increasing its exports by 79.8 percent. In addition, it has expanded its production capacity to 500,000 units and has set up five new manufacturing sites. The company's success in crafting a breakthrough strategy from such unpromising beginnings is based in part on its founder's deep understanding of Chinese markets, and in part on the innovations it has made in its product architecture.

Refrigerators, motorcycles, and cars were the three products most affected by the rise in living standards and purchasing power that followed the economic reforms of the 1980s (Wang, 2008). The Chinese middle class, who buy these goods, are highly price sensitive but also very concerned about the appearance of the product, which is an outward expression of their social status. Geely was able to identify precisely what the consumer wanted but, in addition, was able to develop a new product architecture that allowed it to produce a low-price/low-cost product that was designed to meet specific local needs.

As elsewhere, components from best-selling foreign cars were reverse-engineered and copied, but the approach pioneered by Geely differed from traditional copying in one important respect: the architecture of the copied product was progressively altered in such a way that the high-level mixing and matching of components from different sources became possible.

Geely experienced at least two stages in the development of their product architecture. In the first stage, architectural changes were based on simple imitation. The first model produced in 1998, the Haoqing, was based on the Charade, which was itself the result of technology transfer from Toyota's affiliate, Daihatsu. The Charade was produced by the state-owned FAW Xiali. Initially, around 60 percent of components (including the engine and transmission) were purchased directly from FAW Xiali, with copied components accounting for another 10 percent. Thus, around 70 percent of the components of the Haoqing were interchangable with that of the Charade.

Later, in the second stage, the capability of mixing and matching components was increased. The Maple, which entered production in 2002, was based on the combination of two foreign models already produced in China: the French Citroën ZX and the Charade (originally from Japan). The body and chassis of the Maple were based on the imitation and remodeling of Citroën ZX, while the engine was based on the remodeling of a Toyota engine. From this point of view, the Maple was more of an open-modular design than the Haoqing.

Combining components from cars designed with an integral or closed modular architecture

(the Citroën ZX and Charade) to build a car with a quasi-open modular architecture (the Maple) was a major technical challenge for Geely. Architectural change requires a significantly higher level of technological and engineering capability than copying. The more recent cars produced by Geely have reached a high level of modularity, going well beyond the closed modular model typical of leading Western carmakers. For example, the engine produced by Geely can fit into bodies derived from several different foreign models, each produced by different manufacturers. Additionally, cars produced by Geely can also accommodate a number of other engines that can be bought in the open market. A senior manager at Geely explains:

> During the design period, enough space has been reserved for an engine. We've tried to assemble different engines on the same car, and all of them work without the need to change the rest of the car's architecture.

In short, the interface between the engine and the rest of the car has been designed to allow the manufacturer to mix and match major components in a flexible and efficient way. This architectural innovation, both at the level of the engine and that of the whole car, has helped Geely to significantly reduce its costs (Wang, 2008). For example, Geely's MR4790Q engine can be produced at one-third of the price of a Toyota engine because the components of Toyota's engine have become "imitation-turned-versatile" parts that can be produced at low costs and in large volumes. In terms of total cost, Geely's plant manager observed:

> If our competitors are selling their vehicles (of the same category) at prices as low as ours, they are losing money, whereas we still make profit.

The final element in Geely's breakthrough is that it has enabled the creation of innovative interfirm relationships that support its overall strategy. A high percentage (around 70 percent) of components, including parts of the engine, are outsourced; consequently, Geely and its suppliers need to work very closely together. Geely strives to lower the price but must also maintain an acceptable level of quality to meet the local market's needs. To achieve this goal, it has built on its links with its suppliers from its motorcycle business who are experienced in high-volume production at low costs. This category accounts for 50 percent of its total number of suppliers. To ensure quality is maintained, the suppliers of big companies such as Volkswagen, Toyota, PSA, Nissan, and General Motors are also integrated into the sourcing system. Having Geely, as the customer helps those suppliers realize economies of scale because of the higher production volume. Thus, the architectural innovation that has taken place at Geely, is now contributing to a wider change at the industrial level (Figure 5).

CONCLUSION: IMPLICATIONS FOR THE AUTOMOBILE GIANTS

Attaining low-cost production is a perennial challenge for most manufacturers. The current incremental approach toward cost reduction using existing product architectures, which predominates in the Western car industry, seems to be reaching its limits; only a radical architectural change in product design will allow a company to lower its costs so significantly that its competitors will find the move hard to follow. In just a single decade, through its innovative use of product architecture, Geely has moved from having no experience of carmaking to a position where it is the ninth-largest carmaker in China and is

able to produce and sell cars that are significantly cheaper than its foreign counterparts. In 2009, Geely announced a sales growth of 25 percent and no job cuts despite the financial crisis and a global economic downturn.

Although Geely's progress has been dramatic, it is by no means an exceptional case in China's car industry. Other local carmakers, including Chery, BYD, and Great Wall are making similar progress using similar methods. We estimate that cars featuring quasi-open architectures now represent around 30 percent of total production in China. In addition to the carmakers, developments among component suppliers are reinforcing the move toward quasi-open architectures. For example, Mitsubishi is selling its engines to at least 21 different carmakers in China and Delphi's engine management system has become modular so that it can be used with any Mitsubishi engine in order to increase its sales. In short, the Chinese market has become the crucible from which a new product architecture for automobiles has begun to emerge: local consumers, carmakers, and leading component suppliers are all contributing to expansion of the quasi-open architectural paradigm.

Leading carmakers in other parts of the world are confronting multiple challenges to their position; so far, the response seems to have been to continue to adhere to closed product architectures. However, technological advances such as greater fuel efficiency or the development of

Figure 5   Three Gears Model in the Chinese Automobile Industry

User Understanding
A low-price car with an appearance that corresponds to the social status of emerging middle class

Concept Visualization
"Me too" strategy
Decent design, low costs with local customization

Strategic Business Design
Quasi-open modular architecture
OEM and suppliers jointly work on the new product architecture

technically complex hybrid or other forms of so-called green cars have failed to stimulate sales in mature markets due to their high price. Abandoning the low-cost bottom of the pyramid, as the market in developing countries is sometimes referred to, to local manufacturers could be a strategic mistake, as these are exactly the markets where the innovations that seem set to produce low-cost strategic breakthroughs appear to be happening.

Developments such as the quasi-open architecture found in Chinese car manufacturing seem to have the potential to produce cars of comparable quality to those of the established carmakers, but at a significantly lower cost. Mainstream Western carmakers may have the edge on new technology, but this alone seems unlikely to give them the strategic breakthrough they need. The current carmaking giants and others need to be fully aware of the strategic potential of innovations in product architecture, both as a potential driver of breakthrough strategy and as a threat to the current position. Manufacturers based in the mature markets of the United States and Europe ignore the lessons of low-cost production through innovations in product architecture that are beginning to emerge from China at their peril.

REFERENCES

Baldwin, C. Y. and Clark, K. B. (1997), "Managing in an age of modularity," *Harvard Business Review,* Vol. 75 No. 5, pp. 84–93.

Fraser, H. M. A. (2007), "The practice of breakthrough strategies by design," *Journal of Business Strategy,* Vol. 28 No. 4, pp. 66–74.

Fujimoto, T. (2002), "Thinking about the China's manufacturing industry from the perspective of product architecture," *Keizai Sangyo Janaru,* pp. 34–7.

Fujimoto, T. (2007), "Architecture-based comparative advantage: a design information view of manufacturing", *Evolutionary and Institutional Economics Review,* Vol. 4 No. 1, pp. 55–112.

Langlois, R. N. (2002), "Modularity in technology and organization," *Journal of Economic Behavior and Organization,* Vol. 49 No. 1, pp. 19–37.

Markides, C. C. (2000), *All the Right Moves: A Guide to Crafting Breakthrough Strategy,* Harvard Business School Press, Boston, MA.

Wang, H. (2008), "The innovation in the product architecture: a study of Chinese automobile industry," *Asia Pacific Journal of Management,* Vol. 25 No. 3, pp. 509–35.

Yin, R. K. (2003), *Case Study Research: Design and Methods,* Sage, Thousand Oaks, CA.

Managing Strategic Alliances: What Do We Know Now, and Where Do We Go from Here?

Prashant Kale
Rice University

Harbir Singh
University of Pennsylvania

EXECUTIVE OVERVIEW

Alliances present a paradox for firms. On the one hand, firms engage in a large number of alliances to secure and extend their competitive advantage and growth; on the other hand, their alliances exhibit surprisingly low success rates. In this paper, we discuss how firms can address these failures by identifying some of the primary drivers of alliance success. First, we discuss how firms can achieve success with any individual alliance by considering critical factors at each phase of the alliance life cycle. Second, we show how firms can increase their overall alliance success by developing and institutionalizing firm-level capabilities to manage alliances. Third, we highlight emerging issues in the alliance context, including the need to recognize a new class of alliances between firms and not-for-profit organizations or individuals, the benefits of taking a "portfolio approach" to alliance strategy and management, and the opportunity to transfer one's alliance capabilities to the effective management of other interfirm relationships, including acquisitions.

THE ALLIANCE PARADOX

In the last two decades, alliances have become a central part of most companies' competitive and growth strategies. Alliances help firms strengthen their competitive position by enhancing market power (Kogut, 1991), increasing efficiencies (Ahuja, 2000), accessing new or critical resources or capabilities (Rothaermel & Boeker, 2008), and entering new markets (Garcia-Canal, Duarte, Criado, & Llaneza, 2002). By the turn of this century many of the world's largest companies had over 20 percent of their assets, and over 30 percent of their annual research expenditures, tied up in such relationships (Ernst, 2004). A study by Partner Alliances reported that over 80 percent of Fortune 1,000 CEOs believed that alliances would account for almost 26 percent of their companies' revenues in 2007–08 (Kale, Singh, & Bell, 2009). Nevertheless, alliances also tend to exhibit high failure rates (Dyer, Kale, & Singh, 2001). Studies have shown that between 30 percent and 70 percent of alliances fail; in

other words, they neither meet the goals of their parent companies nor deliver on the operational or strategic benefits they purport to provide (Bamford, Gomes-Casseres, & Robinson, 2004). Alliance termination rates are reportedly over 50 percent (Lunnan & Haugland, 2008), and in many cases forming such relationships has resulted in shareholder value destruction for the companies that engage in them (Kale, Dyer, & Singh, 2002).

This creates a paradox for firms. On the one hand, companies face significant obstacles in ensuring sufficient success with alliances. On the other hand, they need to form a greater number of alliances than before, and must increasingly rely on them as a means of enhancing their competitiveness and growth. If this is indeed the case, managers need a better understanding of what really underlies alliance success and how firms can manage alliances better. This paper takes a step in addressing these questions by drawing on insights gained from prior and current research on this subject. We examine these issues at two different levels of analysis.

First, we focus at the level of a single alliance between two or more firms, investigating the major factors that explain the success of a given alliance; this has been the primary focus of most alliance research until recently. Second, we focus on a firm as a whole that is engaged in not just one but multiple alliances over time, and we explain how it can get better at managing them. In other words, how can it develop a firm-level "alliance capability" so as to enjoy greater and repeatable success across all its alliances? Scholars have begun studying the latter issue only recently, but it is particularly important as, in a world where firms rely more than ever on alliances, having a superior capability to manage them is in itself a source of competitive advantage.[1]

We conclude the paper by discussing both emerging opportunities and challenges at both levels of analysis. First, at the alliance level firms need to recognize the growing importance of a new class of alliances in addition to the traditional firm-to-firm alliance: alliances between firms and not-for-profit entities, including non-governmental organizations (NGOs), and alliances between firms and individuals (such as Procter & Gamble's Connect + Develop relationships established to foster and accelerate innovations). Second, at the firm level, companies need to develop another kind of capability in the alliance context apart from the capability to enable greater and repeatable success across their set of alliances—firms also need to learn how to manage their alliance portfolio as a whole. We term this "alliance portfolio capability," and later in this paper we describe some of its constituents. Third, we suggest that if firms have a capability to manage alliances successfully they have an opportunity to leverage this proficiency to effectively manage acquisitions, which are traditionally considered to be a different mode of inorganic growth from alliances. In doing so, we highlight some opportunities for fruitful synthesis between alliances research and acquisitions research, which otherwise have

been pursued as distinct and separate streams of research.

WHAT DETERMINES THE SUCCESS OF A SINGLE ALLIANCE?

A strategic alliance is a purposive relationship between two or more independent firms that involves the exchange, sharing, or codevelopment of resources or capabilities to achieve mutually relevant benefits (Gulati, 1995). A strategic alliance can span one or more parts of the value chain and have a variety of organizational configurations typically based on the absence or presence of equity in the relationship (for example, joint ventures represent one type of an equity-based alliance). Figure 1 provides an overview of the range of interfirm relationships that can be categorized as strategic alliances. The success of any single alliance depends on some key factors that are relevant at each stage of alliance evolution (Gulati, 1998). These include (a) the formation phase, wherein a firm deciding to initiate an alliance selects an appropriate partner, (b) the design phase, wherein a firm (and its partner) set up appropriate governance to oversee the alliance, and (c) the postformation phase, wherein a firm manages the alliance on an ongoing basis to realize value (Schreiner, Kale, & Corsten, 2009). Given the hundreds of articles that have studied these issues over two decades, it is not feasible to examine every aspect in detail. Therefore, we briefly review only those factors that prior research considers most important. Figure 2 provides an overview of the main phases of the alliance life cycle and factors in each phase that are critical to alliance success. In the process, we also extend prior work by highlighting conditions under which some of these factors have a stronger impact on alliance success, and/or the relationships between them.[2]

Alliance Formation Phase: Partner Selection and Fit

Previous research has focused extensively on partner selection during alliance formation and its

Figure 1   **Scope of Interfirm Relationships**

Source: Adapted from Yoshino and Rangan, 1995.

Figure 2   **A Single Alliance: Key Success Factors**

implications for alliance success. A review of more than 40 studies (Shah & Swaminathan, 2008) showed that the following partner traits have a positive influence on alliance performance: partner complementarity, partner commitment, and partner compatibility or fit. Partner complementarity is the extent to which a partner contributes non-overlapping resources to the relationship, such that one partner brings those value-chain resources or capabilities the other lacks and vice versa (Dyer & Singh, 1998; Harrigan, 1988; Mowery, Oxley, & Silverman, 1996). Resource-based theories suggest that the greater the complementarity between partners, the greater the likelihood of alliance success, and many studies have found support for this.

However, partner complementarity alone is insufficient for alliance formation and success. A partner firm must be compatible with the focal firm (Beamish, 1987) and committed to the relationship. Partner compatibility refers to the fit between partners' working styles and cultures, whereas commitment includes the willingness of a partner not only to make resource contributions required by the alliance but also to make short-term sacrifices to realize the desired longer-term benefits (Gundlach, Achrol, & Mentzer, 1995).

While all three partner attributes—complementarity, commitment, and compatibility—are vital to the success of an individual alliance, emerging research shows that managers need to appreciate under which conditions some of these attributes are more critical to alliance success than others. To illustrate, partner complementarity seems to have greater impact on alliance success when one partner is relatively younger than the other (Rothaermel & Boeker, 2008), or when the alliance is such that it is difficult for partners to fully specify the exact outcomes expected from that alliance. In the latter case partner complementarity is important, as it provides assurance that due to extant complementarity of resources or products outcome benefits are likely to be positive even if it is difficult to fully assess them (Shah & Swaminathan, 2008). Often, complementarity implies greater interdependence between alliance partners. In that case, complementarity positively affects alliance success only when partners establish the processes necessary to manage those interdependences (Dyer & Singh, 1998).

On the other hand, commitment seems particularly critical in alliances where partners have identified the specific benefits they expect to gain by coming together, but remain relatively unclear about the exact processes necessary to achieve them. In these alliance relationships, partner commitment is more important than usual, as partners must be willing to dedicate costly resources to the relationship and pledge to work with each other even when they realize that some adaptation might be required in the future in light of the uncertainty that exists. Overall, managers need to pay attention to such contingencies while selecting partners that are generally complementary, compatible, and committed.

Alliance Design Phase: Choice and Implementation of Alliance Governance

An alliance exposes a firm to several transaction or coordination hazards that can adversely affect the firm itself or its partner. Thus, how a firm constructs alliance governance during the design phase of the alliance life cycle is crucial to alliance success. Literature has highlighted three primary mechanisms to address governance issues in an alliance.

First, transaction costs theory has proposed that equity ownership is an effective mechanism to govern alliances (Williamson, 1985). In an alliance, a firm can expose itself to opportunistic behavior by its alliance partner if it has invested in relationship-specific assets in order to derive expected benefits, or if there is uncertainty regarding market conditions facing the relationship. In such situations, creating an equity-based alliance (wherein one partner takes an equity stake in the other, or both partners create a new, independent venture wherein both take a stake) is critical to success, as equity has three governance properties to address the hazards involved. First is the property of "mutual hostages," in which shared equity aligns the mutual interests of the partners (Hennart, 1988); by owning equity, partners are required to make ex ante commitments toward the alliance, and their concern for their investment reduces the possibility of future opportunistic behavior. Second, equity facilitates hierarchical supervision to monitor day-to-day functioning of the alliance and address contingencies as they arise (Kogut, 1988). And third, equity ownership creates a basis for each partner to receive a share of the returns from the alliance in proportion to its level of ownership. This in turn creates an incentive for partners to cooperate with one another. Numerous studies have provided evidence for the effectiveness of equity in governing alliances (David & Han, 2004).

Contractual provisions in the alliance agreement represent the second mechanism of effective governance (Mayer & Argyres, 2004; Poppo & Zenger, 2002; Reuer & Arino, 2007), but this aspect has received attention in research only recently. Contracts help manage exchange hazards in a variety of ways. A contract clearly sets forth mutual rights and obligations of partners by specifying each firm's inputs to the alliance, processes by which exchanges will occur and disputes will be resolved, and expected outputs from the relationship. Contracts also limit information disclosures by partners during the operation of the alliance, specify how each partner will interact with third parties, and outline ways in which the alliance will end. Two more aspects that increase contractual effectiveness in governing alliances are enforcement provisions that relate to IP protection and the specification of breaches that might necessitate termination or adjudication, and informational provisions that facilitate required coordination between alliance partners (Reuer & Arino, 2007).

Self-enforcing governance, relying on goodwill, trust, and reputation (Granovetter, 1985; Gulati, 1995; Uzzi, 1997), is the third mechanism of effective alliance governance. At times, it is referred to as "relational governance." Relational governance enhances the likelihood of alliance success by reducing transaction costs in several ways: (a) Contracting costs are minimized because firms trust their partners to behave fairly; (b) monitoring costs are lower because external, third-party monitoring is not required; and (c) costs of complex adaptation are lowered because partners are willing to be flexible in response to unforeseen circumstances. In addition, relational governance enables partners to work together in implementing value-creation initiatives that need sharing of tacit knowledge between partners, exchanging resources that are difficult to price, and offering responses that are not explicitly called for in the contract (Zajac & Olsen, 1993). Finally, if relational governance is based on some resource dependence between partners, it acts as an effective means to monitor and control partner behavior (Filatotchev, Stephan, & Jindra, 2008).

However, in making choices about alliance governance, it is important to understand some of the subtle relationships between the various governance mechanisms. First, as recent work (Reuer & Arino, 2007) has shown, contractual complexity does not vary across equity and nonequity alliances. This finding implies that

equity alone is insufficient to guarantee successful alliance governance and that these mechanisms might actually complement each other in driving alliance success. Second, there are different views of the relationships between formal governance (based on equity ownership or contracts) and informal governance (based on trust). One school of thought suggests that one type of mechanism substitutes or crowds out the other such that informal relational governance reduces the need for formal governance (Bradach & Eccles, 1989; Gulati, 1995), or that inclusion of formal governance mechanisms actually hinders the development of relational governance in alliances (Ghoshal & Moran, 1996). A second school of thought sees these mechanisms as being complementary in enhancing alliance success such that relational governance amplifies the positive effects of formal governance further (Poppo & Zenger, 2002) and enables partners to more easily accept formal contractual governance despite the incomplete and ambiguous nature of contractual clauses (Gulati & Nickerson, 2008). Recent work by Puranam and Vanneste (2009) takes a further step in outlining conditions affecting the nature of the relationships (negative or positive) among these different mechanisms. They show how the nature of these relationships actually varies based on whether a manager makes governance choices in alliances by selecting a particular level of governance complexity to *match* the need for safeguards based on expected hazards, or whether she tries to maximize alliance performance given the attributes of the transactions involved.

Postformation Alliance Management: The Roles of Coordination and Trust

Appropriate decisions linked to partner selection and alliance governance positively affect the likelihood of success of every alliance. However, to realize the expected benefits, firms must also proactively manage an evolving entity such as an alliance *after* it is up and running. Two factors are especially important during the postformation phase of the alliance life cycle: managing coordination between partners and developing trust between them.

Alliance partners must coordinate their actions to manage their interdependence and realize the benefits of their relationship. But severe coordination problems can result from the lack of sufficient knowledge about how one's actions are interdependent with the other's, what decision rules a partner is likely to use, how to allocate resources, or how information should be handled (Gulati, Lawrence, & Puranam, 2005; Gulati & Singh, 1998; Schreiner et al., 2009). Coordination problems refer to the difficulties of aligning actions between partners. These problems can arise even when partners' interests are fully aligned with each other. To manage coordination successfully, alliance partners can use any or all of three classic mechanisms: programming, hierarchy, and feedback (Galbraith, 1977).

Programming is the least complex of the three mechanisms. It involves developing clear guidelines on what specific tasks need to be carried out by each partner, who exactly is accountable for each task, and a timetable for implementing them. This mechanism facilitates coordination by improving the clarity and predictability of partner actions, reducing frustration, and increasing decision-making speed. Use of interfirm knowledge-sharing routines (Dyer & Singh, 1998) to share critical task-related information is another dimension of this aspect.

The use of hierarchy, the second coordination mechanism, includes the creation of a formal role or structure with authority and decision-making ability to oversee ongoing interactions between partners and to facilitate information and resource sharing. As an example, a firm can appoint a separate dedicated alliance manager to manage this, or both partners can create an alliance review committee to play this role. Finally, in cases where partners need to regularly inform each other of their respective actions or decisions, or they must periodically evaluate the evolving nature of their interdependence and adapt to it, feedback mechanisms such as joint teams and collocation are helpful in order to quickly process pertinent information and mobilize resources accordingly. Of course, the exact nature of various coordination mechanisms and the extent to which they are required depends on the nature of interdependence between partners. Alliances with reciprocal interdependence generally need the greater and more complex coordination mechanisms of the

ones listed above as compared with those with either sequential or pooled interdependence (Gulati et al., 2005; Gulati & Singh, 1998).

Many studies find that trust between partners is critical to alliance success, not only because it facilitates alliance governance, as described earlier, but also because it helps partners work more cooperatively. Trust comprises two parts: a structural component, which refers to a type of expectation that one's partner will not act opportunistically due to a mutual hostage situation (Bradach & Eccles, 1989), and a behavioral component, which refers to the degree of confidence a firm has in its partner's reliability and integrity (Madhok, 1995). The former type of trust is akin to deterrence-based trust, which arises from the use of governance mechanisms such as shared equity or contractual agreements (Gulati, 1995), and the latter to knowledge-based trust, which gradually emerges as two partners interact and develop norms of reciprocity (Zaheer, McEvily, & Perrone, 1998) and fairness. The behavioral component of trust is particularly critical to effective functioning of the alliance during the postformation phase.

However, if it is so important, *how can firms create trust in their relationships, and how exactly does it help?* Trust develops through a cyclical process of bargaining, interaction, commitment, and execution between the concerned firms (Ring & Van de Ven, 1994). Based on this idea, scholars have identified several trust-building mechanisms. A firm can build trust by demonstrating that it trusts its partner firm by making large, unilateral commitments. By voluntarily placing itself in a position of vulnerability, a firm invites the alliance partner to reciprocate in kind, and interfirm trust gradually develops between the two (Mayer, Davis, & Schoorman, 1995). A second way is to demonstrate one's own trustworthiness (instead of being just trusting) by scrupulously honoring all commitments, and making sure to commit to only those actions that are within a firm's power and ability to execute. By making commitments and living up to the expectations, a firm can earn its partner's trust (Zaheer & Harris, 2006). A third driver of interfirm trust is interpersonal trust, sometimes referred to as "relational capital" (Kale, Singh, & Perlmutter, 2000). Such interpersonal trust most often develops between the individuals from the two firms that interact with each other at the alliance interface. It is linked to the social bonds that develop between these individuals as they work regularly with each other, understand each other's working style, and are stable in their respective roles (Schreiner et al., 2009). Finally, interfirm trust also depends on institutional factors including the location or national culture of the concerned firms (Dyer & Chu, 2003), or the existence of industry-level arrangements to facilitate interactions between them (McEvily, Perrone, & Zaheer, 2003).

Developing trust during the postformation phase of an alliance is critical to its success in many ways. It facilitates greater information sharing between partners (Dyer & Chu, 2003), lowers perceptions of relational risk, and promotes the willingness of partners to adapt the alliance to evolving contingencies (Doz, 1996). Trust between partners also enables them to simultaneously achieve two objectives generally considered mutually exclusive: Trust not only enables them to share valuable know-how with their alliance partner but also protects against the opportunistic acquisition of proprietary knowledge by the partner (Kale et al., 2000). Apart from these positive outcomes, studies show that trust also leads to increased partner satisfaction with the alliance and the achievement of joint action and goal fulfillment (Schreiner et al., 2009). Consequently, the scope and longevity of the alliance increase (Jap & Anderson, 2003).

HOW TO BUILD A FIRM-LEVEL CAPABILITY FOR ALLIANCE SUCCESS?

Turning our attention to the level of the firm gives rise to another important question in light of the alliance paradox highlighted earlier: If most firms engage in multiple alliances over time, and their overall alliance success rates are generally low, how does a firm develop its capability to manage alliances to achieve greater, repeatable alliance success than others? In an environment where alliances are an important part of a firm's strategy, having a firm-level alliance capability to manage alliances would indeed be a source of competitive advantage (Gulati, 1998). Only recently has this subject received attention. We review this research and highlight three main building blocks underlying the development of alliance capability in firms: prior alliance experience, creation of a dedicated alliance function, and implementation of firm-level processes to accumulate and leverage alliance management know-how and skills. Figure 3 provides an overview of these factors and their relationship to one another.

Building Alliance Capability through Experience

Quite simply, a firm can develop its alliance capability by having greater experience in doing alliances.

Figure 3   Drivers of Firm-Level Alliance Capability

Implicit feedback from alliance experience helps build alliance management skills through tacit "learning by doing." Researchers have recently found empirical support for the role of experience in explaining a firm's alliance capability and success. Anand and Khanna (2000) conducted one of the first studies in this domain and found that firms with greater alliance experience received a more positive response from stock markets when they formed or announced a new alliance. According to them, favorable market reaction suggests that firms with greater alliance experience presumably have greater alliance capability and hence are more likely to succeed with the new alliance they have formed. Others have found that prior experience leads to greater alliance success not only in terms of creating shareholder value but also in the focal firm's ability to achieve its stated objectives in future alliances (Kale et al., 2002).

Creating an Alliance Function to Build Alliance Capability

Although experience is a useful mechanism for building a firm's alliance capability, Anand and Khanna (2000) found that this does not fully explain why some firms enjoy greater success with alliances than others do. Emerging research addresses this gap by highlighting the role of a second mechanism in building firm-level alliance capability. The adoption of higher-order organizing principles, such as creating a separate structure or entity that is responsible for coordinating and managing a firm's overall alliance activity, is critical in this regard (Kale et al., 2002). A separate organizational unit to manage alliances, commonly referred to as a "dedicated alliance function," is vital in building an organization's alliance capability. Companies such as Hewlett-Packard (Alliance Analyst, 1996), Eli Lilly (Dyer et al., 2001; Gueth, 2005), and Philips Electronics (Kale et al., 2009) have demonstrated the successful use of this mechanism.

The dedicated alliance function provides several benefits to firms (Dyer et al., 2001; Kale et al., 2002). First, it is a focal point for capturing and storing alliance management lessons and best practices from the firm's own prior and current alliance experiences as well as leveraging that knowledge throughout the organization as

time and occasion warrant. The managers in this function become repositories of alliance management know-how by virtue of their repeated involvement in the various alliances of the firm. Second, the dedicated alliance function enhances the visibility and awareness of a firm's alliances among external stakeholders (investors, customers, government), thus enlisting their buy-in and support. Third, a dedicated alliance function provides legitimacy and support for a firm's alliances and helps garner internal resources necessary for alliance success. Fourth, it acts as a mechanism to monitor the performance of the firm's alliances in order to identify potential trouble spots before they become an issue. The dedicated alliance function can then take necessary action in a timely manner to escalate or resolve those conflicts. Empirical studies (Hoang & Rothaermel, 2005; Kale et al., 2002) have shown a positive link between the existence of a dedicated alliance management function and a firm's alliance capability and overall alliance success. Firms that have a dedicated alliance function to coordinate their alliance activities enjoy a much greater alliance success rate (around 70 percent) than firms without one (around 40 percent). Moreover, these studies have found that the alliance function is relatively more important than prior experience in building a firm's alliance capability. Firms can establish this function in many different ways—they can organize it around key partners, businesses, functions, geography, or some combination of the same based on which of these dimensions is most important.

Establishing Learning Processes to Build Alliance Capability

New research provides insight into a third mechanism used to develop alliance capability in firms (Kale & Singh, 2007). Building on the knowledge-based view of the firm (Grant, 1996), which suggests that organizations improve their skills to manage a given task by accumulating and applying knowledge relevant to that task, this work emphasizes the role of certain learning processes in building alliance capability. Firms can implement four deliberate processes to learn, accumulate, and leverage alliance management knowledge either from their own alliance experience or from that of others. Usually, individual managers in a firm are the primary repository of useful alliance management experience and knowledge gained from prior or current alliance experience. As such, a firm can undertake efforts to help individual alliance managers articulate their personally held know-how of alliance management. By doing so, the firm can capture and externalize that knowledge so other managers in the firm can learn from those experiences.

A firm can go a step further and codify its accumulated alliance management know-how in the form of usable knowledge objects, such as alliance management guidelines, checklists, and manuals, that incorporate best practices to manage the different phases and decisions in the alliance life cycle. Hewlett-Packard and Eli Lilly were some of the early adopters of this practice—they developed such codified tools and templates to help managers assess the fit of potential alliance partners, draw up alliance agreements, assess alliance performance, and so on. The codification process facilitates the replication and transfer of alliance best practices within a firm, creating what is essentially a toolkit for managers. Figure 4 provides examples of various codified resources that some alliance-capable firms have developed for personal use.

It is important to note, however, that it is not possible to articulate or codify *all* know-how,

especially knowledge that is tacit or personal in nature (Winter, 1987). However, a firm can leverage such alliance know-how by having knowledge-sharing processes to exchange tacit and individually held alliance management know-how across the organization. Creating communities of personal interaction (Seely Brown & Duguid, 1991), such as cross-company alliance committees, task forces, or other forums, to exchange alliance experience and best practices among alliance managers is one of the means companies have used to achieve this goal (Draulans, deMan, & Volberda, 2003; Kale & Singh, 2007).

Finally, some companies use a fourth process to help individual managers internalize and absorb relevant alliance management know-how that exists in different parts of the firm, through formal and informal means. This internalization process stresses "learning how," wherein the recipient focuses on acquiring a recipe of how to undertake a specific alliance-related task or decision rather than just conceptually understanding why it works. In practical terms, when some firms have adopted this process they have created an "alliance apprenticeship" in which newer managers work with experienced alliance managers and soak up useful knowledge from them. Other firms send their managers to formal alliance training programs that are conducted either internally by the firm or by outsiders.

Figure 4 **Examples of Codified Tools to Manage Alliances**

CODIFIED ALLIANCE MANAGEMENT TOOLS

Alliance Planning	Alliance Formation	Alliance Design	Post-Formation Management	Alliance Evaluation
• Value Chain Analysis Form • Tool to Decide Partnering Need and Form	• Partner Screening Form • Technology and Patent Domain Maps • Cultural Fit Evaluation Form	• Negotiations Matrix • Needs vs. Wants Checklist • Alliance Contract Template • Alliance Structure Guidelines • Alliance Metrics Framework	• Problem Tracking Template • Trust Building Worksheet • Alliance Contact List • Alliance Communication Infrastructure	• Relationship Evaluation Form • Yearly Status Report • Termination Checklist • Termination Planning Worksheet

Collectively, the four learning processes we have described are directed toward building and institutionalizing a firm's alliance capability through articulating, codifying, sharing, and internalizing alliance management know-how and skills to help the firm manage its future alliances more effectively. Kale and Singh (2007) equated these learning processes to a higher-order dynamic capability (Eisenhardt & Martin, 2000; Zollo & Winter, 2002) that helps firms extend, modify, and improve their organizational capability to manage alliances. The empirical evidence shows that these processes have a strong influence on a firm's alliance capability and overall alliance success.

When Do These Mechanisms Really Matter and How Do They Relate to One Another?

Alliance experience, a dedicated alliance function, and organizational processes to learn and leverage alliance management know-how are three important mechanisms to develop and institutionalize an organizationwide capability in alliance management. However, it would be useful for managers to know the specific conditions under which some of these mechanisms are more effective in developing alliance capability, and the relationships among them. Emerging research has begun to shed light on some of these issues, but others remain unresolved.

Concerning alliance experience, it seems that prior experience is more useful in developing capabilities to manage certain kinds of alliances than others. In their work, Anand and Khanna (2000) found that prior experience with joint ventures is useful in developing skills to manage future joint ventures, but this does not hold true for contractual nonequity alliances. This may be because, as an alliance form, joint ventures show greater similarity in terms of structure, design, and governance issues across different situations (which makes it possible to transfer learning) as compared to contractual nonequity alliances. Sampson (2005) observed that prior experience helps develop alliance skills when that experience is more recent, as the benefits derived from experience depreciate over time. The usefulness of experience also varies by the degree of its specificity; experience in alliances with a particular

partner help a firm build its capability to manage future alliances successfully with that same partner, whereas general alliance experience is less useful in this regard. This research seems to suggest that, even though experience is a critical mechanism for building alliance capability, its relevance varies by its type, specificity, and timing.

The relevance of the dedicated alliance function also seems to vary across different business or firm conditions. We find that a dedicated alliance function helps develop alliance skills more effectively in larger firms than in smaller ones (Rothaermel & Boeker, 2008). This is plausible as the use of organizing principles to collect and disseminate relevant knowledge is perhaps more necessary in larger firms, where the knowledge has to be collated from and shared with diverse sources/individuals. This may not be the case in smaller firms where key individuals interact directly and frequently with each other. The use of this function also depends on the extent of functional relatedness across different alliances of a firm and the know-how required for managing them (Kale et al., 2002). But many other questions related to the creation and usefulness of the alliance function remain unanswered: If a firm were to create such a function, where exactly should it be located in the organizational setup, who should head it, who should it report to, what should be the composition of the individuals who comprise it, and how does its role evolve and change over time? Given the cost and effort involved in setting up a dedicated alliance function, future research must study these questions in detail. Similar questions arise about the alliance learning processes described earlier. While the literature has observed the efficacy of these processes, the following issues are worth examining: Will continual use of these processes turn them into "rituals" that are routinely followed, without the deliberate effort necessary to learn from them? Will implementation of these processes create a bureaucracy whose costs outweigh the resultant benefits?

The investigation of relationships among the three primary mechanisms used to develop alliance capability (alliance experience, a dedicated alliance function, and alliance learning processes) is necessary as well. Some scholars have suggested that the use of explicit mechanisms, such the dedicated alliance function or specific processes to articulate or codify alliance know-how, enhances the direct effect of implicit mechanisms such as alliance experience (Zollo & Winter, 2002) in building a firm's alliance capability. In other words, these mechanisms interact with and moderate each other in explaining a firm's alliance capability and success. However, more recent research has shown (Kale & Singh, 2007) that these mechanisms are actually mediating in nature—that is, the dedicated alliance function mediates the impact of alliance experience on a firm's alliance capability and overall alliance success. In turn, alliance-learning processes of articulation and codification further mediate the effect of the dedicated alliance function in building a firm's alliance capability.

Creating Capabilities: Time Frames and Challenges

In recent applied work we explored the actual time required to implement alliance capability development in an organization. In a multiyear collaboration with Dr. John Bell (he was the previous vice president of corporate alliances for Philips, and is a management scholar who studies alliances), we tracked the development of alliance capability within Philips, a large multinational with operations in more than 150 countries and a range of businesses in electronics (music systems, televisions, etc.), lifestyle products (shavers, coffee makers, lighting fixtures), and health care (large-scale medical imaging products, patient monitoring systems). Observing that Philips had myriad interfirm relationships without organized coordination, Bell conceived of and implemented an alliance capability development process that started in 2001. He set up the Corporate Alliance Office at Philips and over the next seven years his team, armed with a strong mandate from the CEO and board, implemented a set of decisions and management processes to improve Philips's alliance capability. Bell implemented many of the practices and processes discussed in the previous section of this paper. Several key observations worth discussion emerged from that experience.

First, the process of building alliance capability in a large corporation is a slow and multiyear process. It took Bell more than seven years to gradually and informally introduce some of the alliance management processes we have described. It was only in the latter portion of the

seven years that he created a well-defined process and codified the firm's accumulated alliance know-how into usable tools and templates. Second, as in most organizations, creating capabilities that rest on knowledge-based processes requires consistent sponsorship and support from senior management. This is a factor worth noting particularly because it is one that often remains unmeasured in large sample studies, as the nature of top management commitment does not lend itself to easy empirical representation. Third, the impact of the alliance function is easier to observe with rich, multifaceted data in a single firm than in a more reduced form or larger sample study. By studying a single organization like Philips over an extended period, we were able to observe how the organization was able to derive increased revenues or greater new product introductions through its alliances. We were also able to see how line managers increasingly embraced alliance relationships as a vehicle to pursue growth opportunities after they became more proficient in managing alliances. As such, it was possible to identify the effectiveness of the dedicated alliance function. Through it all, it became clear that alliance capability building is time-consuming and draws on intangible assets such as knowledge and decision/management processes. On the positive side, and in justification of the time, effort, and resources required, building alliance capability provides enduring benefits to a firm.

EMERGING ISSUES IN ALLIANCES: WHERE DO WE GO FROM HERE?

Extant literature provides valuable insights into successful alliance management. But scholars also need to address new issues that emerge on the alliance frontier. In the next section, we outline some of these issues and offer preliminary suggestions on how to think about them.

From Firm-to-Firm Alliances to a New Class of Alliances

Extant alliance literature has focused mainly on alliances between two or more commercial or for-profit firms. Today, many firms are engaging in two new types of alliances: those with not-for-profit entities and/or nongovernmental organizations, and formal collaborations with individuals. Partnerships with the former type of entity are becoming important in several situations. In today's evolving business environment, society views firms as entities that are responsible for serving not only the interests of their shareholders but also the interests of other stakeholders within the community. Often, commercial firms are unable to meet this obligation on their own, and hence they collaborate with not-for-profit entities or NGOs that might be better positioned to understand the needs of these other stakeholders. Further, to accelerate their growth many firms are expanding in emerging economies by serving poor consumers at the so-called bottom of the pyramid. These efforts require unconventional means and business models to address this new class of customer (Prahalad, 2006), and NGOs and grassroots organizations that interact directly with these customers might understand them better than commercial firms do. Thus, commercial firms often partner with such organizations to address this large untapped market. Finally, in their quest to tap new and innovative ideas from outside their own organizations, firms are collaborating not only with other organizations (of any kind) but also directly with single persons or individuals. Initiatives including P&G's Connect $\leqq$ Develop (Houston & Sakkab, 2006) and "open innovation" (Chesbrough, 2005) are prominent examples of this kind.[3]

Both types of collaboration, those with nonprofits or NGOs and those with individuals, represent a new class of alliances quite different from the traditional interfirm alliances studied in academic literature. We consider them alliances because in both cases, the entities involved in the relationship bring distinct but valuable resources to meet mutually beneficial objectives, and they are often required to make investments that are specific to the concerned relationship. Nevertheless, these alliances are different, not only because the objective function of a firm's alliance partner is different (as compared to a traditional for-profit organization) but also because the concerned partner has a different set of skills and organizational culture. Thus, the challenges of managing such alliances and the factors and best practices that lead to success may also be different from

what we know from our study of traditional interfirm alliances. Current academic research has very little to say about how to successfully manage this emerging class of alliances. Hence, future research must investigate this issue in greater depth.

From Individual Alliances to Alliance Portfolios

It is beneficial to know the best practices of managing a single alliance between two or more firms. However, firms could also benefit significantly by assuming a portfolio approach to alliances in the future. As discussed earlier, most firms today engage in more than one alliance. For example, a pharmaceutical firm might have one alliance with partner A to source a new technology, a second alliance with partner B to facilitate its entry into a new geographical market, a third alliance with partner C to jointly manufacture a core compound, and so on. Even when it comes to sourcing a new technology, a firm may have alliances with more than one partner to achieve the same objective. Each individual alliance is important, and a firm certainly needs to have a sound strategic logic for its alliance and adopt appropriate best practices in each stage of its life cycle. Nevertheless, a firm can gain additional advantages by considering its entire set of individual alliances as one portfolio, and managing it as such.

In shifting the level of analysis to the entire alliance portfolio and away from each individual alliance within that portfolio, though, new issues arise. A firm needs to know how to configure its alliance portfolio (Hoffmann, 2007) along several dimensions. It must first assess the extent to which its portfolio is complete such that collectively all its alliances meet its strategic needs. Second, in building the alliance portfolio, firms must guard against competition that might arise between individual alliances in that portfolio. If a firm undertakes more than one alliance for the same purpose, greater overlap in the benefits offered by each individual alliance may increase to the extent that one alliance rivals another alliance in the portfolio. This in turn can lead to significant adversities that might ultimately outweigh the benefits. Third, some alliances in a firm's portfolio may actually complement, rather than compete with, each other such that the benefits they offer are extra-additive in nature. For example, a pharmaceutical firm may have one alliance with a firm to in-source a new molecule for a drug that targets a particular disease, and at the same time have a second alliance with another firm to get a specific technology to test the efficacy of that molecule in a speedy and cost-effective way. In this scenario, the benefits derived from the first alliance are accentuated because of the second alliance in the firm's portfolio, and vice versa. The greater the existence of such complementarity between individual alliances in a firm's portfolio, the greater will be the firm's opportunity to generate extra-additive benefits from those alliances.

For the reasons outlined above, conceptually it is useful to take a portfolio approach to alliances. Thus far, however, very few academics (Hoffmann, 2007; Lavie, 2006) have paid attention to it. In practice too, the portfolio approach to alliance strategy and management is still in its infancy. In a survey of 76 companies, we found that only 30 percent of them consider or manage their alliances as a portfolio in building their alliance strategy; even among those firms that do, most look only at the degree of competition that exists between different alliances in the portfolio. Only a small proportion of firms consider completeness of the alliance portfolio, and an even smaller number assess the extent of complementarity across individual alliances in the portfolio. This implies that most firms still focus mainly on each individual alliance, and they do not fully exploit synergy benefits that might exist across their individual alliances by considering them as part of one portfolio.

The capabilities necessary to manage alliances as a portfolio are different from the alliance capability discussed earlier. So far, in conceptualizing alliance capability scholarly literature has focused primarily on the constituent skills required to successfully manage a single alliance through the different stages of its life cycle (e.g., partner selection skills, alliance governance skills, skills to create trust between partners in a given alliance), and recent literature has now also shown how a firm can develop an organizationwide alliance capability for repeatable and greater alliance success. Nevertheless, looking ahead we think it is important to distinguish between a firm's alliance capability, which refers to the firm's ability to manage each single alliance successfully, and a firm's alliance *portfolio* capability, which refers to its ability

to manage its set of alliances as a portfolio. In our view, alliance portfolio capability comprises multiple dimensions, including the skills to configure an alliance portfolio (to create a set of complete, noncompetitive, and complementary alliances), to foster and maintain trust across different alliance partners in the portfolio, to resolve conflicts between alliances in the portfolio, to coordinate strategies and operations across alliances in the portfolio, to create routines to share operational know-how across individual alliances in the portfolio, to monitor the extra-additive benefits (and costs) that arise due to interaction between different individual alliances in the portfolio, and so on. So far, little academic research has been done on this subject (Sarkar et al., forthcoming), and more work in this direction would be beneficial.

A Relational Organization: From Managing Alliances to Managing Acquisitions

In a strategic alliance two or more firms come together to access or exchange resources and capabilities to enhance their competitive advantage or growth while retaining their respective independence and identity (Gulati, 1995). However, instead of doing an alliance, a firm can also use a very different mode to access resources of another firm: It can acquire that firm. In an acquisition, the focal company (i.e., the acquirer firm) purchases control rights over the assets and operations of another firm (i.e., the acquired firm), and in the process the two companies usually become one organization to realize the desired benefits of coming together. Quite rightly, most scholars generally consider alliances to be a very different organizational mode than acquisitions, given differences in terms of the control, ownership, and independence of the firms involved in each case. Consequently, two separate research streams have evolved to study issues associated with these two very distinct organizational modes. But looking ahead we believe there is an opportunity to share insights from the world of alliances, in terms of both research and practice, with respect to managing certain kinds of acquisitions. Here's why. The success of an acquisition relies on how an acquirer manages the acquired firm after completing the transaction (Haspeslagh & Jemison, 1991).

During the postacquisition management phase, the acquirer has to make decisions on two critical aspects: the extent to which it integrates the acquired firm with itself, and the extent to which it replaces managerial resources of the acquired firm (Zollo & Singh, 2004). Research shows that in most cases, an acquirer fully integrates the acquired organization within itself, combining the boundaries of the two firms. Consequently, the acquired company loses its separate identity and independence in the market; this approach to integration is referred to as absorption or structural integration. The acquirer typically also replaces most of the acquired firms' senior executives with its own, and even in cases where it chooses to retain them it limits their decision-making freedom.

However, recent studies show that some acquirers take a very different approach to managing their acquisitions in certain settings: when large companies acquire small entrepreneurial firms for their technological or knowledge-based skills (Puranam & Srikanth, 2007), or when firms from emerging economies acquire larger firms in developed economies to enhance their global presence or competitiveness (Kale & Singh, 2008). In both of these cases, most acquirers leave the acquired firm structurally separate so that the latter maintains its identity in the market. The acquirer also retains most senior employees in the acquired firm and gives them operating freedom in running the acquired company. There are several reasons for taking this approach to acquisitions. By not integrating the acquired company into itself, an acquirer minimizes the complexities that arise during the postacquisition period and avoids the disruption of resources and routines that results when two companies attempt to combine their operations. Maintaining a separate organization is also beneficial if the acquired firm has a unique identity in the minds of its key stakeholders (customers, regulators, shareholders) and maintenance of that identity generates business value for the firm. Retaining senior executives of the acquired firm and giving them independence and autonomy creates a positive climate within the acquired firm and sends a positive, symbolic signal to its stakeholders. It also allows the acquirer firm to retain the industry- or context-specific expertise of the acquired firm's management/ employees and leverage their human and social capital for mutual gains. This is relevant when an acquirer buys a target for its intellectual capital and expertise. At the same time, the two companies still need to coordinate some of their activities and operations to realize potential synergies that exist between them.

The aforementioned description suggests that, although the concerned transactions are an acquisition from an ownership standpoint, the manner in which an acquirer manages them makes them more like an alliance between two firms. The Renault-Nissan relationship, Cisco's acquisitions of some small technology companies, and the Tata Group's acquisition of Corus Steel in the United Kingdom are examples of such transactions. This is because, unlike in a traditional acquisition, in this approach both the acquirer and acquired firms remain independent and relatively autonomous—and yet, how do they then interact with each other to achieve some of the desired benefits of coming together? To manage such acquisitions the acquirer needs to recognize the issues and best practices discussed earlier as important in the postformation phase of an alliance. First, the acquirer needs to choose appropriate coordination mechanisms to leverage the interdependence between the two separate firms. Second, it needs to build trust between the two firms such that employees in each firm work in the interests of both firms and are willing to share relevant know-how with each other for mutual benefit. Third, it needs to establish appropriate mechanisms to resolve or escalate any conflicts that might arise.

We term this approach a "partnering approach to acquisitions." What it implies is that if a firm is skilled in managing alliances and has a collaborative capability or mindset, that firm could be equally effective in managing acquisitions that call for such an approach to handling postacquisition integration. Therefore, firms can extend their alliance capability into a broader relational capability that can sometimes be leveraged to manage certain other interfirm relationships, such as acquisitions, too. Thus far, very few academics or practitioners have recognized this opportunity, let alone studied or addressed it, but we hope that will change in the future. From a practical standpoint, taking this approach may call for some changes in how firms are organized internally. As we mentioned before, in our fieldwork we have studied many companies that have created a dedicated alliance team or function to oversee their overall alliance activity. Some of the firms we have observed have an additional team to oversee and coordinate their acquisition activity. In the majority of cases, these two teams are structurally separate and operate in their own silos. However, if alliance management capabilities are useful in managing some kinds of acquisitions, there exists a need for learning or capability transfer between these teams, and it would be helpful if they worked in close concert with one another and had relevant mechanisms to enable that. Cisco is one of the few companies that seem to have taken this step.

CONCLUSION

Alliances are widespread in today's business landscape. In the face of growing competition, the high rate of technological change, and discontinuities within most industries, firms pursue a large number of alliances to access new resources, enter new markets or arenas, or minimize their risk. Yet there is a paradox: They frequently fail to reap the anticipated benefits of most of their alliances. In this paper we have discussed how firms can address this paradox to improve their likelihood of alliance success by focusing on two different levels of analysis: (a) the level of an individual alliance a firm engages in, and (b) the level of the firm as a whole that is engaged in more than one alliance over time. At the level of a single alliance of a firm, we highlighted how certain factors at each stage of the alliance life cycle are critical to alliance success. If a firm selects a complementary, compatible, and committed partner at the time of alliance formation, and makes relevant choices with respect to alliance design in terms of equity or contractual or relational governance, the alliance is more likely to succeed. During the postformation stage,

alliance success depends on the effective use of relevant coordination mechanisms to manage the interdependence between the two firms and the successful development of trust between partners as the alliance evolves. We also highlight specific conditions when the above-mentioned aspects are more pivotal to alliance success.

In settings where alliances are a central element of strategy and firms engage in more than one alliance over time, they stand to benefit by building their alliance capability. The idea, supported by empirical evidence, is that firms improve their overall alliance success if they take systematic action to develop processes and talent in support of alliance management. Alliance capability requires attention to both a dedicated alliance function within a firm and a set of institutionalized processes to accumulate and leverage alliance management know-how across the firm. These soft factors underlying a firm's overall alliance success perform better when championed by a firm's leaders; frequent restructuring and inconsistent support are recipes for the loss of accumulated learning. Yet the path to development of alliance capabilities remains both uncertain and time-consuming. As we saw in the example of a large corporation, despite strong championing by the CEO and a sustained effort to incorporate alliance management processes within the firm, building effective alliance capability can take between 5 and 10 years. This may well be a window into the development of capabilities in general.

Looking into the future, managers face new challenges and issues with respect to alliances. Firms need to learn how to manage certain new types of alliances, generate incremental value by taking a portfolio approach to managing their alliances, and realize gains by extending their alliance capabilities to become relational organizations that are adept at successfully managing other interfirm relationships too, including acquisitions.

ENDNOTES

[1] A vast literature examines a firm's network of interorganizational relationships, including alliances. We acknowledge the importance of the network perspective in providing useful insights regarding alliances. However, given its broad scope a detailed incorporation of the network perspective is beyond the scope of this paper.

[2] Joint ventures are also a form of alliance. Hence, many of the alliance success factors we discuss are relevant to success in joint ventures as well. However, because joint

ventures also entail the creation of a separate entity by the partners concerned, which is not the case in other types of alliances, they have certain unique issues and challenges worth addressing. For a more complete review of the issues that are unique to joint venture management, please refer to a recent article by Beamish and Lupton (2009).

[3] Most companies have traditionally relied on internal innovation, where new products and services are developed by the companies' in-house R&D teams. But in these two approaches to innovation, which are a radical alternative to the internal innovation model, companies connect with external sources for new ideas: university and government labs, Web-based talent markets, suppliers, and even individual inventors. Companies then develop these new ideas, sourced from external partners, into new and refined profitable products—swiftly and cheaply—by using their firm's own R&D and other resources.

REFERENCES

Ahuja, G. (2000). Collaboration networks, structural holes and innovation: A longitudinal study. *Administrative Science Quarterly, 45*(3), 425–456.

Alliance Analyst. (1996). *Managing alliances: Skills for the modern era.* Philadelphia: PA.

Anand, B., & Khanna, T. (2000). Do firms learn to create value? The case of alliances. *Strategic Management Journal, 21*(3), 295–315.

Bamford, J., Gomes-Casseres, B., & Robinson, M. (2004). *Envisioning collaboration: Mastering alliance strategies.* San Francisco: Jossey-Bass.

Beamish, P. (1987). Joint ventures in LDCs: Partner selection and performance. *Management International Review, 27*(1), 23–27.

Beamish, P., & Lupton, N. (2009). Managing joint ventures. *Academy of Management Perspectives, 23*(2), 75–94.

Bradach, J., & Eccles, R. (1989). Price, authority and trust: From ideal types to plural forms. *Annual Review of Sociology, 15*(1), 97–112.

Chesbrough, H. (2005). *Open innovation: The new imperative for creating and profiting from technology.* Cambridge, MA: Harvard Business School Press.

David, R. J., & Han, S. K. (2004). A systematic assessment of the empirical support for transaction cost economics. *Strategic Management Journal, 25*(1), 39–58.

Doz, Y. (1996). The evolution of cooperation in strategic alliances: Initial conditions or learning processes? *Strategic Management Journal, 17*(7), 55–83.

Draulans, J., deMan, A., & Volberda, H. (2003). Building alliance capability: Management techniques for superior alliance performance. *Long Range Planning, 36*(2), 151–166.

Dyer, J., & Chu, W. (2003). The role of trustworthiness in reducing transaction costs and improving performance. *Organization Science, 14,* 57–68.

Dyer, J., Kale, P., & Singh, H. (2001). How to make strategic alliances work. *Sloan Management Review, 42*(4), 37–43.

Dyer, J., & Singh, H. (1998). The relational view: Cooperative strategy and sources of interorganizational competitive advantage. *Academy of Management Review, 23*(4), 660–679.

Eisenhardt, K., & Martin, J. (2000). Dynamic capabilities: What are they? *Strategic Management Journal, 21*(10–11), 1105–1121.

Ernst, D. (2004). Envisioning collaboration. In J. Bamford, B. Gomes-Casseres, & M. Robinson (Eds.), *Mastering alliance strategies.* San Francisco: Jossey-Bass.

Filatotchev, I., Stephan, J., & Jindra, B. (2008). Ownership structure, strategic controls and export intensity of foreign invested firms in emerging economies. *Journal of International Business Studies, 39*(7), 1133–1148.

Galbraith, J. (1977). *Organization design.* Reading, MA: Addison-Wesley.

Garcia-Canal, E., Duarte, C., Criado, J., & Llaneza, A. (2002). Accelerating international expansion through global alliances. *Journal of World Business, 37*(2), 91–107.

Ghoshal, S., & Moran, P. (1996). Bad for practice: A critique of the transaction cost theory. *Academy of Management Review, 21*(1), 13–34.

Granovetter, M. (1985). Economic actions and social structure: A theory of embeddedness. *American Journal of Sociology, 91*(3), 481–510.

Grant, R. (1996). Toward a knowledge-based theory of the firm. *Strategic Management Journal, 17,* Winter Special Issue, 109–122.

Gueth, A. (2005). Entering into an alliance with big pharma: Benchmarks for drug delivery contract service providers. *Pharmaceutical Technology, 25*(10), 132–135.

Gulati, R. (1995). Does familiarity breed trust? The implications of repeated ties for contractual choice in alliances. *Academy of Management Journal, 38*(1), 85–112.

Gulati, R. (1998). Alliances and networks. *Strategic Management Journal, 19*(4), 293–317.

Gulati, R., Lawrence, P., & Puranam, P. (2005). Adaptation in vertical relationships: Beyond incentive conflict. *Strategic Management Journal, 26*(5), 415–440.

Gulati, R., & Nickerson, J. (2008). Interorganizational trust, governance form and exchange performance. *Organization Science, 19*(5), 688–710.

Gulati, R., & Singh, H. (1998). The architecture of cooperation: Managing coordination costs and appropriation concerns in strategic alliances. *Administrative Science Quarterly, 43*(4), 781–814.

Gundlach, G., Achrol, R., & Mentzer, J. (1995). The structure of commitment in exchange. *Journal of Marketing, 59*(1), 78–92.

Harrigan, K. (1988). Joint ventures and competitive strategy. *Strategic Management Journal, 9*(2), 141–158.

Haspeslagh, P., & Jemison, D. (1991). *Managing acquisitions.* New York: Free Press.

Hennart, J. (1988). A transaction cost theory of equity joint ventures. *Strategic Management Journal, 9*(1), 36–74.

Hoang, H., & Rothaermel, F. (2005). The effects of general and partner-specific experience on joint R&D project performance. *Academy of Management Journal, 48*(2), 332–345.

Hoffmann, W. (2007). Strategies for managing a portfolio of alliances. *Strategic Management Journal, 28*(8), 827–856.

Houston, L., & Sakkab, N. (2006). Connect and develop: Inside Procter and Gamble's new model for innovation. *Harvard Business Review,* March, 1–8.

Jap, S., and Anderson, E. (2003). Safeguarding interorganizational performance and continuity under ex post opportunism. *Management Science, 49,* 1684–1701.

Kale, P., Dyer, J., & Singh, H. (2002). Alliance capability, stock market response and long-term alliance success: The role of the alliance function. *Strategic Management Journal, 23*(8), 747–767.

Kale, P., & Singh, H. (2007). Building firm capabilities through learning: The role of the alliance learning process in alliance capability and success. *Strategic Management Journal, 28*(10), 981–1000.

Kale, P., & Singh, H. (2008). Emerging multinationals: A partnering approach to acquisitions. *Strategic Management Society India Conference.* Hyderabad: India.

Kale, P., Singh, H., & Bell, J. (2009). Relating well: Building capabilities for sustaining alliance networks. In P. Kleindorfer & Y. Wind (Eds.), *The network challenge: Strategies for managing the new interlinked enterprise.* London: Pearson Press.

Kale, P., Singh, H., & Perlmutter, H. (2000). Learning and protection of proprietary assets in strategic alliances: Building relational capital. *Strategic Management Journal, 21*(3), 217–237.

Kogut, B. (1988). A study of the life cycle of joint ventures. *Management International Review, 28,* 39–52.

Kogut, B. (1991). Joint ventures and the option to expand and acquire. *Management Science, 37*(1), 19–34.

Lavie, D. (2006). The competitive advantage of interconnected firms: An extension of the resource-based view. *Academy of Management Review, 31*(3), 638–658.

Lunnan, R., & Haugland, S. (2008). Predicting and measuring alliance performance: A multidimensional analysis. *Strategic Management Journal, 29*(5), 545–556.

Madhok, A. (1995). Revisiting multinational firms' tolerance for joint ventures: A trust-based approach. *Journal of International Business Studies, 26*(1), 117–137.

Mayer, K., & Argyres, C. (2004). Learning to contract: Evidence from the personal computer industry. *Organization Science, 15*(4), 394–410.

Mayer, R., Davis, J., & Schoorman, F. (1995). An integration model of organizational trust. *Academy of Management Review, 20,* 709–734.

McEvily, B., Perrone, V., & Zaheer, A. (2003). Trust as an organizing principle. *Organization Science, 14*(1), 91–104.

Mowery, D., Oxley, J., & Silverman, B. (1996). Strategic alliances and interfirm knowledge transfer. *Strategic Management Journal, 17*(Winter Special Issue), 77–91.

Poppo, L., & Zenger, T. (2002). Do formal contracts and relational governance function as substitutes or complements? *Strategic Management Journal, 23*(8), 707–725.

Prahalad, C. K. (2006). *The fortune at the bottom of the pyramid.* Upper Saddle River, NJ: Wharton School Publishing.

Puranam, P., & Srikanth, K. (2007). What they do vs. what they know: How acquirers leverage technology acquisitions. *Strategic Management Journal, 28*(8), 805–825.

Puranam, P., & Vanneste, B. (2009). Trust and governance: Untangling a tangled web. *Academy of Management Review, 34*(1), 11–28.

Reuer, J., & Arino, A. (2007). Strategic alliance contracts: Dimensions and determinants of contractual complexity. *Strategic Management Journal, 28*(3), 313–330.

Ring, P., & Van de Ven, A. (1994). Developmental processes of cooperative interorganizational relationships. *Academy of Management Review, 19*(1), 90–118.

Rothaermel, F., & Boeker, W. (2008). Old technology meets new technology: Complementarities, similarities and alliance formation. *Strategic Management Journal, 29*(1), 47–77.

Sampson, R. (2005). Experience effects and collaborative returns in R&D alliances. *Strategic Management Journal, 26*(8), 1009–1031.

Sarkar, M., Aulakh, P., & Madhok, A. (2009). Process capabilities and value generation in alliance portfolios. *Organization Science, 20*(3), 583–600.

Schreiner, M., Kale, P., & Corsten, D. (2009). What really is alliance management capability and how does it impact alliance outcomes and success? *Strategic Management Journal, 30*(13), 1395–1419.

Seely Brown, J., & Duguid, P. (1991). Organizational learning and communities-of-practice: Toward a unified view of working, learning, and innovation. *Organization Science, 2*(1), 40–56.

Shah, R., & Swaminathan, V. (2008). Factors influencing partner selection in strategic alliances: The moderating role of alliance context. *Strategic Management Journal, 29*(5), 471–494.

Uzzi, B. (1997). Social structure and competition in interfirm networks: The paradox of embeddedness. *Administrative Science Quarterly, 42*(1), 35–67.

Williamson, O. (1985). *The economic institutions of capitalism: Firms, markets, relational contracting.* New York: Free Press.

Winter, S. G. (1987). Knowledge and competence as strategic assets. In D. J. Teece (Ed.), *The competitive challenge: Strategies for industrial innovation and renewal.* New York: Harper Collins.

Yoshino, M., & Rangan., S. (1995). *Strategic alliances: An entrepreneurial approach to globalization.* Boston: Harvard Business School Press.

Zaheer, A., & Harris, S. (2006). Inter-organizational trust. In O. Shenkar & J. J. Reuer (Eds.), *Handbook of strategic alliances.* Thousand Oaks, CA: Sage Publications.

Zaheer, A., McEvily, B., & Perrone, V. (1998). Does trust matter? Exploring the effects of interorganizational and interpersonal trust on performance. *Organization Science, 8*(1), 141–159.

Zajac, E., & Olsen, C. (1993). From transaction cost to transactional value analysis: Implications for the study of inter-organizational strategies. *Journal of Management Studies, 30*(1), 131–147.

Zollo, M., & Singh, H. (2004). Deliberate learning in corporate acquisitions: Post-acquisition strategies and integration capabilities in US bank mergers. *Strategic Management Journal, 25*(13), 1233–1256.

Zollo, M., & Winter, S. (2002). Deliberate learning and the evolution of dynamic capabilities. *Organization Science, 13*(3), 339–351.

How to Win in Emerging Markets

Satish Shankar
Bain & Co.

Charles Ormiston
Bain & Co.

Nicolas Bloch
Bain & Co.

Robert Schaus
Bain & Co.

Vijay Vishwanath
Bain & Co.

Village roads can be impassable, home cooking is still a way of life, product prices can be below the cost of production in developed markets, and local products often have generations of loyal customers. Nevertheless, emerging markets in Asia, Latin America, and Eastern Europe are delivering some of the strongest revenue and profit growth for global makers of fast-moving consumer goods—everything from snacks to toothpaste—despite concerns that lower prices translate into lower profits.

Emerging-market leaders like Coca-Cola, Unilever, Colgate-Palmolive, Groupe Danone, and PepsiCo earn 5 percent to 15 percent of their total revenues from the three largest emerging markets in Asia: China, India, and Indonesia. The story is similar in Russia and Eastern Europe, where these companies often dominate their target categories and routinely exceed internal corporate benchmarks for profitability. And the trend is likely to continue: The gross domestic product of emerging markets equaled the gross domestic product of advanced nations for the first time in 2006, with much of the growth coming from the "BRICET" nations—Brazil, Russia, India, China, Eastern Europe, and Turkey.

Until the past few years, emerging markets were a relatively low priority for the leading consumer products companies with a few exceptions, even though these markets are home to about 85 percent of the world's population. The obstacles are still real—in emerging markets, multinationals compete on unfamiliar terrain dominated by local players, sell at price points below those in their home countries, and wrestle with deep-seated social and cultural customs. But with growth slowing in the mature markets of North America, Japan, and Western Europe, some consumer goods companies have figured out how to tap into the purchasing power of a new and growing middle class—which has rising income, credit cards, and access to personal loans—in these emerging markets. The fast-moving consumer goods market leaders have proved that, when armed with the right strategies, they can beat domestic competitors. But what separates the winners from the losers?

Flexible thinking, to begin with. Successful companies are willing to break away from business as usual. They reconfigure global products to compete with consumers' preferences for popular local brands, both in price and taste. Or, as with Rossiya—the leading chocolate brand in Nestlé S.A.'s Russian portfolio—companies skillfully steer acquired brands with 50 years of tradition under their own umbrella. They adapt Western

Figure 1   Keys to Emerging-Market Success

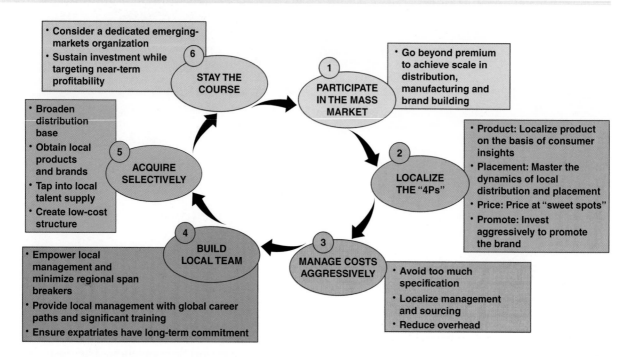

marketing and business management practices to local customs. And they develop the resourcefulness to overcome inevitable barriers. For example, where the transportation infrastructure is poor, they might develop workarounds to distribute their products, as Unilever Group did with its fleet of motorcycles to reach customers in remote villages in Indonesia.

For those that surmount the obstacles, the rewards can be great. In some consumer product categories, growth in emerging markets is three times that of developed markets. While each market requires different adaptations, the emerging-market winners share six common practices. (See Figure 1, "Keys to Emerging-Market Success.")

THEY ENTER THE MASS MARKET TO ACHIEVE SCALE IN DISTRIBUTION, BRAND BUILDING, AND OPERATIONS

Historically, multinationals in developing nations targeted niche premium segments—those that

traditionally delivered the highest profit margins. Typically, these companies could not bring their costs low enough to sell to less affluent consumers, many of whom still lived in the countryside. The multinationals often were stuck with low growth, while local players were expanding rapidly in the low-end segments. And local players—making the most of their low costs, better distribution, and increasing sophistication—also began launching brands in the premium segment as the middle class started to grow.

A good example is the cigarette business in Indonesia, where foreign players were limited to less than 10 percent of the market with brands like Marlboro, Dunhill, and Lucky Strike. In 2003, one local player, PT Hanjaya Mandala Sampoerna Tbk., launched A Mild, a kretek (clove-and-tobacco) cigarette for the premium segment. The success of that brand propelled local players like PT Djarum to attack the premium and near-premium segments with brands like L.A. Lights.

As local companies moved into the premium and near-premium market segments, multinationals realized that the mass-market opportunity was too big and important to ignore—they needed to enter the mass market for both the opportunity and to play defense. What's more, participating in the mass segment allows multinationals to drive down the costs of their premium products by achieving economies of scale in raw materials purchasing, manufacturing, sales, distribution, and brand building.

In 2005, for example, Philip Morris International Inc. purchased family-owned Sampoerna in a $5.2 billion transaction. It was the largest deal by a foreign investor in Indonesia. In addition to the many benefits that come with achieving scale, the acquisition will help Philip Morris and Sampoerna make the most of distribution synergies that can help them expand both companies' brands in Indonesia and in markets like Malaysia, Singapore, Brunei, and Brazil. Said Sampoerna president director Martin King, "In Indonesia, Sampoerna has an unparalleled distribution network, whereas Philip Morris has a very good distribution system and sales force in many other countries around the world." Among the first offspring from the corporate marriage: In July 2007, Philip Morris introduced Marlboro Kretek Filter, a new cigarette aimed at extending the Marlboro brand in Indonesia's market for clove-and-tobacco cigarettes.

The Philip Morris–Sampoerna acquisition has been an enormous success—the combined company's volume jumped 9.1 percent in the first year, and market share rose 1.5 percent, to more than 28 percent, enabling it to overtake Jakarta-based PT Gudang Garam Tbk. as market leader.

THEY LOCALIZE AT EVERY LEVEL

Homegrown competitors have several incumbent advantages, including consumer understanding and loyalty, lower costs and home court advantages with government regulators. But by taking the time to learn and master local market complexities, multinationals can gain a competitive edge. That often requires fundamental changes to the product offering—switching to significantly smaller pack sizes, using unconventional distribution channels, and developing products in local flavors, to name a few.

For its part, Procter & Gamble Co. knew that winning over Chinese toothpaste consumers meant catering to local preferences and health beliefs. After extensive research, P&G rolled out a reformulated version of Crest. Chinese consumers can find the Crest brand in fruit and tea flavors, with herbal elements, and there's even a salt version, catering to the Chinese belief that salt promotes whiter teeth. P&G's approach to localization helped boost its toothpaste sales in China from nearly zero in 1997 to 25 percent of the market in 2007.

The Coca-Cola Co. accelerated its growth in the Russian soft drinks market by acquiring the second-largest Russian fruit juice maker, Multon, through its Greek subsidiary, Coca-Cola Hellenic Bottling Co. S.A., in 2005. It thus positioned itself to ride the local preference for fruit juice drinks. Russia is the largest producer and consumer of fruit juice in Eastern Europe, where fruit juice sales shot up 64 percent between 1998 and 2003. Coca-Cola credited the acquisition, along with a marketing push, with helping deliver an above-average sales increase of 7 percent in 2005 across North Asia, Eurasia, and the Middle East.

Unilever has used innovative distribution solutions to tap the consumer market in rural India. It trained more than 25,000 Indian village women to serve as distributors, extending its reach to 80,000 villages. The program generates about $250 million yearly from villages that otherwise would be too costly to serve.

Localizing also means taking an aggressive approach to brand building. That was the foundation for Coca-Cola's dramatic success in China, where it leads all carbonated soft-drink sales, with a 51 percent market share led by its Coke and Sprite brands against PepsiCo's 30 percent share. Coca-Cola's sales maintained a 16 to 17 percent annual growth rate in the latest five years, and it even hit 18 percent in the second quarter of 2007. By spending twice as much as PepsiCo on advertising and promotion—including sponsoring sports events in China, Chinese Olympic teams and Beijing's 2008 Olympic bid—Coca-Cola eclipsed domestic and multinational competitors alike to attain the number one position. Now, China is Coca-Cola's fourth-largest market, approximately 5 percent of its worldwide sales.

At the crux of all localization strategies is pricing. Global marketers cannot beat out local brands unless they find the local pricing sweet spot—a price that is competitive in the local marketplace and that also delivers a profit. (See Figure 2, "Can Mass Yield Profits?") Finding that

Figure 2   Can Mass Yield Profits?

Price points in India are low, but players still make reasonable profits.

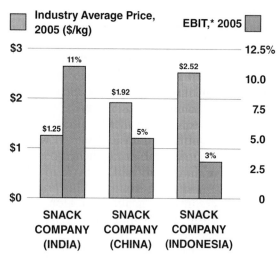

*Earnings before interest and taxes.

Sources: AC Nielsen Corp. data: Bain & Co. Inc. analysis.

Figure 3   Subsidiaries Growing

Equity markets are rewarding the Indian subsidiaries of multinationals with high market caps.

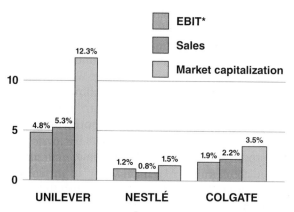

*Earnings before interest and taxes.

Sources: Annual reports: Bloomberg; Reuters; market cap numbers for India from last fiscal year end to match EBIT and sales data.

affordable price point usually requires reconfiguring existing products or creating new ones specific to a market. For example, Singapore-based Petra Foods Ltd., the world's fourth-largest chocolate maker, prices its popular chocolate treat for Indonesian consumers at two pricing sweet spots— 500 and 1,000 rupiahs (approximately 5 and 10 U.S. cents). Those prices coincide with the pocket money typically given to children for treats.

THEY DEVELOP A "GOOD-ENOUGH" COST MENTALITY

Between the traditional premium and low-end market segments is the large and flourishing market for what we call "good-enough" products, with higher quality than low-end goods but affordable prices that still generate profits. Feeding the good-enough market requires aggressive management of costs. Among the techniques: taking advantage of used capital equipment or more labor-intensive production processes, using

local suppliers, and outsourcing. For example, a major multinational food company discovered that it could source capital equipment from India at a third of the price it paid to European suppliers without compromising its stringent quality standards. Cost discipline also means reducing overhead and localizing management.

Winners look at everything they can control to shift the competitive dynamics in their favor— from changing the specifications for packaging material to imposing greater operating efficiency to lowering overhead and using local equipment.

For multinationals catering to the premium end of the market, a strategic acquisition can help slash costs enough to make them competitive. (See Figure 3, "Subsidiaries Growing.") For example, in 2000, Colgate-Palmolive Co. invested $21 million for a 40 percent stake in Sanxiao, a low-cost toothpaste brand in China. The domestic company had a 30 percent cost advantage over Colgate. By localizing manufacturing at a Sanxiao facility, Colgate was able to reduce its costs by 60 percent, which allowed the company to lower the price of its goods by an equal percentage and thus expand into the good-enough segment. Colgate's benefits multiplied when it started using the factory as a worldwide distribution center.

THEY THINK GLOBALLY, HIRE LOCALLY

Too often, multinationals count on expatriates to guide their entry into emerging markets, an approach that can backfire. Expatriates can drive up costs and frequently fail to deliver the deep market understanding offered by local managers. Instead of parachuting in expert expatriates on short assignments, winning multinationals cultivate world-class local management teams that provide a competitive edge in product design, promotion and distribution. The primary role of expatriates shifts from managing to developing local talent and transferring knowledge.

Market leaders foster loyalty by empowering local teams and providing them with global opportunities. It's a talent pool they can tap when entering other emerging markets. Procter & Gamble, the most successful consumer products company in China, has staked its future on its Chinese recruits, who represent nearly all of its employees in China—with one-quarter of them holding Chinese university degrees. When companies do hire expatriates, they make sure there's a long-term commitment.

But the tight local management pools also require creativity, flexibility and commitment. Fast-moving consumer goods players risk becoming the training ground for their local competitors, which are sometimes ready to promote faster and pay better than traditional pay scales allow. A sales force turnover exceeding 50 percent per year can result.

THEY MAKE SURE LOCAL ACQUISITIONS HAVE A STRONG BUSINESS FIT

A strategic acquisition can accelerate a multinational's entry into an emerging market by adding popular local brands to its product lineup, broadening its reach with a stronger distribution network, providing a local talent pool and lowering operating costs. In July 2007, Coca-Cola acquired the Russian beverage group Aquavision, giving itself state-of-the-art, expanded production capabilities. The move builds on Coca-Cola's previous purchase of Multon, the leading Russian fruit juice maker, strengthening the multinational's position in Eastern Europe's hotly contested soft drinks market.

In India, Frito-Lay Inc. increased its market share—and profits—when it bought the local brand Uncle Chipps in 2000. The Indian chips complemented Frito-Lay's brand portfolio, both in price and flavors. After the acquisition, Frito-Lay relaunched the Uncle Chipps brand at a lower price, positioning it as cheaper than Lay's, its flagship potato chip brand. Instead of competing against each other, Frito-Lay has two products targeted at different consumer segments. It also trimmed the number of Uncle Chipps flavors, dropping one that was similar to its saucy ketchup offering. Again, the goal was to have complementary, not competing, flavors. To reduce manufacturing costs, Lay's moved production to a local plant.

Gillette, which was acquired by P&G in 2005 and is the world's largest battery maker, scored a major coup in 2003 by acquiring the Fujian Nanping Nanfu Battery Co. Ltd., the major Chinese rival to its Duracell batteries. The acquisition gave Gillette much more than just a hot-selling Chinese battery brand. The deal had hidden assets: a state-of-the-art manufacturing plant and a distribution network with over three million retailers throughout China. With Nanfu's low-cost factory, Gillette was able to reduce production costs and use the retailing network to extend the reach of its Duracell product line. Gillette protected both Duracell's and Nanfu's brands in their respective segments. The dual branding, cost synergies, sales growth, broadened product portfolio, economies of scale and superior distribution access to more than three million retail outlets in China enabled Gillette to increase its operating margins in the country significantly.

THEY ORGANIZE FOR EMERGING MARKETS

The leaders maximize their investments by building dedicated emerging-market capabilities. This enables them to approach each emerging market with strategies crafted to distinguish the characteristics they find there from the established practices they pursue in developed economies.

For example, British American Tobacco PLC, one of the most successful consumer goods companies in emerging markets, has long had a stable of international management talent that it deploys across Asia, Africa, and Latin America.

A U.K. multinational has taken this a step further by creating a formal emerging-markets organization separate from its other international operations. By putting the emerging-markets operations under one tent, it expects to sharpen management's focus and improve managers' ability to evaluate the relative risk-return trade-offs across its emerging-markets portfolio. This will also promote cross-market learning about what works and what doesn't—crucial lessons that otherwise might be lost if emerging-market insights were blurred in a vast global operation.

Groupe Danone, the French food conglomerate, has substantial presence in major emerging markets in Asia such as India, Indonesia, and China, which share several common characteristics—huge geographic area; a high proportion of mom-and-pop outlets, especially in rural areas; and low price points. The company has learned a lot from operating in these markets, such as positioning brands to appeal to local consumers, using low-cost Asian production equipment, keeping a tight lid on overhead, and changing the specifications for packaging and raw materials to produce "good-enough" products. These lessons have been effectively cross-pollinated across the various emerging markets in which Danone operates.

With consumer markets in Asia and Eastern Europe growing at double-digit rates, multinationals are moving fast to build their brands—and the expertise to manage them in emerging markets. Indeed, succeeding in emerging markets is essential if multinationals are to defend—and increase—their share of the global market. How they fare in emerging markets is a critical indicator of how they will fare in the world.

Why Is Synergy So Difficult in Mergers of Related Businesses?

Sayan Chatterjee

Case Western Reserve University

The belief in potential synergy by merger adherents has not diminished very much over the last twenty years despite a record of extravagant promises, mixed successes, and many outright disasters. Often the proponents of new mergers justify them by describing how the value chains of the merging firms "fit" together and how there is potential for rapid growth via cross-selling. As a famous example, in the early 1980s United Airlines acquired Hertz car rental, Westin Hotels, and a few other service businesses with the idea that they could cross-sell travel customers. These mergers were considered "related" because these firms shared some customers. But growth and profits from the expected cross-selling never materialized and eventually the acquired companies were spun out. In a more recent example, AOL and Time Warner merged to benefit from cross-selling synergies created by combining complementary functions. After the merger, AOL's subscribers were bombarded with pitches for Time Warner products, such as broadband access and music by Time artist Brandy, which did not have the expected success. So instead of creating valuable synergy, the merger led to the loss of enormous shareholder value for Time Warner.

Even with such striking failures in the news, until relatively recently not many managers questioned the likelihood of merger synergy between related companies.[1] Likewise there exists voluminous but inconclusive academic research that seeks to justify synergy as a valid reason for undertaking mergers. However, one of the earliest empirical studies of this genre questioned the validity of synergy in related mergers[2] (as contrasted with horizontal-business or same-business mergers). So how do the drivers of merger success—from due diligence, to valuation, to integration—promote synergy between related business? And what evidence is there that supports or contradicts what the adherents of synergy believe? And what types of related mergers are more likely to fail?

Synergy, the golden prize of related mergers, flourishes when the combination of disparate parts within the new organization can lead to more revenues, more efficiency, or more of both than what the individual parts could muster as stand-alone units. Such synergy is difficult to achieve merely by adding new technology or talented employees, especially when the process by which the interconnected activities increase efficiency, or value to customers, is complex—such as the supply chains of Dell or Walmart.[3] In almost all cases, such complex business operations were developed internally and often over a long period of time. There have been many mergers, such as AOL/Time-Warner, that have tried to create these complex interactions following the merger. Among these, the ones that get the most attention are synergistic mergers of equals. Another reason such unions grab headlines is because these are often a bet-the-company gamble. In contrast, the acquisition of a small company is unlikely to change the business model of the acquiring firm significantly and so is less newsworthy.[4] While mergers of equals can sometimes lead to spectacular successes, such as

Reprinted from *Strategy & Leadership* 35, no. 2 (2007), pp. 46–52.

Kraft-General Foods and Novartis, we argue the odds are heavily stacked against them. Perhaps the most significant obstacle to a merger of equals, or large complex mergers in general, is that these are difficult to integrate.[5]

SYNERGY AND INTEGRATION

Synergistic mergers may, at least in theory, create competitive advantage when their complexity makes imitation difficult by would-be competitors. But this same complexity can also lead to integration problems. The acquiring firm in a synergistic merger is typically looking at an idiosyncratic situation and, therefore, its inability to draw upon previous experience often leads to an underestimation of the integration issues and difficulties. Consider a synergistic merger that is studied as a classic of this genre: AOL/Time Warner. This deal was sold to the shareholders on a promise of cross-selling and other synergies. If AOL had thoroughly explored the organizational constraints and cultural differences during due diligence, then they would have been a little less optimistic about achieving some of the synergies. Consider these events:

> On Valentine's Day (2001), AOL Time Warner Inc.'s America Online service hosted an online chat with movie star Keanu Reeves. . . . As part of the chat, AOL set up links to other online sources on Mr. Reeves, including an article created by People.com, the online version of *People* magazine, which is published by the company's Time Inc. unit. According to people familiar with the details, AOL asked People.com to edit out the phrase "He may not be Oscar material (so far, at least)," because it wasn't Keanu friendly. People.com editors refused, and AOL didn't link to the story during the chat.[6]

Soon after this, much to the reluctance of AOL management, they were forced to add "editorial independence" as prominently in their list of company values as "teamwork"—a prerequisite for synergy.[7]

There are numerous other such instances of planned synergy that failed to materialize. Consider the cross-promotion that was supposed to bring in more revenues. One market that Time Warner had targeted was the Internet radio

stations accessible to AOL subscribers. The basic idea was to increase the royalties for Time Warner's recording artists played over the Internet radio stations. Time expected these radio stations to go along with the royalty increase because of AOL's subscriber base. Instead the Internet radio stations severed their links with AOL. AOL's subscribers ended up with only AOL radio stations. It seems the issue of royalty conflicts was not carefully reviewed during the negotiation stage before this source of revenue was booked as synergy. The clearest admission that the merger synergy was abandoned came from the 2002 directive by the new CEO Richard Parsons: each individual unit would focus on what they are good at individually. Overemphasizing the potential for collective good is a common mistake in synergistic mergers, and AOL is not alone in misjudging the opportunities.

SYNERGISTIC MERGERS AND VALUATIONS

There is research evidence that the premiums paid in mergers perceived to be synergistic by managers (termed "related mergers" in the strategy literature) are higher[8] than purely financial (unrelated) mergers as well as horizontal (same-industry) mergers. However, there is also evidence the acquiring firms in "related" mergers do not benefit or are actually worse off compared to unrelated as well as horizontal mergers.[9] Our interviews with practicing managers confirm this research evidence. In a related merger, the seller knows much more of the true value than the buyer, even though the buyer may think that it knows what it is buying.

Consider the case of Kellogg's acquisition of Lender's Bagels. In late 1990s, Kellogg bought Lender's Bagels (a maker of frozen bagels) from Kraft in a desperate effort to get into a high-growth market—bagels. However, the true growth market was in fresh bagels and not the frozen bagels that Lender's sold. To compound this mistake, Kellogg saw Lender's as a related business because Kellogg was selling Eggo waffles in the grocery freezer. In sum, Kellogg did not know the entire bagel business. To paraphrase a former Kellogg executive: "Kraft got a good deal out of the sale."

It should be common sense that mergers that are dependent on coordination of partially familiar activities (complex or otherwise) by two former independent entities will be more difficult to value. Our advice to managers who are contemplating so-called related mergers: it is absolutely imperative to have much more clarity with these mergers than you think you have. The fact that parts of the acquired business are related to yours can lull you into complacency, which can be disastrous. On top of that, if the coordination of the integration is complex, this unwarranted confidence increases the risk even more. In three well-documented mergers—AT&T/NCR, Quaker Oats/Snapple, and AOL/Time Warner—the acquirers all assumed that they could precisely predict the revenue increases that would only arise from such complex coordination of activities of the merging firms. Moreover, they thought that they could achieve these increases very quickly. It turns out they were very wrong.

HOW TO REDUCE THE VALUATION RISKS OF A SYNERGISTIC MERGER

Managers should expect synergistic mergers to be difficult and success elusive. For one reason, they tend to be one-off initiatives, and thus unique. Because of this, it is very difficult to develop a repeatable acquisition process. Thus, synergistic mergers or acquisitions are likely to be excessively costly and to experience integration problems.

The following checklist—based on our assessment of problematic mergers and on conversations with successful acquirers—may enable potential purchasers to avoid some of the major pitfalls:

- *Avoid high-pressure deals.* If the combination is truly unique, then it avoids a major pitfall for all acquisitions—a high-pressure competitive bidding process. Further, negotiations of such deals are more likely to be friendly and transparent. Leadership's goal should be to manage one-off synergistic mergers much the same way that serial acquirers such as Danaher or RPM do deals. These firms often pursue a target for years and even decades. Not only does their long-term perspective give these acquirers much better insight into what they are buying, but they often receive favorable treatment from the seller because of the long-standing relationship.

- *Same industry mergers are less risky.* Travelers/Citicorp and Hewlett-Packard/Compaq mergers were secretly negotiated over a long period of time, which allowed all the participants to develop realistic expectations. In both cases, all the parties were in the same industry, so everyone understood the business and the industry dynamics. Surprisingly, both mergers exceeded their basic goals.

- *Synergies in cost reductions are easier than revenue increase.* Based on a survey of academic research, interviews and anecdotal evidence, it is my conclusion that it is much easier to achieve success when the stated goal of a merger is its potential for cost reduction rather than its potential to increase revenue. For example, following its disastrous acquisition of Lender's, Kellogg's next purchase was the frozen vegetarian burgers unit of Worthington Foods. However, with this acquisition Kellogg fared much better because they focused on the cost side of the synergy and did not assume that the market would grow by itself.[10] Likewise, the Hewlett-Packard/Compaq merger was largely predicated on a consolidation of capacity that could be accurately measured. Despite Carly Fiorina's sudden departure before integration was complete, all the cost targets of the merger were met earlier than predicted. HP had established an objective of achieving $1.3 billion in cost savings by November 2003. Yet within a year, according to Forrester Research, HP had posted savings of $3.7 billion, and acquired new strength in servers and IT services.[11]

The previous observation also solidifies our belief about mergers in the same industry faring better than related mergers. In a merger or acquisition driven solely by consolidation of capacity in a market or industry, the revenue increase would come from simple supply–demand dynamics that are much easier to understand. In contrast, the typical related merger expects revenue increases from complicated cross-selling and other interfunctional coordination. In general, there is strong and uniform academic evidence that horizontal industry consolidations, motivated by capacity reduction, are one of the few merger categories that seem to succeed.[12]

- *Clarify the source of revenue increase.* On the other hand, the evidence regarding related (as opposed to horizontal) mergers that can lead to new revenue opportunities is extremely mixed. Consider, for example, AT&T's effort to develop a broadband strategy by acquiring the leading cable companies TCI and MediaOne in the early 1990s. This was an entry strategy that required paying an excessive premium to overcome the entry barriers. As time has shown, AT&T's rival, Comcast, became the beneficiary when this strategy failed and it acquired all of AT&T's cable assets at fire-sale prices.

  In sum, it is very difficult to come to a definitive conclusion in advance about the potential for revenue increase, especially for related (as opposed to financial or unrelated) mergers. This makes it highly risky to establish revenue increase as the primary justification for such mergers. As one former Kellogg executive commented on the failed Lender's Bagel merger, "Very often you do not know what you do not know."

  So how can managers mitigate this risk? An alternative approach is to seek a merger as a last resort and instead try to determine if the synergies can be obtained through contractual mechanisms. For example, in the case of United's merger with Hertz car rentals and the Westin hotel chains, United could have reaped the significant benefits of cross-selling between its car-rental and hotel partners by simply referring customers to each other without getting into a merger[13]—as most airlines do at present.

- *Do not make a bad situation worse.* In 1999, Prudential acquired the boutique Silicon Valley investment bank Volpe Brown Whelan in order to get into the booming Internet firm's underwriting business. This is a classic "fit"-driven merger where the acquiring firm buys a complementary resource.

During its negotiations with Volpe, Prudential's dealmakers drew up a list of 12 bankers and analysts considered critical to the firm's value. Yet many of these vital personnel left when Prudential closed Volpe's trading desk and integrated the trading operations with Prudential's own. Prudential was trying to extract cost synergy. Yes, Prudential paid a premium to buy the underwriting business. However, trying to recover the premium by consolidating the trading desk was the wrong integration priority. Instead, Prudential may have been able to generate the cost savings it sought through the merger by integrating the trading desk, if they did not hurry the process and antagonize the key traders. These traders were the first line of contact with the customers. The cost reduction was not worth losing these key personnel.

The case of the Volpe acquisition by Prudential illustrates an important lesson. Let's suppose that your firm has acquired a profitable business. You have paid a premium for it. Now you realize that it is difficult to achieve the synergy and you probably will not recover the premium. Our advice is not to try to squeeze the acquisition to produce a quick profit. Trying to force the issue may well lead to the target firm losing ground to its competitors. This is exactly what happened when Rubbermaid acquired Little Tikes in 1984 and wanted to integrate it with its other product lines. The end result was that the founder of Little Tikes quit Rubbermaid, and started step 2, a company that effectively competed with Little Tikes. As a result, the Little Tikes division suffered a string of annual losses and was divested in November 2006. As these cases show, in certain situations the mishandled acquisition of a relatively small target can lead to painful consequences for the acquiring firm.

TWO TYPES OF SPECIAL CASES

Opportunistic Acquisitions

The problem with opportunistic acquisitions, whether they are synergistic or not, is that they are likely to be ad hoc ventures that cannot draw upon previous experience. Research suggests that, as a defense, decision makers must try to develop an in-depth understanding of the acquisition's market. A case in point, in 1993 Merck wanted to use the disease management database of the leading pharmaceutical benefit management company, Medco, to get into the formularies of the managed care companies. Merck's investment paid off in the 1990s mainly because Merck had invested in in-house disease management programs before making the $6 billion hostile bid for Medco. Thus, it had a slight information/knowledge advantage over pharmaceutical companies that acquired pharmaceutical benefit management companies in the wake of the Merck/Medco acquisition. Any kind of information advantage will be a buffer against paying too much. As another method of defense against overpaying, Cisco routinely tries to develop products in-house first before making an acquisition.

Hostile Bids

What about hostile bids? The Medco acquisition ultimately ended up as a friendly merger, but there are acquisitions that remain hostile to the end. Many hostile bids are not built around synergy but rather a short-term opportunity to create value by restructuring or breaking up the acquired company, a common ploy in the 1980s. These acquirers motivated by restructuring did not really suffer from an information disadvantage because they could not care less about the internal goings-on of the acquired company. They simply applied their skill at restructuring and breaking up companies over and over again—so in some sense they benefited from repetition. For this reason, restructuring acquisitions also have a good track record.[14]

A hostile bid can also be justifiable if the value proposition and the value extraction processes are understood by the purchaser. Consider Oracle's hostile bid to acquire PeopleSoft. Oracle was willing to pay $6 billion (an initial offer that was subsequently raised) simply to buy PeopleSoft's 3,000 customers. There was no information

disadvantage because Oracle made the calculation that the market power that it would generate by removing PeopleSoft as a competitor (or of avoiding the formation of a stronger competitor through the merger of PeopleSoft and J. D. Edwards) was worth $6 billion.[15] Note that, there was no complicated plan to integrate PeopleSoft with Oracle. In sum, hostile bids that have a purely financial goal are likely to work, provided the acquiring firm has done its homework and has complete clarity about the viability of the value proposition.

However, hostile bids that expect to create value by a complex melding of the acquiring and acquired firm are much less likely to succeed. Commenting on AT&T's hostile bid for NCR in 1990, NCR chairman Chuck Exley said that AT&T was "like an electricity company that wants to get into the Mixmaster business!"[16] In fact, the NCR acquisition was an unmitigated disaster. Our advice: never attempt a synergistic hostile takeover.

SOME FINAL ADVICE TO LEADERS

Research shows that acquiring firms that rely on a repeatable acquisition process have the highest probability of success. The reverse is also true: occasional acquirers that seek synergy or a unique opportunity have to contend with all the impediments to acquisition success and are less likely to succeed. Even experienced acquirers should approach synergistic mergers with great care and not put too much faith in their prior success record. Phillip Morris found out that its success with the Miller acquisition did not help it when it undertook the *ad hoc* acquisition of 7UP. Similarly, Quaker Oats' experience acquiring Gatorade did not ensure success when it attempted the opportunistic acquirement of Snapple. Our conclusion: managers should be extremely circumspect when contemplating one-off mergers or acquisitions.

ENDNOTES

[1] Mark L. Sirower (1997). *The Synergy Trap: How Companies Lose the Acquisition Game,* The Free Press, New York, NY. This book summarizes a stream of research starting with Sayan Chatterjee's article "Types of synergy and economic value: the impact of acquisitions on merging and rival firms," *Strategic Management Journal,* Vol. 7, pp. 119–139 (1986).

[2] Chatterjee (1986) op. cit.

[3] This is in effect a "merger" of the procurement activity of Dell/Walmart with the manufacturing activity of their vendors. The reason that competitors have not been able to imitate these supply chains is because of their complexity.

[4] This complexity can be a problem even for smaller acquisitions—the types that we have previously argued are more likely to pay off. However, the previous sections deal with an increase in the productivity of the small target's assets and not synergy from a comprehensive combination of the acquirer and acquired companies' activities. In fact, sometimes these smaller firms targeted as synergistic acquisitions can become a money pit if the acquired

firm is not careful (Joseph L. Bower "Not all M&As are alike—and that matters," *Harvard Business Review,* March 2001, Vol. 79 No. 3, pp. 92–101). Recall AT&T's acquisition of NCR and Quaker Oats' acquisition of Snapple.

[5] Chatterjee (1986) op. cit. hinted at this possibility but did not provide any evidence.

[6] Julia Angwin and Matthew Rose, "Creating a 'new media' concept," *Wall Street Journal,* Eastern Edition, 03/09/2001, Vol. 237 No. 48, p. B1, p. 1

[7] Angwin and Rose op. cit.

[8] Singh, H. and Montgomery. C. (1987), "Corporate acquisition strategies and economic performance," *Strategic Management Journal.*

[9] Anand and Singh. (1997) op. cit. Lubatkin (1987), "Merger strategies and stockholder value," *Strategic Management Journal,* pp. 25–37. D. J. Flanagan (1996), "Announcements of purely related and purely unrelated mergers and shareholder returns: Reconciling the relatedness paradox," *Journal of Management,* pp. 823–835. Chatterjee (1986) op. cit. E.B. Eckbo (1983), "Horizontal mergers, collusion,

and stockholder wealth," *Journal of Financial Economics,* pp. 241–273.

[10] According to the Kellogg executive who integrated the Worthington merger, the revenue estimates were not borne out.

[11] Charles Rutstein, with Galen Schreck (2003), "A year later: HP can claim integration success," Forrester Research, May 9.

[12] Chatterjee (1986); Anand and Singh (1997) op. cit.

[13] The principles for deciding between a contractual arrangement versus an organizational arrangement were well developed in the mid-1960s by Oliver Williamson.

[14] Michael E. Porter (1987), "From competitive advantage to corporate strategy," *Harvard Business Review,* May/June, Vol. 65 No. 3, pp. 43–59.

[15] Porter (1987) op. cit. calls it the better-off test.

[16] Paul Carroll, "Is it synergy or just sin?" *Context,* Winter 2002/2003.

When Managers Pressure Employees to Behave Badly: Toward a Comprehensive Response

Bennett J. Tepper
Georgia State University

UNETHICAL BEHAVIOR IN WORK ORGANIZATIONS

It is an unfortunate but inescapable fact of business life that working people engage in unethical work behaviors which threaten the legitimate interests of organizational stakeholders. Everyday, working people falsify data to support new product innovations, engage in kickback schemes, fudge time sheets, overlook safety defects in new products, and remain silent when they have knowledge about instances of discrimination or harassment. Estimates of the costs of these and other forms of unethical work behavior vary, but it is fair to characterize even the most conservative estimates as staggering.

When events like these transpire, it is natural to look for explanations that make sense to us. A good explanation provides some solace that even if we can't undo what has happened, we can nevertheless develop policies and procedures that make the frequency of such behavior less likely in the future. But if the spate of unethical work behavior that has made national headlines over the last 15 years is reflective of an underlying trend, it is that unethical behavior is by no means becoming less frequent. We would like to think that in the wake of serious violations of the public trust (e.g., Enron, Arthur Andersen), organizational policy makers would inoculate their organizations by developing and rolling out interventions that reduce the occurrence of unethical work behavior. The more recent events at AIG Insurance, Fannie Mae, and other firms can be interpreted to mean that we have not accurately diagnosed the triggers of unethical behavior or that we have not done a good job of translating what we know into effective interventions, or both.

AN OVERLOOKED TRIGGER: MANAGERIAL PRESSURE TO BEHAVE UNETHICALLY

In this article, I focus on a precursor of unethical workplace behavior that gets less attention than it should: pressure organizational authorities put on employees to perform unethical acts. According to estimates, 56% of U.S. workers experience pressure from superiors to behave unethically in the furtherance of organizational objectives and 29% are forced to behave unethically in order to achieve promotion (Lonkevich, 1997). Via interviews conducted with former MBA students, Badaracco and Webb (1995) found that many had been ordered to act unethically by their immediate supervisor. One well known example is the pressure authorities at Brown and Williamson Inc. brought to bear on one of its employees, Dr. Jeffery Wigand, to not disclose some of the tobacco giant's unethical inner workings. Johnson (2009) nicely sums up the scope of the problem:

Bennett J. Tepper, "When Managers Pressure Employees to Behave Badly: Toward a Comprehensive Response," *Business Horizons* 53:6 (November 2010), pp. 591–598. Copyright © Kelly School of Business, Indiana University. Reprinted with permission of Elsevier Science.

"Examine nearly any corporate scandal—AIG Insurance, Arthur Andersen, Enron, Health South, Sotheby's Auction House, Fannie Mae, Hollinger International, Marsh & McLennan, Quest, and you'll find leaders who engaged in immoral behavior and encouraged their followers to do the same" (p. 265).

Society has two noteworthy expectations when evidence suggests that the organizational leaders we count on to serve as moral exemplars are instead the driving force behind employees' unethical behavior. The first expectation is that these leaders will be punished for the injury their betrayal causes. This is entirely appropriate. The second expectation is that rank-and-file employees will display moral courage; that they will resist pressure to behave unethically by just saying "no." But the philosophy embodied in this expectation is likely to produce disappointment. At the risk of sounding cynical, we cannot be surprised when working people follow the orders of their superiors to perform unethical acts; disgusted, perhaps, but not surprised. This is particularly true when workers are made to choose between performing acts that hurt others and protecting the livelihood on which they and their loved ones depend. A compelling body of empirical research evidence suggests that it is disturbingly easy for authority figures to put their direct reports in positions where unethical choices are preferred over ethical choices. Consider, for example, Stanley Milgram's obedience studies, in which research subjects complied with an authority's request to deliver painful and life-threatening electrical shocks to targets whose only transgression was that they failed to provide the correct response on an experimental, word-association task (Milgram, 1974).

Many are of the opinion that those who comply with unethical requests are inherently flawed; that their behavior reflects fundamental short-comings and that to attribute any responsibility for their misdeeds to situational factors is to absolve perpetrators of responsibility for what they have done. Classic experimental research suggests that individuals may be held accountable for unethical behavior even when it is coerced, and observers may view sanctions as justified even when actors' accountability is low (Shaw & Sulzer, 1964). Hence, the excuse, "I was just following orders," does not hold water with many observers.

That some people are given to unethical behavior cannot be disputed. But it is also true that otherwise decent people can be made to do horrible things. And although we have selection tools that can identify some individuals who are inclined toward immoral behavior, those tools are far from perfect. It would, therefore, be foolhardy to fail to address the situational influences that move working people in the direction of immorality. Accordingly, in this article, I introduce a comprehensive intervention to combat one such situational factor: managerial pressure on employees to behave unethically (hereafter referred to as PBU). The intervention I will describe is rooted in the best available scientific evidence. It is not my intention to catalog the many reasons why efforts to combat unethical behavior have coincided with a proliferation of such behavior. While that kind of exercise would be instructive, and undertaking it could help managers separate strategies which have more promise from those which have less, that is not my intent here. Rather, my goal is to present a portfolio of evidence-based strategies: approaches that are informed by scholarly research from the fields of organizational psychology and organizational behavior.

TACKLING PBU IN A COMPREHENSIVE FASHION

My analysis and recommendations draw on the framework of Patterson, Grenny, Maxfield, McMillan, and Switzler (2008), which accounts for the many influences on individuals' inclination to execute destructive acts ranging from practicing unsafe sex to criminal recidivism. This framework also provides a blueprint for instilling in individuals a repertoire of more desirable choices and corresponding behavior. Patterson et al.'s model identifies three sources of influence on human behavior—personal, social, and structural—and, within each of the three sources, distinguishes between the motivation and ability to execute specific behaviors. The resulting cross-classification of the three sources of influence with motivation and ability produces a framework that captures six influences: personal motivation, social motivation, structural motivation, personal ability, social ability, and structural ability. Figure 1 depicts the role that these influences play in the occurrence of PBU, and Table 1 summarizes the recommendations for combating PBU by leveraging the six influences. In the remainder of this article, I describe each influence, explain the link between the six influences and PBU, and outline the steps that can be taken to leverage the six influences to discourage PBU.

Personal Motivation: Making PBU Inherently Distasteful

The first of Patterson et al.'s (2008) influences is personal motivation, which captures the satisfaction that individuals derive from performing a particular activity. Activities are characterized as *intrinsically motivating* when carrying them out is, in and of itself, satisfying. For example, if playing a musical instrument is pleasurable for a person, we would say that the person is intrinsically motivated to play that instrument. People at play—whether it be a child drawing pictures or singing to herself, or an adult shooting baskets—are performing these activities for the intrinsic satisfaction they engender automatically. This is a powerful source of motivation because organizational authorities need not rely on external inducements (i.e., the promise of reward or the

Figure 1   Six Factors That Encourage Managerial Pressure to Behave Unethically

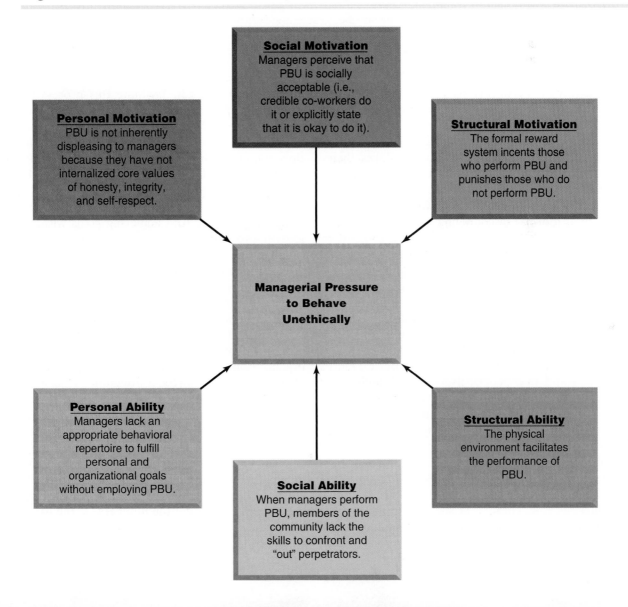

Social Motivation
Managers perceive that PBU is socially acceptable (i.e., credible co-workers do it or explicitly state that it is okay to do it).

Personal Motivation
PBU is not inherently displeasing to managers because they have not internalized core values of honesty, integrity, and self-respect.

Structural Motivation
The formal reward system incents those who perform PBU and punishes those who do not perform PBU.

Managerial Pressure to Behave Unethically

Personal Ability
Managers lack an appropriate behavioral repertoire to fulfill personal and organizational goals without employing PBU.

Social Ability
When managers perform PBU, members of the community lack the skills to confront and "out" perpetrators.

Structural Ability
The physical environment facilitates the performance of PBU.

Table 1   Ways of Warding Off Managerial Pressure to Behave Unethically

Target	Recommendation
Personal Motivation	Develop managers' intrinsic motivation to eschew PBU by establishing honesty, integrity, and self-respect as core organizational values and by making it clear that these values are every bit as important as organizational and personal success.
Social Motivation	Identify the opinion leaders—the managers that other managers look to for guidance—and persuade them to embrace the core organizational values of honesty, integrity, and self-respect.
Structural Motivation	Closely scrutinize the reward system to identify instances in which PBU is inadvertently encouraged; as a last resort, reward managers for eschewing PBU and punish perpetrators.
Personal Ability	Employ training programs in which managers develop moral awareness and practice ethical leader behaviors that are incompatible with PBU.
Social Ability	Equip employees with scripts to resist PBU when they are targets, confront perpetrators when they observe PBU, and call out serious and habitual perpetrators.
Structural Ability	Identify the environmental circumstances in which PBU is highly likely or highly unlikely; scrutinize these cases to identify the structural forces that facilitate or inhibit PBU.

threat of punishment) to prompt intrinsically motivated individuals to perform desired activities or eschew undesirable ones. Indeed, there are circumstances in which offering inducements to intrinsically motivated individuals reduces their intrinsic motivation (Lepper, Greene, & Nisbett, 1973); I return to this point later when I describe some of the limitations of reward and punishment as tools for discouraging PBU.

How can we use this knowledge to reduce the occurrence of PBU? The objective is to make performing PBU inherently displeasing; to leverage the remarkable ability people have to punish or censure themselves for failing to live up to moral standards (i.e., to see themselves as unworthy, irresponsible, and so on). It is this capacity to self-censure that prevents individuals from behaving in ways that violate moral standards. But we must understand that people also have the ability to convince themselves that moral standards do not apply in specific situations; that there are occasions when the victims of our transgressions deserve what they get, that injurious behavior is not terribly harmful, or that we're only doing what we've been ordered to do (Bandura, 1999). It is through cognitions like these that perpetrators justify computer hacking, cheating at sports, and inhumane behavior against those from different ethnic backgrounds. Reducing PBU involves reconnecting managers' behavior to their moral values.

Organizations can facilitate this process by emphasizing *how* organizational members achieve performance goals is just as important as actually achieving those goals. When the organization embraces values such as honest achievement, responsibility, and self-respect, performing PBU becomes intrinsically dissatisfying; managers will avoid these behaviors because doing them brings displeasure. And achieving goals without resorting to PBU becomes a matter of personal significance to managers. Just as winning a game of cards is more personally rewarding for a player who does not peek at the opposition's hand, achieving work goals without resorting to PBU is more personally rewarding for managers than is achieving the same goals by co-opting those who are dependent on the manager. That these are the organization's core values should be made clear at hiring, and reinforced throughout a person's tenure.

This recommendation is also a warning. Making no effort to connect employees' behavior to moral standards sends the tacit message that the organization is not concerned with the means by which employees accomplish their goals. In most organizations, employees get the message that "making the numbers" is the route to personal success. If this is not accompanied by the equally robust message that *how* employees make the numbers is no less valued, we can expect employees to push their moral motivations aside and we can expect PBU from the managerial ranks. This is not to say that no managers find intrinsic satisfaction in eschewing PBU; indeed, many managers take pride in their ability to get the job done the right way without their employer pointing them in that direction. My point here is that in most work organizations, the push for performance is unambiguous and in that push, many managers lose their moral compass.

Social Motivation: Leveraging Peer Pressure

Patterson et al.'s (2008) second influence, social motivation, refers to the social drivers of behavior. People look for cues from others when determining whether specific behaviors are acceptable or unacceptable. Organizational members come to believe that unethical behavior such as PBU is socially acceptable when credible and trusted others explicitly indicate that such behavior is acceptable, or implicitly communicate that it is acceptable by performing those behaviors. This phenomenon is illustrated in the behavior of the energy traders at Enron, who were encouraged by superiors and by each other to find creative ways of manipulating energy prices. A comprehensive approach to deterring PBU involves harnessing the power of peer pressure to create the perception that PBU is socially unacceptable. This entails enlisting credible organizational members who will be listened to when they transmit the message that PBU is unacceptable.

Who, then, are the credible organizational members who can facilitate the adoption of an organizational culture that embraces the core values of honesty, integrity, and self-respect (these being the core values that, when internalized, inhibit PBU)? In any community undergoing change we can identify the *opinion leaders*, individuals who others look to when deciding whether or not to support the change (Rogers, 1995). The opinion leaders constitute a minority of any population, less than 15%, but they exert considerable influence on the behavior of everyone else. Others will not embrace a significant social change if the opinion leaders do not embrace it; indeed, if the opinion leaders are opposed to an innovation, the change will be resisted.

Organizations can leverage the social motivation to eschew PBU by identifying the opinion leaders and winning them over to the aforementioned core values. We can identify opinion leaders by asking the managers whose behavior we're trying to change to name the managers whose opinions they value. Those who receive the most nominations are the managers that other managers look to for guidance when it comes to accepting or rejecting a change effort. It is critically important that these opinion leaders be persuaded to embrace the core ethical values. If the opinion leaders resist internalizing the core values, it is unlikely that other managers will do so. There is nothing more threatening to the effort to reduce PBU than the presence of opinion leaders who practice PBU or otherwise send the message that PBU is not unacceptable. Ideally, the opinion leaders already embrace the core values; if they do not, however, winning them over is essential.

Structural Motivation: The Judicious Use of Carrots and Sticks

The third source of motivation that Patterson et al. (2008) describe is structural motivation, which captures the roles that reward and punishment play in individuals' inclination to perform desirable and undesirable acts. Managers will apply pressure on employees to behave unethically when it is personally rewarding to do so. Hence, for example, we can expect PBU from managers whose career prospects or status within the organization are likely to improve if their employees perform unethical acts. To the extent that the reward system formally or simply inadvertently encourages PBU, managers will perceive that failing to perform PBU is implicitly punished; that by withholding PBU, they will fall behind managers who pressure their employees to behave badly.

Just how common is it for organizations to employ systems of reward and punishment that inadvertently discourage desired behaviors while encouraging undesired behaviors? In a classic scholarly work, Steve Kerr (1975) pointed out that fouled-up reward systems are common and that most of us are affected by these systems at some point in our working lives. As examples, organizations that would like for employees to work well together in teams often use reward systems that emphasize individual accomplishment, and organizations in which candor is valued may reward employees who report only good news or who always agree with the boss.

What can we do to ensure that managers are not inadvertently incented to target rank-and-file employees with PBU? The first step is to create an incentive map: a comprehensive analysis of the consequences of the specific rewards and punishments that are associated with an organization's incentive system. This can begin by assessing the desired and undesired behaviors that are performed in an organization and then tracing those behaviors back to the organization rewards and punishments that are associated with each. In the specific case of discouraging PBU, we would be on the lookout for organizational rewards provided to managers that encourage PBU. The next step is to cut the links that connect PBU performance and valued rewards. Organizations must get rid of messages—including awards, images, and slogans—which imply that being successful at all costs is valued.

Should these be replaced with rewards for withholding PBU (e.g., managerial bonuses to those who display a high level of task and ethical performance), or punishment for performing PBU (e.g., a zero-tolerance policy)? For a number of reasons, organizational authorities must be cautious when it comes to using reward and punishment to discourage undesired behavior. As I mentioned earlier, using rewards can drive out intrinsic motivation, and we must be careful not to eliminate the intrinsic satisfaction that managers derive from achieving performance goals without employing PBU. Using punishment is complicated because it can lead to undesirable outcomes that may be difficult to predict. For example, if a manager is punished for performing PBU, will other managers stop performing PBU, or will they simply become more careful in their use of PBU so as to avoid detection?

It is not my position that organizational authorities should never use carrots and sticks to address managerial PBU, but rather to be sure that they have a good sense of the effects rewards and punishments will have before using them. To the extent possible, organizational authorities should decrease the motivation to perform PBU by

encouraging intrinsic motivation (i.e., connecting managers' behavior to core ethical values) and social motivation (i.e., identifying and co-opting the opinion leaders), and by disconnecting extrinsic rewards from PBU. If these methods are unsuccessful, using rewards and punishment to encourage PBU-free managerial behavior should be the last option authorities avail themselves of.

Personal Ability: Developing the Capacity to Recognize and Respond to Ethical Dilemmas

By leveraging the three sources of motivation discussed thus far, we can inhibit managers' motivation to perform PBU. But motivation is only part of the story; managers must also know how to meet their task-related goals without resorting to PBU. It is to ability as a source of influence that I now turn my attention, beginning with what Patterson et al. (2008) refer to as personal ability, which captures an individual's capacity to execute desired behaviors. Many managers apply pressure on employees to behave unethically because it does not occur to them to do otherwise, or because they do not know *how* to do otherwise. Inhibiting the PBU of these managers will involve developing their moral awareness and training them to execute an incompatible behavioral repertoire.

Every day, people make decisions or take actions that have ethical implications, without recognizing them as such. Consider Apple computer's failure to recognize the problem of consumers inappropriately disposing of their iBooks, iPods, and iPhones; another example is Ford Motor Company's decision to not recall the Pinto automobile, which had defective gas tanks that made them susceptible to explosion during rear-end collisions (Johnson, 2009). The first step on the road to behaving ethically is to recognize that one's behavior and decisions have moral implications.

Developing moral awareness is, therefore, an essential feature of training for managers who perform PBU unconsciously. Training in moral awareness involves frank discussion whereby those in managerial positions describe decisions they have made or actions they have taken, and colleagues and trained session leaders provide honest feedback about the potential negative consequences of their actions. Via this technique, managers become more sensitive to the possible negative effects of their actions when they practice analyzing their own behavior and the behavior of other managers for ethical implications.

As for executing an incompatible behavioral repertoire, a useful framework comes from Brown, Trevino, and Harrison (2005), who have identified the core features of ethical leadership: listening to employees, establishing trust, employing fair decision making processes, communicating decisions in a sensitive manner, and disciplining employees who behave unethically. A promising approach to instilling this repertoire in managers is *justice training*. Justice training involves teaching a number of specific techniques that supervisors can use to reduce psychological distance with employees, promote the perception that employees have "voice," equitably apply decision making criteria, and recognize and suspend bias in their decision making. The specifics of justice training are described elsewhere, and I encourage those who are interested to read more on the topic; see Skarlicki and Latham (2005) for a recent review. What I can say here is that in mastering the techniques of justice building, managers develop a behavioral tool chest (i.e., personal ability) that is incompatible with PBU.

Social Ability: Accessing the Knowledge and Skills of Others

Patterson et al.'s (2008) fifth influence, social ability, refers to knowledge regarding how to prevent PBU that is embedded in the larger community of which managers are members. Different group members possess unique knowledge and skills, and when there are strong interconnections among these individuals, each person benefits from the capabilities of all the others. The value that is embedded in the connections among members of a social network is referred to as *social capital*. Organizations have access to a valuable source of social capital if the collective has the knowledge and skills to discourage employees from performing undesirable behaviors. That social capital goes unexploited when individuals experience social pressure to conform to unethical courses of action, such

as when decision making bodies are affected by *groupthink*. In such cases, groups make reaching unanimous agreement a priority over reasoned decision making (Janis, 1982). Examples include the decision making processes leading up to the Bay of Pigs invasion and the launch of the space shuttle Challenger.

When it comes to addressing PBU, leveraging social ability involves giving organization members the skills to resist managerial PBU when they are targeted and the skills to confront and/or "rat-out" perpetrators when they observe PBU occurring. Employees can be trained to use three kinds of scripted responses to PBU: *resistance* scripts, for those who find themselves the target of PBU; *confrontation* scripts, for those who observe others being targeted; and *calling-out* scripts, for habitual offenders whose behavior must be brought to the attention of higher authorities. Scripts can be developed with assistance from the opinion leaders. These high status organizational members are likely to have a good idea what combination of words will be most effective in helping employees say "no" to a powerful manager whose moral compass is off (i.e., the resistance script), letting perpetrators know that what they are doing has not gone unnoticed and that it is not acceptable (i.e., the confrontation script), and blowing the whistle on serious transgressors (i.e., the calling-out script).

Mastering these kinds of scripts is by no means easy. Most people are content to avoid—rather than confront—difficult individuals and situations, and some might find the calling-out script to be unsavory; indeed, they might believe that developing these abilities in employees creates a culture of "snitching." But those who remain silent when they see PBU occurring are enablers of a problem that threatens the legitimate interests of an organization's many stakeholders. We must remember that these recommendations are responses to a culture where wrongdoing is actively encouraged by those in positions of power and where unethical activity may be inextricably intertwined with the organization's business model (e.g., predatory lending). The philosophy of keeping quiet while fellow members erode an organization's legitimacy is the blueprint for derailment and organizational failure. Whatever we may think of calling out the perpetrators of PBU, we must keep in mind the costs of their misbehavior upon an organization's many internal and external stakeholders.

Structural Ability: Engineering PBU Out of the Environment

The sixth source of influence, structural ability, refers to environmental factors that facilitate or inhibit the performance of particular behaviors. To the extent possible, an intervention designed to discourage PBU will make it physically impossible to perform PBU. Of course, PBU manifests in different ways in different industries, organizations, and leadership situations. PBU could involve pressuring an employee to deceive a customer, alter accounting information, or keep quiet when they become aware of transgressions perpetrated by the manager or others. Even within each of these categories, the ways in which PBU manifests may vary; deceiving customers could involve making untenable promises regarding product delivery targets, withholding information about product defects, making false claims about product performance, and so on.

What generally applicable recommendations can we make to address structural ability if how PBU manifests depends on employees' job responsibilities, the scope of the manager's influence, and other idiosyncratic features of the work environment? A useful strategy is to look for what Patterson et al. (2008) refer to as instances of *positive deviance:* situations where an undesirable behavior should be occurring, but is not. In this case, we would be on the lookout for instances in which the motivation to perform PBU is present, but managers are logistically unable to follow through. What features of the environment facilitate or inhibit PBU in these cases? Are there work policies or procedures that inhibit certain forms of PBU? Does the setup of the environment—for example, the physical layout; the presence or absence of certain kinds of equipment; or, the proximity to specific co-workers—discourage PBU?

Identifying the environmental features that play a role in PBU performance is not a simple matter. Over time, we come to ignore most of our surroundings. Our brains are not suited to process each and every detail of our environment and, to make things more efficient, we take note of the few things that are salient to us and ignore everything else. This complicates the search for behavioral triggers because we don't "see" a substantial percentage of what's out there. The key, then, is to be deliberate about *noticing,* seeing as much of the environment as possible.

Once organizational authorities have identified the environmental features that play a role in PBU performance, they can turn their attention to making changes to those features. This could involve changing technology, work processes, reporting relationships, and so on. It might also involve littering the environment with cues that keep managers attuned to the importance of adhering to the core values that are incompatible with PBU; for example, appending to all electronic and paper communications a slogan that espouses the core value.

CLOSING THOUGHTS

Herein, I have proposed a comprehensive solution to a difficult problem: managing the frequency with which those in leadership positions pressure employees to behave unethically. The approach I have advocated targets managers' motivation and ability to avoid PBU. The motivation to avoid PBU should be developed by:

1. Establishing core values of honesty, integrity, and self-respect as no less important than the usual performance goals;
2. Persuading the opinion leaders to embrace the core values; and
3. Decoupling formal rewards from PBU.

The ability to eschew PBU should be addressed by:

4. Improving managers' ability to recognize moral dilemmas and to practice behaviors that are incompatible with PBU;
5. Equipping employees with scripts for resisting PBU, confronting perpetrators, and blowing the whistle on perpetrators; and
6. Redesigning the environment to make PBU logistically impossible, or to keep the avoidance of PBU at the top of all managers' minds.

It may be tempting to treat my recommendations as a menu of options from which would-be eliminators of PBU might pick and choose. This would be a mistake. In their review of the roles that the six sources of influence play in discouraging undesirable behavior, Patterson et al. (2008) make clear that big problems require complex solutions and that when it comes to reducing the occurrence of costly organizational misbehavior the most efficacious strategy is one that involves a comprehensive intervention. If the goal is to eliminate PBU, a haphazard approach—one that leverages sources of influence that happen to be easier to implement—is destined to produce disappointing outcomes. Tackling PBU requires a multifaceted intervention that targets all possible sources of influence simultaneously.

REFERENCES

Badaracco, J. L., & Webb, A. P. (1995). Business ethics: A view from the trenches. *California Management Review, 37*(2), 8–28.

Bandura, A. (1999). Moral disengagement in the perpetration of inhumanities. *Personality and Social Psychology Review, 3*(2), 93–209.

Brown, M. E., Trevino, L. K., & Harrison, D. (2005). Ethical leadership: A social learning perspective for construct development and testing. *Organizational Behavior and Human Decision Processes, 97*(2), 117–134.

Janis, I. (1982). *Groupthink* (2nd ed.). Boston: Houghton Mifflin.

Johnson, C. E. (2009). *Meeting the ethical challenges of leadership: Casting light or shadow* (3rd ed.). San Francisco: Sage.

Kerr, S. (1975). On the folly of rewarding A while hoping for B. *Academy of Management Journal, 18*(4), 769–783.

Lepper, M. R., Greene, D., & Nisbett, R. E. (1973). Undermining children's extrinsic motivation with extrinsic reward: A test of the "Over-Justification Hypothesis." *Journal of Personality and Social Psychology, 28*(1), 129–137.

Lonkevich, D. (1997). Flexibility urged in profits and ethics demands. *National Underwriter: Property and Casualty/Risk and Benefits Management Edition, 101*(17), 8–10.

Milgram, S. (1974). *Obedience to authority*. New York: Harper & Row.

Patterson, K., Grenny, J., Maxfield, D., McMillan, R., & Switzler, A. (2008). *Influencer: The power to change anything*. New York: McGraw-Hill.

Rogers, E. (1995). *Diffusion of innovations* (4th ed.). New York: Free Press.

Shaw, M. E., & Sulzer, J. L. (1964). An empirical test of Heider's levels in attribution of responsibility. *Journal of Abnormal and Social Psychology, 69*(1), 39–46.

Skarlicki, D. P., & Latham, G. P. (2005). How can training be used to foster organizational justice? In J. Greenberg & J. A. Colquitt (Eds.), *Handbook of organizational justice* (pp. 499–522). Mahway, NJ: Lawrence Erlbaum.

How to Do Well *and* Do Good

Rosabeth Moss Kanter

Harvard Business School

Can companies do well by doing good? That question is asked frequently—but beware of false choices when considering it. In business, there is not a strict dichotomy between doing well and doing good; it is not an either-or proposition. Instead, social good and profitability are among the criteria by which companies make choices. In reality, any company is better off creating both bottom-line and societal benefits—and creating synergies between them.

That does not mean executives should lose sight of the goals and mission of the business, however. There is no reason certain kinds of good works—say, merely giving away money to areas unrelated to the business—should provide particular strategic advantage for a company. But if a company can integrate the benefits that it offers society more closely into its existing business, that integration can be very sensible and beneficial for the business. For example, people within the organization may recognize internal capabilities which they can build and develop to address a problem in society while simultaneously enlarging the company's market.

As I describe in my book *Supercorp*, some smart companies are finding that including a focus on benefiting society in their mission can help yield competitive advantage. These companies, which are in the vanguard of creating a new business model, have discovered that a commitment to tackling societal problems can be one aspect of creating a corporate culture that leads to high performance and profits. (However, it is important to note that no company exemplifies this aspirational approach to management completely; all companies have flaws, and none live up to their ideals all of the time.)

There are a number of reasons why incorporating social good into strategy can help a company's long-term performance. For one thing, it can help strengthen a company in the eyes of a number of important constituencies: its customer base, its employee base and the general public. In particular, a mission that includes serving society can help motivate employees—especially a younger generation of employees who seek meaning in work. Having strong values and a mission that incorporates social good can also help a multinational corporation maintain a cohesive culture despite a diverse global workforce, mergers and acquisitions, and fast-changing markets for the company's products or services. (In other words, if a company has strong values, what exactly the company sells may change, but what it stands for does not.) Finally, thinking about societal problems can help spark innovative thinking by exposing employees to new ideas and perspectives.

The Procter & Gamble Company (P&G) provides a good example of how thinking about societal problems can help a company innovate within its traditional lines of business. P&G turned around and grew its business in Brazil by having employees live in and observe low-income households (an untapped market for P&G in Brazil at the time), creating numerous new products and product modifications, such as affordable, environmentally friendly and hands-friendly detergent for those without washing machines who hand-washed clothes. The ideas spread to other countries and influenced the introduction of Tide Basic in the U.S. P&G employees attributed this success to the need to live up to the company's purpose of creating products that "improve the lives of the world's consumers"—which motivated them to see how they could contribute to improving the lives of lower-income consumers in their country.

More generally, the reason many companies now want to enter emerging markets is because those markets are growing. But companies are discovering that there are so many social and environmental needs in emerging markets that those needs can be a good source of new product or service ideas that people will pay for, such as the ability to have access to banking services through a cell phone. Providing such services is good business—and yet also helps develop society.

In the long run, companies have to do some good for society to continue doing well financially. Fundamentally, companies that are not somehow doing good will eventually hit problems. Those problems may not be immediate, but one of the things technology has done is make information about a company's behavior anywhere in the world more readily available to people all around the globe. We have more public awareness of what's going on all over the world, and, in the Internet age, problems with a company's behavior can get aired again and again.

If companies take a proactive approach, they can turn this increased consumer awareness into a benefit. Take Seattle-based Starbucks Corp. A number of years ago, some consumers began asking questions about the conditions in which coffee was grown and urging the company to carry fair-trade coffee. Since then, Starbucks has benefited greatly by consumers knowing that the company offers fair-trade coffee—and that Starbucks has a reputation for social responsibility.

The importance of benefiting society is not, however, a new phenomenon in business. Historically, businesses have always done well by doing good. If a company sold defective cars, it would not stay in business very long, so instead, car companies sell safety as one of their benefits, and safety is a societal good. Today, we take for granted many of the societal goods that companies supply.

Offering societal benefit does not necessarily mean doing things outside the realm of your business—and it is not restricted to only some types of companies. Consider the example of London-based Diageo plc, one of the world's largest producers of alcoholic beverages, in Kenya, where Diageo's East African Breweries Limited subsidiary launched a new beer that brought societal benefits. Traditionally thought of as part of a "sin industry," beer does not seem like an obvious candidate for helping address social problems. But in Kenya, beer is popular, and cheap; unregulated home brews accounted for more than half of national alcohol consumption. Unfortunately, home brews using impure water and sometimes even laced with ethanol or battery acid had became a serious public health problem, causing lost productivity and even blindness because of the dangerous additives sometimes used. As a result, after it successfully introduced "Senator," a popular, inexpensive beer brewed to international standards, Diageo was recognized in Africa for contributing to lower rates of blindness and increased workplace productivity.

For business leaders, thinking about creating societal benefits through business should be part of setting strategy; in today's complex world, it has become part of a manager's toolkit for growing and developing a business over the long term. It is no longer a sideline activity or an afterthought, but a mainstream imperative that influences every aspect of the business. If, as a business leader, you start thinking deeply about growing your company in the future—and where new markets are going to be—that means thinking about unsolved problems and unmet needs. Solving some of those problems and addressing some of those needs can, if done well, benefit both your company and the larger world.

The Secrets to Successful Strategy Execution

Gary L. Neilson
Booz & Company

Karla L. Martin
Booz & Company

Elizabeth Powers
Booz & Company

A brilliant strategy, blockbuster product, or breakthrough technology can put you on the competitive map, but only solid execution can keep you there. You have to be able to deliver on your intent. Unfortunately, the majority of companies aren't very good at it, by their own admission. Over the past five years, we have invited many thousands of employees (about 25 percent of whom came from executive ranks) to complete an online assessment of their organizations' capabilities, a process that's generated a database of 125,000 profiles representing more than 1,000 companies, government agencies, and not-for-profits in over 50 countries. Employees at three out of every five companies rated their organization weak at execution—that is, when asked if they agreed with the statement "Important strategic and operational decisions are quickly translated into action," the majority answered no.

Execution is the result of thousands of decisions made every day by employees acting according to the information they have and their own self-interest. In our work helping more than 250 companies learn to execute more effectively, we've identified four fundamental building blocks executives can use to influence those actions—clarifying decision rights, designing information flows, aligning motivators, and making changes to structure. (For simplicity's sake we refer to them as decision rights, information, motivators, and structure.)

In efforts to improve performance, most organizations go right to structural measures because moving lines around the org chart seems the most obvious solution and the changes are visible and concrete. Such steps generally reap some short-term efficiencies quickly, but in so doing address only the symptoms of dysfunction, not its root causes. Several years later, companies usually end up in the same place they started. Structural change can and should be part of the path to improved execution, but it's best to think of it as the capstone, not the cornerstone, of any organizational transformation. In fact, our research shows that actions having to do with decision rights and information are far more important— about twice as effective—as improvements made to the other two building blocks. (See Figure 1, "What Matters Most to Strategy Execution.")

Take, for example, the case of a global consumer packaged-goods company that lurched down the reorganization path in the early 1990s. (We have altered identifying details in this and other cases that follow.) Disappointed with company performance, senior management did what most companies were doing at that time: They restructured. They eliminated some layers of management and broadened spans of control. Management-staffing costs quickly fell by 18 percent. Eight years later, however, it was déjà vu. The layers had crept back in, and spans of

**Figure 1   What Matters Most to
Strategy Execution**

When a company fails to execute its strategy, the first thing managers often think to do is restructure. But our research shows that the fundamentals of good execution start with clarifying decision rights and making sure information flows where it needs to go. If you get those right, the correct structure and motivators often become obvious.

Relative Strength (out of 100)

control had once again narrowed. In addressing only structure, management had attacked the visible symptoms of poor performance but not the underlying cause—how people made decisions and how they were held accountable.

This time, management looked beyond lines and boxes to the mechanics of how work got done. Instead of searching for ways to strip out costs, they focused on improving execution—and in the process discovered the true reasons for the performance shortfall. Managers didn't have a clear sense of their respective roles and responsibilities. They did not intuitively understand which decisions were theirs to make. Moreover, the link between performance and rewards was weak. This was a company long on micromanaging and second-guessing, and short on accountability. Middle managers spent 40 percent of their time justifying and reporting upward or questioning the tactical decisions of their direct reports.

Armed with this understanding, the company designed a new management model that established who was accountable for what and made the connection between performance and reward. For instance, the norm at this company, not unusual in the industry, had been to promote people quickly, within 18 months to two years, before they had a chance to see their initiatives through. As a result, managers at every level kept doing their old jobs even after they had been promoted, peering over the shoulders of the direct reports who were now in charge of their projects and, all too frequently, taking over. Today, people stay in their positions longer so they can follow through on their own initiatives, and they're still

around when the fruits of their labors start to kick in. What's more, results from those initiatives continue to count in their performance reviews for some time after they've been promoted, forcing managers to live with the expectations they'd set in their previous jobs. As a consequence, forecasting has become more accurate and reliable. These actions did yield a structure with fewer layers and greater spans of control, but that was a side effect, not the primary focus, of the changes.

THE ELEMENTS OF STRONG EXECUTION

Our conclusions arise out of decades of practical application and intensive research. Nearly five years ago, we and our colleagues set out to gather empirical data to identify the actions that were most effective in enabling an organization to implement strategy. What particular ways of restructuring, motivating, improving information flows, and clarifying decision rights mattered the most? We started by drawing up a list of 17 traits, each corresponding to one or more of the four building blocks we knew could enable effective execution—traits like the free flow of information across organizational boundaries or the degree to which senior leaders refrain from getting involved in operating decisions. With these factors in mind, we developed an online profiler that allows individuals to assess the execution capabilities of their organizations. Over the next four years or so, we collected data from many thousands of profiles, which in turn allowed us to more precisely calibrate the impact of each trait on an organization's ability to execute. That allowed us to rank all 17 traits in order of their relative influence. (See Figure 2, "The 17 Fundamental Traits of Organizational Effectiveness.")

Ranking the traits makes clear how important decision rights and information are to effective strategy execution. The first eight traits map directly to decision rights and information. Only 3 of the 17 traits relate to structure, and none of those ranks higher than 13th. We'll walk through the top five traits here.

1. *Everyone has a good idea of the decisions and actions for which he or she is responsible.* In companies strong on execution, 71 percent of

Figure 2   The 17 Fundamental Traits of Organizational Effectiveness

From our survey research drawn from more than 26,000 people in 31 companies, we have distilled the traits that make organizations effective at implementing strategy. Here they are, in order of importance.

RANK	ORGANIZATION TRAIT	STRENGTH INDEX (OUT OF 100)
1	Everyone has a good idea of the decisions and actions for which he or she is responsible.	81
2	Important information about the competitive environment gets to headquarters quickly.	68
3	Once made, decisions are rarely second-guessed.	58
4	Information flows freely across organizational boundaries.	58
5	Field and line employees usually have the information they need to understand the bottom-line impact of their day-to-day choices.	55
6	Line managers have access to the metrics they need to measure the key drivers of their business.	48
7	Managers up the line get involved in operating decisions.	32
8	Conflicting messages are rarely sent to the market.	32
9	The individual performance-appraisal process differentiates among high, adequate, and low performers.	32
10	The ability to deliver on performance commitments strongly influences career advancement and compensation.	32
11	It is more accurate to describe the culture of this organization as "persuade and cajole" then "command and control."	29
12	The primary role of corporate staff here is to support the business units rather than to audit them.	29
13	Promotions can be lateral moves (from one position to another on the same level in the hierarchy).	29
14	Fast-track employees here can expect promotions more frequently than every three years.	23
15	On average, middle managers here have five or more direct reports.	19
16	If the firm has a bad year, but a particular division has a good year, the division head would still get a bonus.	13
17	Besides pay, many other things motivate individuals to do a good job.	10

BUILDING BLOCKS
☐ Decision rights ☐ Information ☐ Motivators ■ Structure

individuals agree with this statement; that figure drops to 32 percent in organizations weak on execution.

Blurring of decision rights tends to occur as a company matures. Young organizations are generally too busy getting things done to define roles and responsibilities clearly at the outset. And why should they? In a small company, it's not so difficult to know what other people are up to. So for a time, things work out well enough. As the company grows, however, executives come and go, bringing in with them and taking away different expectations, and over time the approval process gets ever more convoluted and murky. It becomes increasingly unclear where one person's accountability begins and another's ends.

One global consumer-durables company found this out the hard way. It was so rife with people making competing and conflicting decisions that it was hard to find anyone below the CEO who felt truly accountable for profitability. The company was organized into 16 product divisions aggregated into three geographic groups—North America, Europe, and International. Each of the divisions was charged with reaching explicit performance targets, but functional staff at corporate headquarters controlled spending targets—how R&D dollars were allocated, for instance. Decisions made by divisional and geographic leaders were routinely overridden by functional leaders. Overhead costs began to mount as the divisions added staff to help them create bulletproof cases to challenge corporate decisions.

Decisions stalled while divisions negotiated with functions, each layer weighing in with questions. Functional staffers in the divisions (financial analysts, for example) often deferred to their higher-ups in corporate rather than their division vice president, since functional leaders were responsible for rewards and promotions. Only the CEO and his executive team had the discretion to resolve disputes. All of these symptoms fed on one another and collectively hampered execution—until a new CEO came in.

The new chief executive chose to focus less on cost control and more on profitable growth by redefining the divisions to focus on consumers. As part of the new organizational model, the CEO designated accountability for profits unambiguously to the divisions and also gave them the authority to draw on functional activities to support their goals (as well as more control of the

About the Data

We tested organizational effectiveness by having people fill out an online diagnostic, a tool comprising 19 questions (17 that describe organizational traits and two that describe outcomes).

To determine which of the 17 traits in our profiler are most strongly associated with excellence in execution, we looked at 31 companies in our database for which we had responses from at least 150 individual (anonymously completed) profiles, for a total of 26,743 responses. Applying regression analysis to each of the 31 data sets, we correlated the 17 traits with our measure of organizational effectiveness, which we defined as an affirmative response to the outcome statement, "Important strategic and operational decisions are quickly translated into action." Then we ranked the traits in order, according to the number of data sets in which the trait exhibited a significant correlation with our measure of success within a 90 percent confidence interval. Finally, we indexed the result to a 100-point scale. The top trait—"Everyone has a good idea of the decisions and actions for which he or she is responsible"—exhibited a significant positive correlation with our success indicator in 25 of the 31 data sets, for an index score of 81.

---

budget). Corporate functional roles and decision rights were recast to better support the divisions' needs and also to build the cross-divisional links necessary for developing the global capabilities of the business as a whole. For the most part, the functional leaders understood the market realities—and that change entailed some adjustments to the operating model of the business. It helped that the CEO brought them into the organizational redesign process, so that the new model wasn't something imposed on them as much as it was something they engaged in and built together.

2. *Important information about the competitive environment gets to headquarters quickly.* On average, 77 percent of individuals in strong-execution organizations agree with this statement, whereas only 45 percent of those in weak-execution organizations do.

Headquarters can serve a powerful function in identifying patterns and promulgating best practices throughout business segments and geographic regions. But it can play this coordinating role only if it has accurate and up-to-date market intelligence. Otherwise, it will tend to impose its own agenda and policies rather than defer to operations that are much closer to the customer.

Consider the case of heavy-equipment manufacturer Caterpillar.[1] Today it is a highly successful $45 billion global company, but a generation ago, Caterpillar's organization was so badly misaligned that its very existence was threatened. Decision rights were hoarded at the top by functional general offices located at headquarters in Peoria, Illinois, while much of the information needed to make those decisions resided in the field with sales managers. "It just took a long time to get decisions going up and down the functional silos, and they really weren't good business decisions; they were more functional decisions," noted one field executive. Current CEO Jim Owens, then a managing director in Indonesia, told us that such information that did make it to the top had been "whitewashed and varnished several times over along the way." Cut off from information about the external market, senior executives focused on the organization's internal workings, overanalyzing issues and second-guessing decisions made at lower levels, costing the company opportunities in fast-moving markets.

Pricing, for example, was based on cost and determined not by market realities but by the pricing general office in Peoria. Sales representatives across the world lost sale after sale to Komatsu, whose competitive pricing consistently beat Caterpillar's. In 1982, the company posted the first annual loss in its almost-60-year history. In 1983 and 1984, it lost $1 million a day, seven days a week. By the end of 1984, Caterpillar had lost a billion dollars. By 1988, then-CEO George Schaefer stood atop an entrenched bureaucracy that was, in his words, "telling me what I wanted to hear, not what I needed to know." So he convened a task force of "renegade" middle managers and tasked them with charting Caterpillar's future.

Ironically, the way to ensure that the right information flowed to headquarters was to make sure the right decisions were made much further down the organization. By delegating operational responsibility to the people closer to the action, top executives were free to focus on more global strategic issues. Accordingly, the company reorganized into business units, making each accountable for its own P&L statement. The functional general offices that had been all-powerful ceased to exist, literally overnight. Their talent and expertise, including engineering, pricing, and manufacturing, were parceled out to the new business units, which could now design their own products, develop their own manufacturing processes and schedules, and set their own prices. The move dramatically decentralized decision rights, giving the units control over market decisions. The business unit P&Ls were now measured consistently across the enterprise, as return on assets became the universal measure of success. With this accurate, up-to-date, and directly comparable information, senior decision makers at headquarters could make smart strategic choices and trade-offs rather than use outdated sales data to make ineffective, tactical marketing decisions.

Within 18 months, the company was working in the new model. "This was a revolution that became a renaissance," Owens recalls, "a spectacular transformation of a kind of sluggish company into one that actually has entrepreneurial zeal. And that transition was very quick because it was decisive and it was complete; it was thorough; it was universal, worldwide, all at one time."

3. *Once made, decisions are rarely second-guessed.* Whether someone is second-guessing depends on your vantage point. A more senior and broader enterprise perspective can add value to a decision, but managers up the line may not be adding incremental value; instead, they may be stalling progress by redoing their subordinates' jobs while, in effect, shirking their own. In our research, 71 percent of respondents in weak-execution companies thought that decisions were being

second-guessed, whereas only 45 percent of those from strong-execution organizations felt that way.

Recently, we worked with a global charitable organization dedicated to alleviating poverty. It had a problem others might envy: It was suffering from the strain brought on by a rapid growth in donations and a corresponding increase in the depth and breadth of its program offerings. As you might expect, this nonprofit was populated with people on a mission who took intense personal ownership of projects. It did not reward the delegation of even the most mundane administrative tasks. Country-level managers, for example, would personally oversee copier repairs. Managers' inability to delegate led to decision paralysis and a lack of accountability as the organization grew. Second-guessing was an art form. When there was doubt over who was empowered to make a decision, the default was often to have a series of meetings in which no decision was reached. When decisions were finally made, they had generally been vetted by so many parties that no one person could be held accountable. An effort to expedite decision making through restructuring—by collocating key leaders with subject-matter experts in newly established central and regional centers of excellence—became instead another logjam. Key managers still weren't sure of their right to take advantage of these centers, so they didn't.

The nonprofit's management and directors went back to the drawing board. We worked with them to design a decision-making map, a tool to help identify where different types of decisions should be taken, and with it they clarified and enhanced decision rights at all levels of management. All managers were then actively encouraged to delegate standard operational tasks. Once people had a clear idea of what decisions they should and should not be making, holding them accountable for decisions felt fair. What's more, now they could focus their energies on the organization's mission. Clarifying decision rights and responsibilities also improved the organization's ability to track individual achievement, which helped it chart new and appealing career-advancement paths.

4. *Information flows freely across organizational boundaries.* When information does not flow

horizontally across different parts of the company, units behave like silos, forfeiting economies of scale and the transfer of best practices. Moreover, the organization as a whole loses the opportunity to develop a cadre of up-and-coming managers well versed in all aspects of the company's operations. Our research indicates that only 21 percent of respondents from weak-execution companies thought information flowed freely across organizational boundaries whereas 55 percent of those from strong-execution firms did. Since scores for even the strong companies are pretty low, though, this is an issue that most companies can work on.

A cautionary tale comes from a business-to-business company whose customer and product teams failed to collaborate in serving a key segment: large, cross-product customers. To manage relationships with important clients, the company had established a customer-focused marketing group, which developed customer outreach programs, innovative pricing models, and tailored promotions and discounts. But this group issued no clear and consistent reports of its initiatives and progress to the product units and had difficulty securing time with the regular cross-unit management to discuss key performance issues. Each product unit communicated and planned in its own way, and it took tremendous energy for the customer group to understand the units' various priorities and tailor communications to each one. So the units were not aware, and had little faith, that this new division was making constructive inroads into a key customer segment. Conversely (and predictably), the customer team felt the units paid only perfunctory attention to its plans and couldn't get their cooperation on issues critical to multiproduct customers, such as potential trade-offs and volume discounts.

Historically, this lack of collaboration hadn't been a problem because the company had been the dominant player in a high-margin market. But as the market became more competitive, customers began to view the firm as unreliable and, generally, as a difficult supplier, and they became increasingly reluctant to enter into favorable relationships.

Once the issues became clear, though, the solution wasn't terribly complicated, involving little

more than getting the groups to talk to one another. The customer division became responsible for issuing regular reports to the product units showing performance against targets, by product and geographic region, and for supplying a supporting root-cause analysis. A standing performance-management meeting was placed on the schedule every quarter, creating a forum for exchanging information face-to-face and discussing outstanding issues. These moves bred the broader organizational trust required for collaboration.

5. *Field and line employees usually have the information they need to understand the bottom-line impact of their day-to-day choices.* Rational decisions are necessarily bounded by the information available to employees. If managers don't understand what it will cost to capture an incremental dollar in revenue, they will always pursue the incremental revenue. They can hardly be faulted, even if their decision is—in the light of full information—wrong. Our research shows that 61 percent of individuals in strong-execution organizations agree that field and line employees have the information they need to understand the bottom-line impact of their decisions. This figure plummets to 28 percent in weak-execution organizations.

We saw this unhealthy dynamic play out at a large, diversified financial-services client, which had been built through a series of successful mergers of small regional banks. In combining operations, managers had chosen to separate front-office bankers who sold loans from back-office support groups who did risk assessments, placing each in a different reporting relationship and, in many cases, in different locations. Unfortunately, they failed to institute the necessary information and motivation links to ensure smooth operations. As a result, each pursued different, and often competing, goals.

For example, salespeople would routinely enter into highly customized one-off deals with clients that cost the company more than they made in revenues. Sales did not have a clear understanding of the cost and complexity implications of these transactions. Without sufficient information, sales staff believed that the back-end people were sabotaging their deals, while the support groups considered the front-end people to be cowboys. At year's end, when the data were finally reconciled, management would bemoan the sharp increase in operational costs, which often erased the profit from these transactions.

Executives addressed this information misalignment by adopting a "smart customization" approach to sales. They standardized the end-to-end processes used in the majority of deals and allowed for customization only in select circumstances. For these customized deals, they established clear back-office processes and analytical support tools to arm sales-people with accurate information on the cost implications of the proposed transactions. At the same time, they rolled out common reporting standards and tools for both the front- and back-office operations to ensure that each group had access to the same data and metrics when making decisions. Once each side understood the business realities confronted by the other, they cooperated more effectively, acting in the whole company's best interests—and there were no more year-end surprises.

CREATING A TRANSFORMATION PROGRAM

The four building blocks that managers can use to improve strategy execution—decision rights, information, structure, and motivators—are inextricably linked. Unclear decision rights not only paralyze decision making but also impede information flow, divorce performance from rewards, and prompt work-arounds that subvert formal reporting lines. Blocking information results in poor decisions, limited career development, and a reinforcement of structural silos. So what to do about it?

Since each organization is different and faces a unique set of internal and external variables, there is no universal answer to that question. The first step is to identify the sources of the problem. In our work, we often begin by having a company's employees take our profiling survey and consolidating the results. The more people in the organization who take the survey, the better.

Once executives understand their company's areas of weakness, they can take any number of actions. Figure 3, "Mapping Improvement Tactics to the Building Blocks," shows 15 possible steps that can have an impact on performance. (The options listed represent only a sampling of the dozens of choices managers might make.) All of these actions are geared toward strengthening one or more of the 17 traits. For example, if you were to take steps to "clarify and streamline

Figure 3 Mapping Improvements to the Building Blocks: Some Sample Tactics

Companies can take a host of steps to improve their ability to execute strategy. The 15 here are only some of the possible examples. Every one strengthens one or more of the building blocks executives can use to improve their strategy-execution capability: clarifying decision rights, improving information, establishing the right motivators, and restructuring the organization.

- ☐ **Focus corporate staff on supporting business-unit decision making.**
- ☐ **Clarify and streamline decision making at each operating level.**
- ☐ **Focus headquarters on important strategic questions.**
- ☐☐ **Create centers of excellence by consolidating similar functions into a single organizational unit.**
- ☐☐☐ **Assign process owners to coordinate activities that span organizational functions.**
- ☐☐ **Establish individual performance measures.**
- ☐ **Improve field-to-headquarters information flow.**
- ☐ **Define and distribute daily operating metrics to the field or line.**
- ☐☐ **Create cross-functional teams.**
- ☐ **Introduce differentiating performance awards.**
- ☐ **Expand nonmonetary rewards to recognize exceptional performers.**
- ☐☐ **Increase position tenure.**
- ☐☐ **Institute lateral moves and rotations.**
- ☐ **Broaden spans of control.**
- ☐ **Decrease layers of management.**

| BUILDING BLOCKS | ☐ Decision rights | ☐ Information | ☐ Motivators | ☐ Structure |

decision making" you could potentially strengthen two traits: "Everyone has a good idea of the decisions and actions for which he or she is responsible," and "Once made, decisions are rarely second-guessed."

You certainly wouldn't want to put 15 initiatives in a single transformation program. Most organizations don't have the managerial capacity or organizational appetite to take on more than five or six at a time. And as we've stressed, you should first take steps to address decision rights and information, and then design the necessary changes to motivators and structure to support the new design.

To help companies understand their shortcomings and construct the improvement program that will have the greatest impact, we have developed an organizational-change simulator. This interactive tool accompanies the profiler, allowing you to try out different elements of a change program virtually, to see which ones will best target your company's particular area of weakness. (For an overview of the simulation process, see the box "Test Drive Your Organization's Transformation.")

To get a sense of the process from beginning to end—from taking the diagnostic profiler, to formulating your strategy, to launching your organizational transformation—consider the experience of a leading insurance company we'll call Goodward Insurance. Goodward was a successful company with strong capital reserves and steady revenue and customer growth. Still, its leadership wanted to further enhance execution to deliver on an ambitious five-year strategic agenda that included aggressive targets in customer growth, revenue increases, and cost reduction, which would require a new level of teamwork. While there were pockets of cross-unit collaboration within the company, it was far more common for each unit to focus on its own goals, making it difficult to spare resources to support another unit's goals. In many cases there was little incentive to do so anyway: Unit A's goals might require the involvement of Unit B to succeed, but Unit B's goals might not include supporting Unit A's effort.

The company had initiated a number of enterprisewide projects over the years, which had been completed on time and on budget, but these often had to be reworked because stakeholder needs hadn't been sufficiently taken into account. After launching a shared-services center, for example, the company had to revisit its operating model and processes when units began hiring shadow staff to focus on priority work that the center wouldn't expedite. The center might decide what technology applications, for instance, to develop on its own rather than set priorities according to what was most important to the organization.

In a similar way, major product launches were hindered by insufficient coordination among departments. The marketing department would develop new coverage options without asking the claims-processing group whether it had the ability to process the claims. Since it didn't, processors had to create expensive manual work-arounds when the new kinds of claims started pouring in. Nor did marketing ask the actuarial department how these products would affect the risk profile and reimbursement expenses of the company, and for some of the new products, costs did indeed increase.

To identify the greatest barriers to building a stronger execution culture, Goodward Insurance gave the diagnostic survey to all of its 7,000-plus employees and compared the organization's scores on the 17 traits with those from strong-execution companies. Numerous previous surveys (employee-satisfaction, among others) had elicited qualitative comments identifying the barriers to execution excellence. But the diagnostic survey gave the company quantifiable data that it could analyze by group and by management level to determine which barriers were most hindering the people actually charged with execution. As it turned out, middle management was far more pessimistic than the top executives in their assessment of the organization's execution ability. Their input became especially critical to the change agenda ultimately adopted.

Through the survey, Goodward Insurance uncovered impediments to execution in three of the most influential organizational traits:

*   *Information did not flow freely across organizational boundaries.* Sharing information was never one of Goodward's hallmarks, but managers had always dismissed the mounting anecdotal evidence of poor cross-divisional information flow as "some other group's problem." The organizational diagnostic data, however, exposed such plausible deniability as

an inadequate excuse. In fact, when the CEO reviewed the profiler results with his direct reports, he held up the chart on cross-group information flows and declared, "We've been discussing this problem for several years, and yet you always say that it's so-and-so's problem, not mine. Sixty-seven percent of [our] respondents said that they do not think information flows freely across divisions. This is not so-and-so's problem—it's our problem. You just don't get results that low [unless it comes] from everywhere. We are all on the hook for fixing this."

Contributing to this lack of horizontal information flow was a dearth of lateral promotions. Because Goodward had always promoted up rather than over and up, most middle and senior managers remained within a single group. They were not adequately apprised of the activities of the other groups, nor did they have a network of contacts across the organization.

• *Important information about the competitive environment did not get to headquarters quickly.* The diagnostic data and subsequent surveys and interviews with middle management revealed that the wrong information was moving up the org chart. Mundane day-to-day decisions were escalated to the executive level—the top team had to approve midlevel hiring decisions, for instance, and bonuses of $1,000—limiting Goodward's agility in responding to competitors' moves, customers' needs, and changes in the broader marketplace. Meanwhile, more important information was so heavily filtered as it moved up the hierarchy that it was all but worthless for rendering key verdicts. Even if lower-level managers knew that a certain project could never work for highly valid reasons, they would not communicate that dim view to the top team. Nonstarters not only started, they kept going. For instance, the company had a project under way to create new incentives for its brokers. Even though this approach had been previously tried without success, no one spoke up in meetings or stopped the project because it was a priority for one of the top-team members.

• *No one had a good idea of the decisions and actions for which he or she was responsible.* The general lack of information flow extended to decision rights, as few managers understood where their authority ended and another's began. Accountability even for day-to-day decisions was unclear, and managers did not know whom to ask for clarification. Naturally, confusion over decision rights led to second-guessing. Fifty-five percent of respondents felt that decisions were regularly second-guessed at Goodward.

To Goodward's credit, its top executives immediately responded to the results of the diagnostic by launching a change program targeted at all three problem areas. The program integrated early, often symbolic, changes with longer-term initiatives, in an effort to build momentum and galvanize participation and ownership. Recognizing that a passive-aggressive attitude toward people perceived to be in power solely as a result of their position in the hierarchy was hindering information flow, they took immediate steps to signal their intention to create a more informal and open culture. One symbolic change: the seating at management meetings was rearranged. The top executives used to sit in a separate section, the physical space between them and the rest of the room fraught with symbolism. Now they intermingled, making themselves more accessible and encouraging people to share information informally. Regular brown-bag lunches were established with members of the C-suite, where people had a chance to discuss the overall culture-change initiative, decision rights, new mechanisms for communicating across the units, and so forth. Seating at these events was highly choreographed to ensure that a mix of units was represented at each table. Icebreaker activities were designed to encourage individuals to learn about other units' work.

Meanwhile, senior managers commenced the real work of remedying issues relating to information flows and decision rights. They assessed their own informal networks to understand how people making key decisions got their information, and they identified critical gaps. The outcome was a new framework for making important decisions that clearly specifies who owns each decision, who must provide input, who is ultimately

Test-Drive Your Organization's Transformation

You know your organization could perform better. You are faced with dozens of levers you could conceivably pull if you had unlimited time and resources. But you don't. You operate in the real world.

How, then, do you make the most educated and cost-efficient decisions about which change initiatives to implement? We've developed a way to test the efficacy of specific actions (such as clarifying decision rights, forming cross-functional teams, or expanding nonmonetary rewards) without risking significant amounts of time and money. You can go to www.simulator-orgeffectiveness.com to assemble and try out various five-step organizational-change programs and assess which would be the most effective and efficient in improving execution at your company.

You begin the simulation by selecting one of seven organizational profiles that most resembles the current state of your organization. If you're not sure, you can take a five-minute diagnostic survey. This online survey automatically generates an organizational profile and baseline execution-effectiveness score. (Although 100 is a perfect score, nobody is perfect; even the most effective companies often score in the 60s and 70s.)

Having established your baseline, you use the simulator to chart a possible course you'd like to take to improve your execution capabilities by selecting five out of a possible 28 actions. Ideally, these moves should directly address the weakest links in your organizational profile. To help you make the right choices, the simulator offers insights that shed further light on how a proposed action influences particular organizational elements.

Once you have made your selections, the simulator executes the steps you've elected and processes them through a Web-based engine that evaluates them using empirical relationships identified from 31 companies representing more

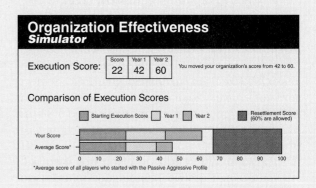

than 26,000 data observations. It then generates a bar chart indicating how much your organization's execution score has improved and where it now stands in relation to the highest-performing companies from our research and the scores of other people like you who have used the simulator starting from the same original profile you did. If you wish, you may then advance to the next round and pick another five actions. What you will see is illustrated above.

The beauty of the simulator is its ability to consider—consequence-free—the impact on execution of endless combinations of possible actions. Each simulation includes only two rounds, but you can run the simulation as many times as you like. The simulator has also been used for team competition within organizations, and we've found that it engenders very engaging and productive dialogue among senior executives.

While the simulator cannot capture all of the unique situations an organization might face, it is a useful tool for assessing and building a targeted and effective organization-transformation program. It serves as a vehicle to stimulate thinking about the impact of various changes, saving untold amounts of time and resources in the process.

accountable for the results, and how results are defined. Other longer-term initiatives include:

- Pushing certain decisions down into the organization to better align decision rights with

the best available information. Most hiring and bonus decisions, for instance, have been delegated to immediate managers, so long as they are within preestablished boundaries relating to numbers hired and salary levels.

Being clear about who needs what information is encouraging cross-group dialogue.

- Identifying and eliminating duplicative committees.
- Pushing metrics and scorecards down to the group level, so that rather than focus on solving the mystery of *who* caused a problem, management can get right to the root cause of *why* the problem occurred. A well-designed scorecard captures not only outcomes (like sales volume or revenue) but also leading indicators of those outcomes (such as the number of customer calls or completed customer plans). As a result, the focus of management conversations has shifted from trying to explain the past to charting the future—anticipating and preventing problems.
- Making the planning process more inclusive. Groups are explicitly mapping out the ways their initiatives depend on and affect one another; shared group goals are assigned accordingly.
- Enhancing the middle management career path to emphasize the importance of lateral moves to career advancement.

Goodward Insurance has just embarked on this journey. The insurer has distributed ownership of these initiatives among various groups and management levels so that these efforts don't become silos in themselves. Already, solid improvement in the company's execution is beginning to emerge. The early evidence of success has come from employee-satisfaction surveys: Middle management responses to the questions about levels of cross-unit collaboration and clarity of decision making have improved as much as 20 to 25 percentage points. And high performers are already reaching across boundaries to gain a broader understanding of the full business, even if it doesn't mean a better title right away.

Execution is a notorious and perennial challenge. Even at the companies that are best at it—what we call "resilient organizations"—just two-thirds of employees agree that important strategic and operational decisions are quickly translated into action. As long as companies continue to attack their execution problems primarily or solely with structural or motivational initiatives, they will continue to fail. As we've seen, they may enjoy short-term results, but they will inevitably slip back into old habits because they won't have addressed the root causes of failure. Such failures can almost always be fixed by ensuring that people truly understand what they are responsible for and who makes which decisions—and then giving them the information they need to fulfill their responsibilities. With these two building blocks in place, structural and motivational elements will follow.

ENDNOTE

1. The details for this example have been taken from Gary L. Neilson and Bruce A. Pasternack, *Results: Keep What's Good, Fix What's Wrong, and Unlock Great Performance* (Random House, 2005).

Six Sigma at Your Service

Peter Guarraia
Bain and Company

Gib Carey
Bain and Company

Alistair Corbett
Bain and Company

Klaus Neuhaus
Bain and Company

Lean Six Sigma is justly famous for making a better car or widget. Since 1986 at least (the roots of the movement go back to the early 1900s), the Six Sigma process—made popular by companies such as Motorola, Toyota, and General Electric—has become a time-tested methodology for repeatedly producing products while using the most exacting tolerances for quality control. But now service companies are pushing this defect-reduction methodology to a new level. Banks are trying to use it to jump-start growth, telecommunications giants are aiming it at costs, and even retailers are trying it out to serve their customers better.

There's only one trouble: diffused too far and wide, even the best quality control initiative can become a scattershot technique without a focus on major results. All too often, companies train and deploy cadres of Lean Six Sigma experts, known as "black belts," only to see few major improvements from their work. Proof of this comes in a recent Bain & Company management survey of 184 companies. A full 80 percent of executives say their Lean Six Sigma efforts are failing to drive the anticipated value. Moreover, 74 percent say they are not gaining the expected competitive edge because they haven't achieved their savings targets.

Worse yet, unfocused Six Sigma efforts actually *slow* improvement efforts. When managers are unsure how best to deploy the Lean Six Sigma, black belts treat all problems, big and small, with the same approach. Attacking problems piecemeal is virtually guaranteed to yield less than optimal solutions.

And because of this ground-up perspective, it is also almost certain to miss those critical, company-wide improvements that will make the biggest difference.

Such a lack of focus becomes even more critical today, when a sharp fall-off in business needs to be addressed with bold, extremely targeted measures—measures that can substantially increase cost savings, trim the most waste, and boost revenues. In other words, it is management's job to know exactly where to put black belts to work, not let them wander off on their own quests.

A BUSINESS X-RAY?

Some services companies have discovered the solution to this lack of focus. They've added a step at the beginning of the Lean Six Sigma process—something we call a diagnostic X-ray—that allows them to identify the biggest opportunities for gains. Performed by a small advance team of black belts, the diagnostic X-ray consists of three steps.

First, the X-Ray team starts with a procedure called "value-stream mapping." This reveals the largest sources of wasted time and materials in current processes, which also yields the best places for reducing costs.

Next, the team checks the efficiency of company processes (such as bill collecting) by measuring actual performance against internal and external benchmarks, including competitors. The test allows the team to gauge shortcomings and establish improvement targets.

Finally, they set priorities, focusing on process improvements that will have the biggest impact.

Once let loose on the thorniest problems, black belts can then do what they do best: improving inefficient or poorly designed processes through Lean Six Sigma's famed DMAIC sequence—define, measure, analyze, improve, and control. Simply put, these steps are now sighted on the targets of highest opportunity.

Some may find it surprising that a quality-improvement technique can "translate" from a factory floor to, say, a claims office. And it's equally surprising that service firms are helping perfect this methodology. But when you consider that the goal of pleasing valuable customers—whether it's the buyer of a Lexus or a holder of a large annuity—is the same for all businesses, it's understandable how Lean Six Sigma can fit the bill. Indeed, as Lean Six Sigma spreads, it is helping a growing range of companies meet a vast range of new objectives—everything from spending less on equipment to redesigning stores for efficiency to performing a better job of stocking and replenishing inventory. In fact, perhaps the best way to see how Six Sigma is reshaping the services industry is to take a quick tour of an array of companies who have made quality the hallmark of providing a service instead of building a product.

NEW CLAIMS TO FAME: AN INSURANCE COMPANY FINDS PROFITS IN ITS CLAIMS PROCESSES

A laser-guided approach to Six Sigma, for example, recently paid off for a major UK insurance company that found itself at a crossroads. Fast-changing market conditions were jeopardizing the insurer's ambitious plans to grow its market share by 150 percent. And that wasn't the worst of it. The insurer also estimated that if it did nothing, half its profits were at risk. Management knew in its bones that the root problem was inefficient internal processes, but various random efforts to streamline them had failed. So the company decided to try a different approach: perform a diagnostic X-ray of its business to know where to focus its efforts.

Instead of spreading out all over the company, the X-ray team's first move was to develop a map of the insurer's claims processes. That exercise revealed the largest problem in high definition: costs were out of control. The reason? Too many activities. There were, in fact, 189 separate ones, by actual count. The team's creation of a business-process fact base that involved looking at every step in the claims process, from account setup to claims handling, revealed this jumble.

Analysis showed that the claims process could be broken down into seven major steps. Each step was then broken out so that the team could look at time spent and staffing levels. This breakdown helped the company zero in on major inefficiencies. It also resulted in a significant discovery; the insurer was spending the same amount of time and money on each and every claim—be it for a highly valued customer such as a global corporation or a single individual.

But while the team could now clearly see where to improve costs, it still needed to know by how much. In other words, what was the ultimate goal of the Six Sigma process? For that, they turned to benchmarking. Looking internally, they found both the best-in-process efficiency—and the worst. For example, in one unit, the claims-handling process represented 11 percent of total costs, while at another business unit it was only 6 percent.

The X-ray team also found that the placement process—gathering customer information, placing insurance, issuing certificates, handing over processing to the back office, and chasing client payments—took twice as long in one business unit as it did in another. Armed with this knowledge, the firm began to develop standardized processing times.

Benchmarking also helped the team track its costs by activity—an insight that allowed the insurer to better understand client risk. The company was able to see where it made money, exposing the most- to least-profitable business units. This cost curve starkly showed how the company could tailor service to better align its costs to what clients actually value. It also allowed the insurer to break its customers into three value segments based on overall profitability.

But a management question remained: Were all the possible changes literally worth the effort? Or were some more lucrative than others? Data to determine that would be developed in the final phase of the X-ray team's work, in which the group came up with solid numbers for adopting each of the various solutions. Out of this investigation came a list of the top three opportunities for boosting revenues and cost savings, while simultaneously better meeting customer needs.

This critical winnowing process—skipped in the past in the rush to deal with myriad problems—set the stage for unleashing the entire horde of trained black belts. Not only did they now have their marching orders, the black belts also had a set of priorities. What were they?

First, they set out to re-price some policies—charging more to clients who were expensive to serve and raising prices for smaller clients who demanded tailored service. Within the first year, re-pricing alone earned the insurer an additional 10 percent of the company's profits.

Second, the black belts worked on a series of organizational changes, such as standardizing the processing times across business units—boosting profits by an additional 10 percent.

Third, over a span of 30 months, the insurer invested in technology upgrades that included sophisticated cost-modelling tools. This investment allowed business units to calculate such details as how many hours employees need to spend on gold-standard clients versus other customer segments. The cost analysis also challenged staffing assumptions, such as how large a sales team it needed. Ultimately, the IT investments helped deliver an additional 30 percent profit increase.

CREDIT WHERE CREDIT IS DUE: A BANK SPEEDS ITS CREDIT PROCESSES

In a case that sounds like a foreshadowing of today's financial turmoil, a major Australian commercial bank not long ago found itself in need of just such a Lean Six Sigma diagnostic X-ray when its local residential-property market suddenly cratered in an economic downturn. Moving quickly, it shifted its focus to its robust commercial banking division—and grew handily.

To make the transition, the bank knew that it needed to overhaul credit processes at every level—from loan handling to credit policies to the sales force and credit approval teams. Unfortunately, its existing loan-approval procedure did not set speed records; in fact, it plodded. The unfortunate result: new investments from valued customers who needed—and expected—quick action were going elsewhere. In a nutshell, the bank had to become more agile, increasing the speed, accuracy, and efficiency of credit processes and decision making.

Beyond identifying the problem, the diagnostic X-ray team pinpointed major trouble spots. Among these was a lack of uniformity in loan application approvals. This institutional randomness resulted in delays and errors requiring costly rework. Compounding the problem, credit officers too often made lending decisions based on personal judgement. Long-standing institutional lending policies were observed in the breach. On top of that, all loans—large and small—had to move through the same initial layers of approval, causing even more delays.

This glacial pace was not true throughout the bank; the diagnostic team discovered this fact after benchmarking different bank branches. For example, the team found that one branch expedited loan application decisions by simply assigning a credit officer to work alongside loan managers on the bank floor. With mapping and benchmarking results in hand, the X-ray team then prioritized a small list of big opportunities. One of the most effective was to develop a fast track for processing lower-risk loans. Today, nearly half of all loan applications get expedited treatment, and errors requiring rework have dropped by 25 percent. As a result, even as its real estate loan operations continue to languish, new commercial business is fuelling growth at 2.5 times the market.

HOLDING THE PHONE: A MOBILE PHONE COMPANY MAKES MORE OF ITS CALL CENTER

Lean Six Sigma can help companies not only on the ground in real estate but over the airways. A leading European mobile phone company was bleeding customers. It knew exactly why it had the problem, if not exactly how to fix it: the company's customer service center was abysmal. Swamped with calls, the center's operators had racked up a poor track record for resolving customer problems. And, with its limited budget, the center wasn't likely to provide its own solution.

The company thus had to devise a two-pronged solution: a new call-center strategy that would transform the facility from a cost center into a revenue generator, and the ability to zero in on the most critical initiatives to improve customer service. The diagnostic X-ray laid the groundwork for the Lean Six Sigma work that led to the twin solutions. The X-ray showed that the biggest cost saver (and customer boon) would be to redesign systems so operators could resolve problems on the first call. This not only allowed the company to eliminate hand-offs but also made it possible to reduce staff count.

To turn the call center into a revenue generator, the X-ray process conducted customer and competitor surveys to create three distinct customer groups, based on their customer value. That ultimately led to devising service plans for each customer segment. And who better to sell that than someone who has just created a satisfied customer? Indeed, by knowing exactly where to focus its efforts, the mobile phone company's new call-center strategy has improved customer service and started generating revenue. Thanks to its newly empowered operators, the company is on track to save 25 percent of its operating costs in less than three years.

A BEAUTIFUL MARRIAGE: A BANK INTEGRATES MERGED OPERATIONS

Six Sigma can also be applied to a company's culture. Indeed, a company's personality not only affects how it treats, or mistreats, customers, it can threaten the success of mergers. So discovered a major U.S. financial institution faced with a culture clash after an acquisition.

The story is common enough in the world of mergers and acquisitions. In this case, when a U.S. merchant bank acquired its major competitor, management was divided on how to run the merged business. The vastly different business practices generated friction that drove a number of top performers from the acquired company out the door. Hardly a defect-reduction problem, one might think. Yet management deployed the diagnostic X-ray to build a consensus around how best to integrate operating practices and quickly identify top areas for improvement. In effect, the tool moved the discussion from personalities to processes.

In the value-stream mapping phase, the diagnostic team compared loan-approval processes. What became immediately apparent was that while the merchant bank was better at assessing larger, riskier deals, its approvals took much longer. On the other hand, the acquired bank was faster and delivered better customer service—but its deals typically were smaller. The team's follow-up benchmarking of competitor practices showed that the merchant bank had many unnecessary approval steps, which frustrated its best customers—new and old.

To quickly plug the brain drain, the team prioritized dramatic improvements that all could buy into. At the top of the list was a loan approval system with a fork in the path: lower-risk deals would take a simpler route, while harder deals would go through a more rigorous, but standardized, process. The solution incorporated the best of both cultures: the acquired bank's speed and predictability with the acquiring bank's sophistication for handling larger deals.

Ultimately, the merger stayed intact. And the solution allowed the merged entity to accelerate approvals and increase its average deal size by 35 percent.

SWEATING THE DETAILS: A RETAILER BECOMES MORE CUSTOMER-FRIENDLY

While attacking big problems with Lean Six Sigma produces the most dramatic results, sometimes that overall picture is composed of a welter of details. In the United States, one big-box retail market leader figured it needed to wade into the minutiae of store activities to stave off inroads from general merchandise discounters and to keep its strong growth on track.

The cost of its initial solution—making stores more customer friendly—was skyrocketing faster than it was delivering results. The retailer needed a customer-focused strategy that it could afford over the long haul. Like its namesake, the preliminary X-ray had to reveal what was below the surface.

The X-ray team laboriously mapped more than 100 operations in store after store to determine how many hours were spent each week on routine tasks—everything from opening and closing stores to pricing, taking inventory, restocking shelves, and filling orders placed through the retailer's website. Mundane tasks that consumed lots of time went to the top of list for streamlining. The members also compared the workings of individual outlets and their efficiency.

No process was too small for review. One time waster that emerged was the requirement that employees fill out a lengthy form each time a customer requested price matching. What for? Employees reported that the form was never looked at again. Also on the list: the haphazard system for filling online orders. While the retailer was encouraging customers to place online orders for pickup at a nearby store, nobody at the store necessarily knew where the merchandise was. The team found out why: unless an employee was stationed at a computer, the store had no way of knowing when an order arrived. Also, items were stacked virtually anywhere, causing delays as employees searched for the right product.

The X-ray team unearthed another important failing: the stocking system was supposed to keep high-profit items on store shelves. Indeed, it was more important to have a $100 high-margin core item in stock than a $5 accessory. But by watching employees and checking merchandise holes on shelves, the team realized that workers weren't following the high-margin inventory plan. Why not? Employees said the plan was too detailed to follow.

Back at corporate headquarters, the team prioritized these minuscule findings that added up to huge savings. Once the black belts were dispatched, they eventually generated an incredible $50 million in annual cost reductions from a variety of small process tweaks and from simply revamping systems for inventory restocking and online order pickups.

BLACK BELTS REQUIRED?

A "black belt" is an employee trained in Six Sigma approaches and technology with deep experience using the techniques to deliver change to the business. Sometimes the diagnostic X-ray is enough in itself; you don't always need to send in black belts to fix a problem. Black belts are often most valuable when attacking well-defined opportunities, but may not be ideal for leading the X-ray process. Also, small efforts requiring less analytical or process rigor might not require a blackbelt's experience. That's exactly what a UK energy company found when it sought ways to curb operating costs that had ballooned to some $1 billion annually.

When the X-ray team mapped and benchmarked costs related to all aspects of customer service—from pursuing new customers, and setting up accounts, to measuring energy use and collecting payments—it unearthed several cost-saving opportunities. But the biggest one was a total surprise. The company discovered that nearly 50 percent of its meter-reading expenses were avoidable, largely by reducing the number of times it reads a meter. No team of black belts was needed to simply change the schedules.

But that didn't mean they were totally unnecessary. As the energy provider ranked other cost-saving opportunities, it found additional quick wins. In the end, the detailed X-ray of the energy provider's major processes showed how it could reduce 30 percent of its total costs while at the same time more effectively competing for new customers and improving customer service. When the black belts were set to work on these initiatives, challenges worthy of allocating their valuable time and skills, the energy leader was back on track to achieve stronger cost performance.

AT YOUR SERVICE

Looking to the future, service companies' increasing adoption of quality-improvement techniques that have already been in use for at least five decades (in the case of Toyota) may have other surprising outcomes. This is especially likely as new sources of energy are developed in the face of wildly fluctuating petroleum costs and global warming. After all, Chevrolet, which plans to introduce its all-electric Volt vehicle in 2010, has already begun negotiations with electric utilities to ensure enough inexpensive electricity is available to power them. That tremendous demand for electricity will certainly test current procedures in the utility industry (in both senses of "current") and probably employ a lot of black belts. But in the broader perspective, the convergence of Lean Six Sigma across industries may be arriving just as many industries converge into a new and better model for operating in the 21st century.

RESOURCES

Sandra L. Furterer (editor), *Lean Six Sigma in Service,* CRC Press, 2009.

Mismanaging Pay and Performance

Rupert Merson
London Business School

Performance measurement and management mechanisms, and reward systems in particular, are cornerstones of every management system. Not surprisingly, they are the focus of much thinking under the heading of corporate governance and the subject of many rules, regulations and guidance notes in the governance codes. But they are not just subjects of corporate governance, they are levers for delivering governance as well. Rules and regulations are imposed by external agencies; but, for governance to have real impact and influence, it needs to be internalised. Managers need to mean it, not just say it and write it.

There are two fundamental premises here: (1) that measurement is a key, if not the key, component of a control system, and (2) that people respond to remuneration systems (if you pay them to do something, they are more likely to do it than if their pay is actually determined by something else). The first premise is summed up in a maxim: "If you cannot measure it, you cannot manage it." Switch this around and we have a recipe for perfect management: make sure you have the right measurement tools and you can manage anything.

However, what is true of rules—that they struggle to capture the detail of reality in a meaningful and manageable way—is also true of management and measurement systems. The more we wrestle with our businesses, the more we seek to perfect the dashboards and the indicators that tell us how our businesses are performing. And the more we try to deduce actionable conclusions from them, the more it becomes evident that much of what really matters within the business continues to escape our attention, despite the increasingly sophisticated measurement tools at our disposal. Businesses are always far too complicated to be reduced to the easily measurable. Indeed, it is almost as if what really matters cannot be measured at all! This is because businesses at heart are about people, and people refuse to respond logically to management stimuli in the way they are supposed to.

UNREAL COMFORTS

There are many instances of managers seeking unreal comforts in the easily measurable and coming, as a consequence, to unfortunate ends. One particularly meaningful illustration has come to be called "McNamara's fallacy," after Robert McNamara, U.S. Secretary of Defence at the time of the Vietnam war, who was reduced to measuring military success in terms of the ratio of Viet Cong casualties to U.S. casualties. Logical reductionism of this type has led decision takers down all sorts of management blind alleys. As Charles Handy outlines it: "The first step down the alley is to measure whatever can be easily measured. This is OK as far as it goes. The second step is to disregard what cannot be easily measured or to give it an arbitrary quantitative value. This is artificial and misleading. The third step is to presume that what cannot be measured is not really important. This is blindness. The fourth step is to say what cannot be measured does not exist. This is suicide."

Rupert Merson, "Mismanaging Pay and Performance," *Business Strategy Review* 21:2 (Summer 2010), pp. 54–57. Reprinted with permission of John Wiley & Sons, Inc.

That measurement misses aspects of business performance that are critical or can foster distorted behaviour is well known—not that such knowledge stops managers from inventing mechanisms for measuring performance. In October 2006, the UK Healthcare Commission reported that there were serious and significant failings in the way that Stoke Mandeville Hospital in Aylesbury, Buckinghamshire, had dealt with Clostridium difficile infections. It noted that managers had not learned from the first outbreak; and, consequently, when the second occurred, senior managers did not bring it quickly under control because they focused on objectives such as the government's targets on waiting times in the accident and emergency departments. Infected patients were kept in or put on open wards rather than in isolation facilities, and several died.

One of the most common, and increasingly controversial, manifestations of a connection between measurement and management is performance-related remuneration. Unfortunately, the mechanics of connecting pay to performance are difficult to establish effectively. If you want individuals to be influenced by their remuneration, then you have to avoid making their incentive packages too complicated.

The fact is that most senior team members' roles are complicated, and the individuals who hold them are responsible for dozens of variables, many of which sit uncomfortably with each other. To connect remuneration to all aspects of such an individual's performance is an impossible task. To connect remuneration to just a selection of the most important of an individual's deliverables is to invite dysfunctional behaviour, as staff will be encouraged to focus on those aspects of their roles that will increase their incomes at the expense of those that do not.

For any senior role, therefore, it can be difficult to develop individually tailored performance targets. For those at the top, rather than look for personal targets, the sensible thing for many is to look for corporate targets. If the business does well, then the individual will do well. This takes us right into the heart of corporate governance, of course: if what you really want is to align the interests of directors and the interests of the businesses they lead, make sure directors are rewarded when these businesses do well. But determining when a business does well can, in itself, be difficult. Determining profit is an art, not a matter of fact. Seemingly healthy profits one year might be bought at the cost of the long-term health of the company.

The tidiest way of connecting a director's remuneration to the interests of the business or the interests of shareholders is to give shares and to require the director to hold them for an extended period of time. Cash is inherently short term, while equity surely rewards the long-term performance that shareholders seek. Equity should be used to foster or reward commitment.

PREPARED TO PAY?

If you are looking to recruit or reward knowledge or experience, you should be prepared to pay for it when you use it—with cash. Many businesses are not this discriminating. Equity is now an expected component of the package of a senior member of any business, big or small, public or private. But equity as remuneration is better in theory than it is in practice. Directors can do very well; but, in a bear market, the value of shares will go down anyway. Conversely, many a fool has been rewarded for being lucky enough to ride off the back of a bear market. It is also a little presumptuous to assume that equity-based remuneration will align directors and shareholders. The problem is not necessarily the directors. Pinning down the motives of the ultimate shareholders in a listed company, in which blocks of shares are controlled by institutions on behalf of individuals, is difficult; and even if you assume that all such shareholders want is a decent return, then this in itself is difficult to reconcile with the real decisions that directors have to take every day, laden with uncertainty, risk and the pressures of entrepreneurship.

Giving and receiving shares in a private company has its own complications. Being given a slice of the equity of an unlisted company is not the same as being given equity in a business whose shares have a ready market. To be given equity inevitably begs questions about when those shares might be sold and in what circumstances. A new member of the management team with equity is thus likely to have half an eye on a financial strategy that will enable him to realise his investment—which might have very little to do with the interests, long or short term, of the other shareholders. Hopefully, equity or equity-based remuneration should force a discussion about the alignment of personal and corporate objectives, but it might not guarantee the alignment in itself. Indeed, it might provoke the opposite. As one observer claims, "If you want managers to act in their shareholders' interests, take away their company stock." Perhaps less extreme is the perception that many owner-managers use equity-based remuneration as a strategy for not paying market salaries in the first place.

In recent years, executives have received options over equity as an important component of their remuneration packages. For many businesses thinking about equity as an incentive, share options can look like another way of having your cake and eating it. Assuming options are granted at least at current business value, an option will only become a share if the business increases in value. It is easy to be cynical about options. Dotcoms in their boom years shed share options like confetti, which did little to improve their credibility. Option schemes are inherently complicated and expensive to establish. Also, because the individual probably will not have to give much (if anything) for them at the outset, it is easy to see option schemes as all gain and no pain, and therefore not so great a motivation as they might at first appear. Additionally, as with equity, options are only meaningful if the holder can at least imagine a time when they are realisable.

But the real truth about options is that neither companies giving them, nor shareholders receiving them, have really thought of them as aligning the interests of shareholders and management. When options sink "under water" (that is, the price of the shares subject to the option declines in value to a position at which it would be cheaper to buy the shares on the market rather than via the option), some companies have been only too quick to reprice the options using the lower share price as a reference point, arguing that managers still need an "incentive" even though their performance to date has only resulted in the share price declining. Actions of this sort on the part of companies demonstrate that, for many, an option is really a deferred performance-related bonus masquerading as a mechanism for aligning managers with shareholders. As with most fudges, it often achieves neither objective.

BONUSES DESPITE PERFORMANCE

If a manager's performance does not warrant a bonus, the manager should not receive a bonus and should be disappointed. To give out bonuses when performance is poor is "shameful," as U.S. President Barack Obama has put it. That a company believes it needs to give bonuses despite poor performance suggests that base pay is wrong and options are being used as an excuse for not paying properly to start with, that remuneration is connected to the wrong measure of performance, or that the reward has nothing to do with performance in the first place. Re-pricing options has the effect, therefore, of alienating managers from shareholders, not aligning them.

Much of the governance fuss about remuneration has been generated not so much by the nature of the remuneration given to directors as by the amount. It is only too easy to pick examples, there being so many. Let's take one of the more obvious—Richard Fuld, erstwhile CEO of Lehman Brothers. In one interchange, U.S. House of Representatives Oversight Committee Chairman, Henry Waxman, reeled off details of Mr Fuld's large art collection, several houses and what he said was the "half a billion dollars" that the Chief Executive had taken home over his time at the helm of the company. He then asked Fuld to compare all this with the losses faced by shareholders and the damage done to the wider economy. "Is that fair?" Mr. Waxman asked. Mr. Fuld answered: "The majority of my compensation came in stock. The vast majority of stock I got I still owned at the point of our filing. . . . The $500 million number is not accurate, although it is still a large number." When an individual is earning as much from a listed business as Fuld was from Lehman Brothers, even if a large part of the remuneration is in the form of shares, it is misleading to suggest that his interests were being aligned with those of his shareholders. Fuld's remuneration was at the expense of his shareholders—and that was even before the bank he led went bust. The Combined Code of the UK's Financial Reporting Council states:

> Levels of remuneration should be sufficient to attract, retain and motivate directors of the quality required to run the company successfully, but a

company should avoid paying more than is necessary for this purpose. A significant proportion of executive directors' remuneration should be structured so as to link rewards to corporate and individual performance.

Every element of this prescription is a tall order. However, a few questions are worth asking. What does "sufficient" mean? At what level is a company paying "more than is necessary"? What is a "significant proportion"? And does linking performance to reward work anyway?

Management thinker Alfie Kohn argues that performance-based reward ultimately acts as a disincentive. The concept operates all right in the short term; but, in the long term, performance-based reward just does not work. Kohn even argues that performance-based reward discourages risk taking: individuals will do what they need to do to get the reward, and then no more.

INTRACTABLE PROBLEM

Unfortunately for Kohn's thesis, people do have to get paid something, and his book is much weaker when making recommendations for remuneration strategies that do not punish. Remuneration continues, therefore, to be an intractable problem for those responsible for governance frameworks inside and outside organisations. These individuals should at least:

- Appreciate the complex nature of the problem they are dealing with;
- Recognise and protect their companies and their stakeholders from the consequences of an over-powerful director and her influence on her own remuneration;
- Recognise how reward for achievement is different from incentive for performance not yet delivered; and
- Appreciate how, at a level that differs from individual to individual, incentive turns into greed, something that is quite different and in nobody's interests.

Establishing the right remuneration levels in a small business brings challenges all its own. The first finance director in a business, the recruitment of whom marks a key stage in the evolution of governance in a growing business, can seem particularly expensive. He is quite likely to be the highest-paid employee in a young business—but as one venture capitalist put it: "I always tell companies we're looking to invest in that a quality finance director will more than pay for himself within a year." It is not just the fact that accountants are expensive that accounts for the differential salary. More than money motivates a founding entrepreneur, but any senior manager recruited to an established business has motivations inherently different from those of the founder. Money will almost inevitably mean more. Many businesses without a decent finance director will argue that they cannot afford one and will leave the recruitment of a finance director until it's too late—when the control of the most important governance element in the business is in the hands of someone who is unqualified and unable to add serious value.

Not surprisingly, many founders of new businesses look for ways of structuring a remuneration package that allows the business to keep the cake while giving the candidate the illusion of eating it. Giving directors options, or equity, is often seen as a route to making them very rich. In smaller businesses it is more likely to be an excuse for not paying them properly in the first place.

It can be forgotten that performance management is not just a matter of remuneration. Appraisal, assessment, training and development should be key components of any governance framework, as should forms of non-financial recognition such as title, promotion, status and authority.

Appraisal, training and development are live issues. The costs of not taking them seriously far outweigh the time and financial costs required to invest in them properly. Professional institutes and organisations acknowledge this and oblige their members to comply with continuing professional development. The day may come when the profession of management will benefit by establishing similar requirements.

COMPANY INDEX

A

A. T. Kearney, 163, R-41
A&E networks, 335
A&W, 282
ABB, 250
ABC network, 199, 335
Aber Diamond, 230
Accenture, 163, 267, 286
Accor, 205
Acer, 192
Adelphia Communications, 347, 450
Adidas, 86, 362
Aer Lingus, 217
Aerospatiale, 267, 392
Affiliated Computer Services, 297
Agilent Technologies, 328
Ahold, 116
AIG Insurance, 347, R-85, R-86
Air France, R-45
Air France–KLM, 362
Airbus industries, 259, R-16
Alberto-Culver Company, 438
  corporate culture, 439
Alcan Aluminum, 416
Aldi, 116
Allegro Manufacturing, 305
Allstate Insurance, 232
Amazon.com, 194, 382, 384, 416,
    421, 423, 448, 455, R-33, R-34,
    R-38, R-46
  first-mover advantage, 224
America Movil, 51, 214
American Airlines, 239
American Express, 236
American Lock, 309
American Productivity and Quality
    Center, 164, 413
America Online, R-79
AM-FM, Inc., 230
Amgen, motivation and rewards at,
    427
Am Tran Technology, 203
Anaheim Angels, 335
Anheuser-Busch Companies, 117, 186
Animal Compassion Foundation, 365
AOL/Time Warner, R-79, R-80, R-81

Apple Inc., 51, 56, 57, 82, 145, 148,
    152, 157, 198, 216, 231–232, 236,
    301, 340, 448, R-33, R-34, R-35,
    R-38, R-49, R-90
  Supplier Code of Conduct, 341
  supplier problems, 341
Aprica strollers, 310
Arsenal Digital Solutions, 267
Arthur Andersen, 349, R-85, R-86
Aston Martin, 201
AT&T, 295, R-81, R-82, R-83
Audi, 207, R-50
Avon Products, Inc., 82, 198, 457
  financial statements, 176–178

B

Bain & Company, R-73, R-107
Banana Republic, 127
B&Q, 358
Bank of America, 227, 229, 236, 299,
    416
Barnes & Noble, R-46
Bata, 192
BBC, 198
Beaird-Poulan, 304
Bell helicopters, 309
Ben & Jerry's Homemade, 151, 366
Benchmarking Exchange, 163, 412
Benchnet, 163
Berkshire Hathaway, 311
Bernard L. Madoff Investment
    Securities, 349
  investment fraud, 350–351
Bernzomatic, 310
Best Buy, 64, 203, 211, 427
Best Practices, LLC, 163, 412–413
BHP Billiton, 51
Biotherm, 334
Black & Decker, 305
BMW, 75, 145, 194, 207, 212, 252,
    362, 416
Body Shop, 366
Boeing Company, 267, 392, 416, R-16
Bonefish Grill, 334
Booz & Company, R-96
Boston Beer Company, 231

Boston Consulting Group, 418
BP Amoco, 261
Braun, 328
Brennan's Restaurant, R-28
Bridgestone Corporation, 246
Bridgestone/Firestone, 116
Bright House Networks, 238
British Aerospace, 267
British Airways, 217, 420
British American Tobacco plc, R-78
British Petroleum (BP), 422
British Sky Broadcasting, 228
British Telecommunications, 295, 357
Broadcom, 391
Brown and Williamson Inc., R-85
BTR, 324
Burger King, R-17
Burghy, 299
Business Roundtable, 356
BYD, R-47, R-53

C

Cadillac, 207
Callaway Golf Company, 168
Calphalon, 310
Canon, 386
Carrabba's Italian Grill, 333
Carrefour, 115, 116, 167
Carrier, 334
Castrol, 261, 269
Caterpillar, 79, 362, 416, R-99–R-100
CBS network, 199
CEMIG, 362
Ceridian Corporation, 338
Cessna, 309
Chamak, R-6, R-7
Chanel, 127, 194, 275
Charles Schwab Corporation, R-14
Chery, R-47, R-53
Chevrolet Volt, 367, R-112
Chevron, 94, 392
Chicago Tribune, 56
Chik-Fil-A, 365
Chopin Vodka, 167
ChotuKool, R-4, R-8
Christie's, R-48

Chrysler Corporation, 229, 239, 259
Ciba Vision, 418
Cirque du Soleil, 219
Cisco-Nokia-Siemens alliance, 267
Cisco Systems, 228, 237, 244, 267, 274, 328, 362, 382, 384, 448, R-33, R-40, R-68, R-83
Citicorp, R-81
Citigroup, 324, 347
Citizen Holding Company, 302
Citroën, R-50, R-52
Classic Sports Network, 335
Clear Channel Communications, 239
   mergers and acquisitions, 230
Clear Channel Worldwide, 229
Clearwire, 238
Coach, 232, 236
Cobra Golf, 168
Coca-Cola Company, 51, 145, 196, 228, 229, 358, 362, 363, 367, R-43, R-73, R-75, R-77
   strategic vision, 73
Coca-Cola Hellenic Bottling, R-75
Colgate-Palmolive Company, 235, R-73, R-76
Comcast, 238, R-82
Compaq Computer, R-81
Conair Corporation, 305
Continental Airlines, 239, 430
Continental Tires, 116
Coors, 117
Corning, 302
Corus Steel, R-68
Costco Wholesale, 203, 211
Countrywide Financial, 450
Courvoisier, 309
Craftsman, 109
Craigslist, R-38
Cray, 386
Credit Suisse, 416
CSR Europe, 360
Ctrip, defense against rivals, 285
CVS, 201
Cyworld, R-35

D

Dacia, R-42
Daihatsu, R-52
Daimler AG, 79, 229, 237, 239, 388
Daimler-Benz Aerospace, 267
DaimlerChrysler, 237, 266
Danaher, R-81
DeBeers Group, 230, 299

Deer Park Refinery, 237
Dell, Inc., 94, 121, 188, 197, 214, 236, 239, 286, 304, 349, 382–384, 392, R-42, R-79
   in China, 282–283
Deloitte Touche Tohmatsu, R-14
Delphi, R-53
Delta Air Lines, 239
DePuy International, 343
Deutsche Bank, 227
DHL, 420
Diageo plc, R-95
Dillard's, 127
Disney Automation, 239
Disney Channel, 335
Disney Cruise Line, 335
Disneyland Paris, 272
Disney Radio, 335
Disney Store chain, 335
Dollar Rent-a-Car, 228
Dollar Thrifty, 228
Domino's Pizza, 203
Doritos, R-40
Ducati Motorcycles, 194, 197, 232, 255, 401
Dunkin' Donuts, 56
DuPont, 416
Duracell, 305, 328, R-77

E

E. & J. Gallo Winery, 391
East African Breweries Limited, R-95
EasyJet, R-45
eBay, 56, 201, 421, 448, R-48
Electronic Arts, 146
Electronic Data Systems, 286, 382
Eli Lilly, R-62, R-63
Emerge Logistics, 284
Emerson Electric, 304, 416
Enron Corporation, 91, 347, 348–349, 351–352, 450, R-85, R-86, R-89
Entergy Corporation, 436
Epson, 60
Ernst & Young, 364
ESPN, 335
ESPN2, 335
Etap Hotels, 205
European Aeronautic Defense and Space Company, 267
Expedia, 239, 285
ExxonMobil, 261
EzTravel, 285

F

Facebook, 201, R-34, R-35, R-38
Fannie Mae, 89, R-85, R-86
   failure of corporate governance, 90–91
FAW Xiali, R-52
Federal Express, 57, 75, 167, 194, 219, 403, 416, 420, 442
Fendi, 127
Ferrari, 202, 203, 255
Fiat-Chrysler, 229
Fiat, 259
First Energy, R-9
Fleming's Prime Steakhouse & Wine Bar, 334
Flickr, R-34, R-36, R-38
Focus Media, 286
Folgers, 305
FootJoy, 309
Ford Motor Company, 207, 218, 229, 259, 281, 388, R-18, R-19
Formule1 Hotels, 205
Forrester Research, R-81
Fortune Brands, 309
Four Seasons Hotels and Resorts, 57
Fox network, 199, 228, 331
Fox News, 228
Fox Sports, 228
Fox Studios, 228
FOXTEL, 228
Freddie Mac, 89
   failure of corporate governance, 90–91
Frito-Lay Inc., 442, R-77
Fuji, R-43
Fujian Nanping Nanfu Battery Company Ltd., R-77
Fuji-Xerox, 162
FX, 228

G

Gap Inc., 127
Garner, 334
Gatorade, R-83
Geely, R-47, R-51, R-52, R-53
Genentech, 239
General Electric, 82, 89, 155, 292, 309, 311, 312, 352, 362, 367, 382, 413–414, 416, 417, 425, 438, 455, 457, R-19, R-39, R-42, R-107
   corporate culture, 353–354
   talent development, 383–384

General Electric Capital, 309
General Electric Capital Mortgage, 416
General Electric Healthcare, 331
General Electric Leadership Development Center, 383
General Mills, 148, 302, 358
General Motors, 207, 218, 259, 267, 287, 386, 388, 395, 449, R-18, R-30, R-53
Gilbey's gin, 309
Gillette Company, 60, 305, 328, R-77
Giorgio Armani, 334
Glaceau, 228
GlaxoSmithKline, 357
Global Crossing, 91
Global Reporting Initiative, 361
Godiva Chocolates, 54, 202
Godrej & Boyce, R-3, R-4, R-8
Goldman Sachs, 382
Goodyear, 116, 232
Google Inc., 51, 216, 238, 382, 384, 416–417, 438, 448, 460, R-33, R-34, R-38, R-39
 corporate culture, 439
 motivation and rewards, 426
Grand Mercure Hotels, 205
Great Wall, R-53
Green Mountain Coffee Roasters, 364
Greenpeace, 73
Groupe Danone, R-73, R-78
Grupo Bimbo, 158
Gucci, 127, 194

H

H. J. Heinz Company, 117, R-40
Haägen-Dazs, 202
Haier, 192
Hallmark, 413
Hamilton Sundstrand, 334
Handy Dan Home Improvement, 217
Hanson Trust, 310
Harley-Davidson, 166, 232, 300
Harris Corporation, 408
HealthSouth, 347, 349, 450, R-86
Helena Rubinstein, 334
Hero Group, 289
Hertz Rent-A-Car, 228, R-79, R-82
Hewlett-Packard, 60, 76, 236, 239, 286, 328, 410, R-62, R-63
Hewlett-Packard/Compaq, R-81
Hillenbrand, 217

Hilton Hotels Corporation, 79, 93, 261, 264
Hindalco, 286
Hollinger International, 450, R-86
Home Depot, 187, 212, 217, 283–284, 358
Hometel, 201
Honda Motors, 109, 194, 207, 222, 252, 276, 386, 408, R-47
Honeywell International, 374
Hotmail, 225
HousingMaps.com, R-38
HSBC, 324
Hugo Boss, 392
Huiyuan Juice Group, 229
Hulu, 239
Hyundai Heavy Industries, 51, 57

I

IBM, 182, 235, 236, 239, 286, 362, 421, R-33, R-34, R-35, R-38, R-42, R-49, R-50
IKEA, 51, 64, 167, 194, 214, R-42
Inditex, 232
Infosys Technologies, 286
ING Insurance, 194, 392
Innosight Venture, R-2
Intel Corporation, 94, 113, 238, 239, 362, 382, 460, R-50
International Paper Company, 232
Internet Security Systems, 267
Intuit, R-33
iPad, 152
iPhone, 152, 194
iPod, 152

J

J. D. Edwards, R-83
J. D. Power & Associates, 207
J. D. Power Asia Pacific, 283
Jaguar, 207, 229
Jani-King International, 264
Japan Airlines, 261, 392
Jiffy Lube International, 56–57
Jim Beam, 309
JM Family Enterprises, 426
John Deere, 109, 358
 corporate social responsibility, 359–360
John F. Welch Leadership Development Center, 383

Johnson & Johnson, 56, 194, 328, 343, 357, 362, 460
 managing diversification, 329
 product lines, 334
Jollibee Foods, 286
Just Coffee, 158, 175–176
 value chain, 160

K

Kaiser Permanente, 421
Kellogg's, 281, R-80, R-81, R-82
Kentucky Fried Chicken, 80, 113, 264, 272
Kiehl's, 334
KinzCash, R-39
Kiva, R-40
KLM Royal Dutch Airlines, 266, 362, R-45
Kmart, 57, 127, R-30
Koch Industries, 68
Kohl's, 127
Komatsu, R-99
Kraft Foods, 227
Kraft-General Foods, R-80
Kroger, 116, 191

L

Lancôme, 334
Land Rover, 229
La Roche–Posay, 334
Lego, R-39–R-40
Lehman Brothers, R-115
Lender's Bagels, R-80, R-81, R-82
Lenovo, 286
Lenox, 310
Levelor, 310
Levi Strauss & Company, 73
Lexmark, 60
LGT Asset Management, 338
Lifetime channel, 335
Lincoln automobile, 207
Lincoln Electric Company, 149, 222
 motivation and rewards at, 426
Lipton Tea, 364
Little Tikes, R-82
Liz Claiborne, Inc., 460
Long John Silver's, 80, 282
L'Oréal, 302, 334, 403
Lotus Connections, 421
Louis Vuitton, 167
Lowe's, 212, 239

Lucent Technologies, 344
Lufthansa, 94, 420
LVMH, 299

M

Macy's, Inc., 127, R-9
Mahindra and Mahindra, 283
Maple Leaf Foods, 230
Marriott Hotels, 158, 261
Marriott International, 365, 456
Marsh & McLennan, 450, R-86
Maruti-Suzuki, 281
Marvel Comics, 301
Mary Kay Cosmetics, 68
Maserati, 255
Maybelline, 334
Mayo Clinic, 73
McAfee, 57
McDonald's, 51, 53, 64, 75, 113, 252,
    263, 264, 272, 281, 283, 286, 299,
    357, 392, 410, 456, 457, R-17
  company objectives, 80
  strategy, 55–56
McKesson, R-40
McKinsey & Company, 382, 425
Medco, R-83
MediaOne, R-82
Mercantec, 267
Mercedes-Benz, 56, 194, 207, 229, R-3
Merck & Company, R-83
Mercure Hotels, 205
Merrill Lynch, 229, 299
Metro AG, 115, 395
Mexx chain, 460
MGallery resorts, 205
Michelin, 116, 194, 252
Microsoft Corporation, 51, 65,
    74–75, 113, 226, 228, 239,
    267, 357, 370, 382, 408, 442,
    R-17–R-18, R-50
  company objectives, 80
  competition with Red Hat, 61
Microsoft Office, 194, 198
Microsoft TV Internet Protocol
    Television, 228
Microsoft Windows, 148
Microsoft Xbox 360, 217
Mighty Ducks NHL franchise, 335
Minute Maid, 228
Mitsubishi, 266, R-53
Moen faucets, 309
Motel 6, 205
Motobecane, 201

Motorola, 285, 416, R-107
M-PESA, R-5, R-7
Mr. Rooter, 113
Multon, R-75, R-77
MySpace, 239, R-38

N

Nano, R-3
National Hockey League, 214
National Tyre Services, 324
NBC network, 199, 331
NCR, R-81, R-83
Neiman Marcus, 127, 128
Neopets, R-35
Nestlé, 146, 202, 227, 252, 370, R-73
  differentiation strategy, 204–205
Nestlé Research Center, 74
Netscape, R-40
Newell Company, 388
Newell Rubbermaid, 310
NewsCorp, 228, 232, 250
Nextel, 229, 238
Nike, Inc., 73, 86, 361, 366, 382, 391
Nikki, 261
Nintendo, 51, 75, 246, R-18
Nintendo Wii, 217, 246
Nissan Motor Company, 82, 239,
    R-53, R-68
Nokia, 75, 239, 252, 285, 362, 416
Nokia Siemens Networks, 267
Nordstrom, 127, 134, 410, 438, 442
  motivation and rewards at, 426
Northwest Airlines, 239, 266
Northwest Water, 414
Norwest Corporation, 228
Novartis, 362, R-80
Novotel, 205
NTT Communications, 267, 295
Nucor Steel Corporation, 167, 188,
    190, 430, 453
  incentives and strategy, 429

O

Odwalla, 228
Oklahoma Gas & Electric, R-39
Oracle Corporation, 229, 267, R-83
Orbitz, 239
OSI Restaurants, 333–334
Osram, R-42
Otis Elevator, 272, 334, 421
Outback Steakhouse, 333
Owens Corning, 416

P

Pacific Gas & Electric, 363
Pactiv, 292
Pandora, 239
Papa John's Pizza, 203
Parmalat, 347, 450
Partner Alliances, R-55
Patagonia, 366
PayPal, R-48
Pemex, 237, 347
Pennzoil, 261
PeopleSoft, R-83
PepsiCo, 145, 186, 187, 196, 329, 362,
    363, 367, 382, 436, R-73, R-75
Perrigo Company, 201
Petra Foods Ltd., R-76
Pets.com, 224
Pfizer, Inc., 150
Philip Morris International, R-75,
    R-83
Philips Electronics, 416, R-42, R-62,
    R-65
Pillsbury, 148, 302
Ping Golf, 168
Pirelli, 116
Pizza Hut, 80, 113, 263–264
Polo/Ralph Lauren, 127
POM, R-43
Porsche, 203
Prada, 197
Pratt & Whitney, 334
Procter & Gamble, 51, 75, 188, 227,
    304, 305, 328, 360, 362, 382,
    R-43, R-56, R-66, R-75, R-77,
    R-94–R-95
  supplier to Walmart, 191
PSA, R-53
PT Djarum, R-74–R-75
PT Gudang Garam Tbk., R-75
PT Hanjaya Mandala Sampoerna
    Tbk., R-74–R-75
Pullman resorts, 205
Puma, 366

Q

Quaker Oats, R-81, R-83
Quaker State, 261
Qualserve Benchmarking
    Clearinghouse, 164
QuanJuDe, R-24–R-25
Qwest Communications, 91, 450,
    R-86

R

Radisson Hotels, 113
Rainforest Alliance Certified Farms, 364
Ralph Lauren, 127, 197, 232, 334
Red Bull GmbH, 194, 201
Red Hat, 60
  competition with Microsoft, 61
Refco, 450
Renault-Nissan, R-68
Rio Tinto, 94
Rite-Aid, 201, 347, 450
Ritz-Carlton Hotels, 57, 167
Roche AG, 362
Rolex, 56, 128, 194, 197, 275
Rolls-Royce, 197, 202
Ronald McDonald House, 357
Rossiya, R-73
Roto-Rooter, 264
Royal Bank of Scotland, 324
Royal Dutch Shell, 76, 347, 352, 365
  mission and core values, 77–78
Roy's Restaurant, 334
RPM, R-81
Rubbermaid, 388, R-82
Ryan Air, 167, 217, R-45

S

Safaricom, R-5, R-7
Safeway, 191, 201
Sage Software, R-9
SAIC-GM-Wulung Automotive Company, 267
SAIC (Shanghai Automotive Industrial Corporation), 267
Saks Fifth Avenue, 127, 128, 158
Sam's Club, 203, 211
Samsonite, 232
Samsung Electronics, 75, 239, 243, 274, 285, 362
  strategic vision, 73
Samsung Group, 243
Samuel Adams, 231
SAP, 414
Satyam Computer Services, 286
Schneiders, 230
Scotland Yard, 74
Scotty Cameron, 309
Sears, 127
Seat, R-50
7-Eleven Stores, 113, 264
7UP, R-83

Shanda, 284
Sharpie, 310
Shell Oil Company, 75, 237, 261
Sheraton Hotels, 261
Shu Uemura, 334
Siemens AG, 79, 267, 343, 416, 450
Sikorsky, 334
Singapore Airlines, 178, 420
Skoda, R-50
Sky Deutschland, 228
Sky Italia, 228
Sky News, 198
Smart cars, 229
Smucker's, 304
Snapper, 109
Snapple, R-81, R-83
Sofitel, 205
Sony Corporation, 74, 239, 301, 362, R-17–R-18
Sony PlayStation 3, 217
Sotheby's Auction House, R-48, R-86
Southwest Airlines, 51, 56, 163, 188, 190, 382, 420, 443, R-45
Sprint, 229, 238
St. Jude Children's Research Hospital, 351
Standard and Poor's, 368
Stanford Financial Group, 349, 450
  investment fraud, 350–351
Stanford International Bank, 350–351
Staples, 361, 367
STAR, 283
Starbucks Corporation, 56, 82, 86, 196, 219, 358, 367, 399, 456, R-46, R-95
Step2, R-82
Stihl, 212
Stoke Mandeville Hospital, R-114
Strategic Planning Institute, 163
Summers Group, 324
Sundaram Fasteners, 286–287
Sun Microsystems, 229, 267
Suzuki, 283

T

Taco Bell, 80, 264, 282
Taiwan Semiconductor, 391
Target Stores, 57, 127, 157, 305
Tata Group, R-42, R-68
Tata Motors, 94, 229
Tata Nano, 267
TATA SKY, 228

TCI, R-82
Telcel, 214
Televisa, 286
Telmex, 214
Tencent, 285
Tesco, 115, 395
Tesla Motors, 239
Tesler Roadster, 367
Textron, 309
Thalassa sea & spa resorts, 205
Therma-Tru, 309
3M Corporation, 150, 151, 167, 194, 362, 417–418, 457, R-19
Thrifty Rent-a-Car, 228
Tiffany & Company, 157, 197, 230, 256, 275
Time Warner, 331, R-79
Time Warner Cable, 238
Timex, 128
Titleist, 309
T.J. Maxx, 127
Toon Disney, 335
TopCoder, R-38
Toro, 109
Toshiba Corporation, 239, 436, R-17
Toyota Motor Corporation, 163, 192, 206, 217, 218, 239, 364, 386, 426, R-29, R-30, R-47, R-52, R-53, R-107
  best-cost provider strategy, 207
  production system, 387–388
Toyota Prius, 197
Trader Joe's, 202
Travelers/Citicorp, R-81
Travelocity, 239, 285
Trip Advisor, R-34
Tupperware, 457
Twentieth Century Fox, 228, 232
Twitter, R-34
Tyco International, 347, 348, 450
Tyson Foods, 367

U

UBS, strategic vision, 73
Ukrop's Food Group, R-14
  motivation and rewards at, 427
Uncle Chipps, R-77
Unifreight India Pvt., 403
Unilever Group, 151, 227, 281–282, 363–364, R-74
United Airlines, 239, R-79, R-82
United-Continental merger, 226
United Parcel Service, 79, 420

United Parcel Service Store, 264
United Technologies, 334
UTC Fire & Security, 334
UTC Power, 334

V

Vector Products, 305
Verio, 267
Viacom, 331
Vichy Laboratories, 334
Village Laundry Service, R-6, R-7
Virgin Airlines, R-18
Vitamin Water, R-43
Vivendi Universal Entertainment, 331
Vizio, Inc., 201
  low-cost strategy, 203
Vodafone, 392, R-5
Volkswagen, 259, 388, 416, R-50, R-53
Volpe Brown Whelan, R-82

W

W. L. Gore, 202, 456
  motivation and rewards at, 427
Wachovia Bank, 229

Walgreens, 201
Walmart, 51, 54, 55, 56, 57, 115, 116, 127–128, 149, 157, 188, 189, 190–192, 201, 203, 216, 217, 252, 305, 358, 395, 438, 453, 455, 456, R-30–R-31, R-79
  Procter & Gamble as supplier to, 191
  strategic vision, 73
Walt Disney Company, 57, 272, 276, 292, 301, 331, 456
  businesses owned by, 335
Weather Channel, 57
Webkinz World, R-39
Wegmans, motivation and rewards at, 426
Wells Fargo & Company, 228–229, 364
Westin Hotels & Resorts, R-9, R-79, R-82
Whirlpool Corporation, 275, 277, 392, 416
  Six Sigma at, 417
Whole Foods Market, 365, R-5
Woolworths, 115
WorldCom, 91, 349, 450
Worthington Foods, R-81
Wulung, 267

X

Xerox Corporation, 162–163, 297, 416
Xing, R-36–R-37

Y

Yamaha, 301
YouTube, 203
Yum! Brands, 263–264, 281
  in China, 282
  company objectives, 80

Z

Zara, 225, 232
Zipcar Inc., 220
Zopa, R-39
zShops, R-38

NAME INDEX

A

Aaronson, Susan Ariel, 372
Abkowitz, Alysa, 351
Achrol, R., R-58, R-71
Adamy, Janet, 56
Agle, Bradley R., 372
Ahlstrand, Bruce, 95
Ahmed, P. K., R-23, R-32
Ahuja, G., 336, R-70
Aitken, J., R-26, R-31
Alexander, Marcus, 292, 336
Ambroz, Milan, 433
Amit, R., 179, R-22, R-31
Amsden, Davida M., 433
Amsden, Robert T., 433
Anand, B., R-62, R-64, R-70, R-84
Anand, J., 290
Anderson, E., R-61, R-71
Angwin, Julia, R-84
Anslinger, Patricia L., 336
Antony, Jiju, 433
Argandoña, Antonio, 371
Argyres, C., R-58, R-71
Arino, A., R-58, R-71
Arnold, David J., 291
Ascari, Alessio, 433
Ash, Mary Kay, 68
Aulakh, P. S., 291, R-72
Avery, Gayle C., R-9, R-10, R-13, R-15

B

Badaracco, Joseph L., 461, R-85, R-93
Baetz, M. C., R-10, R-15
Bailey, Wendy J., 371
Bain, J. S., 135
Baldwin, C. Y., R-49, R-50, R-54
Bamford, James, 248, R-55, R-70
Band, David C., 434
Bandler, James, 351
Bandura, A., R-88, R-93
Bareilles, Sara, 239
Barkema, H., 336, 405
Barnevik, Percy, 250
Barney, Jay B., 179, 461

Barrett, Amy, 329
Barringer, Bruce, 95
Bart, C. K., R-10, R-15
Barthélemy, Jérôme, 248, 405
Bartlett, Christopher A., 179, 248, 291, 404, 405, 462
Basu, Kumal, 338
Bates, K. A., R-25, R-32
Baum, J. Robert, 405, R-10, R-12, R-15
Beamish, P., R-58, R-70
Beauchamp, T. L., 371
Beckett, Ron, 433
Beckhard, Richard, 405
Bell, H., R-55
Bell, John, R-65, R-71
Benner, Katie, 351
Bergen, Mark E., 179, 248
Bettcher, Kim Eric, 372
Bezos, Jeff, 224, 423, 455
Bhattacharya, Arindam K., 285, 291
Birchall, David W., 180
Birinyi, Laszlo, 96
Blank, Arthur, 217
Bleeke, Joel, 248, 291
Bloch, Nicolas, R-73
Bluedorn, Allen C., 95
Blum, Justin, 351
Boeker, W., R-55, R-58, R-64, R-72
Boen, H. K., R-29
Bogan, Christopher E., 433
Bontis, Nick, 180
Bossidy, Larry, 374, 404, 462
Bou-Llusar, J. C., R-26, R-28, R-31
Bowen, H. K., R-32
Bower, Joseph L., 248, R-84
Bowie, N. E., 371
Boyink, Jeffrey L., 384
Bradach, J., R-59, R-60, R-70
Brady, D., 384
Brandy, R-79
Brin, Sergey, 439
Brinkman, Johannes, 372
Briscoe, Jason, 433
Brohan, Mark, 224
Bromley, Philip, 95
Brown, David, 372
Brown, M. E., R-91, R-93

Brown, Robert, 95
Brown, Shona L., 66
Brugmann, Jeb, 372
Brush, T., 336
Bryce, David J., 247
Buckley, P. J., 290
Burcher, Peter, 433
Burke, Doris, 351
Burke, Ronald J., 433
Burnah, Philip, 405, 434
Burns, Lawton R., 433
Burton, R. M., 405
Byrne, John, 404
Byrnes, N., 429

C

Caliguiri, Paula M., 434
Calkins, Laurel Brubaker, 351
Camp, Robert C., 180
Campbell, Andrew, 292, 336, 405
Cannella, A., 336
Capron, L., 290, 404
Carasco, Emily F., 461
Carey, Gib, R-107
Carroll, Archie B., 372
Carroll, Lewis, 68
Carroll, Paul, R-84
Carter, John C., 462
Carver, John, 95
Cavanagh, Roland H., 433
Cha, Sandra E., 461
Chadha, A., 291
Chambers, John, R-40
Champy, James, 213, 433
Chandler, Alfred D., Jr., 405
Chapman, J., R-10
Charan, Ram, 374, 404, 462
Chatain, O., 248
Chatham, Jennifer A., 461
Chatterjee, Sayan, 336, R-79, R-84
Chen, C., 371
Chen, Ming-Jer, 248
Chen, R., 371
Cheney, Glenn, 372
Chesbrough, Henry, R-66, R-70
Chittoor, R., 291
Christensen, Clayton M., 66, 434

Christopher, M., R-26, R-31
Chu, W., R-61, R-70
Clark, Delwyn N., 179, 461
Clark, H. B., R-49, R-50
Clark, K. B., R-54
Clark, Robert C., 95
Collins, James C., 95, 374, 404
Collins, John, 214
Collis, David J., 66, 95, 336, 337
Colquitt, J. A., R-93
Cool, K., R-22, R-31
Cooper, Robin, 180
Copeland, Thomas E., 336
Corbett, Alistair, R-107
Cordon, Carlos, 405
Corson, D., R-10
Corsten, D., R-56, R-72
Courtney, Hugh, R-18
Covin, Jeffrey G., 95, 248
Coyne, Kevin P., 248
Criado, J., R-55, R-70
Cristie, James R., 91
Crosby, Philip, 433
Cua, K. O., R-23, R-31
Cucuzza, Thomas G., 180
Cullen, J. B., 248
Cummins, Chip, 372
Cusumano, M. A., 248

D

D'Aveni, Richard, 247
Daft, R. L., R-10, R-14
Darr, Eric D., 434
Das, T. K., 248
Dash, Eric, 91
David, R. J., R-58, R-70
Davidson, Hugh, 72, 95
Davidson, Wallace N., 372
Davies, E., 434
Davis, J., R-60, R-71
Davis, Scott, 248
Dawar, Niroj, 291
Dayton, Nick A., 434
Deal, Terrence E, 461
DeCarlo, Scott, 91
Dechant, Kathleen, 372
Delios, A., 290
Dell, Michael, 214
DeMan, A., R-63, R-70
Derfus, Pamela J., 135
Deshpardé, Rohit, 372
Devinney, Timothy M., 372
Dhanaraj, C., 290
Dienhart, John W., 355

Diericks, I., R-22, R-31
DiMicco, Daniel, 429
Dinur, A., 290
Disney, Walt, 374
Donaldson, Gordon, 95
Donaldson, Thomas, 371
Dosi, G., 404, R-23, R-31
Doz, Yves L., 248, 267, 291, 336, R-61, R-70
Dragonetti, Nicola C., 180
Dranikoff, Lee, 337
Draulans, J., R-63, R-70
Drucker, Peter F., 138, 336, 337
Duarte, C., R-55, R-70
Duguid, P., R-63, R-72
Dunfee, Thomas W., 371, 372
Dussauge, P., 290, 404
Dutta, Soumitra, 433
Dyer, Jeffrey H., 247, 248, 249, 291, R-55, R-57, R-60, R-61, R-62, R-70

E

Eccles, R., R-59, R-60, R-70
Eckbo, E. B., R-84
Eichenwald, Kurt, 372, 462
Eisenhardt, Kathleen M., 66, 180, 249, 336, R-30, R-31, R-64, R-70
Eisenstat, Russell, 179, 404
Eisner, Michael, 292
El-Jelly, Abuzar, 372
Elfenbein, Hillary A., 372
Emerson, Ralph Waldo, 63
English, Michael J., 433
Enrico, Roger, 436
Ernst, David, 248, 291, R-55, R-70
Escrig-Tena, A. B., R-26, R-28, R-31
Exley, Chuck, R-83
Eyring, Matthew J., R-2

F

Fahey, Liam, 248
Farkas, Charles M., 462
Fastow, Andrew, 349–349
Fawcett, Stanley E., 405, 433, 434
Ferratt, Thomas W., 433
Ferrier, W. J., 247
Fiegenbaum, Avi, 136
Filatochev, I., R-59, R-70
Fiorina, Carly, R-81
Flanagan, J., R-84
Fliedner, D., R-26, R-31

Florentino, Amy E., 361
Floyd, Steven W., 404
Flynn, Barbara B., R-22, R-23, R-31
Foote, Nathaniel, 179, 404
Forbes, Malcolm, 406
Franklin, Benjamin, 338
Franko, Lawrence G., 336
Fraser, H. M. A., R-48, R-54
Froese, F., 291
Frost, Tony, 291
Fujimoto, Takahiro, R-48–R-50, R-54
Fuld, Richard, R-115
Furterer, Sandra L., R-112

G

Galbraith, J., R-60, R-70
Galunic, Charles, 336
Garcia-Canal, Esteban, R-55, R-70
Garrette, B., 290
Garvin, David A., 95
Gavetti, G., 213
Genge, M., R-10
George, S., 433
Ger, Guitz, 291
Geroski, Paul A., 248
Gerstner, Lou, 182
Ghemawat, Pankaj, 291
Ghoshal, Sumantra, 179, 248, 291, 404, 405, 462, R-59, R-70
Gibbon, Henry, 248
Glaister, K. W., 290
Glass, Kathryn, 351
Glover, J., 336
Goeritz, L., 291
Goffee, Robert, 461
Golden, Timothy D., 372
Goldsmith, Marshall, 405
Goleman, Daniel, 462
Gomes-Casseres, B., R-55, R-70
Goodland, Robert, 372
Goodman, Paul S., 434
Goold, Michael, 292, 336, 405
Gordon, Joseph, 433
Gordon, M. Joseph, Jr., 433
Gordon, Mary Ellen, 136
Govindarajan, Vijay, 180
Graham, Jefferson, 427
Granovetter, M., R-59
Grant, R., 404, 405, R-22, R-32, R-62
Greenberg, Duncan, 351
Greenberg, J., R-93
Greene, D., R-88, R-93
Greenfield, W. M., 371
Grenny, J., R-86, R-93

Grewal, R., R-22, R-29, R-32
Griffin, M. A., R-10
Grimm, Curtis M., 135, 247
Guarraia, Peter, R-107
Gueth, A., R-62
Gulati, R., R-29, R-56, R-59, R-60, R-61, R-67, R-70
Gundlach, G., R-58, R-71
Gunnarson, Sarah K., 462
Gupta, Nandini Sen, 267

H

Hall, Gene, 433
Hallinger, Ph., R-10
Hambrick, Donald C., 248, 336
Hamel, Gary, 182, 248, 267, 291, 336, 404
Hamm, Steve, 291
Hammer, Michael, 213, 433
Han, S. K., R-70
Handschuh, Martin, R-41
Handy, Charles, R-113
Hanson, Hames, 310
Hariharan, S., 136
Harreld, J. B., R-22, R-32
Harrigan, Kathryn R., 248, R-57, R-71
Harris, S., R-60, R-72
Harrison, D., R-91, R-93
Hart, A., R-10
Haspeslagh, P., 336, R-71
Haugland, S., R-55, R-71
Hayes, R. H., R-30, R-32
Hayes, Robert H., 138, 404
Hayibor, Sefa, 372
Hayward, M. L. A., 336
Heeley, Michael B., 248
Hegarty, W. H., R-25, R-26, R-27, R-29, R-32
Heifetz, Ronald A., 462
Heikkiiä, Jussi, 405
Heineman, Ben W., Jr., 354
Helfat, C. E., 180, 404, R-31
Hendricks, Kevin B., 95
Hennart, J., R-58, R-71
Henriques, Adrian, 372
Herrera, Tilde, 372
Herzberg, Frederick, 406
Heskett, James L., 434, 461, 462
Hess, A. M., R-32
Hess, David, 372
Hess, O. M., R-23
Hesselbein, Frances, 405
Hewlett, Bill, 76

Hill, Ronald Paul, 357
Hilmer, F., 405
Hindo, Brian, 433
Hoang, H., R-62, R-71
Hobday, M., R-23, R-31
Hodgetts, Richard M., 434
Hoffmann, W. H., R-66, R-67, R-71
Holpp, Larry, 433
Horn, John T., 248, R-18
House, Charles H., 95
Houston, L., R-66, R-71
Hout, Thomas M., 462
Hubbell, Victoria, 461
Hughes, Jonathan, 248, 249
Hull, G., 405
Humble, John, 461
Hurd, Jonathan, 248
Hyland, Paul, 433

I

Iacobucci, Dawn, 180
Iansiti, Marco, 191
Immelt, Jeffrey, 331, 353, 383, 384
Inkpen, A. C., 248, 290, 291

J

Jackson, David, 461
Jacobsen, Kristine, 180
Janis, I., R-91, R-93
Jap, S., R-61, R-71
Jassawalla, Avan R., 461
Jemison, D., 336, R-67, R-71
Jickling, Mark, 91
Jindra, B., R-59, R-70
Jobs, Steven, 82
Johnson, C. E., R-85, R-90, R-93
Johnson, J. L., 248
Johnson, Mark W., 66, R-2
Jones, D. T., R-30, R-32
Jones, Del, 433
Jones, Gareth, 461
Jonk, Gillis, R-41
Jung, Andrea, 82
Junttila, M. A., R-25, R-32
Juran, Joseph M., 433

K

Kahaner, Larry, 136
Kale, Prashant, 248, 249, 291, R-55, R-56, R-59, R-60, R-64, R-65, R-68, R-70, R-71, R-72

Kamprad, Ingvar, 214
Kanazawa, Michael T., 462
Kantabutra, Sooksan, R-9, R-10, R-13
Kanter, Rosabeth Moss, 248, 291, 405, 462, R-94
Kaplan, Nancy J., 248
Kaplan, Robert S., 95, 180
Kar, Jayanti, R-18
Karim, S., 404
Katila, R., 336
Kaufman, Rhonda, 95
Kaufman, Stephen P., 95
Keeble, Justin, 372
Keith, Jonathan D., 160
Kelley, D., R-23, R-30, R-32
Kennedy, Allan A., 461
Kerr, Steven, 434, R-89, R-93
Khanna, Tarun, 291, R-62, R-64, R-70
Kim, Jane J., 351
Kim, W. Chan, 66, 95, 138, 248
Kimberly, John R., 433
Kimble, Chris, R-47
King, Martin, R-75
Kirkpatrick, S. A., R-10
Kleindorfer, P., R-71
Kleisch-Eberl, M., R-22, R-23, R-32
Knight, Phil, 366
Koch, Charles G., 68
Kogut, B., 290, 404, R-58, R-71
Kohn, Alfie, R-116
Kolakowski, Nicholas, 341
Koller, Tim, 337
Kotler, Philip P., 248
Kotter, John P., 72, 434, 461, 462, R-10, R-14
Koza, M., 248
Kramer, Mark R., 372
Kulashekaran, Mukund, 267
Kumar, N., 291
Kwak, Mary, 247

L

Lachenauer, Rob, 247, 248
Lampel, Joseph, 66, 95
Langlois, R. N., R-50, R-54
Lanzolla, Gianvito, 248
Latham, G. P., R-91, R-93
Latour, Almar, 372
Laurie, Donald L., 462
Lavie, D., R-67, R-71
Lawrence, Anne T., 371
Lawrence, P., R-60, R-71

Lee, H., R-23, R-30, R-32
Lee, Hau L., 180
Lee, Terry Nels, 433
Lee, Timothy E., 267
Leithwood, Kenneth, R-10
Lemak, David J., 434
Leonard, Wayne, 436
Leonard-Barton, D., 179, R-23, R-32
Lepper, M. R., R-88, R-93
Levering, A. E., R-10
Levering, R., R-10
Levesque, Lynned C., 95
Levicki, C., 405
Levien, Roy, 191
Lewin, A., 248
Lieberthal, K., 291
Liedtka, Jeanne M., 336, 405
Little, Arthur D., 372
Little, Royal, 309
Llaneza, A., R-55, R-70
Locke, Edwin A., R-10
Lonkevich, D., R-85, R-93
Lorsch, Jay W., 95, 462
Lubatkin, M., 336
Lunnan, R., R-55, R-71
Lupton, N., R-70
Lyles, M. A., 290
Lynn, B. C., 136

M

MacMillan, Ian C., 248
Madhok, Anoop, 248, R-60, R-71,
    R-72
Madoff, Bernard L., 349, 350, 354
Maggitti, Patrick G., 135
Magretta, Joan, 66
Main, Jeremy, 180, 291
Majchrzak, Ann, 433
Mannix, E., 405
Marcus, Bernie, 217
Marengo, L., R-23, R-31
Margolis, Joshua D., 372
Markides, Constantinos C., 66, 138,
    248, 336, 337, R-54
Martin, J. A., 180, R-30, R-31, R-64,
    R-70
Martin, Karla L., 404, R-96
Marx, Matt, 434
Mauborgne, Renée, 66, 95, 138, 248
Maxfield, D., R-86, R-93
Mayer, K., R-58, R-60, R-71
Mays, Lowry, 230
McCauley, B., R-22, R-32
McCawley, Tom, 372

McClellan, S., 439
McCombs, Billy Joe, 230
McCone, K. E., R-23
McEvily, B., R-60, R-61, R-71, R-72
McGee, Ken, R-21
McGrath, Rita Gunther, 248
McIvor, Ronan, 248
McKone, K. E., R-31
McMillan, R., R-86, R-93
McNamara, Robert S., R-113
McNerney, James, 417–418, R-19
McQuillen, Bill, 351
Melnyk, Steven, R-22
Menkes, Justin, 404
Menor, Larry, 95
Mentzer, J., R-58, R-71
Merson, Rupert, R-113
Meyer, K. E., 291
Michael, David C., 285, 291
Miles, Morgan P., 95
Miles, Robert H., 462
Milgram, Stanley, R-86, R-93
Miller, Danny, 179, 404
Milne, George R., 136
Mintz, Jenni, 434
Mintzberg, Henry, 66, 95, 338, 405
Mitchell, W., 290, 404
Mittal, V., R-22, R-32
Mizrahi, Isaac, 57
Mohammad, 344
Mokwa, Michael P., 136
Montgomery, Cynthia A., 66, 95,
    136, 179, 336, 337, R-84
Montgomery, David, R-21
Montgomery, Joseph C., 434
Moore, Marian Chapman, R-21
Moran, P., R-59, R-70
Moren, Dan, 341
Morgan, C. David, 80
Morse, Andrew, 341
Moskowitz, M., R-10
Mowery, D., R-57, R-71
Mroz, John Edward, 405
Mullaly, Alan, R-19
Muller, Joanne, 267, 291
Murdoch, Rupert, 250
Murphy, Patrick E., 461
Mustapha, Aishah, 434

N

Nadler, David A., 95
Nair, Hari, R-2
Nazareth, Rita, 336
Neilson, Gary L., 404, R-96, R-106

Nelson, R., 404
Ness, Joseph A., 180
Neuhaus, Klaus, R-107
Neuman, Robert P., 433
Nichols, P. M., 372
Nickerson, J., R-59, R-71
Niewiem, Sandra, R-41
Niles-Jolly, Kathryn, 462
Nisbett, R. E., R-88, R-93
Noble, Charles H., 136
Nohria, Nitin, 462
Nordhielm, Christie, 180
Norton, David P., 95

O

Obama, Barack, R-35, R-36, R-55,
    R-115
O'Bannon, Douglas P., 372
Obel, B., 405
Ohinata, Yoshinobu, 433
Ohmae, Kenichi, 96
Ohni, Taiichi, 388
Okamura, Tadashi, 436
Olian, Judy D., 434, 462
Olie, R., 291
Olsen, C., R-59, R-72
Olsen, E., 405
Olusoga, S. Ade, 136
O'Reilly, Charles A., 433, R-22,
    R-32
Ormiston, Charles, R-73
Osegowitsch, Thomas, 248
Ososo, Emi, 388
Owens, Jim, R-99, R-100
Oxley, J., R-57, R-71

P

Pablo, E, 291
Page, Larry, 439
Pagonis, William G., 406
Paine, Lynn Sharpe, 291, 372, 461
Palepu, Krishna G., 291
Pan, Y. G., 249
Pande, Peter S., 433
Parise, Salvatore, 248
Parsons, Richard, R-80
Pasternack, Bruce A., R-106
Patterson, K., R-86, R-87, R-89,
    R-90, R-92, R-93
Peel, Michael, 371
Perlman, Lawrence, 338
Perlmutter, H. V., R-60, R-71
Perrone, V., R-60, R-61, R-71, R-72

Peteraf, Margaret A., 66, 179, 180, 404
Pettit, A., 290
Pfeffer, Jeffrey, 434, 462
Phoenix, 239
Pisano, Gary P., 138, 180, 248, 404, 405, R-23, R-30, R-32
Poe, Edgar Allen, R-29, R-32
Poppo, L., R-58, R-59, R-71
Porras, Jerry I., 95
Portanger, Erik, 371
Porter, Michael E., 66, 96, 103, 135, 136, 159, 162, 180, 182, 184, 187, 195, 213, 248, 254, 290, 291, 336, 372, 462, R-84
Post, James C., 371
Powell, Thomas C., 434
Powers, Elizabeth, 404, R-96
Prahalad, C. K., 182, 248, 291, 372, 404, 405, R-66, R-71
Premji, Azim, 50
Preston, Lee E., 372
Price, Raymond L., 95
Priem, Richard L., 213
Pruthi, S., 291
Puranam, P., R-59, R-60, R-68, R-71

Q

Quelch, John A., 291
Quinn, James Brian, 405, 433, 462
Quittner, Josh, 224

R

Rafferty, A. E., R-10
Raines, Franklin, 90
Rangan, S., R-57, R-72
Rao, Ashkay R., 248
Raubitschek, R., 404
Ray, S., 291
Reed, John, 371
Reed, Richard, 66, 434
Reeves, Keanu, R-80
Reid, Joanne, 461
Reuer, J. J., 249, R-58, R-59, R-71
Rhoads, Gary K., 405, 434
Richardson, Sandy, 95
Ridderstråle, Jonas, 404
Ring, P., R-60
Rivkin, Jan, 66
Robert, Michel, 72, 95
Roberts, Sarah, 372
Robinson, M., R-55, R-70
Rock, Melinda, 433

Rockwood, K., 291
Rogers, E., R-89, R-93
Rogovsky, Nikolai, 372
Roll, R., 336
Roman, Ronald M., 372
Roos, D., R-30, R-32
Roos, Goran, 180
Rose, Matthew, R-84
Rosenthal, Jim, 433
Rothaermel, Frank T., R-23, R-32, R-55, R-58, R-62, R-64, R-71, R-72
Rothschild, William E., 248
Rui, H., 291
Rukstad, Michael G., 66, 95
Rutstein Charles, R-84
Rynes, Sara L., 434, 462

S

Sakakibara, S., R-23, R-31
Sakano, T., 248
Sakkab, N., R-66, R-71
Sampson, R., R-64, R-72
Sanyal, Rajib, 371
Sarkar, M. B., 291, R-67, R-72
Sashittal, Hemant C., 461
Sasson, Lisa, 248
Satchell, M. J., 371
Sathe, Vijay, 461
Scanlan, Gerald, 434
Schaal, Dennis, 285
Schaefer, George, R-99–R-100
Schaus, Robert, R-73
Scherer, F. M., 135
Schermerhorn, John R., 355
Schmidt, Eric, 416–417
Schneider, Anton, 337
Schneider, Benjamin, 462
Schoemaker, P. J. H., 179, R-22, R-31
Schoonhoven, C. B., 249
Schoorman, F., R-60, R-71
Schreck, Galen, R-84
Schreiner, M., R-56, R-60, R-61, R-72
Schreyogg, G., R-22, R-23, R-32
Schroeder, R. G., R-23, R-25, R-28, R-31, R-32
Schultz, Howard, 82
Schwartz, Mark S., 371, 461
Seely Brown, J., R-63, R-72
Senge, P. M., R-10
Seth, A., 290
Shah, Amit J., 372
Shah, R., R-57, R-58, R-72

Shank, John K., 180
Shankar, Satish, R-73
Sharifi, H., R-26, R-32
Shaw, Gordon, 95
Shaw, M. E., R-86, R-93
Shaw, Warren, 338
Shielfer, A., 336
Shih, Willy C., 248, 405
Shimizu, Norihiko, 388
Shin, Annys, 91
Shortell, S. M., R-29
Shuen, Amy, 180, R-23, R-32, R-33, R-35, R-36, R-55
Sieber, Sandra, R-33
Silverman, B., R-57, R-71
Simons, Robert, 338, 405, 434
Sims, Ronald R., 372
Singh, Harbir, 248, 249, 291, R-55, R-58, R-60, R-62, R-63, R-64, R-65, R-68, R-70, R-71, R-84
Sinha, Jayant, 291
Sirower, Mark L., R-84
Skarlicki, D. P., R-91, R-93
Slater, S., 405
Slevin, Dennis P., 248
Slim, Carlos, 214
Slotegraaf, R. J., R-22, R-29, R-32
Smith, Iain, 357
Smith, Ken G., 135, 247
Smith, Kennedy, 433
Smith, N. Craig, 372
Somerville, Iain, 405
Song, K., 290
Spear, S. J., R-29, R-32
Speth, J. G., 372
Spicer, Andrew, 371
Srikanth, K., R-68, R-71
Stalk, George, Jr., 247, 248
Stanford, R. Allen, 350
Steensma, H. K., 290
Stephan, J., R-59, R-70
Stephens, Debra, 357
Stevenson, Howard, 434
Stone, Reuben E., 180
Stroh, Linda K., 434
Stuckey, John, 248
Suarez, Fernando, 248
Sull, Donald, 180
Sulzer, J. L., R-86, R-93
Sundaram, A., 291
Sunderraman, G., R-8
Swaminathan, V., R-57, R-72
Swift, Taylor, 239
Swink, M., R-25, R-26, R-27, R-29, R-32

Switzler, A., R-86, R-93
Syron, Richard, 90–91
Szulanski, Gabriel, 290, 404

T

Takeuchi, Hirotaka, 388
Tata, Ratan, R-3, R-6
Teece, David J., 180, R-23, R-26,
    R-29, R-30, R-32, R-72
Teng, B. S., 248
Tepper, Bennett J., R-85
Thomas, Howard, 136
Thomas, Terry, 355
Thompson, Arthur A., 372
Thomson, Alan, 461
Tomlinson, D., R-10
Tovstiga, George, 180
Towill, D., R-26, R-31
Trevino, L. K., R-91, R-93
Tse, D. K., 249
Tushman, Michael L., 433, R-22,
    R-32
Twer, Doran, 434

U

Ungan, Mustafa, 433
Upton, David M., 138, 404, R-30,
    R-32
Urbany, Joel, R-21
Uzzi, B., R-59

V

Van de Ven, A., R-60, R-72
Van Marrewijk, Marcel N. A., 372
Van Putten, Alexander B., 248
Vanneste, B., R-59, R-71
Varchaver, Nicholas, 351

Veiga, John F., 372, 434
Vermeulen, F., 336
Vishny, R., 336
Vishwanath, Vijay, R-73
Vogelstein, Fred, 434, 462
Vokurka, R. J., R-26, R-31
Volberda, H., R-63, R-70

W

Wade, Judy, 433
Wakean, Jason, 248
Wally, S., 405
Walsh, J. P., 336
Walston, Stephen L., 433
Walton, M., 433
Walton, Sam, 455
Wambold, Richard, 292
Wang, C. L., R-23, R-32
Wang, Hua, R-47, R-51, R-52, R-54,
    R-60
Wang, Qianwei, 433
Watanabe, Katsuke, 387
Waterman, Robert H., Jr., 250
Waters, J. A., 66
Watson, Gregory H., 180
Waxman, Henry, R-115
Webb, Allen P., 461, R-85, R-93
Weber, James, 371
Weiss, Eric, 91
Weiss, Jeff, 248, 249
Welch, Jack, 50, 292, 383, 404, 455
Welch, Suzy, 404
Wernerfelt, Birger, 136, 179, 336
Wesley, Norm, 309
Wessel, Godecke, 433
Westphal, J. D., R-29, R-30
Wetlaufer, Suzy, 462
Wheelwright, Steven C., R-29, R-32
White, David, 248
White, Gordon, 310

Wiedman, Christine, 95
Williamson, Oliver E., 405, R-34,
    R-58, R-72, R-84
Williamson, Peter J., 138, 213, 336
Wind, Yoram, R-71
Wingfield, Nick, 341
Winter, Sidney G., 180, 290, 404,
    R-63, R-64, R-65, R-72
Womack, J. P., R-30, R-32
Woodridge, Bill, 404
Woods, Tiger, 385
Worrell, Dan L., 372
Wright, M., 291
Wu, Sarah Jinhui, R-22

Y

Yin, R. K., R-51, R-54
Yip, George S., 136, 291
Yoffie, David B., 136, 213, 247, 248
Yoon, Sangwon, 291
Yoshino, M., R-57, R-72

Z

Zaheer, A., R-60, R-61, R-71, R-72
Zajac, E., R-59, R-72
Zander, U., 404
Zbaracki, Mark J., 433
Zeitz, G., R-22, R-32
Zemsky, P., 248
Zeng, Ming, 213
Zenger, T., R-58, R-59, R-71
Zetsloot, Gerald I. J. M., 372
Zhang, Z., R-26, R-32
Zollo, M., 180, 249, 404, R-64, R-65,
    R-68, R-72
Zook, Chris, 336

SUBJECT INDEX

A

Abandoned strategy elements, 58–59
Abductive reasoning, R-48
Ability, 386
Abstract vision, R-12
Access, R-4–R-5
Accounting fraud, 349–351
Acquisition(s), 226; *see also* Mergers
   and acquisitions
  to access resources and capabilities,
    296
  to acquire capabilities, 388–389
  as alliances, R-68
  business fit, R-77
  cross-border, 252
  definition and purpose, R-67
  for diversification, 296–297
  hostile bids, R-83
  by local companies, 286
  managing, R-67–R-69
  necessitating restructuring, 331
  opportunistic, R-82–R-83
  partnering approach, R-68–R-69
  Philip Morris–Sampoerna, R-75
  that fail to deliver, 297
  transaction costs, 296, 299–300
  of undervalued companies, 310
  vs. localization strategy, R-75
Acquisition strategies, 264
Action agenda, 86–87
Action plan, 52
Activities, intrinsically motivating,
   R-87–R-88
Activity-based costing, 160
Activity ratios, 143
Adaptation costs, R-59
Adaptive cultures
  accepting change, 447
  dominant traits, 447–448
  examples, 448
Adaptive strategies, 58–59
Affordability, R-4
Agency problems, R-19
Aggressive price-cutting, 193
Agility, R-26, R-29
Airline industry, low-cost carriers,
   R-45

Air pollution, 363
Alliance apprenticeship, R-63
Alliance capability, R-56
  built through experience, R-61–R-62
  creating an alliance function for,
    R-62
  learning process for, R-62–R-64
  versus portfolio capability, R-67
  time needed to create, R-64
Alliance design phase, R-58–R-59
Alliance formation, R-56–R-58
Alliance management tools, R-63
Alliance portfolio, R-66–R-67
Alliance portfolio capability, R-56
Ambidextrous organizations, 418
Analyze, 414
Asia, major emerging markets in,
   R-78
Assets
  effects of value chain, 158–160
  reconfiguring, R-26
Asymmetric competition, R-17
Audit committee, 91
Authoritarian structure, 397–399
Automobile industry
  bargaining power, 116
  in China, R-50–R-51
  and globalization, R-42–R-43
  impact of financial crisis, R-40
Average collection period, 143
Awards, 424

B

Backward integration
  cost-saving strategy, 231
  definition, 230
  differentiation-based advantage,
    232
  to enhance competitiveness,
    231–232
  in-house activities, 231–232
  and supplier bargaining power, 115
  threat by buyers, 117
Balanced scorecard
  definition, 79
  examples, 79
  for financial objectives, 78–79

Banking regulation, 328
Banks and banking
  in financial crisis of 2008, 309
  in Kenya, R-4–R-5, R-7
Bargaining power; *see also* Buyer
    bargaining power; Supplier
    bargaining power
  in auto industry, 116
  of companies with suppliers, 187
  of retailers, 116
  of supermarkets, 116
Barriers to entry
  brand preferences, 108
  conditions for, 107
  cost advantage of incumbents, 108
  customer loyalty, 108
  distributor network, 108
  in diversification decisions, 299
  economies of scale, 107
  high capital requirements, 108
  and industry growth rate, 121
  learning curve advantage, 107
  network effects, 108
  restrictive government policies,
    108–109
  securing retail space, 108
  for start-up companies, 295–296
Barron's, 229
Beer industry, 131
  in Kenya, R-95
Beliefs, in corporate culture, 440
Below-market pricing, 279–280
Benchmarking
  for accessing costs of rivals, 163
  for assessing value chain activities,
    162–163
  for best practices, 412–413
  capturing full value of, 419–420
  databases for, 412–413
  definition, 162
  and ethics, 164
  to focus on continuous
    improvement, 456
  inadequate for complete
    competitive situation, 168
  information sources for, 163
  objectives, 162
  operational practices, R-25

Best-cost provider strategies, 57
  definition and characteristics,
    205–206
  distinguishing features, 208–209,
    228–229
  as hybrid, 206
  versus low-cost providers, 206
  market position, 183
  resources and capabilities, 206
  risks, 207–208
  target market, 206
  at Toyota, 207
  when successful, 206
Best practices
  adapted to circumstances, 412
  benchmarking for, 412–413
  capturing full value of, 419–420
  definition, 411
  to focus on continuous
    improvement, 456
  identifying, 162–163, 411–413
  to improve efficiency, R-31
  lacking universal application, R-30
  and sustainable competitive
    advantage, R-31
Better-off test, 296
  for unrelated diversification, 307,
    308
Big-box discounters, 57
Black belt experts, in lean Six Sigma,
    R-107, R-111
Blue-ocean strategy
  characteristics, 219
  examples, 219–220
  view of market space, 219
Board of directors
  appraisal of company direction and
    strategy, 88
  audit committee, 91
  compensation committee, 89
  executive compensation plan, 89
  fiduciary duty, 89
  inside directors, 91
  leadership evaluation, 88–89
  negligent, 89
  outside directors, 91
  oversight of financial accounting
    and reporting, 89–91
  qualities for effectiveness, 91
Bonuses, despite poor performance,
    R-115–R-116
Bottom-of-the-pyramid
  entrepreneurs, R-40
Boycotts, 366
Brain drain, after mergers and
    acquisitions, R-110

Brand building by localization,
    R-75
Brand loyalty, for first-movers, 222
Brand management activities, 196
Brand names
  exploiting common use of, 301
  global, 271, 276
Brand preferences, as barrier to entry,
    108
Brand recognition, establishing, 108
Brand reputation, in global
    competition, 261
Brands, 145–146
  corporate, 309
  and customer loyalty, 196
  not transferable, 277
  umbrella, 309
Brand switching, rivalry and cost of,
    105
Brazil
  exchange rates, 258
  growth potential, R-2
  market growth potential, 286
Breakthrough strategies
  company example, R-48
  at Geely Automobile Company,
    R-51–R-53
  key concepts, R-47–R-48
  and product architecture,
    R-48–R-49
  and product design, R-48
Bribes
  payment of, 342–343
  permitted or forbidden, 345
  and social contract theory, 346
BRICET nations, R-73
Broadband technologies, R-33
Broadly diversified companies, 313
Brutal rivalry, 106–107
Budget-conscious buyers, 206
Budget proposal reviews, 407
Budget reallocation, 408
Building blocks for strategy
    execution, R-96, R-102
Business base, broadening, 327–328
Business ethics
  bribes and kickbacks, 342–343
  business case for, 354–355
  and child labor, 342
  context of generalized ethics,
    339–340
  and corporate social responsibility,
    356–362, 364–368
  cosmetic approach to, 347
  definition, 339

and drivers of unethical strategies,
    348–352
  and ethical relativism, 343–344
  failure of suppliers at Apple, 341
  implied social contract, 365
  integrated social contracts theory,
    345–346
  and law, 347
  moral case for, 354
  and strategy, 346–347
  sustainability strategies, 362–368
Business-level strategy
  in diversified companies, 293
  in multidivisional structure, 396
  and scope of the firm, 226
Business model(s)
  Ctrip in China, 285
  customer value proposition, 59
  definition, 59
  for emerging markets
    areas of future growth, R-2
    basic components, R-5–R-7
    challenges, R-2
    customer value proposition,
      R-3–R-5
    defining consumer needs, R-3
    need for systematic process, R-2
    product innovation, R-8
    strategies of start-ups, R-2–R-3
    target marketing, R-3
    testing and implementing,
      R-7–R-8
  examples, 60
  integration of elements of, R-5–R-7
  for local companies, 284
  Microsoft vs. Red Hat, 61
  modified for developing countries,
    282–283
  of multinational corporations, R-2,
    R-4
  profit formula, 59–60
  relevance of, 60
  and strategy, 59–60
  of telecommunication companies,
    R-33, R-34
  Web 2.0 empowered, R-33
  of Xing, R-36
Business process reengineering
  capturing full value of, 419–420
  description, 413–414
  focus on operating excellence,
    455–457
Business risk
  reduction in, 123
  spread in foreign markets, 253
  in vertical integration, 233

Business strategy, 83
  consistent with operations strategy, R-30
  definition, 84
  and principles of design, R-48
  single-business enterprise, 85
Business units
  cash cows, 323–324
  cash hogs, 323–324
  competitive strength
    calculating, 317–318
    interpreting scores, 318–319
    nine-cell matrix for portraying, 319–321
  divesting, 325
  pressure to achieve excellence, 455–457
  ranking performance prospects, 325–326
  strategic interdependence, R-16
Buyer bargaining power
  in auto industry, 116
  conditions for, 115
  determinants, 115–116
  discretion to delay purchases, 117–118
  factors affecting, 117
  few relative to number of sellers, 116
  increased by Internet, 122
  lacking for individual consumers, 116
  and low-cost providers, 192
  low switching costs, 116
  price sensitivity, 118
  product information, 116–117
  of retailers, 115–116
  from shift in demographics, 121–122
  standardized/weak differentiation, 116
  of supermarket chains, 116
  threat of backward integration, 117
  and types of buyers, 118
  weak demand, 116
Buyer demographics, 121–122
Buyer expectations, unmet, 223
Buyer patronage, increased, 366
Buyer-related activities, 274–275
Buyers; see also Consumers; Customers
  budget-conscious, 206
  lower overall costs, 197
  price-conscious, 206
  unenthusiastic about differentiation, 200
  value-conscious, 206

Buyer's market, 106
Buyer tastes or preferences
  cross-border differences, 259–260
  flexibility in shifting, 233
  reduced risk exposure to, 236

C

Calling-out scripts, R-91–R-92
Cannibalization, R-45
Capabilities; see also Operational capabilities
  added by outsourcing, 392
  adequate for diversification, 325
  aggressive spending on, 191–192
  alliance vs. portfolio, R-67
  avoiding overtaxing, 325
  basis of competitive attack, 216
  for best-cost provider strategy, 206
  categories of, R-17
  co-created, R-33
  competitive assets, 141–150
  competitively superior, 149
  competitively valuable, 57
  cross-border sharing, 275–277
  cross-functional, 147
  cutting-edge, 150
  definition, 145
  diverse kinds of expertise, 237
  in diversification decisions, 298–299
  durable value, 150
  dynamic, 150, 385
  empirically validated, R-23
  gradual emergence, R-23–R-24
  hollowing out, 237
  identifying, 137–147
  knowledge-based, 146
  of local companies to compete, 286–287
  to manage alliance portfolio, R-67
  needed in vertical integration, 234
  path-dependent, R-23
  rare, 148
  reason for mergers and acquisitions, 229
  related to functions, 147
  relation to value chain, 167–168
  resource bundles, 147
  specialized vs. generalized, 301–303
  in strategic management literature, R-22–R-23
  for successful differentiation, 198
  tacit, R-23
  from testing resources, 146–147
  and threat of new entrants, 109

  at Toyota, 387–388
  updating and remodeling, 386
  used in foreign markets, 252–253
Capabilities-based matrix structure, 397
Capabilities-motivated acquisitions, 388–389
Capacity, unused, 106
Capacity-matching problems, 144
Capacity utilization rate, 186–187
Capital requirements
  as barrier to entry, 108
  for exporting, 262–263
Cash cows, 323–324
  surplus funds from, 325–326
Cash flow, in diversified company, 323–324
Cash hogs, 323–324
Causal ambiguity, 149
Cell phone manufacturers, 196
Centralized companies, R-19
Centralized decision making
  versus decentralized decision making, 398
  pros and cons, 397–399
CEOs; see also Executives; Managers; Top executives; Top-level executives
  board of directors evaluation, 88–89
  leading strategy-making, 81–82
Ceremonies, 442
Challenging vision, R-12
Change
  acceptance of, 447–448
  hostility to, 449
  linked to vision, R-10
Change-resistant cultures, 448
Channel allies, coordinating with, 196
Channel conflict, 233
Charitable contributions, 357
Child labor, extent of, 342
China
  automobile industry
    BYD, R-53
    Chery, R-53
    Geely Automobile Company, R-51–R-53
    Great Wall, R-53
    innovation from product architecture, R-47
    low-cost strategy, R-47
    quasi-open modular architecture, R-48, R-51–R-54
    reverse engineering by, R-50
    size of, R-47
    three gears model, R-53

China—*Cont.*
  Coca-Cola Company in, R-75
  Dell's experience in, 283
  export strategies, 263
  Gillette Company in, R-77
  growth potential, R-2
  largest economy, 281
  largest online travel agency, 285
  market growth potential, 286
  market potential, 259–260
  market size, 281
  outdoor advertising in, 286
  population, 259, 281
  Yum! Brands in, 282
China Learning Center, 384
Cigarette business, in Indonesia,
    R-74–R-75
Clear vision, R-12
Closed-integral product architecture,
    R-49
Closed-modular product architecture,
    R-49, R-50
Codes of ethics, 346–347
Coffee industry, 204–205
Collaboration with external partners,
    400–401
Collaborative innovation, R-34
Collaborative partnerships, to access
    capabilities, 389
Collateralized debt obligations, 347
Collective user value, R-35–R-36
Combination related-unrelated
    diversification, 313
Combination structure, 396–397
Command-and-control paradigm,
    397–399
Commercial specialization, R-41
Communication systems, for low-cost
    providers, 188
Companies; *see also* Diversified
    companies
  ambidextrous organizations, 418
  assessing competencies, 151–152,
    154
  bargaining with suppliers, 187
  benefits of profit sanctuaries,
    277–279
  board responsibilities, 88–91
  business model and strategy, 59–60
  codes of ethics, 346–347
  competitively important resources
    and capabilities, 141–150
  competitiveness of prices and costs,
    156–168
  conclusions from SWOT analysis,
    155–156

conglomerate, 307
corporate governance, 88–91
corporate social responsibility
    strategies, 358–360
corrective adjustments, 87–88
cost drivers, 186–187
cost-shifting by, 368
crafting strategy, 81–82
cross-market learning, R-78
diverse strategies, 53
dominating depth, 276
emerging-market leaders, R-73
entering emerging markets
    achieving scale, R-74–R-75
    business fit of acquisitions, R-77
    flexible thinking, R-71–R-74
    "good enough" cost mentality,
      R-76
    keys to success in, R-74
    localization strategies,
      R-75–R-76
    organizing for, R-77–R-78
    versus slow-growth mature
      markets, R-73
    think globally, hire locally, R-77
entry and exit of, 122–123
future direction, 52
game plan, 52
global giants vs. local companies,
    284–287
going on the offensive, 215–216
with incompatible subcultures, 450
internal universities, 389–390
long-lived success, 51
low-cost leadership, 185
macroenvironment, 98–100
managerial pressure to behave
    unethically, R-85–R-86
mission statements, 74–75
nullifying external threats, 150–156
performance evaluation, 87–88
present situation, 52
profitability with social benefit,
    R-94–R-95
recognized for triple bottom line,
    362
responsibilities of, 339
restructuring, 310
at risk from old assumptions,
    R-41–R-42
scope of the firm, 84, 225–226
seizing market opportunities,
    150–156
set apart from rivals, 53
setting objectives, 76–81
strategic balance sheet, 152

strategic intent, 86
strategic issues to be addressed, 173
strategic plan, 85–86
strategic vision, 70–74
strategies for competitive
    advantage, 54–57
strategy execution, 86–87
how strategy is working, 140–141
strategy-making hierarchy, 82–84
stronger or weaker than rivals,
    168–172
SWOT analysis, 150–155
timing of strategies, 221–225
tradition-steeped, 441
undervalued, 310
value chain, 157–163, 165–167
values, 75–76
weak strategy execution,
    R-96–R-97
winning strategy tests
    competitive advantage test, 61–62
    fit test, 60
    performance test, 62
Company culture, 146, 149, 188; *see
    also* Corporate culture
  driver of unethical strategies,
    351–352
  at General Electric, 353–354
  with high ethical principles, 352
Company image, 145–146
Company opportunity, 153
Company-to-company innovation,
    R-35
Company-to-user innovation, R-35
Companywide restructuring,
    330–332
Comparative advantage, 321–322
Comparative cost, 299–300
Compensation; *see also* Executive
    compensation; Incentive
    compensation
  lavish for executives, 349–351
  low-wage countries, 256
  pay for performance for executives,
    R-114–R-116
  for top executives, 89
Compensation committee, 89
Competence, 151–152
Competencies
  assessing, 151–152
  conceptual differences among, 152
  core, 151–152
  distinctive, 151–152
Competition
  between alliances, R-66
  asymmetric, R-17

basis of, in emerging markets, R-5–R-7
basis of competitive advantage, 54
five-forces model, 102–103
increased by globalization, 121
industry attractiveness and intensity of, 317
and quality spectrum, 157
symmetric, R-17
varying among strategic groups, 128
Competitive advantage
connected to profitability, 57
cost-based, 56, 167
definition, 54
differentiation-based, 167, 232
in differentiation strategy, 198
in diversified companies, 293
from dynamic capabilities, R-33
from environmentally sustainable strategies, 364–365
in focused differentiation strategy, 201–202
in focused low-cost strategy, 201
in global competition, 261
in international marketing
cross-border coordination, 277
sharing and transferring resources, 275–277
using location, 273–275
limited in unrelated diversification, 311–312
loss in strategic alliances, 268
from operational capabilities, R-25
protecting
blocking avenues open to challengers, 220–221
signaling retaliation, 221
in related diversification, 306
from resources and capabilities, 147–150
strategic approaches
best-cost provider, 57
differentiation features, 56
low-cost provider, 56
market niche focus, 56–57
strategy as quest for, 53–57
from strategy execution, 390
sustainable, 54
at Toyota, 387–388
translating value chain activities into, 166–167, 169
Competitive advantage test, 62
Competitive analysis
costs of value chain activities, 161
inadequate, 168

key success factors, 170
quantitative strength rankings, 169–170
weighted assessment, 170–173
Competitive assets, 144, 152
caliber of, 147–148
Competitive attack
based on strategic assets, 216
strategic options
continuous innovation, 217
cost-based advantages, 216–217
hit-and-run guerrilla tactics, 217–218
improving ideas of rivals, 217
next-generation technologies, 217
pre-emptive strike, 218
time to yield results, 218
Competitive battles, 102–104
Competitive capabilities, 385–390
Competitive deficiency, 152
Competitive environment; *see also* Industry environment
ideal for profits, 119
information flow about, R-99–R-100
Competitive forces
buyer bargaining power, 115–118
effect of Internet, 122
and industry change, 120
key success factors, 130–131
matching strategy to, 119
price sensitivity, 115–118
prospects for profitability, 118–119
rivalry among competing sellers, 102–103
sellers of substitutes, 111–112
supplier bargaining power, 112–115
threat of new entrants, 107–110
Competitive intelligence
about rival's strategies, 129
sources, R-20–R-21
Competitive liabilities, 152
Competitively superior strength, 151–152
Competitively unattractive industry, 118–119
Competitively valuable resources, 148
Competitiveness
backward integration to enhance, 231–232
effect of globalization, 251
forward integration to enhance, 232–233

Competitive position
defensive strategies
blocking avenues open to challengers, 220–221
signaling retaliation, 221
first-mover advantages, 221–223, 224
first-mover disadvantages, 223
horizontal merger and acquisitions strategies, 226–229
late-mover advantages, 223
and mutual restraint, 234
options for improving, 214–220
basis for competitive attack, 216–218
blue ocean strategy, 219–220
choosing rivals to attack, 218–219
outsourcing strategies, 235–236
pros and cons for first movers, 224–225
strategic alliances/partnerships, 237–244
strengthening scope of operations, 225–226
vertical integration strategies, 229–235
Competitive pressures
from existing industry members, 110
favoring some/hurting others, 128
Competitive strategy, resource-based, 210
Competitive strength, 62
business unit scores
calculating, 317–318
interpreting, 318–319
of countries, 253
nine-cell matrix for, 319–321
quantifying factors, 318
weighted scores, 318, 319
Competitive success, 53
Competitor analysis
and agency problems, R-19
and asymmetrical competition, R-17
of competitor decision makers
front-line employees, R-19
general managers, R-19
owners, R-18–R-19
stakeholders, R-18–R-19
top-level executives, R-19
competitor-insight loop, R-20
decentralized vs. centralized companies, R-19
after financial crisis, R-16–R-17
game theory, R-19

Competitor analysis—*Cont.*
  at individual level, R-16–R-17
  information-sharing with partners, R-21
  latest competitive intelligence sources, R-20–R-21
  learning from mistakes, R-20
  at organizational level, R-16
  resource-based view of strategy, R-17–R-18
  scenario planning, R-20
  and symmetrical competition, R-17
  and unlikely competitor moves, R-20
  video-game console business, R-17–R-18
  war games, R-20
Competitor-insight loop, R-20
Competitors
  anticipating strategy of, R-16
  bases for attack on, 216–220
  exploiting weaknesses of, 216
  incumbent advantages, R-75
  rivalry and diversity of, 106
  rivalry and number of, 106
Components, self-manufacturing, 115
Composite structure, 396–397
Computer-aided design, 188
Computer manufacturers, R-42
Concise vision, R-12
Confrontation scripts, R-91–R-92
Conglomerate, 307
Consumer needs; *see* Customer needs
Consumers; *see also* Buyer *entries;*
    Customer *entries*
  as buyer group, 116
  discovering unmet needs of, R-8
  in emerging markets, R-3
  lack of bargaining power, 116
  selling direct to, 189
Consumer tastes/preferences
  global convergence, 262
  in local markets, 285
Continuous improvement, 387
  focus on, 456
  process management tools, 411–420
  in quality, 195–196
Continuous product innovation, 217
Contracting costs, R-59
Contracts, in strategic alliances, R-58–R-59
Control, 415
  advantages in greenfield ventures, 264–265
  lacking in outsourcing, 237

Coordination
  in alliances, R-68
  costs of, R-33–R-34
Coordination problems
  definition, R-60
  management of
    by feedback mechanisms, R-60
    by hierarchy, R-60
    by programming, R-60
    by trust between partners, R-60–R-61
Copy cats, 199–200
Core business, concentration on, 237
Core competencies, 151–152
  building and straightening
    from acquisitions, 388–389
    through collaborative partnerships, 389
    internal development, 386–388
    upgrading, 389–390
  for foreign markets, 252
  leveraged across borders, 276
  preserved in outsourcing, 235
Core values; *see also* Values
  in corporate culture, 440–441
  definition, 75
  number of, 75
  in practice, 75–76
  retention of, 442
  Royal Dutch Shell, 77
  transformed into cultural norms, 441–442
Corporate brands, 309
Corporate citizenship, 358
Corporate culture; *see also* Company culture
  adaptive cultures, 447–448
  at Alberto-Culver, 439
  change-resistant, 448–449
  characteristics, 437
  core values and ethics in, 440–441
  definition, 438
  evolution of, 443
  in fast-growing companies, 443
  at Google, Inc., 439
  high-performance cultures, 446–447
  with incompatible subcultures, 450
  insular and inwardly focused, 449
  key features, 438–440
  leadership role in changing
    at Chrysler, 454
    making a case for change, 451–452
    substantive actions, 452–453
    symbolic actions, 453–454
    time it takes, 454

and lean Six Sigma, R-110
matched to strategy execution, 445
and operational capabilities, R-30
origin of, 440
politicized, 449
role of stories, 341
in strategy-execution process, 445–450
strong-culture companies, 443–444
and total quality management, 414
in tradition-steeped companies, 441
transforming values into norms, 441–442
with unethical behavior, R-85–R-93
unethical and greed-driven, 449–450
ways of perpetuating, 442–443
weak-culture companies, 444–445
Corporate fraud; *see* Corporate scandals
Corporate governance; *see also* Business ethics
  basic principle, 89
  board of director roles, 88–91
  failure at Fannie Mae and Freddie Mac, 90
  financial scandals, 91
  and reward systems, R-113
  versus self-dealing, 348
  self-enforcing, R-59
  in strategic alliances, R-58–R-59
Corporate Knights, 360
Corporate parenting
  administrative resources, 309
  definition, 308
  examples, 309
  high-level oversight, 308–309
Corporate responsibility, 358
Corporate Responsibility Magazine, 360
Corporate restructuring, 330
Corporate scandals, 91, 347, 450
  Bernard L. Madoff Investment Securities, 350
  Dell Computer, 349
  Enron, 348–349, 352–353
  HealthSouth, 349
  Royal Dutch/Shell, 353
  Stanford Financial Group, 350–351
  Tyco International, 348
  WorldCom, 349
Corporate social responsibility; *see also* Smart partnering
  definition, 356
  diverse workforce, 358

environmentally sustainable business practices, 365–368
environmental protection, 358
ethical strategy, 356
at John Deere, 359–360
philanthropic initiatives, 357
profitability along with, R-94–R-95
and sustainability strategies, 364–365
and triple bottom line, 360–362
work environment, 358
Corporate social responsibility strategies, 358–360
reporting criticism of, 361
Corporate strategy; *see also* Strategy/ Strategies
definition, 82–84
facets in diversified companies
actions to boost combined performance, 294
cross-business value chain activities, 293
investment priorities, 293–294
picking industries to enter, 293
Corporate venturing, 297–298
Corrective adjustments
challenges of, 458
to strategy execution, 87–88
success in, 457–458
time frame, 457
Cost(s)
of acquisitions, 296–297
of acquisition strategies, 264
in adjoining markets, 123
competitive with rivals, 156–168
effects of value chain, 158–160
of rivals, 163
of switching brands, 104
of transferring resources and capabilities, 276
of unethical behavior, 354–355
value chain analysis, 158–161
Cost advantage
as barrier to entry, 107–108
failing to recognize avenues of, 193
Cost-based advantages, 216–217
Cost-based competitive advantage, 56, 167
Cost competitiveness, 160
Cost-cutting methods
advanced production technology, 188
company bargaining power, 187

economies of scale, 186
full capacity operation, 186–187
gaining advantages over rivals, 188–189
information technology, 188
learning-curve effects, 186
lower input costs, 187
motivating employees, 188
outsourcing, 188
supply chain efficiency, 187
vertical integration, 188
Cost disadvantages, strategic options, 163–166
improving distribution, 166
improving internally performed activities, 165
improving supplier-related activities, 165–166
Cost drivers
definition, 186
types of, 187
Cost information, and buyer bargaining power, 116–117
Cost-of-entry test, 295–296, 299
for unrelated diversification, 307
Cost reduction
in foreign markets, 252
too fixated on, 193
Cost saving, in backward integration, 231
Cost-shifting, 368
Coverage ratio, 143
Creativity, stifled by Six Sigma, 416–418
Credit crunch, R-16
Credit rating, 324
Cross-border acquisitions, 252
Cross-border alliances, 252
Cross-border coordination, 277
Cross-border subsidization
definition, 279
and price-cutting, 279–280
Cross-border tactics, 280
Cross-business allocation, 309–310
Cross-business strategic fit, 304, 329, 400
competitive advantage potential, 321–322
Cross-business value chain activities, 293
Cross-country strategic fit, 315
Cross-country variations
demand conditions, 253–254
factor conditions, 254–255

firm strategy, structure, and rivalry, 255
related-and supporting industries, 255
Cross-functional capabilities, 147
Cross-functional teams, business process reengineering, 413
Cross-market learning, R-78
Cross-network effects, R-37
Crowdsourcing, R-34–R-35
Cultural differences, 242
in acquired companies, 450
ethical relativism, 342–345
integrated social contracts theory, 345–346
think-local, act-local approach, 270–271
Cultural due diligence, 450
Cultural fit, 329–330
Cultural norms
practicing and enforcing, 451–452
strictly enforced, 442
transforming values and ethics into, 441–442
Culture, cross-country variations, 259–260
Culture change; *see* Corporate culture
Culture-induced peer pressures, 445
Current ratio, 52
Customer demand; *see* Demand
Customer-friendly stores, R-111
Customer loyalty
as barrier to entry, 108
to brands, 196
Customer needs, R-48
and collective user value, R-36
and differentiation strategy, 193–194, 197
in local markets, 285
meet efficiently and effectively, 54
Customers
commercial specialization for, R-41
product creation, R-39–R-40
Customer satisfaction
from company vision, R-10
from intangible features, 197–198
from tangible features, 197
Customer segmentation
limitations of, R-46
and value chains, R-43–R-45
Customer service
capability for, 386
improvements, 195
strategic fit, 305

Customer value, R-26
Customer value proposition
  ability to deliver, R-5
  access, R-4–R-5
  affordability, R-4
  competitiveness in, 157
  and demand, R-3–R-5
  value chain analysis, 158
Customization, R-28
  for foreign markets, 260
  in local markets, 285
Custom-order manufacturers, 195
Cut-rate pricing attack, 279
Cutthroat rivalry, 106–107

D

Data sharing, 188
Days of inventory ratio, 143
Debt-to-assets ratio, 143
Debt-to-equity ratio, 143
Decentralized companies, R-19
Decentralized decision making
  capturing strategic fit, 400
  versus centralized decision making, 398
  pros and cons, 399–400
Decision making
  centralized, 397–399
  and corporate objectives, R-18
  decentralized, 399–400
  to empower employees, 425
  second-guessing, R-100
  in strategic alliances, 242
Decision rights
  at Caterpillar, R-99–R-100
  for strategy execution, R-97–R-99
Dedicated alliance function, R-62, R-64–R-65
Defects
  dealing with, 387
  Six Sigma for reducing, 415–418
Defensive strategies
  blocking avenues open to challengers, 220–221
  late-mover advantage, 223–224
  signaling retaliation, 221
Define, 414
Delegation of authority, 456
  centralized decision making, 397–399
  decentralized decision making, 399–400
Deliberate strategy, 58–59
Delivery time, 189

Demand
  and buyer bargaining power, 116
  conditions in foreign markets, 253–254
  cultural influences, 260
  customer value proposition, R-3–R-5
  and exit barriers, 121
  increased by globalization, 121
  and rivalry, 105
  and shift in buyer demographics, 121–122
  strong network effects in, 108
Demand-side network effect, R-37
Democratized innovation, R-34
Demographic market segment, 101
Demographics
  of buyers, 121–122
  cross-country variations, 259–260
  definition, 100
  think-local, act-local approach, 270–271
Departmental structure, 395
Design features, 194
Design for manufacture procedures, 188
Developing countries
  local defenses against global giants
    acquisitions and rapid-growth strategies, 286
    business models, 284
    cross-border transfer of expertise, 286–287
    local workforce, 285–286
    understanding customer needs, 285
  major nations, 281
  population of, 281
  purchasing power, 259
  strategies for competing in, 280–284
    avoid impractical markets, 283–284
    business model modification, 282–283
    changing local market, 283
    low-price basis, 281–282
    tailoring products for, 281
Diamond model of national advantage, 251, 254
Differentiation
  buyer bargaining power forcing, 116
  competition based on, R-5–R-7
Differentiation-based competitive advantage, 167, 232

Differentiation strategies, 56; *see also* Focused differentiation strategy
best conditions for
  diverse buyer needs, 199
  fast-paced technological change, 199
  followed by few rivals, 199
  many ways of differentiating, 199
delivering superior value
  approaches difficult to duplicate, 198
  intangible features, 197–198
  lowering buyer's costs, 197
  from resources and capabilities, 198
  signals of value, 198
  tangible features, 197
distinguishing features, 208–209, 228–229
effects on firms, 194
enhancing profitability, 194
examples, 194
incentive system in, 428
managing value chain to create, 194–196
market position, 183, 184
pitfalls to avoid
  overspending, 200
  possible rapid imitation, 199–200
  timidity, 200
  too high a price, 200–201
  too many features, 200
  unenthusiastic buyers, 200
reasons for failure, 194
revamping value chain
  coordinating with channel allies, 196
  coordinating with suppliers, 197
strong vs. weak, 200
successful, 193–194
unique customer value proposition, 194
uniqueness drivers
  continuous improvement, 195–196
  high-quality inputs, 196
  human resource management activities, 196
  improved customer service, 195
  innovation, 195
  marketing and sales activities, 196
  research and development, 195
  superior features, design and performance, 194
  technological advances, 195

Direct network effect, R-37
Direct selling, 189, 233
Discount stores; *see* Wholesale clubs
Disruptive environmental change, 150
Disruptive innovation, R-8
Distinctive competencies, 198
Distribution
    definition, 159
    in emerging markets, R-74–R-75
    strategic fit, 305
    value chain activities, 161
Distribution channels, low-cost, 189
Distribution networks
    as barrier to entry, 108
    local, 284
Distribution-related value chain
    activities, 166
Distributors
    avoiding costs of, 189
    coordinating with, 196
Diverse workforce, 358
Diversification; *see also* Related
    diversification; Unrelated
    diversification
    to add shareholder value
        better-off test, 296
        cost-of-entry test, 295–296
        industry attractiveness test, 295
    barriers to entry, 299
    circumstances for, 295
    combination related-unrelated, 313
    comparative cost, 299–300
    critical resources and capabilities,
        298–299
    four main options after, 327
    at Johnson & Johnson, 329
    speed, 299
    strategies
        acquisition of existing business,
            296–297
        corporate venturing, 297–298
        internal development, 297–298
        joint ventures, 298
    timing of, 294–295
Diversification strategy
    alternatives for using, 314
    and multidivisional structure,
        395–396
Diversified companies, 293
    broadening business base, 327–328
    broadly diversified, 313
    conglomerates, 307
    crafting new strategy moves,
        326–332
    divesting or retrenching, 328–330

dominant-business enterprises, 313
    internal capital market, 323
    narrowly diversified, 313
    parenting advantage, 311
    ranking performance prospects,
        325–326
    restructuring, 330–331
    sticking with existing business line,
        326–327
    strategy analysis
        business unit competitive
            strength, 317–321
        competitive advantage potential,
            321–322
        industry attractiveness, 314–317
        resource fit, 322–325
        steps, 313–314
    turnaround capabilities, 310
    unrelated groups of related
        businesses, 313
Divesting, 294, 327
    candidates for, 331
    causes leading to, 330
    of marginal units, 325
    reasons for, 328–329
    useful guide for, 330
Dividend payout ratio, 144
Dividend yield on common stock,
    143
Divisional structure, 395
DMADV (define, measure, analyze,
    design, and verify) Six Sigma,
    415
DMAIC (define, measure, analyze,
    improve, and control) sequence
    in lean Six Sigma, R-108
    in Six Sigma, 415–416
Dominant-business enterprise, 313
Dominating depth, 276
Domini 400 index, 368
Dow Jones Large Cap Index, 368
Dow Jones Sustainability Index, 368
Dow Jones Sustainability World
    Index
    companies recognized by, 362
    composition of, 361
Dow Jones Total Market Index, 368
Dow Jones World Index, 361
Downstream partners, 196
Drivers of change
    assessing impact of, 124–125
    favoring some/hurting others, 128
    identifying, 120–124
    most common, 124
    strategy to deal with, 125

Dumping, 156–157
    definition, 279
    reason for appeal of, 279
    retaliation against, 279–280
    unfair, 279
    World Trade Organization on, 280
Dynamic capabilities, 150, 385
    definition, R-33
    examples of success, R-39–R-40
    multiplying
        activate network effects, R-37
        build on collective user value,
            R-35–R-37
        through social networks,
            R-37–R-38
        by syndication, R-38
    new collaborative matrix, R-34–R-35
    new relevance of, R-34
    and Web 3.0, R-40
    of Web 2.0 applications, R-34–R-40
Dynamic fit, 60
Dynamic industry analysis, 121, 122
    value of, 125
Dynamic management of resources,
    149–150

E

Earnings per share, 142
Ease of Doing Business Index (World
    Bank), R-2
Economic conditions; *see also*
    Financial crisis of 2008
    banking crisis of 2008, 309
    definition, 100
    reason for broadening business
        base, 328
Economic indicators of growth
    opportunities, 101
Economic risks, 257
Economies of scale
    as barrier to entry, 107
    from centralizing production, 263
    cost-cutting method, 186
    versus economies of scope, 306
    in foreign markets, 252
    location-based, 274
    from standardization, 260
    from technological change, 122
    and vertical integration, 144
Economies of scope, 306
Economist, R-2, R-5
Effectiveness
    definition, R-30
    versus efficiency, R-30–R-31

Efficiency
in adjoining markets, 123
definition, R-30
versus effectiveness, R-30–R-31
Electronic score cards, 422
E-mail, and industry change, 122
Emergent strategy, 58–59
Emerging-market capabilities,
R-77–R-78
Emerging markets
achieving scale in, R-74–R-75
Asian geographic area, R-78
bases of competition, R-5–R-7
BRICET nations, R-73
business fit of acquisitions, R-77
flexible thinking for entering,
R-73–R-74
functional expertise in, R-8
"good enough" cost mentality,
R-76
keys to success in, R-74
localization strategies, R-75–R-76
lower price and profits, R-73
new business models
areas of future growth, R-2
basic components, R-5–R-7
challenges, R-2
customer value proposition,
R-3–R-5
defining consumer needs, R-3
need for systematic process, R-2
product innovation, R-8
strategies of start-ups, R-2–R-3
target marketing, R-3
testing and implementing,
R-7–R-8
organizing to enter, R-77–R-78
versus slow-growth mature markets,
R-73
social and environmental needs,
R-95
think globally, hire locally, R-77
Empire-building managers, 449
Empirically validated capabilities,
R-23
Empirically validated operational
capabilities, R-25
Employee motivation, 188
Employee recruiting, 366–367
Employees; *see also* Human resource
management
acting on ideas from, 424–425
developing capabilities in, 381–390
in high-performance cultures, 447
incentives extended to all, 428

misconceptions about strategy,
375–376
monitoring performance of, 423
perpetuating corporate culture,
442–443
recruiting and training, 382–385
rewards and incentives for,
423–430
sharing information with, 425
in strong-culture companies,
445–446
treated as valued partners, 456
on weak strategy execution, R-96
work environment, 358
Employee satisfaction, from company
vision, R-10, R-15
Employee skills, 196
upgrading, 389–390
Empowerment, 387, 399, 423, 425,
456
Enterprise resource planning, 188
Enterprise Resource Planning
software, 414
Entrepreneurs, bottom-of-the-
pyramid, R-40
Entry of major firms, 122–123
Environment, 362
engineering PBU out of, R-92
Environmentally sustainable
strategies
business case for, 366–368
and buyer patronage, 366
competitive advantage, 364–365
and corporate social responsibility,
364
and cost reductions, 366–367
versus cost-shifting, 368
definition, 363
forms of, 364
implied social contract, 365
moral case for, 365
and procurement policies, 365
reducing risk of reputation-
damaging incidents, 366
revenue enhancement, 367
shareholder interests, 367–368
workforce retention, 366–367
Environmental protection, 358
Environmental regulation, 358
Equity-based alliances, R-58
Equity-based pay, R-114–R-115
Esprit de corps, 456
Ethical dilemmas, R-90–R-91
Ethical leadership, R-91
Ethical principles, 356

Ethical relativism
breakdown of
local standards, 344
rudderless standards, 344
bribes and kickbacks, 342–343
definition, 342
and multinational corporations,
344–345
multiple sets of standards,
343–344
use of underage labor, 342
Ethical standards
conflicting for multinational
corporations, 344–345
impact on strategy, 346–347
local, 344–345
multiple sets of, 344–345
rudderless, 344
Ethical strategy, 356
business case for, 354–355
moral case for, 354
reasons for, 352
Ethical universalism, 340–342
Ethics, 339; *see also* Business ethics;
Pressure to behave unethically
in benchmarking, 164
in corporate culture, 440–441
ethical relativism, 342–344
ethical universalism, 340–342
integrated social contracts theory,
345–346
transformed into cultural norms,
441–442
Evolving strategy, 57–58
Exchange rates
decline of dollar, 258–259
favorable shift, 259
fluctuating, 258
risks of adverse shifts, 257–259
strength of euro, 259
unpredictable, 259
Execution-critical activities,
consistency in, 410
Executive compensation
board responsibility for, 89
incentive, 329
lavish, 349–351
need for reform, 89
Executives
as agents for shareholders, 89
board of directors evaluation,
88–89
pay for performance, R-114–R-116
Existing business lineup, sticking
with, 326–327

Exit barriers
effect of demand, 121
and strength of rivalry, 106–107
Exit of major firms, 122–123
Expatriates vs. local hiring, R-77
Experience
alliance capability from, R-61–R-62
prior, R-64
Experience, benefits in single
location, 274
Experience curve, 107, 186
Expertise
competitively valuable, 57
diverse kinds of, 237
transferred to cross-border markets, 286–287
transferring, 301
Export strategies
and cost competitiveness, 263
disadvantages, 263
to enter foreign markets, 262–263
vulnerability, 263
External fit, 60

F

Factor conditions, foreign markets, 254–255
Fast-changing market, 153
Fast-growing market, and rivalry, 105
Fast-moving consumer goods, R-43
Faulty oversight, 348–349
Federal Home Loan Mortgage
Corporation; *see* Freddie Mac
Federal National Mortgage
Association; *see* Fannie Mae
Feedback, from alliance members, R-63
Fiduciary duty, 89
Field employees, information needed
by, R-101–R-102
Fierce rivalry, 107
Financial accounting, board of
directors oversight, 89–91
Financial crisis of 2008, 347
credit crunch, R-16
impact on auto industry, R-47
need for competitor analysis after, R-16–R-17
and strategic interdependence, R-16
Financial incentives
at Amgen, 427
components, 424
fringe benefits, 424

high-powered motivation, 424
at Lincoln Electric, 426
major piece of total compensation, 428
at Nordstrom, 426
perks, 424
at Ukrop's Super Markets, 427
Financial integration, R-68
Financial objectives, 76–78
Financial options for allocating
financial resources, 326
Financial performance
benefits of sustainability strategies, 367–368
measures of
balanced scorecard, 78–79
lagging indicators, 78
leading indicators, 78
pursuing strategic outcomes, 79
ratios for, 142–144
of rivals, 129
Financial ratios
activity ratios, 143
dividend payout ratio, 144
dividend yield, 143
free cash flow, 144
internal cash flow, 144
leverage ratios, 143
liquidity ratios, 142
price-earnings ratio, 144
profitability ratios, 142
Financial reporting, 89–91
Financial Reporting Council, United
Kingdom, R-115–R-116
Financial resource fit
adequate financial strength, 324
business unit inadequacy, 324
cash flow considerations, 323–324
good credit rating, 324
internal capital market, 323
Financial resources, 145–146
cross-business allocation, 309–310
options for allocating, 326
Financial scandals, 91
Financial strain, 324
Financial strength, 324
Firm-specific capabilities, R-23
Firm-specific operational capabilities, R-24
Firm strategy, structure, and rivalry, 255
First-mover advantages
at Amazon.com, 224
create brand loyalty, 221–222
create switching costs, 222

definition, 221
hard questions for, 223
learning curve, 222
property rights protection, 222
pros and cons, 224–225
requirements, 223
setting technical standard, 222–223
First-mover disadvantages
costly pioneering, 223
definition, 221
market uncertainties, 223
not meeting buyer expectations, 223
opening for fast followers, 223
rapid market evolution, 223
"First-order" ethical norms, 345
Fit test, 60
Five-forces model of competition
as analytical tool, 103
definition, 102
using, 102
Fixed costs, and intensity of rivalry, 106
Flat structure, 394
Flexible manufacturing systems, 195
Fluctuating exchange rates risks, 258–259
Focused differentiation strategy
attractiveness, 202–203
characteristics, 201–202
distinguishing features, 208–209, 228–229
at Nestlé, 204–205
risks, 203–205
at Vizio, Inc., 203
Focused low-cost strategy
attractiveness, 202–203
characteristics, 201
distinguishing features, 208–209, 228–229
risks, 203–205
Focus group analysis of operational
capabilities, R-26–R-27
Focus strategies, 56–57
market position, 183
Forbes, 229, 350
Foreign Corrupt Practices Act, 343
Foreign markets
in developing countries, 281–284
exploit core competencies, 252
impractical to enter, 283–284
lower costs, 252
options for entering
acquisition strategies, 264
export strategies, 262–263
franchising, 263–264

Foreign markets—*Cont.*
    greenfield ventures, 264–265
    joint ventures, 265–269
    licensing strategies, 263
    risks of alliances, 266–268
    strategic alliances, 265–269
    when alliances are unnecessary,
        268–269
    reason for broadening business
        base, 328
    reasons for entering
        access to new capabilities,
            252–253
        access to new customers, 252
        spread business risk, 253
Foreign partners, risks of alliances
    with, 266–268
Fortune, 229, 331, 349, R-10,
    R-13–R-14, R-55
Forward integration
    and channel conflict, 243
    definition, 230
    direct selling, 243
    to enhance competitiveness,
        232–233
Franchising strategies, 263–264
Free cash flow, 144
Frills, stripping, 188–189
Fringe benefits, 424
Frontline employees/managers, 85
    and competitor analysis, R-19
Full capacity operations, 186–187
Full integration, 230–231
Function, basis of alliance capability,
    R-62
Functional-area strategies, 83, 84
Functional structure, 394–395
Functions related to capabilities,
    147
Funding
    reallocating, 408
    too little or too much, 407

G

Game theory, R-16, R-19
General administration, 159
Generalized resources and
    capabilities, 301–303
    low value, 312
    in unrelated diversification, 308
Generally accepted accounting
    principles, 89–91
General managers, and competitor
    analysis, R-19

Generic competitive strategies
    attractiveness of focused
        differentiation strategy, 202–203
    attractiveness of focused low-cost
        strategy, 202–203
    best-cost provider strategy, 205–208
    contrasting features of, 197–210
    differentiation strategies, 193–201
    focused differentiation strategy,
        201–202
    focused low-cost strategy, 201
    low-cost provider strategies, 184–193
    and market position, 184
    purpose, 183
    resource-based, 210
    risks in focused differentiation
        strategy, 203–205
    risks in focused low-cost strategy,
        203–205
Geographic boundary lines, 101
Geographic coverage, 227
Global brand names, 271, 276
Global competition
    competitive advantage, 261
    convergence of tastes, 262
    definition, 261
    transition from multidomestic
        competition, 261–262
    types of market segments, 261
Global forces, 100
Global giants
    versus competitive abilities of local
        companies, 286
    disadvantages in developing
        countries, 284
    lacking local workforce, 285–286
    and local company expertise,
        286–287
    versus local orientation, 285
    strategies for local companies
        against, 284–287
Globalization
    accelerating pace of, 251
    leading to industry change, 121
    low-cost players, R-42–R-43
    and specialization, R-41
Global market leadership, 241
Global strategy
    advantages/disadvantages, 273
    definition, 271
    drawbacks, 272
    standardization, 271–272
    think-global, act-global approach,
        271
Global warming, 363

Glocalization, 272
Goal conflict, 398
"Good enough" cost mentality, R-77
Government
    hostile to business, 257
    pro-business environment, 256
Government policies
    as barrier to entry, 108–109
    cross-country variations, 256–257
    and industry change, 123
Greed-driven culture, 449–450
Greenfield ventures
    control advantage, 264–265
    learning by doing, 264
    problems, 264
Greenhouse gases, 363
Gross profit margin, 142
Groupthink, R-91
Growth
    in emerging markets, R-2
    opportunities for, 101
    wrong reason for diversification,
        312
Growth rate, long-term changes,
    120–121
Guerrilla offensive, 217–218
Guggenheim Museum, New York,
    194
Guidelines for activities, 409–410

H

Heads Up (McGee), R-21
Healthcare Commission, United
    Kingdom, R-114
Higher-order organizational
    principles, R-62
High-performance cultures, 446–447
High-powered motivation, 424
High-tech companies, 382–384
Hiring; *see* Recruitment
Hit-and-run guerrilla offensive,
    217–218
Home mortgage problem, 347
Horizontal mergers and acquisitions,
    226–227
Horizontal scope, 226
Hostile bids, R-83
Human assets, 145–146
Human resource management
    and differentiation strategy, 196
    value chain activity, 159
Human rights, commitment to, 344
Hybrid strategy, 206
Hybrid value chains, R-43–R-45

I

Imitation, rapid, 199–200
Implied social contract, 365
Improve, 415
Incentive compensation, 329
  communicating and explaining, 430
  guidelines
    extended to all employees, 428
    financial incentives, 428
    performance targets and
      outcomes, 429–430
    results not effort rewarded, 430
    scrupulous administration, 429
    timing of rewards, 430
  high vs. average performance, 428
Incentive maps, R-90
Incentives
  based on results, 427–430
  financial, 424
  for high-performance standards,
    456–457
  nonmonetary, 424–425
  piece-rate plan, 429
  and strategy execution at Nucor,
    429
  strategy execution objectives, 423
Incentive system, 145–146, 149,
  187–188
Incompatible subcultures, 450
India
  Frito-Lay in, R-77
  growth potential, R-2
  market caps of subsidiaries, R-76
  market growth potential, 286
  prices and profits in, R-76
  products tailored for, 281–282
  women as distributors, R-75
Indirect network effect, R-37
Indoctrination of new employees, 442
Indonesia
  cigarette business, R-74–R-75
  mergers and acquisitions in, R-75
Industries/Industry
  changed conditions over time, 57–58
  competitively unattractive, 118–119
  convergence of, 228
  differences among, 101
  for diversified companies, 293
  globally competitive, 261
  high exit barriers, 106–107
  key success factors, 130–131
  profit prospects, 132–133
  strategic groups, 126
  value chain system for, 161–162

Industry attractiveness, 119
  cross-country strategic fit, 315
  and diversification strategy, 315
  evaluating
    questions required, 314–315
    scores for ranking, 315–317
  key indicators, 315
  nine-cell matrix for portraying,
    319–321
  and profit prospects, 132–133
  resource requirements, 315
Industry attractiveness scores
  calculating, 315–316
  difficulties of calculating, 317
  interpreting, 316–317
  weighted, 316
Industry attractiveness test
  for related diversification, 295
  for unrelated diversification, 307
Industry change
  analyzing industry dynamics, 120
  effect of competitive forces, 120
  environmental scanning for, 120
  identifying drivers of change
    cost and efficiency in adjoining
      markets, 123
    diffusion of technological know-
      how, 123
    exit or entry of firms, 122–123
    globalization, 121
    Internet, 122
    lifestyle changes, 123–124
    long-term growth rate, 120–121
    product market innovation, 122
    reduction in uncertainty, 123
    regulatory influences, 123
    shift in buyer demographics,
      121–122
    societal change, 123–124
    technological change, 122
  impact of drivers of change,
    124–125
  most common drivers of, 124
  strategy to deal with, 125
Industry competitiveness, cross-
  country variations
    demand conditions, 253–254
    factor conditions, 254–255
    firm strategy, structure, and
      rivalry, 255
    related and supporting industries,
      255
Industry environment; *see also*
  Competitive environment
  buyer bargaining power, 115–118

  characteristics, 58
  growth opportunities, 101
  kinds of competitive forces
    rivalry among sellers, 102–107
    threat of new entrants, 107–110
  pressure from price sensitivity,
    115–118
  profitability prospects, 118–119
  sellers of substitutes, 111–112
  strategic thinking about, 100–101
  supplier bargaining power, 112–115
Industry life cycle, 101
Industry opportunity, 153
Industry position, 241
Industry rivals
  competitive intelligence about, 129
  likely strategic moves, 128–130
  questions to ask about, 129–130
  strategic group mapping, 125–128
    assessing market position, 126–127
    benefits of using, 127–128
    definition of groups, 126
    guidelines, 126–127
    procedures, 126
    some positions more attractive,
      128
    variables for, 126–127
    varying profit prospects, 128
Industry standard, 222–223
Industry transformations, R-40
Information
  about competitive environment,
    R-99–R-100
  flow across organizational
    boundaries, R-100–R-101
  flow to line and field employees,
    R-101–R-102
  shared with employees, 425
Information systems
  areas covered by, 422
  electronic score cards, 422
  to monitor employees, 423
  real-time, 422
  for strategy execution, 420–422
Information technology
  for low-cost providers, 188
  outsourcing projects, R-38
Infrastructure, developing countries,
  284
Innovation
  in consumer goods market, R-43
  democratized, R-33
  disruptive, R-8
  loss in outsourcing, 237
  operational, R-27–R-28

Innovation—*Cont.*
  platform, R-35
  rapid, 199
  recombinant, R-35
  reversed sequence of, R-40
  stifled by Six Sigma, 416–418
  striving for, 195
Inputs
  high-quality, 196
  lower-cost, 187
Inside directors, 91
Insular, inwardly-focused cultures, 449
Intangible assets, 145–146
Intangible features, 197–198
Integrated social contracts theory
  cross-cultural differences, 345–346
  guidance for managers, 346
  imposing limitations, 345
  and local standards, 345
  and major religions, 346
  and "second-order" norms, 346
  universal "first-order" norms,
    345–346
Integration problems in synergistic
    mergers, R-80
Intellectual capital, 145–146
Internal capital market, 309, 323
Internal cash flow, 144
Internal cost structure, 160–161
Internal development
  of core competencies, 386–388
  diversification by, 297–298
Internal entrepreneurship, 447
Internal fit, 60
Internally performed value chain
    activities, 165
Internal universities, 389–390
International Labor Organization, 342
International marketing, 250–287
  cross-border subsidization, 279–280
  cross-border tactics, 280
  cross-country variations, 253–255
  demographic differences, 259–260
  in developing countries, 280–284
  economic risks, 257
  exchange rate risks, 257–259
  global competition, 262
  global strategy, 271–272
  impact of government policies,
    256–257
  local defenses against global giants,
    284–287
  locating value chain activities,
    255–256
  multidomestic competition,
    260–262

  multidomestic strategy, 269–271
  options for entering foreign
    markets, 262–269
  political risks, 257
  profit sanctuaries, 277–278
  quest for competitive advantage,
    273–277
  reasons for entering foreign
    markets, 252–253
  strategy complexity, 253–260
  transnational strategy, 272–273
International rivals
  cross-border tactics against, 280
  mutual restraint, 280
International Standards
    Organization, 360
International strategy
  advantages and disadvantages, 273
  definition, 269
  global, 270–272
  multidomestic, 269–271
  transnational, 272
International trade
  dumping strategy, 279
  and exchange rates, 258–259
Internet
  effect on competitive forces, 122
  and industry change, 122
  use in China, 282–283
  versus Village Store, R-41
  Voice-over Internet Protocol
    (VoIP), 122
Internet retailing; *see* Online retailing
Introductory low prices, 192
Inventory turnover ratio, 143
Investment
  industry attractiveness test, 295
  priorities for diversified companies,
    293–294
  socially responsible, 368
Investment fraud, 350–351
Ireland, pro-business environment,
    256
Iron Chef, R-28
ISO 9000 standard, 196, 287

J

Japan
  export strategies, 263
  kaizen, 414
  as profit sanctuary, 277–278
Joint ventures, R-56
  to access capabilities, 389
  cross-border, 252

  definition, 239
  diversification by, 298
  to enter foreign markets, 265–269
  examples, 239–240
  facilitating resource and risk
    sharing, 265–266
  learning and added expertise, 267
  risks
    conflicting objectives, 266
    loss of competitive advantage,
      268
    overly dependent on partners, 268
    transaction costs, 266
  value of prior experience, R-64
  when unnecessary, 268–269
Justice training, R-91
Just-in-time delivery, 189–190
Just-in-time systems, 274, 387, R-23
  to improve efficiency, R-31

K

Kaizen, 414
Kenya
  banking services, R-4–R-5, R-7
  beer industry, R-95
Key success factors
  in beer industry, 131
  and company strategy, 130–131
  for competitiveness analysis, 170
  correctly diagnosing, 130–131
  definition, 130
  for entering emerging markets, R-74
  number of, 131
  questions for, 131
  in single strategic alliance, R-57
Kickbacks
  payment of, 342–343
  permitted or forbidden, 345
  and social contract theory, 346
Know-how, codified, R-63
Knowledge-based capabilities, 146
Knowledge-based view of firms,
    R-62–R-64
Knowledge resources, upgrading,
    389–390

L

Labor costs, country differences, 121
Lagging indicators, 78
Late-mover advantages
  buyer expectations, 223
  and costly pioneering, 223
  market uncertainties, 223

pros and cons, 224–225
rapid market evolution, 223
Lead by example, 453
Leaders, vision defined by, R-10
Leadership; *see also* Management;
  Managers
  to change problem cultures
    difficulties, 450
    making a case for change,
      451–452
    questions needed for, 450–451
    steps, 452
    substantive actions, 452–453
    symbolic actions, 453–454
    time it takes for, 454
  ethical, R-91
  linked to vision, R-10
  in strategy execution
    making corrective adjustments,
      457–458
    management by walking around,
      455
    managerial actions, 454–455
    pressure for excellence, 455–457
    role of top executives, 454–455
  visionary, R-9, R-10
Leadership in Energy and
  Environmental Design
  standards; *see* LEED certified
  construction
Leading indicators of financial
  performance, 78
Lean Six Sigma, R-107–R-112
  Australian bank, R-109
  benchmarking, R-108
  black belt experts, R-107, R-111
  and collapse of home values,
    R-109
  for corporate culture, R-110
  cost modeling tools, R-109
  diagnostic X-ray process
    DMAIC sequence, R-108
    efficiency check, R-107–R-108
    meeting new objectives, R-108
    set priorities, R-108
    value-stream mapping, R-107
  flawed from lack of focus, R-107
  future of, R-111–R-112
  insurance claim processes,
    R-108–R-109
  in mergers and acquisitions, R-110
  mobile phone company,
    R-109–R-110
  for retailing, R-110–R-111
Leapfrogging competitors, 217
Learning by doing, R-62

Learning curve, 107
  benefits in single location, 274
  from centralizing production, 263
  from foreign markets, 252
Learning-curve effects, 186
Learning process, in strategic
  alliances, 242
Learning processes
  for alliance capabilities, R-62–R-64
    alliance apprenticeships, R-63
    codified know-how, R-63
    internalization process, R-63
    knowledge-sharing, R-63
    management experience, R-63
  as rituals, R-64
  turned into bureaucracy, R-64
Legal factors, 100
Leverage ratios, 143
Licensing
  as barrier to entry, 108–109
  versus diversification, 300
Licensing strategies, 263
Lifestyles
  changes, 123–124
  national differences, 277
Lighting industry, R-42–R-43
Line-and-staff structure, 394
Line employees, information needed
  by, R-101–R-102
Liquidity ratios, 142
Loans; *see* Mortgage lending
Local companies, defenses against
  global giants
  acquisitions and rapid-growth
    strategies, 286
  business models, 284
  customized products, 285
  knowing customer needs, 285
  local workforce, 285–286
  transfer of company expertise,
    286–287
Local-country ethical norms, 346
Localization strategies in emerging
  markets
  brand building, R-75
  pricing, R-75–R-76
  product reformulation, R-75
Local market, making changes in, 283
Local network effects, R-37
Local workforce, 285–286
Location, to build competitive
  advantage, 273–275
  concentrated, 274
  dispersed, 274–275
Location-based economies of
  scale, 274

Lodging industry; *see* Hotel
  industry
Long-term debt-to-capital ratio, 143
Long-term debt-to-equity ratio, 143
Long-term growth rate changes,
  120–121
Long-term objectives, 79–81
Lowballing on price, 217–218
Low-cost advantage
  achieving, 185–186
  over rivals, 185
Low-cost distribution channels, 189
Low-cost leadership, 185
Low-cost production, in China's auto
  industry, R-53
Low-cost providers
  distinguishing features, 208–209
  in globalization, R-42–R-43
Low-cost provider strategies, 56
  to achieve cost leadership, 185
  advantages over rivals, 185
  avenues to achieving, 185–190
    cost-efficient value chain,
      186–189
    revamp value chain, 189–190
  best conditions for
    buyer bargaining power, 192
    few ways to differentiate, 192
    low switching costs, 192
    price cuts, 192
    products identical, 192
    same product use, 192
    vigorous price-cutting, 192
  compared to best-cost providers,
    216
  compared to focused low-cost
    strategy, 201
  corporate examples, 192
  distinguishing features, 228–229
  features and services, 185
  incentive system in, 428
  keys to success
    scrutinize cost-cutting activities,
      190–191
    spend on resources and
      capabilities, 191–192
  market position, 183
  pitfalls to avoid
    aggressive price-cutting, 193
    failure to emphasize cost
      advantage, 193
    fixation on cost reduction, 193
  strategic target, 185
Low-price strategy, for developing
  countries, 281–282
Low-wage countries, 256

M

Macroenvironment
  components, 98–99
  demographics, 100
  general economic conditions, 100
  global forces, 100
  immediate and competitive
    environment, 99
  natural environment, 100
  political, legal, and regulatory
    forces, 100
  rapid or slow changes in, 99
  social forces, 100
  strategically relevant, 98–99
  technological factors, 100
Make-or-buy decision, 115
Management
  action agenda, 86–87
  demands on, in unrelated
    diversification, 311
  to develop core competencies, 388
  as good strategy execution, 62–63
  of greenfield ventures, 265
  locally hired in emerging markets,
    R-77
  style in foreign markets, 255
Management by walking around,
  455
Management innovation, R-33
Management team
  assembling, 381–382
  critical mass of talented managers,
    382
  at General Electric, 383–384
  main considerations, 381–382
  situational differences, 381
Managerial motives, wrong reason
  for diversification, 312–313
Managers; see also Leadership
  and competitor analysis, R-19
  empire-building, 449
  frontline, 85
  in high-performance cultures, 447
  involved in strategy-making,
    81–86
  issues meriting attention of, 173
  pressure to behave unethically,
    R-85–R-86
  pressure to meet short-term targets,
    349–351
  questions faced by, 52
  self-dealing, 348
  strategy execution procedures,
    409–411

  in strong-culture companies,
    443–444
  "worry list" of problems, 173
Managing by the numbers, 311
Manufacturing
  concentrated in few locations, 274
  country variations, 255–256
  cross-border coordination, 277
  dispersed, 274–275
  export strategies, 262–263
  global competition, 261–262
  incentive compensation, 329
  lower costs in some locations, 274
  multidomestic competition,
    260–261
  strategic fit, 305
Manufacturing execution system, 188
Market(s)
  as competitive battleground,
    102–103
  with growing demand, 104
  oversupplied, 106
Market conditions
  cross-country variations, 259–260
  deterioration of, 328–329
  external fit, 60
  think-local, act-local approach,
    270–271
Market demand, 109
Market evolution, rapid, 223
Marketing
  in differentiation strategy, 196
  incentive compensation, 329
  strategic fit, 304–305
  value chain activity, 159
Marketing environment, strategy
    mismatch, R-29
Marketing innovation, 122
Marketing strategy, 84
Market leaders
  attack on, 218–219
  global vs. domestic, 251
Market niche focus, 56–57
Market niche strategy; see Focus
    strategies
Market opportunities
  emerging and fast-changing
    markets, 153
  factor in shaping strategy, 152–153
  identifying, 152–153
  industry vs. market opportunity,
    153
  list of, 154
  new, 228
Market pioneers, 221–222

Market position
  and acquisition, 296
  defensive strategies, 220–221
  of generic competitive strategies,
    184
  mergers and acquisitions, 226–229
  outsourcing strategies, 235–237
  reason for broadening business
    base, 328
  and scope of the firm, 225–226
  strategic alliances, 237–240
  strategic group mapping for,
    125–128
  strategic offensives, 216–221
  and timing of strategies, 221–225
  vertical integration, 229–235
Market potential in China, 259–260
Market segments in global
    competition, 261–262
Market share
  and costs, 157
  reason for mergers and acquisitions,
    227
  relative, 318
  and total profit, 193
Market shocks, 153–155
Market size, 101
Market space, types of, 219
Market standing, 62
Market uncertainties, 223
Mash-ups, R-38–R-39
Mass-customization
  from technological change, 122
  in transnational strategy, 272
Massively multiplayer online role-
    playing games, 284
Mass market opportunities in
    emerging markets, R-74–R-75
Materials handling, reducing,
    189–190
Matrix structure
  advantages and disadvantages, 397
  capabilities-based, 397
  definition, 396
  modern form, 396
  multiple reporting relationships, 396
  terms for, 396–397
Measure, 414
Mergers
  definition, 226
  related vs. unrelated, R-80–R-82
Mergers and acquisitions; see also
    Acquisitions; Synergistic mergers
  to acquire capabilities, 388–389
  benefits of, 227

Clear Channel Communications, 230
and cultural compatibility, 450
failures
  AOL/Time Warner, R-79, R-80
  United Airlines, R-79
horizontal, 226–229
and horizontal scope, 226
to increase scale and scope, 226–227
and lean Six Sigma, R-110
market leadership from, 228–229
much-used option, 226
outcomes aimed at
  access to new technologies, 228
  convergence of industries, 228
  expanding geographic coverage, 227
  increasing market share, 227
  increasing scale of operations, 227
  new product categories, 227–228
  new resources and capabilities, 228
reasons for failure, 229
recent failures, 228–229
and specialization, R-45
versus strategic alliances, 237–238, 243–244
to strengthen competitiveness, 227
synergy from, R-80
M-forms, 395
Mission, for societal benefit, R-94–R-95
Mission statement
definition, 74
descriptive nature of, 75
flawed examples, 75
Microsoft, 75
Royal Dutch Shell, 77
Sony Corporation, 74
Mobile money-transfer, R-5
Mobile phone, 197
Mobile technologies, R-33
Moderate rivalry, 107
Modular-integral dimension of product architecture, R-49
Modular value chains, R-43
Monitoring costs, R-59
Moral free space, 345
Motivation
at Amgen, 427
to avoid PBU, R-92–R-93
of employees, 188
from financial incentives, 424
at Google, Inc., 426

for high-performance standards, 456–457
high-powered, 424
at JM Family Enterprises, 426
at Lincoln Electric, 426
from nonmonetary incentives, 424–425
at Nordstrom, 426
personal, R-87–R-89
at Ukrop's Super Markets, 427
at W. L. Gore, 427
at Wegmans, 426
Multidivisional structure
definition, 395
and diversification strategy, 395–396
versus functional structure, 396
related diversification problems, 396
vertically integrated firms, 396
Multidomestic competition
features of, 260–261
transition to global competition, 261–262
Multidomestic strategy
advantages/disadvantages, 273
definition, 269
drawbacks, 271
think-local, act-local approach, 269–271
Multinational corporations
business models in emerging markets, R-2, R-4
in emerging markets, R-73
hiring locally, R-77
less need for alliances, 268–269
local acquisitions, R-77
payment of bribes and kickbacks, 342–343
Multiple alliances, R-65–R-66
Mutual restraint, 280

N

Narrowly diversified companies, 313
Natural environment, 100
Natural resources, 362, 363
Near-term performance targets, 86
Needs, unmet, R-8
Net profit margin, 142
Net return on sales, 142
Network convergence, R-40
Network effects, R-34
activating
  cross-network, R-37
  demand-side, R-37

  direct, R-37
  indirect, R-37
barrier to entry, 108
cause of, R-37
social and local, R-37
in Webkinz, R-39
workable, R-37
Network structure, 401
New collaborative matrix
changing rules of business, R-34
crowdsourcing, R-34–R-35
democratized innovation, R-34
platform innovation, R-35
recombinant innovation, R-35
New customers, in foreign markets, 252
New employees
and corporate culture, 442–443
screening, 442
New entrants
and barriers to entry, 107–109
competitive pressures from threat of, 107–110
effect on market, 107
existing industry members, 110
factors affecting threat of, 110
from growing demand, 109
from high profit potential, 109
from lower trade barriers, 121
pool of potential entrants, 109–110
quality level of products, 157
reaction of incumbent firms, 106
test of weakness or strength, 109
Newly emerging markets, 153
New product categories, 227–228
New products, speeding to market, 386
New venture development, 297–298
Next-generation products, 199, 237
Next-generation technologies, 217
Nine-cell matrix
for competitive strength, 319–321
to portray industry attractiveness, 319–321
Nonfinancial resource fit
avoid overtaxing, 325
resources and capabilities, 324–325
Nongovernmental organizations, in strategic alliances, R-56, R-66
Nongovernmental stakeholders, R-18–R-19
Nonmonetary incentives
acting on employees' ideas, 424–425
attractive office space, 425
awards and recognition, 424

Nonmonetary incentives—*Cont.*
  information-sharing, 425
  promotion from within, 424
  strategic vision, 425
  work atmosphere, 425
Normal rivalry, 107
Norms, 340
  in corporate culture, 441–442

O

Objectives
  at all organizational levels, 79–81
  balanced scorecard for, 78–79
  of benchmarking, 162
  characteristics, 76
  of company owners, R-19
  corporate examples, 91
  financial, 76–78
  long-term, 79–81
  merits of strategic objectives, 79
  setting, 76–81
  short-term, 79–81
  strategic, 78
  top-down process, 81
  as yardsticks, 76
Office of Federal Housing Enterprise
    Oversight, 90
Office space, 425
Online retailing
  advantages, 233
  and channel conflict, 233
Online syndication, R-38–R-39
Online training, 390
Open-closed dimensions of product
    architecture, R-49
Open-modular product architecture,
    R-49, R-50
Operating excellence, 455–457
Operating flexibility, 233
Operating funds, reallocating, 408
Operating profit margin, 142
Operating statistics, 423
Operating systems
  corporate uses, 420–421
  for strategy execution, 422–423
Operational capabilities
  agility and flexibility, R-26
  and best practices, R-30
  in changing external environment,
    R-26
  competitive advantage, R-25
  and corporate culture, R-30
  definition, R-23

differentiated from resources and
    practices, R-23
  embedded in organizational fabric,
    R-29
  emergence over time, R-24
  emergent, R-25–R-26
  empirically validated, R-24–R-25
  firm-specific, R-24
  focus group analysis, R-26–R-27
  functions, R-23
  hidden in plain view, R-29–R-30
  kinds of, R-25
  linked to resources and practices,
    R-30
  operational cooperation, R-26, R-28
  operational customization,
    R-25–R-26, R-28
  operational improvements, R-27
  operational innovation, R-27–R-28
  operational reconfiguration, R-29
  operational responsiveness,
    R-28–R-29
  path dependent, R-24
  process responsiveness, R-26
  resource reconfiguration, R-26
  restaurant kitchen example,
    R-23–R-24
  tacit, R-24
  and total quality management,
    R-29–R-30
  types of fit, R-30
Operational cooperation, R-26, R-28
Operational customization,
    R-25–R-26, R-28
Operational improvement, R-27
Operational innovation, R-27–R-28
Operational practices
  compared to operational
    capabilities, R-23
  easily perceived and duplicated,
    R-29
  easily transferred, R-25
  linked to operational capabilities,
    R-30
  purpose, R-24
Operational reconfiguration, R-29
Operational responsiveness,
    R-28–R-29
Operations, 159
  business process reengineering,
    413–414
  component of value chain, 158
  reason for mergers and acquisitions,
    227
Operations management system,
    R-29

Operations strategy, 83
  and best practices, R-31
  confusion over concepts, R-31
  definition, 84–85
  efficiency vs. effectiveness,
    R-30–R-31
  goal of, R-30
  and just-in-time systems, R-31
  and marketing environment, R-29
  and total quality management, R-31
Opinion leaders, R-89
Opportunistic acquisitions,
    R-82–R-83
Opportunities; *see also* SWOT
    analysis
  industry vs. company, 153
  for related diversification, 301
Orchestration, R-33
Organizational bridges, 400–401
Organizational capabilities; *see*
    Capabilities
Organizational culture; *see* Company
    culture; Corporate culture
Organizational resources, 145–146
Organizational structure
  aligned with strategy, 393
  benefits of good design, 393
  centralized decision making,
    397–399
  collaboration with external
    partners, 400–401
  decentralized decision making,
    399–400
  definition, 393
  in foreign markets, 255
  functional, 394–395
  matrix, 396–397
  multidivisional, 395–396
  network structure, 401
  simple, 394
  strategy-critical activities as
    building blocks, 393–394
Organization-building activities
  core competencies, 380, 385–390
  organizing work effort, 380, 390–401
  staffing, 380–385
Organization for Economic
    Cooperation and Development
    antibribery standards, 343
Organizations; *see also* Companies
  information about competitive
    environment, R-99–R-100
  information flow in, R-100–R-101
  need for objectives at all levels,
    79–81
  opinion leaders, R-89

pressure to behave unethically in, R-85–R-93
social capital, R-91
strategy-making at all levels, 81–86
test-driving transformation of, R-105
testing effectiveness of, R-99
traits for strategy execution, R-97–R-102
transformation program, R-102–R-106
Osmanabad, India, R-4
Outside directors, 91
Outside specialists, 235
Outsourcing
  to access capabilities, 389
  advantages of, 188
    concentration on core business, 237
    diverse kinds of expertise, 237
    not crucial for competitive advantage, 235
    outside specialists, 235
    reduced risk exposure, 236
    speed time to market, 235–236
  definition, 235
  drawbacks, 392–393
  of information technology projects, R-38
  risks in
    hollowing out capabilities, 237
    lack of direct control, 237
    weakened innovation, 237
  of value chain activities, 392–393
Outsourcing decisions, 226
Overspending, 200
Owners, in competitor analysis, R-18–R-19

P

Parenting advantage, 311
Parenting capabilities, 308
Partial integration, 231
Partner commitment, R-57–R-58
Partner complementarity, R-57–R-58
Partnering approach to acquisitions, R-68–R-69
Partner relation and fit, R-56–R-58
Partners, from syndication, R-38–R-39
Partnerships; see Joint ventures; Strategic alliances
Path-dependent capabilities, R-23

Path-dependent operational capabilities, R-24
Pay for performance
  bonuses, R-115–R-116
  challenges of, R-116
  complications, R-114
  as disincentive, R-116
  equity-based, R-114–R-115
  nature vs. amount of, R-115–R-116
  stock options, R-115
PBU; see Pressure to behave unethically
Peer-based control, 423
Peer pressure, to ward off PBU, R-89
Performance
  better-off test, 296
  combined, 294
  linked to vision, R-10, R-11–R-13
  prospects for business units, 325–326
  rewards linked to, 427–430
  short-term earnings targets, 349
  short-termism, 351
  strategy moves to improve, 326–332
Performance evaluation, 87–88
Performance indicators
  competitive strength, 62
  market standing, 62
  profitability, 62
Performance measurement
  and corporate governance, R-113
  examples of failure, R-113–R-114
  for incentive compensation, 329
  and pay for performance, R-114–R-116
  triple bottom line, 361
Performance targets, 81, 428
  to enhance individual commitment, 429–430
  near-term, 86
  results vs. efforts rewarded, 430
  and timing of rewards, 430
Performance test, 62
Perks, 424
Personal ability, and PBU, R-90–R-91
Personal motivation, and PBU, R-87–R-89
Philanthropic activities, 357
Physical resources, 145–146
Piece-rate incentive plan, 429
Pioneering
  to build brand loyalty, 222
  for firm's reputation, 222
  more costly than imitation, 223
  risks in, 221
Platform innovation, R-35

Plug 'n play value chains, R-43
Political factors, 100
Political risks, 257
Politicized cultures, 449
Ponzi scheme, 349, 350
Poor, the, in emerging markets, R-3
Population
  cross-country variations, 259
  of developing countries, 281
Portfolio approach
  to alliances, R-66–R-67
  to financial fit, 323–324
Portfolio capability, R-67
Positive deviance, R-92
Postformation alliance management; see Strategic alliances
Powerful visions, R-12
Practices, in corporate culture, 440
Pre-emptive strike, 218
Press releases, 129
Pressure groups, 366
Pressure to behave unethically
  company examples, R-85
  and corporate scandals, R-86
  developing motivation to avoid, R-92–R-93
  extent of worker experience, R-85
  factors encouraging, R-87
  and influences on behavior
    personal ability, R-90–R-91
    personal motivation, R-87–R-89
    social ability, R-91–R-92
    social motivation, R-89
    structural ability, R-92
    structural motivation, R-89–R-90
  and justice training, R-91
  made distasteful, R-87–R-89
  managerial pressure for, R-85–R-86
  and obedience studies, R-86
  scripted responses to, R-91–R-92
  and societal expectations, R-86
  ways of warding of manager pressure
    assessing knowledge and skills of others, R-91–R-92
    engineering out of environment, R-92
    leveraging peer pressure, R-89
    personal motivation, R-87–R-89
    recognizing ethical dilemmas, R-90–R-91
    using carrots or sticks, R-89–R-90
Price(s)
  below-market pricing, 279–280
  competition based on, R-5–R-7
  competitive with rivals, 156–168

Price(s)—*Cont.*
dumping strategies, 156–157
lowballing, 217–218
low introductory, 192
of substitutes, 113
Price competition, 192
Price-conscious buyers, 206
Price-cutting
aggressive, 193
and cross-market subsidization,
279–280
Price-cutting offensive, 216–217
Price-earnings ratio, 144
Price gouging, 200
Price information, 116–117
Price premium, 200–201
Price sensitivity, and buyer
bargaining power
with low profit or income, 118
product performance, 118
purchase as large fraction of
budget, 118
Pricing, as localization strategy,
R-75–R-76
Primary value chain activities,
157–158
distribution, 159
operations, 159
sales and marketing, 159
service, 159
supply chain management, 159
Prior experience, R-64
Private-equity firms, R-18
Proactive strategies, 58–59
Pro-business environment, 256
Process innovation, 188
Process management tools
benchmarking, 412–413
best practices, 411–413
business process reengineering,
413–414
capturing benefits of, 419–420
Six Sigma quality programs,
415–418
total quality management, 414
Process responsiveness, R-26
Procurement policies, 365
Product(s)
continuous innovation, 217
diverse needs and uses of buyers,
199
essentially identical, 192
identical or differentiated,
104–105
next-generation, 199, 237

superior features, design, and
performance, 194
tailored for developing countries,
281–282
too many features, 200
Product architecture
cost reductions, R-53
definition and description,
R-48–R-49
forms of, R-49
Geely Automobile Company case,
R-51–R-53
IBM example, R-49–R-50
implications for auto giants,
R-53–R-54
modular-integral dimension, R-49
move to open-modular architecture,
R-50
open-closed dimension, R-49
source of competitive advantage,
R-49
and strategic positioning, R-49
taxonomy of, R-49
Product development strategy, 84; *see
also* New product development
Product differentiation
in beer industry, 131
in best-cost provider strategy, 206
and degree of rivalry, 104–105
effect on switching costs, 106
few ways of achieving, 192
in multidomestic strategy, 269
from technological change, 122
Product information, and buyer
bargaining power, 116–117
Product innovation, 122
Production capacity, 106
Production costs
in China's auto industry, R-53
and industry change, 123
lower costs in some locations, 274
Production research and development
activities, 195
Production technology, advanced, 188
Product life cycle, extended in foreign
markets, 252
Product line, limited, 189
Product research and development,
159
Product "versioning," 195
Professional online networks,
R-37–R-38
Profit
in emerging markets, R-3, R-76
lower in emerging markets, R-73

from niche premium segments,
R-74
requirement in unrelated
diversification, 308
Profitability, 62
connected to competitive
advantage, 57
cost-of-entry test, 295–296
enhanced by differentiation, 194
eroded by overspending, 200
identifying threats to, 153–155
in related diversification, 307
slow in developing countries, 284
with social benefit, R-94–R-95
and strength of competitive forces,
118–119
Profitability ratios, 142
Profit margin, 158
Profit potential, and threat of new
entrants, 109
Profit prospects
factors in analyzing, 132–133
and industry attractiveness, 132–133
varying among strategic groups, 128
Profit sanctuaries
as competitive asset, 279
and cross-market subsidization,
279–280
definition, 277
to deter rivals, 280
domestic-only companies, 278
Japan, 277–278
part-international company, 278
worldwide company, 278
Promotion from within, 424
Proprietary knowledge, 231–232
Public recognition, 424
Punishment, 425–427
Purchase, buyer discretion to delay,
115–118
Purchasing power
in developing countries, 259
in foreign markets, 252
Pursuit of personal gain, 348–349

Quality
ISO 9000 standard, 196
of products, 157
Quality control
in franchises, 264
Six Sigma program, 415–418
total quality management, 414

Quality control process, 195–196
Quality spectrum, 157
Quantitative strength ratings, 169–170
Quasi-open modular architecture,
    R-47, R-50–R-51, R-52,
    R-53–R-54
Quick-service restaurant industry, 55

R

Rapid-growth strategies, 286
Raw materials, 253
Realized strategy, 58–59
Recession of 2008–2009; *see also*
    Financial crisis of 2008
Recombinant innovation, R-35
Reconfiguration, R-29
Reconfiguring resources, R-26
Recruitment, local, in emerging
    markets, R-77
Reengineering
    value chain activities, 414
    work effort, 413
Regulatory factors
    definition, 100
    and industry change, 123
Related and supporting industries
    in foreign markets, 255
    location near, 274
Related businesses, 300
Related diversification
    based on value chain matchup, 301
    definition, 300–301
    economies of scope, 306
    gains in shareholder value, 306–307
    and multidivisional structure,
        395–396
    path to competitive advantage, 306
    satisfying better-off test, 307
    specialized resources and
        capabilities, 301–303
    strategic fit, 300–303
    value chain activities, 303
Related mergers, R-80–R-82
Relational governance, R-59
Relational organization, R-67–R-69
Relationship managers, 401
Relationships, 145–146
Relative market share, 318
Religious beliefs
    and bribery and corruption, 346
    and ethical standards, 342
Reputational assets, 145–146
Reputation-damaging incidents, 366

Reputation of firm, for first-movers,
    222
Research and development
    for emerging markets, R-8
    strategic fit, 305, 400
    value chain activity, 159
Resistance scripts, R-91–R-92
Resource allocation assigning priority
    for, 325–326
Resource and capability analysis, 168
    dynamic management, 149–150
    identifying resources and
        capabilities, 144–147
    to produce competitive advantage,
        147–150
    purpose, 144
    tests of competitive power, 148–149
Resource-based competitive
    strategies, 210
Resource-based view of strategy,
    R-17–R-18
Resource bundles, 147, 168
Resource fit
    definition, 322
    in diversified companies, 322–325
    financial, 323–324
    nonfinancial, 324–325
    related diversification, 322–323
    unrelated diversification, 322–323
Resources
    adequate for diversification, 324–325
    aggressive spending on, 191–192
    avoiding overtaxing, 325
    basis of competitive attack, 216
    for best-cost provider strategy, 206
    better in some locations, 274
    categories of, R-17
    causal ambiguity, 149
    competitive assets, 141–150
    competitively superior, 149
    contrasted with capabilities, R-23
    cross-border sharing, 275–277
    cutting-edge, 150
    definition, 148–149
    in diversification decisions, 298–299
    durable value, 150
    easily perceived and duplicated,
        R-29
    easily transferred, R-25
    intangible, 145–146
    linked to operational capabilities,
        R-30
    of local companies to compete,
        286–287
    as passive and reactive, R-24

reason for mergers and acquisitions,
    229
relation to value chain, 167–168
requirements for diversification,
    315
social complexity, 148–149
specialized vs. generalized, 301–303
for successful differentiation, 198
tangible, 145–146
tests of competitive power
    available substitutes, 149
    competitively valuable, 148
    hard to copy, 148–149
    rarity, 148
used in foreign markets, 252–253
Restructuring, 327
    companywide, 330
    corporate, 330
    through divesting and new
        acquisition, 330–332
    examples, 332
    following divestiture, 331
    necessitated by large acquisition,
        331
    undervalued companies, 310
    at VF Corporation, 331
Results-oriented work climate,
    456–457
Retailers
    bargaining power, 115–116
    coordinating with, 196
    franchising strategies, 263–264
    vision studies of, R-11–R-14
Retailing, lean Six Sigma for,
    R-110–R-111
Retail space, barrier to entry, 108
Retaliation
    for below-market pricing, 279–280
    signaling, 221
Retraining, 389–390
Retrenching, 327
    to narrow diversification base,
        328–330
Return on invested capital, 142
Return on investment, R-34, R-36
Return on sales, 142
Return on total assets, 142
Revenue, from emerging markets,
    R-73
Revenue enhancement, 366–367
Reverse engineering, in China's auto
    industry, R-50
Rewards
    balanced with punishment, 425–427
    company examples, 426–427

Rewards—*Cont.*
  in corporate culture, 442
  linked to performance, 427–430
  scrupulous administration of, 429
  strategy execution objectives, 423
  for success, 457
Reward systems
  and corporate governance, R-113
  equity remuneration, R-114–R-115
  with pay for performance,
      R-114–R-116
  and PBU, R-89–R-90
  stock options, R-115
Risk reduction, wrong reason for
    diversification, 312
Risks
  best-cost provider strategy, 207–208
  of exchange rate shifts, 257–259
  focused differentiation strategy,
      203–205
  focused low-cost strategy, 206
  political, 257
  in synergistic acquisitions,
      R-81–R-82
Rivalry
  and buyer demand
    cost of brand switching, 104
    in fast-growing markets, 104
  cutthroat, 107
  and diversity of competitors, 106
  factors affecting strength of, 105
  fierce or strong, 107
  in foreign markets, 255
  in globally competitive markets, 106
  and high exit barriers, 105–107
  identical vs. differentiated products,
      104–106
  moderate or normal, 107
  as number of competitors increases,
      106
  and unused production capacity, 106
  varying by industry, 103
  weak, 107
Rivals; *see also* Competitors;
    Industry rivals
  accessing costs of, 163
  adopting or improving ideas of, 217
  chosen for attack, 218–219
  competitive battles among, 102–104
  competitive intelligence on, 129–130
  competitive weapons, 104
  cost advantage over, 188–189
  costs and prices competitive with,
      156–168
  deterred by profit sanctuaries, 280

following differentiation, 199
  low-cost advantage over, 185
  signaling retaliation, 221
  strategy for competitive edge over,
      102
  ways of competing, 102–103
Robotic production, 188
ROI; *see* Return on investment
Runner-up firms, attack on, 219
Russia
  McDonald's experience in, 283
  soft-drinks market, R-75

S

Sales
  in differentiation strategy, 196
  incentive compensation, 329
  Six Sigma program for, 416
  smart customization approach,
      R-102
  strategic fit, 304–305
  value chain activity, 159
Sarbanes-Oxley Act, 346
Scale, in emerging markets,
    R-74–R-75
Scenario planning, R-16, R-20
Scope of the firm
  decisions, 225–226
  horizontal, 226
  outsourcing decisions, 226
  vertical, 226
"Second-order" ethical norms, 346
Securities and Exchange
    Commission, 90, 346
  failure in Madoff fraud, 349
  and Tyco International, 348
Self-dealing, 348
Self-enforcing governance, R-59
Self-managed work groups, 423
Self-manufacturing, 115
Sellers, number of, in relation to
    buyers, 116
Separation of ownership and control;
    see Ownership and control
Serious Fraud Office, United
    Kingdom, 343
Service enterprises
  franchising strategies, 263–264
  value chain activity, 159
Shareholders
  benefits of sustainability strategies,
      367–368
  effect of unethical behavior, 355
  executive as agents for, 89

Shareholder value
  justification for diversification
    better-off test, 296
    cost-of-entry test, 295–296
    industry attractiveness test, 295
  in related diversification, 306–307
  from unrelated diversification
    acquiring undervalued
        companies, 310
    corporate parenting, 308–309
    cross-business allocation of
        financial resources, 309–310
    requirements, 310–311
    restructuring, 310
Short-term earnings targets, 349–351
Short-termism, 351
Short-term objectives, 79–81
Signaling retaliation, 221
Signaling value, 198
Simple structure, 394
Single-business company, 141
Six Sigma quality programs, 413,
    R-19; *see also* Lean Six Sigma
  blended approach, 418
  capturing full value of, 419–420
  companies using, 416–418
  compared to business process
      reengineering, 418
  compared to total quality
      management, 418
  definition, 415
  DMADV type, 415
  DMAIC type, 415–416
  to focus on continuous
      improvement, 456
  innovation stifled by, 416–418
  underlying principles, 415
  at Whirlpool, 417
Skills
  needed in vertical integration, 234
  for operational cooperation, R-28
  for operational customization, R-28
  for operational improvement, R-27
  for operational innovation,
      R-27–R-28
  for operational reconfiguration,
      R-29
  for operational responsiveness,
      R-28–R-29
  upgrading, 389–390
Slogan, vision expressed as, 73–74
Small companies
  simple structure, 394
  strategic plans, 86
Small firms, attack on, 219

Smart customization approach to sales, R-102
Smart meters, R-39
Smartphone, 199
Social ability, and PBU, R-91–R-92
Social capital, R-91
Social complexity of resources, 148–149
Social conscience, 356
Social contract theory, 345–346
Social forces, 100
Social lending, R-39
Socially responsible investments, 368
Social motivation, and PBU, R-89
Social network effects, R-37
Social networking, R-37–R-38
Societal benefit, R-94–R-95
Societal concerns, changing, 123
Software development, R-38
South Korea, export strategies, 263
Specialization
  commercial, R-41
  from mergers and acquisitions, R-45
  modular value chains, R-43
Specialized assets, 307
Specialized resources and capabilities, 301–303
Specialized value chains
  competitive playing field, R-45–R-46
  developing, R-45
  dimensions of, R-45
  versus hybrid value chains, R-43–R-45
Specifications, lower, 188
Speed, factor in diversification, 299
SS United States, 344
Stabilization, wrong reason for diversification, 312
Stable vision, R-21
Staffing
  recruiting and training employees, 382–385
  scope of, 380
  strong management team, 381–382
Stakeholders, 89
  benefits of sustainability strategies, 365
  in competitor analysis, R-18–R-19
  and corporate social responsibility, 356
Standard and Poor's index, 368
Standardization
  for foreign markets, 260
  in global strategy, 271–272

Standardized goods, 116
Star businesses, 324
Start-up companies
  barriers to entry, 295–296
  strategies of, R-2–R-3
Stock options, R-115
Storage costs, 106
Stories, role in corporate culture, 442
Strategic alliances
  to access capabilities, 389
  acquisition management, R-56
  advantages over mergers and acquisitions, 237–238
  advantages over vertical integration, 237–238, 243–244
  alliance portfolios, R-66–R-67
  capturing benefits of
    decision-making process, 242
    keeping commitments, 242
    managing learning process, 242
    mutual benefit, 242
    picking a good partner, 242
    sensitive to cultural differences, 242
  as central element of strategy, R-69
  codified management tools, R-62–R-64
  compared to acquisitions, R-67
  contractual arrangements, R-57
  contractual provisions, R-58–R-59
  dedicated alliance function, R-62
  definition, 238
  definition and characteristics, R-56
  and diversification costs, 300
  drawbacks
    culture clash, 243
    integration problems, 243
    losing proprietary knowledge, 243
  drivers of firm-level capabilities
    creating capabilities, R-65
    dedicated alliance function, R-62
    experience, R-61–R-62
    institutionalization, R-64–R-65
    learning processes, R-62–R-64
  to enter foreign markets, 265–269
  equity arrangements, R-57
  equity-based, R-58
  evolution of strategy, R-56
  examples, 239–240, 267–268
  facilitating resource and risk sharing, 265–266
  failure rate, R-55
  for global market leadership, 241
  governance mechanism relationships, R-59

growth and revenue increases, R-55
joint ventures, 239
key advantages, 244
learning and added expertise, 267
life cycle, R-67
long-lasting, 243
managing acquisitions, R-67–R-69
multiple, R-65–R-66
new class of, R-56, R-65–R-66
with nongovernmental organizations, R-56, R-66
number of failures, 244
paradox of, R-55–R-56, R-69
portfolio management, R-56
postformation management, R-59–R-61
  coordination, R-60
  feedback mechanisms, R-60
  hierarchy, R-60
  programming, R-60
  trust between partners, R-60–R-61
qualifications for, 239
reasons for, 241
requirements for effectiveness, 244–245
risks
  conflicting objectives, 266
  loss of competitive advantage, 268
  overly dependent on partners, 268
  transaction costs, 266
scope of interfirm relationships, R-57
self-enforcing governance, R-59
single alliance success factors
  design and governance, R-58–R-59
  formation phase, R-56–R-58
  illustrated, R-57
  partner selection and fit, R-56–R-58
  postformation management, R-59–R-61
single vs. multiple, R-56
for strong industry position, 241
time for building capabilities, R-65
when unnecessary, 268–269
Strategically relevant environmental factors, 98–100
Strategic assets, 216
Strategic balance sheet, 152
Strategic business design, R-48
Strategic choices, 53

Strategic fit
  competitive advantage, 306
  cross-business, 321–322, 329
  cross-country, 315
  versus cultural fit, 329–330
  in decentralized structure, 400
  definition, 300–301
  economies of scope, 306
  examples of opportunities, 301
  lacking in unrelated diversification,
    312
  of operational capabilities, R-30
  profitability and shareholder value,
    306–307
  specialized resources and
    capabilities, 301–303
  along value chain
    customer service, 305
    distribution, 305
    manufacturing-related, 304
    research and development, 304
    sales and marketing, 304–305
    supply chain activities, 304
    technology, 304
  value chain matchup, 301
Strategic group mapping, 125–128
  competing and noncompeting
    groups, 127–128
  definition of groups, 126
  example, 127
  prevailing competitive pressures, 128
  procedures, 126
  profit prospects, 128
  variables, 126–127
Strategic groups, 126
Strategic intent, 86
Strategic interdependence, R-16
Strategic management, central
  concept of, R-31
Strategic Management Journal, R-33
Strategic management process
  corrective adjustments, 87–88
  mission statement, 74–76
  performance evaluation, 87–88
  setting objectives, 76–81
  strategic vision, 70–74
  strategy execution, 86–87
  strategy-making, 81–86
Strategic objectives, 78
Strategic offensives
  basis for competitive attack,
    216–218
  block avenues open to challengers,
    220–221
  blue-ocean strategy, 219–220
  choosing rivals to attack, 218–219

  for competitive advantage, 216
  to exploit competitor weakness, 216
  first-mover advantages, 221–223
  late-mover advantage, 223–224
  principal options, 217–218
  principles for, 216
  signaling retaliation, 221
  timing of, 215–216
Strategic options
  for allocating financial resources,
    326
  after diversification, 327
Strategic plan, 85–86
Strategic positioning, and product
    architecture, R-49–R-50
Strategic vision
  communicating
    easily stated, 72
    expressed as slogan, 74
    to lower-level managers, 71
  corporate examples, 73
  definition, 70–71
  developing, 70–71
  distinctive, 71
  inspirational, 425
  and mission statement, 74–75
  payoffs, 74
  specific, 71
  winning support for, 71–72
Strategies/Strategy; see also
    Breakthrough strategies;
    Corporate strategy; Ethical
    strategy; Unethical strategies
  abandoned elements, 58–59
  adaptive reactions, 58–59
  anticipating, of competitors, R-16
  blue-ocean strategy, 219–220
  and business model, 59–60
  for competitive edge, 102
  complexity in international
    marketing
    cross-country variations, 253–255
    demographics, 259–260
    economic conditions, 256–257
    exchange rate risks, 257–260
    impact of government policies,
      256–257
    locating value chain activities,
      254–256
  components, 52
  components for single-business
    company, 141
  crafting and executing, 62
  definition, 52
  deliberate, 58–59
  emergent, 58–59

  employee misconceptions, 375–376
  evolution over time, 57–58
  indicators of success, 140–141
  issues meriting manager attention,
    173
  key to successful, 57
  levels of
    business, 84
    corporate, 82–84
    functional-area, 84
    operating, 84–85
  likely moves of rivals
    from financial performance, 129
    from press releases, 129
    from public documents, 129
    questions to ask about, 129–130
  linked to vision, R-10
  for local companies against global
    giants, 284–287
  for long-lived success, 51
  market opportunity factor,
    152–153
  matched to competitive conditions,
    60, 119
  matched to industry, 60
  at McDonald's, 55–56
  mismatch with marketing, R-29
  proactive, 58–59
  quest for competitive advantage,
    53–57
  reactive, 58–59
  realized, 58–59
  resource-based view, R-17–R-18
  to set company apart, 53
  for small companies
    for competing in developing
      countries, 281–284
    in developing countries, 284–287
  stages in crafting and executing,
    69–70
  of start-ups, R-2–R-3
  tests for winning strategy
    competitive advantage test,
      61–62
    fit test, 60
    performance test, 62
  types of action and approaches, 54
  what not to do, 53
  as work in progress, 58
  "worry list" of problems, 173
Strategy-critical activities
  benefits of focus on, 392
  building blocks of organizations,
    393–394
  consistency in, 410
  hindrances to, 413

Strategy execution
  without added expense, 408
  assessment of companies, R-96
  building block improvements, R-102
  building blocks, R-96
  building on capabilities, 379–380
  for competitive advantage, 390
  and corporate governance, 88–91
  devising action agenda, 378
  effect of structural measures,
    R-96–R-97
  employee skills and knowledge for,
    389–390
  framework for, 376–379
  fundamentals of, R-97
  and good management, 62–63
  impact of ethical standards,
    346–347
  information systems for, 420–422
  internal fit, 60
  in large organizations, 378–379
  leadership roles, 454–458
  long-term initiatives, R-105–R-106
  management challenges, 376
  new management model, R-97
  operating systems for, 422–423
  operations-driven activity, 375
  organizational traits for
    creating transformation program,
      R-102–R-106
    decision rights, R-97–R-99
    fundamental for effectiveness,
      R-98
    information about competitive
      environment, R-99–R-100
    information flow across
      boundaries, R-100–R-101
    information need by employees,
      R-101–R-102
    no second-guessing decisions,
      R-100
  organization-building activities
    core competencies, 380, 385–390
    organizing work effort, 380,
      390–401
    staffing, 380–385
  paramount actions for, 390
  policies and procedures
    consistency in critical activities,
      410
    prescribed vs. independent
      activities, 411
    top-down guidance, 409–410
    work climate, 410
  poor, 375
  principal aspects, 87

  principal components, 377–379
  prior requirements, 407
  process management tools, 411–420
  process steps, 454
  proficient, 88
  relevance of corporate culture
    adaptive cultures, 447–448
    change-resistant cultures, 448–449
    changing problem cultures,
      450–454
    clash of culture with execution,
      446
    high-performance cultures,
      446–447
    incompatible subcultures, 450
    insular and inwardly focused
      cultures, 449
    politicized cultures, 449
    strong-culture companies,
      445–446
    unethical greed-driven cultures,
      449–450
    ways of implementation, 445–446
    weak-culture companies, 445
  resource allocation for, 407–408
  and resource shifts, 408
  in small organizations, 379–380
  summary on, 458
  ten basic tasks of, 378
  testing company transformation,
    R-105
  tied to rewards and incentives,
    423–430
  time-consuming, 86
  for whole management team, 376
  work involved in, 376–377
Strategy-making, 52–53
  at all organizational levels, 81–85
  bases of, 375
  collaborative team effort, 85
  and corporate governance, 88–91
  diversity in, 53
  ethical, 354
  at General Electric, 82
  impact of ethical standards,
    346–347
  led by CEOs, 81–82
  on-the-scene managers, 82
  in single-business enterprise, 85
  strategic plan from, 85–86
  summary of process, 81, 458
Strategy-making hierarchy, 83
Strategy options, to improve
    corporate performance
  broadening business base, 327–328
  divesting or retrenching, 328–330

  restructuring, 330–332
  sticking with business lineup,
    326–327
Strengths, 151; see also SWOT
    analysis
Stretch objectives, 76, 79, 425, 456
Strong-culture companies, 443–444
  effects on strategy execution,
    445–446
  ingrained values and norms, 444
  senior management in, 444
Strong rivalry, 107
Strong vs. weak differentiation, 200
Structural ability, and PBU, R-92
Structural motivation, and PBU,
    R-89–R-90
Struggling firms, attack on, 219
Subcultures, incompatible, 450
Subsidiaries, market caps in India,
    R-76
Substantive culture-changing actions,
    452–453
Substitutes
  available for resources, 149
  competitive pressure from sellers of,
    111–112
  creating a price ceiling, 111
  factors affecting competition from,
    112
  identifying, 113
  market indicators of competitive
    strength, 111–112
  pricing of, 111
  switching costs, 111
  from technological change, 122
Sudden-death threat, 153–155
Supercorp (Kanter), R-94
Supermarkets, bargaining power, 116
Supplier bargaining power
  competitive pressures from,
    112–115
  decreased by globalization, 121
  determining strength of, 113–115
  factors affecting, 114
  Microsoft and Intel, 113
  versus small-scale retailers, 113
Supplier Code of Conduct, Apple,
    Inc., 341
Supplier-related value chain activities,
    165–166
Suppliers
  company bargaining power with,
    187
  coordinating with, 189, 197
  expanding internationally, 253
  located near company, 189–190

Suppliers—*Cont.*
  partnering with, 187
  value chain activities, 161
Supply chain, R-26
Supply chain activities, 305
Supply chain efficiency, 187
Supply chain management, 159
Support value chain activities,
    157–158
  general administration, 159
  human resource management, 159
  research and development, 159
  systems development, 159
  technology, 159
Sustainability, means of, 362
Sustainable business practices, 79
  definition, 363
  at Unilever, 363–364
Sustainable competitive advantage
  definition, 53, 148
  in operational capabilities, R-30
  from resources and capabilities,
    147–150
  strategic approaches for, 54–57
Sustainable differentiation advantage,
    198
Switching costs
  and buyer bargaining power, 116
  created by first-movers, 222
  and differentiation strategy, 198
  kinds of, 104
  and low-cost providers, 192
  and product differentiation, 106
  to substitutes, 113
SWOT analysis
  conclusions from, 155–156
  definitions, 150–151
  identifying opportunities, 152–153
  identifying strengths, 151–152
  identifying threats to profitability,
    153–155
  identifying weaknesses, 152
  questions answered by, 156
  steps involved, 155
  what to look for, 154
Symbolic culture-changing actions
  ceremonial events, 453–454
  lead by example, 453
Symmetric competition, R-17
Syndication, R-38–R-39
Synergistic mergers
  advice on acquisitions, R-83
  and hostile bids, R-83
  integration problems, R-80
  opportunistic acquisitions,
    R-82–R-83

reducing valuation risks, R-81–R-82
  valuations, R-80–R-81
Synergy, 296
  cost reduction vs. revenue increase,
    R-81
  difficulties in achieving, R-79–R-80
  merger failures
    AOL/Time Warner, R-79, R-80
    United Airlines, R-79
Synergy-by-merger adherents, R-80
Systems development, 159

T

Tacit capabilities, R-23
Tacit knowledge, 146, 388
Tacit knowledge-sharing, R-59
Tacit operational capabilities, R-24
Tangible assets, 145–146
Tangible features, 197
Tapered integration, 231
Target marketing
  for best-cost provider strategy, 206
  in emerging markets, R-3
  foreign, 252
Tariffs, barrier to entry, 109
Taxability, R-26
Technical know-how
  diffusion of, 123
  in licensing strategies, 263
Technological advances/change
  fast-paced, 199
  and industry change, 122
  striving for, 195
  in vertical integration, 233
Technological assets, 145–146
Technological factors, 100
Technological standard, set by first-
    movers, 222–223
Technology
  for decentralized decision making,
    399
  next-generation, 217
  reason for mergers and acquisitions,
    229
  strategic fit, 305
  value chain activity, 159
Technology companies, adaptive
    cultures, 448
Telecommunications industry
  innovation, R-33
  new business models, R-33
Terrorist attack of 2001, 153–155
Think-global, act-global approach,
    271

Think-global, act-local approach, 272
Think-local, act-local approach,
    269–271
Threats; *see* SWOT analysis
Time
  to develop operational capabilities,
    R-24
  required for culture change, 454
Times interest earned ratio, 143
Time to market, 235–236
Timing of offensive or defensive
    strategies, 221–225
Top-down process of setting
    objectives, 81
Top-level executives; *see also* CEOs;
    Executives
  with centralized decision making,
    397–399
  and competitor analysis, R-19
  with decentralized decision making,
    399
  incentive compensation, 329
  role in strategy execution, 454–455
Total quality management, 413, R-23
  capturing full value of, 419–420
  compared to business process
    reengineering, 418
  compared to Six Sigma, 418
  description, 414
  to focus on continuous
    improvement, 456
  with high and low performers,
    R-29–R-30
  to improve efficiency, R-31
Trade barriers
  and acquisition strategies, 264
  as barrier to entry, 109
  threat of entry from lowering, 121
Tradition-steeped companies, 441
Training, 389–390
Transaction costs, R-33–R-34
  in acquisitions, 299–300
  in strategic alliances, 266
Transaction cost theory, R-58
Transformative collaboration, R-33
Transnational strategy
  advantages/disadvantages, 273
  definition, 272
  drawbacks, 272
  leveraging skills and capabilities,
    272
  mass-customization in, 272
Triple bottom line
  companies recognized for, 362
  and corporate social responsibility
    strategies, 361

definition and scope, 360–361
measures of performance, 361
mutual fund companies, 361
Triple-bottom-line reporting, 361
Trust between alliance partners,
    R-60–R-61
Turnaround capabilities, 310

U

U-forms, 395
Umbrella brands, 309
Uncertainty, reduction in, 123
Underage workers, 342
Undercapitalized firms, 324
Undervalued companies, 310
Unethical and greed-driven culture,
    449–450
Unethical behavior; *see also* Pressure
    to behave unethically
    costs of, 354–355
    managerial pressure for, R-85–R-86
Unethical strategies
    corporate scandals, 347, 348–353
    drivers of
        company culture, 351–352
        faulty oversight, 348–349
        pressure to meet short-term
            targets, 349–351
        pursuit of personal gain, 348–349
Uniqueness drivers, 194; *see also*
    Differentiation strategies
Unitary structure, 395
United Auto Workers, R-18
United Kingdom
    Financial Reporting Council,
        R-115–R-116
    Healthcare Commission, R-114
United States, Foreign Corrupt
    Practices Act, 343
United States dollar, decline in value,
    258–259
Unrelated businesses, 300
Unrelated diversification
    better-off test, 308
    building shareholder value
        acquisition of undervalued
            companies, 310
        corporate parenting, 308–309
        cross-business allocation of
            financial resources, 309–310
        generalized resources and
            capabilities, 308
        requirements, 310–311
    criteria for, 307

drawbacks
    demands on management, 311
    limited competitive advantage,
        311–312
    focus of, 307
    inadequate reasons for
        growth, 312
        managerial motives, 312–313
        risk reduction, 312
        stabilization, 312
    and multidivisional structure,
        395–396
    parenting advantage, 311
Unrelated groups of related
    businesses, 313
Unrelated mergers, R-80–R-82
User-to-company innovation, R-34,
    R-35
User-to-user innovation, R-34

V

Valuation
    means of reducing risks in
        synergistic mergers, R-81–R-82
    in synergistic mergers, R-80–R-81
Value
    differentiating to add, 199
    from differentiation strategy,
        197–198
    provided to customers, 157
    signaling, 198
Value chain
    definition, 157
    at Dell Inc., R-42
    globalization effects, R-42–R-43
    hybrid vs. specialized, R-43–R-45
    at Just Coffee, 160
    limits of customer segmentation,
        R-46
    low-cost players, R-42–R-43
    managed for differentiation, 194–196
    modular, R-43
    operations component, 158
    profit margin component, 158
    revamped to increase
        differentiation, 196–197
    rising costs, 158–160
    risk of old assumptions, R-41–R-42
    specialization challenges, R-45
    and strategic alliances, R-56
    tying up assets, 158–160
Value chain activities
    activity-based costing, 160
    benchmarking, 162–163

for competitive advantage, 166–167,
    169
and competitiveness, 161
cost-efficient management
    advanced production technology,
        188
    company bargaining power, 187
    cost advantage over rivals,
        188–189
    economies of scale, 186
    full capacity operation, 186–187
    information technology, 188
    learning-curve effects, 186
    lower input costs, 187
    motivating employees, 188
    outsourcing, 188
    supply chain efficiency, 187
    vertical integration, 188
of distribution channel, 161
in foreign markets, 255–256
in global strategy, 271
improving
    distribution-related activities, 166
    internally performed activities,
        165
    supplier-related activities, 165–166
kinds of primary activities, 159
kinds of support activities, 159
for low-cost providers, 186–189
management at Walmart, 191
in outsourcing, 235–237
performed internally vs.
    outsourcing, 392–393
primary, 157–158
reengineering, 414
in related diversification, 303
relation to resources and
    capabilities, 167–168
revamped to lower costs
    coordination with suppliers, 189
    direct selling, 189
    nearby supplier location, 189–190
    at Nucor Corporation, 190
    at Southwest Airlines, 190
of suppliers, 161
support, 157–158
Value chain analysis
    comparison of rival companies, 158
    customer value proposition, 158
    inadequate for complete
        competitive situation, 168
    internal cost structure, 158–161
Value-chain mapping, R-107, R-110
Value chain matchup, 293
    in related diversification, 301,
        304–305

Value chain specialization
  assessment, R-45–R-46
Value chain system
  for entire industry, 161–162
  scope of, 161
Value-conscious buyers, 206
Value creation, R-26
  Web-based businesses, R-36
Values; *see also* Core values
  of companies
    definition, 75
    linked to vision and mission,
      75–76
  in corporate culture, 440
Value statement, 76
  Royal Dutch Shell, 77
Variables in strategic group mapping,
  126–127
Vertical integration, 229–235
  advantages, 188, 231–233
  at American Apparel, 236
  backward or forward, 230
  disadvantages
    capacity-matching problems, 234
    economies of scale unrealized,
      234
    impaired flexibility, 233
    increased business risk, 233
    less flexibility in buyer
      preferences, 233
    need for new business capabilities,
      234
    need for new skills, 234
    slow to embrace technological
      advances, 233
  to expand activities, 230
  full integration, 230–231
  in multidivisional structure, 396
  partial integration, 231
  versus strategic alliances, 237–238,
    243–244
  tapered integration, 231
  weighing pros and cons, 234–235
Vertically integrated firm, 229
Vertical scope, 226
Videoconferencing, 122
Video game console business,
  R-17–R-18
Village Store, Internet metaphor,
  R-41
Vision
  abstractness, R-12
  challenging, R-12
  clarity, R-12

compared to mission, R-9
conciseness, R-12
and customer satisfaction, R-10
defined by leaders, R-10
effective, R-9–R-10
effect on customers and staff, R-13
future orientation, R-12
guidelines for developing, R-15
impact on employees, R-10
and job satisfaction, R-15
linked to results, R-14
and organizational performance,
  R-11–R-13
powerful, R-12
stable, R-12
strong vs. weak, R-10
study and findings on, R-11–R-14
and venture growth, R-12
workable
  factors affecting realization, R-11
  needed characteristics, R-11
Visionary leadership, R-9, R-10
Vision content, R-13
Vision realization factors, R-13
Vision sharing, R-13, R-14
Vision statement
  analysis of, R-13–R-14
  dos and don'ts, 72
  incorporating all characteristics,
    R-13
  purpose, 71
  varying characteristics, R-9
Visualization, R-48
Voice-over Internet Protocol (VoIP),
  122

W

Wages
  country differences, 121
  low-wage countries, 256
War games, R-20
Weak-culture companies
  lack of employee allegiance, 444
  and strategy execution, 445
Weakness, 151; *see also* SWOT
  analysis
Weak rivalry, 107
Web-based businesses
  business models, R-33
  future of, R-40
  multiplying dynamic capabilities,
    R-35–R-36

new collaborative matrix,
  R-34–R-35
success stories, R-39–R-40
Web 3.0, R-40
Web 2.0
  business models, R-33, R-34
  and changing rules of business,
    R-34
Weighted competitive strength
  assessment
  description, 168–171
  implications, 172
Weighted competitive strength scores,
  318, 319
Weighted industry attractiveness
  scores, 316
Wholesale distributors, 108
Winning strategy tests
  competitive advantage test, 61–62
  fit test, 60
  performance test, 62
Women, as distributors in India,
  R-75
Work atmosphere, 425
Work climate, 410
  results-oriented, 456–457
Work effort
  aligning structure and strategy,
    393–397
  collaboration with partners,
    400–401
  delegation of authority, 397–400
  to fit business lineup, 401
  for good strategy execution,
    390–391
  internal vs. outsourced value chain,
    391–393
  reengineering, 413
Work environment, 358
Workforce; *see also* Employees;
    Human resource management
  empowerment, 456
  local, 285–286
Workforce diversity, 358
Workforce retention, 366–367
Working capital ratio, 52
Work organization, 387–388
World Bank, Ease of Doing Business
  Index, R-2
World Trade Organization, and
  dumping, 280
World Wide Web, effects on business
  and collaboration, R-33
"Worry list" of problems, 173